To Fetch Some Golden Apples

READINGS IN INDO-EUROPEAN MYTH, RELIGION, AND SOCIETY

Edited by
Roger D. Woodard

KENDALL/HUNT PUBLISHING COMPANY
4050 Westmark Drive Dubuque, Iowa 52002

ISBN 13: 978-0-7575-2160-7
ISBN 10: 0-7575-2160-6

Printed in the United States of America
10 9 8 7 6 5 4 3 2 1

à la mémoire d' Émile Benveniste et Georges Dumézil

and

for Calvert Watkins
Doktorgroßvater

Preface

Heracles, that consummate Greek strongman and slayer of monstrous beasts, was sent by Eurystheus—the master for whom he was compelled to perform a dozen labors—to a distant western locale in order to fetch certain golden apples that hung upon a tree within the garden of the Hesperides (the daughters of Evening). This he accomplished successfully, slaying in the process the dragon Ladon, which guarded the tree, and for a while, shouldering the cosmic burden of the titanic giant Atlas. Apollodorus, the ancient Greek mythographer, relates the story for us in part 3, chapter 13, of this volume.

Of the tree-fruits that were known by those prehistoric peoples that we call the Proto-Indo-Europeans—the linguistic and cultural ancestors of the historically attested Indo-European peoples—it is possible to reconstruct with confidence the denotation of the "apple"—**abel-* being the Indo-European root. How can we know this? How is it possible to gain knowledge of linguistic forms of a language that was never written down (according to received opinion—surely not *attested* in any written form)? How can we identify tree-fruits known by a prehistoric people whose archaeological identity has yet to be identified with any certainty?

Such specific information about the world in which the prehistoric Indo-Europeans lived and the language with which they negotiated that world is retrieved by application of the remarkable scientific procedure dubbed the *comparative method of historical linguistics* (discussed in more detail in part 1). By comparing related forms (*cognates* is the technical term) in documented, descendent Indo-European languages—such as Latin *Abella* (name of an Italian town famed for its apples), Old Irish *ubull*, Crimean Gothic *apel*, Old High German *apful*, Old Church Slavic *ablŭko* (all meaning 'apple')—the parent, Proto-

Indo-European, root **abel-* can be reconstructed, working backwards through linguistic time. The method works because of an equally remarkable characteristic of language evolution, commonly expressed as the dictum "sound change is regular"; thus, for example, as illustrated by the Gothic form cited above, *apel*, Proto-Indo-European **b* regularly changes into *p* in the evolution of the Germanic languages, one component of a set of changes described by *Grimm's Law* (or the *First Consonant Shift*). An additional change in High German, the so-called *Second Consonant Shift*, results in the further development of Proto-Germanic **p* to *pf*, as in Old High German *apful*.

Two linguistic events here conspire—one an analytic technique of reconstruction, the other a natural, essentially biological, phenomenon of evolution—to produce a dialectic process, a hand-in-hand dance backwards and forwards through the history of a language. The dialectic operates under the constraints of rigorous structural comparison, and the continuous back-and-forth method provides a constant check on the accuracy of the process.

In the following pages the reader will encounter works produced by several investigators whose scholarship cuts across numerous disciplinary boundaries and spans most of the twentieth century, and continues, in some cases, in the twenty-first. The readings presented herein, however, flowed predominantly from the pens of three of the twentieth—and twenty-first—century's most ardent and eminent practitioners of Indo-European linguistic and cultural study: Émile Benveniste (1902–1976), Georges Dumézil (1898–1986), and Calvert Watkins. While the three scholars may not have found themselves in mutual agreement at all points and at all times, a commonality of method and goal unites their work. All three—especially Benveniste and Watkins—have masterfully practiced the science of the comparative method of historical linguistics. Of equal significance for the present collection, all three have assiduously applied the comparative method to the study of Indo-European culture and society, including the study of Indo-European myth and religion—especially Dumézil. By adapting linguistic comparison to an examination of recurring cultural, social, and ideological patterns—cognates, in effect—under the rigorous constraint of cross-cultural structural (including linguistic) agreement, Watkins, Benveniste, and Dumézil demonstrate the efficacy of this method for reconstructing ancestral Indo-European sociocultural structures. What is more, reconstruction of such ancestral structures effects the elucidation of common inherited traditions among descendent Indo-European peoples—traditions whose relatedness has become obscured by cultural evolution. The latter procedure is admirably demonstrated, for example, by Dumézil's analysis of the Roman goddess Mater Matuta (see part 4, chapter 20).

Back to apples: the motif of "golden apples" is broadly disseminated among early Indo-European peoples of Europe, suggesting that the tradition may possibly have been inherited from ancestral Indo-European myth, though the traditions are quite variable. Gamkrelidze and Ivanov (1995, *Indo-European and the Indo-Europeans*, Part 1, Berlin: Mouton de Gruyter, pp. 553–554) nicely summarize the evidence. Aside from the apples of the Hesperides that Heracles was sent to fetch, there is a Norse tradition about apples of gold kept by Idun, wife of Bragi, the god of poetry—apples that kept the gods ever youthful and that were stolen by the giant Thjazi. Golden apples also figure in the mythology of the Baltic and Slavic Indo-European peoples, associated with, among other figures, the Serbo-Croatian lightning deity.

Regardless of the status of the apple of gold in primitive Indo-European mythic tradition, there are golden apples waiting for the fetching in the ancient texts and scholarly works that follow. Like Heracles, let's pick some fruit.

Acknowledgments

I wish to express my appreciation to each of the following for their help and support in bringing this work into the light of day: to Christopher Dadian of the Center for Hellenic Studies, for salvific guidance at a critical stage; to Kerri Sullivan, for expertly compositing a tedious typescript; to Jessica Weaver, for unflagging commitment in poring over proofs; to Michael Funke and Stefani DeMoss of Kendall/Hunt, for doing the right thing; and to Paul and Katherine, for Greek and grace.

Note to Readers

Many of the essays in this collection are excerpted from larger works. Introductory remarks that precede each reading are intended to provide a measure of context for such excerpted selections. Even so, the reader may still encounter within some readings references to ideas that fall outside of the excerpted passages, ideas that may be unfamiliar. In most instances this should cause no difficulty. If, however, the reader's curiosity is peaked, or there remains some nagging uncertainty regarding the significance of such references, the reader is urged to explore the selections within the broader context of their originally published form.

Within many of the essays, references occur to pages, sections and chapters of the works in which they originally appeared. So that readers will not misconstrue such references as referring to pages, etc., within the present volume, these references have been enclosed within angled brackets (i.e., < and >).

Contents

PART 1: THE INDO-EUROPEANS

PART 2: ROME AND ITALY

PART 3: GREECE

PART 4: INDIA

PART 5: IRAN

PART 6: IRELAND AND THE CELTS

PART 7: SCANDINAVIA AND THE GERMANIC TRIBES

Select Bibliography

Supplementing references appearing in individual articles and providing suggested resources for further reading

Abbreviations

ANET	Pritchard 1969
ANF	*Arkiv för nordisk filologi*
BSL	*Bulletin de la Société de Linguistique de Paris*
DIE	Dumézil 1952
DL	Dumézil 1956
EWA	Mayrhofer 1986–
Hér.	Dumézil 1949
Idéol.	Dumézil 1958
IF	*Indogermanische Forschungen*
IR	Dumézil 1969
JAOS	*Journal of the American Oriental Society*
JMQ	Dumézil 1941–1948
KEWA	Mayrhofer 1956–1980
ME	Dumézil 1995
MV	Dumézil 1998
NA	Dumézil 1945
NR	Dumézil 1944
P.-W.	*Pauly-Wissowa, Real-Encyclopädie*
QII	Dumézil 1959–1961
REL	*Revue des études latines*
RhM	*Rheinisches Museum für Philologie*
RHR	*Revue de l'histoire des religions*
RIER	Dumézil 1954
RPh.	*Revue de philologie, de littérature et d'histoire anciennes*
RVV	*Religionsgeschichtliche Versuche und Vorarbeiten*
Tarpeia	Dumézil 1947

Citations

Anderson, J. G. C. 1938. *Tacitus: Germania.* Oxford: Oxford University Press.
Armstrong, John. 1985. "A Glossarial Index of Nouns and Adjectives in *IGT* II–IV." *Proceedings of the Harvard Celtic Colloquium* 5:187–410.

Bader, Françoise. 1976. "Un nom indo-européen de l'homme chez Homère." *Revue de Philologie* 50:206–12.

Benveniste, Émile. 1973. *Indo-European Language and Society*. Translated by Elizabeth Palmer. Coral Gables, Florida: University of Miami Press (translation of Benveniste 1969).

——. 1970. "Les valeurs économiques dans le vocabulaire indo-européen." In *Indo-European and Indo-Europeans*, edited by G. Cardona, H. Hoenigswald and A. Senn, 307–20. Philadelphia: University of Pennsylvania Press.

——. 1969. *Le vocabulaire des institutions indo-européennes*. 2 vols. Paris: Minuit.

——. 1966–74. *Problèmes de linguistique générale*. 2 vols. Paris: Gallimard.

——. 1949. "Don et échange dans le vocabulaire indo-européen." *L'année sociologique*, 3e série, 7–20.

——. 1945a. "Symbolisme social dans les cultes gréco-italiques." *Revue de l'histoire des religions* 129:5–16. Reprinted as "Social Symbolism in Greco-Italic Cults" in Loraux, Nagy and Slatkin 2001, 439–47. Translated by Arthur Goldhammer.

——. 1945b. "La doctrine médicale des Indo-Européens." *Revue de l'histoire des religions* 130:5–12. Reprinted as "The Medical Tradition of the Indo-Europeans" in Loraux, Nagy and Slatkin, 2001, 422–27. Translated by Arthur Goldhammer.

——. 1938. "Traditions indo-iraniennes sur les classes sociales." *Journal asiatique* 230:529–49.

——. 1936. "Liber et Liberi." *Revue des études latines* 15:51–58.

Benveniste, É., and L. Renou. 1934. *Vr̥tra et Vr̥θragna: Étude de mythologie indo-iranienne*. Cahiers de la Société Asiatique 3. Paris: Impremerie Nationale.

Bergin, Osborn. 1970. *Irish Bardic Poetry*. Dublin: Institute for Advanced Study.

——. 1955. "Irish Grammatical Tracts 5: Metrical Faults." *Ériu* 17 Supplement, 259–93.

——. 1939. "The Native Irish Grammarian." *Proceedings of the British Academy* 24:205–34.

Bierbaumer, P. 1976. "Der botanische Wortschatz des Altenglischen." *Grazer Beiträge zur englischen Philologie* 2:127–28.

Binchy, Daniel A. 1940. *Críth Gablach*. Dublin: Institute for Advanced Study.

Bömer, Franz. 1957–58. *Die Fasten*. 2 vols. Heidelberg: Carl Winter.

Boyce, Mary. 1984. *Textual Sources for the Study of Zoroastrianism*. Totowa, New Jersey: Barnes and Noble Books.

——. 1975–91. *A History of Zoroastrianism*. 3 vols. Leiden: Brill.

Boyle, Anthony J. and Roger D. Woodard. 2004. *Ovid: Fasti*. Rev. ed. London: Penguin Books.

Breatnach, Liam. 1987. *Uraicecht na Ríar: The Poetic Grades in Early Irish Law*. Dublin: Institute for Advanced Study.

Buck, Carl Darling. 1928. *The Greek Dialects*. Chicago: University of Chicago Press.

Calame, Claude. 2003. *Myth and History in Ancient Greece*. Translated by Daniel Berman. Princeton: Princeton University Press.

Campanile, Enrico. 1987. "Indogermanische Dichtersprache." In *Studien zum indogermanischen Wortschatz*, edited by W. Meid, 21–28. Innsbruck: Innsbrucker Beiträge zur Sprachwissenschaft.

——. 1977. *Ricerche di cultura poetica indoeuropea*. Pisa: Giardini.

Carruba, Onofrio. 1969. "Die Chronologie der heth. Texte." *Zeitschrift der Deutschen Morgenländischen Gesellschaft*. Supplementband 1:226–49.

Clay, Jenny Strauss. 2003. *Hesiod's Cosmos*. Cambridge: Cambridge University Press.

Cockayne, T. O. 1961. *Leechdoms, Wortcunning and Starcraft of Early England*. Reprint ed. London: Holland.

Cowgill, Warren. 1980. "The Etymology of Irish *guidid* and the Outcome of *g^wh in Celtic." In *Lautgeschichte und Etymologie*, edited by M. Mayrhofer, M. Peters and O. E. Pfeiffer, 49–78. Wiesbaden: Reichert.

Dandekar, Ramchandra N. 1974. "The Two Births of Vasiṣṭa: A Fresh Study of Rigveda 7.33.9–14." In *Antiquitates Indogermanicae: Gedenkschrift Hermann Güntert*, edited by M. Mayrhofer et al., 223–32. Innsbruck: Innsbrucker Beiträge zur Sprachwissenschaft.

Davies, Malcolm. 1991. *Poetarum Melicorum Graecorum Fragmenta*. Oxford: Oxford University Press.

Detienne, Marcel. 2006. *Comparative Anthropology of Ancient Greece*. Cambridge, Massachusetts: Harvard University Press.

——. 1986. *The Creation of Mythology*. Translated by Margaret Cook. Chicago: University of Chicago Press.

Dobbie, Elliot van Kirk. 1942. *The Anglo-Saxon Poetic Records VI: The Anglo-Saxon Minor Poems*. New York: Columbia University Press.

Doniger O'Flaherty, Wendy. 1981. *The Rig Veda*. London: Penguin Books.

Dryden, John. 1932. *Plutarch's Lives of the Noble Grecians and Romans*. Revised by Arthur H. Clough. New York: Dodd, Mead.

Dumézil, Georges. 2000. *Mythes et dieux de la Scandinavie ancienne*. Paris: Gallimard.

——. 1998. *Mitra-Varuna*. Translated by Derek Coltman. New York: Zone Books.

——. 1995. *Mythe et épopée*. 3 vols. Rev. ed. Paris: Gallimard.

——. 1986. *Loki*. 3rd ed. Paris: Flammarion.

——. 1983. *The Stakes of the Warrior*. Translated by David Weeks. Berkeley and Los Angeles: University of California Press.

——. 1980. *Camillus*. Translated by A. Aronowicz and J. Bryson. Berkeley and Los Angeles: University of California Press.

——. 1975. *Fêtes romaines d'été et d'automne*. Paris: Gallimard.

——. 1973a. *Gods of the Ancient Northmen*. Edited by Einar Haugen. Berkeley and Los Angeles: University of California Press.

——. 1973b. *The Destiny of a King*. Translated by Alf Hiltebeitel. Chicago: University of Chicago Press.

——. 1970. *Archaic Roman Religion*. Translated by Philip Krapp. Chicago: University of Chicago Press.

——. 1969a. *The Destiny of the Warrior*. Translated by Alf Hiltebeitel. Chicago: University of Chicago Press.

——. 1969b. *Idées romaines*. Paris: Gallimard.

——. 1961. "Quaestiunculae indo-italicae 8–10." *Latomus* 20:253–65.

——. 1960. "Quaestiunculae indo-italicae 4–6." In *Hommages à L. Herrmann*, 315–29. Brussels: Collection Latomus.

——. 1959. "Quaestiunculae indo-italicae 7." *Revue des études latines* 37:94–101.

——. 1958. *L'idéologie tripartie des Indo-Européens*. Brussels: Collection Latomus.

——. 1956. *Déesses latines et mythes védiques*. Brussels: Collection Latomus.

——. 1954. *Rituels indo-européens à Rome*. Paris: Klincksieck.

——. 1952. *Les dieux des Indo-Européens*. Paris: PUF.

——. 1949. *L'héritage indo-européen à Rome*. Paris: Gallimard.

——. 1947. *Tarpeia*. Paris: Gallimard.

——. 1945. *Naissance d'archanges*. Paris: Gallimard.

——. 1944. *Naissance de Rome*. Paris: Gallimard.

——. 1943. *Servius et la Fortune*. Paris: Gallimard.

——. 1942. *Horace et les Curiaces*. Paris: Gallimard.

——. 1941–48. *Jupiter, Mars, Quirinus*. 4 vols. Paris: Gallimard and PUF.

——. 1939. *Mythes et dieux des Germains*. Paris: PUF.

Durante, Marcello. 1958. "Prosa ritmica, alliterazione e accento nelle lingue dell'Italia antica." *Ricerche Linguistiche* 4:61–98.

Edmunds, Lowell, ed. 1990. *Approaches to Greek Myth*. Baltimore: Johns Hopkins University Press.

Evans, David. 1979. "Agamemnon and the Indo-European Three-fold Death Pattern." *History of Religions* 19:153–66.

Fontenrose, Joseph. 1980. *Python*. Reprint ed. Berkeley and Los Angeles: University of California Press.

Forssman, Bernhard. 1966. *Untersuchungen zur Sprache Pindars*. Wiesbaden: Harrassowitz.

Foster, B. O. 1919. *Livy: History of Rome, Books I-II*. Cambridge, Massachusetts: Harvard University Press.

Fox, Anthony. 1995. *Linguistic Reconstruction*. Oxford: Oxford University Press.

Fraser, M. J. 1915. "The First Battle of Moytura." *Ériu* 8:1–63.

Fraser, P. M. and E. Mathews. 1987. *A Lexicon of Greek Personal Names*. Oxford: Oxford University Press.

Frazer, J. G. 1951. *The Golden Bough*. 3rd ed. New York: Macmillan.

——. 1921. *Apollodorus: The Library*. Cambridge, Massachusetts: Harvard University Press.

Gamkrelidze, Tamaz V. and Vjačeslav V. Ivanov. 1995. *Indo-European and the Indo-Europeans*. Translated by Johanna Nichols. Berlin: de Gruyter (translation of Gamkrelidze and Ivanov 1984).

——. 1984. *Indoevropejskij jazyk i indoevropejcy*. Tbilisi: Izdatel'stvo Tbilisskogo Universiteta.

Gercenberg, Leonid G. 1972. *Morfologičeskaja struktura slova v drevnix indoiranskix jazykax*. Leningrad: Nauka.

Gershevitch, Ilya. 1969. "Amber at Persepolis." In *Studia Classica et Orientalia A. Pagliaro Oblata II*, 167–251. Rome: Herder.

Gerstein, M. R. 1974. "Germanic *Warg*: The Outlaw as Werewolf." In *Myth in Indo-European Antiquity*, edited by G. J. Larson, 131–56. Berkeley and Los Angeles: University of California Press.

Gordon, E. V. 1949. *An Introduction to Old Norse*. Reprint ed. Oxford: Oxford University Press.

Graf, Fritz. 1993. *Greek Mythology: An Introduction*. Translated by Thomas Marier. Baltimore: Johns Hopkins University Press.

Güntert, Hermann. 1914. "Über die ahurischen und daēvischen Ausdrücke im Avesta." *Sitzungsberichte der Heidelberger Akademie der Wissenschaften*, Bd. 5, Nr. 11.

Hamilton, J. N. 1970. "Phonetic Texts of the Irish of North Mayo." *Zeitschrift für Celtische Philologie* 31:125–60.

Hamp, Eric P. 1985. "An Archaic Poetic Statement." *Živa Antika* 35:85–86.

——. 1961. "Albanian *be, besë*." *Zeitschrift für Vergleichende Sprachforschung* 77:252–53.

Harris, Joseph. 1985. "Die altenglische Heldendichtung." In *Neues Handbuch der Literaturwissenschaft, Bd. 6. Europäisches Frühmittelalter*, edited by K. von See, 238–46. Wiesbaden: Aula.

Heaney, Marie. 1994. *Over Nine Waves*. London: Faber and Faber.

Hoffman, Karl. 1975. *Aufsätze zur Indoiranistik*. Wiesbaden: Reichert.

Hoffner, Harry. 1990. *Hittite Myths*. Atlanta: Scholars Press.

Huld, Martin E. 1984. *Basic Albanian Etymologies*. Columbus: Slavica.

Jamison, Stephanie. 1991. *The Ravenous Hyenas and the Wounded Sun: Myth and Ritual in Ancient India*. Ithaca: Cornell University Press.

Jeffery, Lillian, and A. Morpurgo Davies. 1970. "ΠΟΙΝΙΚΑΣΤΑΣ and ΠΟΙΝΙΚΑΖΕΝ." *Kadmos* 9:118–54.

Kellens, Jean. 1974. *Les noms-racines de l'Avesta*. Wiesbaden: Reichert.

Kelly, Fergus. 1976. *Audacht Morainn*. Dublin: Institute for Advanced Study.

Klaeber, Fredrick. 1950. *Beowulf*. 3rd ed. Lexington: Heath.

Krapp, George P. and Elliot van Kirk Dobbie. 1936. *The Anglo-Saxon Poetic Records III: The Exeter Book*. New York: Columbia University Press.

Latte, Kurt. 1960. *Römische Religionsgeschichte*. Munich: C. H. Beck'sche Verlagsbuchhandlung.

Lazard, Gilbert. 1984. "La métrique de l'Avesta." In *Orientalia* (*Acta Iranica, 9*), 285–300. Leiden: Brill.

Lazzeroni, Ricardo. 1971. "Su alcuni deverbali greci e sanscriti." *Studi e Saggi di Linguistica* 11:40–50.

Leo, Friedrich. 1913. *Geschichte der römischen Literatur*. Berlin: Weidmann.

Lerza, Paola. 1982. *Stesicoro*. Genoa: Melangolo.

Littleton, C. Scott. 1982. *The New Comparative Mythology*. 3rd ed. Berkeley and Los Angeles: University of California Press.

——. 1970. "The 'Kingship in Heaven' Theme." In *Myth and Law among the Indo-Europeans*, edited by Jaan Puhvel, 83–121. Berkeley and Los Angeles: University of California Press.

Loraux, Nicole, Gregory Nagy and Laura Slatkin, eds. 2001. *Antiquities*. New York: The New Press.

Lühr, Rosemarie. 1982. *Studien zur Sprache des Hildebrandliedes*. Frankfurt-am-Main: Lang.

MacCana, Proinsias. 1970. *Celtic Mythology*. London: Hamlyn.

Malandra, William. 1983. *An Introduction to Ancient Iranian Religion*. Minneapolis: University of Minnesota Press.

Mallory, J. P. 1989. *In Search of the Indo-Europeans*. London: Thames and Hudson.

Mallory, J. P. and D. Q. Adams, eds. 1997. *Encyclopedia of Indo-European Culture*. London and Chicago: Fitzroy Dearborn.

Mannhardt, Wilhelm. 1963. *Wald- und Feldkulte*. Reprint ed. Darmstadt: Wissenschaftliche Buchgesellschaft.

Martinet, André. 1972. "Des labio-vélares aux labiales dans les dialectes indo-européens." In *Indo-Celtica: Gedächtnisschrift A. Sommerfelt*, edited by H. Pilch, 89–93. Munich: Hueber.

Mayrhofer, Manfred. 1986–. *Etymologisches Wörterbuch des Altindoarischen*. Heidelberg: Carl Winter.

——. 1966. *Die Indo-Arier im Alten Vorderasien*. Wiesbaden: Harrassowitz.

——. 1956–80. *Kurzgefaßtes etymologisches Wörterbuch des Altindischen*. Heidelberg: Carl Winter.

Meid, Wolfgang. 1984. "Bemerkungen zum indogermanischen Wortschatz des Germanischen." In *Das Germanische und die Rekonstruktion der indogermanischen Grundsprache*, edited by J. Untermann and B. Brogyanyi, 91–112. Amsterdam: Benjamins.

Meillet, Antoine. 1925. *La méthode comparative en linguistique historique*. Paris: Champion.

Melchert, H. Craig. 1993. *Cuneiform Luvian Lexicon*. Chapel Hill: self-published.

Meroney, Howard. 1944. "The Nine Herbs." *Modern Language Notes* 59:157–60.

Much, Rudolf. 1959. *Die Germania des Tacitus*. Heidelberg: Carl Winter.

Nagy, Gregory. Forthcoming. "Homer and Greek Myth." In Woodard forthcoming b.

——. 1999. *The Best of the Achaeans*. Rev. ed. Baltimore: Johns Hopkins University Press.

——. 1990a. *Pindar's Homer*. Baltimore: Johns Hopkins University Press.

——. 1990b. *Greek Mythology and Poetics*. Ithaca: Cornell University Press.

——. 1974. *Comparative Studies in Greek and Indic Meter*. Cambridge, Massachusetts: Harvard University Press.

Norden, Eduard. 1939. *Aus altrömischen Priesterbüchern*. Lund: Gleerup.

Page, Denis L. 1973. "Stesichorus: The *Geryoneïs*." *Journal of Hellenic Studies* 93:138–54.

——. 1972. *Supplementum Lyricis Graecis*. Oxford: Oxford University Press.

——. 1962. *Poetae Melici Graeci*. Oxford: Oxford University Press.

Pavese, Carlo 0. 1966. "ΧΡΗΜΑΤΑ, ΧΡΗΜΑΤ' ΑΝΗΡ ed il motivo della literalità nella seconda Istmica di Pindaro." *Quaderni Urbinati di Cultura Classica* 2:103-42.

Pokorny, Julius. 1959. *Indogermanisches Etymologisches Wörterbuch*. Bern: A. Francke.

Poultney, James Wilson. 1959. *The Bronze Tables of Iguvium*. American Philological Association: Baltimore.

Pritchard, James B. 1969. *Ancient Near Eastern Texts Relating to the Old Testament*. 3rd ed. Princeton: Princeton University Press.

Puhvel, Jaan. 1987. *Comparative Mythology*. Baltimore: Johns Hopkins University Press.

Reichelt, Hans. 1968. *Avesta Reader*. Reprint ed. Berlin: de Gruyter.

Rees, Alwyn and Brinley Rees. 1989. *Celtic Heritage*. Reprint ed. London: Thames and Hudson.

Schlerath, Bernfried. 1974. "Gedanke, Wort und Werk im Veda und im Awesta." In *Antiquitates Indogermanicae. Gedenkschrift Hermann Güntert*, 201–22. Innsbruck: Innsbrucker Beiträge zur Sprachwissenschaft.

Schmitt, Rüdiger. 1967. *Dichtung und Dichtersprache in indogermanischer Zeit*. Wiesbaden: Harrassowitz.

Schwyzer, Eduard. 1960. *Dialectarum graecarum exempla epigraphica potiora*. Reprint ed. Hildesheim: Olms.

Seebold, Elmar. 1980. "Etymologie und Lautgeschichte." In *Lautgeschichte und Etymologie*, edited by M. Mayrhofer, M. Peters and O. E. Pfeiffer, 435–84. Wiesbaden: Reichert.

——. 1967. "Die Vertretung idg. *$g^w h$* im Germanischen." *Zeitschrift für Vergleichende Sprachforschung* 81:104–33.

Singer, Charles. 1920. *Early English Magic and Medicine*. London: Oxford University Press.

Soysal, Oğuz. 1989. "Der Apfel möge die Zähne nehmen!" *Orientalia* 58:171–92.

Starobinsky, Jean. 1971. *Les mots sous les mots: Les anagrammes de Ferdinand de Saussure*. Paris: Gallimard.

Terry, Patricia. 1990. *Poems of the Elder Edda*. Philadelphia: University of Pennsylvania Press.

Thurneysen, Rudolf. 1946. *A Grammar of Old Irish*. Translated by D. A. Binchy and Osborn Bergin. Dublin: Institute for Advanced Study.

Tolkien, J. R. R. 1938. "Beowulf: The Monsters and the Critics." *Proceedings of the British Academy* (1936), 245–95.

Toporov, Vladimir Nikolaevič. 1981. "Die Ursprünge der indoeuropäischen Poetik." *Poetica* 13:189–251.

van Buitenen, J. A. B. 1973–1978. *The Mahabharata*. 3 vols. (Books 1–5). Chicago: University of Chicago Press.

Vernant, Jean-Pierre and Pierre Vidal-Naquet. 1988. *Myth and Tragedy in Ancient Greece*. Translated by Janet Lloyd. New York: Zone Books.

Wackernagel, Jakob. 1953. *Kleine Schriften*. Göttingen: Vandenhoeck & Ruprecht.

Warde Fowler, W. 1899. *The Roman Festivals of the Period of the Republic*. London: Macmillan and Co.

Watkins, Calvert. 2000. *The American Heritage Dictionary of Indo-European Roots*. 2nd ed. Boston: Houghton Mifflin.

——. 1995. *How to Kill a Dragon: Aspects of Indo-European Poetics*. Oxford: Oxford University Press.

——. 1993. "Another Thorny Problem." *Linguistica XXXIII. Bojan Čop septuagenario in honorem oblata*. Ljubljana.

——. 1990. "Some Celtic Phrasal Echoes." In *Celtic Language, Celtic Culture: Festschrift for Eric P. Hamp*, edited by A. Matonis and D. Melia, 47–56. Van Nuys: Ford and Bailie.

——. 1989. "New Parameters in Historical Linguistics, Philology, and Culture History." *Language* 65:783–99.

——. 1987. "Two Anatolian Forms: Palaic *aškummāuwa*, Cuneiform Luvian *wa-a-ar-ša*." In *Festschrift for Henry Hoenigswald on the Occasion of His 70th Birthday*, edited by G. Cardona and N. Zide, 399–404. Tübingen: Narr.

——. 1979a. "NAM.RA GUD UDU in Hittite: Indo-European Poetic Language and the Folk Taxonomy of Wealth." In *Hethitisch und Indogermanisch*, edited by E. Neu and W. Meid, 269–87. Innsbruck: Innsbrucker Beiträge zur Sprachwissenschaft.

——. 1979b. "*Is tre fír flathemon*: Marginalia to *Audacht Morainn*." *Ériu* 30:181–98.

——. 1976. "The Etymology of Irish *dúan*." *Celtica* 11.270–77.

West, M. L. 1997. *The East Face of Helicon*. Oxford: Oxford University Press.

——. 1978. *Hesiod: Works and Days*. Oxford: Clarendon Press.

——. 1966. *Hesiod: Theogony*. Oxford: Clarendon Press.

Wikander, Stig. 1947. "Pāṇḍavasagan och Mahābhāratas mytiska förutsättningar." *Religion och Bibel* 6:27–39.

Wissowa, Georg. 1971. *Religion und Kultus der Römer*. Reprint ed. Munich: C. H. Beck'sche Verlagsbuchhandlung.

Woodard, Roger D. Forthcoming a. "Hesiod and Greek Myth." In Woodard forthcoming b.

——, ed. Forthcoming b. *The Cambridge Companion to Greek Myth*. Cambridge: Cambridge University Press.

——. 2006a. *Indo-European Sacred Space*. Urbana and Chicago: University of Illinois Press.

——. 2006b. *Indo-European Myth and Religion: A Manual*. Rev. 2nd ed. Dubuque: Kendall/Hunt.

——, ed. 2004. *The Cambridge Encyclopedia of the World's Ancient Languages*. Cambridge: Cambridge University Press.

Woodbury, Leonard. 1968. "Pindar and the Mercenary Muse: *Isthmian* 2.1–13." *Transactions of the American Philological Association* 99:527-42.

Wünsch, R. 1916. "Hymnos." *Pauly-Wissowa, Real-Encyclopädie* 17.141–83.

PART 1

THE INDO-EUROPEANS

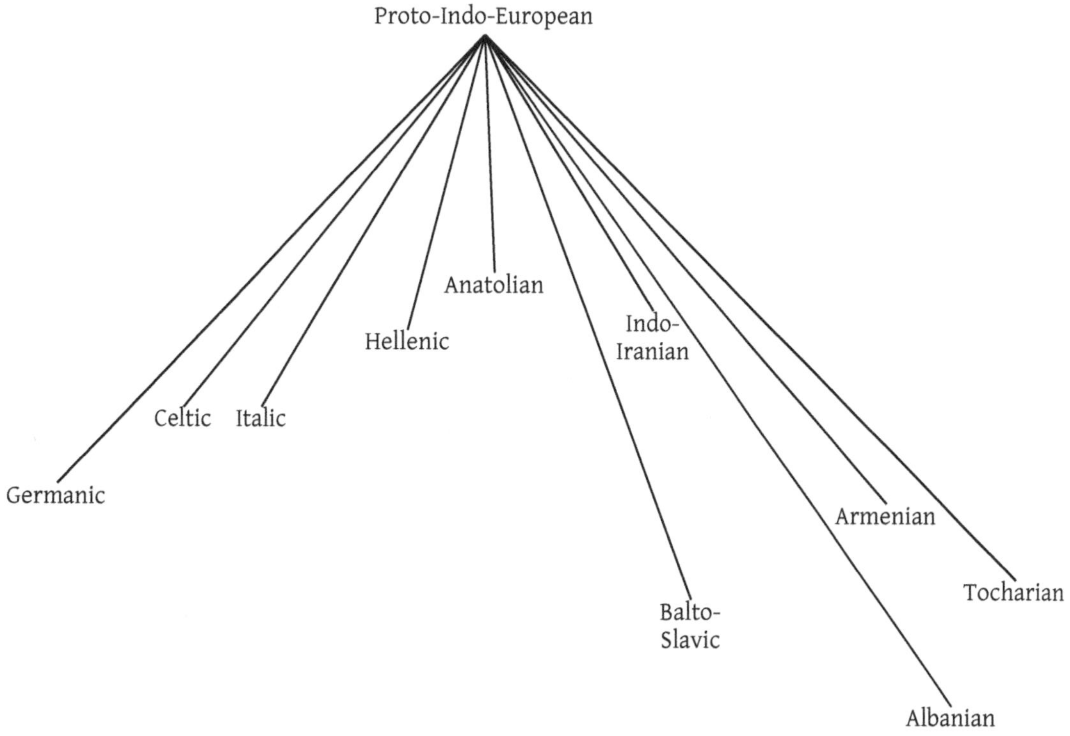

1. Indo-European and the Indo-Europeans

Who are the Indo-Europeans? What constitutes an Indo-European language? In the ensuing excerpt from his introductory chapter appearing in The American Heritage Dictionary of Indo-European Roots, *Calvert Watkins presents an overview of early developments in the scholarly discipline of Indo-European linguistics, beginning with the eighteenth-century British jurist Sir William Jones (1746–1794). Watkins then provides his readers with a survey of the language groups that comprise the Indo-European language family: Anatolian, Indo-Iranian, Hellenic, Italic, Celtic, Germanic, Armenian, Tocharian, Balto-Slavic, Albanian, as well as so-called "minor Indo-European languages," such as Phrygian and Messapic.* (RDW)

INDO-EUROPEAN AND THE INDO-EUROPEANS

Calvert Watkins

Indo-European is the name given for geographic reasons to the large and well-defined linguistic family that includes most of the languages of Europe, past and present, as well as those found in a vast area extending across Iran and Afghanistan to the northern half of the Indian subcontinent. In modern times the family has spread by colonization throughout the Western Hemisphere.

A curious byproduct of the age of colonialism and mercantilism was the introduction of Sanskrit in the 18th century to European intellectuals and scholars long familiar with Latin and Greek and with the European languages of culture—Romance, Germanic, and Slavic. The comparison of the classical language of India with the two classical languages of Europe revolutionized the perception of linguistic relationships.

Speaking to the Asiatick Society in Calcutta on February 2, 1786, the English Orientalist and jurist Sir William Jones (1746–1794) uttered his now famous pronouncement:

> The Sanskrit language, whatever be its antiquity, is of a wonderful structure; more perfect than the Greek, more copious than the Latin, and more exqui-

> sitely refined than either, yet bearing to both of them a stronger affinity, both in the roots of verbs and in the forms of grammar, than could possibly have been produced by accident; so strong, indeed, that no philologer could examine them all three, without believing them to have sprung from some common source, which, perhaps, no longer exists.

Jones was content with the assertion of a common original language, without exploring the details. Others took up the cause, but it remained for the German philologist Franz Bopp (1791–1867) to found the new science of comparative grammar, with the publication in 1816 of his work *On the Conjugational System of the Sanskrit Language, in Comparison with that of the Greek, Latin, Persian, and Germanic Languages*. He was 25 years old when it appeared.

It has been rightly said that the comparatist has one fact and one hypothesis. The one fact is that certain languages present similarities among themselves which are so numerous and so precise that they cannot be attributed to chance and which are such that they cannot be explained as borrowings or as universal features. The one hypothesis is that these languages must then be the result of descent from a common original. Certain similarities may be accidental: the Greek verb "to breathe," "blow," has a root *pneu-*, and in the language of the Klamath of Oregon the verb "to blow" is *pniw-*, but these languages are not remotely related. Other similarities may reflect universal or near-universal features of human language: in the languages of most countries where the bird is known, the *cuckoo* has a name derived from the noise it makes. A vast number of languages around the globe have "baby talk" words like *mama* and *papa*. Finally, languages commonly borrow words and other features from one another, in a whole gamut of ways ranging from casual or chance contact to learned coinages of the kind that English systematically makes from Latin and Greek.

But where all of these possibilities must be excluded, the comparatist assumes genetic filiation: descent from a common ancestor. In the case of Indo-European, as Sir William Jones surmised over two centuries ago, that ancestor no longer exists.

In the early part of the 19th century scholars set about systematically exploring the similarities observable among the principal languages spoken now or formerly in the regions from Iceland and Ireland in the west to India in the east and from Scandinavia in the north to Italy and Greece in the south. They were able to group these languages into a family that they called *Indo-European* (the term first occurs in English in 1813, though in a sense slightly different from today's). The similarities among the different Indo-European languages require us to assume that they are the continuation of a single prehistoric language, a language we call *Indo-European* or *Proto-Indo-European*. In the words of the greatest Indo-Europeanist of his age, the French scholar Antoine Meillet (1866–1936), "We will term *Indo-European language* every language which at any time whatever, in any place whatever, and however altered, is a form taken by this ancestor language, and which thus continues by an uninterrupted tradition the use of Indo-European."

The dialects or branches of Indo-European still represented today by one or more languages are Indo-Iranian, Greek, Armenian, Balto-Slavic, Albanian, Celtic, Italic, and Germanic. The present century has seen the addition of two branches to the family, both of which are extinct: Hittite and other Anatolian languages, the earliest attested in the Indo-European family, spoken in what is now Turkey in the second and first millennia B.C.; and the two Tocharian languages, the easternmost of Indo-European dialects, spoken in Chinese Turkestan (modern Xinjiang Uygur) in the first millennium A.D. (An outline of all the branches is provided further below in the text.)

It should be pointed out that the Indo-European family is only one of many language families that have been identified around the world, comprising several thousand different languages. We have good reason, however, to be especially interested in the history of the Indo-European family. Our own language, English, is its most prevalent member, the native language of nearly 350 million people and the most important second language in the world. The total number of speakers of all Indo-European languages amounts to approximately half the population of the earth.

English is thus one of many direct descendants of Indo-European: one of the dialects of the parent language became prehistoric Common Germanic, which subdivided into dialects of which one was West Germanic; this in turn broke up into further dialects, one of which emerged into documentary attestation as Old English. From Old English we can follow the development of the language directly, in texts, down to the present day.

This history is our linguistic heritage; our ancestors, in a real cultural sense, are our linguistic ancestors. But it must be stressed that linguistic heritage, while it may tend to correspond with cultural continuity, does not imply genetic or biological descent. The transmission of language by conquest, assimilation, migration, or any other ethnic movement is a complex and enigmatic process that this discussion does not propose to examine—beyond the general proposition that in the case of Indo-European no genetic conclusions can or should be drawn.

Although English is a member of the Germanic branch of Indo-European and retains much of the basic structure of its origin, it has an exceptionally mixed lexicon. During the 1400 years of its documented history, it has borrowed extensively and systematically from its Germanic and Romance neighbors and from Latin and Greek, as well as more sporadically from other languages. At the same time, it has lost the great bulk of its original Old English vocabulary. However, the inherited vocabulary, though now numerically a small proportion of the total, remains the genuine core of the language; all of the 100 words shown to be the most frequent in the Corpus of Present-Day American English, also known as the Brown Corpus, are native words; and of the second 100, 83 are native. A children's tale like *The Little Red Hen*, for example, contains virtually no loanwords.

Yet precisely because of its propensity to borrow from ancient and modern Indo-European languages, especially those mentioned above but including nearly every other member of the family, English has in a way replaced much of the Indo-European lexicon it lost. Thus, while the distinction between native and borrowed vocabulary remains fundamentally important, more than 50 percent of the basic roots of Indo-European as represented in Julius Pokorny's *Indogermanisches Etymologisches Wörterbuch* [*Indo-European Etymological Dictionary*] (Bern, 1959) are represented in modern English by one means or the other. Indo-European therefore looms doubly large in the background of our language.

After the initial identification of a prehistoric language underlying the modern Indo-European family and the foundation of the science of comparative linguistics, the detailed reconstruction of Proto-Indo-European proceeded by stages still fascinating to observe. The main outlines of the reconstructed language were already seen by the end of the 1870s, but it was only during the course of the 20th century that certain of these features received general acceptance. The last decades of the 20th century have happily witnessed a resurgence of Indo-European studies, catalyzed by advances in linguistic theory and an increase in the available data that have resulted in a picture of the reconstructed protolanguage that is, in a word, tighter. The grammar of Indo-European today is more thoroughly organized and more sharply focused, at all levels. There are fewer loose ends, fewer hazy areas, and those that remain are more clearly

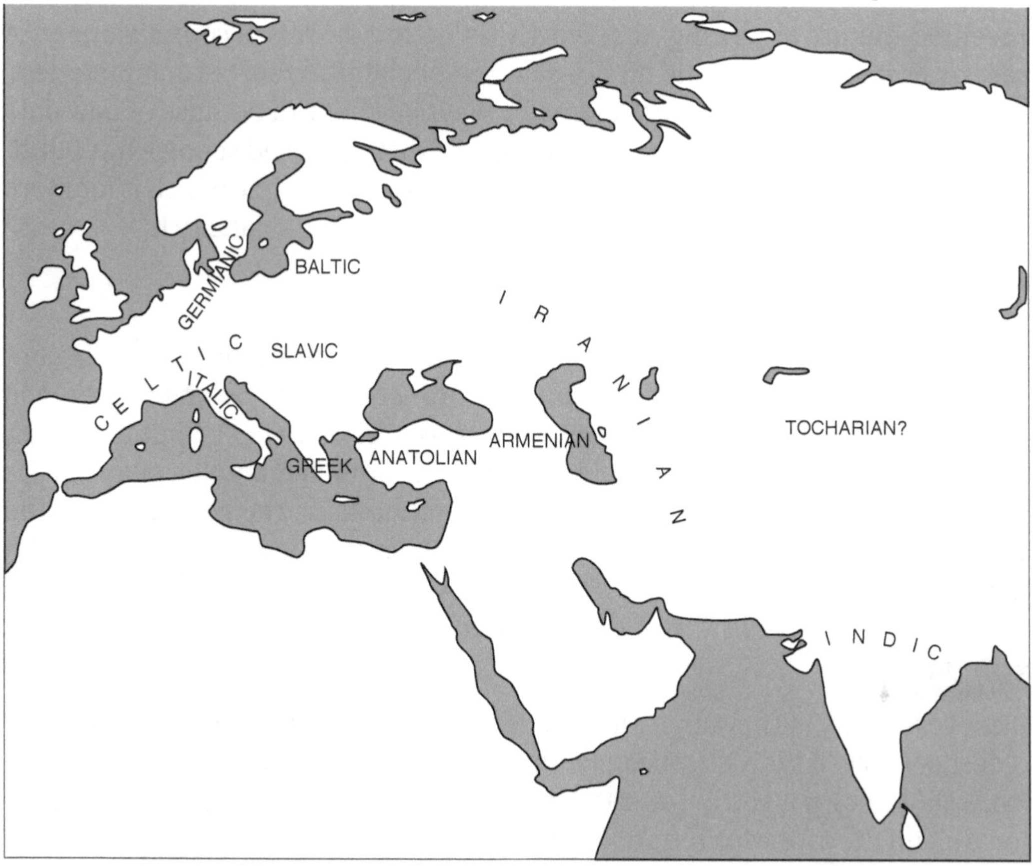

Geographical distribution of the major Indo-European peoples in the first millennium B.C.

identified as such. New etymologies continue to be made, new roots are recognized, and older etymologies undergo revision to incorporate new evidence or better analyses. The attention to detail in reconstruction in this newly revised *Dictionary of Indo-European Roots* reflects these ongoing developments in the field: Indo-European studies are alive with excitement, growth, and change.

The comparative method—what we have called the comparatist's "one fact and one hypothesis"—remains today the most powerful device for elucidating linguistic history. When it is carried to a successful conclusion, the comparative method leads not merely to the assumption of the previous existence of an antecedent common language but to a reconstruction of all the salient features of that language. In the best circumstances, as with Indo-European, we can reconstruct the sounds, forms, words, even the structure of sentences—in short, both grammar and lexicon—of a language spoken before the human race had invented the art of writing. It is worth reflecting on this accomplishment. A reconstructed grammar and dictionary cannot claim any sort of completeness, to be sure, and the reconstruction may always be changed because of new data or better analysis. But it remains true, as one distinguished scholar has put it, that a reconstructed protolanguage is "a glorious artifact, one which is far more precious than anything an archaeologist can ever hope to unearth."

The Branches of Indo-European

According to the most widely accepted model, the Indo-European family contains ten principal branches. Some of the branches likely belong together in larger subgroupings, but the details are controversial and need not detain us. A general outline of the historical settings of the branches is given below in the order of their earliest attestation, with an emphasis on the geographical and temporal locations of the relevant peoples. <This outline is meant to complement the chart of the family on pages 148–149, to which the reader is referred for a comprehensive listing of the individual languages.>

ANATOLIAN

Discovered only in the 20th century, the extinct Anatolian branch contains the oldest preserved Indo-European languages, spoken in what is now Turkey and Syria. Best known is Hittite, attested in over 10,000 clay tablet fragments in Babylonian cuneiform script found in Boğazköy (central Turkey) and dating from ca. 1700–ca. 1200 B.C. Cuneiform Luvian and the closely related Hieroglyphic Luvian were spoken in southern and western Anatolia. A form of Luvian was probably the language of Troy and the Trojans. Hieroglyphic Luvian continued to be attested in monumental and other inscriptions in southeast Turkey and northern Syria until ca. 750 B.C. Inscriptions in other Anatolian languages, in a variety of scripts, date to as late as the fourth century B.C.

INDO-IRANIAN

The Indo-Iranian branch includes various ancient and modern languages of a large part of central and southern Asia. The original homeland of the Indo-Iranians is not certain, but by the early second millennium B.C., Indic and Iranian peoples had migrated southward into Afghanistan and the eastern Iranian plateau. The Iranian tribes remained or moved westward and would later spread out over vast stretches of western and central Asia. An Indo-Aryan group apparently established itself as a ruling class among speakers of Hurrian (a non-

Indo-European language of the ancient Near East), perhaps in Iran, who later migrated into eastern Anatolia where they established the kingdom of Mittanni (the details are conjectural). The Mittanni in Anatolia would eventually die out, but not before leaving us (via Hittite) the first remains in an Indic language—a number of words and names preserved in Anatolian inscriptions from ca. 1500 B.C. The oldest preserved literature in both Indic and Iranian is in the form of orally-composed hymns: the Rig-Veda in the Indic language Sanskrit, probably dating from the latter half of the second millennium B.C.; and the songs traditionally attributed to Zarathustra (Zoroaster) in the Iranian language Avestan, more or less contemporary with the Rig-Veda. These texts were not written down until long after they were composed. The oldest written Indic texts are in Middle Indic (Pali) from about the fifth century B.C., and the oldest Iranian texts are in Old Persian, found in monumental inscriptions from the Achaemenid dynasty (sixth to fourth centuries B.C.), notably those of Darius and his son Xerxes. Iranian is continued by the modern languages of Iran and Afghanistan and by languages spoken by minorities in Iraq and Turkey; Indic is continued by Hindi-Urdu and the other Indo-Aryan languages of southern Asia.

GREEK (HELLENIC)

The sole member of the Hellenic branch is Greek, the European language with the longest recorded history (over 3000 years down to the present). It has at various times been spoken not only in Greece but also in colonies in Asia, Africa, and Italy. The oldest Greek inscriptions, in the Mycenaean dialect, are written in a non-alphabetic script called Linear B that was not deciphered until 1952; they date from about the 13th century B.C. The oldest alphabetic Greek is the poetry of Homer, originally oral compositions that reached something like their present form by the eighth century B.C.

ITALIC

The Italic branch is inscriptionally attested in central and southern Italy from the sixth or seventh century B.C. At that time it consisted of many languages and dialects of limited geographic distribution (such as Oscan, Umbrian, and Faliscan), most of them known only from meager remains. One of these local languages, however, would eventually eclipse all the rest and spread throughout the Mediterranean basin: Latin, the language of Rome. The other Italic languages died out, at least in written form, by the dawn of the Christian era. The descendants of Latin are the modern Romance languages.

CELTIC

The Celtic branch and most of its speakers are now restricted geographically to parts of the British Isles and northern France; but the Celts once were the most powerful and widespread people of western Europe. By the latter half of the first millennium B.C., Celtic territory stretched from the Iberian peninsula north through France and east through southern Germany, Switzerland, northern Italy, Austria, the former Czechoslovakia, and the Danube plain, with some groups as far east as Galatia in central Anatolia. The extinct Celtic languages of continental Europe, forming the Continental Celtic branch, are attested inscriptionally from the sixth or seventh century B.C. to the third century A.D.; best known of these is Gaulish. The Celtic languages of the British Isles (Insular Celtic) first appear inscriptionally around 400 A.D. with the earliest Irish stone carvings in the ogham alphabet. The surviving Insular Celtic languages of culture, Irish, Welsh, and Breton (brought to Brittany by migration from Britain), are now the only branch of Indo-European threatened with extinction.

GERMANIC

Germanic dialects were spoken prehistorically by tribes occupying an area of northern Europe east of the Rhine and stretching north through Denmark into parts of Norway and Sweden. Successive waves of migration in the first millennium A.D. resulted in a great expansion of Germanic-speaking territory. The earliest Germanic inscriptions, in a language called Runic, are from Scandinavia and are written in the runic alphabet; they date from the early third century A.D. The oldest extensive text in a Germanic language is a translation of the New Testament written in Gothic (now extinct) in the fourth century A.D. Of the living Germanic languages, English has the longest recorded history, with incriptions dating to the fifth century A.D. and literature to the eighth.

ARMENIAN

The oldest Armenian text dates from the fifth century A.D., a Bible translation in Classical Armenian; but Armenians are present in the historical record from much earlier, having probably already settled in eastern Turkey by the mid-second millennium B.C. Today Armenian is spoken in diverse dialects in Armenia and surrounding areas of Turkey, the Caucasus, and the Near East, and, following the 20th-century diaspora, in Europe and the Americas.

TOCHARIAN

Like Anatolian, Tocharian was not discovered until the 20th century and is an extinct branch of the family. The two Tocharian languages, termed A and B, are preserved in Buddhist writings from ca. 600–800 and were unearthed in Chinese Turkestan (now Xinjiang Uygur in western China).

BALTO-SLAVIC

Slavic languages have been spoken since prehistoric times in areas of eastern Europe that were bordered on the west by territories inhabited by Germanic peoples. Christian missionaries from Byzantium converted the Slavs in the ninth century and introduced writing; the earliest surviving text is an Old Church Slavonic translation of the Bible, also from the ninth century. The closely related Baltic languages, spoken (also apparently since ancient times) to the north, first appear in writing with words and phrases in the extinct Old Prussian from the 14th and 16th centuries. The two living Baltic languages, Lithuanian and Latvian, were written down starting in the 16th century.

ALBANIAN

Albanian, spoken now in Albania and parts of Italy in two dialects, northern (Gheg) and southern (Tosk), is not attested until the 15th century. The prehistory of Albanian is controversial; the language is considered by some to be the descendant of a very poorly known ancient Balkan language, Daco-Mysian.

OTHER BRANCHES

Besides these ten branches, a number of scantily attested (and not well understood) ancient languages are known that are clearly Indo-European but of uncertain filiation within the family: Phrygian in Anatolia, Thracian in the Balkans, Venetic and Messapic in Italy. They are preserved in short inscriptions mostly from the first millennium B.C.

2. Linguistic Reconstruction

The linguistic method used for reconstructing earlier, unattested forms of languages and language systems, such as the parent language of the Indo-European language family, Proto-Indo-European, is called the comparative method of historical linguistics. *In the following introduction to his book* Linguistic Reconstruction, *Anthony Fox presents an overview of this method—one of the most remarkable scientific achievements to come out of the nineteenth century. As Watkins noted above, the inception of the scientific discipline of comparative grammar is commonly attributed to the German scholar Franz Bopp (1791-1867). Prominent roles in the early development of the comparative method were played by, among others, Bopp's fellow countryman Jacob Grimm (1785-1863), perhaps more readily recognized for the collection of German "fairy tales" that he assembled together with his brother, Wilhelm Grimm (1786-1859), and by the Danish scholar Rasmus Rask (1787-1832)—both of whom applied the comparative method to the study of the Indo-European languages. Significant advances in the reconstruction of primitive Indo-European were made by the German August Schleicher (1821-1868) in the middle of the nineteenth century, and in the second half of that century by that group of scholars known as the Neogrammarians, most notably Hermann Osthoff (1847-1909) and Karl Brugmann (1849-1919).*

Within French-speaking Europe in the nineteenth century, comparative grammar was no less the object of scientific exploration. Michel Bréal (1832-1915) facilitated the spread of Bopp's ideas about comparative grammar in France with his translation of Bopp's four-volume work, Vergleichende Grammatik, *into French. While in Germany the Neogrammarians were elevating the reconstruction of primitive Indo-European to new levels of precision, Bréal was turning his attention to a different sort of comparative venture, the study of Indo-European religion and myth. Upon his retirement from the École des Hautes Études in Paris, Bréal was succeeded by a young Swiss scholar, Ferdinand de Saussure (1857-1913). At an early age, Saussure had produced a remarkably sophisticated comparative study of the Indo-European vowel system, but he is undoubtedly best known as the founder of the modern study of synchronic language structures, often dubbed the "father" of the discipline of general linguistics. Among Saussure's students was Antoine Meillet (1866-1936), who would become what Watkins above (in the preceding reading) terms "the greatest Indo-Europeanist of his age." Benveniste, Dumézil, and Watkins are all three the intellectual heirs of Meillet, with his exacting precision, and of Bréal, with his extension of comparativism to the realm of the social constructs of religion and myth.* (RDW)

LINGUISTIC RECONSTRUCTION

Anthony Fox

Why Reconstruction?

Languages are not static, but are constantly changing: the latest slang comes and goes, our own language is subtly, but noticeably, different from that of our grandparents, and the further back we go in time the more remote and incomprehensible the language seems to be. Shakespeare's language is difficult for us; Chaucer's even more so; and should we be bold enough to peruse the writings of King Alfred, who lived in the ninth century, we will barely understand a word, even though he wrote in 'English'. At the same time, we also notice that some foreign languages, such as German or Dutch, have some similarities to English, which we assume to be the result of the common origins of English and these languages. Over the course of time the languages have diverged, to the point where they are mutually incomprehensible. How and why did these changes come about, and what means can we use to find out?

It is one of the tasks of linguistics, and specifically historical linguistics, to attempt to answer these questions. Historical linguists study these developments, documenting the changes that have taken place, and are still taking place, in the pronunciation, grammar, and vocabulary of the languages of the world, and relating them to the historical and cultural context in which they occur. They examine the characteristics of related languages, and try to determine the scope and nature of their relationships, and the historical connections between them. And, finally, they attempt to go beyond the history of individual languages, to an understanding of the general principles which underlie *all* language change. To pursue such broad aims, it is necessary to examine a wide range of evidence, from ancient inscriptions and manuscripts to the results of dialect surveys; from the rhyming schemes of poets to the remarks of writers and grammarians; from historical relics within languages themselves to evidence provided by comparison with other related languages. These different kinds of data demand a variety of different methods of analysis and interpretation.

It is helpful to draw a distinction here between the study of language *history* on the one hand, and its *prehistory* on the other. In the former case we are concerned with changes in languages as reflected in texts, inscriptions, and other documentary evidence; in the latter with changes occurring before the appearance of such evidence. The distinction must not be exaggerated, since the aim—to understand the changes that have occurred in a language or group of languages—remains the same in either case, and it may therefore seem unimportant whether the evidence is derived from historical or prehistoric sources. In any case, the discovery of new evidence, or a new interpretation of existing evidence, may provide documentation for what was previously undocumented, changing prehistory into history. We cannot, therefore, always keep these two perspectives apart. Nevertheless the distinction is a valid and significant one, since the methods, and the status of their findings, are necessarily very different in the two cases.

In the overwhelming majority of instances, study of the documented history of languages is severely limited owing to a lack of available material: most of the world's languages are still unwritten, and documentary evidence is simply non-existent. Even in cases where we are more fortunate, for example with the classical languages of Europe and with the ancient languages of the Near East, documentary evidence can still take us back only a relatively short distance along the path of their historical development. Study of linguistic prehistory is therefore our only means of acquiring adequate knowledge of earlier stages of these languages. Furthermore, it is not merely a desire to trace the source of languages as far back into prehistoric times as possible, legitimate though this may be, that leads us to study the prehistory of languages; the investigation of linguistic prehistory is also prompted by questions that are raised by the historical data themselves and which cannot be answered by historical sources alone. The earliest historically attested forms of languages may contain anomalies and historical fossils, while different languages may show clear affinities which point to historical connections between them. The explanations for these phenomena can generally not be found in documentary historical evidence, but must be sought in undocumented prehistory.

It is in such prehistoric investigation of language and languages that LINGUISTIC RECONSTRUCTION becomes of central importance. This term refers to the practice of creating, on the basis of extant historical evidence, hypothetical language forms from which the actually occurring forms of one or more languages may be systematically derived. Given certain assumptions—to which we shall return below—these hypothetical forms may be equated with earlier forms of the language or languages in question, and hence the procedure can be said to 'reconstruct' such forms, though, as we shall see, not all scholars have considered it necessary, or indeed desirable, to assume historical reality for the reconstructed forms.

In practice, reconstruction can be said to have two roles. On the one hand it can be considered as part of the *process* of investigating historical linguistic data; by reconstructing hypothetical, abstract forms we may relate sets of words or their parts in a language or languages to one another, and such forms can be said to have methodological value as hypotheses about the historical relationships between the languages: they are part of the process of investigating linguistic history. But on the other hand, these forms, which are produced only after careful comparison of the data from specific languages, are also the *products* of the investigation, encapsulating its results. Linguistic reconstruction may therefore become not merely a *tool* in the historical analysis of languages but the *goal* of this analysis: we reconstruct earlier forms of languages not merely to explain historical relationships between present-day languages but in order to find out what the earlier languages themselves were actually like. Again depending on the status we accord to our reconstructions, this in turn may have wider significance, since reconstruction of languages brings with it cultural, social, and ethnological implications relating to the speakers of these languages and to the conditions under which they lived. The rather restricted objective of explaining specific forms of attested languages may thus move naturally to the exploration of remote and unrecorded cultures and peoples.

This prospect is doubtless an attractive one, which offers us the possibility of discovering something of our own origins. However, whether it is a legitimate or even attainable goal of historical linguistics is a matter on which there is some divergence of views, since the re-creation of earlier cultures is not something that can be undertaken using linguistic evidence alone, but requires evidence from other sources, such as archaeology and anthropology. The aims of this book, however, are at once less ambitious and more fundamental: we shall be exploring the *methods* of linguistic reconstruction, the means that linguists actually employ in their study of linguistic prehistory. As in any discipline, the scope and validity of the results that can be obtained are directly dependent on the adequacy and reliability of the methods used. Whatever may be the ultimate objective in reconstructing earlier forms of languages, without an understanding of the nature of these methods, of the assumptions on which they rest and the limitations to which they are subject, no wider conclusions can in any case be drawn.

The Methods of Reconstruction

Although there has probably always been speculation about the origin of individual languages and of language itself, it was only towards the end of the eighteenth century that the historical study of languages became systematic, and it was only gradually, with increased knowledge and increasing confidence in the methods used, that such study could result in serious attempts to reconstruct earlier forms. This is not to say that there had not been earlier attempts of this kind; many of the similarities between the languages of Europe are too evident to have escaped the notice of scholars, and these similarities certainly provoked speculation as to possible relationships between these languages, and possible common sources.[1] But such speculation was more philosophical than linguistic, and it remained unsystematic, without a consistent methodology.

It was nevertheless recognized from an early date that an understanding of the historical relationships between languages demanded *comparison* of those languages. In the course of the nineteenth century such comparison became more systematic, more reliable, and more 'scientific', and by the latter part of the century it was elevated to the status of a scientific procedure: the COMPARATIVE METHOD. Strictly speaking, the Comparative Method and the reconstruction of earlier forms on the basis of such comparison are logically distinct, but from the middle of the nineteenth century the two go hand in hand, reconstruction being the natural result of attempts to relate the forms of attested languages. <We shall consider the Comparative Method in detail in later chapters of this book.>

Improvements in the methodology arose gradually as more became known of the characteristics of language itself (especially in the area of phonetics), and in response to the various problems that were encountered and solved. The major area of application of the 'classical' method was the Indo-European languages, that language family that stretches from western Europe to southern Asia, and includes English and virtually all of the classical and modern languages of Europe, as well as Sanskrit and the languages of northern India; but the method was also applied elsewhere, for example to the Semitic and Finno-Ugrian languages.[2] In the Indo-European field, the basic results of the application of the method were established very comprehensively by the end of the nineteenth century—a notable intellectual achievement, since the whole subject area did not exist a century earlier.

All this was achieved within a conceptual framework which viewed language as essentially a historically determined object, and the study of language itself as in principle a historical discipline. This view was to be maintained well into the present century, but towards the end of the last century there was already an increasing awareness that language could also be seen as a coherent entity in itself, independently of its history. This view, first articulated in a consistent and coherent manner by the Swiss linguist Ferdinand de Saussure in lectures before the First World War,[3] has come to dominate language study in the twentieth century, with the development, first, of STRUCTURALIST linguistics as an essentially non-historical discipline, and more recently of various theories of GENERATIVE GRAMMAR. In the case of structuralist theories the emphasis is on language as an autonomous or independent SYSTEM, with a patterned formal STRUCTURE; the aim of linguistic study is therefore to establish and explore the nature of this system and this structure. In Generative Grammar the focus has been on the GRAMMAR, seen as a set of rules and conditions on rules, which underlies the sentences of a language; here the task is not merely the description of the grammar of individual languages but the explanation of this grammar in terms of the human language faculty. The implications of both these approaches for historical linguistics and for linguistic reconstruction will be followed up later, but the important point here is that in both cases language is seen primarily as a coherent entity existing at a particular time, rather than merely as the product of historical developments.

The rise of linguistics as a non-historical discipline in the twentieth century has inevitably had important consequences for the historical study of language. The point is not so much that this linguistics threatens to supplant historical language study (though institutionally this has occurred to a considerable extent, with the establishment of departments of linguistics in universities and the decline in historically based courses), but rather that we may now recognize two complementary dimensions of language which, following Saussure, are designated the DIACHRONIC (historical) and the SYNCHRONIC (non-historical). For historical linguistics this development has a negative side, inasmuch as historical facts may be relegated to secondary importance, but on the positive side the recognition of these two dimensions opens up new possibilities: first, synchronic linguistics has developed a range of methods and categories which can be used to make more explicit the procedures and concepts used in historical linguistic study; second, and more importantly, it has increased our understanding of the nature of language itself, enabling us to invoke aspects of synchronic language structure in our efforts to understand the diachronic development and to reconstruct earlier forms. In other words, instead of seeing a language as the rather arbitrary and unsystematic product of historical processes, we may view these historical processes themselves as in part the reflection of systematic regularities in the nature and structure of languages.

Given these new insights, it became possible for the Comparative Method, which, though it was the mainstay of historical linguistics in the nineteenth century, was never clearly formalized at that time, to receive more formal and rigorous treatment within the framework of twentieth-century structuralist linguistics. Furthermore, new methods of historical investigation were rendered possible, in particular the method of INTERNAL RECONSTRUCTION, whose origins go back to the late nineteenth century but which developed into a standard tool in the first half of the twentieth. It relies essentially on the historical interpretation of patterned linguistic structure in a way that would hardly have been possible before the development of structuralist linguistics. Unlike the Comparative Method, Internal Reconstruction does not depend on the comparison of related languages to establish hypothetical forms but rather on internal evidence from within a single language. <As we shall see in Chapter 7,> certain systematic regularities within the language are assumed to have a historical origin, so that again we may reconstruct a hypothetical source. Once more the historical status of such reconstructed forms is a controversial matter which will be addressed below.

Although the Comparative Method, and to a lesser degree Internal Reconstruction, remain the most important methods of reconstruction, during the twentieth century a number of other techniques of reconstruction have been devised, <which we shall also examine in later chapters.> A new dimension to reconstruction has been opened up by studies of LANGUAGE UNIVERSALS and LINGUISTIC TYPOLOGY. Here, we make the assumption that there are inherent characteristics of language, and general principles of language change, that are valid for all languages at all times and in all places. By applying such characteristics and principles to prehistoric forms we may attempt to determine the grammars and systems of reconstructed languages, and to recover the changes that they are likely to have undergone. A further avenue that has been explored is the possibility of using QUANTITATIVE criteria, and thus offering a challenge to the QUALITATIVE criteria of established scholarly methods, including the Comparative Method itself. Quantitative methods have been applied primarily by anthropological linguistis concerned with pre-literate cultures, where documentary evidence is insufficient to determine the relationships between languages by other means. Measures of linguistic relationships are established by quantitative comparisons of similarities between the basic vocabularies of languages.

<These methods will be explored and explained in later chapters of this book.> It should be noted, however, that for the most part they do not seek to supplant the 'classical' methods but rather to supplement them in various ways. Furthermore, as we shall see, they remain controversial, and their reliability and validity have not yet been established to the satisfaction of all scholars.

The Status and Limitations of Reconstructions

Although, as we have noted, the methods of reconstruction have been extremely successful, in the sense that they have allowed linguists to reconstruct earlier languages and to establish historical relationships between them, there are nevertheless a number of general reservations that must be made at this stage. It is, of course, inevitable that there will be disagreements among scholars about the justification for this or that reconstruction of a particular form; such disagreements are neither surprising nor particularly damaging. More important are disputes about the validity of the methods of reconstruction themselves. No method in any human discipline is entirely reliable in its application; all methods have gaps and blind spots with which they cannot deal adequately, and it is important to establish the limitations of the methods that are being used. But it is also important to distinguish between limitations which arise from inadequacies of the methods themselves on the one hand, and those which arise from the circumstances in which the methods are applied on the other.

For example, the success of the methods of reconstruction inevitably depends on the quality and quantity of the data to which they are applied, and since in many cases the data on which reconstructions are based are sparse and unreliable, the reconstructions themselves are at best tentative. Clearly, such limitations cannot be attributed to weaknesses in the methods themselves; where the evidence is lost or unavailable, even the most reliable of methods cannot recover it, and little can be done in such cases except to search for more and better evidence. The nature of the evidence will also determine which of the methods of reconstruction can be applied, and in what way. The Indo-European languages constitute a very rich source of data, with a large number of languages, some of which have records stretching back over several millennia; moreover, their history and relationships have been studied intensively for 200 years. The indigenous languages of Africa and America, on the other hand, are very poorly recorded; evidence for their history is scant, and they have only begun to be studied in relatively recent times. Reconstruction of the earlier forms of these languages is therefore a rather different kind of task in each case, even where the same methods are applied. The Comparative Method, which depends on a plentiful supply of well-ordered data, is likely to be rather more successful in the former case than in the latter, for which quantitative techniques might be more appropriate. And even in the case of the Indo-European languages there are differences in the applicability of the methods. The earlier form of the Romance languages, Latin, is amply attested; this does not necessarily make it superfluous to reconstruct it, as the evidence provided by reconstruction complements that of the documentary sources, and the latter also provides a valuable means of testing the method itself.[4] But the situation is very different with the Germanic or the Celtic languages, where no comparable earlier form has been handed down to us. The procedures involved in reconstruction will evidently be somewhat different in these different cases.

More significant are the problems which derive from weaknesses in the methods themselves. All methods of reconstruction are based on a number of assumptions about the nature of the data examined, the kind of changes that can occur, and ultimately about the nature of language itself. If these assumptions are false or inaccurate, the results we obtain from the application of the methods are unlikely to be reliable. <Some of the more specific weaknesses and limitations of the individual methods can only be considered in the light of the more detailed discussion of these methods that will be conducted in later chapters of this book.> We may nevertheless examine one question at the outset which is fundamental to the whole enterprise of linguistic reconstruction: the status of reconstructed forms themselves. This question is of long standing in historical linguistics, and we cannot necessarily expect a clear and definitive answer.

As we have already observed, reconstructed forms are initially hypothetical abstractions which result from attempts to relate attested linguistic forms, whether across different languages (as in the case of the Comparative Method) or within a single language (as in the case of Internal Reconstruction). But are we entitled to claim for such reconstructions the status of earlier linguistic forms? This controversy can be summed up in a confrontation between two views of reconstruction: the FORMULIST and the REALIST. The formulist view regards reconstructions merely as formulae which represent the various relationships within the data, while the less cautious realist view assumes that reconstructions can be taken to represent genuine historical forms of a real language, which happen not to have been recorded. Which of these two views is the more appropriate?

The key to this controversy lies in the relationship between methodology on the one hand and historical reality on the other. As we have observed, reconstruction, either by the Comparative Method or Internal Reconstruction, involves postulating abstract forms—conventionally marked with an asterisk to indicate their hypothetical status[5]—from which the attested forms can be derived. Forms reconstructed by means of the Comparative Method are called PROTO-FORMS, and 'languages' consisting of such forms are PROTO-LANGUAGES. As an illustration consider the reconstruction of the Proto-Indo-European form of the word for *father*. Attested forms in a number of ancient languages are as follows:

Latin	*Greek*	*Sanskrit*	*Old High German*
pater	patɛ:r	pita:	fater

On the basis of data such as these, the 'classical' methods of reconstruction are able to establish a Proto-Indo-European form **pəte:r* from which the data themselves may be derived by a series of regular processes: **ə* is regularly converted to [a] in Latin, Greek, and Old High German, and into [i] in Sanskrit; in Old High German **p* appears as [f], and so on.[6]

What does the form **pəte:r* represent here? In its extreme version the formulist view would regard it as no more than a set of symbols representing these regular relationships between attested languages: **ə* is shorthand for 'Latin, Greek, and Old High German [a] and Sanskrit [i]', **p* for 'Latin, Greek, and Sanskrit [p], and Old High German [f]', and so on. The form **pəteːr* will thus have no status as a word, but merely as a formula. It would therefore be possible to use any arbitrary symbols here, since those that are used do not represent real sounds. In place of *ə we might, for example, use *♠, and reconstruct a proto-form **p♠teːr*, which is, of course, unpronounceable. Furthermore, when we speak of 'deriving' the attested forms from the reconstructed forms we are not speaking in temporal terms but merely in terms of correspondence: Old High German [f] is 'derived' from Proto-Indo-European **p* not in a historical sense but merely in the sense that it belongs to the set of correspondences represented by this symbol.

Consider now the alternative realist view. According to this conception, **pəteːr* is not just an abstract formula but an actual (or at least potential) linguistic form, with all the characteristics that such a form would have in real languages, for example, it is meaningful and pronounceable. We may therefore assume that there once was a word with these characteristics in a real language, used by real people. There is therefore no justification for using arbitrary symbols to represent this form, as such symbols do not represent real sounds and are therefore unpronounceable. 'Reconstruction' is thus to be taken literally, as the *re-creation* of an actual word in a real language, and when we 'derive' attested forms from such a reconstruction, we are likewise claiming that this is a real historical process: **pəteːr* developed historically into the forms given above in the different languages.

Plausible arguments can be advanced in support of both the formulist and the realist positions. We must certainly acknowledge, for example, with the formulists, that reconstructions are abstractions which are dependent on the particular theoretical framework within which they are conceived, and this may lead us to conclude that they have no factual basis. But on the other hand *all* scientific constructs are abstract in this sense, and this does not necessarily prevent us from assuming the reality of the phenomena which they purport to describe. We cannot observe the reality behind, for example, the various subatomic particles postulated by physicists; they are the abstract products of a particular theory. Yet this does not prevent us from accepting them as real. The fact that we have no concrete evidence for our reconstructed forms does not mean, therefore, that they cannot be assumed to have existed. Of course, there must be *some* evidence for our reconstructed forms, just as there is experimental evidence for particles in physics. Here realists may point to many cases where corroborative evidence has subsequently come to light in support of reconstructed forms, and, perhaps most spectacularly, to the evidence of Hittite, whose decipherment early this century provided confirmation of the findings of Internal Reconstruction <(see below, Ch. 7)>. There is, furthermore, the evidence of Latin which, as we have noted, supports reconstructions of Proto-Romance. However, the existence of such corroborative evidence can clearly never be guaranteed.

Further formulist arguments are based on the deficiencies and distortions of the methods used in reconstruction. First, reconstructions are never complete, as we can never know all the details of forms and their uses; more seriously, they are often demonstrably inaccurate, and it is therefore illegitimate to place too much faith in reconstructed forms. The forms of reconstructed Proto-Indo-European have changed out of all recognition as successive generations of scholars have refined and amended their predecessors' work, and this process will continue; we can never be confident, therefore, that we have uncovered the 'truth'. Still more seriously, the methods often rest<, as we shall see in later chapters,> on patently false assumptions about the nature and the mechanisms of language change. All these criticisms lend weight to the formulist view of reconstruction. If our reconstructions are incomplete and inaccurate, and they rest on false premisses, then we apparently have little alternative but to regard them as merely formulae; to treat them as genuine linguistic forms is to distort and misrepresent reality in an unscientific manner.

Such arguments can be counterbalanced by other considerations, however. We might regard the methods, in spite of their acknowledged weaknesses, as necessary idealizations, which are in any case justified by their successes in allowing inferences to be drawn about the forms of unattested languages and the historical relationships between attested ones. Such idealizations are common elsewhere in linguistics, and they do not necessarily detract from the validity of the conclusions drawn. Furthermore, the assumption of historical reality for reconstructions may itself be a methodological requirement for some kinds of reconstruction. Recent work in reconstruction on a typological basis, for example, appeals to the overall internal organization of reconstructed languages as part of its methodology <(see Ch. 10)>. Yet the application of such criteria to these languages naturally assumes that they are indeed languages, with all the various properties that languages possess, including such attributes as meaningfulness, pronounceability, learnability, and so on. Merely to consider them as mathematical or methodological abstractions will not allow us to use criteria of this kind.

Finally, we may invoke the aim and purpose of reconstructions. From the formulist perspective, reconstructions have no historical validity; their value is heuristic (i.e. methodological) rather than historical. But the realist may counter with the claim that there is really little point in doing reconstruction if we are not prepared to ascribe historical reality to our reconstructed 'languages'. In the synchronic domain, linguists routinely introduce abstract concepts in order to explain data, and are prepared to ascribe to these abstractions some form of reality, often of a mental kind.[7] There is no obvious reason to exclude the historical study of language from such general practices.

In spite of the apparent incompatibility of these two positions, there does, in fact, appear to be a way of resolving the conflict between them, which consists in recognizing that there are two distinct, though interrelated aspects of the reconstruction process: the APPLICATION OF THE METHODS on the one hand and the INTERPRETATION OF THE RESULTS on the other. These are rather different procedures, with their own criteria of adequacy, which must not be confused. The methods themselves are not, and by their nature cannot be, concerned with the historical development of language as such. The Comparative Method, for example, simply compares features of different languages, while the method of Internal Reconstruction is concerned with synchronic aspects of a single language; neither is explicitly historical. To have historical relevance, the results must be *interpreted* in a particular way, so that the various relationships and entities are projected on to the historical plane, and given historical significance and validity.

This division is crucial for how we evaluate the methods and their results. Since the methods themselves are not inherently historical, they cannot be properly evaluated in historical terms, but only, as with all methodology, according to their own internal logic and consistency; for interpreting the results, on the other hand, the only relevant criterion is the historical validity of the inferences to be drawn from them. Putting this another way: the methods are formal procedures which produce particular results; these results can be taken as hypotheses about the historical facts; their historical validity will depend on other factors that are relevant to the process of interpretation, such as our knowledge of how languages change and of the principles on which languages are constructed and used, as well as any other historical or circumstantial evidence which may impinge on the interpretation. The evidence from the methods of reconstruction may often be the most important factor in this interpretation, but it is not necessarily the *only* evidence.

Recognition of these two aspects of the reconstruction process goes a long way towards reconciling the formulist and the realist positions, since it will be clear that both of these views are actually valid, but for different stages of the process. Procedurally, it is important to apply the methods consistently, even blindly, treating them, as the formulists would have it, as purely formal procedures with no historical implications. But, as the realists rightly maintain, to be significant the results must be interpretable in historical terms. On the one hand we may see it as merely scientifically prudent to treat our methods as no more than formal procedures, with their own logic, and to evaluate them solely in terms of their internal consistency, but on the other hand these methods must ultimately be answerable to broader external goals: an understanding of the actual changes which the language or languages investigated have undergone. The two perspectives are thus complementary.

<This dualism of method and interpretation will be a constant theme throughout this book.> As we examine the methods of reconstruction we will encounter again and again conflicts and discrepancies between the requirements imposed by the methods and the historical reality which underlies the phenomena themselves. Each of the methods can be seen as an attempt to provide—with varying degrees of success and reliability—evidence which can be interpreted in historical terms; the greater the possibility for historical interpretation of its results, the more useful the method will be. But we must bear in mind that the methods are not in themselves historical, and that the historical truth, in so far as it is obtainable, derives from the interpretation of the results, rather than from the methods themselves.

Notes

1. See especially Droixhe (1978) for discussion of seventeenth- and eighteenth-century ideas on language relationships.

2. There are a number of books available which give information about the various language families of the world. See, for example, Comrie (ed.) (1987), and Ruhlen (1987). It should be noted, however, that the classification of the world's languages is not complete, and is subject to many controversies.

3. Saussure's *Cours de linguistique générale*, compiled by his students from their lecture notes, was published in 1916.

4. In fact, the Romance languages are assumed to be derived not from the well-attested classical Latin but from the popular, but largely undocumented, speech of the Roman Empire. Reconstruction is therefore necessary even in this case. See Hall (1950), Pulgram (1961).

5. Note that this use of an asterisk is somewhat different from the convention in Generative Grammar, where it marks an 'ungrammatical' or impossible form or sentence.

6. Since the aim of the present book is an exposition of the principles of reconstruction and not an introduction to Indo-European linguistics, the forms given here are largely the traditional, conservative ones. <Some of the issues raised by more recent Indo-European studies will be considered in later chapters.>

7. As in the works of Chomsky, e.g. *Language and Mind* (1968), *Rules and Representations* (1980), *Knowledge of Language* (1986), and elsewhere.

Further Reading

GENERAL WORKS ON HISTORICAL LINGUISTICS

Anttila, R. (1972), *An Introduction to Historical and Comparative Linguistics.*

Arlotto, A. (1972), *Introduction to Historical Linguistics.*

Anderson, James M. (1973), *Structural Aspects of Language Change.*

Bynon, Th. (1977), *Historical Linguistics.*

Jeffers, R. J. and Lehiste, I. (1979), *Principles and Methods for Historical Linguistics.*

Hock, H. H. (1986), *Principles of Historical Linguistics.*

Aitchison, J. (1991), *Language Change: Progress or Decay?*

Crowley, T. (1992), *An Introduction to Historical Linguistics.*

Lehmann, W. P. (1992), *Historical Linguistics: An Introduction.*

——— (1993), *Theoretical Bases of Indo-European Linguistics.*

McMahon, A. M. S. (1994), *Understanding Language Change.*

GENERAL WORKS ON RECONSTRUCTION

Meillet, A. (1925), *La Méthode comparative en linguistique historique.*

Bloomfield, L. (1935), *Language*, ch. 18.

Tovar, A. (1954), 'Linguistics and Prehistory'.

Hockett, C. F. (1958), *A Course in Modern Linguistics*, ch. 55–60.

Hoenigswald, H. M. (1960), *Language Change and Linguistic Reconstruction.*

Hass, M. (1969), *The Prehistory of Languages.*

Katičić, R. (1970), *A Contribution to the General Theory of Comparative Linguistics.*

Birnbaum, H. (1978), *Linguistic Reconstruction: Its Potentials and Limitations in New Perspective.*

Lehmann, W. P. (1993), *Theoretical Bases of Indo-European Linguistics.*

ON THE STATUS OF RECONSTRUCTIONS

Meillet, A. (1925), *La Méthode comparative en linguistique historique.*

Bonfante, G. (1945), 'On Reconstruction and Linguistic Method'.

Allen, W. S. (1953), 'Relationship in Comparative Linguistics'.

Pulgram, E. (1959), 'Proto-Indo-European Reality and Reconstruction'.

Hall, R. (1960), 'On Realism in Reconstruction'.

Nehring, A. (1961), 'Zur "Realität" des Urindogermanischen'.

Pulgram, E. (1961), 'The Nature and Use of Proto-Languages'.

Zawadowski, L. (1962), 'Theoretical Foundations of Comparative Grammar'.

Katičić, R. (1970), *A Contribution to the General Theory of Comparative Linguistics.*

Wald, L. (1977), 'Réconstruction et linguistique générale'.

Koerner, E. F. K. (1989), 'Comments on Reconstructions in Historical Linguistics'.

Lass, R. (1993), 'How Real(ist) are Reconstructions?'

3. Indo-European Homeland

J.P. Mallory is well known as the author of an important book on the ancient Indo-European peoples, their cultures, their homeland, and their geographic distribution in historical times, In Search of the Indo-Europeans *(1989, London: Thames and Hudson). In the following article, Mallory focuses specifically on issues relating to the chronology and locale of the earliest Indo-European society. After surveying the history of scholarship treating the problem, and the methods and principles utilized in attempting to identify the Indo-European homeland, Mallory examines the four solutions to the homeland problem that have recently generated the greatest following, or attention: the Baltic-Pontic solution; the Anatolian solution; the Central Europe-Balkan solution; and the Pontic-Caspian solution.* (RDW)

INDO-EUROPEAN HOMELAND

J.P. Mallory

One of the longest standing and still unresolved problems, not only of Indo-European studies but also general prehistoric research, is the time and place of origin of the Indo-European language family and the nature of its dispersal. Solutions to the problem have been derived from the Bible and mythology, linguistics, physical anthropology, genetics, and archaeology.

Background to the Problem

The Indo-European languages begin to appear in the written record in the Bronze and Iron ages. The earliest attested languages are first encountered between Greece and northern India and consist of: Anatolian, the proper names of which are first attested in Akkadian trading documents of *c* 1900 B.C.; Indo-Aryan first emerges in northern Syria in the Mitanni kingdom by *c* 1600–1500 B.C.; and Greek which is known from the palace documents of the Mycenaeans, in the so-called Linear B script, from at least *c* 1300 B.C. By the Iron Age (*c* 700–1 B.C.) we have evidence for the Italic, Messapic, Celtic and Germanic stocks in the west, the Balkan languages such as Thracian, Dacian and Illyrian, Phrygian in Anatolia and first hand evidence of Iranian. The other IE languages, other than occasional parahistorical references, do not appear in written records until the first millennium A.D. or later. Although this evidence allows us to see the full "historical" distribution of the Indo-European languages of Eurasia, there are substantial reasons for rejecting the notion that this distribution had been stable for many thousands of years.

First, there is some evidence for the existence of relic non-IE populations that preceded IE expansions into their territories. In the Iberian peninsula there are Iron Age inscriptions in what would appear to have been two different non-IE languages known as Tartessian and Iberian while the modern (non-IE) Basque language, situated in northern Iberia and southern France, reinforces the notion that Spain and Portugal were the subject and not the source of IE expansions. Similarly, central and northern Italy offers the remains of the Etruscan, a language that is generally, although not quite universally, regarded as a non-IE language, while fleeting inscriptions in a number of other meagerly attested languages (e.g., North Picene) have also been held to reflect the existence of relic non-IE populations in Iron Age Italy. Central Anatolia, the historical seat of the Hittites, was apparently previously occupied by the non-IE Hatti who have left some texts, primarily religious. It is generally accepted that the Hittites themselves established their state in Hattic territory (from whom they borrowed their name) where they absorbed the previous occupants along with sections of their vocabulary pertaining to both the running of the state and religion. Eastern Anatolia, territories historically occupied by the Luvians and Armenians, were previously settled by the non-IE Hurrians and their linguistic cousins, the Urartians, and so this territory is also traditionally excluded from the earliest IE-speakers, as is northern Syria where the earliest attested traces of Indo-Aryan appear among the Hurrian-speaking Mitanni. The Iranian languages emerge beyond the limits of the earliest historical records but expanded southwards into the kingdom of Elam in southern Iran whose language was clearly non-IE. Finally, the Indo-Aryan languages still share the Indian subcontinent with the non-IE Dravidian and Munda language families and their presence indicates that this enormous region was also the subject of later IE expansions. Thus, the written record tends to suggest that the IE languages spread from somewhere north of Iberia, Italy, central and eastern Anatolia, northern Mesopotamia, southern Iran and India-Pakistan.

The second line of evidence is primarily theoretical. There are finite limits to the size of area that any language may occupy without separating into different dialects and gradually unintelligible languages. Language is constantly changing and without a written standard and other artifices of modern media exchange, it is impossible for the various speakers of a language, spread over a broad territory through time, to enjoy sufficient inter-communication that they experience the same course of linguistic change through time. This process is self evident among various IE stocks where Latin and Common Slavic of the early mediaeval period have both differentiated into the modern Romance and Slavic languages respectively. Studies of North American Indian languages suggest that the area they occupied ranged from about 530 to 660,000 sq km, averaging about 19,000 sq km, about the size of the modern state of Israel. The area occupied by a single language will be dependent on many factors such as terrain and the nature (and mobility) of the economy but the probable maximum upper range of a prehistoric language would be on the order of 250,000 to a million sq km (i.e., the size of the United Kingdom to about one and a half times the size of the Ukraine). The theoretical limits then suggest that the IE language family, at some time in its prehistoric existence, should have occupied a territory far more confined than that which is evident in its earliest historically attested distribution.

History of the Problem

Attempts to locate the earliest Indo-Europeans have existed since the discovery of the IE language family itself. Initially, the IE language family was explained by reference to the Bible where Japhet, one of the sons of Noah, was regarded as the source of all those languages neither Semitic (from Noah's son Shem) nor Hamitic (Ham) and hence Mount Ararat in Armenia, the reputed resting place of the Ark, served as a convenient homeland. The rise in interest in the early literature of the Indo-Aryans and Iranians, coupled with an exaggerated conception of their antiquity, encouraged the belief that the earliest IE peoples derived from the territory between the Caspian Sea and Bactria, part of Afghanistan, Uzbekistan and Tadzhikistan, and the cradle of the Indo-Europeans was set variously in mountainous areas such as the Hindu-Kush. Such a homeland stimulated romantic notions of how the earliest Indo-Europeans nurtured their language and culture in isolation and then burst forth from their homeland to spread their higher culture to Europe and the rest of Asia.

The consensus of an Asian homeland, although still widely accepted throughout the nineteenth century, received its first attack in 1851 when the English philologist, Roger Latham, argued on linguistic grounds that an Asian homeland was contrary to the linguistic evidence. Employing the biological model of the relationship between species and genus, Latham argued that the similarity between Indo-Aryan and Iranian, what today we recognize as the Indo-Iranian superstock, is such to suggest that it represented a more recent expansion from Europe where a much greater number of linguistic stocks (species) existed, suggesting that the original territory of the language family (genus) was Europe and not Asia. Although Latham's arguments were not widely accepted, they were augmented during the 1870s and 1880s by a variety of scholars who confused language and race and argued that the earliest Indo-Europeans, now frequently designated with the Indo-Iranian ethnonym "Aryans", must have derived from the lightest pigmented Caucasian physical type. Once the concept of the tall, long-headed, blue-eyed blond Aryan was accepted, the homeland was shifted to southern Scandinavia or northern Germany and a new consensus emerged.

By the turn of the century, this newer consensus began to crack and the various schools of thought emerged and set the course for most of the solutions of the twentieth century. Although Europe was almost universally accepted as the IE homeland, the precise location of the homeland became very much a matter of dispute. The case for northern Europe persisted and the earlier racial arguments were augmented by archaeology that associated the earliest Indo-Europeans with the Corded Ware (Battle-Ax) cultural horizon that covered northern and central Europe. A Baltic origin was further supported by linguists who found in Lithuanian the most conservative IE language. That conservatism suggested, in their opinion, that it had travelled least from the original homeland.

The northern homeland theories (in whatever guise) were opposed by those who became increasingly convinced that the earliest Indo-Europeans were primarily steppe pastoralists and the homeland was variously set to the Ukraine, south Russia, and occasionally as far east as Kazakhstan. Other proposed homelands were within the territory of the Linear Ware culture that spanned the Danubian drainage from the Netherlands and France in the west to the Ukraine in the east or the Neolithic cultures of south-eastern Europe, centered on the northwest corner of the Black Sea and stretching from the Balkans again to the western Ukraine. The only part of Europe universally rejected as potential homeland territory was the Atlantic periphery and the Mediterranean, the former on geographical grounds and the latter on the exclusion principle as it was the one region that possessed evidence of non-IE populations. Now even this latter principle has been partially breached by a number of solutions that seek the IE homeland in Anatolia and Armenia, either on linguistic grounds that the IE language family is closely related to language families of the Near East and southern Caucasus, or on archaeological grounds that the Indo-Europeans should be linked to the earliest spread of agriculture from Anatolia to Europe.

The path to the current indecision has hardly been straight and in addition to the various broad schools of thought, there have been numerous less widely accepted solutions. These range from proposals to set the homeland at both the North and the South poles, North Africa, Egypt, India, and as early as the Neanderthals or as late as *c* 1600 B.C.

Linguistic Solutions

Solutions to the IE homeland problem have often derived from the field of linguistics and these can be categorized into five different approaches.

The first approach involves the external relationships of the IE family. Just as the stocks of a language family may be more or less similar (and presumably once geographically proximate) to one another, so also one may argue that similar relationships exist between different language families. Within the area of homeland studies, these types of relationships are argued either on a one-to-one basis or as part of a larger linguistic entity that itself comprises different language families. For example, there have been frequent attempts to demonstrate that the IE languages share broad grammatical features and individual items of vocabulary with the Semitic, Kartvelian, North Caucasian and Uralic families. The putative "super-family" that would include Indo-European and these other language families is usually called "Nostratic" (derived from Lat *noster* 'our'). On such evidence the location of the homeland has been set to the Black and Caspian sea areas because of the close relationship between Proto-Indo-European and Uralic to its north or North Caucasian to its south or the proposed relationships between IE and Semitic or Kartvelian have been employed to support an IE homeland south of the Caucasus, in Anatolia, or Central Asia. The "ultimate" homeland has even been pulled so far south as Egypt in some solutions to Nostratic origins although they generally lie somewhere in southwest Asia. Since all of these other language families are at least geographi-

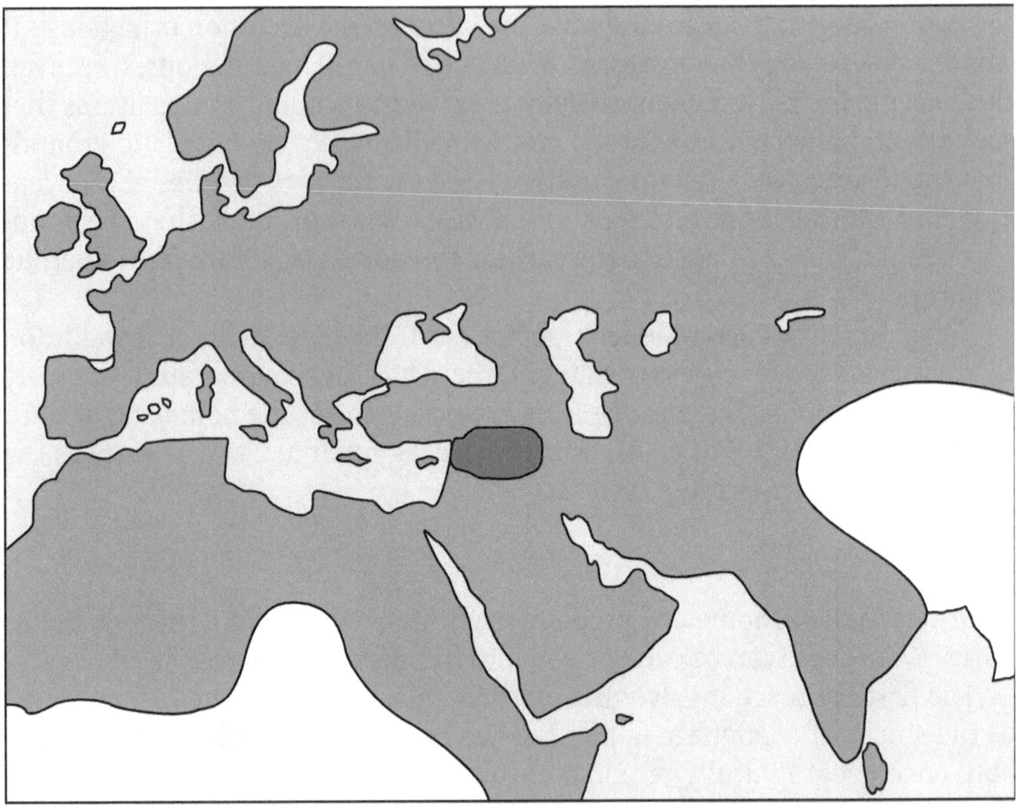

Homeland I

The shaded area indicates the generalized distribution of the Nostratic language family. The darker shaded area indicates the Nostratic homeland c 15,000 B.C. according to Allan Bomhard.

cally proximate to the earliest attested IE languages, the solutions are possible but the levels of similarity which are proposed between the language families fall vastly short of those found between the individual stocks of Indo-European. Lexical items that reputedly link different language families are often dismissed as undemonstrated or the products of widespread borrowing while grammatical similarities are often rejected as hopelessly vague. In short, no extra-familial relationship with Indo-European has been demonstrated at a level that would enjoy anything other than partisan support. The only exception here is that there is clear evidence for some form of substantial contact between the IE and Uralic families but these may have occurred at too late a date (i.e., pre-Proto-Indo-Iranian or later) to be relevant to the homeland problem.

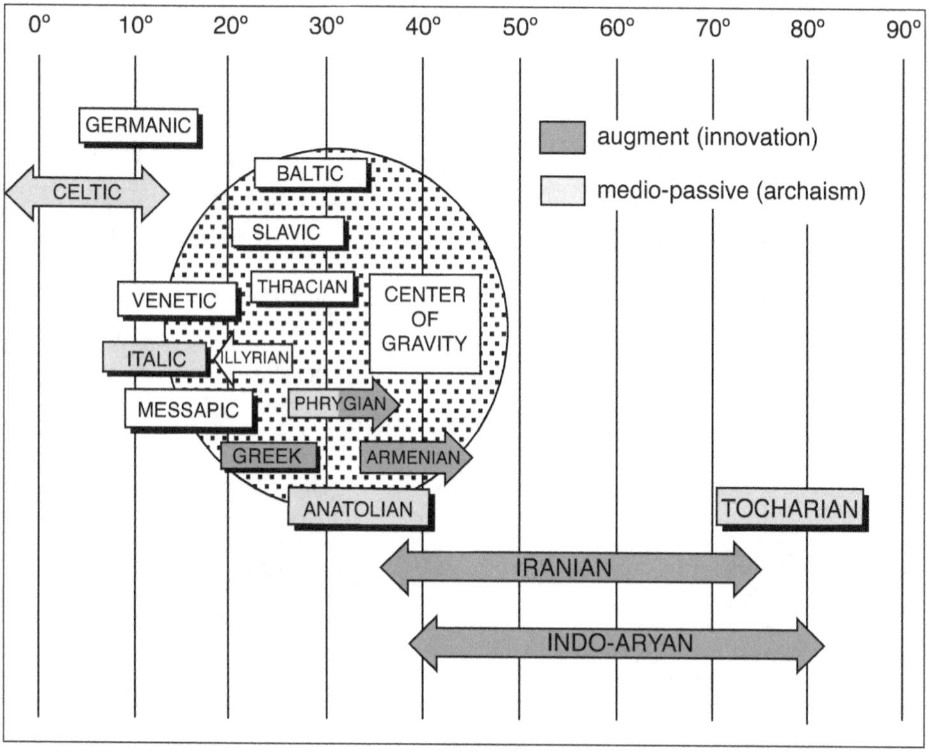

Homeland II

The traditional representation of the "center of gravity" of the IE stocks has often been employed to support a homeland in the Balkans. However, it is filled with languages that are either minimally known, e.g., Venetic, Thracian, Illyrian, Messapic, or whose Balkan origins are assumed rather than demonstrated, e.g., Phrygian, Armenian.

A second linguistic approach derives from an examination of the mutual relationships of the different IE stocks under the assumption that their internal configuration will reveal their original position. Theoretically, such an approach usually embraces the "center of gravity" principle wherein it is assumed that where the IE languages have existed longest, we should expect the greatest differentiation since this would be the area which has had the greatest opportunity to experience language change. The corollary of this is that those stocks who seem to be most similar to one another have probably occupied their relative positions most recently hence their lack of marked differentiation. On the

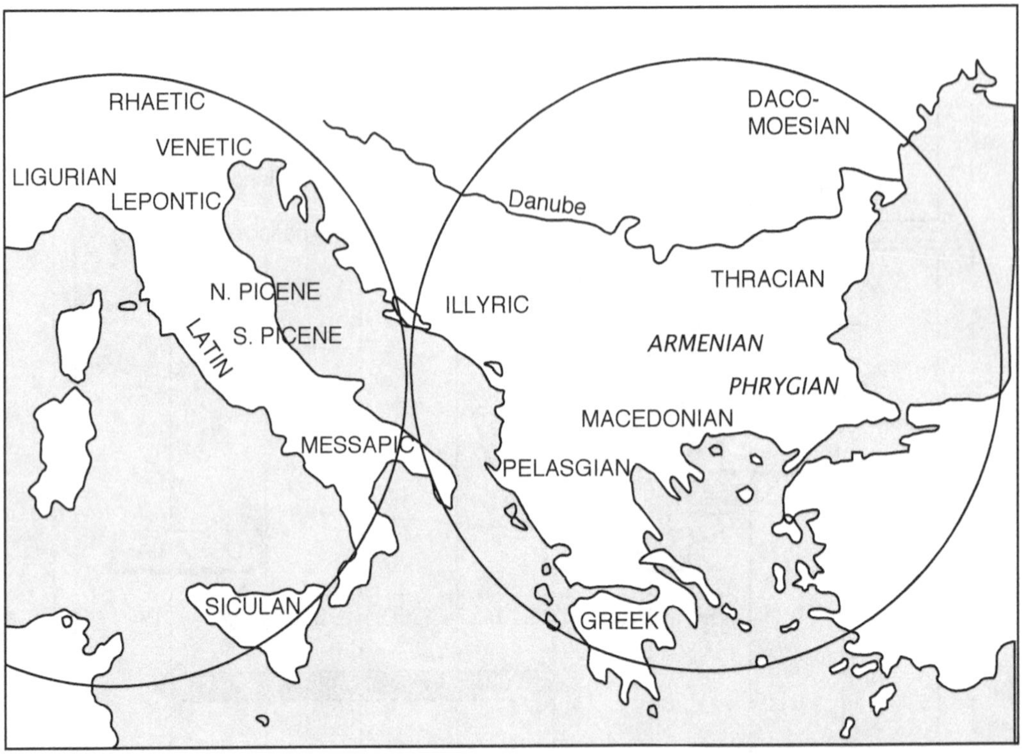

Homeland III

When compared with the Balkans, Italy offers as many ill-attested Indo-European dialects to suggest a different "center of gravity." If the "center of gravity" principle is to be credited with any validity, it must be employed using well attested languages derived from the same time depth.

basis of this, the Indo-Iranian superstock, for example, would be regarded as a relatively recent expansion into their historical seats, presumably during the Bronze Age. Possibly much the same could be said of the Celtic languages that occupied much of western and central Europe during the Iron Age. The greatest density of IE languages seems to appear between about 20 and 40 degrees longitude, the area between Poland and Albania on the west eastwards to the Dnieper to central or eastern Anatolia. This area would appear to be central and, indeed, it tends to be the area where the IE homeland is most often sought with territories to the west and east being regarded increasingly peripheral to the homeland. There are, however, several problems with such a line of argument.

First, while the Indo-Iranian superstock may be regarded as relatively late, it is not specially related to the Tocharian languages to its east which have generally been regarded as more closely associated with the languages from the supposedly central zone. Second, any attempt to employ the "center of gravity" principle should be undertaken with languages that are contemporary with one another which is virtually impossible when studying the IE languages since some languages, e.g., most of the Anatolian stock, were already extinct long before other stocks, e.g., most of the European languages, had emerged in the written record. Very often the "center of gravity" proposed by linguists for Indo-European tends to be a palimpsest of different linguistic periods, particularly for those who argue a Balkans homeland. Here we have numerous marginally attested languages to pile into the IE nucleus. In actual fact, a similar exercise could put the homeland in Italy where the nucleus of (marginally attested) IE languages and stocks is even greater. Finally, the theoretical premise of the arguments rests on the notion that the only or at least primary factor in linguistic differentiation is time, and it therefore ignores other possible reasons for language change, e.g., some would explain the heterogeneity of the Balkan languages with reference to different non-IE substrates or to the mountainous topography that impedes communication and thus hastens linguistic fragmentation.

In addition to time then, another major factor often cited in language change is the impact of foreign substrates on an expanding language. The theoretical assumption is that when a language spreads over an existing population, the native language with its presumably different phonetic and grammatical systems will influence the way its speakers articulate the new language. Conversely, where languages seem to preserve the greatest number of early IE features, this lack of change is credited to their speakers having occupied their home region the longest and involved the incorporation of few if any foreign speakers. The identification of foreign substrates is most easily accomplished when one also has documents in the foreigner's language. Hence the presence of Hattic or Hurrian vocabulary in Hittite suggests foreign contacts in central and east Anatolian while the Armenian language appears to have borrowed terms for their own native environment from Hurrian or Urartian and the occasional Dravidian loanword is uncovered in Old Indic. These examples, however, do not gain much since there is already historical documentation for the various substrate languages in these territories. The evidence of foreign lexical items, however, has also been extended to *Greek* and many of the other languages of Europe where even cognate forms tend to throw up reconstructions that look suspiciously non-IE because of their root structure or (unstable) root vocalism or perhaps because of the instability of the reconstruction that suggests different IE groups adopting a foreign term from a substrate and assimilating it differently from one region to the next. A classic example is the designation for 'hemp'. In the various Indo-European languages where this particular word is attested we have a variety of only partially compatible forms: Lat *cannabis*, ON *hampr*, OE *hænep* (whence NE *hemp*), NHG *hanf*, OPrus *knapios*, Lith *kanãpės*, Grk *κάνναβις*, OInd *śaṇá-*. The Latin, Germanic, and Greek forms might reflect a putative PIE **kannabis* which would be phonologically unusual in the two **a-*'s, the double **-n-* and the presence of the rare **-b-*. Baltic shows **-p-* rather than **-b-* (borrowed from Germanic?) while Old Indic shows a palatal **k̑-* and no labial at all. (Similar words are found in non-Indo-European languages as well, e.g., Turkish *kenevir*, Karakalpak *kenep*.) In addition to primarily lexical arguments, linguists have also proposed substrate influences on the basis of broader linguistic features such as the supposed restructuring of the insular Celtic or Anatolian languages from their IE ancestor, the Germanic sound shift, the abandonment of the free accent in west European languages, etc. Finally, linguists have frequently examined the other side of the coin and sought out the least altered IE language. Most often this distinction is awarded to the Baltic stock, in particular Lithuanian which, although only attested in the last four hundred years, still reveals a remarkable conservatism which has stimulated arguments for an IE homeland in the Baltic region.

Both the logical and methodological premises of the search for foreign substrates is open to serious questions. It assumes that language change is primarily a product of linguistic expansion across foreign substrates but in actual fact language change does not respond so symmetrically to substrate effects, even when they are well known. For example, Old English behaves very much as any other early Germanic language despite the fact that it was superimposed on a native British (Celtic-speaking) population. In any case, reference to possible substrates as agents of linguistic change can only be tested when the substrate is known. When the presumed substrate has been completely replaced long before the supposedly influenced language is recorded, the very existence of the substrate, much less the kinds of influences it may have had, is completely speculative. Moreover, if the mechanisms of language change are really quite variable, then distinctions between supposedly conservative languages such as Baltic and much altered ones such as Albanian may have nothing whatsoever to

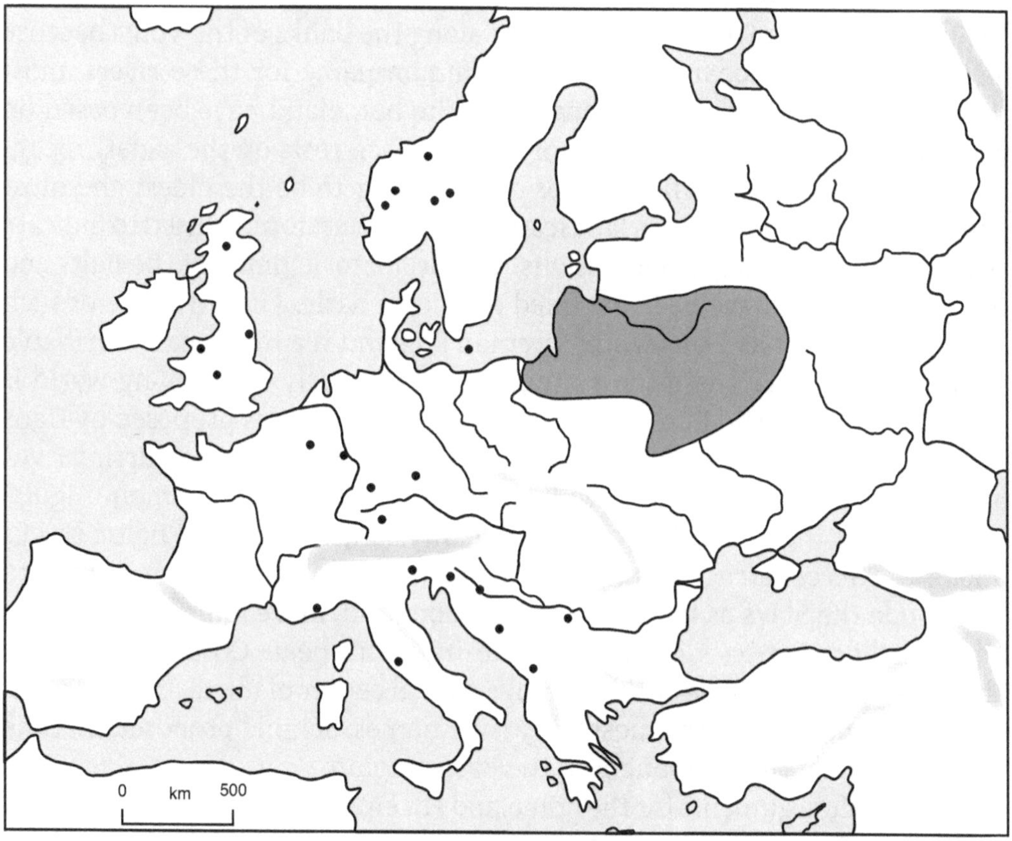

Homeland IV

According to W. Schmid the shaded area bears early "Indo-European" river names while the dots indicate where such "Indo-European" names might be found elsewhere in Europe. Schmid suggested that the concentration of early names in the Baltic region supported this region's claim to have been the Indo-European homeland.

do with the prior location of their linguistic ancestors. Indeed, the principle that a language will remain most archaic where it has existed longest is an apparent contradiction of the previously discussed "center of gravity" approach that would assume that such a language area would have experienced the greatest rather than least linguistic fragmentation.

Finally, some linguists have argued that the most direct testimony of the location of the IE homeland can be found in the examination of river names. Other than a few attempts to situate the earliest Indo-Europeans either between the Kura and Araxes rivers in Armenia or along the banks of the Volga because the Indo-Iranians appeared to share a common name for these rivers, most attempts to employ rivers as indicators of the homeland have been based on systematic hydronomies. The logic of the approach rests on the widely recognized phenomenon that river names often appear to be the oldest and most conservative place names on a landscape and can, therefore, be used to indicate the distribution of earlier populations. The prehistoric limits of the Balts and Celts, for example, have been assigned on such a basis. The existence of such British river names as *Thames* and *Severn* in England is a historically verifiable case in point. The largest such system within the early IE-speaking world is generally known as Old European (*Alteuropäisch*) which was proposed by Hans Krahe. His hydronymic system comprised a series of frequently recurring river names that were believed to have been established by the common linguistic ancestor of the Celtic, Italic, Germanic, Illyrian, Venetic and Baltic stocks *c* 1500 B.C. This construct was then pushed eastwards by Wolfgang Schmid to also include the Slavs as far east as the Dnieper and, more importantly, it was also pushed further back in time to Proto-Indo-European. Observing that the Baltic region seemed to be both the geographical center of the distribution and the territory possessing the most early river names, Schmid proposed that the homeland should then be sought in the Baltic region.

Hydronymic arguments for the homeland are empirically quite controversial since they are based on assuming that similarity of river names in different areas must derive from a common proto-form, a statement with very little hope of verification. Moreover, much of the evidence rests on river names with a root vocalism in *a* which is widely thought to be either late, i.e., not PIE, or a marker of the assimilation of a non-IE word by IE speakers in Europe. Hydronymic evidence for the IE homeland (as opposed to the distribution of individual IE stocks) does not enjoy much currency beyond the limits of those few specialists concerned with such research.

Lexico-geographical Approach

In addition to purely linguistic approaches to resolving the homeland problem, there are also a series of arguments where linguistics is combined with some other discipline such as geography or archaeology to locate the territory of the earliest IE speakers.

Lexico-geographical analysis utilizes the reconstructed vocabulary to determine the geographical borders of the proto-language and is a technique widely applied not only in IE studies but also in determining the location of most other language families, e.g., Uralic, Semitic, Algonquin. The primary data is drawn from the semantic fields concerned with flora and fauna which tend to have restricted ranges. In the search for the IE homeland, special prominence has been accorded to the beech and salmon. The significance of the former is the famous "beech line", the eastern limit of the beech (*Fagus silvatica*) which ran from the Baltic (Kaliningrad/Königsberg) south to the northwest corner of the Black Sea (Odessa). It was widely accepted that the existence of PIE **bhāĝos* 'beech' indicated that the Indo-Europeans could not have originated east of this line. However, this argument loses much of its force when it is noted that the reconstruction of the word is confined to European stocks, that its reconstructed semantic range is not unambiguous (the cognates yield 'elm' in Slavic and 'oak' in both Albanian and Greek), and the range of the Caucasian beech (*Fagus orientalis*) is known from the Caucasus region and could therefore extend the area of a potential homeland east to the Caspian Sea. The second term **loḱs* 'salmon' was generally taken to be the sea salmon (*Salmo salar*) which might only be found in the rivers draining into the Baltic Sea and, therefore, argued for a homeland somewhere between north Germany and Latvia. This argument has proven even less robust than the beech line since the semantic reconstruction would now seem to be the ubiquitous *Salmo trutta*, the trout, that is found widely throughout much of Eurasia, thus denying this term any utility in determining the IE homeland. Other terms that have at least enjoyed some currency in the history of the problem are words for 'eel', which also reputedly demonstrated a north European homeland (despite the fact that it is not strongly ascribed linguistically to PIE nor is it restricted geographically to the Baltic) and the 'tortoise', whose distribution was seen to exclude the far north of Europe. Attempts to employ other environmental terms are numerous but even less consequential. Example can be found in the recent attempts of T. Gamkrelidze and V. Ivanov to assert that since the PIE lexicon shared words for mountains and fast running water, the homeland was most logically set to the Caucasus mountains.

The distribution of cognate sets and shifts in the semantics of reconstructed forms have also been employed to trace the location of the homeland. The reconstruction of a PIE term for the 'birch', **bherh*$_x$*ĝos*, for example, which would exclude Anatolia from the homeland, has been dismissed by one linguist because it is etymologically transparent, i.e., it indicates the 'bright one', and it is a late *o*-stem, therefore, it is ascribed not to the homeland but only to those

Indo-Europeans who had left their Anatolian homeland and entered Europe. On the other hand, semantic shifts in the meanings of reconstructed arboreal terms in Greek and Latin, for example, the Latin cognate for the 'birch' word denotes the 'ash', are employed to demonstrate that the Indo-Europeans originated north of the Mediterranean and when they did not find the same trees in their new environments, they reapplied the inherited names to different trees. The most extensive attempts to employ semantic shifts as a marker of the homeland appeared in the works of Wilhelm Brandenstein who sought to demonstrate that cognate sets between Indo-Iranian and the other European languages indicated that the former preserved the earlier non-agricultural meaning, e.g., OInd *ajra-* 'open field, pasture' but Lat *ager* 'cultivated field', and that the Europeans had innovated with many terms for their new, wetter and more forested environment when they had moved from a homeland in Kazakhstan.

Finally, the lexicon has been employed to provide negative evidence for the location of the homeland where, for example, the presumed absence of terms for 'oil', 'cypress', 'olive', 'ass', 'lion', etc., have been employed to show that the Indo-Europeans did not originally inhabit the Mediterranean or Anatolia while the absence of terms for such items as 'amber' have been used to exclude a Baltic homeland.

Lexico-archaeological Approach

The most direct testimony for the early culture of the Indo-Europeans is the reconstructed vocabulary which provides the only direct bridge between Indo-European as a primarily linguistic concept and the hard data of archaeology. The reconstructed vocabulary for domestic animals ('sheep', 'goat', 'cattle', 'pig', 'dog') and 'grain', coupled with terms for agricultural implements, e.g., 'sickle', 'grinding stone', 'pottery', all attest an agricultural or Neolithic economy which should not have existed anywhere proximate to the Indo-European world prior to *c* 7000 B.C. Other terms suggesting the use of animals for draft or secondary products such as 'wheeled vehicles', 'yoke', 'plow', 'milk', 'wool', as well as 'silver' and the ascription to the PIE community of the domestic 'horse' tend to lower the earliest date for the common IE lexicon to *c* 4000 B.C. This date does not necessarily pertain to the movements of IE-speaking communities but only marks the time by which those communities, whether they had expanded or not, still showed no signs of significant linguistic separation. By *c* 2500 B.C., it is widely regarded that at least some of the IE stocks had already become so significantly different from the reconstructed proto-language that items of vocabulary should be recognized as loan words rather than inherited. In the intervening period, between *c* 4000 B.C. and 2500 B.C. there is hardly an item of culture, diagnostic for the reconstruction of PIE culture, that had not expanded from one end of Eurasia to the other, regardless of where it had first appeared.

The other terms relating to the culture of the earliest Indo-Europeans are not particularly diagnostic. Concepts such as the 'house' or even some form of 'enclosure', 'village' or even 'fortified settlement' are nearly ubiquitous across the Eurasian Neolithic. The PIE arsenal of 'knife', 'spear', 'bow', and 'arrow' are similarly found over all Eurasia while IE social institutions, including the detailed evidence for its kinship system, are not credibly retrievable from the archaeological record.

Assessing Homeland Solutions

One of the major reasons for the abundance of homeland solutions (and scepticism that any of them is correct) is the absence of a commonly agreed upon set of criteria by which one can evaluate the validity of any particular solution. There are, nevertheless, some criteria that appear so widespread that they constitute an essential suite of principles. A homeland solution should be robust enough to satisfy or, at least, not violate the following basic principles.

1. *Exclusion principle.* It is widely argued that the homeland should not be set in an area where there is evidence of prior non-IE occupation. This has generally provided grounds for excluding areas such as Iberia (Tartessian, Iberian, Basque), Italy (Etruscan, ?North Picene), north-central (Hattic) and eastern (Hurrian) Anatolia, the Caucasus, almost the entire Near East (Semitic, Sumerian), southern Iran (Elamite) and much if not all of the Indian subcontinent (Dravidian, Munda). The limitation of this principle is that establishing the presence of non-IE speakers in a particular region does not necessarily establish their priority there, e.g., the current language of Anatolia is Turkic yet we know that it was previously Indo-European (i.e., Greek, Phrygian, and the several Anatolian languages). Generally, the antiquity of our attestations, e.g., for the Bronze Age in Anatolia and the Near East and the Iron Age in Iberia, has suggested that our evidence for non-IE languages is close enough to the date of early IE dispersals that we may assume that they were indeed

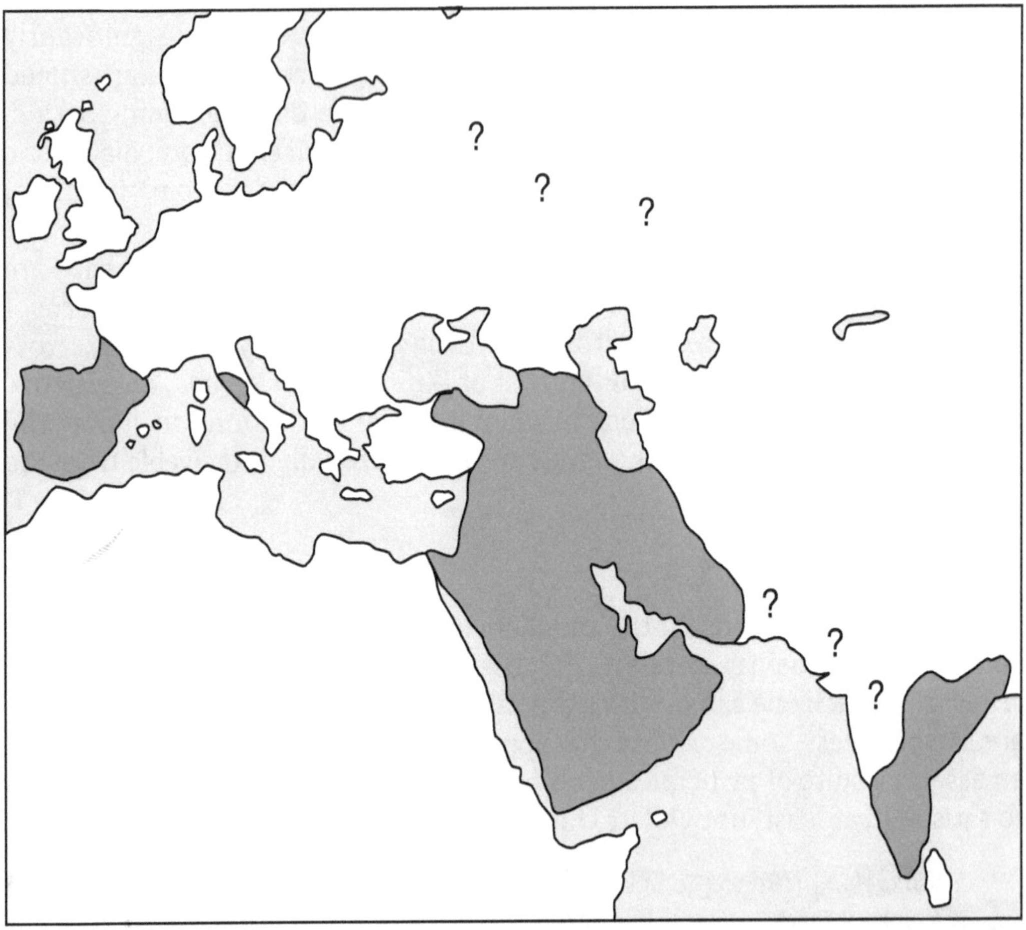

Homeland V

The exclusion principle is indicated in this map of Eurasia which indicates where non-IE languages were solidly attested or presumed to underlie the expansion of the Indo-Europeans. Tartessian, Iberian and the modern Basque generally exclude Iberia. The Etruscans are commonly regarded as non-IE. North and east Anatolia was occupied by non-IE languages during the Bronze Age while to the south and east were the Hurrian, Semitic, Sumerian and Elamite languages, the last of which may be related to the Dravidian of southern India (i.e., Elamo-Dravidian). The Uralic homeland and the early dispersal of the Uralic languages (indicated by question marks) is generally set to the forest zone of either side of the Urals.

"substrates" and not later intruders. This example also emphasizes that the exclusion principle is of limited application because it can only be applied where there is certain evidence of non-IE populations which, for most of Eurasia, could only be known (one way or the other) with the spread of writing in the last centuries B.C. or first centuries A.D. It is impossible to pronounce on whether there were non-IE languages, for example, in the Baltic territory before our earliest evidence for Baltic languages.

2. *Temporal principle.* Any homeland solution should be set within the broad temporal constraints of the lexical-cultural evidence for Proto-Indo-European. The lexico-cultural evidence indicates that the Proto-Indo-European vocabulary cannot predate the Neolithic, i.e., the establishment of a settled way of life based on domesticated plants and animals and the technology associated with such a subsistence base. On the other hand, any date after *c* 2500 B.C. is unlikely to accommodate the degree of linguistic differentiation we already encounter in the second millennium B.C. If the full range of the reconstructed vocabulary is taken into consideration, including those items of material culture that only appear at the end of the Neolithic or early Bronze Age, the date of PIE should be broadly set to the period *c* 4500–2500 B.C.

3. *Relationship principle.* The interrelationships of the IE languages suggest that their dispersal was not unidirectional but appears to involve a series of interrelationships. While the specific nature of the "branching" of the IE stocks is subject to debate, there are certain broad patterns that are generally agreed upon. These would comprise the following:

A. Anatolian would appear to have separated early from the other IE stocks (or the reverse).
B. A core of "Late" IE stocks formed which comprised Greek, Armenian, Indo-Iranian.
C. A "Northwestern" group of languages formed comprising Germanic, Baltic and Slavic.
D. The western stocks of Celtic and Italic seem to be more closely associated with the Northwestern rather than the Late IE stocks.
E. The position of Tocharian is disputed but it does not appear to be in any particular close association with Indo-Iranian.

These broad relationships should be accommodated within any solution to the homeland problem and description of IE dispersals.

4. *Cultural principle.* The minimum cultural and environmental picture derived from the reconstructed PIE lexicon should be accommodated within a homeland solution. In general, much of the reconstructed lexicon attests environmental or cultural features that are found broadly over much of Eurasia and are not particularly diagnostic. In some instances, where we have an animal such as the horse which is both fully reconstructible to PIE (notwith-

standing debate as to whether it was wild or domestic) and appears to have had a limited distribution in the prehistoric record, it may be employed as a test of a solution's plausibility. Such tests, however, are also dependent on time, i.e., although limited in distribution at 4500 B.C., the horse was found over a much broader area of Eurasia by *c* 2500 B.C. Diagnostic cultural items are hence time factored, i.e., they only have meaning if one can control for time as well.

5. *Archaeological principle.* Although ignored in some purely linguistic solutions to the problem, it is difficult to accept any homeland solution that lacks some form of confirming evidence for dispersals in the archaeological record. While archaeologists will freely acknowledge that there is great uncertainty as to what constitutes evidence for population dispersals in the archaeological record (much less how that evidence should be "read" linguistically), the archaeological record does indicate trajectories that require some spatial and social mechanism of explanation and it also can evaluate to some extent the conditions of social change under which linguistic replacement may have occurred. Fragile although it may be, archaeology offers one of the few forms of confirming evidence to purely linguistic arguments.

6. *Total distribution principle.* Probably one of the single greatest reasons for rejecting many solutions to the IE homeland problem are breaches of the total distribution principle. Any homeland solution must account for the dispersal of *all* the IE stocks. Numerous solutions proposed in the nineteenth and early twentieth centuries made vigorous defences of how Indo-Europeans spread from, for example, a Baltic homeland through the rest of Europe without providing the slightest evidence of how dispersals from this area carried IE stocks into Anatolia or Asia; conversely, the Asiatic homelands proposed in the nineteenth century and more recently by some scholars provide no explanation whatsoever how the IE stocks reached Europe. No solution is acceptable unless it explains the distribution of all IE stocks.

Current Homeland Solutions

From the great number of homeland solutions one can select four that enjoy fairly wide currency. Each differs not only with respect to *where* it sets the homeland but also *when* it initiates IE dispersals.

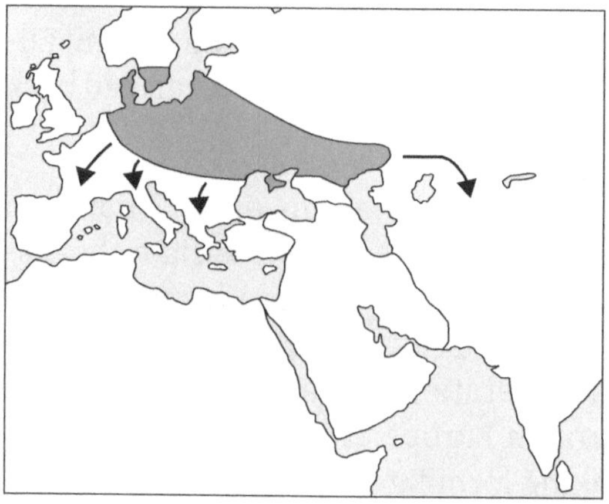

Homeland VI
Baltic-Pontic homeland set to the Mesolithic.

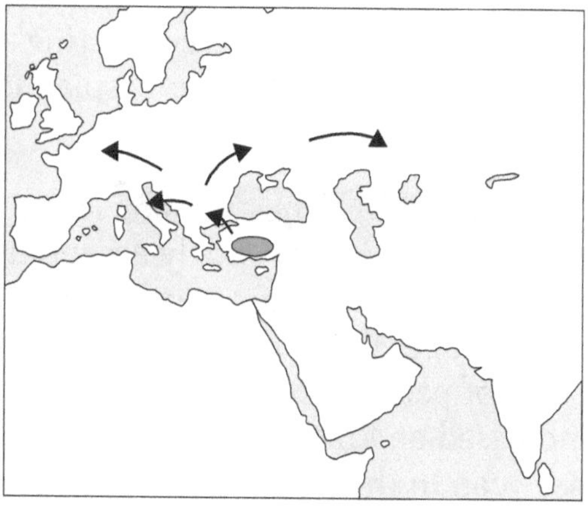

Homeland VII
The Anatolian or Neolithic "wave of advance" model seeks IE origins in Anatolia in the eighth–seventh millennium B.C.

1. The *Baltic-Pontic* solution. This solution argues that a PIE linguistic continuum already existed during the Mesolithic, i.e., *c* 8500–5000 B.C., in the area between the Baltic and Black/Caspian seas. The Neolithic cultures that emerge across this enormous region are then ancestral to their respective regional IE stocks, e.g., the northwest IE languages emerge in the TRB culture of the north European plain, while Indo-Iranian develops in the steppelands of the Ukraine and south Russia and pushes eastwards into Asia. A central tenet of this solution, at least as argued by archaeologists, is that there is a major cultural border between the steppe cultures and those of temperate Europe which provides the foundation for the split between Asiatic and European languages as this cultural border was not seriously transgressed at any period from the Neolithic onwards (except during the Iron Age where the late spread of Iranian nomads to eastern Europe is irrelevant to IE dispersals).

The Baltic-Pontic theory cannot be evaluated according to the *exclusion principle*. It fails both the *temporal* and *cultural* principles in that there is no way that a homeland set among hunter-gatherers can explain the agricultural and specific technological vocabulary reconstructed to PIE. It can accommodate the *relationship principle* but does not fully satisfy the *archaeological* or *total distribution* principles in that, other than the movement of IE-speakers to Asia, it does not account for their spread into the Balkans or Anatolia. In sum, this solution attempts to embrace two conflicting alternative solutions, i.e., the central Europe/Balkan and the Pontic-Caspian solutions, into a single model pushed back further in time.

2. The *Anatolian* solution. There are several variations on an Anatolian homeland. The most widely accepted is that which seeks to associate the dispersal of the Indo-Europeans with the spread of agriculture from Anatolia into Europe. This spread, set to the *c* 7000–6500 B.C., is attributed to a movement of peoples (demic diffusion) over generations as farming populations increased and moved progressively through Europe at about a rate of 1 km per year. In this way putatively IE-speaking farming colonists absorbed (culturally, genetically and linguistically) the previous occupants of Europe as they expanded in a "wave of advance". Expansion into Asia is accounted for in one of two models. One requires that the Neolithic economy spread eastwards from Anatolia into Iran and India. The other model continues that of the first (and all other solutions) by attributing IE dispersals into Asia to populations previously occupying the steppelands of the Black and Caspian seas. In this model, these steppe-nomads are ultimately derived from the same farmers who migrated from Anatolia through the Balkans and then eastwards around the northwest shore of the Black Sea.

This solution comes very close to violating the *exclusion principle* if it does not directly do so since broad areas of central and eastern Anatolia can be attributed to non-IE populations with the emergence of written records within the region from the third millennium B.C. onwards. It might be emphasized that the clearest evidence for a local transition from hunting-gathering to farming occurs in the southeast of Anatolia and that it is just as plausible to assume that if any new language spread to Europe with farming it was probably not an IE language. The solution can avoid violation of the *exclusion principle* only by shifting the IE heartland to western Anatolia where linguistic evidence for non-IE Bronze Age populations is lacking.

The Anatolian solution also seems to be a bit early to accommodate the *temporal principle*. Although Anatolia does produce evidence for basic domestic plants and animals, the cultural reconstructions which appear to date to the end of the Neolithic or early Bronze Age, e.g., wheeled vehicles, plow, wool, cannot be attributed to the seventh millennium B.C. With respect to the *cultural principle*, there is no evidence of the horse (domestic or otherwise) in western Anatolia or in neighboring Greece, the first region "Indo-Europeanized" according to this solution, until *c* 2000 B.C. Even the *relationship principle*, which can normally be satisfied with a little cartographical legerdemain, seems to be violated as this model suggests dispersals that run Anatolia → Greece → Italy, which implicitly suggests linguistic relationships unaccommodated by any linguistic evidence. The model has been adjusted by some who have argued that population movements were limited to the Balkans and central Europe and that later Bronze and Iron Age expansions must account for the distribution of the IE languages on the European periphery.

The *archaeological principle* has been the strongest element in support of this theory in that the spread of agriculture can be followed in the archaeological record and could offer the social conditions for large-scale language replacement. Insofar as the spread to Asia is concerned, the model that ties the Asiatic Indo-Europeans to the initial spread of agriculture seems very unlikely in that the transition to agriculture in Iran and India can be explained by sources far closer than Anatolia. This model falls on just about every possible matter of assessment, e.g., the *exclusion principle* as the area between eastern Anatolia and the Indo-Iranian world was clearly occupied by non-IE language families (Hurrian, Urartian, Semitic, Sumerian, Elamite), it is no better at satisfying the *temporal* and *cultural* principles, it does not explain the relationship between the "late" IE stocks of Greek, Armenian, Indo-Iranian. The alternative model of Asiatic expansions is questionable since there is some evidence that the Pontic-Caspian region received its Neolithic economy not from the Balkans but from the Caucasus.

Other solutions based on an Anatolian homeland are set later, i.e., *c* 5000–2000 B.C. These mitigate the impact of the *temporal* and *cultural* principles but still do not resolve the problem of the *exclusion* principle. Nor is the archaeological evidence for such expansions particularly strong (in some cases it is non-existent).

3. The *Central Europe-Balkan* solution. This theory has generally been driven by recognition that the *exclusion principle* appeared to remove Anatolia and Greece (on the acceptance of the secondary evidence for a non-IE Greek substrate) from consideration and the positive fact that such a homeland fitted the "center of gravity" principle. It places the homeland in central Europe (the Linear Ware culture), including perhaps the Balkans, from the Neolithic onwards. It can be adjusted (if one accepts a late date of *c* 5000–3000 B.C.) to accommodate the *temporal* and *cultural principles* but suf-

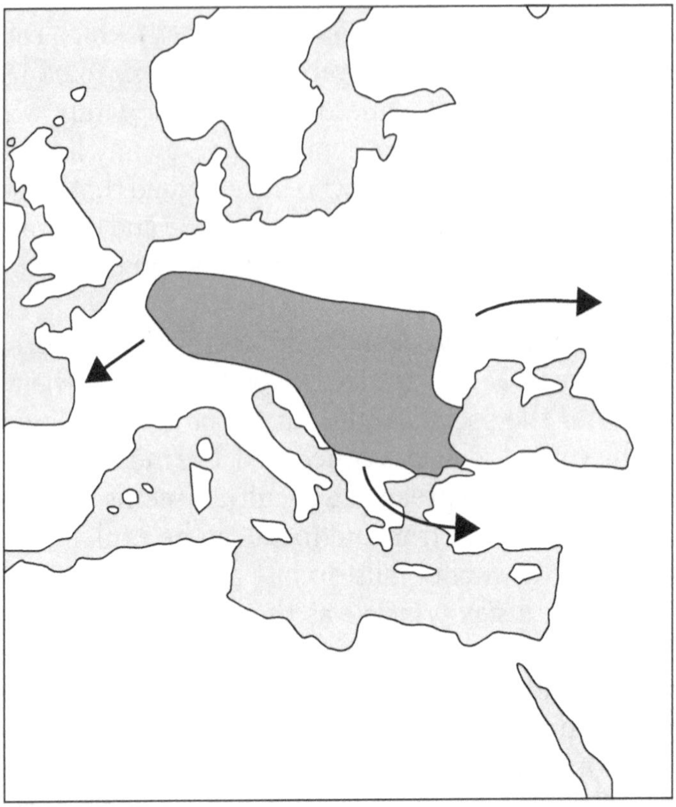

Homeland VIII

The Balkan–central European homeland associates the earliest Indo-Europeans with the Linear Ware culture and early Neolithic cultures of southeast Europe.

fers in terms of the *archaeological* and *total distribution* principles. It is difficult to employ this model to explain the Indo-Europeans of Asia or Anatolia. In fact, by ignoring the relationships between Anatolia and Greece and the Balkans, it unaccountably attributes a non-IE language to the Neolithic cultures of Anatolia and Greece and yet finds grounds to assign an IE identity to their later descendants in the Balkans and central Europe.

4. The *Pontic-Caspian* solution. This is the theory that places IE dispersals in the most recent period, i.e., *c* 4500–2500 B.C. It suggests that the homeland lay among mixed agricultural and increasingly mobile pastoralist tribes that emerged in the steppe and forest-steppe of the south Ukraine and south Russia and then expanded both to the east and west. The western expansion,

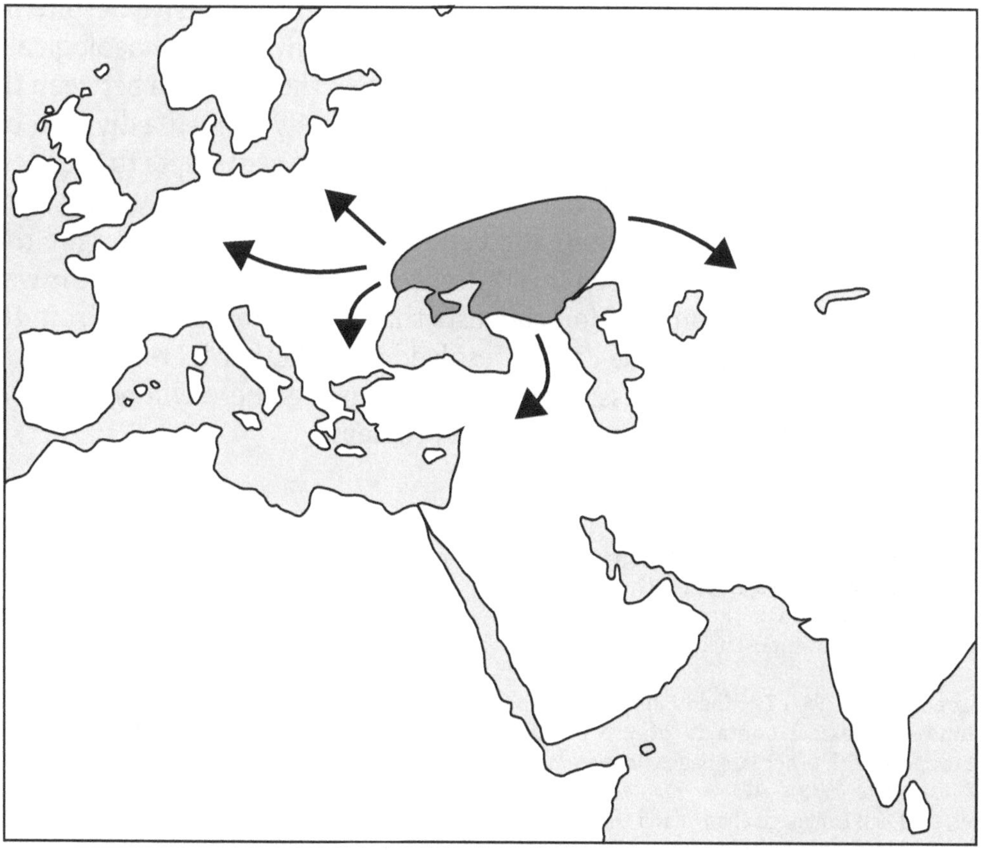

Homeland IX

The "Kurgan solution" seeks the origin of the Indo-Europeans in expansions from the Pontic-Caspian steppelands c 4500–2500 B.C.

seen as the "Kurgan model" of IE origins (the *kurgan* or tumulus is one of the typical markers of this expansion), involves the spread of populations into southeast Europe and their progressive domination or acculturation of non-IE peoples across Europe. This model meets almost all requirements except the *archaeological principle* where many would argue that the evidence for expansions from the steppe was limited (the hard evidence seems to end with the river Tisza in Hungary) and so it is very difficult to explain IE dispersals in much of Europe nor is the evidence for intrusions into either Greece or Anatolia particularly strong.

The solution to the IE homeland problem thus remains elusive despite periodic announcements to the contrary. Geographically and archaeologically, the major issue of dispute appears to occur north of the Black Sea between the rivers Dniester and Dnieper since this has traditionally formed a division between two cultural "worlds". The Baltic-Pontic solution attempts to reconcile this division by retreating back in time to the Mesolithic and drawing a circle around both areas. The Anatolian and central European solutions argue that the Indo-Europeans transgressed this Dniester-Dnieper fault line from the west while the Pontic-Caspian solution suggests that it was transgressed from the east. How this particular issue can be resolved and whether its resolution can accommodate the other assessment principles invoked here will be essential to resolving the Indo-European homeland problem.

Further Readings

Anthony, D. (1991) The archaeology of Indo-European origins. *JIES* 19, 193–222.

Diakonoff, I. (1985) On the original home of the speakers of Indo-European. *JIES* 13, 92–174.

Dolgopolsky, A. (1987) The Indo-European homeland and lexical contacts of Proto-Indo-European with other languages. *Mediterranean Language Review* 3, 7–31.

Evret, C. (1988) Language change and the material correlates of language and ethnic shift. *Antiquity* 62, 564–574.

Gimbutas, M. (1991) *The Civilization of the Goddess.* San Francisco, Harper.

Mallory, J. P. (1989) *In Search of the Indo-Europeans.* London, Thames and Hudson.

Renfrew, C. (1987) *Archaeology and Language.* London, Jonathan Cape.

Sherratt, A. and S. Sherratt (1988) The archaeology of Indo-European: an alternative view. *Antiquity* 62, 584–595.

Zvelebil, M. and K. (1988) Agricultural transition and Indo-European dispersals. *Antiquity* 62, 574–583.

4. The Tripartition of Functions

Benveniste examines terms used to denote social classes in four Indo-European languages: Sanskrit (Indic); Avestan (Iranian); Greek (Hellenic); and Umbrian (Italic). The classificatory equivalences displayed across these languages reveal that Proto-Indo-European society, the common parent society of the Indic, Iranian, Greek, and Italic peoples, was characterized by a hierarchical three-part (tripartite) social division: the "functions" of (1) the priests, (2) the warriors, and (3) the agricultural producers. This tripartition of functions is identical to that proposed by Georges Dumézil for the early Indo-Europeans, but Benveniste did not simply derive his interpretation from that of Dumézil, nor vice versa. The two scholars independently came to the same conclusion concerning primitive Indo-European social structure, with Benveniste's own interpretation first appearing in print in the early 1930s. (RDW)

THE TRIPARTITION OF FUNCTIONS

Émile Benveniste

By parallel series of terms, often of revealing etymology, but which differ from language to language, Iranian, Indic, Greek and Italic testify to a common Indo-European heritage: that of an hierarchical society, structured according to three fundamental functions, those of priests, warriors and tillers of the soil.

According to Indo-Iranian traditions society is organized into three classes of activity, priests, warriors and farmers. In Vedic India these classes were called 'colours', *varṇa*. In Iran, they have as their name *pištra* 'craft', the etymological sense of which is also 'colour'. We must understand the word in its literal sense: they are indeed colours. It was by the colour of their clothes that in Iran the three classes were distinguished—white for priests, red for warriors and blue for farmers, according to a profound symbolism, which is taken from ancient classifications known in many cosmologies, which associates the exercise of a fundamental activity with a certain colour that is itself connected with a cardinal point.

The same classes and the members of these classes are not called by the same terms in India and Iran. Here are the respective words

India	Iran
(1) *brahmán* (*brāhmaṇa-*)	(1′) *āϑravan*
(2) *kṣattriya* (*rājanya*)	(2′) *raϑaēštā*
(3) *vaiśya*	(3′) *vāstrō fšuyant*
(4 *śūdrá*)	(4′ *hūiti*)

These words do not correspond; however, the organization is the same and also the mode of classification rests on the same distinctions. It is in their true meanings, as in their relations within the social system, that we must examine the terms.

Here, briefly, are the lexical meanings of the two series:

India
brahmán: priest, man in charge of what is sacred in religion;
kṣattriya: who has martial power (the power of the *rāj*);
vaiśya: man of the *viś*, the clan, equivalent to 'man of the people'.

Iran
āϑravan: priest (unclear etymology);
raϑaēštā: warrior; literally: one who stands in the chariot, as a chariot fighter;
vāstryō fšuyant: provisional translation: 'he of the pastures' and 'he who occupies himself with livestock'.

We see that both in India and Iran these terms, although distinct, are organized in the same way and refer to the same activities. This social structure was maintained longer in Iran than in India.

This terminology is basic to the problem which dominates the whole organization of Indo-European society. The two groups of terms are different in their lexical character, but they agree in their social reference. The tripartite division of society to which they testify is the oldest to which we can attain. Its survivals in historical times have not always been recognized, especially in Indian society. It was the merit of Emile Senart to show that the Indian castes should not be explained by internal rules but are in fact the continuations of much older divisions which India has inherited and which did not originate on Indian soil. The Indian castes are the much fossilized systematization of divisions which go back certainly to the Indo-Iranian period, if not to Indo-European society itself. The problem is to examine the words which define in India and Iran this division into castes, and then to see if, in other societies of the Indo-European family, we can recognize a similar system.

If we review the various terms, we find that for the most part they can be interpreted directly and have a signification which is still accessible to us. We can show this by taking them in succession.

The Iranian term for 'priest', Avestan *āϑravan*, has its Vedic correspondent in *atharvan* which, to tell the truth, is not quite what one would expect, but the two words can be superimposed without great difficulty, the difference between *-ϑr-* in Iranian and *-thar-* in Indic not constituting any serious obstacle to the comparison. The derivatives are symmetrical in both Indic and Iranian: Av. *aϑauruna-*, which denotes the function of a priest, and Vedic *ātharvaṇá* 'relating to the *atharvan*'; the detail of the structures is evidence for the concordance of the original meanings. Only the etymological analysis of the word remains uncertain.

It has long been thought that *āϑravan-* and *atharvan-* can be explained by the word for 'fire', which is *ātar* in Iranian. Although the connexion is plausible from a formal point of view, we run into great difficulties with the meaning itself: it is by no means certain that *āϑravan* is the fire-priest. In Mazdaean Iran he is responsible for religious ceremonies; in India, the *atharvan* is endowed with magical powers. This conception finds expression in the collection of magical hymns, called precisely the *Atharva-Veda*. The function of this personage is divided thus: in Iran the exclusively religious side is shown, in India we see the magical aspect. But there is nothing we can see in this role which particularly relates to 'fire'. There never existed in Iranian any etymological relationship between *ātar* and *āϑravan*; and, the second difficulty, this word for fire, Av. *ātar-*, is quite unknown in India, where fire as a material concept and as a mythological figure is called *agni-*, a term corresponding to Latin *ignis* and to Old Slav. *ognjĭ*. We cannot therefore regard the connexion between *ātar-* and the word for 'priest' *āϑravan* as anything like certain.

Isolated as it seems to be, this term may nevertheless go back far into history. That it is confined to Indo-Iranian does not prove that it is of recent creation. In any case, to regard it as Indo-Iranian is perhaps to simplify the problem, because even within Indo-Iranian, as we have seen, the forms do not exactly coincide. Their relationship is perhaps not that of common forms which have been inherited in parallel ways by both members. A morphological detail suggests a different and more precise relationship. As against Vedic *átharvan-*, Avestan presents a root with inflectional variation, *āϑravan-* in the strong cases (nominative and accusative), *aϑaurun-* (i.e. *aϑarun-*) in the weak cases (genitive, etc.). If we posit for Iranian a primitive flexion *aϑarvan-* (altered into *āϑravan-*

under the influence of *ātar-*), genitive *aϑarunō*, etc., we get a regular structure, whereas the Vedic declension *átharvan-*, *átharvanaḥ* is not, and seems to have been recast. It would then be possible to regard the Vedic form *átharvan-* rather as a borrowing from Iranian *aϑarvan-* than an authentic Indic correspondent. This would explain better the relative rarity of *átharvan-* in the Rig-Veda as compared with *brahman-*, and also its specialization in the world of charms and deprecatory rites, while the term in Iranian keeps its ancient value as a term for a social class.

To designate the functions and the class of priests in India, the hallowed term is *brahmán*. It raises a problem which is still more difficult. The exact signification and origin of the word has provoked long debates which are not yet at an end.

There are in fact two forms, differentiated by the place of the accent, by their gender, and meaning: *bráhman* (neuter), *brahmán* (masculine), the first designating a thing, the second a person. This shift of the accent from the root to the suffix is a regular procedure which, because the Indo-European tone preserved its discriminatory and phonological function, served to distinguish an action noun from an agent noun.

What is the meaning of the well-known term *bráhman*? It is almost impossible to define it precisely and in a constant fashion; in the Hymns it admits of translation in a disconcerting number of different ways. It is a mysterious fluid, a power of the soul, a magic and mystical power; but it is also a hymn, a religious practice, an incantation, etc. Consequently, how can we characterize with any exactitude the masculine *brahmán* that is 'the person vested with *bráhman*', who is also designated by the derived noun *brāhmaṇa*?

There is nothing in Indian tradition to guide us in a reconstruction either of the form or the notion it designated; what we lack is a concrete sense to which we could attach the diversity of usage. India itself does not supply this firm pointer: *bráhman* is tinged with a meaning of a mystical character; it is one of the notions on which Indian speculation exercised itself at an early period and this obliterated the point of departure. The analysis of the form has fared no better: the origin of *bráhman* is one of the most controversial questions in Indo-European etymology. For a century now the most varied suggestions have succeeded one another and have been the object of dispute. Since the fluid sense of *bráhman* admits of any interpretation the textual exegesis of the Vedic uses itself reflects, as between scholar and scholar, their tentative etymologies. Let us recall the principal ones.

It has been proposed to connect *bráhman* with a group of ritual terms in Indo-Iranian of which the principal ones are Vedic *barhiṣ-* 'sacrificial grass' Avestan *barəziš-* 'cushion', and especially Avest. *barəsman-* 'bundle of branches which the priest holds in his hand during the sacrifices'. There has in fact been a formal proposal to make the etymological equation Ved. *bráhman* = Av. *barəsman-*. However, without even insisting on the difference of the structure in the root syllable, a point which is not without importance, the gap in sense is so marked in Vedic itself between the notion of 'sacrificial strewing' (*barhiṣ-*) and that of *bráhman-*, that it would be vain to attempt to reconcile them. The technique of oblation to which *barhiṣ-* in Vedic and *barəsman-* in Avestan refer has never had any extensions in the abstract sense, religious or philosophical, which is the exclusive sense of *bráhman*. In fact, *barəsman* in Avestan is only a ritual term without religious implications, designating an instrument, the use of which is prescribed along with that of other cult accessories. The characteristic association of *barəsman-* with the verb *star-* 'spread', to which the Vedic phrase *barhiṣaḥ star-* 'to spread out the sacrificial grass' exactly corresponds, shows that these terms had from their origin only a material and strictly technical sense, to which they remained confined. They had nothing in common with *bráhman*.

Of quite a different kind is the ancient connexion between Vedic *bráhman* and Lat. *flāmen*, which once was in considerable favour. In this concordance we were supposed to have evidence of ancient terms preserved both in Latin and Indic; an ancient neuter coined by means of the same suffix *-man*, Lat. *-men* is supposed to have become in both languages the word for a cult officiant. Added to this were supposedly the remarkable resemblances in the functions of *brāhmaṇa* and *flāmen* respectively. But this equation encounters numerous objections. The comparison of the essential element of the form, the root *brah-* in Indic and *flā-* in Latin causes grave difficulties; we should have to posit for Latin **flags-men-*, a form difficult to justify, with the additional disadvantage that it does not yield any precise sense either in Italic or in Indo-European. This is why this equation has been abandoned.

We shall not linger over other attempts which have come to naught, but we think that a new fact has come to light which must put an end to this discussion. We now have at our disposal a firm foothold for the determination of the original sense of *bráhman*. It is the Iranian correspondent which supplies it since in an inscription in Old Persian the word *brazman-* figures, which corresponds exactly to Vedic *bráhman*. The sense of the Old Persian word has been established by W.-B. Henning[1] who has shown that *brazman* develops to *brahm* in Middle Parthian and Middle Persian, and that *brahm* signifies 'form, (decent) appearance' and is applied sometimes to clothing and sometimes to deportment and conduct.

In fact *brazman* in Old Persian refers to cult and may indicate the 'appropriate form', the 'rite' which this cult demands. This would also be the sense of *bráhman* in Vedic; all the usages of the term have in common the notion of 'ceremonial form' in the behaviour of the priest who makes the offering and in the operations of the sacrifice. It is along these lines that we should define the proper sense of the term *bráhman*, which later was charged with mystical and speculative values.

Consequently, the Indic *brahmán* (or *brāhmaṇa-*) is he who ensures the performance of the rites in the prescribed forms. This is the definition which, at the conclusion of this analysis, harmonizes the functions of the cult official with the now assured sense of the fundamental Vedic term *bráhman*, Old Persian *brazman*. The conceptual basis is now established in Indo-Iranian, even if the root of the word does not recur elsewhere.

We are still too poorly informed of the Persian religion of the Achaemenids to assess the role of the *brazman* in cult. There is no proof that this abstract noun ever produced in ancient Iranian an agent noun, parallel to Vedic *brahmán*, to designate the person who knows and carries out the operations of cult. This is one reason for believing that *brahmán* is a purely Indic term which has [for] its equivalent a different term in Iran: the *āϑravan* of the Avesta.

The words for the other two classes are derivatives or compounds which are easy to interpret; they do not give rise to such complex problems as those which were raised by the term for the priest. But each is tied up with an important concept and because of this they deserve a brief comment.

The designation for the warrior class in India is Skt. *kṣattriya, rājanya*. The first word is a derivative form of *kṣattra* 'power', a notion which will be studied in greater detail in the Iranian world;[2] the second, *rājan(i)ya-* 'of royal stock' comes from the word for 'king' *rāj(an)-*. These two words are not applied to dignitaries but to the members of a class and designate them by the privilege attached to their condition. They do not refer to the profession of arms; both evoke the concept 'power', 'royalty'. We discern in these two clear terms the manner in which the word for 'warriors' was orientated in India: if there was a connexion between 'warriors' and 'power', this is because temporal power was not the necessary attribute of the *rāj*.

We shall see in fact that, when examining the concept of *rēx* as it is defined both in ancient Rome and India, that the 'king' was not endowed with the real power.[3] What we learn from the words *kṣattriya* and *rājanya*, is that power, defined by *kṣattra* and *rāj(an)-*, was associated with the profession of arms.

In Iranian society, the equivalent term to *kṣattriya* is, in its Avestan form, *raϑaēštā-*. More frequently, *raϑaēštar-* is encountered, a secondary analogical form of agent nouns in *-tar* (a type corresponding to Gr. -τωρ, -τήρ and Latin *-tor*); for **-star-* as an agent noun from *stā-* is impossible; roots with an intransitive sense, like *stā-* 'to keep upright' do not supply agent nouns. The formation of the compound justifies the analysis *raϑaē-štā-*, which signifies 'he who stands upright in the chariot', just like the corresponding Vedic *ratheṣṭhā*, the epithet of the great warrior god Indra. This descriptive term goes back to an heroic age with its idealization of the warrior and its celebration of the young fighter who, standing upright in his chariot, hurls himself into the fray. Such is the Indo-European conception of the noble warrior. It was not on foot or on horseback that the Indo-European warrior went into battle. The horse is still a draught animal attached to the war chariot. It needed a long history and a number of inventions before the horse could become a mount and so transform the conduct of war. But long after the revolution in technique and culture represented by the appearance of the mounted warrior, the vocabulary was still to testify to the priority of the chariot as compared with equitation. Thus the Latin expression *equo vehi*, that is 'go on horseback' continued to employ the verb *vehere* 'to transport in a vehicle'. The ancient verb which was appropriate to the technique of the chariot was adapted to the new practice of horse-riding. In Homer *eph' hippōn baínō* (ἐφ' ἵππων βαίνω) signifies not 'to mount a horse' but always 'to get into the chariot'. The sole function of the horse was to pull the chariot. To mount a horse was no more conceivable to a warrior of the Indo-European age than to ride an ox would have been for the people of the classical period. In calling the 'warrior' by the term 'fighter in a chariot', Iran was more faithful than India to the Indo-European ideology of the warrior class.

For the third class, the Indic term is *vaiśya*, which literally means 'man of the *viś*', which is approximately 'man of the people'. This establishes a connexion between this last class and membership of a social division, called *viś*.

It is quite different in Iran, where the complex, and not always well understood, designation is composed of two associated words designating one and the same person: *vāstryō fšuyant*.

The first is a derivative from *vāstra* 'pasture', cf. *vāstar* 'herdsman'. These two terms (*vāstra, vāstar*) are very common in the Avesta and are endowed with great importance. We have had occasion elsewhere[4] to analyse the etymology and to study the sense which they assume in the pastoral way of life and the religious ideology of Iran; they are among the most significant words of Zoroastrian doctrine. The second, *fšuyant* is a present participle from the root *fšu-* 'to rear stock'. The class is thus named analytically by a combination of the two words, one of which refers to 'pasturing' and the other to 'stock-breeding'.

A double expression like this belongs to a category of compounds known under the name of *dvandva*. These are double words, the two components of which are in asyndeton, simply juxtaposed, both in the plural or, more frequently, in the dual. The two terms, closely associated, form a conceptual unit. This type is illustrated in Vedic by *Mitra Varunā*, which unites the two juxtaposed gods: *dyāvā pr̥thivī* (*dyaus/pr̥thivī*) 'heaven-earth', and also *mātā-pitarā* (*u*) 'the two, mother and father'. The *dvanda* subsumes the unity of the concept in its two distinct species. It may also appear in looser forms and simply associate two qualifications. For instance in Latin the expression *Patres conscripti* only makes sense if we recognize it as two juxtaposed nouns, *patres* on the one hand, and *conscripti* on the other; that is to say here we have two groups of persons, originally independent, who together constituted the Senate. It is an expression of the same type which we have here in Iranian: the *vāstryō* and the *fšuyant* are two different kinds of persons: one has to do with pastures, the other is in charge of livestock. Then, since each forms part of a single class, a single term serves to indicate them: *vāstryō fšuyant*. This Iranian class has an explicit functional denomination in contrast to the Indic term *vaiśya*, which simply indicates their belonging to a tribe.

For completeness sake we must mention a fourth class which appears in the most recent lists. In India, the fourth estate is called *śūdrá*, the etymological sense of which escapes us; it is applied to people of the lowest category, ethnically mixed, people without a well-defined profession or a precise function.

In Iran, too, after the three traditional classes, one text mentions the *hūiti*, a term which seems to signify 'occupation, craft' and which is applied to artisans. We do not know the date when this new social distinction came about which lumped all the artisans together and made them into a distinct class.

To estimate the importance of this triple classification it should be noted that it did not only apply to groups of human beings. It was extended to the groups of concepts which were thus brought into relation with the several classes. This is not easy to recognize at first sight; it is indirectly revealed in expressions which appear to be of little significance, but which are understood in their full sense once they are brought into connexion with what are essential social concepts. We read in an Achaemenid Persian inscription of Darius the expression for a prayer to avert three calamities from the country: *dušiyārā* 'bad harvest', *hainā* 'the enemy army', *draugā* 'the lie', that is to say the perversion of moral and religious order. This is not a chance formulation. These three calamities correspond to a necessary order. The first, 'bad harvest' ruins the farmer; the second, the attack of the enemy, affects the warrior; the third, the 'lie' concerns the priest. We find here again, transposed into three kinds of misfortune, this same hierarchy of the three classes which we have found implicit in the words for their representatives. Society cannot be conceived, the universe cannot be defined, except by this triple order. Is this division, which embraces the whole people, limited to Indo-Iranian society? It might be thought to be very old, going back to the Indo-European period. In fact, it has left its traces everywhere. We recall in particular in Greek the legendary tradition about the original organization of Ionian society. A reflection of it survived in the myth concerning Ion, the eponym of the race. A legend (preserved by Strabo, 383) attributes to Ion the division of society into four classes:

(1) *geōrgoí*	(2) *dēmiourgoí*	(3) *hieropoioí*	(4) *phýlakes*
(γεωργοί)	(δημιουργοί)	(ἱεροποιοί)	(φύλακες)
'farmers'	'artisans'	'priests'	'guardians'

Plato in the *Critias* also alludes to it when he enumerates:

hiereîs	*dēmiourgoí*	*geōrgoí*	*mákhimoi*
(ἱερεῖς)	(δημιουργοί)	(γεωργοί)	(μάχιμοι)
'priests'	'artisans'	'farmers'	'warriors'

On the other hand we know the names of the four great Ionian tribes, headed by the four sons of Ion. These four proper names may be related to the four social classes. Unfortunately they are cited in a different order in different authors, which makes the comparison difficult and prevents the direct equation of each name with one of the four functions.

Herodotus, V, 66:

Geléōn	*Aigikorées*	*Argádēs*	*Hóplēs*
(Γελέων)	(Αἰγικορέες)	(Αργάδης)	(Ὅπλης)

Euripides, *Ion*, 1579–1580:

Geléōn	*Hóplētes*	*Argádē̂s*	*Aigikorē̂s*

Plutarch, *Solon*, 23:

Hoplîtai	*Ergadē̂s*	*Gedéontes*	*Aigikorē̂s*

The form in which these names have been transmitted has been affected by the interpretation: it is clear, for instance, that Plutarch intends his list to designate the warriors, artisans, farmers and goatherds. All the same, this list of names may well roughly cover the four classes. We can try to establish some correlations, but we must discard Plutarch's interpretation, which is too transparent to be anything but a late adaptation of terms which were no longer understood.

Hóplētes (*hóplēs*) is known from a number of inscriptions: e.g. from Miletus (fifth century B.C.) *hoplḗthōn* (ὁπλήθων), genitive plural with an orthographic variant; in Dacia, we encounter a *phylḗ hopleítōn* (φυλὴ ὁπλείτων). The name is doubtless to be connected with *hóplon*, plural *hópla*, not in the sense of 'arms', which is secondary, but with the proper sense of 'instruments, tools'. On this interpretation the word would designate *artisans*.

Argádēs (confirmed by epigraphic reference from Cyzicus and Ephesus as a name given to a *khiliostús*, a group of one thousand men), has a resemblance to the name of *Argos*, the meaning of which we know. *Argos* signifies τὸ πεδίον 'ground', 'plain' in the language of the Macedonians and the Thessalians, according to Strabo. *Argádēs*, if it refers to the ground or soil, would then designate the farmers. Such is the second identification which we can make with some probability.

Geléōn and *Aigikoreús* would then correspond to the noble functions, and we should expect them to head the list, as in fact they do in Herodotus. For *Aigikoreús* we are struck by the resemblance of this compound to *aigís* the 'aegis' of Athena. It is also relevant to recall that the four classes were respectively put into relation with Zeus, Athena, Poseidon and Hephaistos. We may link the last two classes *Hóplēs* as 'artisans' to Hephaistos, *Argádēs* as 'farmers' to Poseidon, who was patron of agriculture among his other functions. There remain the two classes attributed to Zeus and Athena. The *Aigikoreús* may be linked with the latter. As for *Geléōn*, we recall that he is under the patronage of Zeus according to an inscription (I.G. II^2, 1072), mentioning *Zeus Geléōn*. This testimony associates the last term with the only divine name left at our disposal, that is Zeus.

It is certain that we have here survivals which were no longer understood at the time when this tradition was recorded, and their interpretation remains hypothetical. However, the manner in which the different persons divided the social activities among themselves conforms with the explicit traditions of India and Iran. The fourth activity is that of the artisan, as it is in Iran. Finally, this distribution is regulated by divine order. We may therefore suppose that here, in a legendary form, the old social divisions have survived and this would in itself be a reason for considering it as Indo-European and not merely Indo-Iranian.

This analysis may also find confirmation in the Italic world, notably in the Iguvine Tables, a ritual formulated in the Umbrian language for the use of the Atiedian priests of Iguvium (Gubbio) in Umbria.

The tables describe the ceremonial of the annual lustration performed by the priests; it consists of a circumambulation of the territory of the city. The procession is interrupted by stations at each gateway of the town, each one occasioning oblations and recitations of formulae. Now, in the prayers which are repeated in the form of litanies, certain expressions recur which are worth analysing. They appeal for divine protection over creatures or things which are enumerated in six consecutive words, divided into three groups of two:

nerf *arsmo* *ueiro* *pequo* *castruo* *frif*

The first term, *ner-f* (accusative plural of *ner*) corresponds to Skt. *nar*, Gr. *anḗr* (ἀνήρ); these are the men of war, the chiefs; *arsmo* is the term designating the rites, the sacred; *ueiro* = Lat. *virōs* 'the men'; *pequo* = Lat. *pecus* 'livestock'; *castruo*, which corresponds to Lat. *castra*, designates the cultivated land, the fields: *fri-f* = Lat. *fructus*. We have thus: the chiefs, the priests, the people, the herds; the fields, the products of the earth; three groups of two words or, one might say, three successive *dvandva*. One of these *dvandva, ueiro pequo* 'men-animals' recurs in Iranian, in the Avesta, in the form of *pasu vīra* 'animals-men'; this correspondence, which has been long noted, illustrates the antiquity of the rite and the formulation itself of the Iguvine Tables.

Each of the three groups is concerned with a department of social life: first, the priests and chiefs, then, man and the animals, finally, the earth and its fruits.

This division corresponds, although in a somewhat different manner, to the ancient scheme, with an extension. It mentions not only the society of men, but also the products of the soil. This addition apart, the principle of classification remains the same: the priests, the warriors, the farmers (men and herds).

We limit our study to an enumeration of the proofs of this social organization, where these proofs consist of specific terms or of onomastic data. The other pointers which may be gathered from a study of the religions and mythologies lie beyond the limits of our subject. In any case, it is the domain in which George Dumézil has contributed works of fundamental importance which are too well known to need citation here.[5]

Notes

1. *Transactions of the Philological Society*, 1944, p. 108ff.
2. <Pp. 313ff.>
3. <Pp. 306ff.>
4. *Hittite et indo-européen*, Paris, 1962, p. 98ff.
5. See especially *L'Idéologie tripartie des Indo-Européens* (Brussels, 1958) and *La religion romaine archaïque* (Paris, 1966), where a recasting of earlier work is announced, such as *Jupiter, Mars, Quirinus* (Paris, 1941).

PART 2

ROME AND ITALY

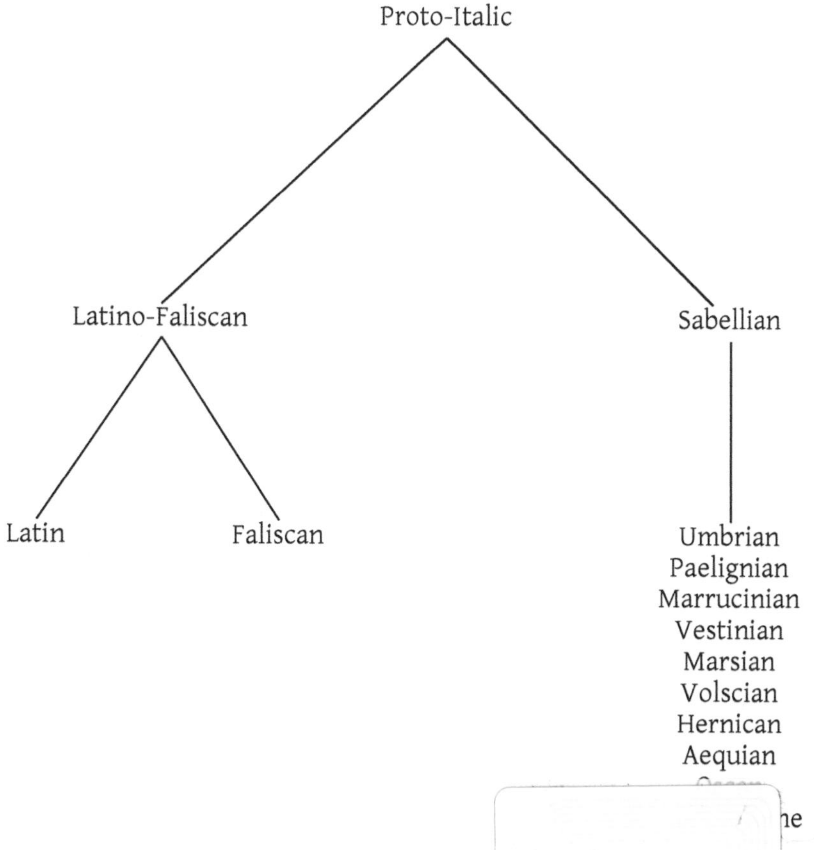

5. *Livy,* History of Rome *1.9.1–1.13.8*

Titus Livy, a native of the northern Italian city of Patavium (modern Padua), lived between 59 B.C. *and* A.D. *17. His great work on the history of Rome,* Ab Urbe Condita Libri, *consisted of 142 books; only about one-fourth of the work has survived. Livy's* History of Rome *spanned the period from the founding of Rome in 753* B.C. *(the traditional date established by the Roman antiquarian Varro) to 9* B.C., *or possibly* A.D. *9.*

Book one of Livy's History *opens with an account of the arrival of the Trojan refugee Aeneas in Italy and the fortunes of his descendants down to the time of Romulus and Remus (1.1.1–1.6.3). Most of the book, however, is devoted to the period of the Roman monarchy (traditionally dated from 753* B.C. *to 509* B.C.*). Rome was said to have been ruled successively by seven kings: Romulus, founder of the city (having a coregent, the Sabine Titus Tatius, during a portion of his reign), Numa Pompilius, Tullus Hostilius, Ancus Marcius, Tarquinius Priscus, Servius Tullius, and Tarquinius Superbus. The era of the monarchy came to an end when the Roman people expelled the last-named, the third of the Etruscan-affiliated Tarquin kings.*

The portion of Livy's Ab Urbe Condita *that appears below details the reign of Romulus, beginning with his abduction of Sabine women. Through auspices, the gods had "revealed" to Romulus that he was to be Rome's king; an angry and defiant Remus challenged Romulus and was killed by him. To grow the population of his new city, Romulus had established a sanctuary on the Capitoline hill, to which large numbers of unsavory types—principally male—had fled for refuge. In order to ensure continued population growth, however, Romulus needed to add a female element to his citizenry—hence the abduction of the daughters of Rome's neighbors, the Sabines.* (RDW)

LIVY, HISTORY OF ROME 1.9.1–1.13.8

Translated by B.O. Foster

IX. Rome was now strong enough to hold her own in war with any of the adjacent states; but owing to the want of women a single generation was likely to see the end of her greatness, since she had neither prospect of posterity at

From *Livy: History of Rome*. First published, 1919.

home nor the right of intermarriage with her neighbours. So, on the advice of the senate, Romulus sent envoys round among all the neighbouring nations to solicit for the new people an alliance and the privilege of intermarrying. Cities, they argued, as well as all other things, take their rise from the lowliest beginnings. As time goes on, those which are aided by their own worth and by the favour of Heaven achieve great power and renown. They said they were well assured that Rome's origin had been blessed with the favour of Heaven, and that worth would not be lacking; their neighbours should not be reluctant to mingle their stock and their blood with the Romans, who were as truly men as they were. Nowhere did the embassy obtain a friendly hearing. In fact men spurned, at the same time that they feared, both for themselves and their descendants, that great power which was then growing up in their midst; and the envoys were frequently asked, on being dismissed, if they had opened a sanctuary for women as well as for men, for in that way only would they obtain suitable wives. This was a bitter insult to the young Romans, and the matter seemed certain to end in violence. Expressly to afford a fitting time and place for this, Romulus, concealing his resentment, made ready solemn games in honour of the equestrian Neptune, which he called Consualia.[1] He then bade proclaim the spectacle to the surrounding peoples, and his subjects prepared to celebrate it with all the resources within their knowledge and power, that they might cause the occasion to be noised abroad and eagerly expected. Many people—for they were also eager to see the new city—gathered for the festival, especially those who lived nearest, the inhabitants of Caenina, Crustumium, and Antemnae. The Sabines, too, came with all their people, including their children and wives. They were hospitably entertained in every house, and when they had looked at the site of the city, its walls, and its numerous buildings, they marvelled that Rome had so rapidly grown great. When the time came for the show, and people's thoughts and eyes were busy with it, the preconcerted attack began. At a given signal the young Romans darted this way and that, to seize and carry off the maidens. In most cases these were taken by the men in whose path they chanced to be. Some, of exceptional beauty, had been marked out for the chief senators, and were carried off to their houses by plebeians to whom the office had been entrusted. One, who far excelled the rest in mien and loveliness, was seized, the story relates, by the gang of a certain Thalassius. Being repeatedly asked for whom they were bearing her off, they kept shouting that no one should touch her, for they were taking her to Thalassius, and this was the origin of the wedding-cry.[2] The sports broke up in a panic, and the parents of the maidens fled sorrowing. They charged the Romans with the crime of violating hospitality, and invoked the gods to whose solemn games they had come, deceived in violation of religion and honour. The stolen maidens were no more hopeful of their plight, nor less indignant. But Romulus himself went amongst them and explained that the pride of their parents had caused this deed, when they had refused their neighbours the right to intermarry; nevertheless the daughters should be wedded and become co-partners in all the possessions of the Romans, in their citizenship and, dearest privilege of all to the human race, in their children; only let them moderate their anger, and give their hearts to those to whom fortune had given their persons. A sense of injury had often given place to affection, and they would find their husbands the kinder for this reason, that every man would earnestly endeavour not only to be a good husband, but also to console his wife for the home and parents she had lost. His arguments were seconded by the wooing of the men, who excused their act on the score of passion and love, the most moving of all pleas to a woman's heart.

X. The resentment of the brides was already much diminished at the very moment when their parents, in mourning garb and with tears and lamentations, were attempting to arouse their states to action. Nor did they confine their complaints to their home towns, but thronged from every side to the house of Titus Tatius, king of the Sabines; and thither, too, came official embassies, for the name of Tatius was the greatest in all that country. The men of Caenina, Crustumium, and Antemnae, were those who had had a share in the wrong. It seemed to them that Tatius and the Sabines were procrastinating, and without waiting for them these three tribes arranged for a joint campaign. But even the Crustuminians and Antemnates moved too slowly to satisfy the burning anger of the Caeninenses, and accordingly that nation invaded alone the Roman territory. But while they were dispersed and engaged in pillage, Romulus appeared with his troops and taught them, by an easy victory, how ineffectual is anger without strength. Their army he broke and routed, and pursued it as it fled; their king he killed in battle and despoiled; their city, once their leader was slain, he captured at the first assault. He then led his victorious army back, and being not more splendid in his deeds than willing to display them, he arranged the spoils of the enemy's dead commander upon a frame, suitably fashioned for the purpose, and, carrying it himself, mounted the Capitol. Having there deposited his burden, by an oak which the shepherds held sacred, at the same time as he made his offering he marked out the limits of a temple to Jupiter, and bestowed a title upon him. "Jupiter Feretrius," he said, "to thee I, victorious Romulus, myself a king, bring the panoply of a king, and dedicate a sacred precinct within the bounds which I have even now marked off in my mind, to be a seat for the spoils of honour which men shall bear hither in time to come, following my example, when they have slain kings and commanders of the enemy." This was the origin of the first temple that was consecrated in Rome.[3] It pleased Heaven, in the sequel, that while the founder's words should not be in vain, when he declared that men should bring spoils thither in the after time, yet the glory of that gift should not be staled by a multitude of partakers. Twice only since then, in all these years with their many wars, have the spoils of honour been won; so rarely have men had the good fortune to attain to that distinction.[4]

XI. While the Romans were thus occupied in the City, the army of the Antemnates seized the opportunity afforded by their absence, and made an inroad upon their territory; but so swiftly was the Roman levy led against them that they, too, were taken off their guard while scattered about in the fields. They were therefore routed at the first charge and shout, and their town was taken. As Romulus was exulting in his double victory, his wife Hersilia, beset with entreaties by the captive women, begged him to forgive their parents and receive them into the state; which would, in that case, gain in strength by harmony. He readily granted her request. He then set out to meet the Crustuminians, who were marching to attack him. They offered even less resistance than their allies had done, for their ardour had been quenched by the defeats of the others. Colonies were sent out to both places, though most of the colonists preferred to enrol for Crustumium on account of the fertility of its soil. On the other hand, many persons left Crustumium and came to live in Rome, chiefly parents and kinsmen of the captured women.

The last to attack Rome were the Sabines, and this war was by far the gravest of all, for passion and greed were not their motives, nor did they parade war before they made it. To their prudence they even added deception. Spurius Tarpeius commanded the Roman citadel. This man's maiden daughter was bribed with gold by Tatius to admit armed men into the fortress: she happened at that time to have gone outside the walls to fetch water for a sacrifice. Once within, they threw their shields upon her and killed her so, whether to make it appear that the citadel had been taken by assault, or to set an example, that no one might anywhere keep faith with a traitor. There is also a legend that because most of the Sabines wore heavy golden bracelets on their left arms and magnificent jewelled rings, she had stipulated for what they had on their left arms, and that they had therefore heaped their shields upon her, instead of gifts of gold. Some say that, in virtue of the compact that they should give her what they wore on their arms, she flatly demanded their shields and, her treachery being perceived, forfeited her life to the bargain she herself had struck.[5]

XII. Be that as it may, the Sabines held the citadel. Next day the Roman army was drawn up, and covered the ground between the Palatine Hill and the Capitoline, but the Sabines would not come down till rage and eagerness to regain the citadel had goaded their enemy into marching up the slope against them. Two champions led the fighting, the Sabine Mettius Curtius on the one side, and the Roman Hostius Hostilius on the other. Hostius held the Romans firm, despite their disadvantage of position, by the reckless courage he displayed in the thick of the fray. But when he fell, the Roman line gave way at once and fled towards the old gate of the Palatine. Romulus himself was swept along in the crowd of the fugitives, till lifting his sword and shield to heaven, he cried, "O Jupiter, it was thy omen that directed me when I laid here on the Palatine the first foundations of my City. The fortress is already bought by a crime and in the possession of the Sabines, whence they are come, sword in hand, across the valley to seek us here. But do thou, father of gods and men, keep them back from this spot at least; deliver the Romans from their terror, and stay their shameful flight! I here vow to thee, Jupiter the Stayer, a temple, to be a memorial to our descendants how the City was saved by thy present help." Having uttered this prayer he exclaimed, as if he had perceived that it was heard, "Here, Romans, Jupiter Optimus Maximus commands us to stand and renew the fight!" The Romans did stand, as though directed by a voice from Heaven, Romulus himself rushing into the forefront of the battle. Mettius Curtius, on the Sabine side, had led the charge down from the citadel, and driven the Romans in disorder over all that ground which the Forum occupies. He was not now far from the gate of the Palatine, shouting, "We have beaten our faithless hosts, our cowardly enemies! They know now how great is the difference between carrying off maidens and fighting with men!" While he pronounced this boast a band of gallant youths, led on by Romulus, assailed him. It chanced that Mettius was fighting on horseback at the time, and was therefore the more easily put to flight. As he fled, the Romans followed; and the rest of their army, too, fired by the reckless daring of their king, drove the Sabines before them. Mettius plunged into a swamp, his horse becoming unmanageable in the din of the pursuit, and even the Sabines were drawn off from the general engagement by the danger to so great a man. As for Mettius, heartened by the gestures and shouts of his followers and the encouragement of the throng, he made his escape; and the Romans and the Sabines renewed their battle in the valley that lies between the two hills. But the advantage rested with the Romans.

XIII. Then the Sabine women, whose wrong had given rise to the war, with loosened hair and torn garments, their woman's timidity lost in a sense of their misfortune, dared to go amongst the flying missiles, and rushing in from the side, to part the hostile forces and disarm them of their anger, beseeching their fathers on this side, on that their husbands, that fathers-in-law and sons-in-law should not stain themselves with impious bloodshed, nor pollute with parricide the suppliants' children, grandsons to one party and sons to the other. "If you regret," they continued, "the relationship that unites you, if you regret the marriage-tie, turn your anger against us; we are the cause of war, the cause of wounds, and even death to both our husbands and our parents. It will be better for us to perish than to live, lacking either of you, as widows or as orphans." It was a touching plea, not only to the rank and file, but to their leaders as well. A stillness fell on them, and a sudden hush. Then the leaders came forward to make a truce, and not only did they agree on peace, but they made one people out of the two. They shared the sovereignty, but all authority was transferred to Rome. In this way the population was doubled, and that some concession might after all be granted the Sabines, the citizens were named Quirites, from the town of Cures.[6] As a reminder of this battle they gave the name of Curtian Lake to the pool where the horse of Curtius first emerged from the deep swamp and brought his rider to safety.[7]

The sudden exchange of so unhappy a war for a joyful peace endeared the Sabine women even more to their husbands and parents, and above all to Romulus himself. And so, when he divided the people into thirty *curiae*, he named these wards after the women.[8] Undoubtedly the number of the women was somewhat greater than this, but tradition does not tell whether it was their age, their own or their husbands' rank, or the casting of lots, that determined which of them should give their names to the wards. At the same time there were formed three centuries of knights: the Ramnenses were named after Romulus; the Titienses after Titus Tatius; the name and origin of the Luceres are alike obscure. From this time forth the two kings ruled not only jointly but in harmony.

Notes

1. The Consualia was a harvest festival, held on August 21. Consus, the true name of the god, is from *condere*, "to store up." From the association of the festival with horses came the later identification of the god with *Neptunus Equester*. See Warde Fowler, *Fest.* pp. 206–9.

2. Plutarch, *Rom.* 15, also gives the story, and observes that the Romans used "Talasius" as the Greeks did "Hymenaeus." See also Catullus, lxi, 134.

3. Jupiter Feretrius (etymology unknown) was the pure Italian Jupiter, whose worship was later overshadowed by the Etruscan god of the great temple on the Capitol. See Warde Fowler, *Fest.* p. 229.

4. The other instances were the victories of Cossus over Tolumnius, king of Veii (iv. 20), and of Marcellus over Viridomarus, king of the Insubrian Gauls. Propertius tells the three stories in iv. 10.

5. According to Dion. Hal. ii. 38, this was the version given by L. Calpurnius Piso. Propertius wrote the best of his aetiological poems (iv. 5) about Tarpeia.

6. *Quirites* probably comes not from Cures, nor (as Varro thought) from the Sabine word *quiris* (*curis*), "spear," but from *curia* <(*cf.* next section)>; it would then mean "wardsmen."

7. For another explanation of the name see vii. 6. Varro, *L. L.* v. 14 ff., assigns this version of the story to Piso, the other to Procilius, adding a third, on the authority of Cornelius and Lutatius, to the effect that the Lacus Curtius was a place which had been struck by lightning in the consulship of a Curtius.

8. The *curia* was a political unit the members of which had certain religious rites in common.

6. From Mythology to History

In the opening section ("Preliminary Remarks") of his Archaic Roman Religion, *from which this selection is drawn, Dumézil argues that the history of the Roman monarchy, as recorded by Livy and other ancient historians of Rome writing in the annalistic tradition, is a mythic history—an inherited Indo-European mythic tradition transposed into historical narrative. The war that Romulus wages with the Sabines, brought on by his abduction of Sabine women, for example, is a Roman reflex of a widely attested Indo-European myth about a conflict between that element of society possessing wealth and fertility (the third function) and those elements defining the realms of magic and power (first/second function). In concluding the conflict, the two elements fuse to form a single, complete society. Here Dumézil makes explicit the cognate equations between Roman and Scandinavian forms of this tradition—both descended from a common tradition of the Indo-European ancestors of the Romans and the Norse (and to which we will return in Part 7).* (RDW)

FROM MYTHOLOGY TO HISTORY

Georges Dumézil

The story of Rome's first war is very well fabricated, but it is plainly a fabrication. In the clearly revealed characters and the advantages held by each side; in the sequence of well-balanced battle episodes, none of which is decisive and which bring into play, one after another, these characters and these advantages; in the unforeseen yet basically logical development which turns a desperate war into something better than an alliance, an intimate fusion; beneath the armed maneuvers and the human passions we see a game of a different kind being unfolded, described, and demonstrated, a rigorous game of concepts. Understood in this way, the story of the formation of the full Roman society is exactly parallel to those accounts, not "historical" but mythical, which are known to other Indo-European peoples. These accounts tell how the full society of the gods was formed, starting with two groups originally juxtaposed, then opposed in a war with alternating victories and defeats, and finally united in a true fusion. I reproduce here the comparative analysis of the Roman and Scandinavian accounts which I published in 1949 in *L'héritage indo-européen à Rome*, summing up earlier works:

I. Here in the beginning, before the war, is the description of the two opposing sides:

1. On one side, Romulus. He is the son of Mars and the protégé of Jupiter. He has just founded the city in ritual form, having received the auspices and marked out the sacred furrow. He and his companions are magnificent youths, strong and brave. This side has two trump cards: it has the great gods with it and partially in it, and it is full of warlike qualities. On the other hand, it has gross deficiencies in terms of wealth and fecundity: it is poor, and it is without women.

2. On the other side, Titus Tatius with his wealthy Sabines. To be sure, they are neither cowardly nor irreligious—quite the contrary—but at this point in history they are defined as rich. Moreover, they possess the women that Romulus and his companions need.

Before they confront each other, before they even dream of confronting each other, the two sides are thus complementary. And it is because they are complementary that Romulus, realizing that his incomplete society cannot survive, has "the Sabine women" carried off in the course of the rustic festival of Consus. He acts in this way both to obtain the women and to oblige the rich Sabines, despite their repugnance, to enter into relations with his savage band.

All the authors agree in stressing and making explicit this conceptual, functional motive of the earliest events. Reread in Livy 1.9.2–4, the instructions which Romulus gives to his ambassadors when, before resorting to violence, he sends them to the surrounding cities. They are charged to tell their future fathers-in-law:

> *"Cities, . . . as well as all other things, take their rise from the lowliest beginnings. As time goes on, those which are aided by their own valor and by the favour of the gods achieve great power and renown. They said they were well assured that Rome's origin had been blessed with the favour of the gods, and that valor would not be lacking; their neighbours should not be reluctant to mingle their stock and their blood with the Romans, who were as truly men as they were."*

Di and *uirtus*, the gods and courage or manly energy, define very well the bases of the first two functions; *opes*, resources, power consisting of property, of the means of action, and also the means of fertility and propagation, here designated by *san-*

guis ac genus, characterize the third equally well. *Di*, meaning the divine ancestry of the two brothers and the promise given by the auspices on the site of the future Rome, constitutes the double supernatural element which they bring as a dowry; as for *uirtus*, they have not yet tested it in actual combat, but they feel it within themselves. *Opes* is the only factor which they do not yet have, either potentially or actually, and which is not ascribed to their nature. When they shall have acquired it and intermingled with it *sanguinem*, the synthesis of the three principles which were originally distributed between the two neighboring peoples will assure Rome of its place in history, *nomen*. And in fact the synthesis will have this result. Another historian, Florus, summing up the war very schematically (1.1), writes that after the reconciliation the Sabines moved to Rome and *cum generis suis auitas opes pro dote sociant*, sharing their hereditary riches, like a dowry, with their sons-in-law.

In the third book of his *Fasti* (lines 178–99) Ovid provides the same conceptual substructure to the event, but in dramatic form. It is the god Mars himself who tells how he inspired his son Romulus with the idea of carrying off the Sabine women:

> "*Wealthy neighbours scorned to take poor men for their sons-in-law; hardly did they believe that I myself was the author of the breed. . . . I chafed and said, 'Thy father's temper, Romulus, I have bestowed on thee. A truce to prayers! What thou seekest, arms will give.'*"

Here once more Romulus's two trumps are first his divine birth, with a god as *auctor sanguinis*, and second, thanks to a direct inspiration from this god, a warlike temperament, *patriam mentem*, and arms, *arma*. His opponents are rich men, *uicinia diues*, who scorn his *inopia*.

Dionysius of Halicarnassus (2.30.2 and 37.2), wordy as always, and following a slightly different tradition (involving not two, but three races, among whom the three trumps are distributed), still expresses the same fundamental structure. Sounded out by Romulus for matrimonial alliances, the Latin cities refuse to join these newcomers "who neither are powerful by reason of their wealth nor have performed any brilliant exploit." For Romulus, thus reduced to his quality as son of a god and to the promises of Jupiter, there remains nothing to do but to rely on professional soldiers, which he does, summoning among other reinforcements Lucumo of Solonium, "a man of action and reputation for military achievements."

Such is the structure of the entire plot: the need, the temptation, the intention, and the action of Romulus all have as their goal the formation of a complete society by imposing on the "wealthy" the necessity of associating with the "brave" and the "godlike."

II. The war itself falls into two episodes. In each, one of the two sides is almost victorious, but each time the original situation is restored, and a final decision is postponed.

1. First there is the episode of Tarpeia. It is told in different ways, sometimes (these are the most beautiful forms: Propertius . . .) with the passion of love as the motive; but it seems to have its purest form in the version adopted by Livy (1.11.5–9). Titus Tatius, the head of the wealthy Sabines, using as a bribe the gold, the bracelets, and the jewels which sparkle on the arms of his men, seduces the daughter of the Roman who is entrusted with guarding the essential position of the Capitoline. Treacherously admitted into this dominant fortress, the Sabines seem about to be victorious.[1]

2. In fact, they almost are, when the second episode occurs. This time it is Romulus who seizes the advantage (Liv. 1.12.1–9). In the course of the battle in the valley of the Forum between Romulus's companions, who have been driven back to the Palatine, and Tatius's Sabines, who control the Capitoline, the former yield and fall back in disorder. Then Romulus raises his sword toward heaven and says, "O Jupiter, it was thy omen that directed me when I laid here on the Palatine the first foundations of my city. . . . But do thou . . . deliver the Romans from their terror, and stay. I here vow to thee, O Jupiter, the Stayer, a temple, to be a memorial to our descendants from the City saved by thy present help."

> *"Having uttered this prayer he exclaimed, as if he had perceived that it was heard, 'Here, Romans, Jupiter Optimus Maximus commands us to stand and renew the fight!' The Romans did stand, . . . and . . . fired by the reckless daring of their king, drove the Sabines before them."*

Thus Romulus counters the criminal bribery (*scelere emptum*) of Titus Tatius with an appeal to the sovereign Jupiter, the greatest god whose auspices have guaranteed the grandeur of Rome. And from this god he obtains an immediate mystical or magical intervention, which against every expectation reverses the morale of the two armies and changes the fortunes of battle.

We see the meaning of these two episodes and the way in which they are applied constitutively to the descriptions of the two sides as they were first presented: the Romans and the Sabines, Romulus and Titus Tatius, engage in battle, and on equal terms, and it is neither courage nor strategic skill which distinguishes one from the other. But each of them, the chief of the wealthy Sabines on one side and the demigod Romulus on the other, has his own way of intervening in the battle and causing victory to incline toward himself. The wealthy man with his riches has recourse to gold, to the shameful trick of corruption, not by means of money at that time but by means of jewels—the kind of corruption most effective with a woman; the demigod obtains from the all-powerful Jupiter the gratuitous miracle which changes a defeat into victory. To understand the logical structure of this entire arrangement, it is only necessary to state the impossibility of imagining that the roles are reversed, that it is Romulus who resorts to bribery and Titus Tatius who obtains the miracle from Jupiter: this would have no meaning. Titus Tatius and Romulus act not only in accordance with their characters, but in accordance with the functions which they represent.

III. How does the war end? No military decision has occurred. The demigod has neutralized the wealthy man, the miracle of the celestial god has balanced the power of gold, and the struggle threatens to go on forever. Then unexpectedly the reconciliation takes place; the women cast themselves between their fathers and their ravishers. And everything turns out so well that the Sabines decide to merge with Romulus's companions, bringing to them as a dowry, as Florus says, *auitas opes*. The two kings become colleagues, and each institutes a cult: Romulus to Jupiter alone, and Titus Tatius to a whole series of gods connected with fecundity and with the soil, among whom Quirinus figures. Never again, either under this double reign or later, will we hear talk of dissension between the Sabine element and the Latin, Alban, "Romulean" element of Rome. The society is complete. A chemist would say that the valences of the diverse elements have saturated each other reciprocally. To use Livy's words again, Romulus's group, which in the beginning had *deos et uirtutem* on its side, has gained what it was lacking, *opes*, as well as the Sabine women, the pledges of national fecundity.

We see that from one end to the other the logical connection, the significative intention, and the necessity of the episodes are clear. Everything is oriented toward a single meaning, everything states and presents a single lesson; it is the history, in three stages, of the formation of a complete city, starting with its presumed preexistent and originally separate functional components. First stage: the presentation of these separate incomplete components, of which at least one, the superior component, is unfulfilled and not viable as such; second stage: the war, in which each component expresses its genius in a characteristic episode (gold on the one side, grand magic on the other, dominating the combat proper); third stage: an association of these components, unforeseen but nonetheless firm and definitive, in a unified society. And the history of Rome begins.

Where did the Romans get this schema from? In principle, one might believe that they got it from nowhere and from nobody, that it is the peculiar product of their genius, that they invented it, in the full meaning of the word. But it is here that a comparison with the traditions of other Indo-European peoples furnishes a light which Latin philology by itself cannot supply and resolves an uncertainty from which literary criticism cannot escape by itself. In fact, other Indo-European peoples also use an articulated history to explain the formation of a complete society in accordance with the system of the three functions, starting with originally disparate elements. I shall confine myself to reproducing briefly the Scandinavian version of this tradition, the account of the war, and then of the reconciliation of the Æsir and Vanir.

We are not concerned here with an ordinary human society, but a divine society, the difference being further heightened by the fact that in at least one of the usable texts the gods composing this divine society turn out to be the ancestors of a human, Scandinavian society, and that we pass insensibly from one to the other. The story is known to us from two texts of the Icelandic scholar Snorri Sturluson and from four strophes of a fine Eddaic poem, the *Völuspá*, "The Prophecy of the Seeress." As we might expect, hypercriticism has attempted to deny all validity to these two testimonies. Eugen Mogk tried to make Snorri a kind of forger, from whose works one can keep nothing but what one knows from other sources; and on the basis of extremely unreliable arguments he claimed to have demonstrated that the four strophes of the *Völuspá* are irrelevant to the whole matter which here concerns us. A double discussion, which there can be no question of reproducing or even of summing up here, has proved the error of the argument based on the condemnation of Snorri and the dismissal of strophes 21–24 of the *Völuspá*. Here, in three stages, is the sequence of events.

I. The Scandinavians recognize two well-characterized tribes of gods, the Æsir and the Vanir. The Æsir are the gods who surround Óðinn and Þórr ("Ásaþórr," as he is sometimes called). Óðinn in particular, their head, is a combination of god, king, and magician, the patron of earthly chieftains and sorcerers, the possessor of magical runes and generally of powers which allow him immediate action in all his domains; Þórr, the god armed with a hammer, is the great heavenly battler, the giant-killer, whose most famous actions are involved with punitive expeditions, and whom one calls on in order to win in single combat. The Vanir on the other hand are the gods of fecundity, wealth, and pleasure; myths and cults indicative of this quality grew up around the three principal gods of the Vanir—Njörðr (whom Tacitus describes in his *Germania* as the goddess Nerthus), Freyr, and Freyja.

Snorri (*Ynglingasaga* 1–2), who anthropomorphizes them to the highest degree, localizes the Æsir and the Vanir, as neighbors but completely separate, in the region of the lower "Tanais," near the Black Sea. One group inhabits Ásaland or Ásaheimr, with Ásgarðr as their castle-capital; the other inhabits Vanaland or Vanaheimr.

II. Second stage (Snorri, *Yngl.* 4, beginning; *Völuspá* 21–24). The Æsir attack the Vanir, and there ensues, as the poem says, "war for the first time in the world." "Óðinn," says Snorri, "marched with his army against the Vanir; but the latter resisted and defended their country; now one side, now the other, was victorious; each devastated the other's country, and they inflicted mutual losses on each other."

From the precipitate, allusive poem we know the two episodes—the only two—of the war:

1. A sorceress named Gullveig "Frenzy (or Power) of Gold," apparently one of the Vanir or sent by them, comes to the Æsir; the latter burn her and then burn her again in Óðinn's hall, but do not succeed in killing her altogether; she continues to live as a witch; in particular, she "is always the delight of wicked women."[2]

2. Óðinn, the great magician-god, chief of the Æsir, hurls his spear at the enemy, making for the first time the magical gesture which several of the texts later attribute to human chieftains, and the intention of which they specify: as is said in a comparable case, the *Eyrbyggjasaga* (44.13), it is a matter of "gaining *heill*, luck, by magic"; and in the *Styrbjarnar þáttr Svíakappa* (chap. 2 = *Fornmanna Sögur* 5: 250), it is Óðinn himself who gives King Eric of Sweden a canestalk and tells him to hurl it over the enemy army while pronouncing the words, "Óðinn possesses you all!" Eric follows the god's advice: in mid-air the stalk turns into a spear, and the enemies flee, seized by a panic fear. It is the prototype of this gesture which Óðinn makes, a gesture which should assure him of victory. Nevertheless, it does not succeed, since the same strophe later describes the breaking of the Æsir's rampart by the Vanir.

III. Worn out by this costly alternation of half-victories, the Æsir and the Vanir make peace. An unforeseen peace, as complete as the war was desperate;

a peace whereby, at first as hostages, then as equals or "nationals," the principal Vanir, the gods Njörðr and Freyr and the goddess Freyja, by the fecundity and wealth which they represent, come to complete the society of the gods of Óðinn. So well do they complete this society that when "King" Óðinn dies (for in the *Ynglingasaga* the gods are a kind of supermen who die like ordinary mortals), it is Njörðr, and after him Freyr, who become kings of the Æsir. Never again, in any circumstance, is there the shadow of a conflict between the Æsir and the Vanir, and the word "Æsir," except when the contrary is specified, designates Njörðr, Freyr, and Freyja as well as Óðinn and Þórr.

There is no need to stress the exact parallelism not only of the ideological values which provide the point of departure but also of the intrigues from the beginning to the end, including the two episodes which describe the war between the rich gods and the magician gods. It seems hardly imaginable that chance should have twice created this vast structure, especially in view of the fact that other Indo-European peoples have homologous accounts. The simplest and humblest explanation is to admit that the Romans, as well as the Scandinavians, received this scenario from a common earlier tradition and that they simply modernized its details, adapting them to their own "geography," "history," and customs and introducing the names of countries, peoples, and heroes suggested by actuality.[3]

Notes

1. On Tarpeia, see my essay at the end of the book bearing this name (1947) and my note, *REL* 38 (1960): 98–99. The theme is definitely borrowed from Greece. A. H. Krappe, *RhM* 78 (1929): 249–67.

2. Quite recently J. de Vries, who approved on the whole of my analysis, has proposed a new exegesis of strophes 21–22 of the *Völuspá*, which seems to me too critical and at the same time too free (*ANF* 77 [1962]: 42–47). Moreover, if he were right, we would still have what the two allusions of these lines tell of the Vanir people on the one side, and Óðinn on the other, each using his characteristic means against the opposing side: the Vanir's *seiðr* and Óðinn's spear. I think, however, that these two strophes need to be clarified and understood with the help of the most continuous forms of the myth: (1) Snorri assures us that the two sides achieve alternating advantages, without any decisive result; (2) the plagiarism of the myth by Saxo Grammaticus (1.7.1), with his account of the golden statue sent to Othinus and of the corruption caused by this gold in the heart of Othinus's wife, is confirmation that we should give the name *Gullveig* its full meaning, and that line 22.4 does not allude to the "incest" of the Vanir, but to the corruption of the Ase woman by her desire for gold. I refer the reader to chapter 7 of my *Saga de Hadingus, du mythe au roman* (1953), especially pp. 105–11 (cf. *Les dieux des Germains* [1959], chap. 1). I still prefer what J. de Vries has said about the war of the Æsir and the Vanir in *Altgermanische Religionsgeschichte* II^2 (1957), pp. 208–14; cf. W. Betz, *Die altgermanische Religion*, in W. Stammler, *Deutsche Philologie im Aufriss*^{2}, cols. 1557–58 and passim. I cannot discuss here Heino Gehrts, "Die Gulveig-mythe der Völuspá," *Zeitschrift für deutsche Philologie* 88 (1969): 321–78. I only remark that there is no internal contradiction (p. 359) in my treatment of Óðinn's

spear-thrust. Of course, the myth is etiological, but what it justifies is not this particular gesture of Óðinn, but the constitution of a complete society; for this reason Óðinn's gesture, which normally could not miss its intended effect, victory, *must* fail in this particular case: just as Romulus, who in all other wars could not miss victory, *must* be unable to win the Sabine war, the end of which *must* be a compromise, a reconciliation.

3. *Hér.* pp. 127–42; <see above, p. 7, n. 3, and below, p. 73, n. 18>.

7. The Three Functions

Among the various priests of archaic Rome were the fifteen Flamines, members of the Collegium Pontificum, *the Pontifical College. Each of the Flamines was dedicated to the service of a particular deity. In this second selection from* Archaic Roman Religion, *Dumézil examines the Pre-Capitoline triad of Roman deities—Jupiter, Mars, and Quirinus—through the offices of their priests, the three* Flamines Maiores, *or Major Flamines: the Flamen Dialis (priest of Jupiter); the Flamen Martialis (priest of Mars); and the Flamen Quirinalis (priest of Quirinus). These three Flamines, in the priestly hierarchy of Rome, were outranked only by the priest called the Rex Sacrorum. Dumézil demonstrates how the three Major Flamines, and the gods they serve, preserve a Roman ideological expression of the ancestral Indo-European tripartition of society.* (RDW)

INTERPRETATION: THE THREE FUNCTIONS

Georges Dumézil

For as long as people have been willing to discuss it, the pre-Capitoline triad has been generally regarded as the result of Rome's precocious history.

Giving a liberal interpretation to the classic legends about the origins of the city, holding especially to the idea of synoecism, of the fusion of two ethnically different populations, Latin and Sabine, certain scholars have admitted, in agreement with one of the two variants, that Quirinus was the god of the Sabine component, a kind of Sabine Mars, who was juxtaposed with the Latin Mars, and that Jupiter, who was shared by the two nations, was diplomatically placed at the head of this compromise. In the course of my "Preliminary Remarks," the weakness of this Sabine thesis is emphasized.[1] It is sufficient to add here that the variant which assigns Quirinus to the Sabines is obviously based on an etymological approximation, a connection with the name of the Sabine city of Cures, which the linguists have been unable to confirm.

Abandoning the Sabine component and ethnic considerations in general, others support the idea of original dualism by basing it on topographical considerations.

From *Archaic Roman Religion* by Georges Dumézil. Reprinted by permission of The University of Chicago Press.

The population of the *collis Quirinalis*, whatever it was and wherever it came from, had Quirinus as its principal god, as the populations of the Palatine had Mars, and it was the joining of these originally independent settlers in a unified city which brought about the juxtaposition of the local gods, Quirinus and Mars, in the pantheon. But as we saw in the "Preliminary Remarks," if the name *collis Quirinalis* actually means "the hill of Quirinus," there is no proof that this denomination antedates the synoecism—or, to be more prudent, let us say the absorption of the *collis* into the *urbs*—and it is possible as well that a "Palatine" god named Quirinus may have seen his cult transferred to this northern outpost, just as the "Palatine" Jupiter was put in possession of the Capitol. In reality, there is no free choice between these theoretically possible theses. The interpretation of Quirinus as a primitive local god collides with a massive fact which condemns any attempt to explain the triad in terms borrowed from the history or the location of Rome, and which, consequently, the authors of these attempts refrain from mentioning. This fact is the existence among the Umbrians of Iguvium, whose pantheon is partially known to us through the famous *Tabulae*, of a completely similar triad.[2] Three gods also appear there, whose grouping in an organic structure proceeds both from their common and exclusive epithet, *Grabouio-*,[3] and from the three parallel rituals in which they figure. These gods, in order, are *Jou-*, *Mart-*, and *Vofiono-*, and their succession, to judge from one important detail, is truly a hierarchy: if each of these gods receives as a sacrifice, with the same ceremonial, three cattle (with the offering to the third specified as *buf trif calersu* "tres boues callidos," that is, with white forehead or face and the rest of the body of another color), in contrast the minor gods who are attached to them receive unequal victims: respectively, three pregnant sows, three suckling pigs, and three lambs. At Rome, in the theory of the consecration of the *spolia opima*, it is notable that the only liturgical circumstance in which we hear of different victims being offered to Jupiter, Mars, and Quirinus, that of Quirinus is an *agnus mas* (as opposed to a *bos* for Jupiter and the *solitaurilia* = *suouetaurilia* for Mars).[4] Finally, the comparison of the three names at Iguvium with those at Rome brings out a remarkable fact: while *Jou-* and *Mart-*, shared by the two lists, are substantives, the third god is designated in both places by an adjective, a derivative in *-no* of a nominal stem.[5] These facts are enough to establish that the two lists are not separable. And this statement has an important consequence.

Neither form of the divine grouping can be the outcome of chance, a historical accident.[6] It is unlikely, for example, that a fusion of inhabitants into a unified whole under different circumstances and with necessarily very different components, should twice have produced, independently, the same religious compromise, expressed in two divine hierarchies which resemble each other so closely. Thus it is certainly a question of a grouping of gods antedating the foundation both of Iguvium and of Rome, imported and maintained by the two groups of founders and inherited from their common past.

If the explanation of the grouping is neither local nor historical, it can only be of another kind. The grouping is meaningful; it outlines by the association of three different and hierarchized divine types a religious conception in three stages. In short, it constitutes a theological structure, and is indeed, as Wissowa said, a *Göttersystem* and not merely a *Götterversammlung*. It is this structure which we must try to understand.

Finally, since we are concerned with a pre-Roman and pre-Umbrian structure, and hence one which was inherited from a stage nearer to the Indo-European unity than is Rome, there will be occasion to compare it with what is known of the oldest theological structures of the other Indo-European peoples. To reject this help, as several specialists do, cannot be justified by any reason of fact or of principle<; the “Preliminary Remarks” of the present volume illustrate its possibility and its usefulness>. Naturally, however, it is on the basis of the Roman data that the interpretation must be formed, with the comparison providing aid and control on delicate points and giving to the whole its true dimensions.

Which Roman data are we to use in this investigation? We shall gradually have to bring in the entire theology of the three gods, as well as their history. For they do have a history. If Mars shows scarcely any development, the Capitoline Jupiter, whose cult was established during the articulation of the *regnum* and the *libertas*, is in certain respects a new type. As for Quirinus, his identification with Romulus in the account of the origins has certainly altered and complicated his definition. To be sure, we must not exaggerate these changes, and we shall see that the Capitoline god preserved a great deal, and, as the identification of Quirinus with Romulus cannot have been entirely arbitrary, the very changes which it produced are apt to reveal the ancient traits of the figures involved. But, for the specific problem in which we are engaged, we must be exacting and must limit ourselves at first to what is taught by the behavior of the three flamens of these gods. On the one hand, as I have said more than once, these *maiores* priests are in fact true fossils, stubbornly resisting change; in the historical period, not one of them was ever charged with new duties;

their number never varied, and their archaic nature is obvious (the rules of the *Dialis*; the *Martialis* and the sacrifice of the October Horse). On the other hand, they themselves form, in the *ordo* and in the cult of Fides, a human triad in which the differential characteristics must not be divorced from those which distinguish the divine triad. At the most, certain social or political facts of the regal period can be connected with this first piece of evidence.

The status of the *flamen Dialis* and of his wife, the *flaminica*, is the best known of the three: containing a great number of strange items, it has interested the antiquaries and the annalists.[7] A certain number of these items are intended solely to assure the continued presence of the priest in Rome and his physical communication with Roman soil (he may not leave Rome; the feet of his bed are coated with a thin layer of mud, and he may not go three days without lying on it), but others clarify the nature of his god.

Certain items refer to the sky, attesting that Jupiter is in the heavens. For example, the *flamen Dialis* may remove his under tunic only in covered places, in order that he may not appear naked under the sky *tanquam sub oculis Jouis*. Again, he is not allowed to remove *sub diuo* the most distinctive part of his costume, the *apex* of his cap. Moreover, it must be admitted that at all times the sky god was the hurler of thunderbolts; if there is nothing in what we know of the behavior of the *Dialis* which corresponds to this trait, that of his wife fills the gap: when she sees a thunderbolt, the *flaminica* is *feriata* "until she shall have appeased the gods" (Macr. 1.16.8).

But this naturalistic aspect is not the only one. The connections of the *flamen Dialis* and the *rex*, which have already been mentioned, are definite, and must date from earlier than republican times. Livy explains their principle, evidently based on the pontifical doctrine, in his chapter on the alleged foundations by Numa, where he sums up so well the essential features of each priest (1.20. 1–2):

> He [Numa] then turned his attention to the appointment of priests, although he performed very many priestly duties himself, especially those which now belong to the Flamen Dialis. But inasmuch as he thought that in a warlike nation there would be more kings like Romulus than like Numa, and that they would take the field in person, he did not wish the sacrificial duties of the kingly office to be neglected, and so appointed a flamen for Jupiter, as his perpetual priest, and provided him with a conspicuous dress and the royal curule chair. To him he added two other flamens, one for Mars, the other for Quirinus.

The curule chair was not the unique sign of a mystical link with power: the only one of the priests with the Vestals, the *flamen Dialis* was preceded by one lictor (Plut. *Q.R.* 113), and he alone had the privilege of sitting in the Senate (Liv. 27.8.8).[8] Through these definitions and symbols we catch sight of a characteristic of the earliest Jupiter: he himself was *rex*, and he protected the human *rex*. Even in republican times, when this title had become suspect and hateful, it remained *fas* to give it to Jupiter, and to him alone (Cic. *Rep*. 1.50; Liv. 3.39.4).

Other rules governing the *flamen Dialis* (principally Gell. 10.15), the most likely interpretation of which is that they extend to the priest the traits of his god, reveal a Jupiter who is above the oath, above the law, completely free. Alone of the Romans, the *flamen Dialis* is exempt from the oath, *iurare Dialem fas nunquam est*. By virtue of his position he suspends the execution of punishments: if a chained man enters his house, he must be set free, and the chains must be carried up to the roof and thrown down from there into the street; if a man who is being led away to be scourged casts himself in supplication at the feet of the *Dialis*, it is a sacrilege to beat him on that day. A personal symbolism confirms this freedom, this absence of ties: the *Dialis* has no knot on his cap or on his girdle or elsewhere; he may not even wear a ring which is not open and hollow.

Differentially, other rules separate him clearly from the warlike area of human activity. He may not see the army, *classem procinctam*, arrayed outside the *pomerium*. The horse is particularly repugnant to him: he must not mount it.

Finally, another group of rules makes the *Dialis* the pure and sacred being par excellence, the incarnation of the sacred. He is *quotidie feriatus*, which means that for him no day is secular. Day and night he keeps on his person some item of costume which expresses his function. No fire but the sacred fire may be carried out of his house. He must always have near his bedposts a casket containing sacred cakes, *strues* and *ferctum*. The most sacred of the marriage forms, the *confarreatio*, besides being demanded of him and his parents, also requires his presence. He avoids contact with everything which may defile, and especially with that which is dead or suggests death: corpses, funeral pyres, and uncooked meat.[9]

Thus, the already complex figure of a personal god emerges at the head of the triad: celestial and fulgurant, but also kingly; active in the areas of power and the law, but not of battle, which, like the horse, is Mars's concern; the most sacred among sacred beings and the source of sacredness. It would be artificial to try to assign a chronological order to the elements of this coherent representation; particularly artificial to claim that in the beginnings this god was merely a Jupiter of the peasants, the master of good and bad weather and the sender of rain, and to assert that the rest of his qualities were later additions. The *regnum*, as we have seen, is also very old, older than Rome, and the functional pair *rex-flamen Dialis* has its counterparts in Ireland as well as in India.[10] Frazer too drastically reduced the Latin *rex* to magico-agricultural duties, and to the role of guarantor of fertility; he was the leader in all things, primarily in the political area, and in earlier times, without doubt, in the religious area: these are the parts of the royal function which Jupiter controlled in the visible world and discharged himself in the invisible world.

We know little about the *flamen Martialis*; he was not involved in a maze of interdictions and obligations, like the *Dialis*, and this was probably an essential part of his nature rather than the result of a slackening of rules. He would not have fulfilled his true function if he had been subjected to rules which had meaning only in the theology of Jupiter.[11] We have no direct knowledge of any of his sacred duties. Nevertheless it is very probable that he was active in a ceremony which goes back to the earliest times and which definitely characterizes the earliest Mars: the sacrifice of a horse to this god, performed on 15 October, on the Field of Mars. If the summary information which we have concerning the *Equus October* does not actually specify the officiating priest, a macabre imitation of it, which was performed in Caesar's time, in which two mutinous soldiers took the place of the horse, was carried out, according to Dio Cassius (43.24.4) "by the pontiffs and the priest of Mars." <Later we shall have to examine this ceremony in detail, or at least what incomplete sources tell us about it,[12]> but here the only important thing is the character of the ritual act in which the *flamen Martialis* participated. This character is clearly warlike. The victim is a "war horse," *ἵππος πολεμιστής*, and moreover has just been the "winner" in a race, *ὁ νικήσας δεξίος*, and it is not immolated with a knife but with the thrust of a javelin *κατακοντίζειν* (Pol. 12.4b).[13]

The role attributed to Mars in the royal legends allows us to glimpse what his place in the ideology then was, his point of entry into the social order. Even though he may be the father of the founding twins he does not at any point act in association with the monarchy. It is not to Mars but to Jupiter that his son Romulus trusts the protection of his work. If it is said of Numa that he created the flamen of Mars and his group of Salii, this is not an indication of affinity but merely the result of the bias which attributes to this king the establishment of all the great priesthoods. During the monarchy he does not play a significant role, but at the end, with the expulsion of the Tarquins and the establishment of the Republic, he is abruptly thrust into the place of honor. The oath normally belongs in Jupiter's province; however, in the annalistic tradition when Brutus, *tribunus Celerum*, that is, the leader of the army, swears to avenge the rape of Lucretia by expelling the kings, it is Mars whom he invokes; and the fallen king's land lying along the Tiber is consecrated to Mars, receiving the name of *campus Martius*. One has the impression, in this insurrection of the Latin military aristocracy against the Etruscan kings and in general against the *regnum*, that Mars is ideologically opposed to the traditional Jupiter, whom the Capitoline dedication has not yet reconciled, on approval, with the *libertas*.

With regard to the first two gods of the triad, we see that the collection of the oldest facts already sets the general tone for what they will continue to be throughout all of Roman history, despite inevitable adaptations to changing circumstances. Even when he assumes military tasks on the Capitol, the celestial and fulgurant Jupiter will be for the consuls and for the state the ruler and the resource which he was for the king, and, with the features of Zeus, he will still remain the most august of the divinities. Mars will always patronize physical force and the spiritual violence whose principal application is war and whose outcome is victory. The career of Quirinus has been less straightforward. What do we learn from the observation of his priest?

We know three circumstances, and only three, in which the *flamen Quirinalis* participated ritually: at the time of the summer Consualia (21 August), at the time of the Robigalia (25 April), and probably at the time of the Larentalia (23 December). Until quite recent times, they had scarcely been doubted. G. Wissowa, who usually had better inspiration, had been the only one to think that they were secondary (p. 155): the meaning and the function of the god having been forgotten, he says, his priest had become idle, and in order to provide employment for this priest he had been given new duties, unconnected with those which he formerly performed and which had also been forgotten. This thesis is definitely untenable. The Romans never treated the traditional priests in this way, particularly not the other major flamens. When the meaning of a priesthood became blurred, along with the theology which supported it, they allowed it to fade away, preserving its honors, and created new priests in order to fill new needs. Moreover, several of the divinities served by the *flamen Quiri-*

nalis are among the most archaic. The name of Consus, among others, bears the mark of great antiquity. Finally, considering the realities of Rome, it is hard to imagine the shift of these few old cults without priests to an old priest without a cult, which Wissowa conjectures. At least Wissowa does not question the facts of the problem. On the contrary, this is exactly what Latte does. Let us consider them in succession, saving the case of the Larentalia for another occasion, since it involves a particular difficulty; however, if it is to be retained, as probably it should be, it can only confirm the other facts.[14]

The calendar contains two feasts of Consus, the god of stored grains (*condere*), on 21 August and 15 December; each is followed, after a similar interval (25 August and 19 December), by a feast of the goddess Ops, the personification of abundance and, in the earliest times especially, of agricultural abundance. This arrangement proves a connection between the two divinities, which is not at all surprising and which confirms the epithet of Ops in the August cult: *Consiua*.[15] As so often happens, we have scanty information concerning the details of the rites. In the case of the Opeconsivia of 25 August, it can be thought that the grand pontiff and the Vestals officiated, but this is only an inference: all that is said in the only text (Varr. *L.L.* 6.21) which speaks of Ops Consiva is that she had a sanctuary in the Regia of the Forum, so sacred that the only ones allowed to enter it were the Vestals and the grand pontiff, who is designated as usual by the phrase *sacerdos publicus*. As for the Consualia of 21 August, an equally unique text (Tert. *Spect.* 5) says plainly that on this day the *flamen Quirinalis* and the Vestal virgins sacrificed at the underground altar which Consus had in the Circus. The two operations are different, and, if the Vestals take part in both—as they definitely do in the Consualia and as they probably do in the feast of Ops Consiva—it is because the two divinities are strictly interdependent and because the affinity of the priestesses for one also involves an affinity for the other. Latte, however, shows no hesitation in setting aside Tertullian's testimony, on the pretext of an alleged "confusion" committed by Tertullian with regard to Consus—a confusion of which in fact he is not guilty.[16] The Christian doctor is then supposed to have made mistake after mistake, and, not being aware of anything but the *opeconsiua dies* of 25 August, to have replaced 25 August by 21 August, the Forum and the Regia by the Circus, Ops by Consus, and finally—one wonders how and why, since the *pontifex* was surely the *mentio facilior*—the grand pontiff by the flamen of Quirinus. The rite of 21 August, expressly affirmed in this text, is thus evaporated to the advantage of the rite of 25 August, which is itself only a reconstruction. If one is not determined in advance to destroy the dossier of the *flamen Quirinalis* item by item, is it not wiser to accept that which is not suspicious, and to continue to think that 21 August, the feast of Consus, had its rites at the altar of Consus, that 25 August, the feast of Ops, had its rites in the sanctuary of Ops, and that it was the *flamen Quirinalis* who celebrated the former?

The Robigalia involve the sacrifice of a dog and a sheep to Robigus, the personification of wheat rust. This is one of the rare malevolent powers to receive a cult. According to the calendar of Praeneste (*CIL*, I^2, 316–17), the feast takes place near the fifth milestone on the Via Claudia. Ovid, who uses poetic license when he names the divinity "Robigo" as the blight itself, is the only one to speak of a *lucus* consecrated to this spirit, and he says that he met the celebrants of the feast when he was returning from Nomentum. This scarcely agrees with the localization given by the calendar, since the traveler coming from Nomentum returns to Rome by the *via Nomentana* and not by the *via Claudia*. From Mommsen (who cites Ov. *Pont.* 1.8.43–44) to Bömer (*Fast.* 2: 287), various plausible ways of reconciling these two statements have been proposed, and of course it is possible, after all, that Ovid was guilty of an oversight on this point. But it is scarcely thinkable that he was mistaken about the salient features in the ceremony: on the one hand, the nature of the victims, of which one, the dog, is unusual, and on the other hand, the sacrificing priest. This priest is the *flamen Quirinalis*, into whose mouth the poet puts a long prayer consistent with a conception of Quirinus which was particularly cultivated by Augustan propaganda<, and which we shall examine later>: that of a peaceable Quirinus. Latte's judgment here seems to hesitate. On page 67 he does not contest the presence of the priest: "At the fifth milestone of the Via Claudia the *flamen Quirinalis* sacrifices a sheep and a dog"; but on page 114, note 1, he decides on the other hand that Ovid's uncertainty regarding the name (*Robigo* instead of *Robigus*) and the difficulties of itinerary caused by the mention of Nomentum completely invalidate his testimony concerning the priest. This is to mix up the incidental detail, in which the poet has taken one or perhaps two small liberties, and the essential fact, in which he could not commit an error without destroying the interest and the usefulness of the whole passage.

Even though the presence of his flamen there is not affirmed, we must cite here the festival of Quirinus himself, the Quirinalia of 17 February, which belong to the most ancient known cycle of annual ceremonies. The only ritual which is indicated for this day is the one which bears the name of *stultorum feriae*, the last part of the Fornacalia (Ov. *F.* 2.513–32).[17] The Fornacalia, the feast of the roasting of grains, were celebrated separately by each of the thirty curiae, but not on a fixed date, which explains the absence of the name in the calendars. Each year the *Curio maximus* decided the days and posted them in the Forum. But there were laggards—the *stulti*—who through carelessness or ignorance allowed the day assigned to their curia to pass. On 17 February they had a "day of catching-up" on which, as a group, they were supposed to set themselves aright. What is the connection between the "feast of fools" and the Quirinalia? Is it a simple coincidence of two independent rituals on the same day? Or were they even identical? This latter view is represented by Festus, p. 412 (cf. p. 361) L^2, and by the eighty-ninth *Roman Question* of Plutarch, and two reasons recommend it. First, there is the fact that if the Quirinalia are not the feast of fools, no Roman writer and no antiquary has given the slightest indication regarding their content; but rituals just do not disappear so completely; on the contrary, at Rome they often survive the loss of their theological justification. Second—but this will not take on interest until after our next considerations of the very meaning of the name of Quirinus—there is the fact that the feast of fools concludes operations which fully involve the structure of the *curiae*, under the authority of the *Curio maximus*. I do not think, therefore, that Latte is correct when he writes (p. 113): "The feast of the Quirinalia, on 17 February, was later so completely forgotten that the final ceremony of the Fornacalia, the *stultorum feriae*, could be set on this day." This is to attribute to the Romans responsible for theology and especially for the cult more freedom than they acknowledged to themselves; moreover, how are we to understand the word "later"? Do not the Fornacalia and their conclusion furnish, in their subject matter and in their curiate organization, the guarantee of their antiquity?

A sensible consideration is enough to render improbable the disqualifications, in the dossier of Quirinus, of the offices of his flamen and the content of his festival: if the duties of the *flamen Quirinalis* at the Consualia and at the Robigalia are, respectively, a mistake by Tertullian and an invention by Ovid, if the coincidence of the Quirinalia and of the last act of the Fornacalia is accidental and without meaning, then by what miracle did these three accidents have as their convergent result the concern of Quirinus with the same thing, namely, with grain, at three important moments in its life as a foodstuff: first, when rust threatens it; then when it is stored in the granaries; and finally when the Romans, organized in the *curiae*, prolong its preservation by roasting it? If we do not have any preconceived ideas, two lessons emerge from this convergence:

it must be part of the definition of Quirinus, in contrast with Jupiter and Mars, that he collaborates closely with other divinities, to the extent of lending them his flamen; and this collaboration concerns grain, insofar as it is harvested and processed by the Romans, to their advantage.[18]

As for the social sector in which the god is interested, the evidence of the Quirinalia confirms what is suggested by the most likely etymology of his name.[19] Since the time of Kretschmer, *Quirīnus* has generally been recognized as a derivative in *-no-* (of the type *dominus*, from *domo-*), formed on an ancient **co-uirio-*, which would have designated the community of the *uiri*, or might even have been the proper name of their habitat ("*Quirium*"). We must probably simplify this etymology by abandoning the imaginary neuter **couirio-* and the equally imaginary hill called **Quirium*, and being satisfied with the feminine **couiria-*, which survives in the form *cūria*, designating the smallest division of each of the primitive tribes.[20] Quirinus may be, not the god of each *cūria* and of its *curiales*, but the god of the whole curiate organization, of the people as a whole, regarded not as an indistinct *moles*, but in its fundamental divisions. Another word, inseparable from these, has had a great career: *Quirites*, from **couirites*, the specific name of the Romans viewed from the standpoint of their civil and political organization. It is certainly not an accident if one of the feminine abstractions which pontifical science gave to Quirinus as an associate was the plural *Virites* (cf. *uiritim*), which might be translated as "the individualities": in other words, the materials of the synthesis (*co-uirites*) over which the masculine Quirinus presides.

Thus, below the celestial, royal, and highly sacred Jupiter, and below the warlike Mars, the older god Quirinus seems to have been the patron of the Roman people, and, whether by himself or by the action of his flamen in the service of specialized divinities, to have watched particularly over the Romans' supply of grain.

The conceptual religious structure which is manifested in these three hierarchized terms is now familiar to Indo-Europeanists. It can be observed, with the special peculiarities of each of the societies, among the Indians and Iranians as well as among the ancient Scandinavians and, with more pronounced alterations, among the Celts. To judge from some survivals which are to be found despite the early reorganization of the traditions, it was also known to several waves of Greek invaders, the Achaeans and the Ionians. I have proposed, for the sake of brevity, to call this structure "the ideology of the three functions." The principal elements and the machinery of the world and of society are here divided into three harmoniously adjusted domains. These are, in descending order of dignity, sovereignty with its magical and juridical aspects and a kind of maximal expression of the sacred; physical power and bravery, the most obvious manifestation of which is victory in war; fertility and prosperity with all kinds of conditions and consequences, which are almost always meticulously analyzed and represented by a great number of related but different divinities, among whom now one, now the other, typifies the whole in formulary enumerations of gods. The "Jupiter-Mars-Quirinus" grouping, with the nuances appropriate to Rome, corresponds to the lists which occur in Scandinavia and in Vedic and pre-Vedic India: Óðinn, Þórr, Freyr; Mitra-Varuṇa, Indra, Nāsatya.

For about thirty years, numerous studies of the whole and of details have been published on this subject by me or by scholars better qualified than I to explore the material in various areas: in the German collection for which this *Roman Religion* was originally written, the books which G. Widengren, J. de Vries, and W. Betz devote to the Iranian, Celtic, and Germanic religions are or will be based on the examination of this structure. For Vedic India,[21] I can only refer the reader to the most recent scrutiny of the subject, "Les trois fonctions dans le *R̥gVeda* et les dieux indiens de Mitani," published in the *Bulletin de l'Académie royale de Belgique, Classe des lettres et des sciences morales et politiques* 47 (1961): 265–98, and to the basic works by Stig Wikander. A provisional critical analysis of what had been proposed up to 1956 has been published under the title *L'idéologie tripartie des Indo-Européens*, Collection Latomus, vol. 24 (1956).[22] The study continues to make progress, to undergo completion and correction, and the constantly renewed discussions which must be carried on contribute to this improvement. In a parallel development, a slower investigation is attempting to determine which societies throughout the world, outside of the Indo-Europeans, have succeeded in formulating and placing at the center of their thought these three needs which are in fact basic everywhere, but which the majority of human groups have been content merely to satisfy, without theorizing about them: sacred power and knowledge, attack and defense, and the nourishment and well-being of all.

In all the ancient Indo-European societies in which this ideological framework exists, it is a problem to know whether, and up to what point, the structure of the three functions is also expressed in the actual structure of society. For there is a difference between making an explicit survey of these three needs and causing a division of social behavior to correspond to them in practice, as men being then more or less exhaustively divided into functional "classes," into *Stände—Lehrstand, Wehrstand, Nährstand*, as it has sometimes been expressed in a phrase which is assonant but inadequate, especially in its first term. It seems certain, in all areas, that the rapid successes of the columns of Indo-European conquerors were due to the existence of specialists in war, notably in chariotry, such as the Indo-Iranian *márya*, of whom the Egyptian and Babylonian chronicles have preserved the terrified memory. The astonishing resemblances which have been pointed out between the druids and the brahmans and between the Irish *rí* and the Vedic *rā́jan* seem likewise to indicate that in at least one part of the Indo-European world the ancient types of the administrator of sacred matters and the trustee of politico-religious power survived long migrations. Thus the two higher functions must have been guaranteed by the differentiated groups of the general population, which was often enlarged by the addition of conquered natives, and on which the third function devolved. But it is also certain that at the end of these great travels, after they had settled down, the greater part of the Indo-European-speaking groups sooner or later, often very soon, abandoned this framework in actual practice. It thus remained only ideological and formed a means of analyzing and understanding the world, but with regard to social organization it offered at best only an ideal cherished by the philosophers and a legendary view of the beginnings. The light of history overtakes Greece at the moment when this change was accomplished almost everywhere, at the point where the functional meaning of the Ionian tribes was no more than a mythical fact. Among the Indo-Iranians themselves, India is the only region in which this archaic division was hardened, through an inverse evolution, in its system of the three arya *varṇa—brāhmaṇa, kṣatriya, vaiśya*—which dominate the non-arya fourth, the *śūdra*. If the Avesta and the Mazdean books which depend on it speak at length about the three estates (or about the four, the fourth being, as in Ionia, that of the artisans), we nevertheless know that human society was not actually divided in this way, at least not in an exhaustive or stable way, either in the Achaemenid empire or in the other Iranian societies of the Near East.

The problem must thus arise at Rome as well. But it arises under almost desperate conditions, since too many centuries elapsed between the origins and the account which the annalists gave of them for us to be able to expect authentic information concerning the earliest social organization. If in the eighth century there was any survival of a division of society into three classes, respectively operating the three functions, its last traces quickly disappeared, at any rate before the end of the regal period. It was probably one of the accomplishments of the Etruscan domination to achieve its destruction. In my "Preliminary Remarks,"[23] I insist upon the fact that the legend about the war between the Latins of Romulus and the Sabines of Titus Tatius and their subsequent fusion was consistent in its development and in the significance of its episodes with the type of story that, in other Indo-European areas, forms the basis of legends concerning the formation of the complete divine society, starting with the original separation and hostility of its future components. This kind of story occurs among the Scandinavians (war, then fusion of the Æsir and Vanir) and among the Indians (conflict, then close association of the higher gods and the Nāsatya): on the one hand are the gods representing the first and second functions, magical power and warlike power, on the other hand the gods of fertility, health, riches, etc.; similarly Romulus, the son of a god and the beneficiary of Jupiter's promises, sometimes joined by his Etruscan ally Lucumon, the expert in war, is originally opposed to Titus Tatius, the leader of the wealthy Sabines and the father of the Sabine women, and then forms with him a complete and viable society. Now, this legend, in which each of the three leaders, with his respective following, is thoroughly characterized in terms of one of the functions—reread in particular lines 9–32 of the first *Roman Elegy* of Propertius—is intended to justify the oldest known division, the three tribes of which these leaders are the eponyms, the companions of Romulus becoming the *Ramnes*, those of Lucumon the *Luceres*, and those of Titus Tatius the *Titienses*. May we assume from this that the three primitive tribes (whose names, be it said in passing, have an Etruscan ring, and thus were either changed or at least retouched under the last kings) had in effect a functional definition, with the Ramnes controlling political government and the cult (like the companions of "Remus" in Propertius 4.1.9–26), the Luceres being specialists in war (like Lucumon in the same text of Propertius, 26–29), and the Titienses being defined by their wealth of sheep (like the Tatius of Propertius, 30)? The question remains open. I have offered a number of reasons for an affirmative answer, but none is compelling.[24] In the fourth and third centuries the fabricators of Roman history had only a very vague idea of the pre-Servian tribes, and it is possible that the Ramnes, the Luceres, and the Titienses had received their functional coloration only from the "legend of the origins," which was inherited from the Indo-European tradition and, as such, was faithfully trifunctional. But for the present study, an analysis of tenacious ideas and not a pursuit of inaccessible facts, this uncertainty is not very serious. It is more important for us to recognize the implicit philosophy, the theory of the world and of society which supports the legends of the origins, than to try to isolate from it the part which belongs to history.

Notes

1. <Above, pp. 60–78.>

2. See my "Remarques sur les dieux Grabovio- d'Iguvium," *RPh* 28 (1954): 225–34, reprinted, with many changes, as *IR*, part II, chap. 2; "Notes sur le début du rituel d'Iguvium (E. Vetter, *Handbuch* . . . 1, 1953, pp. 171–79)," *RHR* 147 (1955): 265–67. See especially I. Rosenzweig, *Ritual and Cults of Pre-Roman Iguvium* (1937); cf. R. Bloch, "Parenté entre religion de Rome et religion d'Ombrie, thèmes de recherches," *REL* 41 (1963): 115–22. Bibliography of the Tables (notably editions and translations of G. Devoto, E. Vetter, V. Pisani, G. Bottiglioni, J. W. Poultney), most recently in A. Ernout, *Le dialecte ombrien* (1961), pp. 5–6 (pp. 14–47, text and Latin translation of the Tables); cf. A. J. Pfiffig, *Religio Iguvina* (1964), pp. 11–31, text and German translation, followed by a most astonishing commentary: the author is one of those who understand Etruscan.

3. On *Grabouio*, see G. Garbini, *Studi linguistici in onore di V. Pisani* (1969), pp. 391–400 ("Grabovius").

4. <Below, p. 240.>

5. V. Pisani, "Mytho-Etymologica," *Rev. des études indo-européennes* (Bucharest) 1 (1938): 230–33, and, independently, E. Benveniste, "Symbolisme social dans les cultes gréco-italiques," *RHR* 129 (1945): 7–9, propose a very probable etymology for *Vofiono-*, which makes it the exact equivalent of **Couirio-no-*: **Leudhyo-no-*. The phonetic correspondences (*l, eu, dh* > *u, o, f*) are entirely regular; for **leudhyo-*, cf. German *Leute*, etc. Other etymologies of *Vofiono-* are not very likely: see my "Remarques . . ." (above, n. 2), p. 226, n. 1.

6. And borrowing is evidently excluded. A detailed discussion appears in my article, "A propos de Quirinus," *REL* 33 (1955): 105–8.

7. Unless otherwise indicated, the data given here occur in Gell. 10.15, *de flaminis Dialis deque flaminicae caerimoniis*.

8. The *flaminica* and the *regina* are the only ones to wear the headdress called (*in*)*arculum*, Serv. *Aen.* 4.137; cf. Paul. p. 237 L^2.

9. On the role of the *flamen Dialis* at the August Vinalia, <see below, pp. 184–85>.

10. <Above, pp. 16–17.>

11. Serv. *Aen.* 8. 552: *more enim uetere sacrorum neque Martialis neque Quirinalis omnibus caerimoniis tenebantur quibus flamen Dialis*. If the *flamen Martialis* may mount a horse (ibid.), it is not because of a relaxation of his statute, but because the horse belongs to the domain of Mars <(below, p. 216)>. That the position proper to the *Martialis* was rather strict appears, for example, in Val. Max. 1.1.2, where we see a grand pontiff preventing a consul who is at the same time a flamen of Mars from going to war in Africa, *ne a sacris discederet*; but the *caerimoniae Martiae* which required his presence are not known.

12. <Below, pp. 215–28,> and "*QII* 17 (Le 'sacrifice humain' de 46 av. J. C.)," *REL* 41 (1963): 87–89. There is no doubt that the manner of execution was taken from the October Horse (it too was performed on the Field of Mars, and the heads were also carried to the Regia); moreover, Dio Cassius specifies that the execution was performed in the manner of a religious ritual ἐν τρόπῳ τινὶ ἱερουργίας. It is certainly to the *Equus October*, the only sacrifice of a horse at Rome, that Pliny refers, *N.H.* 28.146: horse's gall, he says, is regarded as a poison; *ideo flamini sacrorum equum tangere non licet, cum Romae publicis sacris equus etiam immolatur*; the flamen here must be the *Martialis*, and the method of killing (by thrusts of a javelin) allowed him to sacrifice the animal without touching it.

13. In his inaugural lecture at the Collège de France, 4 December, 1945, p. 12 (*Philologica* I, [1946]: 10), A. Ernout ingeniously attributed another, nonwarlike duty to the *flamen Martialis*: ". . . Such was this distich which the *flamen Martialis* pronounced

on the day of the Meditrinalia, a feast in honor of Meditrina 'the healing <goddess>,' in order to dispel illness: *Nouum uetus uinum bibo / nouo ueteri morbo medeor* (Varro *L.L.* 6.21)." I do not believe that this can be deduced from the text: *Octobri mense Meditrinalia dies dictus a medendo, quod Flaccus flamen Martialis dicebat, hoc die solitum uinum nouum et uetus libari et degustari medicamenti causa; quod facere solent etiam nunc multi quum dicant: nouum uetus uinum bibo*, etc. Flaccus, the flamen of Mars, is thus only the *source* of the information. Ernout maintains this interpretation in his edition of Pliny, *N.H.* 28 (1962), p. 125, n. 4.

14. <See below, pp. 268–69.>

15. The connection established by the ferial between Consus and the agricultural Abundance is confirmed by the fact that Consus is one of the old divinities (Seia, Segeta, etc.) of the valley of the Circus, all of them agrarian. The best etymology of his name is still the one which connects it with *condere*. The form *Consualia* may be analogical (*Februalia*, etc.), or it may be based on a verbal substantive in *-u*; there is nothing in it to suggest an Etruscan origin. Contrary opinion in A. Ernout, *Philologica* 2, (1957): 174. <See below, pp. 267–68.>

16. "Religion romaine et critique philologique, 2, le *flamen Quirinalis* aux *Consualia*," *REL* 39 (1961): 91–93.

17. On the Fornacalia, see L. Delatte, *Recherches sur quelques fêtes mobiles du calendrier romain* (1937), pp. 13–22. The character of "god of the dead" which some have tried to draw from the date of the Quirinalia (H. Wagenvoort, *Studies in Roman Literature, Culture, and Religion* [1956], p. 182) is not supported by the facts. Only the calendar of Polemius Silvius places the death of Romulus on 17 February (*Quirinalia, quo die Romulus occisus a suis*); all the other sources associate this legend with 7 July (*Nonae Caprotinae*). Ovid, *F.* 2.481–512, speaks of the transformation of Romulus into Quirinus at the beginning of his treatment of the Quirinalia, but leaves it associated with *Capreae Palus*, thus with the *Nonae Caprotinae* of July.

18. The interpretation of G. Rohde, *Die Kultsatzungen der römischen Pontifices, RVV* 25 (1936): 121–24, is vitiated by the theory which makes Quirinus a god "adopted" when synoecism took place.

19. Among the other ancient explanations of the name of Quirinus, the association with the city of Cures is no longer defended. The etymology based on a Sabine *curis, quiris* "spear" (the authenticity of which is guaranteed by a related Celtic word) is rather unlikely: (1) Sabine *qu* causes difficulty; (2) the spear belongs to Mars rather than to Quirinus; (3) the *Quirites*, as opposed to the *milites*, can scarcely have been defined by the spear or by any other weapon; (4) on the basis of the "spear," how are we to explain *curia*?

20. R. Adrados, *El sistema gentilicio decimal de los Indo-europeos occidentales y las origines de Roma* (1948), pp. 35–59, thinks that the *curia* was not originally a division of the *tribus*, but a direct (military) "mustering"; for him, in primitive times, *curia = decuria*.

21. This is not the place to criticize the volume written by J. Gonda for the same collection, *Die Religionen Indiens*, vol. 1: *Veda und älterer Hinduismus* (1960), in which the author speaks several times of my work. I have also examined his method of discussion several times and I shall probably return to it elsewhere.

22. Cf. also *Les dieux des Germains, essai sur la formation de la religion scandinave* (1959).

23. <Above, pp. 60–78.>

24. This is the matter of chap. 2 of *NR*, pp. 86–127 ("Properce et les tribus," study of the variants with two and three races), and of the second part of *JMQ* 4 (1948): 113–71: "Les trois tribus primitives de Rome," summed up in *Idéol.*, pp. 12–15. See now *ME* 1: 15–16, 290–302, 428–36, and *IR*, pt. II, chap. 5 ("Les trois tribus primitives").

8. Iguvine Tablets VIa 1–VIb 47

Discovered in the Italian city of Gubbio in 1444, the bronze Iguvine tablets record the rites of an ancient Italic priesthood, the Frater Atiieřiur, *or Atiedian Brothers. The documents are written in the Italic language of Umbrian (belonging to the subset of Sabellian languages of the Italic group, rather than the Latino-Faliscan subset) and were probably produced between the third and first centuries* B.C., *though the religious ceremonies and structures that they evidence are far, far older. The passage below describes a ceremony of purification of the Fisian Mount, that is, of the ancient city of Iguvium (modern Gubbio) itself. The rites begin with the taking of auspices by the* adfertor *(the most important of the priestly officiants appearing in the tablets); then follows the offering of various porcine, bovine, and ovine sacrifices to deities such as Jupiter Grabovius, Mars Grabovius, and Vofionus Grabovius.*

The translator of this text is James Wilson Poultney, among the most learned and distinguished practitioners of Italic linguistics that the twentieth century produced. (RDW)

IGUVINE TABLETS VIa 1–VIb 47

Translated by James W. Poultney

(The *adfertor*) shall commence this ceremony by observing the birds, the *parra* and crow in the west, the woodpecker and magpie in the east. The one who goes to observe the messengers, sitting shall call out from the tent to the *adfertor*: "Demand that I may observe a *parra* in the west, a crow in the west, a woodpecker in the east, a magpie in the east, in the east birds, in the east divine messengers." The *adfertor* shall thus demand: "There observe a *parra* in the west, a crow in the west, a woodpecker in the east, a magpie in the east, in the east birds, in the east divine messengers, for me, for the state of Iguvium, for this established ordinance." While he who goes to observe the messengers sits in the seat, during that time no one shall make a noise nor shall any other person sit in the way until he who has gone to observe the birds returns. If a noise is made or any other person sits in the way, he will make (the ceremony) invalid.

The *templum* where the *adfertor* remains for the purpose of purifying the Mount, when established, is bounded thus: from the lowest angle, which is next to the *Ara Divina*, to the highest angle, which is next to the augural seats: thence from the highest angle to the augural seats to the city boundary, from the lowest angle to the *Ara Divina* to the city boundary. Then within the city boundaries he shall make observation in either direction.

The city boundaries are: from the augural seats to the Exit, to the observation-post, to the fore-area of Nurpius, to the Vale, to the Temple of Smurcia, to the house of the gens Miletina, to the third tower of the rampart; and from the augural seats to the avenue of Vesticius, to the garden of Rufer, to the house of the gens Nonia, to the house of Salius, to the avenue of Hoius, to the gate of Padella. Below these limits which are described above, watch for a *parra* in the west, a crow in the west. Above these limits watch for a woodpecker in the east, a magpie in the east. If the messengers sing forth, (the augur) sitting shall thus make announcement from the tent and shall call the *adfertor* by name: "(I have seen) a *parra* in the west, a crow in the west, a woodpecker in the east, a magpie in the east, in the east birds, in the east divine messengers for you, for the state of Iguvium, for this established ordinance." At each of these rites for the lustration of the people and the purification of the mount (the *adfertor*) shall hold a ritual wand. The vessels at the Trebulan Gate which are to be exhibited for the purification of the mount he shall so exhibit as to cause fire to be kindled from fire. Similarly at the Tesenacan Gate, similarly at the Veian Gate.

Before the Trebulan Gate he shall sacrifice three oxen to Jupiter Grabovius. Thus shall he speak after making the libation: "Thee I invoke as the one invoked, Jupiter Grabovius, for the Fisian Mount, for the state of Iguvium, for the name of the mount, for the name of the state. Be thou favorable, be thou propitious to the Fisian Mount, to the state of Iguvium, to the name of the mount, to the name of the state. In the consecration I invoke thee as the one invoked, Jupiter Grabovius; in trust of the consecration I invoke thee as the one invoked, Jupiter Grabovius. Jupiter Grabovius, thee (I invoke) with this perfect ox as a propitiatory offering for the Fisian Mount, for the state of Iguvium, for the name of the mount, for the name of the state. Jupiter Grabovius, by the effect of this (ox) (bring it to pass), if on the Fisian Mount fire hath occurred or in the state of Iguvium the due rites have been omitted, that it be as not intended. Jupiter Grabovius, if in thy sacrifice there hath been any omission, any sin, any transgression, any damage, any delinquency, if in thy sacrifice there be any seen or unseen fault, Jupiter Grabovius, if it be right, with this perfect ox as a propitiatory offering may purification be made. Jupiter Grabovius, purify the Fisian Mount, purify the state of Iguvium. Jupiter Grabovius, purify the name of the Fisian Mount, of the state of Iguvium, purify the magistrates, the priesthoods, the lives of men and of beasts, the fruits. Be favorable and propitious with thy peace to the Fisian Mount, to the state of Iguvium, to the name of the mount, to the name of the state. Jupiter Grabovius, keep safe the Fisian Mount, keep safe the state of Iguvium. Jupiter Grabovius, keep safe the name of the Fisian Mount, of the state of Iguvium, keep safe the magistrates, the priesthoods, the lives of men and of beasts, the fruits. Be favorable and propitious with thy peace to the Fisian Mount, to the state of Iguvium, to the name of the mount, to the name of the state. Jupiter Grabovius, thee with this perfect ox as a propitiatory offering for the Fisian Mount, for the state of Iguvium, for the name of the mount, for the name of the state, Jupiter Grabovius, thee I invoke.

"Jupiter Grabovius, thee with this perfect ox as a second propitiatory offering for the Fisian Mount, for the state of Iguvium, for the name of the mount, for the name of the state (I invoke). Jupiter Grabovius, by the effect of this (ox) (bring it to pass), if on the Fisian Mount fire hath occurred or in the state of Iguvium the due rites have been omitted, that it be as not intended. Jupiter Grabovius, if in thy sacrifice there hath been any omission, any sin, any transgression, any damage, any delinquency, if in thy sacrifice there be any seen or unseen fault, Jupiter Grabovius, if it be right, with this perfect ox as a second propitiatory offering may purification be made. Jupiter Grabovius, purify the Fisian Mount, purify the state of Iguvium. Jupiter Grabovius, purify the name of the Fisian Mount, of the state of Iguvium, purify the magistrates, the priesthoods, the lives of men and of beasts, the fruits. Be favorable and propitious with thy peace to the Fisian Mount, to the state of Iguvium, to the name of the mount, to the name of the state. Jupiter Grabovius, keep safe the Fisian Mount, keep safe the state of Iguvium. Jupiter Grabovius, keep safe the name of the Fisian Mount, of the state of Iguvium, keep safe the magistrates, the priesthoods, the lives of men and of beasts, the fruits. Be favorable and propitious with thy peace to the Fisian Mount, to the state of Iguvium, to the name of the mount, to the name of the state. Jupiter Grabovius, thee with this perfect ox as a second propitiatory offering for the Fisian Mount, for the state of Iguvium, for the name of the mount, for the name of the state, Jupiter Grabovius, thee I invoke.

"Jupiter Grabovius, thee with this perfect ox as a third propitiatory offering for the Fisian Mount, for the state of Iguvium, for the name of the mount, for the name of the state (I invoke). Jupiter Grabovius, by the effect of this (ox) (bring it to pass), if on the Fisian Mount fire hath occurred or in the state of Iguvium the due rites have been omitted, that it be as not intended. Jupiter Grabovius, if in thy sacrifice there hath been any omission, any sin, any transgression, any damage, any delinquency, if in thy sacrifice there be any seen or unseen fault, Jupiter Grabovius, if it be right, with this perfect ox as a third propitiatory offering may purification be made. Jupiter Grabovius, purify the Fisian Mount, purify the state of Iguvium. Jupiter Grabovius, purify the name of the Fisian Mount, of the state of Iguvium, purify the magistrates, the priesthoods, the lives of men and of beasts, the fruits. Be favorable and propitious with thy peace to the Fisian Mount, to the state of Iguvium, to the name of the mount, to the name of the state. Jupiter Grabovius, keep safe the Fisian Mount, keep safe the state of Iguvium. Jupiter Grabovius, keep safe the name of the Fisian Mount, of the state of Iguvium, keep safe the magistrates, the priesthoods, the lives of men and of beasts, the fruits. Be favorable and propitious with thy peace to the Fisian Mount, to the state of Iguvium, to the name of the mount, to the name of the state. Jupiter Grabovius, thee with this perfect ox as a third propitiatory offering for the Fisian Mount, for the state of Iguvium, for the name of the mount, for the name of the state, (I invoke). Jupiter Grabovius, bringing forward the triad of perfect oxen as propitiatory offerings for the Fisian Mount, for the state of Iguvium, for the name of the mount, for the name of the state, Jupiter Grabovius, thee I invoke." He shall pray each (portion) silently. In the same manner he shall make the presentation, make pronouncement upon the parts cut off, add to the parts cut off a *mefa spefa* cake and a *ficla* cake, and offer grain. He shall perform this sacrifice either with wine or with mead. He shall place the ribs on a tray.

Behind the Trebulan Gate he shall sacrifice three pregnant sows to Trebus Jovius for the Fisian Mount, for the state of Iguvium. He shall perform (the sacrifice) upon the ground, offer grain, sacrifice with mead, pray silently, recite the same formulas as before the Trebulan Gate, and add to the parts cut off a *strušla* cake and a *ficla* cake.

Before the Tesenacan Gate he shall sacrifice three oxen to Mars Grabovius for the Fisian Mount, for the state of Iguvium. He shall offer grain, place the ribs on a tray, sacrifice with mead, pray silently, add spelt-cakes and a *ficla* cake to the parts cut off, and recite the same formulas as before the Trebulan Gate.

Behind the Tesenacan Gate he shall sacrifice three sucking pigs to Fisus Sancius for the Fisian Mount, for the state of Iguvium. He shall sacrifice with mead, perform (the sacrifice) upon the ground, offer grain, recite the same formulas as before the Trebulan Gate, pray silently, have a maniple folded double upon his right hand, and add to the parts cut off a *ficla* cake and a *strušla* cake. When he has put the under-parts at the back (of the altar), kneeling he shall offer a libation and a *mefa spefa* cake in a cup to Fisovius Sancius for the Fisian Mount, for the state of Iguvium. Thus shall he pray after pouring the libation: "Thee I invoke as the one invoked, Fisovius Sancius, for the Fisian Mount, for the state of Iguvium, for the name of the mount, for the name of the state. Be thou favorable, be thou propitious to the Fisian Mount, to the state of Iguvium, to the name of the mount, to the name of the state. In the consecration I invoke thee as the one invoked, Fisovius Sancius, in trust of the consecration I invoke thee as the one invoked, Fisovius Sancius." Likewise shall he pray with the mead. Thus shall he pray with the *mefa spefa* cake: "Fisovius Sancius, thee with this Fisovian *mefa spefa* cake for the Fisian Mount, for the state of Iguvium, for the name of the mount, for the name of the state (I invoke). Fisovius Sancius, grant to the Fisian Mount, to the state of Iguvium, to the men and beasts of the Fisian Mount, of the state of Iguvium, (success in) word and deed, before and behind, in private and in public, in vow, in augury, and in sacrifice. Be favorable and propitious with thy peace to the Fisian Mount, to the state of Iguvium, to the name of the mount, to the name of the state. Fisovius Sancius, keep safe the Fisian Mount, the state of Iguvium. Fisovius Sancius, keep safe the name of the Fisian Mount, of the state of Iguvium, keep safe the magistrates, the priesthoods, the lives of men and of beasts, the fruits. Be favorable and propitious with thy peace to the Fisian Mount, to the state of Iguvium, to the name of the mount, to the name of the state. Fisovius Sancius, thee with this Fisovian *mefa spefa* cake for the Fisian Mount, for the state of Iguvium, for the name of the mount, for the name of the state, Fisovius Sancius, thee I invoke. In trust of Fisovius I invoke thee." In the middle of the prayer he shall pour a libation and dance the *tripudium*. When he has presented this (cake) he shall distribute the *erus* of the parts cut off. Then kneeling, from a cup he shall distribute the *erus* of the libation. Then he shall remove from the platter the *mefa* cake and the libation and scatter them down into the fire. Then sitting he shall grind (the cakes) and shall pray with the ground (cakes). He shall move the two loaned bowls, he shall move the two consecrated bowls.

Before the Veian Gate he shall sacrifice three oxen with white foreheads to Vofionus Grabovius for the Fisian Mount, for the state of Iguvium. He shall place the ribs on a tray, sacrifice either with wine or with mead, offer grain, pray silently, and add to the parts cut off a *mefa spefa* cake and a *ficla* cake, and recite the same formulas as before the Trebulan Gate.

Behind the Veian Gate he shall sacrifice three lambs to Tefer Jovius for the Fisian Mount, for the state of Iguvium. He shall sacrifice sitting, he shall sacrifice (the victims) for burial, offer grain, sacrifice with mead, pray silently, add to the parts cut off a *strušla* cake and a *ficla* cake, and recite the same formulas as at the Trebulan Gate. When he has presented the lambs, the same one who has presented the lambs shall offer at his right foot a libation and a pig-*persondro.* He shall make a mound for the bowl; he shall hold it in his left hand until he has poured the libation; he shall set down the bowl. In like manner he shall distribute the *erus* at his foot. Thus shall he pray after making the libation: "Thee I invoke as the one invoked, Tefer Jovius, for the Fisian Mount, for the state of Iguvium, for the name of the mount, for the name of the state. Be thou favorable, be thou propitious to the Fisian Mount, to the state of Iguvium, to the name of the mount, to the name of the state. In the consecration I invoke thee as the one invoked, Tefer Jovius. In trust of the consecration I invoke thee as the one invoked, Tefer Jovius. Tefer Jovius, (I invoke) thee with this pig-*persondro* for Tefer as a propitiatory offering for the Fisian Mount, for the state of Iguvium, for the name of the mount, for the name of the state. Tefer Jovius, by the effect of this (bring it to pass), if on the Fisian Mount fire hath occurred or in the state of Iguvium the due rites have been omitted, that it be as not intended. Tefer Jovius, if in thy sacrifice there hath been any omission, any sin, any transgression, any damage, any delinquency, if in thy sacrifice there be any seen or unseen fault, Tefer Jovius, if it be right, with this pig-*persondro* as a propitiatory offering may purification be made. Tefer Jovius, purify the Fisian Mount, the state of Iguvium. Tefer Jovius, purify the name of the Fisian Mount, of the state of Iguvium, purify the magistrates, the priesthoods, the lives of men and of beasts, the fruits. Be favorable and propitious with thy peace to the Fisian Mount, to the state of Iguvium, to the name of the mount, to the name of the state. Tefer Jovius, keep safe the Fisian Mount, the state of Iguvium. Tefer Jovius, keep safe the name of the Fisian Mount, of the state of Iguvium, keep safe the magistrates, the priesthoods, the lives of men and of beasts, the fruits. Be favorable and propitious with thy peace to the Fisian Mount, to the state of Iguvium, to the name of the mount, to the name of the state. Tefer Jovius, thee with this pig-*persondro* for Tefer as a propitiatory offering for the Fisian Mount, for the state of Iguvium, for the name of the mount, for the name of the state, Tefer Jovius, thee I invoke." In the middle of the prayer he shall dance the *tripudium*.

He shall offer a *persondro* for Stabilis at his left foot: he shall make a mound for the bowl in the same manner, he shall pray in the same manner as in the case of the pig-*persondro* (for Tefer). When he has presented the *persondro*, he shall distribute the *erus* of the parts cut off. Then he shall distribute the *erus* of the libation accompanying the pig-*persondro*, at his right foot, toward the mound, where he has offered the pig-*persondro*. Then (he shall offer) the libation for Stabilis at his left foot, and likewise distribute the *erus*. Then where he has prayed, there he shall place the pig-*persondro* (for Tefer) on the mound and bury it. Then where he has prayed, there he shall place the *persondro* for Stabilis on the mound and bury it. Then, sitting, he shall throw over (his head) the vessels which he has kept with the *persondra*. He shall sit during the interval until he has prayed with the ground (cakes). Anyone at all, sitting, shall grind (the cakes). Sitting, (the *adfertor*) shall pray with the ground (cakes). The sacrifice will have been completed.

At the Grove of Jupiter, while they are placing on a platter (the remains of) the sheep, he shall sacrifice three bull-calves; he shall sacrifice to Mars Hodius for the people of the state of Iguvium, for the state of Iguvium. He shall place the ribs on a tray, sacrifice with mead, offer grain, pray silently, add spelt-cakes and a *ficla* cake to the parts cut off, and recite the same formulas as at the Trebulan Gate.

At the Grove of Coredius he shall sacrifice three bull-calves; he shall sacrifice to Hondus Šerfius for the people of the state of Iguvium, for the state of Iguvium. He shall place the ribs on a tray, offer grain, sacrifice either with wine or with mead, pray silently, add to the parts cut off a twisted cake and a *ficla* cake, and recite the same formulas as at the Trebulan Gate. Then the Mount will have been purified. If there is any interruption of these rites, they shall be invalid; he must take an observation of the birds, return to the Trebulan Gate, and perform the rite anew.

9. Social Symbolism in Greco-Italic Cults

In this article, first published in 1945, Benveniste considers diverse elements of ancient Italic and Greek religion and finds in each of these the preservation of primitive Indo-European conceptions of social tripartition. He examines Umbrian religion, focusing on the gods Jupiter Grabovius, Mars Grabovius, and Vofionus Grabovius, encountered in the previous reading from the Iguvine tablets; a Roman prayer offered to Mars during a rite of agrarian purification (as described by the Latin author Porcius Cato, who lived from 243 B.C. to 149 B.C.), and the triple sacrifice of a pig, sheep, and bull (the suovetaurilia *or* suovitaurilia*) which is associated with that rite as well as with various other Roman rituals; and Greek liquid offerings to the dead.* (RDW)

SOCIAL SYMBOLISM IN GRECO-ITALIC CULTS

Émile Benveniste

The division of society into three classes—priests, warriors, and farmers—was a principle of which the ancient Indo-Iranians were fully aware and which in their eyes possessed the authority and necessity of a natural fact. This classification governed the Indo-Iranian world so profoundly that its actual domain extended well beyond its explicit statement in hymns and rituals. It has been shown[1] that various representations outside the sphere of the social per se were compatible with this principle, to the point where any attempt to define a conceptual totality tended unconsciously to borrow the tripartite framework that organized society. In a series of brilliant studies, Georges Dumézil traced the origin of this classification back to the Indo-European community by detecting its presence in the myths and legends of ancient Western Europe and in particular in Roman religion (this is the subject of his book *Jupiter, Mars, Quirinus*).[2] The purpose of this paper is to add some new observations to this body of research, observations that confer a symbolic significance on certain formulas and practices of the Italic and Hellenic cults and thereby connect those cults to social representations. The data used are generally well known. This is my excuse for the somewhat schematic nature of the text, whose purpose is not to recount the facts yet again in detail but rather to interpret them.

Umbrian Triads

In the Umbrian religion, as we know it from the ritual of Iguvium,[3] the number three is pregnant with meaning: it governs the order of ceremonies, offerings, and invocations, and we have a triple circumambulation of the site, a triple lustrative sacrifice, deities grouped in triads, triple formulas, and so on. This fact is well known and has many parallels.[4] But the undeniable "mystic" virtue of the number three is not the only issue. In several of these groupings, each term in fact refers to a social class, and the entire enumeration reconstitutes the totality of the society.

A clear example of this is: *nerf arsmo ueiro pequo castruo frif pihatu*, [Lat.] *principes et sacerdotes, homines et pecudes, capita*[5] *et fruges piato* ["he (you?) shall ritually purify rulers and priests, humans and cattle, roots and fruit"].[6] The sentence contains three groups of two nouns juxtaposed in *dvandvas: nerf arsmo* designates the representatives of religious kingship; *ueiro pequo* (Av. *pasu vira*), the *uiri* considered as husbandmen in a situation in which divine favor was being asked for the productive forces of the society;[7] *castruo frif*, the fertility of the soil.

In this context we will include a divine triad that poses a broader problem. I am speaking of the three "Grabovian" gods, who, according to their common epithet, share the characteristic of being "gods of the oak,"[8] whatever such a denomination might mean: Jupiter, Mars, Vofionus: *iuue grabouei . . . marle grabouei . . . uofione grabouie*, [Lat.] *Jovi Grabovio, Marti Grabovio, Vofiono Grabovio.* As has long been noted, this Umbrian triad parallels the Roman triad Jupiter, Mars, Quirinus.[9] But if the first two names are identical, the discordance between Quirinus and Vofionus, coupled with the difficulty of specifying the role of the Umbrian god, poses a serious obstacle to comparison of the two groups. Accordingly, Giacomo Devoto limits himself to the following remark: "In trinitate grabovia Vofionus locum tenet quem Quirinus apud Romanos: natura tamen eius bellica probari non potest."[10]

The allegedly "bellicose" nature of Quirinus is no longer tenable. Analysis of his name assigns him a quite different function. *Quirinus* is the god of the *Quirites*, citizens gathered together in a *curia*. These three words have a common base: **couiria*, "meeting of the *viri*," of which a masculine form **co-uirio-* is attested by Volscan *covehriu*, "*conventu*."[11] In contrast to Jupiter and Mars, who represent, respectively, magical kingship and military might, Quirinus embodies a class of citizens, a "third estate," whose work is essentially rural. For a more detailed analysis of its role in the Roman triad, which reflects the threefold nature of Indo-Iranian society, see the previously mentioned work by Georges Dumézil.[12]

What do we do, then, with Vofionus, who occupies a symmetrical place in the Umbrian triad? All we know about him is what we think we can deduce from his name. *Vofion-* is explained etymologically as the god of offerings, of wishes, *qui oblationem votivam facit*, through a comparison with Umbr. *vufru*, "*votivus*," and Lat. *uoueo, uotum*. But what can a god of offerings, or a god laden with offerings, represent? Where do we find such a god, honored with such high rank?[13] This interpretation, which does not appear to be supported by any known parallel, does not touch on the god's essential function and overlooks the relation with the other two gods. A fortiori, therefore, we cannot understand Vofionus's position in relation to Quirinus. Albrecht von Blumenthal correctly noted that the explanation of Vofionus in terms of *deus votorum* failed to take account of the close relationship between the Grabovian triad and the Roman triad.[14]

We shall therefore attempt to give an interpretation of this divine name that takes fuller account of the god's importance and function. The Umbrian form *vofion-* can be based phonetically on the prototype **leudhyon-*. Each feature of this reconstruction can be proven: for the treatment *u-<l-*, cf. *vuku, uocu-* = Lat. *lucus*, and *uaper, uapers-* = Lat. *lapis*; for *o, u*, representing ancient **-eu-*, **-ou-* (confused since common Italic), cf. *tuta, tota* = Gothic *þiuda*, etc.; for *f* <**dh*, cf. *rofu, rofa* = Lat. *rufus*, Gothic *rauda*, [and] *rufru*, "*rubros*," <**reudh-*, Gr. *ἐρυθρός*. Hence there is no reason why *uofion-* cannot be traced back to **leudhyon-* (or **loudhyon-*). More than that, an ancient **leudhyon-* (**loudhyon-*) could not yield anything in Umbrian other than *uofion-*, a derivative of the same type as Lat. *curio*. According to his name, Vofionus must therefore be either a god of "growth," comparable to the Latin *Liber* (**leudheros*),[15] or, what comes to the same thing, a god of the nation, the popular community (Old Slavic *ljudije*, "*gens*," OE *leod*, German *Leute*, etc.). In this role, he would indeed be the equivalent of Quirinus, god of the "people" and a fructifying deity.

If this analysis is correct, we have restored in Umbrian mythology the same triple grouping that attests the survival of the Indo-European structure among the Romans in the form of the trinity Jupiter-Mars-Quirinus. Hence this is an Italic heritage, but one that was adapted early on to differentiated societies. With the changes in social terminology that occurred in the Italic regions and indeed among most Indo-European peoples, the gods of society took on new names without changing their functions. Thus Quirinus and Vofionus, who occupy the same place in the trinitarian hierarchy, symbolize the same activity and the same class despite the difference in their names.

Agrarian Lustration in Rome

We know about agrarian lustration rites in the old Roman religion from a passage in Cato (*De agricultura* 141), which, though frequently cited, is still worth looking at once again. The passage prescribes leading the three animals of the *suovetaurilia* around the field and offering to Mars a prayer whose terms are prescribed. The essential part of this prayer runs as follows:

> Mars pater, te precor quaesoque uti sies volens propitius mihi domo familiaeque nostrae, quoius rei ergo agrum terram fundumque meum suovetaurilia circumagi iussi, uti tu morbos visos invisosque, viduertatem vastitudinemque, calamitates intemperiasque prohibessis defendas auerruncesque; utique tu fruges, frumenta, vineta virgultaque grandire beneque evenire siris, pastores pecuaque salva servassis duisque bonam salutem valetudinemque mihi domo familiaeque nostrae.
>
> Father Mars, I pray and beseech you to be kindly and favorable to me, my home, and my household. For this purpose I have ordered that a *suovetaurilia* be led around my land, ground, and farm so that you will prevent, ward off, and remove seen and unseen illness, barrenness, destruction, disaster, and unseasonable weather, so that you will allow my crops, grain, and vineyards to flourish and turn out well, and so that you will keep my shepherds and flocks healthy and give good health and strength to me, my home, and my household.

This passage abounds in double and triple expressions, which are ordinarily held to be redundancies typical of archaic formularies and their obsession with detail. In fact, the repetitions are quite varied in character. Some of the repetitions in the first part of the prayer are meant to define unambiguously a feeling, act, or object (*volens propitius, precor quaesoque, agrum terram fundumque*). Others are enumerative (*mihi domo familiaeque, fruges frumenta vineta virgultaque*, etc.). But—and this is what I wish to demonstrate—still others establish hierarchies. In them we recognize distinct notions coordinated in a structure that is not merely formal.

The enumeration of woes includes three terms with two members each: *morbos visos invisosque* – *viduertatem vastitudinemque* – *calamitates intemperiasque*. It is no accident that there are also three verbs: *prohibessis defendas averruncesque*. There is every reason to believe that nouns and verbs correspond analytically and that, with respect to the sense of the passage, they constitute units that balance one another. The woes are divided into three distinct species, each of which is symbolic:

morbos visos invisosque, visible or hidden maladies, are matters for the science of the priest-magician. The god is asked to "prohibit" (*prohibessis*) them, and the verb used is one frequently employed in deprecations: *di prohibeant! Jupiter prohibessit!* etc.;

viduertatem vastitudinemque, depopulation and devastation, are ravages caused by war (the old term *viduertas* is properly speaking the act of taking the life of a spouse). Hence the second verb is *defendere*, "to repulse by force of arms"; cf. *defendere hostes*, "to repulse the enemy," in Ennius;

calamitates intemperiasque are clearly scourges that damage the harvest and must be "swept away" or "turned aside" (*averrunces*). In the guise of a redundant formulation, then, what we find in this enumeration is an arrangement ordered in accordance with the social categories. Each class is defined by the particular woe that threatens its representatives. The totality of evil is socialized and decomposed into symbolic species. This representation also takes us back to the Indo-European past. We have already detected it in India and Iran, where it expressed itself in the form of prayers and wishes.[16] In *Taitt. Samh.*, I, 1, 13, 3, we read: *pāhí prásityai pāhí dúristyai pāhí duradmanyaí*, "keep [me] from subjection! keep [me] from wicked offering! keep [me] from bad food!"[17] Darius echoes this when he implores Ahuramazda's protection for his country (inscr. of Perspeolis, *d* § 3): *imām dahyāum ahuramazdā pātuv hačā haināyā hačā dušiyārā hačā draugā*, "may Ahuramazda keep this country from the armed enemy, bad harvest, the spirit of falseness." If there is a difference, it has to do only with the fact that the Sanskrit and Persian formulas have a general value, whereas the Roman prayer is intended in particular to ensure the prosperity of the field and the expression of wishes is adapted to that purpose. With this caveat, one can establish a comparison among the three phraseological series: *morbi visi invisique* corresponds to Skr. "bad offering," to Old Per. "spirit of perversion"; *viduertas vastitudoque* to Skr. "subjection (to the foreigner)," to Old Per. "armed enemy"; *calamitates intemperiaeque* to Skr. "bad food," to Old Per. "bad harvest."

In the second part of the Roman prayer, the same structure reappears, but this time the whole range of desired benefits is analytically enumerated for each item. The hierarchy is identical but reversed: *utique tu fruges, frumenta, vineta virgultaque grandire beneque evenire siris* . . . herald the health of the crop; . . . *pastores pecuaque salva servassis*, that is, in second place as in the Umbrian prayer and with the same expression (see below), the class of "men," in this case husbandmen; . . . *duisque bonam salutem valetudinemque mihi domo familiaeque nostrae*, the last class, that of priests, is represented by the person making the offering, who is in fact the person making the sacrifice, and the favor that he is asking is expressed in a *bona salus* formula, both terms of which are equally pregnant with religious value: *salus* is the Latin expression for the notion of "integrity" that is so important in all religious phenomenology, and the epithet *bona* adds its special force (cf. *boni di, bona fides, bonas preces precari, bene dicere*, etc.). Compare this phrase with the one that begins the prayer: *Mars pater, te precor quaesoque uti sies volens propitius mihi domo familiaeque nostrae*, and it appears that the *bona salus valetudoque* that it is asking, in both sequences, for *mihi domo familiaeque nostrae* will be the proof of the god's favorable dispositions (*volens propitius*). The sacrifice that he is offering will confer upon him the "integrity" that is a sign of divine favor because it is itself a divine virtue.

It can hardly be doubted that Cato's text, with its consecrated form, perpetuated quite archaic concepts that established a symbolic parallel between the society and the ceremonial act. But this prayer was only the first act of a "sacrifice" that also included a solemn ritual, the offering of the *suovetaurilia*.

The Suovetaurilia

The sacrifice offered to Mars consisted of three animals: a pig, a sheep, and a bull. It was consistently designated by the term *suovetaurilia*, which hypostasized in a single word three words in the ablative, fixed and juxtaposed in the form they had in the ritual: *suovetaurilia* is in a sense the nominal transposition of the locution *su ove tauro* (*facere*). Modern historians have always viewed this grouping as a simple fact, and no one to my knowledge has asked whether this choice of animals was somehow necessary. There must be some reason for such a selection, however. Other animals (such as dogs, horses, or birds) might have been sacrificed, or perhaps only one of these three. Why choose precisely these three, why sacrifice all of them, and why offer them up to Mars?

The answer to the first two of these questions can already be found in the analysis I have proposed of the prayer that preceded the sacrifice. By virtue of a necessary liaison, the ritual was governed by the same representations that ordered the invocation. We need only prove that each of the animals did indeed have the symbolic significance that this liaison suggests. Now, it so happens that in light of very ancient data preserved in the religious literature, we can verify the correspondence between each animal and the god to which it was consecrated.[18]

The pig (*sus*) was the sacrifice that belonged to the Earth. Macrobius (*Saturnalia* 1.12, 20) says of Tellus: *sus praegnans ei mactatur, quae hostia propria est terrae.*[19] The ovine, sheep or lamb (*ovis*), was immolated to Jupiter from time immemorial. It will suffice to recall two important pieces of evidence. First, the *ovis Idulis* of which Festus says: *Idulis ovis dicebatur, quod omnibus idibus Jovi mactabatur*. And second, the offering of the *ovis* to Jupiter to consecrate the most solemn form of marriage, the *confarreatio*, over which the *pontifex maximus* and the *flamen Dialis* presided.[20]

Finally, the bull (*taurus*) belonged to Mars, to whom it was solemnly sacrificed at the Capitol and the Forum Augusti. Roman scholars claimed that, apart from Neptune and Apollo, only Mars was entitled to the sacrifice of a bull and that Jupiter in particular was not so entitled.[21]

We are thus assured that the whole social structure was involved in the *suovetaurilia*, with each class taking part in the sacrifice through the animal symbolizing its specific god, while the entire ceremony—prayer and offering—bestowed its benefits on the society as a whole, whether by purifying the people gathered on the Field of Mars or the victorious legions before the triumph or simply the family field.

It is not fortuitous that this sacrifice of three animals also existed in Greece at a very early date. The *τριττύς* or *τρίττοια* include three male animals: bull, ram, boar. In the *Odyssey*, they are immolated together to Poseidon:

> ῥέξας ἱερὰ καλὰ Ποσειδάωνι ἄνακτι
> ἀρνειὸν ταῦρόν τε συῶν τ' ἐπιβήτορα κάπρον (11.130.1)

But the sacrifice could also be offered to other gods: it is mentioned in connection with Apollo, Asclepius, the Dioscuri, etc. It was usually to consecrate a solemn oath, as we learn from the scholiast of a Homeric text (T 197): *πρὸς δὲ τὰ ὅρκια τρισὶν ἐχρῶντο Ἀττικοί, κάπρῳ κριῷ ταύρῳ*. This assertion is corroborated by Demosthenes,[22] who described the oath-taking in a judgment for homicide: *στὰς ἐπὶ τῶν τομίων κάπρου καὶ ταύρου*. It is also corroborated by a prescription of Cos: *τὰ δὲ ὁρκωμόσια ἔστω ταῦρος κάπρος κριός. τέλεια πάντα.*[23] Although the correlation noted above between the sacrifice of certain animals and the cult of a specific god does not obtain in Greece,[24] there can be no doubt that the *τρίττοια* was a survival of the same past to which the *suovetaurilia* belonged and must be interpretable in the same way. When Mars was invoked and honored with the *suovetaurilia*, it was to repel the various kinds of evil that might pose a threat to the society and the fruits of the earth on which it depended.[25] It was the god's warrior functions that were addressed. In the *Odyssey*, moreover, Poseidon receives a triple sacrifice because of his function: the navigator who wishes to escape the perils of the sea owes the god on whom his fate will depend a sacrifice that symbolically sums up the entire human condition. In other circumstances, however, that sacrifice goes to a different god such as Apollo or the Dioscuri, and so on. In each case it is a question of placing the entire society under the protection of the god who is most effective under the circumstances.

The Libation to the Dead

I believe that the same representations can also be detected in yet another practice: the libation that the Greeks offered to the dead, the *χοή*. Traditionally, this consisted of three liquid offerings: wine, honey, milk.[26] Each of these substances has an intrinsic meaning. *Wine*, whether it was called *οἶνος* or *μέθυ*, was the beverage of the strong, of warriors. *Honey* was famous for its purifying and inspirational virtues; the nourishment of seers, it was reputed to confer prophetic gifts and to place the celebrant in a spiritual relationship with his god. *Milk* was the ordinary offering of farmers and shepherds. Hence it is not presumptuous to link exalting wine, purifying honey, and nourishing milk respectively to warriors, priests, and cultivators. Here, again, the offering epitomizes the whole range of figurations in terms of which the society represents itself. If the homage in this case is offered to the dead, the reason is probably to be sought in the relationship between the dead and the living: it was essential that the framework of society be extended to the dead who once lived in that society, and in order to do this one allowed them to partake of the nourishment essential to the living. In return, the society of the living was rejuvenated and solemnized through consecration by the dead. In the Greek religion, which was so profoundly transformed that it offers little for comparatists to grasp, a trait like this one enables us to recognize the same tripartite organization that we know from Ionian and Attic traditions about the beginnings of Hellenic society.[27]

Notes

1. Benveniste 1938.

2. Dumézil, *Jupiter, Mars, Quirinus: Essai sur la conception indo-européenne de la société et sur les origines de Rome* (Paris, 1941).

3. Quotes are from G. Devoto, *Tabulae Iguvinae* (Rome, 1937).

4. See G. Devoto, "Contatti etrusco-iguvini," *Studi Etruschi* 6 (1930): 243 and *Tab. Ig.* 192.

5. Or perhaps *fundos*, ["farms"] as it was customarily translated.

6. VI a 30 (Devoto, "Contatti etrusco-iguvini," 188; cf. 197).

7. In a passage of the *Avesta* (*Yašt* 19.32), *pasu vīra* is also in an intermediary position, between the *dvandva āpa urvaire*, "water and plants," and the unfortunately murky expression *uye* *x^{v}araye*, "the two foods (?)." At issue are the boons of the golden age that the reign of Yama represents in the Mazdean traditions. If *uye x^{v}araye* referred allusively to felicity of a spiritual order, the Avestan sequence would parallel the Umbrian triad, with the same middle term (*pasu vīra-veiro pequo*).

8. P. Kretschmer, *Festschrift Adalbert Bezzenberger* (Göttingen, 1921), pp. 89ff.

9. Devoto, "Contatti etrusco-iguvini," 183.

10. ["Vofonio- occupies the same place in Grabovian triad and Quirinus in the Roman one; yet his bellicose nature cannot be proven"], ibid., 237.

11. Kretschmer, "Lat. *quirites* und *quiritare*," *Glotta* 10 (1919): 147–57.

12. Dumézil, *Jupiter, Mars*, pp. 74ff.

13. We cannot adduce the Roman *Agonius*, who Festus says was *deum praesidentem rebus agendis* in the old ritual; cf. agonia, "*hostia*." In the first place, this is only a distant memory, and if this god existed, it was to watch over a particular aspect of the sacrificial ritual, the killing of the victim, and guide the arm of the priest responsible for the immolation.

14. A. von Blumenthal, *Die Iguvinischen Tafeln: Text, Übersetzung, Untersuchungen* (Stuttgart, 1931), p. 61.

15. On *Liber*, see Benveniste 1936.

16. Benveniste 1936, 540–49.

17. I would not have known this mantra, which is buried in the vast literature of ritualism and which no exegete had noticed, had I not stumbled upon it by chance in the *Altindische Grammatik* of Jakob Wackernagel and Albert Debrunner (Göttingen, 1957), vol. 3, p. 15 d 39, where it is cited along with other grammatical examples in a discussion of the forms of the genitive.

18. All the necessary details about offerings can be found in the very well-informed article by M. Krause, "Hostia," in *Paulys Real-Encyclopädie der classischen Altertumswissenschaft*, ed. Georg Wissowa (Stuttgart, 1931) supp. v. 5, pp. 236–82. There is no need to reproduce the large number of literary and epigraphic references that Krause systematically assembled. See esp. pp. 264ff. on the *suovetaurilia* (and on the equivalent form, *solitaurilia*, whose meaning is less clear).

19. Krause, "Hostia," p. 253.

20. Ibid., pp. 255ff. Note, moreover, that the sacrifice of a sheep figured in numerous magical acts and fertility rites. See N. Thomas, "Animals," in *Encyclopaedia of Religion and Ethics*, ed. James Hastings (Edinburgh and New York, 1908–1915), vol. 1, p. 527.

21. On these offerings, the essential texts are gathered in an old article by P. Stengel, *Neue Jahrbücher für Philologie und Pedagogik* 133 (1886): 329–31. See also the article *Τρίττοια* by L. Ziehen in *Paulys Real-Encyclopädie*, vol. 13, p. 328.

22. *Contra Aristocratem* 68.642.

23. R. Herzog, *Abhandlungen der Preussischen Akademie der Wissenschaften* 6 (1928), p. 14, cited in Ziehen, *Paulys Real-Encyclopädie*, p. 328.

24. See P. Stengel, *Die griechischen Kultusaltertümer* (München, 1920), p. 122. In general, the pig was sacrificed to Demeter and the bull to Poseidon, bull-god. But the sheep was the most common offering and had no specific attribution.

25. On Mars Gradivus and Averruncus, see R. Stark, "Mars Gradivus and Averruncus," *Archiv für Religionswissenschaft* 25 (1939): 139ff.

26. With variants depending on the time and place (e.g., water substituted for wine, mixture of milk and honey, etc.).[. . .]

27. See Dumézil, *Jupiter, Mars*, pp. 252ff. Though beyond the scope of this article, I should like to mention two late medieval survivals of these con-

ceptions. Toward the end of the ninth century, Alfred the Great added this observation to his translation of Boethius: "A populated territory: that is the work with which a king concerns himself. He needs men of prayer, men of war, and men of labor." In the fourteenth century, moreover, one could read this in an English sermon (G. R. Owst, *Literature and Pulpit in Mediaeval England* [Cambridge, 1933], p. 553, quoted along with the previous quotation by H. St. L. B. Moss, *The Birth of the Middle Ages* [Oxford, 1935], p. 271): "God made clerics, knights, and tillers of the soil, but the Demon made burghers and usurers." With the growth of cities, guilds, and commerce, the ancient order in which the preacher saw the natural order came to an end.

10. Some Indo-European Prayers: Cato's Lustration of the Fields

The two Roman ritual elements treated by Benveniste in the preceding article—the suovitaurilia *and, especially, Cato's prayer to Mars—constitute the focus of the following study by Calvert Watkins. Here Watkins considers with great care the triadic structure of the prayer, its syntactic arrangement, and its phonetic quality. Watkins, like Benveniste, emphasizes the great antiquity of the prayer, demonstrating the same by adducing a broad array of comparative Indo-European evidence.* (RDW)

SOME INDO-EUROPEAN PRAYERS: CATO'S LUSTRATION OF THE FIELDS

Calvert Watkins

The ancient Roman ritual of lustration or 'purification' of the fields is described in a passage in Cato, *De agri cultura* 141.1ff. It is prescribed to the landowner to order the set of three animals which constitute the *suouitaurilia*—pig, sheep, and bull-calf—to be driven around the circumference of the fields with the words

cum diuis uolentibus quodque bene eueniat,
mando tibi, Mani, uti illace suouitaurilia
fundum agrum terramque meam
quota ex parte siue circumagi siue circumferenda censeas
uti cures lustrare

That with the gods favorable everything will turn out well,
I order you, NN,[1] to take care of the lustration of my
farm, field, and land, from whatever side you deem these
suouitaurilia should be driven or carried around them.

The syntactic intricacy of these prefatory instructions, accomplished principally by moving *illace suouitaurilia* out of its clause (*quota ex parte . . . censeas*) to a position of prominence before the objects of the verb *lustrare*, indicates that we are already in the world of *concepta uerba*, of Roman formal solemn diction.

The landowner is then enjoined to pronounce a preliminary prayer with a libation to Janus and Jupiter[2] and to address a prayer with fixed wording to Mars. This prayer to Mars had been justly qualified by Risch 1979 as 'the oldest Latin text preserved,' 'actually older than Early Latin literature,' the monuments of authors of the third and second centuries B.C., considerably before Cato's time (ca. 234–149 B.C.).

The thematic and formal structure of this prayer was analyzed with characteristic lucidity by E. Benveniste, in an article of nearly a half-century ago (1945) entitled 'Social symbolism in Greco-Italic cults,' as an illustration of the principle that 'every definition of a conceptual totality tends to borrow the tripartite framework which organizes human society' among the early Indo-European-speaking peoples, that is to say, in the trifunctional schema of G. Dumézil, of which Benveniste's study provides some of the better examples.

The name of the sacrifice itself, the *suouitaurilia*, is tripartite, a three-member compound. Benveniste, following the materials amassed by Krause in the article *Hostia*, P.-W. Suppl. Bd. V, showed that this compound, a nominalization of a phrase *su oue tauro* (*facere*), combined the three animals which were typically sacrificed to Earth (pig), Jupiter (ram), and Mars (bull) respectively. The whole sacrifice is made to Mars to ward off the symbolic 'set of ills which may menace the body politic or the products of the earth' (p. 15). The threefold sacrifice recurs in Greece as the *τριττύς* or *τρίττοια* of the same three animals (in this case adult): bull, ram, and boar. It is first found in the *Odyssey*, in Tiresias' instruction to Odysseus to sacrifice to Poseidon (11.131 = 23.278),

> ἀρνειὸν ταῦρόν τε συῶν τ' ἐπιβήτορα κάπρον
>
> a ram and a bull and a boar who has been to the sows.

Poseidon receives the triple offering as the deity most appropriate, since he controls the fate of the mariner, but the sacrifice 'symbolically subsumes the whole human condition' (*ibid.*).

The scholiast to *Il.* 19.197 informs us that the same threefold sacrifice consecrated the solemn oath: *πρὸς δὲ τὰ ὅρκια τρισὶν ἐχρῶντο Ἀττικοί, κάπρωι κριῶι* 'for oaths the Athenians would use three: boar, ram, bull.' Demosthenes *Contra Aristocratem* § 68, p. 642, describes the oath-taking in a trial for murder, *στὰς ἐπὶ τῶν τομίων κάπρου καὶ κριοῦ καὶ ταύρου* 'standing on the cut parts (= testicles) of a boar and a ram and a bull.'

While the tripartite sacrifice here symbolically expresses a totality, we may still find in the same or similar circumstances a bipartite expression, like Paul. ex Fest. 112 L *mensa frugibusque iurato* 'he shall swear by his stores and grain', a formula which recalls the Umbrian bipartite rhyming *mefa spefa*, name of a sacrificial flatcake < **menssa spenssa* 'measured out (and) consecrated' (?). In the tradition of another Indo-European people we also find an ascending series of single, double, and triple expression in the same context of oath-taking. In the Sanskrit laws of Manu (8.113) the brāhmaṇa priest swears by his *truth* (*satyena*), the kṣatriya warrior by his *chariot* (*and*) *weapons* (*vāhanāyudhais*), and the vaiśya farmer by his *cattle, seed,* (*and*) *gold* (*gobījakāñcanais*), the last a three-member compound linguistically closely parallel to *suouitaurilia.*

This is not the place to debate the validity of the Dumézilian system wholly or in part. As we shall see, the triadic or tripartite organization of the Old Latin text as demonstrated first by Benveniste is a structural fact independent of any conceptual framework one might choose to superimpose upon it. Benveniste was interested above all in the structure of the *content* of Cato's prayer. Its poetic *form* did not engage his attention, and he printed the text without comment as prose, just as it was transmitted in the manuscript. This prayer, however, as I hope to show, is indeed not only the most ancient piece of Latin literature but the oldest Latin poem that we possess. As we shall see in abundant detail, its structure is far more complex than most commentators have presumed. Two characterizations of the prayer were singled out for praise by Norden. These are Leo 1913:13 'Ein Gebet, Hülfe bittend und Übel verbittend', and Wünsch 1916:176: 'Unsegen soll aufhören, Segen soll kommen; dazu sollen die Götter helfen'. Norden's book belies any 'simplicity' of the Ancient Roman priestly books, and the artistic effect both German authors strove for in their antitheses *bittend : verbittend, HÜLFE : ÜBEL, Segen : Unsegen* is itself an accurate rendition of the spirit of the Roman prayer.

In the following the text is printed with line division essentially as in the collective and anonymous collection *Early Roman Poetry* (Oxford 1951) 5–6,[3] but further separated into four *strophes* numbered I–IV.

1 I Mars pater te precor quaesoque
2 uti sies uolens propitius
3 mihi domo familiaeque nostrae:
4 quoius rei ergo

agrum terram fundumque meum
suouitaurilia circumagi iussi

II uti tu
morbos uisos   inuisosque
uiduertatem   uastitudinemque
calamitates   intemperiasque
prohibessis defendas auerruncesque

III utique tu
fruges frumenta   uineta uirgultaque
grandire   (du)eneque[4] euenire siris
pastores pecuaque   salua seruassis
duisque (du)onam salutem   ualetudinemque
mihi domo familiaeque nostrae

IV harunce rerum ergo
fundi terrae agrique mei
lustrandi lustrique faciendi ergo
sicuti dixi
macte hisce suouitaurilibus lactentibus immolandis esto
Mars pater eiusdem rei ergo
macte hisce suouitaurilibus lactentibus esto

I Father Mars, I pray and beseech you
that you be favorable (and) propitious
to me, my house, and our household:
to which end
I have ordered the *suouitaurilia* to be driven around
my field, land, and farm;

II that you
forbid, ward off,   and brush aside
diseases seen   and unseen,
depopulation   and devastation,
storms   and tempests;

III and that you
let grow tall   and turn out well
grains (and) corn   and vineyards (and) shrubwork
and keep safe   shepherds (and) cattle
and give good health   and soundness
to me, my house, and our household.

IV To these ends,
to purify and perform the purification
of my farm, land, and field
so as I spoke
be magnified by these suckling *suouitaurilia* to be sacrificed;
Father Mars, to that same end,
be magnified by these suckling *suouitaurilia*.

We have here clearly a prayer within a prayer in a *nesting* arrangement:

(I (II III) IV).

Strophe I serves as the introduction and invocation, the *captatio benevolentiae*, and strophe IV as the resolution or conclusion, with the final invocation (22–24) serving as a sort of *envoi*, iterated.

I and IV formally belong together as the "wrapping" of II and III, because of their pattern of *responsions*. These verbal responsions are equivalence tokens, and they form the rings which establish I and IV as a frame. They include

Mars pater	1:23	Father Mars,

and the synonymous doubling figures

precor quaesoque	1	I pray and beseech
uolens propitius	2	favorable (and) propitious,
lustrandi lustrique faciendi	20	to purify and perform the purification.

<For the Indo-European antiquity of the stylistic figure of the last see chap. 13.>

Beside (or within) the synonymous doubling figures we have the counterpoint of synonymous or semantically similar tripling figures:

mihi domo familiaeque nostrae	3:17	for me, my house, and our household,

and the mirror-image repetition

agrum terram fundumque meum	5	my field, land, and farm
fundi terrae agrique mei	19	my farm, land, and field.

The last two phrases provide a link to *fundum agrum terramque meam* of the preceding prefatory instructions discussed above. In general part of the art of the whole prayer is the interplay of the bipartite with the tripartite, the doubling with the tripling figure, which creates a unique stylistic rhythm.

Further responsions between I and IV include the single postposition *ergo* in 4 and its triplication in 18, 20, 23, and the presence in I and IV of the first person singular, the persona of the worshipper as agent, in the perfects *iussi*[5] 6 and *dixi* 21.

Finally, the tripartite designation of the sacrifice itself appears only in I and IV: *su-oui-taurilia* 6:22, 24.

By contrast to all these links between strophes I and IV, there is only one link between them and the internal strophes II and III: *mihi domo familiaeque meae* of lines 3 and 17. The phrase in line 17 is neither thematically nor syntactically organic or necessary; its purpose is to link II–III to the farmer's personal family prayer I–IV.

Ring-composition affords a formal proof. The first word of strophe II, *morbos* 'diseases' in line 8, is answered by the last word of strophe III, *ualetudinemque* 'health' in line 16. This responsion by semantic antithesis bounds the poem proper of II–III and proves that it starts at line 8 and stops at line 16.

Strophes I and IV are stylistically careful, artfully elaborated 'ordinary' solemn religious language of 3rd-century B.C. Rome, as we can observe it for example in Plautus.[6] This sort of solemn usage was clearly traditional by that time on the evidence of its striking stylistic contrast with the colloquial speech of the same period.[7]

Yet nested within these outer layers of formal religious language, cradled and protected against the winds of change, lie the real archaisms: strophes II and III. If I and IV represent traditional language and reflect the stylistic usage of, say, a century or more before the 3rd century B.C., then strophes II–III should represent a state of the language traditional already at that time, and perhaps antedating the foundation of the Roman Republic. One must not be misled by the phonological form, which would have been continuously modernized—as was that of the Law of the XII Tables, a composition datable to 450 B.C. The central prayer to Mars, strophes II and III *kann beliebig alt sein*, 'can be as old as you want', as Rudolf Thurneysen once exclaimed over a passage in Early Irish law (fide D.A. Binchy).

For a parallel consider only that right now, toward the end of the 20th century, the basic phraseology of Christianity in the English language remains virtually unchanged from that of the Bible translation of William Tyndale in the early 16th century (New Testament 1525-6). The span is almost half a millennium. It is the text of this Latin prayer to Mars, strophes II and III—and they are indeed strophe and antistrophe—which will henceforth occupy our attention. Its composition too may well antedate by half a millennium its fixation by Cato in *De agri cultura*, ca. 160 B.C.

Benveniste's contribution was to recognize the tripartite conceptual structure of the two strophes and their homology to the hierarchy of the three functions argued for as an ideology by Dumézil. For Benveniste 'every definition of a conceptual totality tends unconsciously to borrow the tripartite framework which organizes human society' (p. 5). We may retain the key word 'unconsciously'. There may have existed an ideological tripartition into the three functions of sovereignty, force, and fecundity, though the tripartition might be simply a cognitive universal. The model might have been—as it clearly was for Benveniste—a social hierarchy, a threefold division of the classes of free males into priests, warriors, and farmers, as we can observe it in India and Iran. But that too, with all the necessary adjustments, might be a cognitive universal. It is certain in any case that the hierarchy of Roman society by the middle of the 1st millennium B.C. was based rather on birth, wealth, clientship, and the like and that the Roman 'farmer' could and did function at the same time as both 'warrior' (the Cincinnatus ideal) and 'priest' (as here in the lustration of the fields).

That said, it remains to be recognized, with Benveniste, that a tripartite hierarchy agreeing with the Dumézilian model is both present and pronounced in these two strophes of the prayer and is indeed the foundation of their grammatical and conceptual structure. The first strophe enumerates a triad of scourges the divinity is asked to avert, conceived as the totality of evils which can menace the body politic or the produce of the earth, and the second strophe (the antistrophe) enumerates a triad of benefits the divinity is asked to grant, also conceived as 'the protection and favor of the whole society'.

We may symbolize the three 'functions', giving them their reductionist Dumézilian labels, as

f_1 sovereignty (including *medicine*)[8]
f_2 force
f_3 prosperity.

The strophe (II) enumerates the evils which threaten the well-being corresponding to each 'function': illness (f_1), devastation (f_2), and natural catastrophe (f_3), each associated with a particular verb of averting. As Benveniste showed, diseases visible and hidden are to be 'forbidden', cf. *Iuppiter prohibessit* Plautus *Ps.* 13f. (and *God forbid*); the devastation of war to be 'repulsed', cf. *defende hostes* Ennius *Scen.* 6 V (IE **g^u̯hen-*); calamity to be 'swept aside', more generally 'averted', cf. *di . . . amentiam auerruncassint tuam* Pacuvius 112 R.[9] Using the symbols N for noun or noun phrase and V for verb or verb phrase, we obtain the following thematic analysis:

II strophe	8	N_1	AVERT
	9	N_2	
	10	N_3	
	11	V_1 V_2 V_3	

morbos uisos	inuisosque
uiduertatem	uastitudinemque
calamitates	intemperiasque

prohibessis defendas auerruncesque

forbid, ward off, and brush aside

diseases seen	and unseen,
depopulation	and devastation,
storms	and tempests.

The antistrophe (III) then presents, in mirror image and reverse order, the set of three benefices prayed for, again corresponding to each 'function': agricultural prosperity, safety from depredation (with *defendas . . . seruassis . . .* compare Ennius *Scen.* 6 V. *serua ciues, defende hostes* 'save the citizens, ward off the foe'), and good health:

III antistr.	13		N_3		GRANT
	14		V_3		
	15	N_2		V_2	
	16	V_1		N_1	

fruges frumenta	uineta uirgultaque
grandire	(du)eneque euenire siris
pastores pecuaque	salua seruassis
duisque (du)onam salutem	ualetudinemque

let grow tall	and turn out well
grains (and) corn	and vineyards (and) shrubwork
and keep safe	shepherds (and) cattle
and give good health	and soundness.

Benveniste's great achievement was to perceive this thematic structure as a whole for the first time. The correspondence is clear, and no other hypothesis accounts for the facts as well. Benveniste gives further a number of thematic parallels in phraseology from other Indo-European traditions; we will come to these presently.

Let us begin now to look at the poetic form of this prayer. How are the three 'functions' in fact expressed? As we stated earlier, the art of the poem is in the counterpoint of tripling and doubling, the threefold and the twofold, tripartite and bipartite. If the thematic structure as a whole is tripartite, each thematic structure point is represented by a grammatical doubling, sometimes doubled again. All of these doublings generate stylistic figures which are prototypical for the Indo-European poetic world. <These categories of Indo-European bipartite noun phrase formulaic figures were discussed earlier in chap. 3.> Note the following:

Argument + Negated Argument:	8	*morbos uisos inuisosque*
Argument + Synonymous Argument:	9	*uiduertatem uastitudinemque*
	10	*calamitates intemperiasque*
	16	*(du)onam salutem ualetudinemque*
Merism (copulative)	13	**fruges uinetaque*
	15	*pastores pecuaque*

The underlying bipartite 13 **fruges uinetaque* has itself undergone a further doubling (by I.2.b. Arg. + Synon. Arg.) to the alliterative (identity of phonic form) and etymological (identity of meaning) *fruges frumenta uineta uirgultaque.*[10]

Grammatical figures are a central component in the art of strophe II and antistrophe III, as is the placement of the enclitic copulative conjunction *-que* 'and'. Both strophes are penetrated by the interplay and tension double/triple and horizontal/vertical; language and the linguistic sign are not arranged only linearly. Using the + sign for 'and' (Lat. *-que*), we may observe that all doublings are A + B (A B-*que*), all triplings A B + C (A B C-*que*). Thus the three verbs of the strophe are arranged horizontally,

	V_1	V_2	+	V_3
11	prohibessis	defendas		auerruncesque.

while the three verbs of the antistrophe are deployed vertically

V_3	siris	14
V_2	seruassis	15
+		
V_1	duisque	16.

Moving the last verb *duis* to the head of its clause ('fronting') is what enables it to carry the critical conjunction *-que*; all the other verbs are clause final.

The verb phrases in strophe II, diseases forbid, devastation ward off, storms brush aside, must be read "vertically":

II
morbos uisos inuisosque
uiduertam uastitudinemque
calamitates intemperiasque
prohibessis defendas auerruncesque.

The result is a structure like an upside down T:

```
  o o
  o o
  o o
 o o o
```

The same "verticality" is carried over into the first member of the triad in the antistrophe, where *fruges frumenta* 'grain' goes with *grandire* 'grow tall' (cf. *grandia farra, camille, metes* 'tall corn, boy, you'll reap' Paul. Fest. 82 L) and *uineta uirgultaque* 'vineyards' with *(du)eneque euenire* 'turn out well' (cf. the god *Bonus Euentus* 'Good Outcome', Varro *R.R.* 1.1.6). Thus

III	fruges frumenta	uineta uirgultaque
	grandire	dueneque euenire siris
	pastores pecuaque	salua seruassis
	duisque duonam salutem	ualetudinemque.

The underlying formula of line 13 is **fruges uinetaque*, a merism 'grain and grape' indexing the totality of the products of the earth. When each noun underwent doubling,

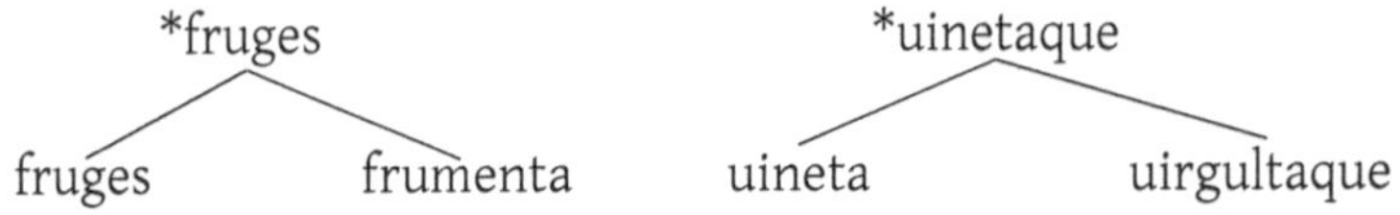

a rule moved the enclitic *-que* from *uineta* to the following *uirgulta* (which misled Benveniste to think of the whole as mere enumeration).

The greater complexity in grammatical figures of antistrophe III is apparent not only in the first member of the triad (13–14), but also in the mirror image order of the noun and verb constituents in the second and third (15, 16): Noun Noun Verb—Verb Noun Noun. Recall finally the ring-composition which by semantic antithesis links the first word of II *morbos* 'sickness' with the last word of III, *ualetudinemque* 'health'.

We have examined the level of theme, where meaning is in play, and the level of grammar, where only grammatical meaning is relevant: the domain of the grammatical figure. We come now to the level of sound alone: the domain of the phonetic figure. Every line of II and III is marked by recurrent sound features, indeed every word is linked to another by such a figure. These equivalence tokens are remarkably varied, ranging over alliteration, homoioteleuton, internal rhyme, and phonic echo. In the following, boldface roman capitals are used for phonetic figures, and boldface italic capitals for figures that are both phonetic and grammatical. The conjunction *-que* is italicized to draw attention to its position in each strophe:

8	morbos ***VISOS***	in***VISOS****que*
9	**V**iduertatem[11]	**V**astitudinem*que*
10	c**A**l**A**mit**A**tes	intemperi**A**s*que*
11	prohibess***IS***defend***AS***	auerrunc***ES****que*,[12]
12	**FRV**ges **FRV**menta	**VI**neta **VI**rgulta*que*
13	grand**IRE**	d**VENE***que* **EVEN-IRE** s**IR*****IS***
14	**P**astores **P**ecua*que*	**S**alua **S**ervass**IS**
15	**DV*****IS****que* **DV**onam sal**VT**em	ualet**VD**inem*que*.[13]

My analysis of the lustral prayer has been hitherto resolutely synchronic and descriptive in character, without attention to external comparison or to diachronic, historical considerations. But the text is as rich in comparative material as it is in figures of sound and form. Let us survey these, beginning again with the thematic level and continuing through to the formulaic, and finally to the phonological level of rhythm and meter.

On the level of theme the most striking comparison in prayers across the Indo-European world is the threefold scourge which is prayed against and—less commonly—the threefold benefice which is prayed for. Beneveniste[14] had already noted the Old Persian prayer of Darius at Persepolis, DPd 15-20 *imām dahạyāum auramazdā pātuv hacā haināyā hacā dušiyāra hacā drauga abiy imām dahạyāum mā ājamiyā mā hainā mā dušiyāram mā drauga* 'May Ahuramazda protect this land from enemy army, from bad harvest, from Deceit. Upon this land may there not come either enemy army or bad harvest or Deceit.'

Benveniste also noted a mantra from the TS 1.1.13.3 *pāhí prásityai pāhí dúriṣṭyai pāhí duradmanyaí* 'protect from bondage, protect from bad worship, protect from bad food.'[15]

Other traditions offer close parallels. In Hesiod's *Works and Days* 225-47, the good consequences of the just ruler—health, peace, and prosperity—are contrasted with the evil consequences of the unjust ruler: famine, plague, and devastation. The genre is that of wisdom literature, and as such may be in large part diffused from Mesopotamia. See the rich discussion in M. L. West's commentary.

I have further compared (Watkins 1979b:189ff.) the threefold scourge in the Hittite prayer of Mursilis II to the Sun Goddess of Arinna, which is in traditional language with an at least Middle Hittite (15th cent. B.C.) archetype (Carruba 1969:240). KUB 24.4 + Ro. 21-2:

> nu=ššan ḫinkan kūrur kaštan *ANA* KUR URUMittanni *ANA*
> KUR URUKizzuwatni *ANA* KUR URUArzawa tarnatten
>
> Loose *plague, war, famine* on the lands of Mittanni,
> Kizzuwatna, Arzawa.

In that study I was concerned with parallels to the 7th-century Old Irish Mirror of Princes text *Audacht Morainn* edited by Kelly (1976), notably the phrase §12, as emended:

> Is tre fír flaithemon mortlithi
> márslóg márlóchet di doínib dingbatar
>
> It is by the ruler's Truth that *plagues*, a *great army*,
> *great lightnings* are warded off men.

As I pointed out there, the tripartite organization of the phraseology in these prayers and similar genres is a fact, whether or not one wishes to interpret them in the light of the theories of Dumézil. The most ardent Dumézilian would probably be reluctant to view as a direct Indo-European inheritance an Irish "prayer" recorded in North Mayo in the 1960's and published in 1970 by J. N. Hamilton. The speaker describes the custom of throwing away the first glass of the singlings (what first passes over in distilling), for the *daoiní maith*', the fairies, when making poteen (*poitín*, home-distilled whiskey). 'And this is what we used to say when we were throwing out the first glass':

> Maith agus sláinte go ndéanaidh sé daoibh,
> Agus toradh agus tairbh' go gcuiridh sé 'ugainn,
> Agus go sábhálaidh sibh aig ár námhaid muid
>
> May it bring you health and goodness,
> and may it bring us good result and profit,
> and may you save us from our enemy.

Of the formulaic figures in Cato's prayer several have close verbal parallels and analogues elsewhere. The figure 'seen and unseen', Argument plus Negated Argument, is grammatically and structurally paralleled by Umbrian (*Tab. Ig.* VI b 59–60)

> nerf śihitu anśihitu
> iouie hostatu anhostatu

chief citizens girt (and) ungirt
young men under arms (and) not under arms,

a sort of "magic square" designating the totality of the four enemy armies cursed. We find the same in the great Hittite prayer of Muwatallis to the Storm God *piḫaššaššiš* (CTH 381, KUB 6.45 iii 4-8):

[DINGIR LÚ^{MEŠ}] DINGIR SAL^{MEŠ} *ŠA* LUGAL-*RI* *Ù* *ŠA*
SAL.LUGAL-*TI* kuieš daran[teš] kuieš *ŪL* daranteš kuetaš
ANA É^{MEŠ} DINGIR^{MEŠ} LUGAL SAL.LUGAL piran EGIR-pa
iyantari kuetaš=a[t] *ANA* É^{MEŠ} DINGIR^{MEŠ} *ŪL* iyantari

[Male gods] and female gods of king and queen, those invo[ked]
and those not invoked, those in whose temples the king and
queen officiate and those in whose temples they do not officiate.

The nominal relative clauses *kueš* (*natta*) *taranteš* recall also the Archaic Latin formula *qui patres qui conscripti* designating the totality of senators, patrician and plebeian (Festus 304 L).[16]

We have even the identical semantics and root of *uisos inuisosque* in the Umbrian formula four times repeated (VIa 28, 38, 48, VIb 30) *uirseto auirseto uas* 'seen (or) unseen ritual flaw', though the morphology is different (*uīsus* < **u̯id-to-*, *uirseto* < **u̯idē-to-*), and with identical semantics but a different root, Atharvavedic *dr̥ṣṭám adŕ̥ṣṭam* (*krímim*) 'seen (and) unseen (worm)' 2.31.2, *dr̥ṣṭā́ṃś ca ghnann adŕ̥ṣṭāṃś ca* 'slaying the seen and unseen (worms)' 5.23.6, *dr̥ṣṭáś ca hanyatām krímir / utā́dŕ̥ṣṭaś ca hanyatām* 'may the seen worm be slain, and may the unseen be slain' 5.23.7. Note in these Latin, Umbrian, and Vedic formulas the three rhythmic variants of the Indo-European bipartite noun phrase: asyndeton *A B*, conjoined *A B-k*$^{\text{u̯}}$*e*, doubly conjoined *A-k*$^{\text{u̯}}$*e B-k*$^{\text{u̯}}$*e*. The relevance of the Vedic to Cato's *morbos uisos inuisosque* was first seen by Durante 1958. The phrase has every right to be considered an Indo-European formula, the more so since in several traditions (Indic, Germanic) 'worm' is a metaphor for 'disease'. <See in greater detail on these part VII.>

We noted above on *defendas ... seruassis* (both V_2) Ennius *Scen.* 6 V *serua ciues, defende hostes* 'save the citizens, repulse the foe'; on *fruges frumenta ... grandire* the agricultural carmen in P. Fest. 82 L *hiberno puluere, uerno luto / grandia farra, camille, metes* 'with winter dust and spring mud, tall corn, boy, you'll reap', and on *beneque euenire* the agricultural god *Bonus Euentus* 'Good Outcome' (Varro, *R. R.* 1.1.6).

The underlying merism **fruges uinetaque* 'grain and grape' (doubled in *fruges fru. uineta ui.*) recurs over the Mediterranean world. From Homer note the flexible formula *Il.* 9.706 etc. *σίτου καὶ οἴνοιο* (*σίτοο καὶ ϝοίνοιο*) 'grain and wine' and numerous variants, as well as *Od.* 4.746 etc. *σῖτον* (-*ος*) *καὶ μέθυ ἡδύ* 'grain and sweet wine.' The earliest Indo-European examples are already in Old Hittite: twice in a fragment concerning Alluwamnas and Harapsilis (KUB 26.77 i 5,8) *n*[*u ḫ*]*alkieš* GEŠTIN$^{\text{ḪI.A}}$-*ešš=a ḫarki*[*r* 'grains and vines perished', and once in the Telepinus edict (§ 20), *n=an kišša*[(ri=*šši ḫalkiuš*) DINGIR^{MEŠ}(-*iš*)] GEŠTIN$^{\text{ḪI.A}}$-*uš* GUD$^{\text{ḪI.A}}$-*uš* UDU$^{\text{ḪI.A}}$-*uš* *Ū*[*L pēter* 'and the gods did not bring (?) grains (and) vines, cattle (and) sheep into his hand'.[17] The context in both is traditional and formulaic: the consequences to the land of the wicked ruler in the *speculum principum* or Mirror of Princes.

Note that in the last passage (and also in the Telepinus myth iv 29–30) we have two inherited formulaic merisms in a row:[18] a recurrent feature of early Indo-European traditional texts, which may indicate that these formulas were learned in groups. <Other instances will be noted further in this work.>

'Grain (and) wine' are of course part of the common and doubtless universal formulaic verb-phrase merism 'eat (and) drink', as in *Il.* 5.341 *οὐ γὰρ σῖτον ἔδουσ', οὐ πίνουσ' αἴθοπα οἶνον* 'for they eat not grain nor drink flaming wine', nominalized in *πόσιος καὶ ἐδητύος* 'drinking and eating' (*passim*). In Old Hittite the formula 'eat (and) drink' is basically equivalent to 'live happily' Telepinus edict § 23 *pāndu=wa=z ašandu nu=wa=za* ***azzikandu akkuškandu*** *idālu=ma=šmaš=kan lē kuiški taggaši* 'Let them go (and) dwell (there); let them eat (and) drink, but let no one do harm to them.' For the condensed banishment formula cf. also KUB 26.77 i 13 (Alluwamnas fragment) *pāntu=war=i apiya aš*[*antu* 'Let them go (and) dwell there.' 'Eat (and) drink' figures in the Old Hittite/old script text KBo 22.1, 28′–30′, where the switch in pronominalization from 2 pl. to 2 sg. indicates the homiletic material (here enclosed in double quotes) is taken from a traditional source: . . . *ta* ^{LÚ}*ḫappinandaš īštēni parna=šša paiši ezši eukši piyanazzi=a=tta* . '. . . You (pl.) do the will of the rich man. "You (sg.) go to his house, you (sg.) eat (and) drink, and he gives you (sg.) presents." '

But it is the phrase *pastores pecuaque salua seruassis* which is the most astonishing in its formulaic wealth and the diachronic developments that lie behind it. These are paradigmatic for continuity and change, retention and innovation in Indo-European formulaic sequences.

The Indo-European formula is

PROTECT MEN (and) CATTLE,

which we may reconstruct lexically as

> **pah$_2$- u̯ih$_x$ro- pek̂u-.*

The history of this formula was given by me in 1979 in the article just cited, building principally on the work of Wackernagel and Benveniste. I briefly recapitulate it here.

The Indo-European folk taxonomy of wealth included inter alia the following branching semantic features:

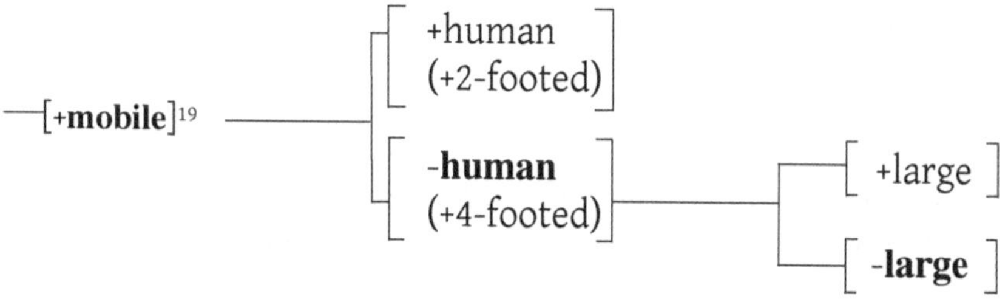

Indo-European **pek̂u-* could denote any of the three in boldface, in increasing order of markedness. Compare RV 3.62.14 *dvipáde/cátuṣpade ca paśáve* '2-footed and 4-footed *paśus*', Umbrian (*Tab. Ig.* VIb 10) *dupursus peturpursus* 'for 2-footed (men) (and) 4-footed (cattle)'.

Eleven times in the Umbrian Iguvine Tables VIa–VIIa we find repeated the triadic strophe

nerf arsmo	magistrates (and) formulations,
uiro pequo	men (and) cattle,
castruo frif	heads [of grain][20] (and) crops,

followed by *pihatu* 'purify' (6×) or *salua seritu* 'keep safe' (7×). As has been known since 1910[21] *uiro pequo* is an Indo-European formulaic merism 'MEN (and) CATTLE', on the comparison of Young Avestan *pasu(.)vīra* 'id.' in the reverse order (Yt. 13.12 etc.), and Gathic *pasu- vīra-* in various cases.[22] The reconstructible **u̯ih$_x$ro- pek̂u-* as a merism corresponds to the middle node of the model of taxonomy of moveable wealth just given. 'Men' as a form of moveable wealth in all these traditions means 'slaves'.[23]

The Latin alliterative merism *pastores pecuaque* is the equivalent and in this formula the replacement of the same merism, as shown by Benveniste.[24] Note also *cum adhibent in pecuda pastores* 'when they bring in shepherds to the sheep' Cicero, *De rep.* 4.1. I later (1979a:275) adduced Varro, *R.R.* 2.1.12 *pecudes minores* 'small cattle' (sheep, goats, pigs), *pecus maius* 'large cattle' (cows, asses, horses)—thus the right-hand node of the model of the taxonomy [+/-large]—and continuing with *tertia pars in pecuaria . . . muli canes* ***pastores*** 'the third sort of cattle . . . mules, dogs, shepherds'. Varro's scholasticism produced this nonsense by combining and expanding two ancient and inherited paired concepts: *pecus minus, pecus maius* on the one hand, *pecus, pastores* on the other.

Benveniste in the two studies cited (1970, 1969) was also the first to recognize that the whole verb phrase of our Latin prayer had an exact cognate in the repeated Umbrian prayer:

pastores pecuaque	salua seruassis
uiro pequo . . .	salua seritu

Both go back to a Common Italic formula, and as I showed (1979a:277–80) this whole formula has correspondents in both Vedic and Avestan, a Common Indo-Iranian formula which together with that of Common Italic goes back to the Common Indo-European prototype. Both Old and Young Avestan preserve the two nouns intact, always in the order *pasu-, vīra-* and with the verb *ϑrā-* 'protect':

Y.50.1 kə̄ mōi pasə̄uš kə̄ mə̄nā ϑrātā vistō

Who has been found to be the protector of my cattle, who of me?

Yt. 13.10 ϑrāϑrāi pasuuå vīraiiå

for the protection of cattle (and) men.

With Y.50.1 *kə̄ . . . ϑrātā* compare the strikingly similar RV 4.55.1, hymn-initial (the Avestan is line 2 of the 1st strophe):

kó vaḥ trātā́ vasavaḥ kó varutā́

who of you is the protector, o good ones, who the keeper?

Rhetorically the Vedic double agent noun parallels the Avestan double object; we may have an Indo-Iranian topos of the language of prayer.

Vedic has replaced the word for 'man' by the alliterative *púruṣa-*. In one example, 'protect' is expressed negatively, 'not harm':

AV 3.28.5,6 sā́ no mā́ hiṁsīt púruṣān paśū́ṃś ca

(refrain) let her not injure our men and cattle.

In another, 'protect' is the verb *trā-*, the cognate of Iranian *ϑrā-*, and the original merism has been expanded:

AV 8.7.11 trā́yantām asmín grā́me
gā́m áśvaṃ púruṣaṃ paśúm

Protect in this village
cow, horse, man, *paśu*.[25]

We may note one important fact in all the languages which attest the formula, however they may vary the order of the constituents and their morphosyntax. The reconstructible Indo-European formula PROTECT MEN (and) CATTLE, **pah_2-u̯ih_xro-peḱu-*, is a whole verb phrase, not just the noun phrase **u̯ih_xro-peḱu-*. It is furthermore as old an Indo-European formula as we can find; it is more securely based on cognates than 'imperishable fame' and syntactically more complex; and the evidence for it is not limited to the Greco-Aryan dialect area.[26] We may display the "stemma" of our formula as follows:

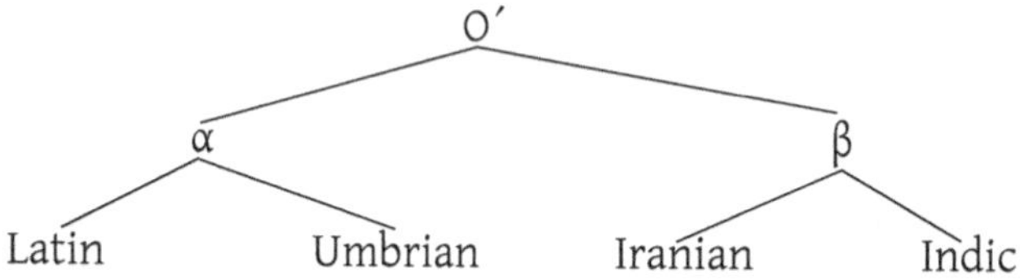

Each of the nodes α and β corresponds to an Indo-European intermediary common language (*langue commune intermédière*): Italic, Indo-Iranian. But more importantly, each is defined by a common innovation (or shared "error") in the transmission of the formula: the replacement of the verb **pah_2-* 'protect' in Italic by the verb phrase *salua ser(u)-* 'keep safe',[27] and the replacement of **pah_2-* in Indo-Iranian by the verb *trā-*, a root confined to this branch. Further innovations ("errors") in the transmission of the formula are the Latin substitution of alliterative *pastores* for 'men' and the Indic substitution of the likewise alliterative *púruṣa-*, as well as the expansion of the original merism in

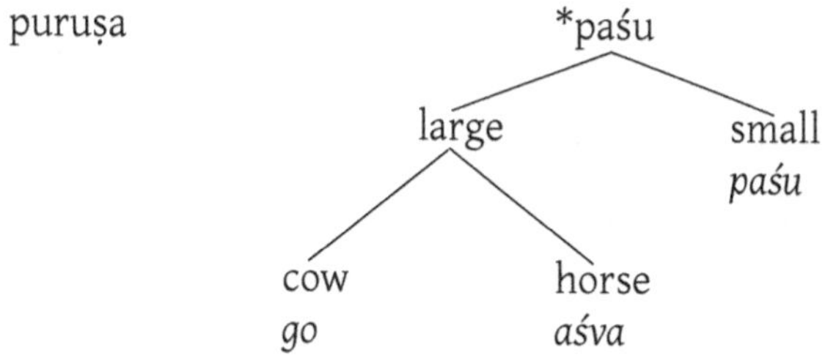

It will be observed that none of the four languages shows a direct reflex of the verb *pah_2- 'protect' in the formula. Neither the Italic phrase *salua seru-* nor the Indo-Iranian *trā-* are of demonstrable Indo-European antiquity. I restore *pah_2- as a likely candidate for the Indo-European lexical expression because it is used in both Indic and Iranian in the traditional trifunctional enumeration of the three scourges in the texts adduced by Benveniste.

More tricky to demonstrate but potentially of great interest are the associative semantics (contiguity relations) of the formula *pah_2- $\hat{u}ih_x$ro- peḱu-* and its various permutations. Latin *pās-tōrēs* may be a formulaic echo of *pah_2-, and the Italic phrase *salua seru-*—note the echoic consonantism **s - lu̯- s - ru̯**—which replaced *pah_2- may have formulaic links with **peḱu-* as evidenced both in Avestan *hauruua. fšu-* with intact livestock' (: *salua*) and Avestan (*spa-*) *pasuš.hauruua-* 'sheep-guarding (dog)' (: *seruassis*). Recall the link *defendere - seruare*, and compare Vergil *Ecl.* 7.47 *solstitium pecori defendite* 'ward off the summer heat from the flock.' To expose such formulaic links, which constitute a potentially vast network, is one of the important tasks of the future for the Indo-European comparatist-littérateur.

Notes

1. Latin *Manius*, the equivalent of our John Doe.

2. *Ianum Iouemque uino praefamino, sic dicito.* The imperative *praefamino* is already a linguistic archaism.

3. 'Edited by a subgroup of the faculty concerned.' The line division there is I believe after W. M. Lindsay.

4. In *(du)ene* here and *(du)onam* 16 I have restored the Old Latin form of later *bene, bonam.*

5. In Cato's time and before the form would surely have been *iousī*, as in the Senatus Consultum de Bacchanalibus of 186 B.C.

6. Both Plautus († ca. 184 B.C.) and Cato (234–149 B.C.) learned to talk in the 3rd century B.C.

7. A good example is Plautus *Trinummus* 39–42 *Larem corona nostrum decorari uolo / uxor, uenerare ut nobis haec habitatio / bona fausta felix fortunataque euenat / —teque ut quam primum possim uideam emortuam.* 'I want our Lar to be adorned with a wreath. Wife, perform your devotions that this home turn out for us well, favorable, prosperous, and fortunate—(aside) and that I see you laid out dead as soon as possible.' The archaic subjunctive *euenat* is metrically sure.

8. Compare the root *med- of Latin *medicina, medērī* 'treat', and Greek *μέδων, μεδέων* 'ruling', *μέδομαι* 'provide for'.

9. The verbs are discussed also by Norden 1939: 126 n. 3.

10. In the latter pair the relation is one of contiguity as well as similarity, the *uirgulta* 'brushwork' grown to support the grapevines.

11. This word is a hapax, found only here; it is properly 'widow(er)hood', 'le fait de rendre veuf (Benveniste). It is, I suggest, formed on the surface analogy of *libertatem*: another term of civil status and, in our context, another parameter of phonic echo. Others (OLD) prefer the model to be *ubertas*, and the meaning 'dearth', from crop failure (so Norden 1939:128). But I think this is excluded by the martial verbs *defendere* and its corresponding *salua seruare.*

12. As transmitted. I think it not unlikely that the text originally had *auerruncassisque* (cf. *auerruncassint* Pacuvius 112) and *defensis* (cf. *bene sponsis = spoponderis* Festus 476 L). The phonetic responsions may be adjusted accordingly.

13. I have not indicated vowel quantities.

Note before the iambic shortening law and with the expected elision, d**VENĒ**qu' **ĒVEN-ĪRE** s**ĪR-ĪS**.

14. 1945:11, reiterated 1969:1.289. Boyce 1982: 2.121 (with references) terms this passage 'traditional', 'three stereotyped evils which might assail society.'

15. The TS 'triad' is actually preceded by *pāhí mā 'dya divaḥ* 'protect me today from the sky (=lightning)' and followed by *pāhí dúścaritād* 'protect from evil deed.' Of the parallel passages in the Yajurveda VS 2.20 begins *pāhí mā didyóḥ* 'protect me from lightning', followed by the triad through 'bad food'; the older KS 1.12 has *pāhi vidyot* 'protect from lightning' with analogical ablative (Wackernagel, AiGr. 3.151) and the triad with the correct genitive-ablatives *prasityāḥ* etc. (ibid. 3.39). But since TS 1.8.14.1 has separate *mṛtyór mā pāhi didyón mā pāhi* (also ŚB 12.8.3.11) 'protect me from death, protect me from lightning', with further parallels elsewhere, the latter phrase may be an addition to the original triad, termed a *Spruch* by Wackernagel loc. cit.

16. Still valuable Benveniste 1966:208–22. esp. 220.

17. For the readings of this passage and for other examples of the phrase in Old and Middle Hittite see Watkins 1979a:283–4.

18. For 'cattle (and) sheep', Gross- und Kleinvieh, the totality of domestic animals, see the paper cited in the preceding note.

19. Compare *Od.* 2.75 *κειμήλιά τε* ***πρόβασίν*** *τε* 'riches which lie and riches which move': Hittite ***iyatar*** *dametar* 'riches which go (and) riches which build' = 'plenty (and) abundance'; English *goods and* ***chattels***, Middle and Early Modern English *goodes and* ***cattel***.

20. Cf. Umbr. *pusti kastruvuf* 'per capita'. For the metaphor in 'heads of grain' compare Old Hittite *ḫalkiaš ḫaršār* . . . ZÍZ$^{\text{ḪI.A}}$-*ašš* = *a ḫaršār* 'heads of grain, heads of spelt', ritual for the Royal Couple (StBoT 8) iv 19–20, cf. 32.

21. Wackernagel 1953:1.280–83, cf. Schmitt 1967.

22. Wackernagel analyzed the Umbrian and Young Avestan forms as dual dvandvas (acc.); the Umbrian could just be neuter plural.

23. Benveniste 1970:308 n. 3, with references to Lüders (Indic), Sittig (Italic), and Gershevitch (Iranian). Whence Greek *ἀνδραπόδεσσι* (Homer +) 'slaves' '2-footed chattels' beside Mycenean *qetoropopi* [k$^{\text{u̯}}$etropopphi] '4-footed chattels'. Note also Vergil *Georgics* 1.118 *hominumque boumque labores* 'the toil of men and oxen', as pointed out to me by Richard Thomas.

24. 1945:6, 11 and more clearly in 1970:309, condensed in 1969:148–50.

25. Here clearly the more highly marked 'small cattle', Kleinvieh, petit bétail.

26. A point also emphasized in another context in a recent work by Campanile (1987).

27. This innovation may be post-Common Italic and attributable to later diffusion in Italy (spread from one of the branches of the Italic family), <as discussed in chap. 18>. But the stemma is unaffected.

PART 3

GREECE

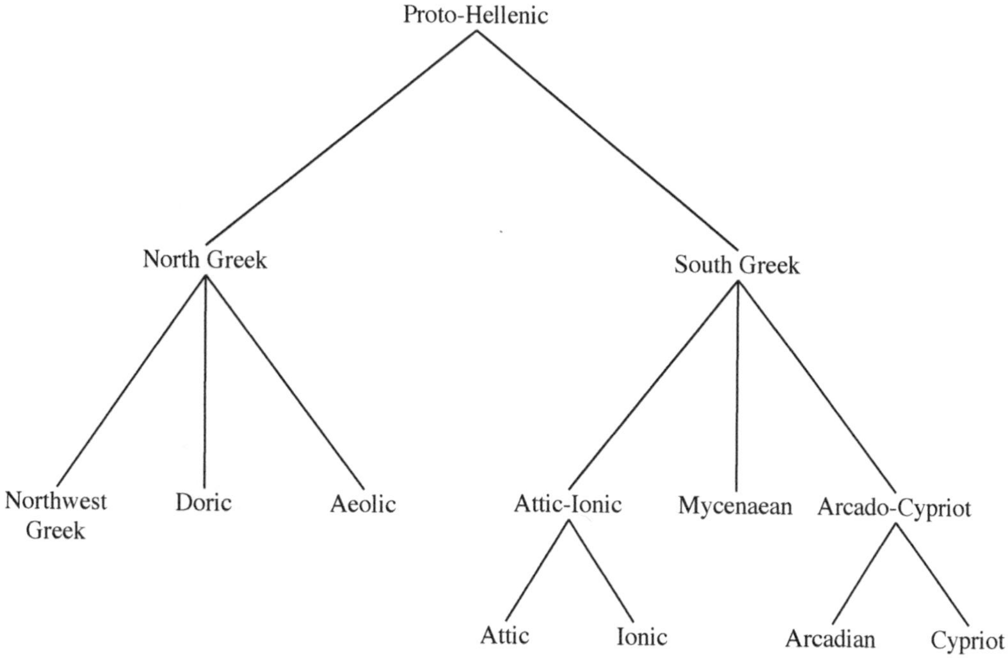
Proto-Hellenic
North Greek
South Greek
Northwest Greek
Doric
Aeolic
Attic-Ionic
Mycenaean
Arcado-Cypriot
Attic
Ionic
Arcadian
Cypriot

11. The "Kingship in Heaven" Theme

The Greek poet Hesiod, composing in the eighth century B.C., preserves in his Theogony *the tale of a series of divine sovereigns who, one after the other, depose the preceding ruler. This Greek tradition finds a close structural parallel in the "kingship in heaven" myth of the Hittites, an ancient Indo-European people of Anatolia. Do the Greeks and their Hittite cousins preserve a tradition that they inherited independently from their common Indo-European ancestors? The tradition is, however, more widely attested, known among other peoples of Europe and Asia, both Indo-European and non-Indo-European. Is the "kingship in heaven" myth then shared by these various peoples as a consequence of cross-cultural borrowing? Could processes of both inheritance and borrowing be at work? C. Scott Littleton here examines the several traditions in an effort to determine the nature and cause of mythic similarities attested from Scandinavia to Iran.* (RDW)

THE "KINGSHIP IN HEAVEN" THEME

C. Scott Littleton

Introduction

By all odds the most important single episode in Greek mythology is the one that begins with the emergence of Ouranos out of Chaos and ends with the final triumph of Zeus over Kronos and his fellow Titans; for on this account of how Zeus came to succeed to the "Kingship in Heaven" depend, directly or indirectly, almost all other Greek myths, sagas, and folktales, to say nothing of their associated rituals and ceremonies. It formed, in the Malinowskian sense, the "charter"[1] that legitimized the position of the Olympians relative to all other classes of natural and supernatural beings, and in so doing provided a firm foundation for the religious beliefs and practices of the ancient Greek-speaking community.

Yet, despite its fundamental importance to the whole structure of Greek myth and religion, the parenthood of these traditions relative to the "Kingship in Heaven" remains obscure. Through archaeological and linguistic research[2] it has become increasingly apparent that the "Kingship in Heaven" theme,[3] as it has come to be called, was in fact quite widely distributed and that it generally served a legitimizing function similar to that served by it among the Greeks. Its presence can be documented in the Hittite and Hurrian "Kumarbi" myths, in the Phoenician "Theogony" of Philo of Byblos, in the Iranian *Shāhnāmeh* or "Book of Kings," as recorded by Firdausi, and, as I attempt to demonstrate, in two Babylonian accounts of the Creation—the well-known *Enūma-Elish*[4] and the newly translated "Theogony of Dunnu"—and in the Norse traditions surrounding the ancestry and ascendance of Odin, as recorded in the *Edda*'s of Saemund and Snorri. In each instance a single pattern of events is present: an existing generation of gods was preceded by two (and in some cases three) earlier generations of supernatural beings, each succeeding generation being presided over by a "king in heaven" who has usurped (or at least assumed) the power of his predecessor. Moreover, there is generally a fourth figure, a monster of some sort, who, acting on behalf of the deposed "king" (in the Iranian and Babylonian versions, as we shall see, the monster became identified with the deposed "king" himself), presents a challenge to the final heavenly ruler and must be overcome before the latter can assert full and perpetual authority.

In considering the source of this "Kingship in Heaven" theme, one question necessarily looms large to the student of comparative Indo-European mythology: despite its apparent absence in the Indic, Balto-Slavic, Italic, and Celtic traditions (discussed later) and its occurrence in a variety of non-Indo-European speaking traditions, is there any possibility that the theme is ultimately derived from one that was present in the Indo-European *Urmythologie*? Perhaps the most ardent advocate of the Indo-European origin theory is the eminent Swedish Iranianist Stig Wikander,[5] who maintains that "l'histoire des Ouranides," as he terms it, reached the non-Indo-European peoples of Mesopotamia and Syria only *after* they had come into contact with the Hittites and Indo-Iranians who penetrated this region after 2000 B.C. This opinion is not shared, however, by most Orientalists. E. A. Speiser,[6] for example, although he suggests that the extant form of the *Enūma-Elish* seems to reflect an immediate Hittite or Hurrian origin, is nevertheless convinced that its roots lie deep in the early Babylonian and Sumerian traditions. A basically similar view has been advanced by the Hittitologist H. G. Güterbock,[7] who asserts that the Hittite version of the theme, from which the Phoenician and eventually the Greek versions appear to derive, is itself based upon Hurrian models, which in turn are probably derived from early Mesopotamian prototypes.

No one, however, has as yet attempted to resolve this question on the basis of a systematic, comparative survey of *all* the mythological materials relative to the "Kingship in Heaven."[8] The purposes of this paper[9] are thus (1) to put into evidence the salient points of similarity and difference between the several versions of the theme in question, among which I include two that heretofore have not generally been recognized as such, the Norse and Babylonian versions, and (2) to consider the question of Indo-European origin in light of the patterns revealed by this survey. I begin with the Greek version which, although it contains neither the oldest[10] nor necessarily the "purest" expression of the theme, is by far the most elaborate, best documented, and most familiar of the versions to be considered and thus can serve as a convenient point of departure.

The Greek Version

Inasmuch as the Homeric epics do not fully express the "Kingship in Heaven" theme and thus, for our purposes, cannot serve as primary sources, the earliest and most important Greek source of data concerning the theme under discussion is to be found in the Hesiodic poems, especially the *Theogony*. Composed during the later part of the eighth century B.C.,[11] the *Theogony* is concerned primarily with the events surrounding and preceding the ascension of Zeus as "king" in heaven. It served as the major source of information about cosmogonic and theogonic matters for most Greek (and Roman) poets, essayists, and dramatists. A second source is to be found in the *Bibliotheca* of Apollodorus, which was composed sometime during the first or second centuries B.C.[12] While drawing heavily upon Hesiod, Apollodorus also includes certain data that are at variance with those contained in the *Theogony*, and therefore, as it may reflect an ongoing popular tradition that was either overlooked by or inaccessible to Hesiod, the *Bibliotheca* must be considered a primary source not only for the Greek version of the "Kingship in Heaven" but for Greek mythological data in general. Our third source is the *Dionysiaca* of Nonnos which, despite its fifth century A.D. date,[13] includes some original materials relevant to the theme not found elsewhere among classical works on myth. Nonnos, as we shall see, is especially concerned with the combat between Zeus and Typhon, and his description of this struggle may reflect a popular tradition unknown to either Hesiod or Apollodorus.

According to both the *Theogony* and the *Bibliotheca*[14] the first "king" in heaven is Ouranos ("Heaven" or "Sky"). In the *Theogony*, Heaven is born of Gaia ("Earth"), who is apparently autochthonous, although she is preceded by the nonpersonified state or condition termed Chaos: "Verily at first Chaos came to be, but next wide-bosomed Earth, the ever sure foundation of all. . . ." Earth or Gaia then gives birth to various beings (e.g., Hills; Pontos ["the Deep"]; *Theogony* 130) who are not specifically important to the theme under consideration. Next, she takes Heaven as a husband: "But afterwards she lay with Heaven . . ." (*Theogony* 135). Thus Hesiod defines the first generation.

In the *Bibliotheca*, these events are simplified: "Sky was the first who ruled over the whole world. And having wedded Earth . . ." (1.1.1). There is no hint of the incestuous situation described in the *Theogony*. To Apollodorus, both Sky and Earth appear to be autochthonous.

At any event, with the marriage of Ouranos and Gaia we may proceed to the second generation, which includes the offspring of this primal pair, the youngest of whom is destined to become the second "king" in heaven. In the *Theogony* (135) Earth has intercourse with Heaven and brings forth first "Okeanos, Koios and Krios and Hyperion and Iapetos, Theia and Rhea, Themis and Mnemosyne . . . Phoibe and . . . Tethys." After these, she bears the so-called Hundred-handed: Kottos, Briareos, and Gyes, termed by Hesiod "presumptuous children" (*Theogony* 145). Then she bears the Cyclopes ("Orb-eyed"): Brontes, Steropes, and Arges;[15] finally, she bears Kronos.[16]

In the *Bibliotheca* these events are similarly reported (1.1.2–4). Here, Apollodorus introduces the terms "Titan" (male) and "Titanide" (female) to refer to these offspring, terms Hesiod uses at a later point (see below).

Ouranos was jealous of his offspring, especially the Cyclopes and the giant Hundred-handed, and "used to hide them all away in a secret place of Earth . . . [Tartaros] . . . so soon as each was born, and would not suffer them to come up into the light . . ." (*Theogony* 155). Apollodorus (1.1.2–4) gives us a similar picture, locating Tartaros as a "gloomy place in Hades as far from earth as earth is distant from the sky." Here he follows Hesiod, who, in a later context (*Theogony* 725) describes Tartaros as so far below the earth that "a brazen anvil falling from earth nine nights and days would reach Tartaros upon the tenth."

Gaia, incensed over the treatment of her children by Ouranos, exhorts them to " '. . . punish the vile outrage of your father; for he first thought of doing shameful things' " (*Theogony* 165). None but Kronos, however, has the courage to take action (*Theogony* 165), and he tells her: " '. . . I will undertake to do this deed, for I reverence not our father of evil name. . . .' " The deed consists of an emasculation of Ouranos, performed with an "element of grey flint" made into a "jagged sickle" (*Theogony* 170), which Apollodorus (1.1.4) terms an "adamantine sickle."[17]

Kronos ambushes his father, cuts off the latter's "members," and casts them into the sea. The blood so spilled impregnates Earth, who gives birth to the Giants (*Theogony* 180) and to the Furies (*Bibliotheca* 1.1.4). The seaborne "members" ultimately reach Cyprus and give birth to Aphrodite.[18]

With the emasculation of Ouranos his power has gone, and Kronos becomes "king in heaven." It is worth noting here for later comparative purposes that Ouranos is *not* killed by Kronos, merely rendered powerless. Kronos is a rebel, but not a parricide.

As regards the nature of this rebellion there seems to be a divergence between the two main sources. Hesiod, as we have seen, gives the impression that it was all accomplished—through guile—by Kronos himself, whereas Apollodorus implies that Kronos was merely the leader of a general attack against the father, one in which all save one of those siblings not previously consigned to Tartaros took part (*Bibliotheca* 1.1.4): "And they, all but Ocean, attacked him . . . and having dethroned their father, they brought up their brethren who had been hurled down to Tartaros, and committed the sovereignty to Kronos." In any case, after his ascension to power Kronos reconsigns all(?) these siblings to Tartaros (*Bibliotheca* 1.1.5): "But he again bound and shut them up in Tartaros. . . ."

Kronos, now firmly seated on the heavenly throne, marries his sister Rhea (*Theogony* 455; *Bibliotheca* 1.1.5). The children produced by this union suffer an unhappy fate, for Kronos, hearing from Heaven and Earth a prophecy that he is destined to be overthrown by his own son (*Theogony* 410, *Bibliotheca* 1.1.5), swallows his offspring as fast as they are born. Here, too, we have an episode that may be used for later comparative purposes: the swallowing of one's offspring.

The swallowed children include first (*Bibliotheca* 1.1.5) Hestia, "then Demeter and Hera, and after them Pluto (Hades) and Poseidon." Finally, pregnant with Zeus, Rhea decides to foil Kronos. As to the birth of Zeus our sources differ slightly. Both Apollodorus and Hesiod claim that the event took place in Crete; just where in Crete has long been a matter of some debate.[19]

A great deal of attention is given to the events surrounding the birth and upbringing of this youngest of Kronos' sons, an attention directed neither to the births of Zeus's siblings nor to those of the preceding generations of gods (or Titans), and several of these events must be mentioned as they have analogues in the versions to be discussed shortly. After hiding her son in Crete, Rhea gives Kronos (*Theogony* 485) "a great stone wrapped in swaddling clothes.

Then he took it in his hands and thrust it down into his belly. . . ." Thus is Kronos deceived by his wife, an event that seems to parallel the duplicity of Gaia in the castration of Ouranos. Apollodorus gives us some information concerning the childhood of Zeus which may also have some comparative value (*Bibliotheca* 1.1.7): "She [Rhea] gave him to the Kouretes and to the nymphs Adrasteia and Ida,[20] daughters of Melisseus, to nurse. So these nymphs fed the child on the milk of Amalthea." This last is apparently either a goat or a cow.[21] We shall have occasion to observe two other cases of this sort, that is, suckling by a goat or a cow, in the Iranian and in the Norse traditions.

Thus, Zeus matures to manhood, being one of the few Greek gods (or Titans) to have a defined childhood.[22] Both Apollodorus (1.2.1) and Hesiod (*Theogony* 490) indicate that this childhood lasted for a fair number of years.

Upon reaching adulthood, Zeus returns to heaven and sets about the overthrow of his father. According to the *Bibliotheca* (1.2.1) he "took Metis, daughter of Ocean, to help him, and she gave Kronos a drug to swallow, which forced him to disgorge first the stone and then the children whom he had swallowed. . . ." In the *Theogony* (495) Zeus is aided by Earth, who, apparently realizing that her son is evil, beguiles Kronos with "deep suggestions" and causes him to vomit up her grandchildren. This time, however, the older generation does not give up without a fight, and there ensues the famous "War of the Titans and Gods," (the latter term now used by both Hesiod and Apollodorus to distinguish the third generation [i.e., that of Zeus, Poseidon, Hera, *et al.*] from the two that preceded it). The war lasts ten years (*Bibliotheca* 1.2.1). On the one side are ranged Kronos and his siblings (save those still bound in Tartaros), and on the other Zeus, his mother,[23] and his siblings. Zeus enlists the aid of the Hundred-handed and the Cyclopes, whom he delivers from their subterranean prison. The latter forge thunderbolts for use against their Titan brethren, and for this they later escape the punishment of Kronos and the rest of the Titans (*Bibliotheca* 1.2.2). It is in this connection that we first see Zeus associated with the sky and with meteorological phenomena, for Zeus's chief weapon is the thunderbolt.

Having defeated the Titans, Zeus now becomes the third and perpetual "king in heaven." As Apollodorus puts it (1.2.2), Zeus "overcame the Titans, shut them up in Tartaros, and appointed the Hundred-handed their guards.[24] According to the *Bibliotheca* (1.2.2), the gods cast lots for the sovereignty, and "Zeus was allotted the dominion of the sky, to Poseidon the dominion of the sea, and to Pluto the dominion in Hades." This lot-casting aspect is not included in the

Theogony; apparently Hesiod merely assumed that Zeus succeeded to the position vacated by his father.

Thus the Olympians, a new breed of supernatural beings, have succeeded to power. But this power is not yet secure; it remains to be confirmed by the conflict between Zeus and a final challenger, the monster Typhon (or Typhoeus).[25]

According to Hesiod, "Typhoeus" is the youngest child of Earth, fathered by a personification of Tartaros at some point following the defeat of the Titans (*Theogony* 820). Apollodorus agrees as to the parentage of the monster, but locates his birth at a somewhat later point, that is, after a successful conclusion of the war of the Olympians against the Giants (offspring of Earth; see above). According to the *Bibliotheca* (1.4.2), "When the gods had overcome the giants, Earth, still more outraged, had intercourse with Tartaros and brought forth Typhon in Cilicia, a hybrid between man and beast." This reference to Cilicia has been used to claim an Oriental origin for the Typhon story; I return to this point shortly when I consider the Phoenician and Hittite traditions.

While there are some minor differences as to details, all three of our Greek sources agree upon one important aspect of Typhon's (or Typhoeus') physical appearance: snakes grow from his body. As Hesiod puts it (*Theogony* 823), "From his shoulders grew a hundred heads of a snake." This aspect of Typhon's appearance will be especially important when we turn to the Iranian version (cf. below, Firdausi's description of the monster Zohak). Also worthy of note here is Nonnos' description of Typhon advancing to battle (*Dionysiaca* 1.266–268), "There stood Typhon in the fish-giving sea, his feet firm on the weedy bottom, his belly in the air and (his head?) crushed in the clouds," which corresponds almost exactly to a similar description in the Hittite version (see below, the description of the monster Ullikummi before Mount Hazzi).

That Zeus defeats this monstrous challenger is agreed upon by all concerned. But between Hesiod and both Apollodorus and Nonnos there are some important divergences when it comes to the manner and location of this defeat. In the *Theogony* the defeat of Typhoeus is accomplished rapidly and apparently with little effort on Zeus's part; the latter merely "leaped from Olympus and struck him (i.e., Typhoeus), and burned all the marvelous heads of the monster about him." This accomplished, "Typhoeus was hurled down, a maimed wreck . . ."; finally, "in the bitterness of his anger Zeus cast him into wide Tartaros" (*Theogony* 850–869). Apollodorus, however, claims that Zeus uses an "adamantine sickle" to inflict a mortal wound upon Typhon, who flees to "Mount Kasios[26] which overhangs Syria." There, however, Typhon is able to wrest the sickle from Zeus and use it(?) to sever the sinews of the latter's hands and feet.[27] Then Typhon lifts Zeus to his shoulders (his power having briefly returned, apparently owing to Zeus's temporary physical incapacity) and carries him to the famous Corycian cave, again in Cilicia. Hiding the sinews, he leaves the "she-dragon Delphyne" to guard his prisoner. Hermes and Aigipan steal the sinews from their bearskin hiding place and, unobserved by the monster, fit them again to Zeus (*Bibliotheca* 1.3.2). There is also a tradition (Oppian, *Halieutica* 3.15–25) wherein Corycian Pan lures Typhon out of the cave with a fish meal. In any event, Zeus regains his power. He pursues Typhon across Thrace and finally to Sicily, where he administers the coup de grâce by burying the monster inside Mount Etna (*Bibliotheca* 1.3.3).

It is clear that this final battle between the chief of the Olympians and the last and most monstrous representative of the old order involves more than is usually involved in most mythological monster slayings. Nonnos underscores this: "No herds of cattle were the cause of that struggle, no flocks of sheep, this was no quarrel for a beautiful woman, no fray for a petty town: *heaven itself was the stake in the fight . . .*" (*Dionysiaca* 2.359–363; italics mine). Thus, having defeated Typhon, Zeus has firmly consolidated the position of his revolutionary Olympian regime. Henceforth, he will rule as perpetual and unchallenged "king" in heaven.

Before leaving the Typhon episode, I should perhaps mention in passing that some years ago F. Vian suggested that it presents a number of interesting parallels to the widespread and quite probably Indo-European tradition wherein a hero (or a triad of heroes) slays a three-headed monster that is menacing the peace and security of the community (cf. the Indian account of the conflict between Indra and the tricephalic son of Tvaṣṭar and the Roman legend of a fight between the three Horatii and the three Curiatii).[28] I shall have more to say about this later on in the context of a general discussion of the possibility that the idea of the divine kingship is Indo-European in origin.

The myths concerning the later exploits of Zeus, his brethren, and his offspring, as well as those that concern the affairs of gods and mortals in subsequent generations (e.g., the Oedipus cycle, the siege of Troy) are not specifically germane to the theme in question, and therefore the delineation of the Greek version is concluded at this point. If I have dwelt here overlong, it is only because in the Greek tradition relative to the "Kingship in Heaven" there is a "model," so to speak, which can be utilized in making comparative statements as I consider the evidence from Anatolia, Phoenicia, Iran, Scandinavia, and Mesopotamia.

The Hurrian-Hittite Version

Since the first study over thirty years ago[29] of the Hittite "Theogony" and the Hittite myth which H. G. Güterbock[30] has labeled the "Song of Ullikummi," there has been a renewed interest in the argument—originally based on the presence of a Phoenician version of the theme under consideration—that the Greek "Kingship in Heaven" tradition just delineated is actually composed of myths having their origin somewhere in the ancient Near East. Indeed, I use the term "Hittite-Hurrian" here because of the indisputable evidence[31] that the Hurrians, who were well established in northern Syria and Mesopotamia by the middle of the second millennium B.C., and whose language appears to have been neither Indo-European nor Semitic, also possessed versions of the myths discussed below.

The texts containing the Hittite and/or Hurrian myths in question date approximately from the thirteenth century B.C. and were translated from a series of cuneiform tablets[32] found at Hattusha, the ancient Hittite capital, the site of which is located near the modern Turkish village of Bogazköy. These tablets are not well preserved and countless interpolations have had to be made in order to arrive at anything like a coherent narrative.[33] That which Güterbock terms the "Theogony"—the Hittite title is unfortunately missing—deals specifically with the "Kingship in Heaven." In it we see four generations of gods. The first is called Alalu, who reigns in heaven nine "years."[34] His future successor, Anu, is described as he who "bows down to his [Alalu's] feet and puts the cups for drinking into his hand" (i.10–11).[35] Although Anu (whose name derives from the Akkadianized form of the Sumerian god An, or 'Sky'[36]) is not specifically identified as Alalu's son, the fact that a god Alala is listed in a Babylonian god list as a father of Anu[37] leaves no doubt as to the filial relationship here. In the ninth "year" of Alalu's reign Anu rebels against him and either drives or hurls him "down to the dark earth" (1.12), the latter expression apparently referring to a subterranean region.[38]

Thus, Anu becomes the second "king in heaven." But he, too, must cope with a rebellious offspring, the "mighty Kumarbi."[39] At first, Kumarbi is described as serving Anu in a manner identical to that in which the latter had served Alalu; however, like his father before him, Anu is only permitted to reign for nine "years," and in the ninth "year" Kumarbi rebels. This time the elder god flees, but Kumarbi "took Anu by the feet and pulled him down from heaven" (i.23–24). Then follows a most interesting passage in light of our Greek "model": "He [Kumarbi] bit his loins[40] [so that] his manhood was absorbed in Kumarbi's interior . . ." (i.25); compare Kronos' emasculation of Ouranos. Indeed, the striking correspondences[41] here between Anu and Ouranos and between Kumarbi and Kronos have been noted frequently (see above).

Subsequent to his deposition and emasculation, Anu informs Kumarbi that by "absorbing" his "manhood" he has been impregnated with five "heavy" divinities: the Weather-god (i.e., the Hurrian Teshub),[42] the river goddess Aranzah (i.e., Tigris),[43] Tashmishu,[44] who is destined to be the vizier of the gods, and two others whose names are not mentioned by Anu.[45] Having thus addressed his successor, Anu "went up to heaven" and, after a visit to Nippur, perhaps to consult its chief deity Enlil about his pregnancy, Kumarbi becomes the third to occupy the heavenly throne.

From here on the text is too fragmentary for a consecutive narrative. It appears that Kumarbi attempts to avoid bearing these unwelcome offspring by spitting out Anu's seed (end of col. i);[46] nevertheless, a fragmentary reference to Kumarbi's failure to count months and the phrase "the ninth month came" clearly indicate that he carried Teshub *et al.* within him for a full term. Güterbock[47] points out that the theme of the mutilated first part of column ii is childbirth and that two of the gods in Kumarbi's "interior," Marduk and KA.ZAL (see n. 45, above), discuss with him several ways in which they might be born. Especially miraculous is the birth of the Weather-god or Teshub[48] (cf. the attention devoted by our Greek sources to the birth of Zeus,[49] to whom, as we shall see, Teshub corresponds in most respects). Then follows a passage that is especially interesting in view of the equivalence between Kumarbi and Kronos. In it someone (Kumarbi?) says "give me the child . . . I shall eat" (ii.42); later there occurs the expression "Kumarbi begins to eat" (ii.52), and prominent mention of the words "mouth" and "teeth" in connection with the Weather-god.

It seems that Teshub and his siblings are able to dethrone Kumarbi, for when we first meet the Weather-god he is already "king in heaven." Just how the rebellion is accomplished is not quite clear. Is it possible that Earth, like her Greek counterpart, conspired with her offspring (if indeed they were such) to bring about Kumarbi's downfall? Considering Earth's probable connection with the birth of Teshub and his siblings, this is quite likely; perhaps we have here a merging of Gaia and Rhea in the person of Earth.

The second Hittite myth relevant to the theme in question is entitled the "Song of Ullikummi" and contains many important parallels to the previously discussed Typhon story.[50] Kumarbi, having been dethroned, has intercourse with a rock; from this unnatural union is produced the Stone-monster[51] (also termed the Diorite after the substance of which the monster is composed), or Ullikummi. Conceived by his father in order to avenge the latter's overthrow, Ullikummi is destined to be a rebel against Teshub.[52] That Typhon was born with a similar purpose in life can be seen from a passage in the *Dionysiaca* (2.565–568) wherein Kronides (an epithet of Zeus), after wounding the monster sorely, chides him saying: "A fine ally has old Kronos found in you, Typhoeus! . . . A jolly champion of Titans!"

The young Ullikummi is placed on a shoulder of the Atlas-like Upelluri and allowed to grow: "In one day one yard he grew, but in one month one furlong he grew . . . when the fifteenth day came the Stone had grown high. And in the sea on his knees like a blade he stood. Out of the water he stood, the Stone . . . , and the sea up to the place of the belt like a garment reached . . . ; he was lifted, the Stone, and up in Heaven the temples and the chamber he reached" (I.23–32). This can be compared to Nonnos' description of Typhon cited earlier, that is, feet in water and head "crushed" against the clouds.

The first of the gods to see Ullikummi is the Sun-god, who reports his terrified observations to Teshub. The latter goes to see for himself, and when he does so he weeps, for apparently he can see no way of overcoming this monster. His sister, Ishtar (Aranzah?) comforts him and tries to enchant Ullikummi by music (cf. Kadmos' charming of Typhoeus while recovering Zeus's sinews [*Dionysiaca* 1.409–534]). Here, however, we learn that the Stone is deaf and blind. So Teshub decides to fight him, but to no avail, for the monster is too powerful. The gods retreat from this battle, fought in the shadow of Mount Hazzi (i.e., Mount Kasios on the Syrian coast), and retire to Kummiya,[53] the city of Teshub. Ullikummi follows, endangering even Teshub's wife Hebat. At this point Tashmishu enters the picture. After climbing a tower to tell Hebat of her husband's defeat, he suggests to Teshub that they visit Ea,[54] the Babylonian god of wisdom and witchcraft (cf. the *Enūma-Elish*, shortly to be discussed, wherein Ea occupies a prominent position), and together they journey to the wise god's home in

Apsuwa (the Babylonian Apsu).[55] Ea, willing to help, first ascertains that Upelluri has no knowledge of what is resting on his shoulder and then orders the "former gods" (i.e., those who ruled in heaven before Alalu, such as Enlil, the Sumerian storm-god) to produce the "ancient tool" (a sickle?) used at one time to separate Earth and Heaven. With this tool Ea cuts Ullikummi from Upelluri's shoulder and thus magically renders him powerless.[56] Here, too, we have a parallel to the Greek tradition, for Apollodorus, as we have seen, described the use of a cutting tool (i.e., the "adamantine sickle") by Zeus in his struggle with Typhon. The same tool, of course, was used against Ouranos by Kronos, and some authorities, both ancient and modern, have interpreted the castration of Ouranos as a symbolic separation of heaven and earth.[57] It is interesting that the Hittites preserve a tradition of a primeval cutting tool once used to separate heaven and earth, and which must later be used to defeat Ullikummi, although no specific tool is mentioned in the account of Anu's castration. Perhaps in the latter case the teeth of Kumarbi have been substituted for the stone "teeth" of a neolithic sickle (i.e., the "ancient cutting tool").

When word reaches the gods that Ullikummi has been rendered powerless, they join together under the leadership of Teshub and attack the monster. From here on the text is unreadable; however, we may assume with Güterbock[58] that Teshub and his fellows are ultimately victorious. For it appears that here, as in the Greek tradition, the new "king in heaven" must meet this final challenger so as to validate his position as perpetual ruler, and there is no doubt that Teshub, like Zeus, is able to accomplish this validation. It should be noted, though, that the conflict here is much more general than in the Greek tradition. Perhaps in the conflict between Teshub and Ullikummi we have a merger of the Titanomachia and the Typhon fight.

The Phoenician Version

In the *Phoenician History* of Herennios Philo of Byblos, known only through the works of Eusebius (*Praeparatio Evangelica*) and Porphyrius (*De Abstinentia*), is contained a version of the "Kingship in Heaven" which closely parallels the two just discussed, a version that has often been regarded as an intermediary between those of the Hittites and the Greeks, Philo's date is uncertain, although the best evidence leads me to believe that he wrote during the latter half of the first century A.D.; Clemen places his birth in the last years of the reign of the Emperor Claudius.[59] Claiming to have obtained his information from the works of a certain Sanchunjathon, a Phoenician scholar who, he asserts, "lived before the Trojan War," Philo attempts to reconstruct the "history" of his city and to trace the origins of its gods. He begins by outlining a four-generational sequence of "kings in heaven," all of whom are intimately associated with the city of Byblos and its environs.

According to Philo, the first "king in heaven" is named Eliun (or Hypsistos "Highest") (I.14),[60] who with his wife Bruth (i.e., Beirut) comes to live in Byblos. They give birth to a son called Ouranos and a daughter named Ge or Gaia. Ge and Ouranos marry and produce four sons: El (who is also referred to as Kronos), Baitylos, Dagon, and Atlas (I.16). A quarrel ensues between Ouranos and his wife, and El (or Kronos) and his siblings side with their mother. Ouranos then tries to destroy his rebellious offspring, but El, on the advice of Hermes, whom he has taken as a counselor, forges a sickle (or spear?) and with it drives out his father. El then becomes "king in heaven" (or at least in Byblos), but turns out to be a bad ruler, casting out his brother Atlas and murdering a son and a daughter. Meanwhile, Ouranos has fled unharmed. He sends Rhea, Astarte, and Dione, his young daughters, to plead his case before El. These three El takes to wife,[61] and by each he produces a number of children. The most important of these is Baal[62] (or Baaltis), who succeeds him.

Thirty-two years later, El lures his father back to Byblos, into an ambush, and castrates him (cf. *Theog.* 175). Thus, the castration theme is present, although it does not accompany the deposition of the "Heaven figure" as it does in the Greek and Hittite-Hurrian versions. Furthermore, what appears to me to be a crucial element is lacking here: the idea that castration is a necessary step in reducing the power of the Heaven figure. In Philo it seems but an afterthought. Castration figures again in Philo's account, although this time it is self-inflicted. For some obscure reason El mutilates himself thirty-two years after so altering his father.

Finally, the fourth generation (in the person of Baal) takes over the heavenly kingship. This transfer of power is apparently made without much conflict, an occurrence unique in the distribution of the theme. Typhon is mentioned by Philo along with the children of El, but there is no mention of a fight.[63] Moreover, the role of the "Zeus figure" (Baal) is minor when compared with that played by him in the Greek and Hittite-Hurrian versions, and in the Iranian, Norse, and Babylonian versions as well.

In view of its late date and the high probability that its author was thoroughly familiar with Hesiod, many scholars have been skeptical of this Phoenician "Theogony," labeling it a poor attempt at syncretism. The discovery of some

Hurrian texts at Ras Shamra, however, wherein the double name El-Kumarbi occurs,[64] has thrown a new light on the matter. As El is clearly identified by Philo with Kronos, it is reasonable to infer that there was some sort of a Kronos-El-Kumarbi syncretism present in northern Syria, at least, as early as 1400 B.C. If this is correct, then it is also quite reasonable to infer with Güterbock that the Phoenician tradition here forms a link between the Hittite-Hurrian version and the later Greek version, and that what formerly appeared as rank syncretism on Philo's part can now be seen as antedating rather than reflecting the Hesiodic version of the theme.[65]

But there still remain other possibilities. That the Phoenicians undoubtedly received elements of the Kumarbi myth from the Hittites as the latter expanded their empire after 1500 B.C. is not questioned here; indeed, the Ras Shamra evidence renders it almost certain. What is questioned, however, is the assumption that the Phoenicians were necessarily the link in a chain of diffusion from northern Syria to Greece. There is always the possibility that the theme reached Hesiod and/or his immediate sources directly from the Hittite-Hurrian region. This alternative is enhanced somewhat by L. R. Palmer's assertion[66] that the Luvians, first cousins to the Hittites, invaded the Peloponnesus and Crete at the beginning of the second millennium B.C., and that the first speakers of Greek arrived several centuries later. If Palmer is correct in this assertion, and there is good reason to believe that he is, then it is remotely possible that the "Kingship in Heaven" theme was taken over by the Greeks along with other aspects of Luvian culture.[67] Another possibility, that the theme was borrowed directly from Babylonia during Mycenaean times, is discussed presently.

The Iranian Version

It was Stig Wikander who, in 1951,[68] first demonstrated the presence of the "Kingship in Heaven"—if indeed the term "heaven" is applicable in this instance—in the Iranian tradition. Bypassing the more ancient and mythological Avestan literature, Wikander pointed out that a threefold set of royal usurpers similar to those present in the Greek, Hittite-Hurrian, and Phoenician traditions occupies a prominent position in Firdausi's *Shāhnāmeh*, which was composed about A.D. 976. Despite its relatively recent date and the high probability that its author was familiar with Greek myth, the *Shāhnāmeh* has long been recognized as a repository of popular traditions not elsewhere represented in Iranian literature. This would certainly appear to be true as far as the theme in question is concerned.

In any event, the three Iranian kings cited by Wikander as comparable with Ouranos, Kronos, Zeus, *et al.*, are Jamshid, Zohak, and Feridun, who occupy, respectively, positions four, five, and six in Firdausi's king list. Jamshid is preceded by three relatively indistinct figures, Kaiumers (equals Gayōmart in the *Avesta*), Husheng, and Tahumers. These three do not seem to be related to their successors in any important sense—Jamshid is made the son of Tahumers, but little else is said about the relationship between them. Thus it is Jamshid who occupies the Ouranos-like position, despite his lack of an autochthonous or truly divine origin.

Jamshid, whose name corresponds to that of Yima Xšaēta[69] in the *Avesta*, is said to have ruled for some seven hundred years, and the early portion of this reign is described as a sort of Golden Age, when men were at peace with one another and the land was bountiful. But this state of affairs did not last. "Then it came about that the heart of Jamshid was uplifted with pride, and he forgot whence came his weal and the source of his blessings."[70] Wikander, in discussing the position of Jamshid, notes that he "règne d'abord sur une humanité heureuse, mais il commet ensuite le premier péché, ce qui amène la perte de la Gloire Royale et sa chute."[71] Wikander also remarks that some texts show Jamshid as having been deceived by "une figure féminine qui aurait inspiré ses transgressions et causé sa chute."[72] Thus, we have some indication that here, too, there is a Gaia-like figure somewhere in the background.[73]

Jamshid is eventually overthrown by Zohak (equals Aži Dahāka in the *Avesta*), who in terms of our model occupies an ambiguous position. He is at once Typhon and Kronos. Both in his physical appearance and in his relationship with the third member of the trio, Feridun, who occupies the position of Zeus figure, Zohak strongly resembles Typhon. Yet he enters the epic occupying the position of a Kronos figure. Like Typhon, his physical appearance is characterized by the presence of snakes growing from his shoulders;[74] yet he is the one who overthrows Jamshid and who commits the inevitable act of mutilation, although in this instance it is not castration but rather a sawing in half.[75]

There are two interesting parallels here to the Phoenician version. Like El, Zohak waits a hundred years before mutilating his deposed enemy: "in the hundredth year [after his overthrow] the impious shah [Jamshid] appeared one day beside the Sea of Chin. Zohak clutched him forthwith, gave him no respite, and, sawing him asunder, freed the world from him and the fear that he inspired."[76] A second parallel can be seen in the fact that Zohak, like El, marries two sisters who stand in close kinship to him—only in this instance they are sisters of the deposed first-generation ruler (Jamshid).

Wikander emphasizes the similarity between the saw that cut Jamshid in half and the sickle that castrated Ouranos. "Azdahak ou un autre ennemi le mutile avec une 'scie' . . . cette 'scie' est évidemment identique à la 'serpe aux dents aigues' d'Hésiode."[77] He also characterizes Zohak as the "neveu" of Jamshid, although nowhere in our reading of the epic is there any clear-cut statement as to the relationship, if any, between the two figures. Zohak is characterized simply as the son of an Arabian king[78] who is invited to come to Iran and replace Jamshid.

Zohak, in his turn, is overthrown by the grandson of Jamshid, Feridun (equals Thraētaona in the *Avesta*), who, like Zeus, has a marvelous childhood. Again we see the theme of the mother hiding away the child from the wrath of the father (in this case Zohak). Zohak, it seems, while having no offspring of his own, has an insatiable desire to consume human beings. Furthermore, the serpent-king dreams that Feridun will someday overcome him (cf. Kronos' foreknowledge of Zeus's coming, and his subsequent swallowing of his offspring), and on the basis of this dream "bade the world be scoured for Feridun."[79] Feridun's mother first places him in the care of a wondrous cow, Purmaieh, who suckles the infant. Then, fearing that Zohak will find this hiding place, she removes him to the care of a shepherd "on the Mount Alberz" (i.e., the Elbruz?), who raises him to manhood. Here we can compare the hiding away of Zeus on Mount Ida (or Aigaion). Finally, Feridun grows to manhood and sets out to overcome his monstrous enemy. Instead of a cutting instrument, Feridun uses a club, the head of which is shaped like a cow—in memory of Purmaieh.[80] The combat between Feridun and Zohak is strongly reminiscent of the conflict between Zeus and Typhon. Again, it is a single-combat situation, not the type of group action which dethroned Kronos.

Feridun overpowers Zohak but does not actually kill him (a fusion, perhaps, of the Typhon and Kronos motifs); rather, he chains the monster to a rock[81] on Mount Demawend(?), and Zohak eventually dies of exposure. After this deed is accomplished, Feridun reigns as king, if not actually "in heaven," then certainly as a divine king in Iran.

While it is certain that the Avestan names Yima Xšaēta, Aži Dahāka, and Thraētaona correspond, respectively, to Jamshid, Zohak, and Feridun, the only clear thematic parallels between the two sets of figures are that both Yima and Jamshid can be seen to be in one respect or another primordial (although both do actually have forebears), that both were "Golden Age" rulers who "sinned," that Aži Dahāka and his later namesake share draconic characteristics, and that both are rendered harmless, respectively, by Thraētaona and Feridun. Even in the latter instance there is an important difference. Thraētaona is characterized as the "smiter" of Aži Dahāka,[82] while Feridun, as we have seen, imprisons Zohak. Thus it can be safely asserted that the theme qua theme, despite some similarities, is not present in the *Avesta*.

Nor is it to be found in the Indic tradition. To be sure, there are some very general parallels, both thematic and philological, between the Avestan figures mentioned above and some of the dramatis personae of the Indic literature. For example, Avestan Yima parallels Vedic Yama; Aži Dahāka is equivalent to the three-headed monster Vṛtra; Thraētaona bears a resemblance to Trita Āptya, the slayer of Vṛtra (also to Indra in this context); and the cow-headed weapon (*gurz*) used by Feridun is linguistically cognate to the thunderbolt *vajra* used in the slaying of Vṛtra. But other than these isolated correspondences, together with one other possibility to be mentioned shortly in connection with the Norse version, there is no evidence for the presence of the theme in question in the *Veda*'s, *Mahābhārata*, and so on.[83] This negative evidence, so to speak, is a most important matter when it comes to the question of possible Indo-European origins, and I return to it later on.

The Norse Version

All too often there is a tendency among students of comparative mythology to equate "Norse" with "Germanic," to assume that the materials contained in the *Edda*'s, *Heimskringla, Gesta Danorum*, and the like, are a true reflection of common Germanic religious beliefs and practices. To make such an equation is, of course, an error; for it is abundantly clear that there were differences in religious outlook among the several branches of the Germanic-speaking peoples. One need only compare Tacitus with Saxo Grammaticus to see examples of these differences. While there are some common figures (e.g., *Tīwaz, probable prototype of Norse Týr, Anglo-Saxon Tiw, and perhaps the figure reflected in

Tacitus' Tuisto),[84] any attempt to draw general conclusions about the nature of Germanic religion from any one region or era must be made cautiously.

Yet, when it comes to cosmogonic and theogonic matters we are necessarily limited to a single region and a single era: Scandinavia (primarily Iceland) in the eleventh and twelfth centuries A.D. Moreover, our chief sources,[85] the *Elder* or *Poetic Edda*, attributed to Saemund Siggfusson, and especially the *Younger*, or *Prose Edda* of Snorri Sturluson, were composed at a time when the old religion was fast giving way to Christianity (Snorri approaches his subject from an explicitly Christian standpoint), and the extent to which non-Norse materials were interwoven with the native tradition is still not wholly clear.

That Saemund and Snorri were aware—albeit dimly—of the mythic traditions of the eastern Mediterranean is entirely possible.[86] It is also possible that whatever parallels may exist between their accounts of the creation and those previously discussed in this paper are wholly or partially the result of independent invention. In any case, all the foregoing must be kept firmly in mind as we proceed to a brief examination of the Norse theogony to see if it contains materials relevant to the "Kingship in Heaven."

In the beginning was Ginnungagap (equivalent to the Greek Chaos), which can be loosely translated as "yawning void." Out of this yawning void were created initially two regions: Muspellheim on the south (i.e., a "Land of Fire") and Niflheim on the north (i.e., a "Land of Mist"). Ice crystals combined with sparks, and out of this combination there was created the first being, called Ymir. Ymir, defined as a giant of enormous proportions, lies down and sleeps. While he sleeps two things happen: first, a second autochthonous creature appears, a cow named Audhumla. While Ymir sleeps the cow nourishes him, at the same time she licks the salty ice and slowly uncovers first the hair, then the body of a third autochthon: Buri. Thus Audhumla serves as a link between these two generationally equivalent Jöntin, or "Giants" (occasionally rendered Etin). Meanwhile, in his sleep, Ymir androgynously gives birth to several offspring (*Lay of Vafthrudnir* 33): "The ice-*etin*'s [i.e., Ymir's] strong arms, beneath there grew both girl and boy, one with the other, the wise *etin*'s shanks begat a six-headed son." The latter is named Thrudgelmir. He, in turn, gives birth to the crafty Bergelmir. Thus, we have one three-generation line of descent from Ymir. As the *Lay of Vafthrudnir* (29) has it: "Ages before the earth was made, Bergelmir came to be. Thrudgelmir was that *thur*'s(?) father. But Aurgelmir [i.e., Örgelmir, or Ymir] oldest of all."

A second three-generational line descends from Buri, who, after emerging from the ice, produces a son: Bör. Bör marries a giantess named Bestla (one of

Ymir's offspring?). They, in turn, produce three sons: Odin, Vili, and Vé (cf. Zeus, Poseidon, Hades). Odin and his siblings (who, unlike their Greek equivalents, become shadowy figures very quickly) are the first of the Aesir (or "Gods" as opposed to "Giants"). Their first act is to overthrow Ymir, and with him Thrudgelmir. Bergelmir they banish (or he escapes) to subterranean Jöntinheim (cf. Tartaros?).[87] Ymir they cut up (the tool involved is not mentioned), forming the world: "of Ymir's flesh the earth was shaped, of his blood the briny sea, of his hair, the trees, the hills of his bones, out of his skull the sky" (*Lay of Grimnir* 40).

There is a parallel to this in *Rig-Veda* 10.90, wherein Indra and others create the world from the flesh and bones of the giant Puruṣa. Another parallel can be seen in the Babylonian *Enūma-Elish*, in the use to which Marduk puts the body of the slain Tiamat. The similarities here, however, may best be explained in terms of a common folkloristic motif which has nothing specifically to do with the theme under discussion. Yet the fact that Odin and his siblings *cut* the primeval figure is significant. It is this feature, rather than the subsequent use of his remains, that is relevant for our purposes.

In any event, it is only after the Jöntin have been defeated that Odin and his brothers create mankind.[88] This, of course, is paralleled in the Greek version (i.e., the human race is only created after the final defeat of the Titans; cf. *Bibliotheca* 1.4.1).

It is our contention that the events just described contain all the essential ingredients of the "Kingship in Heaven" theme: First, there is a three-generational line of descent (although bifurcated); second, there is the mutilation of the first-generation "king" (i.e., Odin's cutting up Ymir); third, there is the banishment of a descendant of this first-generation being by one who has usurped power from him (Bergelmir is the logical inheritor of Ymir); fourth, the final and perpetual holder of power (Odin) is, together with his siblings and offspring, defined as an altogether different sort of supernatural being (i.e., "Gods" or Aesir, as opposed to "Giants" or Jöntin; cf. the Greek distinction between "God" and "Titan"). And finally, there is a battle between these Aesir and the Giants, a battle that seems to be equivalent to that between the Olympians and the Titans[89] (or Giants, too, for that matter).

That the characteristic structure of the theme, as expressed in the Greek and Hittite-Hurrian tradition, is absent, must be admitted. Contained within a broad three-generational framework, however, most of the significant components of this structure are present. To put it another way, the same broad configuration is present in Norse mythology, yet the elements within this configuration are not for the most part structured as they are in the Greek tradition. Indeed, we have seen other cases, generally held to be part of the theme in question, which also deviate from this typological structure, yet which maintain the same broad configuration. We may cite here the Iranian version, wherein Zohak, who most clearly resembles Typhon, appears in the role of a Kronos figure. We may also cite the Phoenician case, wherein Baal does not have to fight his way to power, as is characteristic of the other versions—including the Norse.

It seems fair to assert that the Norse, like the Greeks, Hittites, Hurrians, Phoenicians, Iranians, and Babylonians, knew the "Kingship in Heaven" theme. Whether its presence here can best be explained in terms of diffusion or independent invention is still a moot point, although I believe that the former possibility is the more probable in view of the extremely late periods from which the primary sources date. There is, of course, the alternate possibility that the presence of the theme can be explained in terms of a common Indo-European heritage. Once again, let me defer consideration of this possibility—seemingly quite remote—until I look at the Babylonian versions.

The Babylonian Versions

Like the Norse version, the two Babylonian versions deviate in a number of important respects from that which for convenience sake I have labeled the typological version (i.e., that of the Greeks). Yet these two related accounts of how the gods came to be may well prove to be far closer to the source of the theme in question than any previously considered. Although no extant text of the *Enūma-Elish* is earlier than 1000 B.C., internal evidence alone indicates that its composition probably dates at least from the Old Babylonian period, that is, the early part of the second millennium B.C., and that its content may be considerably older.[90]

The *Enūma-Elish* begins with an account of the primeval state of things: "When on high the heaven had not been named,/Firm ground below had not been called by name,/Naught but primeval Apsu,[91] their begetter,/(And) Mummu-Tiamat,[92] she who bore them all,/Their waters commingling as a single body . . ." (i.1–4).[93] We see here the by now familiar pair of autochthons, in this instance defined as fresh and salt water. From this union several generations of divinities are born, including the figures (for our purposes obscure) Lahmu and Lahamu, Anshar and Kishar, and Anu. Finally, there appears the figure who, together with another shortly to be discussed, occupies the Kronos position, the "all-wise" Ea (or

Nudimmud; cf. Sumerian Enki). Although the exact parentage and birth order of Ea are obscure, by all indications he is the youngest of the lot (who can, for our purposes, be reckoned as a single generation; that is, they band together and act as a generational unit).[94] If this interpretation is correct, then there is an interesting parallel here to the ultimogeniture pattern so clearly evident in the Greek version.

Under the apparent leadership of Ea, the gods of what we may term the second generation (see above) "disturbed Tiamat as they surged back and forth" (i.22). Apsu, too, is annoyed by "their hilarity in the Abode of Heaven" (i.24) and decides to do away with them. His decision is strengthened by the advice of the vizier Mummu,[95] but is opposed by Tiamat, who counsels forgiveness. Nevertheless, the gods discover Apsu's intentions. After putting Apsu to sleep with an incantation (cf. the "deep suggestions" with which Zeus beguiles Kronos[96]), Ea slays him, yet before doing so he tears off the former's tiara or halo (symbolic, perhaps, of sovereignty and the masculine vigor that accompanies it) and puts it on himself (i.60–69). Admittedly, I may be guilty of overinterpretation here, but it does occur to me that the act of tearing off Apsu's tiara is comparable with an act of castration. By so doing, Ea clearly renders his forbear powerless to resist, just as Kronos, Kumarbi, *et al.* render their progenitors powerless by dismembering or "biting" them. In any event, thus passes the first generation.

After having become "king in heaven" Ea[97] takes up residence upon the dead Apsu[98] and is joined by his wife Damkina. In time Damkina gives birth to the great Babylonian divinity Marduk, who is patently the Zeus figure in this version. Many lines follow describing Marduk's brilliance and prowess, for example, "He was the loftiest of the gods, surpassing was his stature,/His members were enormous, he was exceeding tall" (i.97–100). Meanwhile, Tiamat schemes in order to seek revenge for the slaying of her husband. She causes a heretofore unmentioned god, Ea's half-brother, Kingu, to be elevated to command of the Assembly of the Gods, apparently, though the text makes no mention of it, displacing Ea. She then sets about creating a host of monsters (cf. i.126). From this point on Ea fades into obscurity, and the threat presented by Tiamat and Kingu is met by Marduk. A great fight ensues. Marduk eventually slays Tiamat in single combat and destroys her host. He then captures the rebel Kingu and consigns him to Uggae, the god of the dead (iv.119–120). Afterward, Marduk and Ea create heaven and earth from Tiamat's inflated body by splitting it in two[99] (cf. the fate of Ymir). Marduk now reigns perpetually as "king in heaven."[100] He has validated his claim to sovereignty by emerging victorious in the epic duel with Tiamat.

Taken as a whole, the *Enūma-Elish* presents some remarkable parallels to the other versions of the "Kingship in Heaven," although there are, of course, several important structural differences. For one thing, there is a bifurcation of the Kronos figure. Taken together, the careers of Ea *and* Kingu approximate closely that of the typical second generation "king": initially, in the person of Ea, we see him usurping the kingship through a ruse and (perhaps) performing an act of emasculation; later on, in the person of Kingu, we see him defeated by the Zeus figure and consigned to what would appear to be a Tartaros-like place. In the case of Tiamat we have not bifurcation but fusion. She is at once Gaia and Typhon (cf. Zohak, who is both Kronos and Typhon). It is in the latter role, however, that she appears most clearly, and the fight between her and Marduk is strikingly similar to that between Zeus and Typhon, Teshub and Ullikummi, and so on. The relationship between Tiamat and Kingu is, of course, the opposite of that between Kronos and Typhon or Kumarbi and Ullikummi: in the Babylonian account the "king" is a creature of the monster. Yet on balance it seems clear that the theogony contained in the *Enūma-Elish* is akin to those we have previously surveyed. And given its date, it is probably their prototype.

Until recently, the *Enūma-Elish* was the only known Babylonian creation myth that came anywhere near to approximating the idea of the divine kingship. In 1965, however, W. G. Lambert published (with A. R. Millard) and subsequently translated[101] a cuneiform text (BM 74329) which may be termed for convenience' sake the "Theogony of Dunnu."[102]In it we can see essentially the same course of events as described in the *Enūma-Elish*, although the locale and figures involved are for the most part quite distinct. The date of this new text is late. Lambert and Walcot assign it to the Late Babylonian period (i.e., between 635 and 330 B.C.), although it is suggested that it belongs to the earlier phase of this period and that, as in the case of the *Enūma-Elish*, it may contain materials originally composed perhaps as early as the beginning of the second millennium B.C.[103]

Here the action centers on the ancient city of Dunnu, an otherwise obscure place as far as the overall Babylonian tradition is concerned.[104] The text itself is far shorter and more literary than the one just discussed. In this instance the two autochthons are the figures Hain (unknown outside this text)[105] and Earth. Although the first three lines are incomplete, it appears that they give birth first to Sea (cf. Tiamat) by means of a plow, and then in an apparently more normal fashion to the male figure Amakandu (once again we encounter the ultimogeniture pattern). Amakandu is seduced by his mother: "[Earth] cast her eyes on Amakandu, her son,/'Come, let me make love to you' she said to him" (lines 8–9). After marrying his mother, Amakandu slays Hain and lays him to rest in the city of Dunnu, "which he loved" (line 12). He then assumes his father's overlordship of the city (line 13). Subsequently, Amakandu marries Sea (his sister: cf. Kronos and Rhea), who gives birth to a son called Lahar. Lahar in turn slays his father, marries his mother (i.e., Sea), and assumes the kingship. He, too, produces offspring: a daughter, River, and a son, whose first name is unreadable. The latter eventually kills both Lahar and Sea (his mother), marries River (his sister), and assumes power. At this point the text is somewhat obliterated, but the pattern seems to be carried out for at least two more generations. Sons slay their fathers and mothers, marry their sisters, and usurp the sovereignty. The female figures here whose names are readable include Ga'um and Ningeshtinna. There is no clear termination to the text, which is contained on the obverse and reverse of a single tablet, although the last readable line (40) indicates that the seat of power has been transferred to the city of Shupat [or Kupat].

In this "Theogony of Dunnu" can be seen in abbreviated and somewhat redundant form the essential outlines of the theme. The fact that there are five generations rather than three is not a crucial deterrent to putting the text into comparison with the other versions. It will be recalled that both the Hittite-Hurrian version and that of the Phoenicians, to say nothing of the version contained in the *Shāhnāmeh*, all describe one or more generations as existing prior to those upon whom attention is centered. In the present case the replication follows rather than precedes the principal sequence of events. To be sure, there is a major structural problem here in that in all other versions surveyed, including the *Enūma-Elish*, there is a denouement. One figure, be he Zeus, Teshub, Baal, Feridun, Odin, or Marduk, puts a seal on the succession. In the "Theogony of Dunnu," however, Lahar is in turn overthrown, and the series of usurpations is seemingly without end. Nor do we see here any indication of emasculation, although Lambert and Walcot, in comparing the text with Hesiod, suggest, perhaps leaning a bit too heavily upon Freud, that mother lust is equivalent to castration.[106] On this point I suggest that the very brevity and laconic nature of the text perhaps precluded the elaboration of such details as how the sovereignty was transferred (e.g., via emasculation or the "tearing off" of a tiara).

One interesting point of comparison between the Dunnu text and Hesiod's *Theogony* relates to the order in which Sea and River appear. According to Hesiod, the two figures associated with the sea, Pontos and Okeanos, emerge in succeeding generations. Pontos is essentially an autochthon, having emerged from Gaia without benefit of sexual intercourse, while Okeanos is born of Ouranos and Gaia. There is no doubt that Pontos is the sea proper, but Okeanos is more specifically defined as the "father of rivers," the river that circles the earth (cf. *Theogony* 695–696). This order is paralleled in the "Theogony of Dunnu"; Sea is an autochthon, whereas River belongs to the third generation.[107] Lambert and Walcot also point out that there is a parallel to Hesiod in the marital relationships that obtain. The Titans regularly contract sibling marriages (cf. Kronos and Rhea), "but it is only Ouranos and Pontos who practice incest to the extent of mating with their own mother. . . ."[108] Again, in the "Theogony of Dunnu" both Sea and Earth are involved in such marriages, and matings between siblings abound.

These, then, are the Babylonian versions. So far no Sumerian counterpart has come to light, although several important Sumerian divinities are present in the texts just discussed, for example, Enki (Ea) and Anu. I do not mean to suggest that the Greek and other non-Babylonian versions of the "Kingship in Heaven" theme are necessarily based specifically upon the *Enūma-Elish* or the "Theogony of Dunnu." Rather, in one way or another all the previously discussed theogonies[109] may be based upon the immediate sources of these two Babylonian texts, sources that themselves would appear to have been Babylonian and perhaps even Sumerian. This suggestion is strengthened in that we now have two distinct versions of the theme, each dating from the early second millennium B.C., from two distinct centers of Babylonian culture, that is, Babylon proper and Dunnu. The fact that one of these was a minor center adds even more strength.

Conclusions

Most of the principal points of comparison among the several versions which have been noted are summed up in the table on the next page. The question that remains is whether or not the "Kingship in Heaven" theme is Indo-European.

Wikander's assumption that the theme is part of the Indo-European mythological inheritance is based principally upon the concordances among the Greek, Hittite, and Iranian versions. These concordances are in fact present, and there is no doubt that the three versions are part of a single tradition. But

Comparison of Figures in "Kingship in Heaven" Theme

First Generation Figure	*Second Generation Figure*	*Third Generation Figure*	*Monster*
GREEK			
*Ouranos**: autochthon; marries Earth (Gaia); sires	*Kronos*: castrates *Ouranos* with sickle and exiles him; swallows offspring; marries sister (Rhea); sires	*Zeus*: deposes *Kronos*; must validate his position by slaying	*Typhon*: creature or offspring of *Kronos*; is killed in single combat around Mt. Kasios and Cilicia.
HURRIAN-HITTITE			
Anu: son of Alalu; deposes father; sires	*Kumarbi*: castrates *Anu* by biting and deposes him; swallows offspring (?); from *Anu*'s seed and *Kumarbi*'s spittle is born	*Teshub*: deposes *Kumarbi*; must validate his position by rendering powerless with "ancient tool" and slaying (?)	*Ullikummi*: offspring of *Kumarbi*; defeated near Mt. Hazzi (Kasios).
PHOENICIAN			
*Ouranos**: offspring of Eliun; marries Earth (Ge, Gaia); sires	*El* (*Kronos*): drives out *Ouranos* with sickle; later castrates him; kills a son and a daughter; marries his three sisters; sires	*Baal*: deposes *El*; later *El* castrates self. *Baal* reigns perpetually.	Although *Typhon* is mentioned, there is no clear monster figure.
IRANIAN			
Jamshid: preceded by three earlier kings; is overthrown by	*Zohak* (monster-like "nephew" [?]): later saws *Jamshid* in half; marries *Jamshid*'s two sisters; is deposed by	*Feridun* (*Jamshid*'s exiled grandson): reigns triumphantly after defeating	*Zohak*: parallels *Typhon*; after being clubbed in single combat and left enchained, dies on Mt. Demawend (?). Represents fusion of second generation and monster.
NORSE (two lines)			
Buri: autochthon; sires	*Bör*: sires	*Odin*: who reigns perpetually after killing and cutting up *Ymir* and banishing *Bergelmir* to Jöntinheim.	*Ymir*, from whose corpse the universe is formed, represents fusion of first-generation figure and monster.
Ymir: giant autochthon; licked from ice by cow; androgynously begets	*Thrudgelmir*: sires	*Bergelmir*.	
BABYLONIAN			
Enūma-Elish			
*Apsu**: autochthon; marries *Tiamat*; sires	*Ea*: deposes *Apsu*; is apparently supplanted by *Ea*'s half-brother, *Kingu*. *Ea* sires	*Marduk*: deposes *Kingu* and banishes him (to Uggae); reigns perpetually after slaying	*Tiamat*, from whose corpse the universe is formed, represents fusion of first-generation figure and monster.
"Theogony of Dunnu"			
Hain: autochthon; marries Earth; sires	*Amakandu*: slays *Hain*, marries mother (Earth), then sister (Sea); sires	*Lahar*: slays *Amakandu*; marries Sea; deposed eventually by offspring.	No clear monster figure.

* These figures provoke filial rebellion by exiling or attempting to destroy their eventual successors.

the fact that these three Indo-European-speaking communities share a common theogonic theme does not in itself mean that such a theme is part of their common mythological inheritance. By the same token, it can be said that a fair number of Indo-European speaking communities today share a common belief in how the world was created: by a God whose principal attributes are omnipotence and an intense jealousy of all other pretenders to divine status. There is, of course, no doubt whatsoever that this idea was borrowed from the Judaic tradition. We have a clear record of when and where the borrowing occurred. But suppose that we did not have such a record; suppose that a Martian scholar eons hence were to be confronted with this common tradition—present, albeit, among many non-Indo-European speakers as well. Would he not be tempted to view the relationships from a genetic standpoint? Would he not be tempted to reconstruct a common Indo-European cosmogony involving "the hand of God moving across the waters," and so on?

I suggest that those who argue for an Indo-European origin as far as the divine kingship is concerned have most likely fallen into the same trap as our hypothetical Martian. The problem here is that, unlike the spread of the Judaic cosmogony, the spread of the idea of divine kingship cannot be documented. There is no clear record of events to mark its spread from ancient Babylonia to Anatolia, Phoenicia, Iran, Greece, and ultimately, perhaps, to Scandinavia. There is nothing here comparable with the conversion of Clovis or the ministry of St. Patrick. Yet spread it did, from one religious system to another, the initial impetus being perhaps the prestige of the Babylonian tradition. By the time the theme reached Scandinavia (if indeed it did not evolve there independently), the Babylonian roots had long since become obscure, and the prestige would have been that of the Greco-Roman tradition, to which it had diffused perhaps two millennia earlier.

Two of the chief reasons for ruling out an Indo-European origin are the absence, previously noted, of the theme in the Indic tradition and its very late appearance in that of ancient Iran. Also important in this connection is its absence in the ancient Celtic tradition. Admittedly much of our knowledge of Celtic religion is confined to those elements of it that persisted in Ireland; yet even here, given the care taken by the medieval Irish monks to preserve their heritage, one would assume that if the theme had been present before the arrival of Christianity it would have carried over. But only by the most Procrustean of methods can one make a case for its presence in the traditions relating to the Túatha Dé Danann and their predecessors. It is simply not present.

Thus, that neither the *Veda*'s, the *Avesta*, nor the *Lebor Gabála* know the theme is highly significant. With the exception of the Norse, all known versions center upon Mesopotamia. Even Egypt does not seem to have known a clear version of the "Kingship in Heaven."[110] Its diffusion to Greece, usually thought to have been accomplished via Phoenicia,[111] may indeed have been much earlier than heretofore suspected. Lambert and Walcot suggest that the mythical conception of a divine kingship may have diffused directly from Mesopotamia to Greece during the Late Helladic period and cite recent archaeological evidence (e.g., the presence of Babylonian cylinder seals at Thebes) indicative of widespread Mycenaean-Mesopotamian contacts.[112] Its diffusion to the Hittites would probably have been accomplished via the Hurrians, who had come into close contact with the mainstream of Mesopotamian civilization by the middle of the second millennium B.C. Its late diffusion eastward to Iran may reflect more immediately the Hesiodic and/or Phoenician versions rather than the Babylonian versions themselves (cf. the very specific parallels between Zohak and Typhon). But whatever the course taken, its absence in at least three widely separated and important Indo-European traditions, coupled with the early dates of the Babylonian versions, would seem to give powerful support to my contention that it is of Babylonian[113] and perhaps even ultimately of Sumerian origin.

No discussion of Indo-European origins would be complete without reference to Professor Dumézil's theory of a common tripartite social and supernatural system, a system that is clearly evident in most of the ancient Indo-European speaking domain.[114] Dumézil himself has refrained from any attempt to apply the tripartite model to the idea of the "Kingship in Heaven," despite the fact that at first glance, at least, the three-generational sequences would seem to offer a fertile field in this regard. Even Wikander, in many ways Dumézil's most brilliant disciple, and, as we have seen, the chief proponent of the Indo-European origin theory, has refrained from attempting such an application.[115] The closest Dumézil has come to the problem is the suggestion[116] that the proto-Indo-European mythology possibly included a tradition that Heaven was the last and only surviving offspring of a great water deity (probably female), who drowned all but one of her children as soon as they were born. His suggestion is based upon a comparison between the Norse god Heimdallr and the Vedic divinity Dyauḥ. Both are connected with water. Heimdallr is said to have had nine mothers, who were conceived as "sea waves"; Dyauḥ and his seven brothers (the *Vasus*) are linked with the river goddess Gaṅgā (Ganges), who drowns seven of the eight siblings, leaving only Dyauḥ to reach maturity (cf. *Mahābhārata* 1.3843–3963).

Certainly the personifications of sea and heaven play parts in both the Greek and the Babylonian versions of the divine kingship (cf. Pontos, Tiamat), but in neither case do we have any clear identification of the drowning of all but one of their offspring. Moreover, Heimdallr plays no part whatsoever in the Norse version, nor do any of the other traditions surrounding the rather otiose Dyauḥ come anywhere near to approximating the sort of divine succession so crucial to the presence of the theme in question. In short, it would seem to me that, even though Dumézil may well be correct in his suggestions as to the Indo-European roots of the traditions surrounding the births of Dyauḥ and Heimdallr, it would not be germane to the problem at hand. The presence of such a common Indo-European tradition would in no way alter my convictions as to the origin of the theme.

One of the most interesting suggestions yet made from a Dumézilian standpoint is that previously mentioned by F. Vian[117] relative to the Greek Typhon myth. As Vian sees it, Zeus's battle with the monster derives from an isolated story paralleling what Dumézil[118] and others have suggested is the typical Indo-European myth of a fight between a second-function or warrior figure and a tricephalic monster (cf. Indra versus the son of Tvaṣṭar, and the like). This story later fused with a widespread non-Indo-European dragon-slaying account (which had also diffused to the Hittites; cf. the Ullikummi and Illuyanka narratives)[119] that had been introduced into Greece by the Phoenicians in the early eighth century B.C. Thus, according to Vian, by the time of Hesiod the story as it is generally known in Greek mythology had fairly well crystallized. It is interesting that in later versions of the Typhon episode (i.e., those of Apollodorus and Nonnos) the details undergo progressive elaboration and become more and more similar to those of the Hurrian-Hittite version. As noted, the Hittite description of Ullikummi before Mount Hazzi is almost identical with Nonnos' description of Typhon.

If Vian is correct, then some intriguing possibilities present themselves. Perhaps the Hittites, too, grafted the dragon-slaying myth onto an inherited Indo-European three-headed monster tale and, like their Greek cousins a thousand years later, eventually fused this with the Babylonian account of the divine kingship. Thus there would be three distinct strata in both the Greek and Hittite versions: (1) the Indo-European account of the slaying of the tricephalus, (2) the dragon-slaying myth, and (3) the "Kingship in Heaven" theme proper. Of course, it is by no means clear that the monster-slaying episode is disassociated in its origins from the rest of the theme under discussion. It is just as easy to make a case for the presence of this figure in the person of Tiamat—although its presence in the "Theogony of Dunnu" is less clear.

In sum, while it presents some alternative possibilities of interpretation of certain specific episodes associated with the "Kingship in Heaven," I do not feel that Vian's arguments relative to Typhon add anything substantive to the argument favoring an Indo-European origin for the theme as a whole, and I must reiterate my conclusion that it is most probably rooted in the Babylonian tradition.

Notes

1. According to B. Malinowski (*Magic, Science and Religion* [New York, 1955], p. 101), myth is ". . . a vital ingredient of human civilization; it is not an idle tale, but a hard-worked active force; it is not an intellectual explanation or an artistic imagery, but a pragmatic charter of primitive faith and moral wisdom."

2. The first to recognize the basic similarity between the Hittite-Hurrian and Greek versions of the "Kingship in Heaven" theme seems to have been E. O. Forrer; cf. his "Eine Geschichte des Götterkönigtums aus dem Hatti-Reiche," in *Mélanges Franz Cumont, AIPhO*$_4$ (Brussels, 1936), pp. 687–713. A second pioneer work in this area is H. G. Güterbock's *Kumarbi, Mythen vom churritischen Kronos, aus den hethitischen Fragmenten zusammengestellt, übersetzt und erklärt* (Istanbul, 1946). The Phoenician version was first put into its proper perspective by C. Clemen (*Die phönikische Religion nach Philo von Byblos* [Leipzig, 1939]), and the Iranian version was discovered by S. Wikander, "Hethitiska myter hos greker och perser," *VSLÅ* (1951), pp. 35–56.

3. Cf. Güterbock's "Königtum im Himmel"; E. Laroche's "Royauté au Ciel." By *theme* I mean an expression of an idea or set of related ideas rather than a specific type of narrative or tale; cf. S. Thompson's definition of "tale-type:" "... a traditional tale that has an independent existence" (*The Folktale* [New York, 1946], p. 415). It should be noted, however, that in perhaps the majority of instances cognate expressions of a given theme will involve similar patterns of events and consequently may reflect a single tale-type.

4. Literally "When-on-High," from the opening words of the poem.

5. *Op. cit.*; "Histoire des Ouranides," *CS* 36 (314):9–17 (1952).

6. "An Intrusive Hurro-Hittite Myth," *JAOS* 62: 98–102 (1942).

7. "The Hittite Version of the Hurrian Kumarbi Myths: Oriental Forerunners of Hesiod," *AJA* 52: 123–134 (1948).

8. Note should be taken of a doctoral dissertation by Gerd Steiner, *Der Sukzessionmythos in Hesiods 'Theogonie' und ihre orientalischen Parallelen* (University of Hamburg, 1958), as yet unpublished, in which the *Enūma-Elish* is held to be the ultimate source of the theme, although the author does not consider the relevant Norse and Iranian traditions.

9. A shorter version of this paper, "Is the 'Kingship in Heaven' Theme Indo-European?", was delivered at the Third Indo-European Conference, held at the University of Pennsylvania on April 21–23, 1966, under the auspices of the American Council of Learned Societies, the National Science Foundation, and the University of Pennsylvania. It will appear in the proceedings <(cf. p. 263, below)>. I should like to thank Professor Jaan Puhvel for his invaluable advice and encouragement not only as far as the present paper is concerned, but also throughout the entire course of the research upon which it is based. Special thanks are owing as well to Professor H. G. Güterbock of the Oriental Institute of the University of Chicago for his most helpful comments and suggestions.

10. The Hittite-Hurrian version (*ca.* 1400 B.C.) antedates Hesiod by at least 700 years, and the Babylonian versions may well be of much greater antiquity.

11. Cf. H. G. Evelyn-White, *Hesiod, The Homeric Hymns and Homerica* (London, 1914), p. xxvi.

12. Cf. J. G. Frazer, *Apollodorus: The Library* (London, 1921), p. xvi.

13. Cf. W. H. D. Rouse, *Nonnos: Dionysiaca* (London, 1939), p. vii.

14. The numbers enclosed by parentheses refer to lines in the original texts of the *Theogony, Bibliotheca*, and *Dionysiaca*; the translations utilized are those, respectively, of H. G. Evelyn-White, J. G. Frazer, and W. H. D. Rouse.

15. Called, respectively, "Thunderer," "Lightener," and "Vivid One" (cf. Evelyn-White, *op. cit.*, p. 89.).

16. The etymology of Kronos (*Κρόνος*) is obscure (cf. H. Frisk, *Griechisches etymologisches Wörterbuch* [Heidelberg, 1961], II, 24–25; L. R. Farnell, *The Cults of the Greek States* [Oxford, 1896], I, 23). It has been suggested that the name was a variant form of Chronos (*Χρόνος* or 'Time'), though the shift from initial X to K would be difficult, if not impossible, to support philologically (cf. H. J. Rose, *A Handbook of Greek Mythology* [New York, 1959], p. 69). Another etymology has connected Kronos with *κραίνω* and has rendered the meaning as 'ripener' or 'completer.' While both Frisk (*op. cit.*) and Rose (*op. cit.*) consider this equally impossible philologically, the fact that Kronos was inevitably equated with Saturnus by most Latin authors (cf. Vergil, Ovid, Plutarch, *et al.*) should not be overlooked. Saturnus appears originally to have been a harvest god, a god who "ripened" or "completed" crops, and the early and consistent equation of this Roman deity with Kronos may well indicate that the latter once served a similar function. Finally, S. Janez ("Kronos und der Walfisch," *Linguistica* 2:54–56 [Supplement of *Slavistična Revija* 9, 1956] has proposed that the name Kronos be equated with Old English *hrān*, 'whale,' which, according to the first Germanic sound shift, would be philologically acceptable. He points out that the Greeks referred to Gibraltar as *Κρόνου στῆλαι* and compares this to Old English *Hronesnaess* (Beowulf 2805, 3136). Janez suggests that certain "popular superstitions" concerning emasculation of the whale during the sex act may yield a clue to the relationship between Kronos and whales; indeed, in a number of late traditions, especially in the younger Orphic theogonies, Kronos is represented as having been castrated by Zeus (cf. Pauly-Wissowa, *Realencyclopädie der Klassischen Altertumswissenschaft*, vol. 11, p. 2009 [33]: "Zeus den Kronos mit Honig trunken macht und ihn dann im Schlaf fesselt und entmannt"; W. H. Roscher, *Ausführliches Lexicon der griechischen und römischen Mythologie* [Leipzig, 1890], II, 1470–1471). It appears likely, however, that these late traditions were the result of conscious attempts by theologians to harmonize Zeus's overthrow of Kronos with the latter's overthrow of Ouranos, and it seems to me that, if Janez's equation *Κρόνος* = *hrān* be correct, the mere fact that the whale is an obvious symbol of bigness (cf. the English expression "a whale of a ...") may explain the relationship more efficiently; perhaps the name Kronos itself is but the survival of an epithet once applied to a being (a harvest god?) whose proper name had disappeared before Homer's time.

17. Cf. M. P. Nilsson, "The Sickle of Kronos," *ABSA* 46:122–124 (1939). Like Kronos, Saturnus is also associated with a sickle, Greek *ἅρπη*. This seems to be a proto-Indo-European term found also in Balto-Slavic (Lettish *sirpe*, Russian *serp*) and borrowed into Finno-Ugric (Finnish *sirppi*, 'sickle'). Perhaps the "adamantine" blade used by Kronos against Ouranos was originally a tool associated with an Indo-European harvest god ancestral to both Kronos and Saturnus (cf. n. 16, above).

18. Cf. Rose, *op. cit.*, p. 22.

19. Frazer (*op. cit.*, p. 6) sums up this controversy rather succinctly: "According to Hesiod, Rhea gave birth to Zeus in Crete, and the infant god was hidden away in a cave of Mount Aegeum (*Theogony* 468–480). Diodorus Siculus (5.70) mentions the legend that Zeus was born at Dicte in Crete, and that the god afterwards founded a city on the site. But according to Diodorus, or his authorities, the child was brought up in a cave on Mount Ida. . . . The wavering of tradition on this point is indicated by Apollodorus who, while he calls the mountain Dicte, names one of the gods Ida."

20. Cf. *ibid.*

21. Frazer (*ibid.*, p. 7) claims that "According to Callimachus, Amalthea was a goat. Aratus also reported, if he did not believe, the story that the supreme god had been suckled by a goat (Strabo, viii.7.5, p. 387). . . ."

22. Cf. that of Hermes (*Homeric Hymn* 4.17–19):

"At dawn he [Hermes] was born, by noon he was playing on the lyre, and that evening he stole the cattle of Apollo Fardarter. . . ."

23. Although the extent to which Rhea is involved in the conspiracy to dislodge her offspring from Kronos' stomach is unclear, all accounts agree that she sides with Zeus in the ensuing struggle against her husband; cf. W. H. Roscher, "Rhea," in L. Preller, *Griechische Mythologie*, I (Berlin, 1894), 638 f.

24. That Kronos and his fellow Titans escaped eternal punishment in Tartaros is reflected in a number of variant traditions, some of them quite early. In his *Works and Days* (169), Hesiod himself claims that Zeus gave Kronos and his fellows "a living and an abode apart from men, and made them dwell at the ends of the earth . . . untouched by sorrow in the islands of the blessed along the shore of deep swirling Ocean, happy heroes for whom the grain-giving earth bears honey and sweet fruit. . . ." Hesiod also claims (*ibid.*) that "Kronos rules over them; for the father of men and gods [i.e., Zeus] released him from his bonds." The idea that Kronos' ultimate fate is to rule over a group of western Elysian islands (i.e., the "islands of the blessed") is reflected in Pindar (*Olymp. Odes*, 2) and later in Plutarch (*De defectu oraculorum* 420), the latter claiming that Kronos, guarded by Briareos, sleeps peacefully on a sacred island near Britain. Vergil (*Aeneid* 8.319, 355–358) asserts that the defeated Titan fled by sea to Latium, where he founded a city, Saturnia, on the future site of Rome, and that the name of the district stems from Kronos' (i.e., Saturnus') hiding (*latere*) in it (cf. Rose, *op. cit.*, p. 45). The association of Kronos with the West, especially Italy, in the minds of later Greek and Roman writers can be seen in the assertion by Dionysius of Halicarnassus (1.36.1) that the Golden Age, which preceded the ascension of Zeus as "king in heaven," was in Italy under Kronos. It should also be noted that the element of escape or banishment resulting in a sea voyage has an interesting counterpart in the Norse version to be considered presently; cf. the fate of the giant Bergelmir.

25. Hesiod renders the monster's name as "Typhoeus"; Apollodorus and Nonnos render it as "Typhon."

26. The modern Kel Dag or "Bald Mountain," located just south of the mouth of the Orontes River in what is now Turkey.

27. Nonnos also mentions the sinew-cutting episode (*Dionysiaca* 1.482–512). Here Kadmos comes to Zeus's aid instead of Hermes. In a note to his translation of the *Dionysiaca* (*op. cit.*, pp. 40–41) Rouse points out that "the story is obscurely told, and probably Nonnos did not understand it; it is obviously old. By some device or by a well-aimed blow, Typhon had evidently cut the sinews out of Zeus's arms, thus disabling him; Cadmos now gets them back by pretending that he wants them for harp strings." In this version there is no mention of a sickle, adamantine or other.

28. F. Vian, "Le mythe de Typhée et le problème de ses origines orientales", *Éléments orientaux dans la religion grecque ancienne* (Paris, 1960), pp. 17–37. For a discussion of the Indo-European character of the tricephalic monster, see G. Dumézil, *Horace et les Curiaces* (Paris, 1942) and elsewhere.

29. By Forrer, *op. cit.*

30. "The Hittite Version of the Hurrian Kumarbi Myths," p. 124.

31. Primarily in the form of Hurrian god names; cf. *ibid.*, p. 123 and H. G. Güterbock, "Hittite Mythology," in S. N. Kramer, ed., *Mythologies of the Ancient World* (New York, 1961); abbr.: *MAW*.

32. The texts are written in the Indo-European *Nesili* language, which was the official court language of the Hittite kingdom (cf. Güterbock, *MAW*, p. 142), but employ Akkadian cuneiform characters.

33. Güterbock, "The Hittite Version of the Hurrian Kumarbi Myths," p. 124; A. Goetze in J. B. Pritchard, ed., *Ancient Near Eastern Texts Relating to the Old Testament* (Princeton, 1955), p. 121; abbr.: *ANET*.

34. More likely "ages" or "eras" rather than calendar years; cf. Güterbock, "The Hittite Version of the Hurrian Kumarbi Myths," p. 124 n. 11.

35. The numbers enclosed by parentheses refer respectively to columns and lines in the original texts; cf. Güterbock, *Kumarbi*, pp. 6–10, 13–28.

36. Güterbock, *MAW*, p. 160.

37. *Ibid.*

38. Cf. Goetze, *ANET*, p. 120; Güterbock, "The Hittite Version of the Hurrian Kumarbi Myths," p. 134.

39. The name Kumarbi is apparently Hurrian; cf. Güterbock, *MAW*, p. 160, who points out that

Kumarbi is frequently, although not consistently, equated with the great Sumero-Akkadian god Enlil.

40. The approximate meaning "his loins" or "his thighs" seems to fit the reading *paršnuššuš* which various Hittite scholars, including Güterbock (personal communication, and *MAW*, p. 156), now prefer to the earlier emendational interpretation *genuššuš* "his knees" (cf. E. A. Hahn, *JAOS* 85:298–299 [1965]). In either case there is a euphemistic approximation for "male parts." On the widespread sexual connotations of the knee Professor Jaan Puhvel has contributed the following philological note:

Hittite *genu-* means both 'knee' and (secondarily) '[male] genitals' (sometimes combined in anatomical lists with *arraš* [= Old High German *ars*] 'anus': cf. J. Friedrich, "Einige hethitische Namen von Körperteilen," *IF* 41:372–376 [1923]). This usage, however, is not a euphemism but has much more basic implications. Without having to delve deep into folkloristic and psychoanalytical records we find that "knee" is often an expression for sexual potency (cf., e.g., J. Laager, *Geburt und Kindheit des Gottes in der griechischen Mythologie* [Winterthur, 1957], p. 136). As random examples we may refer to the passage in the Old Norse *Flóamannasaga* where a man dreams of leeks (a well-known fertility symbol) growing from his knees (cf. W. P. Lehmann, *Germanic Review* 30:166 [1955]), and quote in translation these lines of Hesiod's *Works and Days* about the "dog days" (582–587; imitated in a drinking song of Alcaeus [*Oxford Book of Greek Verse*, p. 170]): "But when the artichoke blooms and the chirping grass-hopper sits in a tree and pours down his shrill song continually from under his wings in the season of wearisome heat, then goats are plumpest and wine sweetest; women are most wanton, but men are feeblest, because Sirius parches head and KNEES."

In various Semitic languages (e.g., Akkadian, Ethiopic) *b r k* (Akkadian *birku*) means both 'knee' and 'penis,' and then more widely 'strength,' 'family,' or 'tribe' (cf. M. Cohen, "Genou, famille, force dans le domaine chamito-sémitique," *Mémorial Henri Basset* [Paris, 1928], I, 203–210, and more generally W. Deonna, "Le genou, siège de force et de vie," *RA* 13:224–235 [1939]). 'Knee' in the sense of 'offspring,' 'family' is commonly found in Indo-European and Finno-Ugric languages: much as Akkadian *tarbit birkiya* means 'nurseling of my *birku*,' we have the synonymous Old Irish *glūn-daltae*, 'knee-nurseling' (cf. J. Loth, "Le mot désignant le genou au sense de génération chez les Celtes, les Germains, les Slaves, les Assyriens," *RC* 40:143–152 [1923]) and the Sogdian *z'nwk' z'tk*, 'knee-son' (see E. Benveniste, *BSL* 27:51–53 [1926]). Similarly Old English *cnéow*, Old Slavonic *kolěno*, and Finnish *polvi*, 'knee,' also mean 'offspring, generation.'

Some have claimed a connection between IE **ĝenu*, 'knee,' and the root **ĝen-* on the basis of ancient evidence for childbearing labor in a kneeling position (e.g., R. Back, "Medizinisch-Sprachliches," *IF* 40:162–167 [1922]; J. Klek, *IF* 44:79–80 [1927]; and S. Simonyi, "Knie und Geburt," *Zeitschrift für vergleichende Sprachforschung* 50:152–154 [1922]). Yet in spite of the Hittite *genzu*, 'lap,' 'female genitals,' metonymically 'love,' the root of Latin *genus, gignō*, Greek *γένος, γεννάω* means primarily 'beget,' while other words are used for 'bear' (Latin *pariō*, Greek *τίκτω*). Others have argued that in patriarchal society formal recognition of a newborn child on the father's knee was the true means of legal affiliation or adoption, thus 'birth' in a juridical sense (cf., e.g., Old Norse *knēsetningr*, 'adopted son,' and Homeric and Roman practices, and see Benveniste, *op. cit.*, and M. Cahen, "'Genou', 'adoption', et 'parenté' en germanique," *BSL* 27:56–67 [1926]). In archaic Estonian the phrase *lapse põlvede peale tõstma*, 'lift a child on the knees,' is glossed with 'ein Kind gehörig zur Welt bringen' by F. Wiedemann, *Ehstnisch-deutsches Wörterbuch* (2d ed.; St. Petersburg, 1893), p. 864, and *põlwile sāma*, 'come on knees,' is rendered by 'geboren werden' (*ibid.*). Latin *genuīnus* was similarly connected with *genu*, 'knee,' by A. Meillet (*BSL* 27:54–55 [1926]), and IE **gnē*, 'know, recognize,' was brought into play, including the vexed question of its possible original affinity with **ĝen-*, 'beget' (cf. *γνήσιος* 'genuine'). The semantic tangle was further aggravated by R. Meringer ("Spitze, Winkel, Knie im ursprünglichen Denken," *Wörter und Sachen* 11:118–123 [1928]) and H. Güntert (*ibid.*, pp. 124–142, esp. pp. 125–127), who tried to combine both Greek *γόνυ*, 'knee,' and *γένυς*, 'chin,' with *γωνία*, 'angle.'

Even without reference to such inconclusive root etymologies, however, we have unraveled the semantic ramifications of the notion of 'knee' in many languages as comprising 'genitals,' 'potency,' 'offspring,' 'family,' and 'filiation.'

41. Although both Ouranos and Anu are connected with the sky, we refer here of course to functional rather than linguistic correspondences.

42. Although the Hittite reading of the ideogram for weather-god is as yet unknown, it is highly probable that, given this and other contexts (cf. the Ullikummi texts), the Hittite deity in question can be none other than the Hurrian Weather- (or Storm-) god Teshub (cf. Goetze, *ANET*, p. 120; Güterbock, *Kumarbi*, p. 35; *id.*, "The Hittite Version of the Hurrian Kumarbi Myths," p. 124 n. 14; *id.*, *MAW*, p. 158); thus I follow Güterbock and call the Hittite Weather-god by his Hurrian name.

43. Cf. Güterbock, "The Hittite Version of the Hurrian Kumarbi Myths," p. 124 n. 15.

44. *Ibid.*, n. 16.

45. From a reference in column ii it seems that these unmentioned divinities are Marduk (represented by a rare Sumerian name) and one whose name is written with the word sign KA.ZAL, 'lust'; cf. Güterbock, *MAW*, p. 158.

46. Apparently Earth becomes pregnant thereby, although the names of the divinities she bears are unclear.

47. *MAW*, pp. 157–158.

48. *Ibid.*, p. 158.

49. Cf. also the birth of Erichthonios: Hephaistos, desiring to wed a reluctant Athena, struggles with her, and in the course of this struggle his seed falls on the ground; Gaia is thus impregnated and in due time gives birth to Erichthonios (cf. Rose, *op. cit.*, p. 110).

50. Text and translation published by Güterbock, *JCS* 5:135–161 (1951), 6:8–42 (1952).

51. There is an interesting counterpart to this in Phrygian mythology; cf. Arnobius, *Adversus Nationes* 5.55, Pausanias 7.17.10–12. Papas, the Phrygian "Zeus," inseminates a rock called Agdos and begets Agdistis, an indolent hermaphrodite monster who, initially at least, is not unlike Ullikummi in some respects. The Phrygian monster, however, is castrated by the gods and thereby transformed into the mother-goddess figure Cybele. The blood produced by the castration causes a marvelous pomegranate or almond tree to spring up, and the fruit of this tree impregnates Nana, daughter of the river god Sangarios. Nana gives birth to Attis, who later castrates himself out of love for Cybele.

Agdistis' birth and early resemblance to Ullikummi may possibly indicate a relationship between the two traditions. Save for the castration motif, however, which might conceivably be implied in Ullikummi's loss of power after being cut from Upelluri's shoulder, the rest of the story does not have any clear Hittite parallels.

52. Ullikummi is not the only rebel to oppose Teshub's power; there is also a text (Güterbock, *Kumarbi*, pp. 10–13, Text 1; *MAW*, pp. 161–164) which describes the rebellion of a god known to us only by the highly ambiguous word sign KAL (cf. Güterbock, *MAW*, p. 161, who claims that neither the reading Sumerian LAMA, Akkadian *LAMASSU*, nor the Hittite reading Inara [an Anatolian goddess; cf. the Illuyanka myth, *MAW*, p. 151] fits the context). This text presents some interesting, although not conclusive, parallels to the Greek myths concerning Prometheus and his defiance of Zeus. Unfortunately the KAL text (if indeed it is a separate text) is extremely fragmentary; the tablet is broken in such a way that we possess neither the beginning nor the final colophon that would indicate the name of the text and its exact relationship to the other two texts. Nevertheless, the events described almost certainly follow the ascension of Teshub; whether they precede or follow the Ullikummi affair is, however, much less certain.

Unlike Prometheus, KAL actually seems to have assumed the kingship for a time, for when we first meet him he is described as taking "the reins and [the whip] out of the Storm-God's [i.e., Teshub's] hands" (i.18–19). Like Prometheus, however, and unlike Typhon and/or Ullikummi, KAL eventually submits. Addressing the Weather-god as "my lord," he is subjected to some form of bodily punishment involving mutilation; cf. the fate of Prometheus bound to a rock (or mountain) and continually mutilated by an eagle (*Theogony* 521). There are other aspects of KAL's rebellion which also seem broadly similar to that of Prometheus. In the text, one of the chief objections raised against KAL is that he encourages mortals to be lax in their sacrificial duties: Ea, who apparently had appointed KAL to the kingship, later becomes dissatisfied with his protégé's conduct and claims that " 'just as he [KAL] himself is rebellious, so he has made the countries rebellious, and no one any longer gives bread or drink offerings to the gods' " (iii.18,40); Prometheus, too, is accused of encouraging humans to withhold sacrificed food from the gods (cf. *Theogony* 535). While there seems to be no connection here between KAL and either the creation of mankind or man's knowledge of fire, the Hittite rebel can be seen to occupy a role broadly similar to that of Prometheus: a champion of mortals in their dealings with the gods. Furthermore, KAL's downfall, like that of Prometheus, is apparently the result of a plot hatched by the gods and implemented by the chief god's lieutenant (i.e., Teshub's vizier Ninurta [*MAW*, p. 164]; cf. the role played in Prometheus' punishment by Hephaistos [*Theogony* 520]).

53. Apparently located in the mountains of southeast Anatolia; Güterbock suggests (*MAW*, p. 166) that the name Ullikummi itself simply means "Destroyer of Kummiya."

54. Güterbock, "The Hittite Version of the Hurrian Kumarbi Myths," p. 129. In col. iii.19–22 there is the suggestion that Anu wants to make Ea king instead of Teshub; cf. P. Meriggi, "I miti di Kumarpi, il Kronos Currico," *Athenaeum* 31: 101–157 (1953).

55. Güterbock, *op. cit.*

56. *Ibid.*

57. W. Staudacher, *Die Trennung von Himmel und Erde* (Tübingen, 1942), pp. 61 f.

58. Güterbock, *op. cit.*, p. 130.

59. Clemen, *op. cit.*, p. 2.

60. The numbers enclosed by parentheses refer to lines in the original text of the *Phoenician History*; the translation is by Clemen.

61. There is a close parallel to this in the Iranian tradition wherein the "Kronos figure" Zohak marries two of Jamshid's sisters after deposing him. See Wikander, "Hethitiska myter hos greker och perser," p. 52.

62. Cf. the relationship between El and Hadad, the god of thunder and lightning, as delineated in the Ras Shamra texts. The association of Baal and Hadad has long been recognized in the Caananitic tradition; cf. W. F. Albright, *Archaeology and the Religion of Israel* (Baltimore, 1946), pp. 72–74; S. H. Hooke, *Middle Eastern Mythology* (Harmondsworth, 1963), pp. 86–87.

63. Clemen, *op. cit.*, p. 28.

64. Güterbock, "The Hittite Version of the Hurrian Kumarbi Myths," p. 133.

65. A further argument against interpreting Philo wholly in syncretistic terms is that he preserves a "pre-Ouranos" figure, i.e., Eliun; cf. the position of Alalu in the Hurrian-Hittite version.

66. L. R. Palmer, *Mycenaeans and Minoans* (2d ed.; London, 1965).

67. Palmer (*ibid.*) suggests that the name Parnassos is derived from a Luvian form meaning 'place of the temple' (Luvian *parna-*, 'temple,' plus the suffix *-ass-* denoting appurtenance).

68. "Hethitiska myter hos greker och perser."

69. Literally the "first man."

70. Helen Zimmern, *The Epic of Kings* (New York, 1926), p. 4. For a more recent translation, see R. Levy, *The Epic of Kings, Shāh-nāma* (Chicago, 1967).

71. "Histoire des Ouranides," p. 13.

72. *Ibid.*

73. Wikander, "Hethitiska myter hos greker och perser," p. 41.

74. Cf. J. Atkinson. *The Shá Námeh of the Persian Poet Firdausi* (London, 1832), p. 34.

75. Atkinson (*ibid.*) asserts that Jamshid was laid between two planks and sawed lengthwise; see also A. Warner and E. Warner, *The Shāhnāma of Firdausi* (London, 1905), p. 140.

76. *Ibid.*

77. Wikander, "Histoire des Ouranides," p. 13.

78. Warner and Warner, *op. cit.*, p. 142; cf. Wikander, "Histoire des Ouranides," p. 7, Levy, *op. cit.*, p. xvii.

79. Zimmern, *op. cit.*, p. 8.

80. *Ibid.*, p. 12.

81. Or imprisons him in a cave; cf. Wikander, "Hethitiska myter hos greker och perser," p. 47.

82. Warner and Warner, *op. cit.*, p. 171; the Warners suggest (p. 174) that Feridun is actually a coalescence of two Avestan figures, Thraētaona and Thrita (cf. *Yasna* 9.21–30).

83. For a discussion of the possible Vedic parallels here, see Wikander, "Hethitiska myter hos greker och perser," esp. p. 46.

84. Tuisto can be interpreted as meaning 'Twin'; cf. Ymir, possibly cognate with Yama, and Tacitus' Mannus, whom he combines with Tuisto and who

belongs etymologically with Manu; for a discussion of Tuisto and Mannus see H. R. Ellis Davidson, *Gods and Myths of Northern Europe* (Harmondsworth, 1964), pp. 54–61, 196–199; E. O. G. Turville-Petre, *Myth and Religion of the North* (London, 1964), esp. p. 7.

85. The translations utilized are by Lee M. Hollander, *The Poetic Edda* (Austin, 1928), and Jean Young, *The Prose Edda* (Cambridge, 1954).

86. For a discussion of the extent to which Snorri, to say nothing of Saxo Grammaticus, was influenced by the *Aeneid*, see my paper "A Two-Dimensional Scheme for the Classification of Narratives," *JAF* 78:21–27, esp. pp. 24–25.

87. In the *Gylfaginning* Snorri describes Bergelmir's flight as occurring in the context of a universal flood created from the blood that gushed from Ymir after his demise. As this is the only clear reference to a flood in Norse myth, it seems reasonable to infer that Snorri, as a Christian, felt the need of it. This is underscored by the etymology of the word *luðr*, used by him to refer to the "boat" in which Bergelmir and his wife survive the deluge. Although Snorri clearly uses the word in the context of "boat," earlier usages of the term (cf. *Lay of Vafthrudnir* 35) would seem to indicate that it meant 'coffin' or 'bier.' See E. O. G. Turville-Petre, "Prof. Dumézil and the Literature of Iceland," *Hommages à Georges Dumézil* (Brussels, 1960), pp. 211–212; see also H. Petersson, "Aisl. *luðr* 'Trog usw,' " *IF* 24:267–269 (1909), who asserts that the basic meaning here is 'hollowed tree trunk' and proposes a derivation from Indo-European **lu-tró-* (cf. Skt. *lunā́ti*, 'cut, clip').

88. I.e., *askr*, 'ash,' and *embla*, 'elm,' respectively, the first man and woman.

89. I am not the first to make such an observation. Well over a century ago Jakob Grimm, in his *Teutonic Mythology* (translated from the German by J. S. Stallybrass [London, 1883], II, 275), had occasion to observe that "As the Edda has a Buri and Börr before Odinn, so do Uranus and Kronus here come before Zeus; with Zeus and Odinn begins the race of gods proper, and Poseidon and Hades complete the fraternal trio, like Vili and Vé. The enmity of gods and titans is therefore that of ases [Aesir] and giants. . . ."

90. E. A. Speiser, "Akkadian Myths and Epics," *ANET*, p. 60. It should be noted, however, that P. Walcot (*Hesiod and the Near East* [Cardiff, 1966], p. 33), suggests that the rise of Marduk to supremacy among the gods of Mesopotamia was quite late and that the *Enūma-Elish* as we know it was most likely composed around 1100 B.C. He thus concludes that "In terms of chronology, Enuma Elish now seems to stand between the Hattusas tablets and the Theogony. . . ." Nevertheless, this would not preclude earlier Babylonian and/or Sumerian prototypes wherein some other god played the part of Marduk.

91. Sumerian Abzu; see S. N. Kramer, "Mythology of Sumer and Akkad," *MAW*, p. 120.

92. I.e., "Mother" Tiamat; see Speiser, *op. cit.*, p. 61.

93. The translation of the *Enūma-Elish* utilized here is that of Speiser, *ANET*, pp. 61–72.

94. Cf. i.52, wherein Apsu plots "against the gods, his sons"; i.56, wherein Apsu's intentions are made known "unto the gods, their first-born."

95. Not to be confused with the epithet of Tiamat; cf. i.4 and n. 92, above.

96. See Walcot, *op. cit.*, p. 34.

97. M. L. West, in the "Prolegomena" to *Hesiod: Theogony* (Oxford, 1966), p. 23, asserts that Ea's elder sibling (or grandfather) Anshar assumes the kingship. Nowhere in the text is this clearly evident. The only passage that may possibly reflect such a royal status is iii.1 ff., wherein Anshar sends a message to Lahmu and Lahamu via "Gaga, his *vizir*" (italics mine). Otherwise, Anshar appears as but one of the siblings (or forebears) of Ea who plays a prominent albeit essentially supporting role in the deposition of Apsu and the subsequent conflict with Tiamat.

98. There is some confusion here. Kramer suggests (*MAW*, p. 121) that Ea actually takes up residence upon Apsu's corpse. The text itself would seem to indicate that Ea names his place of residence (i.e., the location of his "cult hut"; cf. i.77) *after* his deceased parent.

99. Cf. Kramer, *MAW*, p. 121.

100. "He took from him [i.e., Kingu] the Tablets of Fate, not rightfully his, sealed [them] with a seal and fastened [them] on his breast" (iv.121–122).

101. W. G. Lambert and P. Walcot, "A New Babylonian Theogony and Hesiod," *Kadmos* 4:64–72 (1965). It should be pointed out that Walcot is responsible for the appended "classical commentary" (pp.

68–72); the translation and accompanying commentary are by Lambert.

102. I should emphasize that this is my term, not that of Lambert and Walcot.

103. Lambert and Walcot, *op. cit.*, p. 64.

104. *Ibid.*, pp. 67–68.

105. Lambert and Walcot suggest that the two signs *ḫa-in* may have been miscopied from the one large sign used to write the name of the corn goddess Nisaba (*ibid.*, pp. 66–67).

106. *Ibid.*, p. 72.

107. *Ibid.*, pp. 66, 71.

108. *Ibid.*, p. 72.

109. The Norse version may be only indirectly derived from that which took shape in Babylonia some four thousand years ago; its immediate roots probably lie in the version best known to the Greco-Roman world, i.e., that of Hesiod *et al.*

110. But Lambert and Walcot, *op. cit.*, p. 69, point out that there is an Egyptian tradition according to which Sky devoured her children, quarreled with her husband, Earth, and therefore they were separated; for the relevant text, see H. Frankfort, *The Cenotaph of Seti I at Abydos* (London, 1933), p. 83.

111. Güterbock, "The Hittite Version of the Hurrian Kumarbi Myths," pp. 133–134.

112. Lambert and Walcot, *op. cit.*, p. 72. Walcot, as we have seen (see n. 90), has since modified his views and is convinced that the theme most likely diffused to Greece only after sustained contact had been reestablished with the Near East in the eighth century B.C. (*op. cit.*, p. 47).

113. The historical relationships proposed here are generally congruent with those proposed by Steiner (*op. cit.*, p. 104), who sees the *Enūma-Elish* as the immediate source of two unattested versions of the theme which he labels "X" and "Y." The "Y" version, Steiner suggests, ultimately reached Greece and manifested itself in Hesiod's *Theogony*. The Hurrian-Hittite version reflects both the "X" and the "Y" versions, although the former would seem to be the most immediate source. He also suggests that the "X" version perhaps gave rise to a third unattested version, "Z," which, together with the Hesiodic version, is reflected in Philo's "history." If Steiner is correct, it might be suggested that his hypothetical "Z" version could have diffused to Iran as well as to Phoenicia (cf. the specific correspondences between Philo and Firdausi as noted in the table and elsewhere); the Hesiodic version would be the immediate source of that contained in Snorri's *Edda*.

114. The most succinct statement of Dumézil's theory can be found in his *L'idéologie tripartie des Indo-européens* (Brussels, 1958). For a brief analysis of this theory see my article "The Comparative Indo-European Mythology of Georges Dumézil," *JFI* 1:147–166 (1964); for a more extended discussion of Dumézil's ideas see my *The New Comparative Mythology: An Anthropological Assessment of the Theories of Georges Dumézil* (Berkeley and Los Angeles, 1966).

115. Cf. *ibid.*, pp. 63, 85.

116. "Remarques comparatives sur le dieu scandinave Heimdallr," *EC* 8:263–283 (1959).

117. *Op. cit.*

118. *Horace et les Curiaces*.

119. For a thorough discussion of the dragon-slaying myth, see J. Fontenrose, *Python: A Study of Delphic Myth and Its Origins* (Berkeley and Los Angeles, 1959).

12. *The Medical Tradition of the Indo-Europeans*

In another article that appeared at the end of World War II, Benveniste takes up the question of medical practices among early Indo-Europeans. In one of his Pythic Odes, *the Greek lyric poet Pindar (first half of the fifth century* B.C.*) describes the medical procedures utilized by the Centaur Chiron, a great healer and teacher in Greek tradition. Using his comparative methodology born of historical linguistics, here as elsewhere, Benveniste uncovers a medical lore common to the Greeks and Indo-Iranians, and, hence, one pointing back to an ancestral Indo-European medical "doctrine." This doctrine is revealed to be consistent with the social and ideological tripartition that characterized early Indo-European culture.* (RDW)

THE MEDICAL TRADITION OF THE INDO-EUROPEANS

Émile Benveniste

Did the notion of "medically treating a disease" exist in the common Indo-European language? If proof of such an assertion requires showing that the same term was used in all the Indo-European dialects, doubt would seem to be in order: we find almost as many expressions as there are languages. Yet the Indo-European expression does exist: it is established by the correspondence of Latin *medeor, medicus*, "to heal, healer," and so on, with Avestan *vi-mad-*, "to treat a sick person." However, the forms of the root **med-* elsewhere reveal rather different meanings: Oscan *meddiss*, "judge"; Greek *μέδομαι*, "to care for"; *μέδων*, "lord, chief"; *μήδομαι*, "to decide"; Old Irish *midiur*, "to decide, judge, consider"; Gothic *mitan*, "to measure"; Armenian *mit* (< **mēdi-*), "thought." We must look for the fundamental meaning that might possibly be the origin of senses as diverse as "judging," "governing," and "healing."

A first indication is provided by one of the nominal forms of **med-* in Latin, which best accounts for all the observed facts: *modus*, "measure." Here we have the notion of "measure" but conceived differently than in *metior, mensura*, "to measure, measurement." This is a measure that is *imposed* on things and assumes understanding, reflection, and authority; it is not a measure of mensuration (as in *mensis*, "month") but a measure of *moderation* (cf. *modus: moderor*, "measure, moderate"), applied to that which violates or ignores a rule. This is why *modus* has a moral sense that can be seen clearly in its derivative *modestus*, "moderate, modest," as well as a sense of "reflection," proved by the frequentative *meditor*, "to reflect, consider," and a value of authority, apparently in the verb *moderari*, "moderate, apply restrictions, govern."

In Greek, the senses of "having concern" (*μέδομαι*), being "chief" (*μέδων*), and "to settle on a plan" (*μήδομαι*) all lead back to the idea of "authoritatively taking *measures* appropriate to the situation." This sense also explains why Oscan *med-diss*, literally "he who pronounces the **medo-*," designates the judge, and Oscan *med-* corresponds to Latin *ius* in *iudex*, "judge." It is more attenuated in Gothic *mitan*, "to measure," but it survives, still perceptible, in *us-milan*, "to conduct oneself, to live," *us-mel*, "conduct," which assume a sense such as "to adopt a rule of life." In more recent times all that remains is the notion of "decision, judgment" in Old Irish *midiur*, "I judge, I reflect," and that of "thought, reflection" in Armenian *mit*.

We can now see that the sense "to care for, to heal" in Latin *medeor* and Avestan *vi-mad-* simply restricts the broader sense of **med-*, which can be defined as "to take measures of order with authority and reflection; to apply a deliberate plan to a confused situation." Here we have the point of departure as well as the obvious explanation of the sense "medical." Now, the fact that this technical sense can be found at the two extremities of the zone, in two conservative languages that retained so many vestiges of the common language, is proof that in the Indo-European period the forms of **med-* served to express the notion of "medicine" and that in very early prehistoric times the Indo-European peoples had elaborated a certain technique for the treatment of diseases.

Furthermore, the values that enter into this definition help us to gauge the intellectual level of this technique. It is clear that Indo-European "medicine" assumed reflection, competence, and authority. The "treatment" of diseases called on the same capabilities and required "measures" of the same order as the command of men or the exercise of magistracy. It was quite different from the medicine of primitives. At the level of culture suggested by this lexical analysis, the physician in no way resembles a witch doctor; he is a man of thought.

It is therefore legitimate to ask whether the practice of medicine, which the vocabulary tells us was fairly advanced in the Indo-European era, rested solely on an empirical basis. Was there also a medical *doctrine* common to the Indo-

European peoples? Although the question has yet to be explicitly posed, it is justified by certain historical parallels. Were not the Assyrians and the Chinese familiar, if not with medical "philosophy," then at least with a general notion of diseases, their causes and cures?

In fact, we find a clear statement of such a theory in the Avesta. It is modestly presented as a purely practical classification of curative procedures. These are of three kinds: the "medicine of the knife" (*karəto.baēšaza*), the "medicine of plants" (*urvarō.baēšaza*), and the "medicine of charms" (*mąϑrō.baēšaza*).[1] The fact that three types of disease are here distinguished by specifying the treatment appropriate to each leads us to believe that those who treated patients with the knife, with plants, and with charms were already coordinating their practice in terms of a rudimentary theory.

This inference is confirmed, and the interest of the Iranian example is increased, by the existence of a similar tradition in ancient Greece, which Pindar recorded. This correspondence has been noted previously[2] but without detailed analysis, and over the years it has been forgotten. It is worth taking another look at this important text in *Pythian* 3 (47–55). When Hieron of Syracuse was afflicted with a grave disease, the poet evoked Asclepius, whom his father Apollo plucked as an infant from the pyre where his mother Coronis was to die and entrusted to the Centaur Chiron "so that he might teach him to heal the painful maladies of men" (*διδάξαι πολυπήμονας ἀνθρώποισι ἰᾶσθαι νόσους*). Here are the procedures that Chiron taught Asclepius:

> τοὺς μὲν ὦν, ὅσσοι μόλον αὐτοφύτων
> ἑλκέων ξυνάονες, ἢ πολίῳ χαλκῷ μέλη τετρωμένοι
> ἢ χερμάδι τηλεβόλῳ
> ἢ θερινῷ πυρὶ περθόμενοι δέμας ἢ χειμῶνι, λύσαις ἄλλον ἀλλοίων ἀχέων
> ἔξαγεν, τοὺς μὲν μαλακαῖς ἐπαοιδαῖς ἀμφέπων,
> τοὺς δὲ προσανέα πίνοντας, ἢ γυίοις περάπτων πάντοθεν
> φάρμακα, τοὺς δὲ τομαῖς ἔστασεν ὀρθούς.

> All who came to him with ulcers born within their flesh, wounded somewhere by shining bronze or hurled stone, or with bodies ravaged by the heat of summer or the cold of winter, he delivered each of them from his pain, sometimes by healing them with gentle charms, sometimes by giving them healing potions or by applying various remedies to their limbs, and sometimes he set them on their feet by means of incisions.

Here Pindar reveals an ancient tradition that has all the earmarks of a *school myth* intended to legitimate teaching supposed to be of divine origin. Note, first of all, the internal consistency of this classification. There are three types of disease: the "spontaneous ulcer" that the body engenders by itself; "exhaustion" of the organism from the effects of heat or cold; and "wounds" caused by weapons. There are also three types of treatment, each corresponding to a particular type of disease. "Charms" are applied to "wounds." In the *Odyssey*, for example, the son of Autolykos uses a charm to staunch the flow of blood from Odysseus's wound: *ἐπαοιδῇ δ' αἷμα κελαινὸν ἔσχεθον* (19.457). "Plants" applied to the limbs or imbibed in potions heal the exhaustion of the body. And "incisions" are used for ulcerous sores. Remedies and ailments exhibit a pattern that indicates thoughtful elaboration. Now, it so happens that the medical practice of the Avesta was based on the same classification: the "charm" (*ἐπαοιδή*) corresponds to the *mąϑra-*, "plants" (*φάρμακα*) to *urvara-*, and "incision" (*τομή*) to the "knife" (*karəta-*). Since the treatment procedures are identical, we may conclude that bodily afflictions were classified according to the same categories.

The significance of this concordance is not diminished by the objection that these three procedures are common to all medicine and that people of all ages have resorted to incantations, simples, and knives. In the first place, the problem is not to gauge the originality of Indo-European medicine but to establish that there was one and that it was defined by identical traditions in Greece and Iran. The more important point is that these three procedures, which, taken separately, are indeed found everywhere, are here grouped and coordinated as parts of a *doctrine* that was a distinctive possession of the Indo-European peoples. So far as we know, no other ancient medicine reveals such a hierarchical relationship of three treatments *linked* together in an organic whole encompassing the science of simples, the dexterity of the practitioner, and the curative power of incantations. The originality lies in the classification of methods of treatment, which assumes a unified concept of bodily afflictions.

Together, these two items of evidence would suffice to justify the reconstruction of a common doctrine. We propose to add a third to the list. We find it in the *Rig Veda* (10.39.3), admittedly in a form whose relation to the doctrine in question is not immediately apparent. But the ideas are indeed the same. In a hymn of the Tenth Mandala, the Aśvins are invoked as healing gods in the following terms: . . . "You are the ones, O Nāsatyas, who are called healers of what is blind, of what is meager, and of what suffers from a fracture."[3]

The Nāsatyas are presented as healers of three types of disease whose names, coordinated by *cit-*, in some way cover the whole range of curable ills. These three adjectives were not chosen at random among those denoting infirmity of some kind. Each one corresponds to one of the three treatment procedures mentioned above.

The blind man . . . is afflicted with a malady reputed to be divine, which of course was often taken to be a sign of supernatural sight or poetic inspiration (Tiresias, Homer). Only a god could heal it, or a "charm."

The meager man . . . suffered from a consumption that ate away at his body. The appropriate treatment for his weakness was medication with plants, which nourished and healed.

The "broken" man . . . , that is, the man with a fracture, required the care of a surgeon.

Unintentionally, merely by reproducing what must have been a traditional theme, the Vedic poet has in fact offered us a mirror image of the doctrine contained in Pindar and the Avesta: whereas the latter two sources spoke of remedies while the poet speaks of maladies, both maladies and remedies correspond to the same system of classification. The *Rig Veda* therefore refers, albeit in a brief and remote allusion, to the same Indo-European conceptions, whose antiquity it therefore corroborates.

The doctrine may therefore be considered to have been established by three independent and concordant attestations. It sets forth a series of practices constituting a summa of medical knowledge, a summa that by virtue of its origins is a mythic "totality" embodied by a healing god: Apollo in the legend of Asclepius, Aryaman in Mazdean medicine, and the Aśvins (Nāsatyas) in Vedic medicine.[4] Each of these peoples adapted a doctrine inherited from a common past to its own mythology, a doctrine whose very expression shows that it could not have been reinvented in each case.

Indeed, it is not merely on a priori and empirical grounds that this doctrine should be imputed to the Indo-Europeans. It seems possible to identify deeper relationships that link it to a broader classification. This way of coordinating the afflictions to human life and the remedies that combat them in triplets appears to depend on the same principles that organize the three states of society and, more generally, the tripleness of the universe.[5] Note that each of the three medicines has as its instrument the symbolic attribute of one of the three social classes: the charm (Greek ἐπαοιδή, Avestan *mąϑra*) for the priest-magicians; the knife (Avestan *karəta-*, cf. Greek τομή) for the warriors; plants (Avestan *urvara*, Greek φάρμακα) for farmers. It is hard to believe that these similarities are accidental. Only the figurative values of these three elements are to be considered; their function is of course to heal, not to represent. But the relation between malady and remedy suggests that both are complementary aspects of an *ambivalent* representation of social attributes. Incantations cast spells—or heal them; iron wounds—and removes the cause of the wound; plants poison—or nourish. In each case healing virtue is only half of the power of the attribute, whose very ambiguity is essential to this complex symbolism. With the same arrow Rudra and Apollo can bring either pestilence or salvation. Hence the malady and its corresponding remedy must be considered together in each of the three aspects in which they traditionally figured. Doing so will help us to see better the symbolic relation between the three divisions of the medical doctrine in question and the three divisions in terms of which society organized itself and conceived of its structure.

Notes

1. Vendidad 7.44; cf. also Yašt 3.6 [. . .]

2. J. Darmesteter, *Ormazd et Ahriman, leurs origines et leur histoire* (Paris, 1877). H. Güntert, *Der arische Weltkönig und Heiland* (Halle, 1923). H. Hirt, *Die Indogermanen: ihre Verbreitung, ihre Urheimat und ihre Kultur* (Strassburg, 1905–1907), v. 2, pp. 5-15.

3. See also *Rig Veda* 1.112.8, where similar praise is addressed to the Nāsatyas but in less precise terms: "the rejected(?), the blind, the paralytic."

4. For an etymological interpretation of the name Nāsatyas as healers, see Güntert, p. 259.

5. See my article on this: "Symbolisme social dans les cultes gréco-italiques," *Revue de l'histoire des religions* 129 (1945): 5–16 <[translated in this volume as "Social Symbolism in Greco-Italic Cults," pp. 439–47]>.

13. *Apollodorus,* Bibliotheca *2.5.1–12*

The Bibliotheca, *or "Library," is a singularly valuable work for students of Greek myth. For whatever the work lacks in literary appeal, it compensates in thoroughness of coverage (if often skeletal) of ancient mythic tradition. In composing this work, the author drew upon many literary documents that were at his disposal, some of which have themselves survived, others of which are attested only fragmentarily, if at all. To the latter group belongs the important work of Pherecydes of Athens (fifth century B.C.).*

And who is this Apollodorus to whom the Bibliotheca *is attributed? He was traditionally identified as an eminent scholar of the second century B.C., Apollodorus of Athens, a member of an elite circle of intellectuals who lived and worked in the Greek city of Alexandria in Egypt. Considerations internal to the text of the* Bibliotheca, *however, suggest that the work was composed somewhat later, in the first century A.D., or later still, and that its author is thus some more recent and less well known "Apollodorus" (sometimes dubbed "Pseudo-Apollodorus").*

In the passage below, Apollodorus summarizes for us the "Twelve Labors" of the Greek hero Heracles (Roman Hercules). After murdering his children in a state of madness, Heracles was required to serve his cousin Eurystheus, a king of Argos, for a period of twelve years, during which time he would perform twelve tasks for his master. The selection begins as the Pythia (the priestess of the god Apollo at his oracle in Delphi) has revealed to Heracles his fate of servitude.

The translator of this selection is Sir James Frazer, one of the twentieth century's most distinguished scholars of folklore and myth, perhaps best known for his work The Golden Bough. *(RDW)*

APOLLODORUS, *BIBLIOTHECA* 2.5.1–12

Translated by James Frazer

V. When Hercules heard that, he went to Tiryns and did as he was bid by Eurystheus. First, Eurystheus ordered him to bring the skin of the Nemean lion; now that was an invulnerable beast begotten by Typhon. On his way to attack the lion he came to Cleonae and lodged at the house of a day-labourer, Molorchus; and when his host would have offered a victim in sacrifice, Her-

From *Apollodorus: The Library*, first published 1921.

cules told him to wait for thirty days, and then, if he had returned safe from the hunt, to sacrifice to Saviour Zeus, but if he were dead, to sacrifice to him as to a hero. And having come to Nemea and tracked the lion, he first shot an arrow at him, but when he perceived that the beast was invulnerable, he heaved up his club and made after him. And when the lion took refuge in a cave with two mouths, Hercules built up the one entrance and came in upon the beast through the other, and putting his arm round its neck held it tight till he had choked it; so laying it on his shoulders he carried it to Cleonae. And finding Molorchus on the last of the thirty days about to sacrifice the victim to him as to a dead man, he sacrificed to Saviour Zeus and brought the lion to Mycenae. Amazed at his manhood, Eurystheus forbade him thenceforth to enter the city, but ordered him to exhibit the fruits of his labours before the gates. They say, too, that in his fear he had a bronze jar made for himself to hide in under the earth, and that he sent his commands for the labours through a herald, Copreus, son of Pelops the Elean. This Copreus had killed Iphitus and fled to Mycenae, where he was purified by Eurystheus and took up his abode.

As a second labour he ordered him to kill the Lernaean hydra. That creature, bred in the swamp of Lerna, used to go forth into the plain and ravage both the cattle and the country. Now the hydra had a huge body, with nine heads, eight mortal, but the middle one immortal. So mounting a chariot driven by Iolaus, he came to Lerna, and having halted his horses, he discovered the hydra on a hill beside the springs of the Amymone, where was its den. By pelting it with fiery shafts he forced it to come out, and in the act of doing so he seized and held it fast. But the hydra wound itself about one of his feet and clung to him. Nor could he effect anything by smashing its heads with his club, for as fast as one head was smashed there grew up two. A huge crab also came to the help of the hydra by biting his foot. So he killed it, and in his turn called for help on Iolaus who, by setting fire to a piece of the neighbouring wood and burning the roots of the heads with the brands, prevented them from sprouting. Having thus got the better of the sprouting heads, he chopped off the immortal head, and buried it, and put a heavy rock on it, beside the road that leads through Lerna to Elaeus. But the body of the hydra he slit up and dipped his arrows in the gall. However, Eurystheus said that this labour should not be reckoned among the ten because he had not got the better of the hydra by himself, but with the help of Iolaus.

As a third labour he ordered him to bring the Cerynitian hind alive to Mycenae. Now the hind was at Oenoe; it had golden horns and was sacred to

Artemis; so wishing neither to kill nor wound it, Hercules hunted it a whole year. But when, weary with the chase, the beast took refuge on the mountain called Artemisius, and thence passed to the river Ladon, Hercules shot it just as it was about to cross the stream, and catching it put it on his shoulders and hastened through Arcadia. But Artemis with Apollo met him, and would have wrested the hind from him, and rebuked him for attempting to kill her sacred animal. Howbeit, by pleading necessity and laying the blame on Eurystheus, he appeased the anger of the goddess and carried the beast alive to Mycenae.

As a fourth labour he ordered him to bring the Erymanthian boar alive; now that animal ravaged Psophis, sallying from a mountain which they call Erymanthus. So passing through Pholoe he was entertained by the centaur Pholus, a son of Silenus by a Melian nymph. He set roast meat before Hercules, while he himself ate his meat raw. When Hercules called for wine, he said he feared to open the jar which belonged to the centaurs in common. But Hercules, bidding him be of good courage, opened it, and not long afterwards, scenting the smell, the centaurs arrived at the cave of Pholus, armed with rocks and firs. The first who dared to enter, Anchius and Agrius, were repelled by Hercules with a shower of brands, and the rest of them he shot and pursued as far as Malea. Thence they took refuge with Chiron, who, driven by the Lapiths from Mount Pelion, took up his abode at Malea. As the centaurs cowered about Chiron, Hercules shot an arrow at them, which, passing through the arm of Elatus, stuck in the knee of Chiron. Distressed at this, Hercules ran up to him, drew out the shaft, and applied a medicine which Chiron gave him. But the hurt proving incurable, Chiron retired to the cave and there he wished to die, but he could not, for he was immortal. However, Prometheus offered himself to Zeus to be immortal in his stead, and so Chiron died. The rest of the centaurs fled in different directions, and some came to Mount Malea, and Eurytion to Pholoe, and Nessus to the river Evenus. The rest of them Poseidon received at Eleusis and hid them in a mountain. But Pholus, drawing the arrow from a corpse, wondered that so little a thing could kill such big fellows; howbeit, it slipped from his hand and lighting on his foot killed him on the spot. So when Hercules returned to Pholoe, he beheld Pholus dead; and he buried him and proceeded to the boar-hunt. And when he had chased the boar with shouts from a certain thicket, he drove the exhausted animal into deep snow, trapped it, and brought it to Mycenae.

The fifth labour he laid on him was to carry out the dung of the cattle of Augeas in a single day. Now Augeas was king of Elis; some say that he was a son of the Sun, others that he was a son of Poseidon, and others that he was a son of

Phorbas; and he had many herds of cattle. Hercules accosted him, and without revealing the command of Eurystheus, said that he would carry out the dung in one day, if Augeas would give him the tithe of the cattle. Augeas was incredulous, but promised. Having taken Augeas's son Phyleus to witness, Hercules made a breach in the foundations of the cattle-yard, and then, diverting the courses of the Alpheus and Peneus, which flowed near each other, he turned them into the yard, having first made an outlet for the water through another opening. When Augeas learned that this had been accomplished at the command of Eurystheus, he would not pay the reward; nay more, he denied that he had promised to pay it, and on that point he professed himself ready to submit to arbitration. The arbitrators having taken their seats, Phyleus was called by Hercules and bore witness against his father, affirming that he had agreed to give him a reward. In a rage Augeas, before the voting took place, ordered both Phyleus and Hercules to pack out of Elis. So Phyleus went to Dulichium and dwelt there, and Hercules repaired to Dexamenus at Olenus. He found Dexamenus on the point of betrothing perforce his daughter Mnesimache to the centaur Eurytion, and, being called upon by him for help, he slew Eurytion when that centaur came to fetch his bride. But Eurystheus would not admit this labour either among the ten, alleging that it had been performed for hire.

The sixth labour he enjoined on him was to chase away the Stymphalian birds. Now at the city of Stymphalus in Arcadia was the lake called Stymphalian, embosomed in a deep wood. To it countless birds had flocked for refuge, fearing to be preyed upon by the wolves. So when Hercules was at a loss how to drive the birds from the wood, Athena gave him brazen castanets, which she had received from Hephaestus. By clashing these on a certain mountain that overhung the lake, he scared the birds. They could not abide the sound, but fluttered up in a fright, and in that way Hercules shot them.

The seventh labour he enjoined on him was to bring the Cretan bull. Acusilaus says that this was the bull that ferried across Europa for Zeus; but some say it was the bull that Poseidon sent up from the sea when Minos promised to sacrifice to Poseidon what should appear out of the sea. And they say that when he saw the beauty of the bull he sent it away to the herds and sacrificed another to Poseidon; at which the god was angry and made the bull savage. To attack this bull Hercules came to Crete, and when, in reply to his request for aid, Minos told him to fight and catch the bull for himself, he caught it and brought it to Eurystheus, and having shown it to him he let it afterwards go free. But the bull roamed to Sparta and all Arcadia, and traversing the Isthmus arrived at Marathon in Attica and harried the inhabitants.

The eighth labour he enjoined on him was to bring the mares of Diomedes the Thracian to Mycenae. Now this Diomedes was a son of Ares and Cyrene, and he was king of the Bistones, a very war-like Thracian people, and he owned man-eating mares. So Hercules sailed with a band of volunteers, and having overpowered the grooms who were in charge of the mangers, he drove the mares to the sea. When the Bistones in arms came to the rescue, he committed the mares to the guardianship of Abderus, who was a son of Hermes, a native of Opus in Locris, and a minion of Hercules; but the mares killed him by dragging him after them. But Hercules fought against the Bistones, slew Diomedes and compelled the rest to flee. And he founded a city Abdera beside the grave of Abderus who had been done to death, and bringing the mares he gave them to Eurystheus. But Eurystheus let them go, and they came to Mount Olympus, as it is called, and there they were destroyed by the wild beasts.

The ninth labour he enjoined on Hercules was to bring the belt of Hippolyte. She was queen of the Amazons, who dwelt about the river Thermodon, a people great in war; for they cultivated the manly virtues, and if ever they gave birth to children through intercourse with the other sex, they reared the females; and they pinched off the right breasts that they might not be trammelled by them in throwing the javelin, but they kept the left breasts, that they might suckle. Now Hippolyte had the belt of Ares in token of her superiority to all the rest. Hercules was sent to fetch this belt because Admete, daughter of Eurystheus, desired to get it. So taking with him a band of volunteer comrades in a single ship he set sail and put in to the island of Paros, which was inhabited by the sons of Minos, to wit, Eurymedon, Chryses, Nephalion, and Philolaus. But it chanced that two of those in the ship landed and were killed by the sons of Minos. Indignant at this, Hercules killed the sons of Minos on the spot and besieged the rest closely, till they sent envoys to request that in the room of the murdered men he would take two, whom he pleased. So he raised the siege, and taking on board the sons of Androgeus, son of Minos, to wit, Alcaeus and Sthenelus, he came to Mysia, to the court of Lycus, son of Dascylus, and was entertained by him; and in a battle between him and the king of the Bebryces Hercules sided with Lycus and slew many, amongst others King Mygdon, brother of Amycus. And he took much land from the Bebryces and gave it to Lycus, who called it all Heraclea.

Having put in at the harbour of Themiscyra, he received a visit from Hippolyte, who inquired why he was come, and promised to give him the belt. But Hera in the likeness of an Amazon went up and down the multitude saying that the strangers who had arrived were carrying off the queen. So the Amazons in arms charged on horseback down on the ship. But when Hercules saw them in arms, he suspected treachery, and killing Hippolyte stripped her of her belt. And after fighting the rest he sailed away and touched at Troy.

But it chanced that the city was then in distress consequently on the wrath of Apollo and Poseidon. For desiring to put the wantonness of Laomedon to the proof, Apollo and Poseidon assumed the likeness of men and undertook to fortify Pergamum for wages. But when they had fortified it, he would not pay them their wages. Therefore Apollo sent a pestilence, and Poseidon a sea monster, which, carried up by a flood, snatched away the people of the plain. But as oracles foretold deliverance from these calamities if Laomedon would expose his daughter Hesione to be devoured by the sea monster, he exposed her by fastening her to the rocks near the sea. Seeing her exposed, Hercules promised to save her on condition of receiving from Laomedon the mares which Zeus had given in compensation for the rape of Ganymede. On Laomedon's saying that he would give them, Hercules killed the monster and saved Hesione. But when Laomedon would not give the stipulated reward, Hercules put to sea after threatening to make war on Troy.

And he touched at Aenus, where he was entertained by Poltys. And as he was sailing away he shot and killed on the Aenian beach a lewd fellow, Sarpedon, son of Poseidon and brother of Poltys. And having come to Thasos and subjugated the Thracians who dwelt in the island, he gave it to the sons of Androgeus to dwell in. From Thasos he proceeded to Torone, and there, being challenged to wrestle by Polygonus and Telegonus, sons of Proteus, son of Poseidon, he killed them in the wrestling match. And having brought the belt to Mycenae he gave it to Eurystheus.

As a tenth labour he was ordered to fetch the kine of Geryon from Erythia. Now Erythia was an island near the ocean; it is now called Gadira. This island was inhabited by Geryon, son of Chrysaor by Callirrhoe, daughter of Ocean. He had the body of three men grown together and joined in one at the waist, but parted in three from the flanks and thighs. He owned red kine, of which Eurytion was the herdsman and Orthus, the two-headed hound, begotten by Typhon on Echidna, was the watch-dog. So journeying through Europe to fetch the kine of Geryon he destroyed many wild beasts and set foot in Libya, and proceeding to Tartessus he erected as tokens of his journey two pillars over against each other at the boundaries of Europe and Libya. But being heated by the Sun on his journey, he bent his bow at the god, who in admiration of his hardihood, gave him a golden goblet in which he crossed the ocean. And having reached Erythia he lodged on Mount Abas. However the dog, perceiving him, rushed at him; but he smote it with his club, and when the herdsman Eurytion came to the help of the dog, Hercules killed him also. But Menoetes, who was there pasturing the kine of Hades, reported to Geryon what had occurred, and he, coming up with Hercules beside the river Anthemus, as he was driving away the kine, joined battle with him and was shot dead. And Hercules, embarking the kine in the goblet and sailing across to Tartessus, gave back the goblet to the Sun.

And passing through Abderia he came to Liguria, where Ialebion and Dercynus, sons of Poseidon, attempted to rob him of the kine, but he killed them and went on his way through Tyrrhenia. But at Rhegium a bull broke away and hastily plunging into the sea swam across to Sicily, and having passed through the neighbouring country since called Italy after it, for the Tyrrhenians called the bull *italus*, came to the plain of Eryx, who reigned over the Elymi. Now Eryx was a son of Poseidon, and he mingled the bull with his own herds. So Hercules entrusted the kine to Hephaestus and hurried away in search of the bull. He found it in the herds of Eryx, and when the king refused to surrender it unless Hercules should beat him in a wrestling bout, Hercules beat him thrice, killed him in the wrestling, and taking the bull drove it with the rest of the herd to the Ionian Sea. But when he came to the creeks of the sea, Hera afflicted the cows with a gadfly, and they dispersed among the skirts of the mountains of Thrace. Hercules went in pursuit, and having caught some, drove them to the Hellespont; but the remainder were thenceforth wild. Having with difficulty collected the cows, Hercules blamed the river Strymon, and whereas it had been navigable before, he made it unnavigable by filling it with rocks; and he conveyed the kine and gave them to Eurystheus, who sacrificed them to Hera.

When the labours had been performed in eight years and a month, Eurystheus ordered Hercules, as an eleventh labour, to fetch golden apples from the Hesperides, for he did not acknowledge the labour of the cattle of Augeas nor that of the hydra. These apples were not, as some have said, in Libya, but on Atlas among the Hyperboreans. They were presented by Earth to Zeus after his marriage with Hera, and guarded by an immortal dragon with a hundred heads, offspring of Typhon and Echidna, which spoke with many and divers sorts of voices. With it the Hesperides also were on guard, to wit, Aegle, Erythia, Hesperia, and Arethusa. So journeying he came to the river Echedorus. And Cycnus, son of Ares and Pyrene, challenged him to single combat. Ares championed the cause of Cycnus and marshalled the combat, but a thunderbolt was hurled between the two and parted the combatants. And going on foot through Illyria and hastening to the river Eridanus he came to the nymphs, the daughters of Zeus and Themis. They revealed Nereus to him, and Hercules seized him while he slept, and though the god turned himself into all kinds of shapes, the hero bound him and did not release him till he had learned from him where were the apples and the Hesperides. Being informed, he traversed Libya. That country was then ruled by Antaeus, son of Poseidon, who used to kill strangers by forcing them to wrestle. Being forced to wrestle with him, Hercules hugged him, lifted him aloft, broke and killed him; for when he touched earth so it was that he waxed stronger, wherefore some said that he was a son of Earth.

After Libya he traversed Egypt. That country was then ruled by Busiris, a son of Poseidon by Lysianassa, daughter of Epaphus. This Busiris used to sacrifice strangers on an altar of Zeus in accordance with a certain oracle. For Egypt was visited with dearth for nine years, and Phrasius, a learned seer who had come from Cyprus, said that the dearth would cease if they slaughtered a stranger man in honour of Zeus every year. Busiris began by slaughtering the seer himself and continued to slaughter the strangers who landed. So Hercules also was seized and haled to the altars, but he burst his bonds and slew both Busiris and his son Amphidamas.

And traversing Asia he put in to Thermydrae, the harbour of the Lindians. And having loosed one of the bullocks from the cart of a cowherd, he sacrificed it and feasted. But the cowherd, unable to protect himself, stood on a certain mountain and cursed. Wherefore to this day, when they sacrifice to Hercules, they do it with curses.

And passing by Arabia he slew Emathion, son of Tithonus, and journeying through Libya to the outer sea he received the goblet from the Sun. And having crossed to the opposite mainland he shot on the Caucasus the eagle, offspring of Echidna and Typhon, that was devouring the liver of Prometheus, and he released Prometheus, after choosing for himself the bond of olive, and to Zeus he presented Chiron, who, though immortal, consented to die in his stead.

Now Prometheus had told Hercules not to go himself after the apples but to send Atlas, first relieving him of the burden of the sphere; so when he was come to Atlas in the land of the Hyperboreans, he took the advice and relieved

Atlas. But when Atlas had received three apples from the Hesperides, he came to Hercules, and not wishing to support the sphere [he said that he would himself carry the apples to Eurystheus, and bade Hercules hold up the sky in his stead. Hercules promised to do so, but succeeded by craft in putting it on Atlas instead. For at the advice of Prometheus he begged Atlas to hold up the sky till he should] put a pad on his head. When Atlas heard that, he laid the apples down on the ground and took the sphere from Hercules. And so Hercules picked up the apples and departed. But some say that he did not get them from Atlas, but that he plucked the apples himself after killing the guardian snake. And having brought the apples he gave them to Eurystheus. But he, on receiving them, bestowed them on Hercules, from whom Athena got them and conveyed them back again; for it was not lawful that they should be laid down anywhere.

A twelfth labour imposed on Hercules was to bring Cerberus from Hades. Now this Cerberus had three heads of dogs, the tail of a dragon, and on his back the heads of all sorts of snakes. When Hercules was about to depart to fetch him, he went to Eumolpus at Eleusis, wishing to be initiated. However it was not then lawful for foreigners to be initiated: since he proposed to be initiated as the adoptive son of Pylius. But not being able to see the mysteries because he had not been cleansed of the slaughter of the centaurs, he was cleansed by Eumolpus and then initiated. And having come to Taenarum in Laconia, where is the mouth of the descent to Hades, he descended through it. But when the souls saw him, they fled, save Meleager and the Gorgon Medusa. And Hercules drew his sword against the Gorgon, as if she were alive, but he learned from Hermes that she was an empty phantom. And being come near to the gates of Hades he found Theseus and Pirithous, him who wooed Persephone in wedlock and was therefore bound fast. And when they beheld Hercules, they stretched out their hands as if they should be raised from the dead by his might. And Theseus, indeed, he took by the hand and raised up, but when he would have brought up Pirithous, the earth quaked and he let go. And he rolled away also the stone of Ascalaphus. And wishing to provide the souls with blood, he slaughtered one of the kine of Hades. But Menoetes, son of Ceuthonymus, who tended the kine, challenged Hercules to wrestle, and, being seized round the middle, had his ribs broken; howbeit, he was let off at the request of Persephone. When Hercules asked Pluto for Cerberus, Pluto ordered him to take the animal provided he mastered him without the use of the weapons which he carried. Hercules found him at the gates of Acheron, and, cased in his cuirass and covered by the lion's skin, he flung his arms round the head of the brute, and though the dragon in its tail bit him, he never relaxed his grip and pressure till it yielded. So he carried it off and ascended through Troezen. But Demeter turned Ascalaphus into a short-eared owl, and Hercules, after showing Cerberus to Eurystheus, carried him back to Hades.

14. *The Three Sins of Heracles*

Heracles is the Greek reflex of a far more ancient Indo-European mythic figure, argues Dumézil—a warrior figure who commits three sins, violating each stratum of tripartite Indo-European society. Dumézil here follows the account of Heracles' three sins preserved in the work of Diodorus Siculus, a Greek historian of the first century B.C. *Heracles' twelve-year servitude to Eurystheus was only the first of three "penalties" the hero would suffer, each the consequence of his sin, each bound up with mental or physical ailment. Cognate heroic figures among other Indo-European peoples to whom Dumézil makes reference in this selection are Indra, warrior deity par excellence of India, and Starcatherus, the Danish avatar of a well-known Scandinavian hero (Old Norse Starkaðr), whose tale is preserved in the* Gesta Danorum *of the twelfth/thirteenth-century cleric Saxo Grammaticus.* (RDW)

THE THREE SINS OF HERACLES

Georges Dumézil

Dare one hope that the foregoing considerations will encourage Hellenists to revise—paying attention not only to particular episodes but also to the general structures—the distressing treatment that the story of Heracles has been receiving for several generations?

This hero, the only pan-Hellenic hero, must certainly, in many Greek regions, have given rise to diverse traditions, new episodes, or variants of traditional episodes. But when his career finds him in Argolis, in Thebes, back in Argolis, then in many provinces of Greece, not to mention Lydia and the rest of the world, let us not jump so readily to the conclusion that we have before us Argive legends, Theban legends, etc., arranged artificially, belatedly set end to end, and that the first task of criticism is to disperse them again. It is to be expected that a hero of Heracles' type should be itinerant, that he should carry out many deeds in many places.

When Homer or Pindar make use of only one episode, or a fragment of an episode, and when, in this very fragment, they fail to transcribe some detail

From *The Destiny of the Warrior* by Georges Dumézil, 1970. Reprinted by permission of The University of Chicago Press.

that other versions have led us to expect, let us not immediately conclude that they were unaware of all the other legends about Heracles or even of the particular detail itself. The poet may deliberately have said only what was useful to characterize, to evoke in passing, a personage from ancient times. And when so troublesome a matter as the hero's madness was in question, the poet may have refrained from saying anything.

Finally, let us rid ourselves of philological ingenuity. One of the most intelligent studies of these legends, still useful after three-quarters of a century, is, in my opinion, the *Vorwort* that Ulrich von Wilamowitz-Moellendorff devoted to the "Raging Heracles." After scoffing at the comparative mythology of his time, which he found too facile—twenty years later he would also be able to dismiss the disappointing work of Leopold von Schröder on Heracles and Indra—he gave several detailed examples of the critical method. What confidence and what illusions! For example, with respect to the murder of the children: "Auch hier ist eine mühsame Voruntersuchung nötig, um auf dem zerstreuten Materiale die älteste Gestalt der Geschichte zu gewinnen, die dem Urteil über ihre Bedeutung allein zu Grunde gelegt werden darf" (1.81). *Eine mühsame Voruntersuchung*, "a toilsome preliminary investigation": yes, let us free ourselves from these laborious preparations, which sometimes lack clarity (p. 87), and which are too often designed to give a scientific veneer to a preformed conviction.

With the fear and trembling that accompany such an indiscretion, I will insist only that the most general framework of the legends of Heracles, in its two most systematic presentations (Diodorus of Sicily and the pseudo-Apollodorus of Athens), is clarified and gains plausibility by comparison with that of the legends of Starkaðr the sinner, of Indra the chastised sinner, and generally by reference to the epic theme that we have delineated. The career of Heracles is in fact divided into three and only three parts, each ended by a serious sin which demands an expiation. And following the first two sins is a set of adventures that is presented as its consequence. The aftereffects of these sins bear heavily upon the hero, the first one in his mental health, the second in his physical health, and the third in his life itself. Finally, these sins correspond to the three functions, following the descending hierarchical order, since they involve, in turn, a hesitation before an order of Zeus, the cowardly murder of a surprised enemy, and a guilty amorous passion. Let us follow the account of Diodorus in his fourth book.[1]

The Origin and Functional Value of Heracles [9]

Even before his birth, Heracles—who will not have three lives, but whose conception took three nights to prepare—is officially classified as a hero of the second function. Just before Alcmene's parturition, Zeus, who has sired him at Tiryns, announces in the presence of the gods that the first child about to be born will be king of the Argives. As a result, Hera checks the birth-pains of Alcmene and has Eurystheus born before he is due. Now Alcmene's child will not be king. In compensation, Zeus promises that after having served Eurystheus by performing twelve labors, Heracles will attain immortality. In the scene which follows the birth, the protection which the infant receives from Athena and the hostility he arouses from Hera—Hera the queen, Athena the warrior: let us recall the "trifunctional problem" posed by Hera, Athena, and Aphrodite to the unfortunate Paris[2]—confirm the "second function" character of his destiny.

The First Sin [10.6–11.1]

Heracles is in Thebes. The tremendous services he has rendered have led the king to give him his daughter Megara in marriage.

> ... but Eurystheus, who was ruler of Argolis, viewing with suspicion the growing power of Heracles, summoned him to his side and commanded him to perform Labours. And when Heracles ignored the summons Zeus despatched word to him to enter the service of Eurystheus; whereupon Heracles journeyed to Delphi, and on inquiring of the god regarding the matter he received a reply which stated that the gods had decided that he should perform twelve Labours at the command of Eurystheus and that upon their conclusion he should receive the gift of immortality.
>
> At such a turn of affairs Heracles fell into despondency of no ordinary kind; for he felt that servitude to an inferior was a thing which his high achievements did not deserve, and yet he saw that it would be hurtful to himself and impossible not to obey Zeus, who was his father as well. While he was thus greatly at a loss, Hera sent upon him a frenzy [*λύτταν*],[3] and in his vexation of soul he fell into a madness [*εἰς μανίαν ἐνέπεσε*].

Then follows a whole cycle: the murder of his children, whom he pierces with arrows in his delirium, the painful return to reason, the submission to the will of the gods, the twelve labors accomplished under the order of Eurystheus with many sub-labors added according to circumstance, and finally a long series of exploits taking him throughout the world.

The Second Sin [31.1–4]

> After Heracles had completed his Labours he gave his own wife Megara in marriage to Iolaos, being apprehensive of begetting any children by her because of the calamity which had befallen their other offspring, and sought another wife by whom he might have children without apprehension. Consequently he wooed Iole, the daughter of Eurytus who was ruler of Oechalia. But Eurytus was hesitant because of the ill fortune which had come in the case of Megara and replied that he would deliberate concerning the marriage. Since Heracles had met with a refusal to his suit, because of the dishonour which had been showered upon him he now drove off the mares of Eurytus. But Iphitus, the son of Eurytus, harboured suspicions of what had been done and came to Tiryns in search of the horses, whereupon Heracles, taking him up on a lofty tower of the castle, asked to see whether they were by chance grazing anywhere; and when Iphitus was unable to discover them, he claimed that Iphitus had falsely accused him of the theft and threw him down headlong from the tower. Because of his murder of Iphitus Heracles was attacked by disease [*νοσήσας . . .*].

When Neleus refuses to purify him, he has Deïphobus perform the ceremony; but the disease does not disappear. For the second time he consults the oracle of Apollo, which answers "that he could easily rid himself of the disease if he should be sold as a slave and honorably pay over the purchase price of himself to the sons of Iphitus." And thus we have the sale to Omphale, the bondage in Lydia, and a new series of exploits.

In this episode, Diodorus' account attenuates the fault of Heracles: he has indeed set a trap for Iphitus, his guest, by urging him to climb the tower from which Heracles will easily be able to hurl him; but just as Heracles is about to hurl him, he warns him, even if only by his reproaches, and the surprise is no longer total. In Sophocles' *Trachiniae*, the messenger Lichas offers a better explanation for the divine punishment:

> . . . and when one day Iphitus came to the hill of Tiryns, searching for the tracks of the horses that had strayed, the moment his eyes looked one way, his mind on something else, Heracles hurled him from the top of that flat bastion.
>
> But the King was angry with this act of his, he who is the father of all, Zeus Olympian, and had him sold and sent out of the country, *since this was the only man* [*of all those killed by Heracles*] *he had ever killed by guile* [*ὁθουνεκ' αὐτὸν μοῦνον ἀνθρώπων δόλῳ / ἔκτεινεν*]. If he had taken vengeance openly [*ἐμφανῶς*], [evidently in connection with his adversary], Zeus surely would have pardoned his rightful victory. The gods like foul play no better than do men. [269–80][4]

Thus Heracles' fault is to have violated, contrary to his regular practice, the duty and the honor of the Strong-One by substituting the trap for the duel, by taking a man by surprise who should have been able to regard himself secure in Tiryns, his safety guaranteed by the unwritten pact of hospitality: one can sense how close we are to the episode of Namuci (or Vr̥tra) in the myths of Indra.

The Third Sin and the Death [37.4–38.2]

Heracles has finally found in Deïaneira the lawful wife he had sought and who had been refused him since his separation from Megara. But before dying, the Centaur Nessus has given Deïaneira a little of his blood which is poisoned by the arrow that has been dipped in the Hydra's venom, and has told her that if her husband should be touched by a fabric saturated with this potion, his affection, if one day it were found wanting, would be assured. Soon the hero forgets that he is married.

> . . . as he was leaving the territory of Itonus and was making his way through Pelasgiotis he fell in with Ormenius the king and asked of him the hand of his daughter Astydameia. When Ormenius refused him because he already had for lawful wife Deïaneira, the daughter of Oeneus, Heracles took the field against him, captured his city, and slew the king who would not obey him, and taking captive Astydameia he lay with her and begat a son Ctesipus. After finishing this exploit he set out to Oechalia to take the field against the sons of Eurytus because he had been refused in his suit for the hand of Iole. The Arcadians again fought on his side and he captured the city and slew the sons of Eurytus, who were Toxeus, Molion, and Clytius. And taking Iole captive he departed from Euboea to the promontory which is called Cenaeon.
>
> At Cenaeon Heracles, wishing to perform a sacrifice, dispatched his attendant Lichas to Deïaneira his wife, commanding him to ask her for the shirt and robe which he customarily wore in the celebration of sacrifices. But when Deïaneira learned from Lichas of the love which Heracles had for Iole, she wished him to have a greater affection for herself and so anointed the shirt with the love-charm which had been given her by the Centaur, whose intention was to bring about the death of Heracles. Lichas, then, in ignorance of these matters, brought back the garments for the sacrifice; and Heracles put on the shirt which had been anointed, and as the strength of the toxic drug began slowly to work he met with the most terrible calamity. For the arrow's barb had carried the poison of the Hydra, and when the shirt for this reason, as it became heated, attacked the flesh of the body, Heracles was seized with such anguish [. . . *τοῦ χιτῶνος διὰ τὴν θερμασίαν τὴν σάρκα τοῦ σώματος λυμαινομένου, περιαλγὴς γενόμενος ὁ Ἡρακλῆς* . . .].

Having fallen prey to such increasing and intolerable suffering (*ἀεὶ δὲ μᾶλλον τῇ νόσῳ βαρυνόμενος* [38.3]), the hero dispatches envoys to seek a third and last consultation at Delphi. Apollo responds: Let Heracles be carried onto mount Oete, with all his arms, and a huge pyre be built for him; as for the rest, it should be left to Zeus. And thus we have the pyre, the service of the young and pure Philoctetes who lights it, the bolt of Zeus, and the disappearance of every earthly trace of the man who has attained immortality.

Such is the three-act drama—three sins, three maladies, scanned by three Delphic oracles—which develops, in descending hierarchical order, in accord with the three functions. If the beginning of Heracles' epic (the role of the divinities of the first and second functions) and also its end (the death, suicidal in nature, after the third sin; the demand that a pure young man administer the killing) recall the epic Starcatherus, the details of the second (Iphitus) and the third (Iole) sins are even closer to the second (Namuci) and third (Ahalyā) sins of Indra; in particular, the sin of the third function concerns sexual concupiscence, as with Indra, not venality, as with Starcatherus.[5] Equally close to the Indian conception, in connection with Indra, is the theme of three "losses," which are the consequence of the three sins as well as their punishment: Indra's loss of *tejas* and then of *bala* (psychic force and physical force) after the sins of the first and second functions have the same quality as Heracles' loss of mental health and physical health after his sins of the same levels, with one difference: for Indra the three irreparable losses add themselves together to constitute in their progressive sum the equivalent of an annihilation, whereas for Heracles the first two sins are entirely atoned for, and it is the third, by itself, *ab integro*, which occasions his death. Let us draw no final conclusions about these partial agreements. It is still quite possible that, since the subject matter readily suggests definite oppositions and definite causal connections, one and the same epic framework could have been embroidered in convergent variations by the Indians, the Germans, and the Greeks. But first we must account for the framework, and our actual purpose is only to establish its existence in these three domains. Despite the variants, despite their multiplication in a fashion typical of Greek legends, despite, more especially, the frequent displacements of the Iphitus episode (second sin) in the course of the hero's career, perhaps Hellenists will agree to retain this new element of explanation and accept that fundamentally, at all times, before its further developments, the story of Heracles was marked out by these three ideologically interdependent episodes, either in their present form or equivalent forms.[6] In any case, it is harder to understand how these late compilers could have reinvented such a framework in a period when the memory of the ancient, prehistoric trifunctional structure was surely lost.

Notes

1. Citations from Diodorus are from the translation by C. H. Oldfather, Loeb Classical Library (1935).

2. *ME* 1:581–86.

3. See the excellent observations on the *Λύσσα* of Euripides' *Heracles*, compared to the Alecto of the seventh book of the *Aeneid* (less delicately shaded, "das Böse an sich"), in Vinzenz Buchheit's *Vergil über die Sendung Roms* (1963), pp. 101–2.

4. Michael Jameson, trans., *The Woman of Trachis*, in David Grene and Richmond Lattimore, eds., *The Complete Greek Tragedies*, vol. 2, *Sophocles* (University of Chicago Press, 1959). Italics added.

5. See an analogous pair of variants in my *Tarpeia*, pp. 280–81 (Tarpeia betrays for love of gold, or for love of Tatius); cf. *ME* 1:428–30; 491 and n. 2; 560.

6. In the *Bibliotheca* of Apollodorus (2.4.8–7.7) the "scansion" of the multitude of Heracles exploits by three sins and three curses (*μανῆναι*, 4, 12; *δεινῇ νόσῳ*, 6. 2; *ὁ τῆς ὕδρας ἰὸς τὸν χρῶτα ἔσηπε*, 7.7) is very similar, with several reservations of which the most important bears upon the first sin and its connection with the first malady: (1) the madness in which he kills his children is visited upon Heracles (or rather upon "Alcides," still his name) by Hera, no longer after (and under cover of the depression produced by) an initial sin, but simply *κατὰ ζῆλον*, from jealousy; no matter how involuntary, it is the murder of the children that determines the character of the sin—a sin, moreover, of the "first function" since he defies the sacred ties of blood; (2) at the same stroke, the first consultation at Delphi is displaced: it comes, as is natural, after the event that is the fault in this context, thus *after* the sacrilegious murder of the children (it no longer follows the disobedience of divine orders, given *before* the murder); the question that Alcides puts to the Phythian is "where he should dwell," and it is the priestess, in giving him the name "Heracles," who commands him to go and serve Eurystheus for twelve years and perform ten labors (which will become twelve); (3) the two other sins and the corresponding curses are presented as in Diodorus, but there is a consultation at Delphi only after the second, not after the third: it is on his own that Heracles, his flesh torn away, constructs his pyre (after having charged his legitimate son Hyllus to marry, when he came of age, Iole, Heracles' concubine, his partner in the third sin and the cause of his misfortune; all of which underlines the sexual character of this fault). It will be observed that neither in Apollodorus nor in Diodorus is any of the other acts of violence which Heracles commits in his long career, not even the odious murder of the *Κήρυκες*, the heralds of the king of the Minyans (Diod. 4.10.2; Apoll. 2.4.11)—and the heralds are from Zeus!—considered a fault, nor does any deed entail a divine punishment, sickness or otherwise.

15. Agamemnon and the Indo-European Threefold Death Pattern

Partially in conjunction with Dumézil's identification of the Indo-European triple-sinning warrior, several of Dumézil's disciples have argued for an Indo-European doctrine of a "threefold death"—a death pattern linked to Indo-European tripartite ideology. In the essay that follows, David Evans first provides an overview of earlier research on the topic, summarizing examples of the threefold death as presented in Roman, Greek, Germanic, Slavic, and Celtic sources. Drawing on the work of the Greek tragedian Aeschylus (fifth century B.C.*), Evans then advances an argument for identifying Agamemnon, the leader of the Greek expedition against Troy, as a triple-sinning warrior and, concomitantly, as a sacrificial victim experiencing the threefold death.* (RDW)

AGAMEMNON AND THE INDO-EUROPEAN THREEFOLD DEATH PATTERN

David Evans

Georges Dumézil's discovery of a tripartite Indo-European ideology has provided an extraordinarily useful analytical tool for students of comparative mythology and folklore.[1] Briefly stated, this ideology serves to organize various aspects of culture into three levels or "functions" (to use Dumézil's own term), the first concerned with magico-religious and juridical sovereignty, the second with armed might, and the third with wealth and fecundity. In recent years an Indo-European pattern of threefold death has been identified and discussed in terms of this tripartite ideology by a number of followers of Dumézil, most notably by Donald Ward.[2] The pattern is found in myths and legends of various Indo-European peoples in two main forms. The first of these is a series or grouping of three deaths, each by a different means. The second is a single death by three different means simultaneously. Ward believes that the pattern stems essentially from an Indo-European form of ritual sacrifice. I propose first

From *History of Religions* 19, by David Evans. Reprinted by permission of The University of Chicago Press.

to summarize the evidence for the two forms of this pattern, then to relate the pattern to the death of Agamemnon as described by the Greek tragedian Aeschylus. This ancient Greek evidence should serve as an important link with a number of more modern examples of the pattern and should help to establish more firmly this pattern as a significant embodiment of the Indo-European tripartite ideology.

One of the most important early pieces of evidence for the pattern of three associated deaths is found in the *Commenta* to the Roman poet Lucan's *Pharsalia*, 1.445–46, where it is reported that human sacrifices were made to the Gaulish deity Esus by hanging, to Taranis by burning the victims alive in a large wicker basket, and to Teutates by drowning them in a vat.[3] The weight of evidence suggests that Esus is associated with the first or sovereign function, Taranis with the second or warrior function, and Teutates with the third or fertility function. Thus among the ancient continental Celts we have a pattern of hanging associated with sovereignty, burning with war, and drowning with fertility.

Yoshida has identified a similar pattern of three deaths in an ancient Greek legend.[4] There, however, the deaths consist of two murders and a suicide rather than the ritual sacrifice of the Celts. The first murder is that of Piasus by his daughter Larissa, who drowns him in a vat of wine in revenge for his having raped her. The next murder is of Cyzicus, king of the Pelasgians, to whom Larissa was either married or engaged. He is killed by the Argonauts in a fight caused by a misunderstanding, after he had entertained the Argonauts hospitably when they were driven to his city by a storm. Finally Cleite, who is also described as married or engaged to Cyzicus, hangs herself from a tree out of grief at his death. Yoshida connects all three deaths with the third function, or perhaps we might simply say that the tripartite ideology did not clearly impose itself upon this series of legends.

The richest evidence for this pattern in ancient times comes from Germanic-speaking peoples. Ward has surveyed a great deal of material which suggests that the ancient continental and Scandinavian Germanic peoples had three methods of human sacrifice and criminal execution.[5] These were by hanging, by drowning, and by a weapon. Hanging is in all cases associated with the god Odin, whom Dumézil sees as a representative of the magico-religious portion of the first or sovereign function in the tripartite system. Drowning or its equivalent, burial alive, on the other hand, is shown by Ward to be associated with the third function. The evidence for execution or sacrifice by a weapon is much less extensive among the Germanic peoples than for the other two means, but what evidence there is suggests that this type of death was associated with the war god and hence with the second (warrior) function. There is also some evidence that these three forms of death could occur within the same ritual context. In Adam of Bremen's eleventh-century description of the Swedish pagan temple at Uppsala he mentions both blood sacrifices and hangings of human and animal victims. A scholion to this description adds that there was also at this temple a spring into which live human sacrificial victims were plunged. Adam states that the temple was a cult center for Odin, Thor, and Freyr, deities whom Dumézil and his followers have identified with the first, second, and third functions, respectively. It is thus quite possible that we are dealing here with trifunctional methods of sacrifice.[6]

The pattern of multiple related deaths occurs not only in Germanic ritual and legal practices but also in legend. In a legend complex studied by Dumézil two close friends or kinsmen suffer linked deaths.[7] There are four versions of the legend. In one, reported by Saxo (1.8.27), Hundingus, king of the Swedes, accidentally drowns after falling into a jar full of ale. His friend Hadingus hangs himself in grief. Two other versions are concerned with the deaths of Fjölnir and Sveigdir, as told in the *Ynglingatal* (strophes 1–2) and *Ynglingasaga* (chaps. 11–12). In them Fjölnir, the Swedish king, gets up from a drunken sleep in order to urinate, falls through a hole in the floor into a vat of mead, and drowns. His son Sveigdir then makes a vow to search for the home of Odin and fulfills this by hurling himself into a giant rock which closes around him. Finally, in a nineteenth-century Faroese ballad Veraldur, Odin's son, dies by falling through a hole in the floor into a brewing vat. His father ascends to heaven and remains a king there. Dumézil shows convincingly that the drowned party has clear third-function connections and that the party who is hanged, enclosed in a rock, or ascends to heaven is connected with Odin, a first-function deity. We might add that in the story of Hundingus and Hadingus there is a third death that immediately precedes and partly motivates these other two. This is the murder by Hadingus's men of his son-in-law, who had treacherously tried to kill Hadingus at a banquet (Saxo 1.8.26). This violent death by a weapon would seem to be connected with the second function and would thus complement Hundingus's third-function drowning and Hadingus's first-function hanging.

The other occurrence of linked deaths in Germanic tradition is in the legend of Starkad, also studied by Dumézil in connection with the Indo-European pattern of the three sins of the warrior.[8] The first and third of Starkad's sins are murders, the second being cowardice in battle. The first sin is his killing of King Vikar in a mock sacrifice to Odin when Vikar's ships are delayed by a storm. Vikar is chosen by lot to be a sacrificial victim, but to prevent his death Starkad places a noose of withies around his neck and touches him with a reed. At this point the withies magically become a real noose tightening around Vikar's neck, and the reed becomes a sword. The murder is clearly connected with Odin and the first function. The other sin of Starkad was the treacherous murder of King Olo in his bath, for which Starkad received a reward of gold. His venality connects his act in this case with the third function.

This Germanic pattern of three linked deaths evidently also made its way into Finnish folk tradition through Germany or Sweden. Talley has pointed out a Finnish ballad in which Christ names the three sins of Magdalen, who murdered her children by fire, drowning, and live burial.[9] Christ adds that the children might have grown up to be a knight, a burgher, and a priest, respectively, an evident borrowing of the Indo-European trifunctional pattern expressed in the order of second, third, and first functions. Live burial here replaces the usual hanging as a first-function mode of death.

Evidence for a series of three murders has also been discovered in Slavic tradition by Fisher.[10] One account from the *Chronicle of Henry of Livonia* simply tells us how the Finnic Livonians plotted to kill Bishop Berthold either by burning him in his church, slaying him with a weapon, or drowning him. The other account from the Nestor Chronicle deals with Olga's triple revenge on the Derevlians for the murder of her husband Igor. This may actually represent a Scandinavian intrusion in Slavic tradition, as Olga and Igor are Varangian names. Olga had the first Derevlian contingent buried alive, the second group locked in a bathhouse and burned, and the third group put to the sword at a banquet. These groups of Derevlians are shown by Fisher to be representatives, respectively, of the warriors, nobles, and commoners, or in Dumézil's terms the second, first, and third functions. Their social standing in the Indo-European tripartite scheme is thus not correlated with their manner of death in the usual sense, though there is at least a threefold pattern. Since these are simply historical or pseudo-historical accounts of attempted or real murders, it would seem that any ceremonial or legalistic connections with these deaths had been lost by the time our traditions crystallized around the figures of Berthold and the Derevlians. Hence these traditions do not preserve the relationship of the manner of death to a particular Indo-European functional level as the older Germanic and Celtic material does.

Up to this point we have surveyed evidence for a grouping or series of three different types of death in various Indo-European traditions. There is another Indo-European pattern of myth and folk legend, that of a single death by three different means simultaneously. We have already noted partial examples of this pattern in the story of Starkad, who killed King Vikar by simultaneously hanging and stabbing him and killed King Olo with a weapon in his bath, thus in effect also drowning him. The Germanic prototype for these kinds of multiple death would seem to be the god Odin himself. The *Hávamal* (lines 138–45) clearly states that Odin hung on a windswept tree for nine nights pierced with a spear as a sacrifice to himself for the purpose of obtaining the runes of poetry. In addition to this torture the text states that Odin was "sprinkled with mead" (*ausinn Óðreri*), using as the word for "mead" the name of one of the three vessels, Óðroerir, in which the original mead of poetry was brewed. Thus Odin appears to undergo a symbolic immersion in addition to hanging and spearing, in essence dying a triple death only to be reborn with the wisdom of poetry.

Versions of the motif of a single threefold death found in medieval Irish and Latin literature and a modern European folktale have been surveyed by Ward,[11] and to these we can add a medieval Welsh source. In almost all of the versions the death is the fulfillment of a prophecy. In fact, Starkad's murders of Vikar and Olo are also fulfillments of a prophecy made by Odin himself when Odin gave Starkad three spans of mortal life, in each of which he was to commit a great sin. Odin's own triple death is not said to be the result of a prophecy, but it is obviously a deliberate act on his part whereas all the other deaths in this pattern are unexpected by those who suffer them. Odin could thus be considered to be his own prophet.

The Welsh source for this motif is the Fourth Branch of the Mabinogi, the story of Math son of Mathonwy.[12] As in the case of Odin, the threefold death is not actually prophesied, but instead the victim reveals the unusual manner in which he can be killed. Lleu Llaw Gyffes is the victim, and he tells his treacherous wife Blodeuedd that he can be killed only by a spear that has been fashioned for a whole year during the hours of Sunday mass. He must be struck with the spear while in a bath on a river bank with a thatched frame over the tub and while standing with one foot on the edge of the tub and the other on the back of a he-goat. Blodeuedd conspires with her lover Gronw Bebyr to have him make the spear, and at the end of a year she persuades Lleu to demonstrate to her the manner in which he might be killed. Just as he steps out of the bath onto the he-goat's back, Gronw emerges from hiding and pierces him with the spear. Lleu immediately is transformed into an eagle and flies off screaming. Later he is brought back to good health and human form and wreaks his vengeance upon Blodeuedd and Gronw. While Lleu's "death" may appear on the surface to be only an elaborate form of murder by a weapon, its status as a version of the threefold death motif becomes clear from the evidence adduced below.

The earliest Irish version comes from the seventh-century account of the life of Saint Columba. The saint predicts that Aedh the Black will be wounded in the neck with a spear, fall from a tree into the water, and drown. The prophecy comes true, except that the tree from which Aedh falls becomes a boat. In two twelfth-century poems by Bishop Hildebert of Le Mans a boy learns from Venus that he will die by a noose, from Mars that he will die by a weapon, and from Neptune that he will die by water. In a fall from a tree the boy's sword pierces his breast, and his head is submerged in the river below. Ward interprets the fall from a tree as a metaphorical substitution for the noose. The motif of the threefold death is also associated with the Irish Saint Moling. The saint tells Grag, who has killed Suibhne Geilt, that he will die by a weapon, fire, and drowning. Grag does not believe him, but one day he climbs a tree, is wounded by his spear, falls into a fire below and then into the water where he drowns. In an eleventh-century account of King Diarmaid it is predicted that the king will die by a weapon, burning, and drowning. During a festival he is wounded by a spear, the house is burned over him, and he drowns in a vat of beer where he had sought protection from the flames. Essentially the same story is told of Aidhedh Muirchertaig mac Erca.

The modern European folktale incorporating this motif is classified by Thompson as tale type 934A¹.[13] Variants from eight ethnic traditions stretching from Ireland to Iran have been studied by Brednich as part of a larger study of *Schicksalsfrauen*.[14] In all cases the death is the fulfillment of a prophecy. Typically the victim is bitten by a snake while climbing a tree; he falls and drowns in the water below. Brednich concludes that this tale must have originated in northwestern Europe and migrated from there to the Baltic as well as to the Balkans and Asia.

Ward agrees with Brednich's explanation for most of the variants but points out connections of the medieval legend and modern folktale pattern of the threefold death with older accounts of three related forms of sacrifice or punishment.[15] Ward proposes that we consider the threefold death pattern essentially Indo-European, related to the tripartite ideology, and ultimately derived from a type of sacrificial practice. He believes that the fall from a tree represents a form of hanging and shows that the element of death by fire is a distinctly Celtic one, going back as far as Lucan's description of the sacrifices to the god Taranis. We might add here that the threefold death seems related not only to the Indo-European tripartite ideology of sovereign, warrior, and fertility functions, but that it also seems to express a conception of the natural world as constructed of three essential elements or levels; air, land, and water (or underworld). At the first level the victim hangs in the air, falls through the air, or ascends to heaven. At the second level he dies on the earth, pierced by a weapon. At the third level, he drowns in water or is buried alive under the earth. The Celtic substitution of death by fire, which was also encountered in Baltic and Slavic chronicles, might be viewed simply as an attempt to reconcile a threefold pattern of death with a fourfold view of the natural world as made up of air, earth, fire, and water. It would appear, then, that the essential meaning of the motif of multiple death is that the victim or victims express the idea of death in the most complete manner possible both in the social domain by dying in conformity to the tripartite ideology and in the natural domain by dying in all levels of existence. Such a view would accord well with Ward's contention that the threefold death is ultimately derived from a type of sacrifice.

Evidence from the ancient Greek tradition of the death of Agamemnon helps to confirm Ward's view of the threefold death's Indo-European nature, its relation to the tripartite ideology, and its derivation from a sacrificial practice. The death of Agamemnon also helps to fill several gaps in Ward's chain of evidence.

Agamemnon's death is described in the *Agamemnon* and *Choephoroi* [Libation bearers], which were part of the *Oresteia* trilogy composed by the Athenian dramatist Aeschylus and first performed in 458 B.C. Agamemnon, after returning from an absence of ten years at Troy, is murdered by his wife Clytemnestra in his palace. She kills him in his bath with the sword of her lover Aegistheus after entangling him in a cloth or garment. (Her collusion with a lover to murder her husband is reminiscent of the Welsh story of Lleu's "death.") Aeschylus is the earliest author to attribute clearly such a death to Agamemnon. Homer gives us a much simpler description. In the *Odyssey* 4.534–35, Menelaus tells Telemachus that Agamemnon was killed at a homecoming banquet by Aegistheus. This same story is repeated to Odysseus by the ghost of Agamemnon himself in *Odyssey* 11.405–34. Much later the Roman dramatist Seneca in his *Agamemnon* 867–909 has Cassandra tell how Agamemnon was killed at a banquet with a sword and ax wielded by Aegistheus and Clytemnestra after Agamemnon became entangled in a mantle made for him by Clytemnestra. Seneca does not mention the bath in connection with Agamemnon's death.

Aeschylus, then, is our main source for the threefold-death motif used in connection with Agamemnon. He first describes the death in lines 1125–29 of the *Agamemnon*. Here Cassandra, the blind prophetess whom Agamemnon took captive at Troy, has a vision of Agamemnon entangled in a garment, struck with a weapon by Clytemnestra, and falling into water. Although this water is later described as in a bathtub, Aeschylus here uses words that actually signify a vessel or cauldron (*ἐνύδρῳ τεύχει*, line 1128; *λέβητος*, line 1129). Later in lines 1380–92 Clytemnestra herself describes how she struck Agamemnon with three blows after entangling him with robes. She uses the simile of a fisherman casting an encircling net to describe her strategy. She does not mention the bath in this passage, although the fishnet simile perhaps implies one. The final description in the first play of the trilogy occurs in lines 1529 and 1539–40, where Clytemnestra states that Agamemnon died by the sword and the chorus say that they have seen Agamemnon lying on his funeral bed in a silver-sided bathtub (*ἀργυροτοίχου δροίτης*). In the second play, the *Choephoroi*, Orestes and Electra, Agamemnon's children, build up their courage to kill Clytemnestra and Aegistheus by describing the death of their father. In line 491 Orestes calls to mind the bath (*λουτρῶν*) in which he was slain. In lines 492 and 494 Electra describes the robe in which he was entangled, in each case calling it metaphorically a fishnet (*ἀμφίβληστρον*; *καλύμμασιν*). The final description comes in lines 973–1006 of the *Choephoroi*. Here Orestes stands over the bodies of Clytemnestra and Aegistheus, whom he has just slain, and displays the garment in which his mother had entangled his father, describing her as a poisonous eel or serpent (lines 994–96). Then in a remarkable series of lines (997–1004) he describes the garment, likening it to an animal trap, a shroud for a corpse, a bath curtain, and a snare used by a highway robber.

It is clear that we are dealing in these plays with more than an ordinary murder, if any murder can be called ordinary. In fact, this is much more like the kinds of human sacrifices that we have seen in other Indo-European traditions. The entangling robe or garment can be viewed as the equivalent of the noose. Its description frequently contains the metaphor or simile of a fishnet, and some passages even indicate that it might actually be some kind of netted garment or cloth. At any rate, it serves the purpose of binding the victim just as the noose does. The bathtub too is no ordinary one but is much more like a sacrificial vessel, being described as silver sided and in one passage even being called by the name of a basin for holding purifying water (*Agamemnon* 1129: *λέβητος*). Even the image of Clytemnestra as a serpent, which occurs throughout the trilogy,[16] may be related to the snakebite element that is found in modern European folktale versions of the threefold death. Orestes, in fact, in *Choephoroi* 246–51, uses a simile to compare himself and his sister Electra to the orphaned children of an eagle father, helpless in the coils of a deadly viper. In many of the modern folktale versions of the threefold death the victim is bitten by a snake while seeking bird nests in a tree. We might also note here the fact that in the medieval Welsh version Lleu is transformed into an eagle upon receiving the blow from Gronw's spear as he emerges from his bath.

There can be no doubt that Clytemnestra considers her murder of Agamemnon to be a sacrifice.[17] After she has killed him she states that her deed was done in revenge for the sacrifice of Thyestes' children by his brother Atreus, Agamemnon's father (*Agamemnon* 1497–1504), and for Agamemnon's sacrifice of his own daughter Iphigeneia (*Agamemnon* 1521–29). Before Clytemnestra kills Agamemnon, she invites Cassandra to enter the palace and stand at the altar to partake of the ceremony (*Agamemnon* 1036–38). When Cassandra refuses, Clytemnestra states that she will waste no further time with her, as the sheep are standing at the altar (*Agamemnon* 1055–58). Later she tells the chorus that when she struck the third and final blow, she gave thanks to Hades, Lord of the Dead (*Agamemnon* 1385–87). A few lines later (1432–33) she states that she sacrificed (*ἔσφαξ'*) Agamemnon to her daughter Iphigeneia's Justice, Wrath, and Fury (*Δίκην, Ἄτην Ἐρινύν θ'*). These passages strikingly recall the character of the god Odin, who also underwent a threefold sacrifice (to himself) and was lord of the dead warriors and associated with wrath and fury.[18] There is little doubt, then, that Agamemnon's death must be viewed as a sacrifice. It is furthermore an Indo-European tripartite sacrifice, involving symbols for each of the three functions. The bath is clearly connected with a ritual object, the sacrificial vessel, and hence with the priestly aspect of the first or sovereign function. In fact, as Yoshida has shown,[19] cups and vessels in general tend to be associated with the first function in Greek tradition. The sword that kills Agamemnon is obviously connected with the second or warrior function. The entangling robe, as a symbol of wealth and luxury, a product of feminine handicraft, and metaphorically related to the subsistence activity of fishing, must be connected with the third or fertility function. Hanging as such was rare in Greek tradition, but when it did occur it was generally as a means of suicide used by women. Examples would be the suicide of Cleite, discussed earlier as a third-function death, the suicide of Oedipus's mother Iocasta in remorse for having committed incest, and the attempted suicide of Clytemnestra herself (*Agamemnon* 874–76) after despairing of ever seeing Agamemnon return alive from Troy. All of these instances show that hanging generally has a third function character in Greek tradition. Thus the symbols of drowning and hanging (entanglement) have a meaning in the story of Agamemnon's death that is the reverse of their usual meaning in Germanic and Celtic tradition, where they are connected with the third and first functions, respectively. Until we have more evidence for the threefold death pattern in ancient Greece and other Indo-European peoples, we cannot say whether the Celtic and Germanic pattern of ascribed values for each type of death is typical of all the Indo-Europeans or not.

If Agamemnon's death is related to the Indo-European threefold death pattern, it should be the fulfillment of a prophecy. Evidence for such a prophecy is abundant. First, in a general sense the murder is a partial fulfillment of the curse of Thyestes on the house of Agamemnon's father Atreus, who served up a sacrificial feast to Thyestes of his own children.[20] Thyestes' curse does not specify the manner of Agamemnon's death. It is specified, however, in the vision of Cassandra, a genuine prophetess, who says in *Agamemnon* 1125–29:

> See there, see there! Keep from his mate the bull.
> Caught in the folded web's
> entanglement she pinions him and with the black horn
> strikes. And he crumples in the watered bath.
> Guile, I tell you, and death there in the cauldron wrought.[21]

There is also an ironic premonition of the manner of Agamemnon's death in an earlier passage (lines 866–72) where Clytemnestra tells how the many rumors of Agamemnon's death kept her in a state of continual worry for the last ten years. She states:

> Had Agamemnon taken all
> the wounds whereof the tale was carried home to me,
> he had been cut full of gashes like a fishing net.
> If he had died each time that rumor told of his death,
> he must have been some triple-bodied Geryon
> back from the dead with threefold cloak of earth upon
> his body, and killed once for every shape assumed.

Not only does a fishnet simile occur here as it does elsewhere in the play in connection with the entangling robe, but we also have here an indication that Clytemnestra has a threefold death in mind for her husband. As if to heighten the irony of the fishnet simile, she follows this passage immediately with a statement that she tried many times to commit suicide by hanging but was always saved by her attendants (lines 874–76).

If Agamemnon's death is a ritual sacrifice, it can also be seen as a criminal execution. We have already noticed how in Germanic tradition executions were similar to human sacrifices and how the punishment was often made to fit the crime. It should be no surprise, then, that Agamemnon's triple execution is connected with a threefold crime involving sins against each of the three Indo-European functions. These three crimes or sins are incorporated into the structure of Aeschylus's *Agamemnon* by being described, respectively, in each of the first three choruses that occur in the play before Agamemnon's arrival home. The first chorus (lines 40–257) describes Agamemnon's sacrifice of his daughter Iphigeneia at Aulis in order to obtain wind for the Greek ships sailing to Troy. The chorus calls him sacrilegious (line 220: *ἄναγνον, ἀνίερον*), an indication that this is a crime against the religious aspect of the first or sovereign function. The second chorus (lines 355–488), after condemning Paris's abduction of Helen, tells how Agamemnon caused so many young Greek warriors to be killed over an unfaithful woman and describes the anger of the citizens over the loss of their loved ones. It would appear that Agamemnon is accused here of a crime against the second function by carrying the warrior role to an extreme. The third chorus (lines 681–809) begins with a denunciation of the adulterous Helen and all the grief she caused to both the Greeks and Trojans. Then, after associating Helen with wealth and beauty (lines 741–43), the chorus proceeds to denounce wealth and those who seek to accumulate it. The implication here seems to be that Agamemnon has been immoderate in pursuing wealth (i.e., sacking Troy) and seeking to recover the beautiful Helen. The last part of the third chorus is a welcoming speech to the returned Agamemnon. In it the chorus admits that it had been angry with him for marshalling the army "for Helen's sake" (line 800: *Ἑλένης ἕνεκ'*). Hence Agamemnon has sinned against the third function, which is concerned with wealth and fecundity. The three choruses, then, depict Agamemnon as a trifunctional sinner and prepare us for his tripartite punishment.[22]

It is highly unlikely that Aeschylus was the inventor of the motif of the threefold death as fulfillment of a prophecy, for it occurs elsewhere in Indo-

European tradition and in forms which are so different that they could not possibly be derived from Aeschylus's version. Instead, the traditions of Odin, Agamemnon, and the complex of Celtic legendary and later European folktale versions must go back to a common original Indo-European form of the motif. Aeschylus or his source must have been familiar with a version of this motif and adapted it to the death of Agamemnon. That Aeschylus should have used an Indo-European theme in this manner should not be at all surprising, for, as Strutynski has suggested,[23] Aeschylus used another important Indo-European theme, the conflict between the forces of the third function and those of the first and second combined, elsewhere in this same dramatic trilogy, in the *Eumenides*. As an adaptation of this sort Aeschylus's use of the threefold death motif is extraordinarily successful. The motif has a central organizing role in the play *Agamemnon*, shaping not only the manner of Agamemnon's death but also the prophecies leading up to it, the motivation for Clytemnestra's act as punishment for the three sins of her husband, and the imagery of the eagle, the serpent, and the fishnet, which pervades the entire trilogy.[24] A knowledge of Aeschylus's use of the threefold death motif, then, is a great aid in our understanding of the structure and meaning of his play. His use of this motif is also a great aid for our understanding of the threefold death in general. Not only does it help to confirm the fact that this motif is Indo-European, but it makes clear the relationship of the threefold death to human sacrifice and the Indo-European tripartite ideology. To a great extent all of the other Indo-European traditions of threefold death are brought closer together by Aeschylus's account of the death of Agamemnon.

Notes

Earlier versions of this paper were read at the Annual Meeting of the California Folklore Society at Pitzer College, Claremont, California, on April 24, 1977, and at the University of California, Los Angeles, on June 1, 1977. I would like to express my appreciation to Jaan Puhvel, Udo Strutynski, and Patrick Ford for their helpful criticism.

1. Dumézil summarizes the evidence for this ideology in *L'Idéologie tripartie des Indo-Européens*, Collection Latomus, vol. 31 (Bruxelles: Latomus, 1958). The development of Dumézil's ideas on comparative Indo-European mythology is discussed in C. Scott Littleton, *The New Comparative Mythology: An Anthropological Assessment of the Theories of Georges Dumézil*, rev. ed. (Berkeley: University of California Press, 1973).

2. Donald Ward, "The Threefold Death: An Indo-European Trifunctional Sacrifice?" in *Myth and Law among the Indo-Europeans*, ed. Jaan Puhvel, Publications of the UCLA Center for the Study of Comparative Folklore and Mythology, no. 1 (Berkeley: University of California Press, 1970), pp. 123–42.

3. Ibid., pp. 134–35.

4. Atsuhiko Yoshida, "Piasos noyé, Cléité pendue

et le moulin de Cyzique: Essai de mythologie comparée," *Revue de l'histoire des religions* 168 (1965): 155–64.

5. Ward, pp. 123–34.

6. James L. Sauvé, "The Divine Victim: Aspects of Human Sacrifice in Viking Scandinavia and Vedic India," in *Myth and Law among the Indo-Europeans*, pp. 176–77; Georges Dumézil, *Gods of the Ancient Northmen*, ed. and trans. Einar Haugen, Publications of the UCLA Center for the Study of Comparative Folklore and Mythology, no. 3 (Berkeley: University of California Press, 1973).

7. Georges Dumézil, *From Myth to Fiction: The Saga of Hadingus*, trans. Derek Coltman (Chicago: University of Chicago Press, 1973), pp. 127–53.

8. Georges Dumézil, *The Destiny of the Warrior*, trans. Alf Hiltebeitel (Chicago: University of Chicago Press, 1970), pp. 82–95.

9. Jeannine E. Talley, "The Threefold Death in Finnish Lore," in *Myth and Law among the Indo-Europeans*, pp. 143–46.

10. Robert L. Fisher, Jr., "Indo-European Elements in Baltic and Slavic Chronicles," in *Myth and Law among the Indo-Europeans*, pp. 157–58. I am indebted to Jaan Puhvel for further explication of this material.

11. Ward, pp. 135–42.

12. I am indebted to Patrick Ford for supplying this reference to me.

13. Antti Aarne and Stith Thompson, *The Types of the Folktale*, FF Communications no. 184 (Helsinki: Suomalainen Tiedeakatemia, 1964), p. 329. Actually there are three relevant motifs listed in Stith Thompson, *Motif-Index of Folk-Literature*, rev. ed. (Bloomington: Indiana University Press, 1955–58), 3:233; 5:55. (1) F901.1 Extraordinary threefold death: falling from rock and tree, drowning; (2) F901.1.1 Extraordinary threefold death: wounding, burning, drowning; and (3) M341.2.4 Prophecy: threefold death.

14. Rolf Wilh. Brednich, *Volkserzählungen und Volksglaube von den Schicksalsfrauen*, FF Communications no. 193 (Helsinki: Suomalainen Tiedeakatemia, 1964), pp. 138–45.

15. Ward, pp. 139–42.

16. Anne Lebeck, *The Oresteia: A Study in Language and Structure* (Washington, D.C.: Center for Hellenic Studies, 1971), pp. 13–16.

17. On this point see ibid., pp. 60–63.

18. E. O. G. Turville-Petre, *Myth and Religion of the North* (New York: Holt, Rinehart & Winston, 1964), pp. 35–74.

19. Atsuhiko Yoshida, "Sur quelques coupes de la fable grecque," *Revue des études anciennes* 67 (1965): 31–36.

20. Hugh Lloyd-Jones, "The Guilt of Agamemnon," *Classical Quarterly*, n. s. 12 (1962): 187–99.

21. This and the following translation are taken from Richmond Lattimore, trans., *Aeschylus I: Oresteia* (Chicago: University of Chicago Press, 1953).

22. Although Agamemnon is not treated here as an Indo-European "warrior" figure, his sins have a striking resemblance to the pattern of the three sins of the warrior, particularly the example of Starkad who killed his king in a mock sacrifice conducted for the purpose of gaining wind for the fleet of ships, failed to act like a proper warrior by displaying cowardice in battle, and committed murder in an excessive pursuit of wealth (see Dumézil, *The Destiny of the Warrior*). David J. Cohen has recently added the Irish Suibhne Geilt to the list of Indo-European thrice-sinning warriors in "Suibhne Geilt," *Celtica* 12 (1977): 113–24. Suibhne's murderer Grag, as noted earlier, suffers a threefold death. This link between the careers of Suibhne and Grag seems to offer further evidence for a relationship between the patterns of threefold sin and threefold death. D. A. Miller makes a less convincing attempt to view Agamemnon's murderer Aegistheus as a triple sinner in "A Note on Aegisthus as 'Hero,'" *Arethusa* 10 (1977): 259–68.

23. Udo Strutynski, "The Three Functions of Indo-European Tradition in the 'Eumenides' of Aeschylus," in *Myth and Law among the Indo-Europeans*, pp. 211–28.

24. Lebeck, pp. 8–16, 33–34, 63–68. It is perhaps worth pointing out that these three images correspond to the natural domains of air, earth, and water discussed earlier in connection with hanging, death by a weapon, and drowning.

PART 4

INDIA

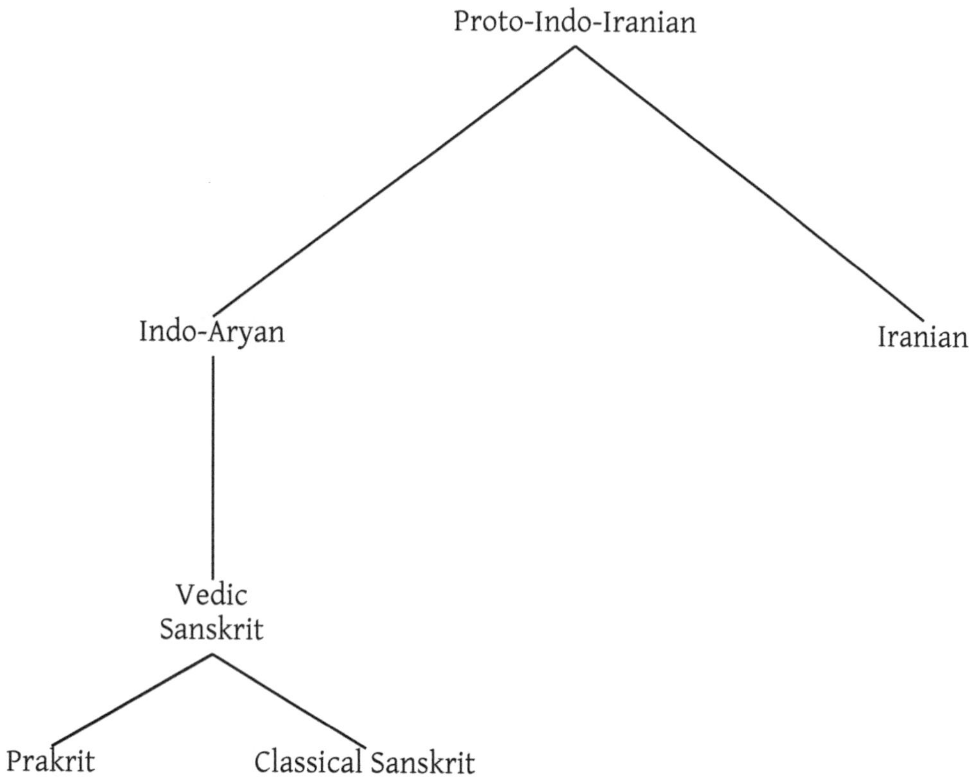
Proto-Indo-Iranian
Indo-Aryan
Iranian
Vedic
Sanskrit
Prakrit
Classical Sanskrit

16. Cities and Communities

In this work examining social relations within and between ancient Indo-European groups, Benveniste explores various terms denoting "people" and related notions. He begins with languages of the Western aspect of the Indo-European speech area in antiquity and then works his way east. The greater part of his investigation focuses upon Indo-Iranian, especially upon the meaning of the thorny Indic term ārya *and its Iranian cognate* arya, *from which are derived, for example, the name of the Indo-Iranian deity Aryaman and the name of the modern Persian state, Iran.* (RDW)

CITIES AND COMMUNITIES

Émile Benveniste

The Western dialects of Indo-European (Celtic, Italic, Germanic, Baltic) have preserved the word *teutā, *derived from a root* *tew- *'to be swollen, powerful', to designate 'the people' as a full development of the social body. Quite naturally, this term, which supplied national ethnics among the Germans* (Teutoni, deutsch) *acquired the opposite meaning when Slavic borrowed it from German: Old Slav.* tŭždĭ *means 'stranger'.*

The Greek pólis *and the Latin* civitas, *which were closely linked in the development of Western civilization, provide a good illustration of the phenomenon of convergence in institutional expressions: nothing could be more different at the outset than the old Indo-European word for 'citadel' (cf. Gr.* akró-polis*) and the Latin derivative* civitas *'the whole body of citizens'.*

Arya, *which signifies 'people' (= my people) in Indic and was the source of the name of Iran* (< aryānām) *is the common ancient designation of the 'Indo-Iranians'. Isolated in Iranian,* arya *can be analysed in Sanskrit as a derivative from* arí; *the latter seems to designate, in contrast to the stranger, the man of my people; perhaps more precisely, the relation by marriage, the member of the other exogamic moiety.*

We have analysed, by means of the terms which express it, the condition of the free man, born and integrated within a society and enjoying full rights that belong to him by birth.

But how does this man imagine the society to which he belongs and how can we form a picture of it ourselves? Do we know of a 'nation', dating from the time of the Indo-European community, which is designated by a single and constant term? How far could an aggregate of tribes conceive of itself as a political entity and call itself a nation?

Let us state straight away that there is no term, from one end of the Indo-European world to the other, which designates an organized society. That is not to say that the Indo-European peoples did not evolve this concept; we must guard against concluding that a deficiency in the common vocabulary implies the absence of the corresponding notion in the dialectal prehistory.

In fact there are a whole series of terms which encompass the whole extent of territorial and social units of varying dimensions. From the beginning these territorial organizations appear to be of great complexity, and each people presents a distinct variety.

There is nevertheless a term which is attested in the Western Indo-European world over a considerable area. In Italic, excluding Latin, this term is represented by the Umbrian word *tota*, which means 'urbs' or 'civitas', 'town' or 'city'. In the great lustration ritual called the Iguvine Tables, which contain a detailed list of sacrificial rites, processions, and prayers, carried out in order to secure the favours of the gods for the city and territory of Iguvium, the formulae *totaper iiouina, tutaper ikuvina*, 'for the city of Iguvium' often recur. No distinction is made between the town and the society: it is one and the same notion. The limits of the habitation of a given group mark the boundaries of the society itself. Oscan has the same word in the form *touto* 'city' and Livy (xxiii, 35, 13) tells us that the supreme magistrate in Campania was called *meddix tūticus* 'iudex publicus'.

We find **teutā* also in Celtic, in Old Ir. *tuath* 'people, country', in Welsh *tud* 'country' (Breton *tud* 'people') and in the Gaulish proper names *Teutates, Teutomatus*, etc.

The corresponding term in Germanic is Gothic *þiuda,* Gr. *éthnos* (ἔθνος), 'people, nation'; an important term because of its date and because it is constant from the oldest Germanic text onwards, important also because of its extent and persistence. <We have seen above (p. 246)> its important derivative *þiudans* 'chief'. From the Old High German form *deot*, German '*Volk*', there was formed by means of the very frequent suffix *-isc-*, the adjective *diutisc* (transcribed in Middle Latin as *theodiscus*), which developed to German *deutsch*. This derivative at first designated the language of the country, the popular language as opposed to the learned language, Latin; then it became the ethnic for a part of the German people. Those who called themselves 'those of the people', to be understood as 'those of the same people as we, those of our community'. Another ethnic formed from the same root is *Teutoni*. It is as well to note that, in the evolution which has produced the ethnic *deutsch*, it was the language to which this description first applied. A curious testimony to the peculiarity of use survives in the shape of the German word *deuten*, which is traced to the same origin as *deutsch*. In fact *deuten*, Old High German *diuten*, comes from a Germanic **þeudjan*, a verb derived from *þeudō-* 'people'; its meaning would then have been 'to popularize, to make accessible to the people' (the message of the Gospels), then generally 'to explain, interpret'.

In this dialectal area Baltic is also included; Lith. *tautà* 'people, race', Old Prussian *tauto* 'country'. Here Old Slavic shows an interesting divergence *vis-à-vis* Baltic, both in the form and the sense of the adjectives *tŭždĭ* and *štŭždŭ*, which signify 'foreign' (Russian *čužoj*). In reality the Slavic forms which represent **tudjo-* and **tjudjo-* do not come from an inherited root; they are derivatives from a Germanic loanword, and this explains the sense of 'foreign'.

It is easy to understand, says Meillet, that an adjective coined from a foreign word signifying 'nation' should become the word for 'stranger'; the Germanic nation was for the Slavs the foreign nation *par excellence*: the *němĭcĭ*, that is the dumb, the *βάρβαρος*, is the German. It is incidentally curious that Lettish *tauta* at an early date meant mainly a foreign people.[1]

Thus the form and sense of Slavic *tŭždĭ* confirms that the term **teuta* characterized the Germanic peoples, in particular in the eyes of the neighbouring Slavs.

Apart from Italic Celtic, Germanic and Baltic, it seems that we must include Thracian and Illyrian among the languages which possessed the word **teutā* to judge by the Illyrian proper names *Teutana, Teuticus*, Thracian *Tautomedes*, a fact which extends this lexical area towards Central and Eastern Europe. But contrary to a widely-held view, we must exclude the Hittite *tuzzi-*, which signifies 'camp', and refers only to the army. Some scholars proposed a different solution and traced back to **teutā-* the Latin adjective *tōtus* 'entire, all'. This connexion has a certain appeal, for it would relate the notion of 'totality' to that of 'society'; it is all the more attractive because another adjective meaning 'all', Skt. *viśva-*, Av. *vispa-*, has been adapted to *viś-* 'tribe'. But this origin for *tōtus* is not admissible except at the cost of a number of indemonstrable hypotheses: (1) that the ō of *tōtus*, instead of the expected **tūtus* is to be explained as a dialect form; (2) that the feminine **teutā* directly produced in Latin an adjective **teutus*, which later disappeared without a trace, whereas in the language in which **teutā* remained alive, it never produced a derivative indicating totality. Thus this affiliation is hardly probable. It seems that *tōtus* must be connected in Latin itself with *tōmentum* 'stuffing' and that the first sense of *tōtus* was, more vulgarly, 'stuffed full, compact', which developed to 'complete, entire'.

The formation of the social term **teutā* is clear. It is a primary abstract in *-*tā* made from the root **teu*- 'to be swollen, mighty'. This root was very productive. Notably, it has given rise in Indo-Iranian to the verb 'to be able', Av. *tav*-, and numerous nominal forms with the same sense. Sanskrit *tavas*- 'strength', *taviṣī*- 'might', Old Persian *tunuvant*- 'mighty', etc.; **teutā* may therefore be explained roughly as 'plenitude', indicating the full development of the social body. An analogous expression is found in Old Slavic *plemę* 'tribe' (Russ. *plemja* 'tribe, people'), which is derived from the root **plē*- 'to be full', like Gr. *plêthos* 'crowd', and perhaps Latin *plebs*.

The group of dialects which have **teutā* (Celtic, Germanic, Baltic, Italic) form a continuous zone in Europe, from which Latin and Greek are excluded to the south and East Slavic, Armenian and Indo-Iranian to the east. This dialect distribution apparently implies that certain ethnical groups, those which were to become the Indo-Iranians, Latins and Hellenes, had become separated from the community before the term **teutā* came into use among a certain number of peoples who became established in the centre and west of Europe. In fact in Latin, Greek and Indo-Iranian different terms are in use to denote the respective societies.

We must take the Greek term *pólis* (*πόλις*) and Latin *civitas* together. Intrinsically they have nothing in common, but history has associated them first in the formation of Roman civilization, in which Greek influence was paramount, and then in the elaboration of modern Western civilization. They are both the concern of a comparative study—which has not yet been attempted—of the terminology and political phenomenology of Greece and Rome. For our purposes two points must be stressed: the Greek *pólis*, even in historical times, still shows the sense of 'fortress, citadel', as Thucydides said: 'the *akrópolis* (citadel) is still today called *pólis* by the Athenians' (II., 15).' This was the prehistoric sense of the word, to judge by its Vedic correspondent *pūr* 'citadel' and Lithuanian *pilìs* 'castle, stronghold'. We have thus here an old Indo-European term, which in Greek, and only in Greek, has taken on the sense of 'town, city', then 'state'. In Latin things are quite different. The word for 'town' *urbs* is of unknown origin; it has been conjectured—but without proof—that it may come from Etruscan. But it is a fact that *urbs*, in the sense of 'town', is not correlative with the Greek *pólis*, but with *ástu* (*ἄστυ*); its derivatives came to have senses which were calques of the corresponding Greek word, e.g. *urbanus* 'of the town' (as opposed to *rusticus* 'of the country'), which came to mean 'fine, polished' after the Greek *asteîos*. To correspond to Gr. *pólis*, Latin has a secondary term *civitas*, which literally indicates the entire body of *cives* 'fellow-citizens'. It follows that the connexion established in Latin between *civis* and *civitas* is the exact reverse of that shown in Greek between *pólis* 'city' and *polítēs* 'citizen'.[2]

In the principal eastern group of Indo-European, in Indo-Iranian, a term of quite a different kind may represent the notion studied here, but in the ethnic aspect rather than the political one: this is *ārya-*, which was at first a social qualification before becoming the designation of the community; it was in use both in India and in Iran from the earliest records.

All terms of an ethnic character were in ancient times differential and oppositive. The names which a people gives itself expresses, either clearly or otherwise, the intention of setting itself off from neighbouring peoples; it affirms that superiority inherent in the possession of a common, intelligible language. This is why the ethnic often forms an antithetic pair with the opposed ethnic. This state of affairs is due to the little noticed difference between modern and ancient societies with regard to the notions of war and peace. The relation between peace and war was once exactly the reverse of what it is today. For us peace is the normal condition, which is interrupted by a state of war; for the ancients, the normal state was war, to which peace puts an end. We have little understanding of anything about the notion of peace and of the vocabulary which designates it in ancient society, if we do not grasp that peace intervenes as a sometimes accidental and often temporary solution to a quasi-permanent state of hostility between towns and states.

The problem of the word *ārya* is of interest because, in the region defined as Indo-Iranian, it is a designation which free men apply to themselves as opposed to slaves, and also because it is the only word which comprises a common nationality, that of those whom we must call 'Indo-Iranians'.

For us, there are two distinct entities, India and Iran. But seen in the light of evolution from the Indo-European parent language, the distinction between 'India' and 'Iran' is inadequate. The word 'India' has never been used by the inhabitants of the country; whereas the Iranians do call themselves 'Iranians'.

This difference is due precisely to the uneven survival, as between one region and the other, of the ancient word *ārya*. The Greeks, to whom we owe our knowledge of India, themselves first knew India through the mediation of Persia. An evident proof of this is the form of the root *India* (Ἰνδία), generally *Indikḗ* (Ἰνδική), which in fact corresponds to the name of the river and of the province called 'Indus', Skt. *Sindhu*. The discordance between the Greek and the Sanskrit is such that a direct borrowing of the indigenous form is out of the question. On the contrary, everything is explained if the Persian *Hindu* was the intermediary, since the initial *h*- corresponds regularly to *s*- in Sanskrit, while the Ionian psilosis accounts for the root *ind*- (ἰνδ-) with loss of the initial aspirate. In the Persian inscriptions of Darius, the term *Hindu* only applies to the province which is today called *Sindh*. Greek usage has extended this name to the whole country.

The Indians, at an early date, gave themselves the name of *ārya*. This form *ārya* is used in Iranian territory as an ethnic term. When Darius lists his ancestry, 'son of Vištāspa, grandson of Aršāma', he adds, to characterize himself, *arya ariyačissa* 'Aryan of Aryan stock'. He thus defines himself by a term which we would now express as 'Iranian'. In fact it is *arya*- which, in the genitive plural form *aryānām*, evolved in a more recent phase of Persian to the form *ērān*, later *īrān*. 'Iranian' is thus the continuation of ancient *ārya* in Persian territory proper.

Very far away, towards the Northwest, enclosed by peoples of Caucasian speech, there is an Iranian enclave in the shape of a people called *Ossetes*, descendants of the ancient *Alani*, who were of Sarmatian stock. They represent the survival of the ancient Scythian peoples (Scythians and Sarmatians) whose territory once comprised the whole of south Russia as far as Thrace and the Balkans. The name of *Alani* goes back to **Aryana*-, which is yet another form of the ancient *ārya*. We have thus a proof that this word is an ethnic description preserved by several peoples belonging to the 'Iranian' family.

In Iranian, *arya* is opposed to *anarya* 'non-*arya*'; in Indic *ārya* serves as the antithetic form to *dāsa*- 'stranger, slave, enemy'. Thus the term confirms the observation made above that there is a fundamental difference between the indigenous, or the 'self', and the stranger.

What does *ārya* mean? This is a very difficult problem which is seen in all its complexity if it is given its place in the Vedic vocabulary; for *Arya* is not isolated in Sanskrit, as it is in Iranian (where it appears as a word not amenable to analysis, serving only to describe those who belong to the same ethnic group). We have in Vedic a coherent series of words, proceeding from the form which is at once the most simple and the most ancient one, *arí*; the group comprises no fewer than four terms: *arí* with its thematic derivatives *árya* and *aryá*, and fourthly, with lengthening of the root vowel, *ārya*. The difficulty is to distinguish these forms by their sense and to recognize their relationship. The basic term, *arí*, presents itself in so confused and contradictory a way that it admits flatly opposed translations. It is applied to a category of persons, sometimes only to one, designated sometimes in a friendly and sometimes in a hostile way. Often the author of the hymn decries the *arí*, from which we may conclude that he regards him as his rival. However, the *arí* as the singer offers sacrifice, distributes wealth; his cult is addressed to the same gods with the same ritual gestures. This is why we find *arí* translated in the dictionaries by 'friend' and by 'enemy' concurrently.

The German Indologist, P. Thieme, devoted a detailed study to this problem in 1938; it is entitled *Der Fremdling im Ṛgveda*, because at the end of a long analysis, the author believes he can translate the root *arí-* as 'stranger'. The two contradictory senses 'friend' and 'enemy' may be compared, he suggests, to the two senses of **ghosti-*: on the one hand Lat. *hostis* 'guest', Got. *gasts* 'guest', on the other Lat. *hostis* 'enemy'. Similarly, *arí* is 'the stranger, friend or enemy'. Based on *arí*, the derivative *arya* would signify 'he who has a connexion with a stranger', hence 'protector of the stranger', German *gastlich* 'hospitable', and also 'master of the household'. Finally, from *arya-* the secondary derivative *ārya* would literally mean 'belonging to the guests'; hence 'hospitable'. The *ārya* called themselves 'the hospitable ones' thus contrasting their humanity with the barbarism of the people who surrounded them.

Following this study, there appeared from 1941 on, a number of works by M. Dumézil, who proposed other interpretations, which tend to establish the social sense and then the ethnic sense of this family.[3]

On the whole our views are close to those of Dumézil. But it will not be possible to justify them here in detail. The examples involve, for the most part, detailed questions of Vedic exegesis, and the discussion would require a whole book of its own. We shall limit ourselves to a few observations and a summary definition.

In such matters, philological criteria must not run counter to intrinsic probabilities. To define the Aryans as 'the hospitable ones' is a thesis remote from all historic reality; at no time has any people whatsoever called itself 'the hospitable ones'.

When peoples give themselves names, these are divided, as far as we can understand them, into two categories; if we exclude names of a geographical character, they are either (1) an ethnic consisting of a complimentary epithet, e.g. 'the valiant', 'the strong', 'the excellent', 'the eminent' or (2) most often they simply call themselves 'the men'. If we start with the Germanic *Ala-manni* and follow the chain of peoples, whatever their origin or their language, to Kamchatka or the southern tip of South America, we encounter peoples by the dozen who call themselves 'the men'; each of them thus presents itself as a community of the same language and the same descent, and implicitly contrast themselves with neighbouring peoples. In a number of connexions we have occasion to insist on this character which is peculiar to many societies.

In these circumstances to imagine that a people, in this case the Aryas, called themselves 'the hospitable ones' would run counter to all historical probability. It is not in this way that a people affirms its individuality vis-à-vis its neighbours, who are always presumed to be hostile. <We had already seen (above, p. 81f) that> the relationship of hospitality is not established either between individuals or between groups except after the conclusion of a pact under special circumstances. Each time a specific relation is established. It is thus inconceivable that a people should proclaim itself as 'the hospitable ones' in general and towards everybody without distinction. We must always determine by precise contexts the original sense of institutional terms such as 'hospitality', which for us has only a moral or sentimental sense.

Without going into the details of the very numerous examples, the exegesis of which is sometimes difficult, we may stress certain features which help us to define the status of the *arí* or the *arya*.

The connotations of the word *arí*, which are sometimes favourable and sometimes unfavourable, do not affect the true sense of the word. It designates a man of the same people as the one who speaks about him. This man is never considered as the member of an enemy people, even if the singer is enraged with him. He is never confused with a barbarian. He takes part in all the cults, he receives gifts which the singer may envy him, but which put him on the same footing. He may be generous or avaricious, friendly or hostile—it is always a personal hostility. At no time can we perceive that the *arí* belongs to a different ethnic group from the author of the hymn.

Further, the *arí* are often associated with the *vaiśya*, that is to say the members of the third social class, which confirms that the *arí* is not a stranger. There is more precise testimony to the social position of the *arí* in the complaint of the daughter-in-law of Indra (*Rig Veda* X, 28, 1): 'All the other *arí* have come (to the sacrifice); only my father-in-law has not come'. Indra is thus counted among the *arí* of his daughter-in-law. If we took the expression in the most literal sense, we should conclude that the *arí* formed the other moiety in an exogamic society. Nothing contradicts this inference, and some facts seem to confirm it. In this way we could understand why the *arí* are sometimes in a relationship of friendship, sometimes of rivalry, and that they together form a social unit: the expression 'all the *arí* (or *ărya*)', often recurs in the *Rig Veda*; it is also known in the Avesta, so that it is an inherited item of Indo-Iranian phraseology.

We must also pay attention to the name and role of the god *Aryaman*, who belongs to the Indo-Iranian pantheon. This name is a compound of *arya-man-* 'of the spirit of *arya*'. Now the god Aryaman in Vedic mythology establishes friendship and, more particularly, he is the god of marriages. For the Iranians, too, Aryaman is a friendly god, but in the different guise of a healer. As a noun, *aryaman-* in the Zoroastrian Gāthās, designates the members of a religious confraternity. In the Persian proper name *Aryarāmna* 'who gives peace to the *arya*', we again find the communal sense of *arya*.

Altogether, we can disentangle from the brief mentions and often fleeting allusions in the Vedic texts some constant features which enable us to form a probable idea of what the word meant: the *arí* or *arya* (we cannot always distinguish the two forms) form what was doubtless a privileged class of society, probably entering into the relation of exogamic moieties, and maintaining relationships of exchange and rivalry. The derivative *ārya*, which at first designated the descendants of the *arí* (or the *arya*), indicated that they belonged to the *arí*, and it soon came to serve as a common denominator for the tribes who recognized the same ancestors and practised the same cults. These comprise at least some of the components of the notion of *ārya*, which among both the Indic people and the Iranians, marks the awakening of a national conscience.

It remains to determine what the stem of *ari, arya-* properly signifies, and to decide whether the form *ari-* belongs to the Indo-European vocabulary or whether it is limited to Indo-Iranian. Scholars have often suggested that *ari* may be connected with the prefix *ari-*, which in Sanskrit denotes a degree of excellence and may correspond to the Greek prefix *ari-* (ἀρι-), which also indicates excellence; and since this Greek prefix *ari-* probably connects up with the group of *áristos* 'excellent, supreme' this would suggest for *ari-*, *arya-* some such sense as 'eminent, superior'. But these etymological connexions are far from certain. In any case, to return to our point of departure, the idea of mutual behaviour (whether friendly or hostile) is more strongly felt in the uses of *ari-*, *arya-* than any suggestion of eulogy. Only a more profound analysis based on new facts would permit us to make any pronouncement on the etymology.

Notes

1. Meillet, *Etudes sur l'étymologie et le vocabulaire du vieux-slave*, Paris, 1902–1905, p. 175.
2. This point is developed in an article contributed to a collection of *Mélanges* offered to C. Levi-Strauss.
3. Theses and antagonistic interpretations: on the one hand, P. Thieme, *Der Fremdling im R̥gveda*, 1938; *Mitra und Aryaman*, 1958; on the other, G. Dumézil, *Le troisième souverain*, 1949; *L'idéologie tripartie des Indo-Européens*, 1958, p. 108ff.

17. Rig Veda *1.32*

Indra, the preeminent warrior deity of ancient India, is praised again and again in the Rig Veda *for his destruction of the cattle-thieving, drought-bringing dragon called Vṛtra (meaning 'resistance'). While the* Rig Veda *often alludes to the feat, commonly through the use of Indra's epithet of Vṛtrahan ('slayer of Vṛtra'), only in hymn 1.32 is the deed rehearsed in any sort of detail. The dragon-slaying motif is not unique to India but occurs broadly across the ancient Indo-European world. What is the function of this widespread myth with primitive Indo-European roots? Calvert Watkins puts it this way in his masterful work,* How to Kill a Dragon *(1995, Oxford University Press, p. 299): "The dragon symbolizes Chaos, in the largest sense, and killing the dragon represents the ultimate victory of Cosmic Truth and Order over Chaos"; and again (p. 300), "The dragon symbolizes finally everywhere the chaos of destruction, the threat to life and property, the ravager of man and beast, which we find formulaically expressed . . . in a variety of traditions throughout the Indo-European world."*

Wendy Doniger O'Flaherty here provides a lively, annotated translation of the hymn of the heroic dragon slayer Indra. Curiously, after the doing of his doughty deed, Indra flees in fear. Indra has his less heroic side, as we shall see. (RDW)

THE KILLING OF VṚTRA

Translated by Wendy Doniger O'Flaherty

1 Let me now sing the heroic deeds of Indra, the first that the thunderbolt-wielder performed. He killed the dragon and pierced an opening for the waters; he split open the bellies of mountains.

2 He killed the dragon who lay upon the mountain; Tvaṣṭṛ[1] fashioned the roaring thunderbolt for him. Like lowing cows, the flowing waters rushed straight down to the sea.

3 Wildly excited like a bull, he took the Soma for himself and drank the extract from the three bowls in the three-day Soma ceremony.[2] Indra the Generous seized his thunderbolt to hurl it as a weapon; he killed the first-born of dragons.

4 Indra, when you killed the first-born of dragons and overcame by your own magic the magic of the magicians, at that very moment you brought forth the sun, the sky, and dawn. Since then you have found no enemy to conquer you.

5 With his great weapon, the thunderbolt, Indra killed the shoulderless Vṛtra, his greatest enemy. Like the trunk of a tree whose branches have been lopped off by an axe, the dragon lies flat upon the ground.

6 For, muddled by drunkenness like one who is no soldier, Vṛtra challenged the great hero who had overcome the mighty and who drank Soma to the dregs. Unable to withstand the onslaught of his weapons, he found Indra an enemy to conquer him and was shattered, his nose crushed.

7 Without feet or hands he fought against Indra, who struck him on the nape of the neck with his thunderbolt. The steer who wished to become the equal of the bull bursting with seed, Vṛtra lay broken in many places.

8 Over him as he lay there like a broken reed the swelling waters flowed for man.[3] Those waters that Vṛtra had enclosed with his power—the dragon now lay at their feet.

9 The vital energy of Vṛtra's mother ebbed away, for Indra had hurled his deadly weapon at her. Above was the mother, below was the son; Dānu[4] lay down like a cow with her calf.

10 In the midst of the channels of the waters which never stood still or rested, the body was hidden. The waters flow over Vṛtra's secret place; he who found Indra an enemy to conquer him sank into long darkness.

11 The waters who had the Dāsa[4] for their husband, the dragon for their protector, were imprisoned like the cows imprisoned by the Paṇis.[4] When he killed Vṛtra he split open the outlet of the waters that had been closed.

12 Indra, you became a hair of a horse's tail when Vṛtra struck you on the corner of the mouth. You, the one god, the brave one, you won the cows; you won the Soma; you released the seven streams so that they could flow.

13 No use was the lightning and thunder, fog and hail that he[5] had scattered about, when the dragon and Indra fought. Indra the Generous remained victorious for all time to come.

14 What avenger of the dragon did you see, Indra, that fear entered your heart when you had killed him? Then you crossed the ninety-nine streams like the frightened eagle[6] crossing the realms of earth and air.

15 Indra, who wields the thunderbolt in his hand, is the king of that which moves and that which rests, of the tame and of the horned.[7] He rules the people as their king, encircling all this as a rim encircles spokes.

Notes

1. Tvaṣṭṛ is the artisan of the gods, sometimes an enemy of Indra (cf. 4.18) but here his ally.

2. Cf. 10.14.16.

3. Manu was the eponymous ancestor of mankind; the verse may refer to the waters that flowed at the time of the great flood, when Manu alone was saved, or to the waters that flowed for the sake of mankind at the time of the piercing of Vṛtra (cf. 1.165.8). The latter seems more likely—or both at once.

4. Dānu is the mother of Vṛtra and of other demons called Dānavas; Dāsa is another name for Vṛtra and also, in the sense of 'slave', for other human and demonic enemies of Indra; the Paṇis are a group of such enemies, said to have stolen and penned up the cows until Indra released them (see 3.31 and 10.108).

5. 'He' is Vṛtra, trying his magic in vain against Indra's (cf. v. 4).

6. Possibly the eagle (Indra in disguise) that stole the Soma (4.26–7).

7. According to Sāyaṇa, the 'tame' are animals that do not attack, such as horses and donkeys, while the 'horned' are fierce animals like buffaloes and bulls.

18. Indra the Sinner
and
The Sins and Losses of Indra

In part 2, we encountered Dumézil's analysis of Heracles as the Greek expression of the Indo-European warrior who sins against each of the three realms of society. India likewise knows such a sinner, inherited from the common Indo-European culture that is ancestral to Greeks and Indo-Aryans alike: he is the warrior god Indra, contends Dumézil, the very god lauded for his slaying of the monstrous serpent Vṛtra. Indra's three sins are the slaying of a three-headed monster (Triśiras, the "Tricephal") called Viśvarūpa—said to be a Brahmin among the gods and the cousin of the gods—with the assistance of one Trita Āptya (first-function sin); the cowardly murder of his former demonic opponent, the asura *Namuci, with whom he had made a pact of friendship (second-function sin); and the seduction of Ahalyā, wife of the Brahmin Gautama (third-function sin).*

This role of the war god as sinner finds little expression in the collection of hymns that is the Rig Veda*, that most ancient of Sanskrit documents; though the* Rig Veda *makes an apparent cursory reference to Indra having killed his own father (*RV *4.18.12). In "Indra the Sinner," Dumézil addresses this silence. In the* Brāhmaṇas*, commentaries on the* Vedas*, and the epics, the* Mahābhārata *and the* Rāmāyaṇa*, however, Indra the sinner is depicted. Dumézil rehearses a particular expression of Indra's three sins in "The Sins and Losses of Indra" and explores ancient connections made between these sins and the persons of the sons of Pāṇḍu, heroes of the* Mahābhārata*.* (RDW)

INDRA THE SINNER

Georges Dumézil

In the *Brāhmaṇa* and the Epics, Indra is a sinner. He is not, however, so designated in the *ṚgVeda*. Hanns Oertel's efforts (1898)[1] to discover, in some passages from the hymns, a trace of censure, an allusion to what is later to be denounced as criminal or shocking, have come up with nothing convincing.

From *The Destiny of the Warrior* by Georges Dumézil, 1970. Reprinted by permission of The University of Chicago Press.

When *R̥gVeda* 6.47.16–17 shows Indra sometimes inclined to help one person and sometimes another, abandoning his initial friends to take new sides, we need only refer to the context in order to understand that what the poet senses here is simply a manifestation, which he registers with neither blame nor complaint, of the *independence*, the necessary and wholesome *autonomy*, of the warrior god.[2] It is mere artifice to see here, as does Oertel, the breaking of the word which we encountered, on the level of the Brāhmaṇa, in the story of Namuci.

When *R̥gVeda* 6.46.3 calls Indra *sahasramuṣka*, "of a thousand testicles," this epithet surely alludes to the supervirility which every people readily attributes to its human and divine warriors: the songs of soldiers, century after century, continue to draw together the diverse offices of the male, just as the Avestan Vərəθragna, the god called upon for victory—in part homologous to Indra Vr̥trahan—is also invoked to obtain *ərəzōiš xå̄, fontes testiculorum*. But here there is no reason to look, as Sāyaṇa does, for a precise reference to the sexual sins, the adulteries, of Indra which the epic literature will expose with such relish.

As to 5.34.4, the verse probably does not say what Oertel and many others have tried to make it say. The symmetry induces one to translate the *kílbiṣāt* of the last verse as an objective ablative, referring not to a fault of Indra, to which there will be no echo in the remainder of the hymn, but to the fault of a man with whom Indra, despite this fault, enters into a relationship. Accordingly, the meaning gains in both force and beauty:

> From the one, whose father or mother or brother he, the strong one, has killed, from that one he does not remove himself; making an arrangement, he seeks even his offerings. From the fault he does not remove himself, he, the giver of boons.[3]

"From the fault" means "from the guilty party." The intention of this verse as of the entire strophe is to remind us that Indra, in contrast, for example, to Varuṇa, keeps no tight accounts, acknowledges no blind paths of justice. He is not held back in his relations with men at that point where the two sovereigns must check themselves perforce. This strong god, who upon occasion kills (that is his mission), is ready to become reconciled with the sons or brothers of his victims; and he does not automatically excommunicate the sinner.

There remains, in the hymn of Indra's painful "births" (4.18), the famous verse in which it is said that he killed his father (str. 12, v. 4). This would be grave indeed, if only we knew what was involved. But this dreadful crime has caused very little commotion, which seems strange when one thinks of the zeal of the Brāhmaṇa and epics in spreading the worst and least of rumors about Indra. Moreover, in the strophe where it is mentioned, the crime is presented under such conditions that it comes out incoherent, nonsensical. One is strongly tempted to adjust the person of the verb: by changing a single letter, one will fall back on a theme of story and novel that is recognizable and clear, that of the future hero—such as Batraz of the Ossets—persecuted at his birth in every way and, in particular, left an orphan. The poet, full of commiseration, asks the unfortunate infant:

> Who has made your mother a widow?
> Who wished to kill you, lying still or moving?
> Which god was compassionate with you . . .[4]

and then adds, in the fourth verse, against every expectation:

> . . . when you seized your father by the feet and caused him to perish?

The strangeness of this last question is more than obvious: by what right can this child who has committed the worst of murders expect the pity of the gods? A paternal persecution, a sequence of the same type as that of the Ouranides, has been supposed, but that is gratuitous. The question initially posed in the first verse suggests rather that the persecutor "who has made your mother a widow" is unrelated to the family and that the father has been the victim of the same enemy or enemies as the mother and child. The strangeness disappears if, in the fourth verse, it is "someone" who killed his father, as, in the second verse, "someone" wished to kill Indra himself. We need only read *ákṣinan* (3d. plur.), "they [the enemies] caused to perish," or *ákṣināt* (3d. sing.), "he [the persecutor designated by the "who" of verses 1 and 2] caused to perish" in place of *ákṣināḥ*, "you caused to perish." Whatever scruples one may have about tampering with the Vedic textual tradition, one must sometimes resign oneself to doing so.[5]

Thus, in the *R̥gVeda*, Indra has no criminal record. But let us not rush to proclaim him innocent, or to conclude that the fuss made about his sins must come from later times. Though Oertel does not succeed in his quest, he does at least, from the first page, wisely perceive its reduced importance.

> If the Vedic hymns offer but little material of this kind, this fact is simply due to the character of these poems. They are invocations and songs of praise—*nahī́ nv àsya mahimā́nam indriyáṁ svàr gr̥ṇánta ānaśúḥ* (*RV* 8.3.13)—in which allusions of this sort would be manifestly out of place. An argumentum ex silentio would therefore here be patently wrong.

That is entirely true. The Vedic poets could hardly give a bad role to the very god they considered most useful, of such usefulness as is attested quite adequately by statistics alone. Courageously, as good servants, they would rather have assumed his more questionable responsibilities along with him. <One example of this attitude has been shown in the earlier part of this book.> In all later literature, the murder of the Tricephal entails a strain. The monster is at once both a brahman, chaplain of the gods, from a tradition that is probably post-Vedic, and the gods' first cousin, a feature that is certainly archaic. Now we have seen how the *R̥gVeda* mentions only a single time, and with a light touch only, with a single word, those social relations between the murderer and the murdered that make the slaying juridically questionable. Indra, according to 2.11.19, has delivered into Trita's hands the son of Tvaṣṭr̥, the son of "the one united [with him] by bonds of friendship," *sākhyásya*. One seeks in vain, if one examines the context, for any trace of blame: it is for our sake, for us men, *asmábhyam*—in the person of Trita—that Indra has performed this delivery, and if the poet recalls it, it is to ask the god to continue the good work, as the inverted syntax of the phrase does indicate: "May we be able to triumph, to conquer all enemies, the barbarians, with your aid, with the arya [that is, probably, with you, the god of the arya], us unto whom you have formerly delivered . . ., etc." When one makes one's addresses to the divine striker, one cannot dictate the manner in which he strikes.

Having explained the *R̥gVeda's* silence, and by the same token eliminated the objection which one might draw from it as to the antiquity of the representation of Indra's sins, one can only share Oertel's observation on the extent and importance which come to be attached to the theologem of Indra the Sinner, and even to the systematization of his sins, when we come to the *Brāhmaṇa* and the ritual treatises. Indeed, the authors have arranged his faults in lists which, with slight variations, can be found in the texts of various schools, and which allude to adventures which we know of only in part. Oertel cites *AitareyaBrāhmaṇa* 7.28:

> When the gods shunned Indra, saying: "He hath intrigued against Viśvarūpa, Tvaṣṭr̥'s son [that is, the Tricephal]; he hath slain Vr̥tra; he hath given the Yatis to the sālāvr̥ka-wolves; he hath killed the Arurmaghas; he hath interrupted Br̥haspati," then was Indra excluded from the soma-draught.

In *KauśitakīUpaniṣad* 3.1, it is Indra himself who classifies his misconduct:

> I killed the three-headed son of Tvaṣṭr̥; I gave the Arunmukhas, the Yatis to the sālāvr̥ka-wolves; transgressing many a covenant [*bahvīḥ saṃdhā atikra-*

> *mya*], I smote in heaven the Prahlādīyas, in the atmosphere the Paulomas, on earth the Kālakāñjas.

To these Oertel added a long passage (2.134) from *JaminīyaBrāhmaṇa*, that precious text from which he then published many extracts and made a special study:

> The creatures condemned Indra, saying: "He hath killed the three-headed son of Tvaṣṭṛ, he hath given the Yatis to the sālāvṛka-wolves, he hath killed the Arurmukhas, he hath interrupted Bṛhaspati, transgressing the covenant he had covenanted [*saṃdhāṃ saṃhitām atītya*] he cut off the head of the asura Namuci." From these sins against the gods [*etebhyo devakilbiṣebhyaḥ*] he walked away into the forest not descending [?] to the gods. He said to the gods: "Perform a sacrifice for me." "No," they said, "these agreements thou hast transgressed, thou hast committed those sins against the gods. We will not perform a sacrifice for thee." Now Agni might have been called his best friend; so among the gods he spoke to Agni: "Sacrifice for me." "Yes," he said, "but I desire some one among the gods with whom I may sacrifice for thee." He did not find any among the gods with whom he might sacrifice for him. He said: "I cannot find any one among the gods with whom I might sacrifice for thee." "Then do thou alone sacrifice for me." "Yes." Agni by himself succeeded. He performed this *agniṣṭut*. With that he sacrificed for him. With it he at once burned away all his [Indra's] evil. As a serpent would get rid of its skin, as one would pull the blade of the reed-grass out of the sheath, even so he got rid of all his evil.

This text is interesting in many respects, especially because it says in its own way that only fire could cleanse, could atone for this career in which sins were mingled with services. Here we have an optimistic version of what is also the lesson, with different nuances, of the pyre of Heracles, the burning of the impious Tullus by the bolt of Jupiter, and, in Iranian tradition, the moving dialogue with the god Fire, by which Zoroaster, in the other world, obtains pardon for Kərəsāspa,[6] the Iranian Hercules.

Even more than the *Brāhmaṇa*, the epic will also obligingly take note of the sins of the god Indra. But a particular type of sin comes to take on increased importance: the sexual sin, adultery, and especially adultery committed by seduction, surprise, or deception with the wife of a brahman. The prototype for this regrettable sin is surely the god's adventure with Ahalyā. Of this the *Brāhmaṇa* have little to say, but here again the *argumentum ex silentio* cannot be trusted; as early as 1887, Albrecht Weber remarked that in certain important ritual formulas, those by which the soma sacrifice is announced on a fixed day to the gods (*subrahmaṇyā*) and which, in particular, refer to Indra by a series of vocatives that allude to his qualities or his adventures, the following salutation is to be found: *Ahalyāyai jāra, Kauśika brāhmaṇa, Gautama bruvāṇa*, "spouse for Ahalyā, brahman Kauśika, named Gautama." It is thus certain that in the definitely early period when this ritual was fixed, the story of Ahalyā was known: wife of the brahman Kauśika Gautama, she was approached by Indra, as Alcmene was by Zeus when the god passed himself off as her husband. If the *Brāhmaṇa* do not incorporate this into the canonical list of the god's sins, one reason, at least, can be found. As sacerdotal literature, in contrast to epic, it would probably seek to avoid drawing attention to a type of conduct declared sinful yet glorified by an august divine example, which could easily establish an awkward precedent for the powerful of this world. It seems that one of the concerns of the brahman caste from its very beginnings as a caste, as can be seen from *R̥gVeda* 10.109, has been to protect its women from the schemes of princes and warriors.

Even if we did not have the evidence provided by the *subrahmaṇyā* formulas, we could scarcely doubt the antiquity of this type of excess: the warrior everywhere takes liberties with the codes by which the *seniores* seek to discipline the ardor of young men, everywhere lays claim to "unwritten rights" to other men's wives, to maidenly virtue. Stig Wikander, in the first two chapters of his *Der arische Männerbund* (1938), established that even in Indo-Iranian times this sexual note clung to the conception of the *márya*, "young man of the second function," and that it counted for a great deal in the condemnation thrust upon the *márya* by the Zoroastrian reform (Avestan *mairya*, Pehlevi *mērak*).[7] In other parts of the Indo-European world, on the level of legend, let us recall the rape of the Vestal Ilia by Mars, of Lucretia by the soldier Tarquin, the scandals which fill the histories of the Scandinavian *berserkir*, the *contubernales* of King Frotho (Saxo Grammaticus 5.1.11),[8] and the innumerable bastards sired by Heracles.

Notes

1. "*Indrasya kilbiṣāṇi*," *Journal of the American Oriental Society* 19:118–25.

2. <See above, pp. 61–62.>

3. Karl F. Geldner's version: "Der Mächtige geht dem nicht aus dem Wege, dessen Vater, dessen Mutter, dessen Bruder er erschlagen hat. Er fordert sogar noch Geschenke von ihm, wenn er Vergleich macht. Er scheut vor keinem Unrecht zurück, der Verschenker des Gutes."

4. Geldner: "Welcher Gott fand Gnade vor dir . . . ." This interpretation of *te* appears to contradict the attitude of the gods toward Indra as indicated in the second verse of the preceding strophe, well rendered by Geldner (the words of the infant

Indra's mother): "Mein Sohn, jene Götter lassen dich im Stich." Moreover, everywhere else in the *RgVeda*, the gods are givers, not beneficiaries of *mārdīká*, "pity, favor, grace" (root *mr̥d-* "to pardon, to spare, to be favorable").

5. One could object to these considerations on the grounds that, on the contrary, we should keep *ákṣiṇāḥ*, since it is the *lectio difficilior*. If one chooses this alternative, the fact remains that no other passage in the hymnal mentions the parricide of Indra, and the enormous crime appears in none of the lists of Indra's sins recorded in Vedic prose literature.

6. Henrik S. Nyberg, "La légende de Kərəsāspa," *Oriental Studies in Honor of Cursetji Erachji Pavry* (1933), pp. 336–43; in the first text published

(*Dēnkart* 9, analysis of *Sūtkar Nask*, 14), Kərəsāspa repents of "having killed men without number"; but his principal sin, for which Ōhrmazd reproaches him and the god Fire demands the punishment of hell, is having "struck the fire."

7. After numerous discussions, often misdirected, this interpretation of *márya*, like the general thesis of the book, has gained credence: Manfred Mayrhofer, *Kurzgef. etym. Wörterbuch des Altindischen* s.v., 2 (1957): 596–97. Louis Renou, who in *Études védiques et pāṇinéennes* 4 (1958): 49 justly defined *márya* "terme mi-érotique mi-guerrier" (for *RV* 8.54.13), was less inspired when he deleted the second element in ibid., 10 (1962): 64 (for *RV* 1.64.2).

8. <See below, pt. 3, chap. 4 at n. 9.>

THE SINS AND LOSSES OF INDRA

Let us now turn our attention to a relatively recent text, in which the theory of Indra's sins appears in a remarkable form: book 5 of the *MārkaṇḍeyaPurāṇa*.

At the beginning of this Purāṇa, Jaimini, a disciple of Vyāsa, seeks out Mārkaṇḍeya to get him to resolve some difficulties concerning the *Mahābhārata*. The sage refers him to certain birds, as famous for their intelligence as for their sacredness, and so it is that, in the fourth section, we learn of the four points which trouble Jaimini about the great epic: What led Janārdana, or Viṣṇu, to assume human form? How did Kr̥ṣṇā, or Draupadī, become the common wife of the five Pāṇḍava brothers, the principal heroes of the poem? How was Baladeva, or the third Rāma, the brother of Kr̥ṣṇa, expiated for the murder of a brahman? How could the sons of Draupadī all die before being married? By the end of the fourth section we are enlightened as to the incarnations of Viṣṇu, and the fifth takes up the truly delicate problem of the polyandric marriage of Draupadī.[1]

I have already alluded to Stig Wikander's memorable article published in 1947, "The Legend of the Pāṇḍava and the Mythical Basis of the Mahābhārata," and its important findings.[2] These five brothers, engendered successively by the functional gods in the wombs of the two wives of Pāṇḍu, have an ordered relationship of their own, forming a hierarchized functional team. In numerous epic passages their respective modes of behavior, whether they are acting alone or together, offer an excellent definition of the three functions which are at the base of the Vedic, Indo-Iranian, and Indo-European ideology. Thus, in total independence of the system of *varṇa* or strict social classes (brahmans, kṣatriya, vaiśya)—which is an essentially Indian development, a hardening of the social structure around the principle of the three functions—and with traits that are almost more Iranian, in any case more Indo-Iranian, than Vedic (for example, the role of Vāyu within the warrior function, which is very nearly effaced in the *Veda*), vast sections of the *Mahābhārata* present themselves as a series of variations on the theme of the three functions and as a projection on the human plane, in heroic adventures, of the ideology which gave life to that grouping of gods which is like an axis for the Indo-Iranian pantheon: the sovereigns Mitra-Varuṇa, the warriors Vāyu and Indra, and the beneficent twin Nāsatya.

Yudhiṣṭhira, the eldest, is the son of Dharma, "Law, Order," a rejuvenation of the concept of Mitra. Of the five, he alone is king, a thoroughly just and virtuous king.

Next come two warriors of very different natures: Bhīma, son of Vāyu, "the wind," is a brutal and not very intelligent Hercules, one who acts readily on his own, armed with a simple mace, but above all sustained by his colossal force; Arjuna, Indra's son, is the warrior-knight, leader of the army, master of the bow and of all classic weapons.

The group is completed by a pair of twins, Nakula and Sahadeva, sons of the twin Nāsatya; beautiful, amiable, servitors devoted to their brothers, they are also, as a characteristic episode demonstrates, specialists in the care of cattle and horses.

We have only begun to take stock, for the interpretation of the *Mahābhārata*, for the history of Indian thought, for the detailed analysis of the Indo-Iranian ideology, and even, by contrast or by analogy, for the study of the Persian Book of Kings, of the consequences of this discovery, which, now that it has been made, looks easy and obvious, but which no one had made before Wikander.[3] As to the shocking nature, from the *arya* standpoint, of the figure of Draupadī, the common wife of the five brothers, Wikander immediately succeeded in proposing the first simple and satisfactory explanation. In Indo-Iranian mythology, to judge from the Vedic and Avestan materials that have been conserved, the team of the functional gods is completed by a single goddess, who ideologically is not confined to any of the three functions, but is situated, and operates, within them all. Her nature is thus synthetic, as is probably signified by the curious triple name which the *Avesta* gives such a goddess: "The Humid (third function), the Strong (second), the Pure (first)," Arədvī Sūrā Anāhitā.[4] The Indian epic has expressed this fundamental idea dramatically, on the human plane, by matching the trifunctional team of the five Pāṇḍava with a single woman, their common wife.

It is this archaic theory of the three functions, expressed in the group of Pāṇḍava, which we are now about to see the *MārkaṇḍeyaPurāṇa* connect and adjust to the theory of the sins and punishments of Indra, presenting the latter at the same stroke in a systematic and trifunctional form. Here follows the literal version of the text, hardly poetic but tightly constructed, which I have divided into its natural sections, indicating the numbers of the twenty-four distichs.

I. (A) *The First Sin*

1 Once, when he had killed the son of Tvaṣṭṛ [that is, the Tricephal], oh brahman, the majesty [*tejaḥ*] of Indra, overpowered by this brahmanicide, underwent a considerable diminution;

2 It entered the god Dharma, this majesty of Śakra [= Indra], because of this fault; and Śakra found himself deprived of majesty [*nistejāḥ*], when his majesty went over into Dharma.

(B) *The Second Sin*

3 Then Tvaṣṭṛ, lord of creatures, learning that his son had been killed, tore out one of the chignons he wore as an ascetic, and said:

4 Let the three worlds with their divinities today see my force! Let him see it, the brahmanicide of evil thoughts, the punisher of the demon Pāka [= Indra],

5 by whom my son, devoted to his duty, has been killed!" Thus having spoken, eyes red with anger, he placed his chignon on the fire as an offering.

6 Out of that Vṛtra, the great asura, came forth, amidst garlands of flames, with great stature and enormous teeth, comparable to a mass of ground collyrium.

7 Enemy of Indra, of immeasurable essence, fortified by the energy [or majesty: again *tejaḥ*] of Tvaṣṭṛ, he grew each day the length of a bowshot, he, the being with the great force.

8 Seeing that Vṛtra, this great demon, was destined to kill him, Śakra, wishing for peace, sick with fear [*bhayāturaḥ*], sent the seven sages to him,

9 who, between him and Indra, made friendship [*sakhyam*] and agreements [*samayān*], they, the sages of pious soul, devoted to the welfare of all beings.

10 When, in violation of the agreement [*samayasthitim ullaṅghya*], Vṛtra had been killed by Śakra, then, overwhelmed by the murder [he had committed], his physical force [*balam*] declined.

11 This physical force, having escaped from Indra's body, entered Māruta [another name for the Wind, Vāyu] who penetrates all, invisible, the supreme divinity of physical force [*balasya . . . adhidaivatam*].

(C) *The Third Sin*

12 And when Śakra, having assumed the appearance [*rūpam*] of Gautama, had violated Ahalyā, then he, the Indra of the gods, was despoiled of his beauty [same word as for "form, appearance": *rūpam*]:

13 The gracefulness of all his limbs, which charmed so many souls, abandoned the tarnished Indra of the gods and entered the two Nāsatya.

II. *The World's Distress*

14 Having learned that the king of the gods was abandoned by his justice and his majesty [*dharmeṇa tejasā tyaktam*], deprived of physical force [*balahīnam*], and without beauty [*arūpinam*], the sons of Diti [demons] undertook to conquer him.

15 Desirous of conquering the Indra of the gods, the Daitya, extremely strong, oh great muni, took birth in the families of kings of immeasurable vigor.

16 Some time thereafter the Earth, oppressed by its burden, went to the summit of mount Meru, where the denizens of heaven have their abode.

17 Crushed by so much burden, she told them the origin of her suffering, caused by the Daitya, Danu's sons:

18 "These asura with vast strength, whom you had overthrown, have all come to be born in the world of men, in the houses of kings;

19 their armies are numerous and, oppressed by their weight, I am sinking down. See now, you thirty [= the gods], that I find relief."

III. *Birth of the Heroes*

20 Then, with portions of their energy [*tejaḥ*], the gods descended from the sky to the earth, for the service of creatures and to lift the burden from the earth.

(A) *21* The male [Dharma] himself set free the majesty [again *tejaḥ*] which had come to him from the body of Indra, and in Kuntī (the queen, Pāṇḍu's wife) he engendered the King, Yudhiṣṭhira of great majesty [*mahātejaḥ*].

(B, B′) *22* The Wind then set free the physical force [*balam*], and Bhīma was born; and from the half [the remainder] of the vigor [*vīryam*] of Śakra, Pārthi Dhanañjaya (or Arjuna) was born.

(C) *23* The pair of twins [*yamajau*] [Nakula and Sahadeva, engendered by the Nāsatya] came into the world in [the womb of] Mādrī [second wife of Pāṇḍu], endowed with Śakra's beauty [*rūpam*], adorned with great luster;

(D) *23* [In continuation] Thus the blessed Śatakratu [or Indra] descended [and incarnated himself, *avatīrṇaḥ*] in five parts,

24 and his most fortunate wife Kṛṣṇā [or Draupadī] was born from the Fire: [consequently] she became the wife of Śakra alone, and of no other.

Whoever the author and whatever the epoch when it was established, this complex account is admirably trifunctional.

The functional values of the five Pāṇḍava, recognized by Wikander, are covered here not only by the names of their divine fathers, but by abstract substantives which fittingly characterize the essence of each function: *tejas*, a somewhat vague term, taken even here with diverse connotations, but one which always indicates, in opposition to the force of the body, a power of the soul, correlates with the god and the hero of the first function, Dharma and Yudhiṣṭhira. Two varieties of physical force, *bala* and *vīrya*, the first certainly more athletic and brutal, are attributed to the two gods and the two heroes of the second function, Vāyu and Indra himself, Bhīma and Arjuna. And beauty, *rūpa*, comes from the pair of divine Nāsatya to adorn the human twins, Nakula and Sahadeva.

But these various elements, these powers whose harmonious incarnation produces the team of the Pāṇḍava, are only transmitted to the sons from the gods, their fathers. On their part, the gods have received them from a sort of three-staged disintegration of Indra, resulting from three sins. The substratum of the three functions can be discerned just as clearly in these three sins as in the three losses that follow them:

1. The loss of *tejas*, spiritual force or majesty, is provoked by a sacrilege and by an outrage against the social structure at its most exalted level: a *brahmanicide*.

2. The loss of *bala*, physical force, is provoked by a sin which, while remaining a breach of contract, is also considered *cowardly*, since the conclusion of the pact was provoked by fear before a superior force.

3. The loss of *rūpa*, beauty of form, is provoked by an *adultery* committed with the help of the shameful fraud of changing into another's form.

Brahmanicide, fear bringing about a dishonorable act, and adultery: the three sins, like their punishments, are situated respectively in the domains of the religious order, the warrior ideal, and well-regulated fecundity.

Given the literary genre in which it appears, one is inclined to see in this systematization of the faults of Indra a late arrangement, made by an intelligent author, of the older, less-organized traditions concerning Indra's sins. This is possible. But it must be acknowledged that if it was conceived in a period when Aryan India no longer meditated on the *functions* as such and knew only the guidelines of the three *social classes*, the arrangement still presents, on the third level, a conception that arises from the Indo-Iranian or Indo-European third function, and not from the third social class of India. By no Indian thinker was beauty thought of as characteristic of the class of breeders and agriculturists, the vaiśya, and, for that matter, neither was sensuality and the sins it entailed. In classical India, such men were defined solely by their planting and stock-raising activities. In contrast, in Indo-European times, and still in the Vedic period (the Aśvin were "masters of beauty"), the third function, along with opulence and fecundity, included other attributes, beauty and sensuality among them, with their own conditions and consequences.[5] These latter were not lost by the Scandinavian gods Freyr and Freyja; nor does the functional goddess Aphrodite neglect them in the well-known legend in which, as the competitor of Hera, giver of sovereignty, and of Athena, giver of victory, she offers Paris nothing less than "the most beautiful woman."[6] So in the Pāṇḍava legend, beauty, just as much as competence in matters of breeding and an aptitude for service, is the characteristic of the twins, a trait which, like the identity and importance accorded to the god Vāyu, roots this legend directly in the Indo-Iranian and Indo-European ideology. We must therefore suppose, at the very least, that the author of this late arrangement had exceeded the ideology of his contemporaries and reconstituted the rich "third function" of former times.

His treatment of the second sin, the violation of the pact concluded with Vṛtra (substituted here, as often in the epic, for Namuci), is no less archaic. It lends authority to one element that the ancient forms of the episode could not eliminate, since it is fundamental to them, but which they could scarcely proclaim: though Indra had concluded the initial agreement and this dubious friendship with the demon, instead of treating him at the outset as the warrior god must treat every demon, it was because he did not feel himself equal to the task, because he was afraid. All that follows is merely the result of this defect in the essential vocation of the warrior, in his force and his pure bravery. The author of our text makes this element explicit: at the very beginning of the scene, he says (distichs 8–9): "Seeing that Vṛtra, this great demon, was destined to kill him, Indra, wishing for peace, sick with fear, sent the seven sages to him, who, between him and Indra, made friendship and agreements. . . ." And Indra's punishment is exacted in the loss of this physical force, *bala*, in which, for once, he did not dare put his trust.

These archaic, even fossil-like treatments of the third and second level are better explained if we assume that the theme of the three sins that the warrior commits within the framework of the three functions already existed before the author of the Purāṇa applied it to Indra.[7]

As for the idea that guides this whole development, it too is ancient: the warrior, by his actual weaknesses, loses his virtual powers, and from these lost powers, new beings are born. In the story of Namuci, inasmuch as it is the myth that justifies the *sautrāmaṇī*, the *ŚatapathaBrāhmaṇa* presents an analogous disintegration, though it is only in the animal, vegetable, and mineral realms that the lost powers are productive, and not in terms of gods or men.[8]

In the *Avesta* a very similar theme can be found, but there it is applied not to a god or hero homologous to Indra—Vərəϑrağna or Kərəsāspa, for example—but to the complex, total, trifunctional personage of Yima, the most illustrious of the "first kings." Immediately after presenting Yima in his majesty and power, *Yašt* 19—the "*Yašt* of the Earth," actually almost entirely dedicated to the sovereign power, the *x^varənah*, a sign which may assume diverse forms, which appears on the prince designated by God, accompanies him in his actions, and leaves him when he has become unworthy—warns us, at the end of verse 33, that this good fortune will last only until Yima should begin to give himself over "to the deceitful, false world." Yima, indeed, sins gravely. One could even expect to see him commit three sins, since the *x^varənah* leaves him three times or, if we translate literally, since three *x^varənah* leave him in succession. This is not the case. There is never more than one sin: in the *Avesta*, it is the lie, the greatest sin of Mazdaism; in later texts, it is pride and revolt against God, or even the usurpation of divine titles, all sins against the rules and proprieties of the *first* function.[9] The consequences of the sins, however, are set in a triple structure; and this structure, in the two known variants, is as clearly trifunctional as that of the incarnations of Indra's lost powers.

According to *Yašt* 19.34–38, the first of the three *x^varənah* of Yima comes to reside in Miϑra, "the lord-of-land of all lands, which Ahura Mazdāh has made, of all the *yazata* of the world of spirits, the most suited for the *x^varənah*"; the second in Θraētaona, "son of the clan of the Āϑwya," who killed the Tricephal; the third in "Kərəsāspa of heroic soul," "the strongest of strong men," the Iranian Hercules, whose labors, here as so often, are obligingly enumerated. It is clear, as Darmesteter recognized, that Miϑra and Kərəsāspa represent the first and second functions respectively. The attribution of the third—agricultural prosperity—to Θraētaona raised a difficulty which Darmesteter began to alleviate, and which<, in the first part of the present book,> has been completely eliminated.[10] In any case, no such difficulty can be pointed to in the explicit affirmation of the second variant, from *Dēnkart* 7.1.25–32–36, which says that one third of Yam's *x^varr* (the Pehlevi form of Avestan *x^varənah*), related to agriculture, passed into Frētōn (Θraētaona), who immediately eliminated plague and sickness by medical treatment; one-third, relating to the warrior estate, passed into Karšāsp (Kərəsāspa); and one-third—that of the "sovereign function," although this time the word itself is not declared—passed into Ōšnar (Aošnara), who is presented in these terms (§§36–37; from the translation by Marijan Molé):

> In the same epoch it [= the "transmission of the word"] returned, thanks to the Glory [*x^varr*] of Yam, to Ōšnar who was very wise, when he was in the womb of his mother. Speaking from his mother's womb, he taught her several wonders. At his birth, he struck the Evil Spirit and refuted the propositions [*frāsnān*] of *mar* Fračya, worshipper of the *dēv*.

He became minister for Kayus and administered the seven continents under his dominion. He discovered [and] taught the art of ordering speech and several other sciences useful to men; and the non-Arya were defeated in debate. He lavished the wisest counsels in the lands of the arya.

It can be seen that the three functions are presented clearly, regularly, and in ascending order: the agricultural function and the warrior function are properly depicted and the first function is abundantly described, joining the faculty of intelligence with the science of administrative technique on the highest level, and also with certain more precise features of this class of "scribes," who often attempted to create an advantageous place for themselves on the social ladder. The test of intelligence in which the demon-debater is conquered by Ōšnar takes its place beside the Vedic practices attested, among the priests, by the important contests of enigmas, to which Louis Renou has recently drawn attention, and the ordeal by questions, in the *Mahābhārata*, to which Dharma, himself invisible, submits the Pāṇḍava, and to which, naturally, only his own son, "the Pāṇḍava of the first function," can respond.[11]

The plan and object of this legend accord well with the plan and object of the fifth book of the *MārkaṇḍeyaPurāṇa*. In both cases an eminent figure, a ṛṣi or a god, commits certain sins—one here, three there—which deprive him in three stages of the three factors of his eminence. And these factors are defined by the three fundamental functions: Yima loses three *x^{v}arənah*, or the three parts of his *x^{v}arənah*, one related to the sacred and the intelligence, one to the warrior force, and one to agriculture and health; Indra, for his part, first loses majesty or spiritual force, then physical force, and then beauty, as a consequence of his three sins—against the sacred, against bravery, and against the conjugal bond. But these factors of eminence are not lost: the three *x^{v}arənah*, lost by Yima, inspire three heroes; and the three advantages lost by Indra pass over into the functional gods who correspond to them, whereby, each in its turn, these advantages are enabled to engender the team of functional heroes in whom Indra finally, in fragmented form, is revived.

Notes

1. This text has been treated differently, from the viewpoint of Draupadī, and in connection with *Mbh* 1.189.1–40 (= Calcutta 197.7275–7318), in *ME* 1:103–24.

2. <See above, pt. 1, chap. 1, n. 1.>

3. This is the subject of the first part of *ME* 1:31–257.

4. <See above, pp. 16–17.>

5. In a scene, surely archaic, from the ritual of the *aśvamedha*, the Vedic horse sacrifice, the

cause-and-effect connection between beauty and fecundity is set forth clearly: *Śat.Brāhm.* 13.1.9.6; cf. *ME* 1:59 (and, for opulence and sensual gratification, p. 491 and p. 560, n. 2).

6. "Les trois fonctions dans quelques traditions grecques," *Eventail de l'histoire vivante = Mélanges Lucien Febvre* 2 (1953), pp. 25–32; now see *ME* 1: 580–86 and the parallel cases, pp. 586–601, and on a question of method, "L'idéologie tripartie, MM. W. Pötscher and M. van der Bruwaene," *Latomus* 20 (1961): 524–29.

7. See the passage from the first book of the *Mahābhārata*, <cited above, chap. 7, n. 1.>

8. See *Tarpeia*, p. 123.

9. In the third part of *ME* 2, I shall examine, going beyond the parallel described here, the record concerning the "sin of the sovereign," different from the "sins of the warrior."

10. <See above, pp. 17–19.>

11. *ME* 1:62.

19. Śiśupāla

Indra is not, however, the only triple-sinning warrior known in Indic tradition. This prehistoric Indo-European mythic figure also finds expression in Śiśupāla, the warrior who commands the army of Magadha, a rival kingdom that emerges as a threat to the Pāṇḍava king Yudhiṣṭhira, early in his reign. After the threat is neutralized by the slaying of Jarāsaṁdha, king of Magadha, a great ceremony of royal consecration is held on behalf of Yudhiṣṭhira, at which Kṛṣṇa, cousin and companion of the sons of Pāṇḍu, openly proclaims five atrocities that Śiśupāla has committed—sins that span the three functions of Indo-European society. The tale is told in Book Two of the Mahābhārata. (RDW)

ŚIŚUPĀLA

Georges Dumézil

The Birth and Destiny of Śiśupāla

Śiśupāla is, in the *Mahābhārata*, an incidental character.[1] Close kinship ties exist and hostile relations develop between him and Kṛṣṇa, but he has no blood relation nor alliance with the Pāṇḍavas, and does not have to intervene, on one side or the other, in the conflict in which all the great names of the epic confront each other; he is put to death beforehand in Book Two. Still, according to the rules of the game, this apparently wholly human being is the incarnation of a being from the beyond, the powerful demon who in several previous lives has already confronted other incarnations of Viṣṇu: Hiraṇyakaśipu, whom the god fought and slew in the guise of the man-lion; later Rāvaṇa, over whom Viṣṇu-Rāma prevailed with difficulty.[2] These antecedents barely enter into the plot of the poem, simply justifying that Śiśupāla should be by nature a determined adversary of Kṛṣṇa-Viṣṇu. But, in accord with another rule of transposition, this deep causality is replicated on the earthly level by another, more immediate and more novelistic one.

Śiśupāla is introduced in the following way. After their childhood, and despite their already serious conflicts with their cousins, the hundred sons of

Dhṛtarāṣṭra (and especially with the eldest, Duryodhana), the Pāṇḍavas have not as yet known their great misfortunes, as it is only at the end of Book Two, the *Sabhāparvan*, that Duryodhana's malice and Dhṛtarāṣṭra's weakness will arrange the fateful dice-game which, by fleecing Yudhiṣṭhira and his brothers and forcing them into thirteen years of exile, begins a conflict between the two groups of cousins that will be settled only in the bloody battle of the "field of the Kurus," *Kurukṣetra*, from Book Six to Book Ten. To all appearances, at the moment, things are on the way to turning out otherwise: Yudhiṣṭhira's rights to kingship seem to be recognized by everyone, including the blind uncle and the maniacal Duryodhana; he has received the first visit from his cousin Kṛṣṇa, who is none other than Viṣṇu incarnate (as Yudhiṣṭhira himself is either the son, or the incarnation of a portion of Dharma),[3] and Kṛṣṇa has begun the part which he will play throughout the poem, that of faithful, lucid, discreet and resourceful counsellor. Yudhiṣṭhira has been discussing with him the advisability of celebrating a *rājasūya*, the ceremony of royal consecration, or "sprinkling," here curiously conceived as an imperial ceremony, bestowing on the recipient not only royalty, *rāṣṭra*, but *sāmrājya*, "universal kingship" and *pārthivya*, "earthly sovereignty," implying in consequence recognition by all other kings of a more or less effective sort of supremacy.

A first obstacle has already been averted, or rather eliminated. Another prince, Jarāsaṁdha the king of Magadha, had launched the same claim to sovereignty as Yudhiṣṭhira, and had begun to back it up with cruelty and indeed barbarity, backed by the support of the god Rudra-Śiva. In the presence of Kṛṣṇa, on his advice and almost on his orders, two of Yudhiṣṭhira's brothers have disposed of this competitor under dramatic circumstances which we will examine later.[4]

Yudhiṣṭhira has then dispatched his four younger brothers to the four corners of the world to secure, and if need be to compel, the consent of the kings. Without much trouble these missions have succeeded and the kings have poured into Yudhiṣṭhira's capital to attend the ceremony and thus to confirm their allegiance. The Pāṇḍavas have before them truly a gallery of kings, seemingly well disposed, among them Vasudeva, accompanied by his son Kṛṣṇa, that is to say again, Viṣṇu incarnate.

Things get off to a good start, with the usual ceremonies of hospitality, particularly the *arghya*, the offering presented to the guests of honor. But very quickly there arises a serious problem, an unexpected quarrel which remotely recalls the Irish legends, where the "hero's portion" regularly provokes competitions and battles. In this case it has to do not with such a portion, but with a supplementary *arghya*, an *arghya* of excellence, which Bhīṣma (the great-uncle, tutor, and counsellor of the whole family of the Bhāratas, the sons of Dhṛtarāṣṭra and those of Pāṇḍu alike) proposes to offer to the most worthy of those present (1330). Yudhiṣṭhira agrees and asks Bhīṣma himself to designate the one to be so honored. Bhīṣma does not hesitate and responds, with good reasons: Kṛṣṇa (1332–1334). The assembled kings would surely accede to this award without grumbling when one of them rises and protests vehemently; it is Śiśupāla, the king of Cedi. He refuses to accept that, in an assembly of kings, a special honor should go to an individual who is not a king.

His protest rapidly occasions an ever more lively exchange of words and the old Bhīṣma, who has lived through three generations and harbors much knowledge, is led to explain to Bhīmasena, the second of the Pāṇḍavas who is not exactly well-informed and whom Śiśupāla has taken personally to task, who this spoilsport is, how he came into the world, what fate weighs upon him, and also why up to this moment Kṛṣṇa has shown so much patience towards him (1494–1522). The tale of his beginnings follows.

Śiśupāla was well-born in the royal family of the Cedis, the son of the reigning king. But he was born monstrous: he had three eyes and four arms (*tryakṣaḥ caturbhujaḥ*), and uttered inarticulate cries like an animal (1494). His distraught parents were all set to abandon him, *tyāgāya kurutām matim* (1495), when a disembodied voice, *vāg aśarīriṇī*, made itself heard to the king, his wife, and his assembled ministers. The voice said (1497–1498):

> "King, he is born your son, illustrious and powerful, therefore be not afraid of him, but guard your child anxiously. You are not to be his death, nor has this Time yet come. His death, his slayer by the sword, has been born, lord of men."

Hearing this speech which came from the invisible, *vākyam antarhitam*, the mother speaks, tormented by the affection she feels, in spite of everything, for this small monster, her son (*putrasnehābhisantaptā*) (1500–1501):

> "I bow with folded hands to him who has spoken this word concerning my son. Now let him also speak further. I want to hear who shall be the death of this son!"

Then the invisible being speaks again (1502–1503):

> "He upon whose lap his two extra arms will both fall on the ground like five-headed snakes and that third eye in the middle of the child's forehead will sink away as he looks at him—he shall be his death."

Thus the prophecy is twofold, but unambiguous: one day, placed in someone's lap, the monstrous child will lose his excesses, two arms and the central eye, and will become normal; but the Deliverer who will work this anatomical miracle will also later be the cause of his death.

Rumor of such a remarkable occurrence travels fast, and all the kings of the earth, drawn by curiosity, *didṛkṣavaḥ*, come to the country and the palace where it took place. The king of Cedi receives them all with honor and places his baby upon the lap of each, *ekaikasya nṛpasyāṅke putram aropayat tadā*, and on the knees of every single one, *pṛthak*, of these thousands of kings, *rājasahasrāṇām*, but the spectacle, the expected miracle never occurs, *śiśur aṅke samārūḍho na tat prāpa nidarśanam.*

So it goes until there arrive from the town of Dvāravatī, attracted by the reports, two princes, who have moreover excellent reasons for coming, since the small monster's mother is their paternal aunt. These two princes are the Yādavas Kṛṣṇa and his older brother Balarāma. They too are received with honor, and the queen personally has just placed her son on Kṛṣṇa's knees, *putram dāmoda-rotsaṅge devī saṃvyadadhāt svayam* (1510). Then finally, the miracle occurs (1511):

> ". . . No sooner was he placed on his lap than the two extra arms fell off and the eye in his forehead sank away."

Seeing this, the mother is troubled and begins to tremble (*vyathitā, trastā*), and understandably: according to the disembodied Voice, the man whose touch has worked this transformation will also be the *mṛtyu*, the (cause of) death of the small being restored to human form. She asks a favor of her nephew (1512–1513):

> "Give a boon to me, Kṛṣṇa, who am sick with fear, strongarmed one, for you are the relief of the oppressed and grant safety to those that are afeared!"

Kṛṣṇa answers (1514–1515):

> "Do not fear. . . . What boon must I give you, or what should I do, my aunt? Whether it can be done or not, I shall obey your word!"

Then the queen makes her appeal (1516):

> "Pray pardon, strong man, the derelictions of Śiśupāla!"

Kṛṣṇa answers (1517):

> "I shall forsooth forgive a hundred derelictions of your son, paternal aunt, even though they may be capital offenses. Do not sorrow."

Thus the fate of Śiśupāla was sealed. We shall soon learn that the account of these hundred offenses, the *aparādhāḥ* to be tolerated, is exhausted and even overdrawn. Released from the promise to his aunt, Kṛṣṇa will in the end be able to punish Śiśupāla.

Rudra, Kṛṣṇa and Śiśupāla

Before proceeding further, let us ponder this monstrous birth, this correction of shape and this boon linking *facinora* and longevity.

India is more familiar than Scandinavia with persons with extra arms, not only among babies, but adults as well, including the greatest of them—*caturbhuja* 'four-armed' is a frequent Hindu epithet of Viṣṇu as well as of Śiva, and there come immediately to mind the figures of Indian gods who seem to have more arms, all gracefully and symmetrically arrayed, than the Hydra of Lerna had heads. The *Mahābhārata* mentions other births of children, even quite human ones, with several arms, which occasion no such alarm nor grief. Here, the fear is immediate: the father and mother can think only of abandoning the infant, and would do so if the Voice of an unseen being did not intervene. We are faced with a peculiar case.

But this is not what is most important. Long ago it was noted that the second congenital deformity of the "little one," the third eye in the middle of his forehead, *lalāṭajaṃ nayanam*, clearly marks him as a human replica of Rudra-Śiva. It is this god, and he alone—and very early, if the epithet *tryambaka* means, at least by connotation, "having three pupils"—who enjoys the privilege of having three eyes, the third between the two normal ones in the middle of the forehead: *tricakṣus, tryakṣa* are epithets of Śiva.[5]

Along the same line it has been pointed out that the name of Śiśupāla, for which the *Mahābhārata* (1497) suggests an obviously postfabricated etymology,[6] is a transposition, to the level of the "small" (*śiśu-*), of the already Vedic epithet of Rudra, and frequently later of Rudra-Śiva, *paśupati; paśupati* is "lord of animals"; *śiśupāla* is "protector (and also "king, prince") of the small."

Finally, in a previous episode—which he himself recalls within the present one—Śiśupāla manifests a particular attachment, to the extent of being his "army chief," to King Jarāsaṁdha, who will occupy us later and who is presented as the favorite of Rudra-Śiva, endowed with the privilege of seeing Rudra-Śiva with his own eyes, and who offers kings in sacrifice to Rudra-Śiva.[7]

These reasons oblige us to conclude, as did John Muir more than a century ago (1864),[8] that Śiśupāla is, as solidly by nature as he is ephemerally in form, a hero "on the side of Rudra-Śiva," a transformation of this Rudra-Śiva whose own incarnation is another of the poem's fearsome heroes, Aśvatthāman.[9]

And this is of great interest because the one who delivers him from his superfluous arms and eye, and with whom he will nonetheless remain to the end in a state of violent hostility, is Kṛṣṇa-Viṣṇu, a god of a completely different sort. In more than one regard the "opposite" of Rudra-Śiva, he will even be, in the Hindu trinity, his polar partner. Śiśupāla is thus found, from his earliest youth, in contradictory relationships with the two great gods.

At the same time that, miraculously, by the mere touch of Kṛṣṇa-Viṣṇu, he is restored to human shape, Śiśupāla receives from the same Kṛṣṇa a true "fate," which by defining a postponement completes what the unknown Voice had imposed on him at birth. The Voice had said that death would come to him from his very normalizer, to be precise, that his normalizer "would be his death." When it is discovered that the normalizer is Kṛṣṇa-Viṣṇu, the latter undertakes to delay this death. He does not define the reprieve in terms of absolute or lived time, he does not say, for example, "a hundred years" or "three average human lives"; rather he sets down a kind of sliding scale which ties the young being's life span to his behavior: "I will tolerate, without killing him, a hundred offenses, *aparādhaśatam*, any of which would deserve death." This number can reassure the mother; even between people who hate each other, to commit a hundred offenses each of which merits death requires a certain amount of time, and especially since the interested party will be forewarned, it will be up to him not to exhaust his credit and to avoid overstepping the limit by a hundred and first offense. In fact it comes out in the episode of Book Two that Śiśupāla has wasted no time; he has carried on like a prodigal son, squandering his store of impunity, and he is still young when here, before us, he overdraws his account, by an offense which will bring on his death. It is no less remarkable that the boon granted him concerning the length of his life should be limited and conditioned by a counting of *aparādhāḥ*, that is, of *facinora* committed against someone.

A final remark will serve to tie together the two preceding statements. It is at the mother's request that Kṛṣṇa grants this gift to the baby, and by asking for it moreover in a very general way (to tolerate his offenses, without specifying a number) she shows that she has no doubt of the enmity that will prevail between normalizer and normalizee, the latter's aggressiveness being exerted consistently at the expense of the former. Has she recognized Rudra-Śiva in the one as she knows that the other is Viṣṇu? In any case, one could not wish for a better expression of the "conflict of divinities" which, from the foreordained immunity until the hundredth offense, will dominate the career of Śiśupāla.

The Offenses

Let us return to the biography of the hero. The texts are not prolix either about his exploits or his crimes: undoubtedly they were the subject of specific, well-known tales, and only allusions are made to them here. The exploits of Śiśupāla must have been numerous, since he commanded the armies of another king of whom it is said expressly that he had conquered a large part of the world (574):

> The mighty king Śiśupāla, having indeed gone over completely to this Jarāsaṁdha's side, has become his marshal (*senāpatiḥ*).

Regarding the hundred personal affronts deserving of death, *vadhārha* (1517), which Kṛṣṇa has undertaken to forgive, we do not have the complete list either. At the moment of the final settling of accounts, Kṛṣṇa gives merely a sampling of them, recalling only five, in five *ślokas*. All have been committed against members of Kṛṣṇa's family, the Yādavas, but in view of familial solidarity they ought to be considered as in effect directed against him and consequently charged to the current account of patience on which the offender keeps drawing (1516). What are these examples (1566–1572)?

> 1. "Knowing that we had gone to the city of Prāgjyotiṣa, this fiend, who is our cousin, burned down Dvārakā [= Dvāravatī, our capital], kings."
> 2. "While the barons of the Bhojas were at play on Mount Raivataka, he slew and captured them, then returned to his city."
> 3. "Malevolently, he stole the horse that was set free at the Horse Sacrifice and surrounded by guards to disrupt my father's sacrifice."

4. "When she was journeying to the country of the Sauvīras to be given in marriage, the misguided fool abducted the unwilling wife-to-be of the glorious Babhru."

5. "Hiding beneath his wizardry, the fiendish offender of his uncle abducted Bhadrā of Viśāla, the intended bride of the Karūṣa!

For the sake of my father's sister I have endured very great suffering; but fortunately now *this* is taking place in the presence of all the kings. For you are now witnesses of the all-surpassing offense against me; learn also now the offenses he has perpetrated against me in concealment."

It is easy to verify that these sample offenses are distributed, in the order II (first and second offenses), I (third offense), and III (fourth and fifth offenses), across the framework of the three functions, and constitute a new example of the theme of the "three sins of the warrior":

In 1 and 2, Śiśupāla, instead of fairly and openly giving battle, waits until he knows a king is absent to burn down his capital, and surprises *rājanyas* in the midst of disporting themselves to massacre or kidnap them: this cowardice is on the same level as that of the second sin of Indra and Herakles slaying an adversary by a foul trick, instead of confronting him in equal combat.

In 3, Śiśupāla attacks the king in the area of religion by preventing him from celebrating the most solemn of royal sacrifices.

In 4 and 5, Śiśupāla abducts a noble married woman—in 5, disguising himself as her husband—committing a sexual sin entirely similar to the third sin of Indra, and as serious as the third sin of Herakles.

The great similarity of the two first and the two last offenses makes it probable that this list has been inflated—India has little taste for conciseness—and that more originally each type of sin was illustrated by only one example. Taking this tack, it is tempting to suppose also that the number "one hundred" has been substituted, for the same reason, for the simple number "three," and that what is presented here as a sampling of the offenses—or rather what this sampling was before the development of the three crimes into five—originally constituted their complete inventory.

In any case, directly or indirectly, all these sins are directed against the king. The first three, those of the second and first function, are direct, attacking the king in his capital, his servants, his religion; the two sexual sins attack women belonging to the king's family or placed under his protection. Rhetorically speaking, therefore, in this final quarrel where Śiśupāla claims to defend royal majesty and where he tries, we shall see, to incite the assembly of kings against Kṛṣṇa and the Pāṇḍavas, this enumeration of crimes committed against a king, in the three functional areas of royal activity, is very timely, and will in the end have on the audience the effect which Kṛṣṇa is hoping for.

Śiśupāla and the Kings

The dispute during which at first Bhīṣma, then Kṛṣṇa himself, reveal the past and unveil the nature of their adversary, develops at length and occasions several speeches by Śiśupāla. While they do not become more and more violent, for the first is already extremely so, they rather lead gradually up to the desperate defiance at the end. Their subject is, from beginning to end, the defense of the majesty of kings, purported to have been violated because the supplementary *arghya* has been accorded not to one of them, but to Kṛṣṇa, who is no king: Śiśupāla makes himself the champion of this outraged assembly.

The theme is stated from the outset (1338), when Bhīṣma hears him say:

> "This Vārṣṇeya does not deserve regal honor as though he were a king, Kauravya, while great-spirited lords of the earth are present!"

It is on *dharma* that he bases himself, he says quickly, in a haughty, didactic tone, to the Pāṇḍavas who are astounded at this effrontery (1340):

> "You are children, you don't know! For the Law is subtle, Pāṇḍavas!"

And the flood is loosed (1342):

> "How can the Dāśārha, who is no king, merit precedence over all the kings of the earth so that he should be honored by you?"

Growing angrier, he lists the kings and other heroes who are present, and praises their virtues—beginning with this very Bhīṣma whom he attacks as if guilty of lese majesty; how, he asks, can they distinguish and honor Kṛṣṇa when there are present Aśvatthāman, Duryodhana, Kṛpa, Druma, Karṇa, and many others (1347–1353)?

> "If you must honor Madhusūdana, why bring these kings here—to insult them, Bhārata?
>
> It was not out of fear for the great-spirited Kaunteya that we all offered him tribute, nor out of greed or to flatter him. He wanted the sovereignty and proceeded according to Law; so we gave him tribute and now he does not count us! What but contempt moves you, if in an assembly of kings you honor Kṛṣṇa with the guest gift, while he has not attained to the title? . . . Not only is there

> delivered an insult to these Indras of kings, the Kurus have also shown you up for what you obviously are, Janārdana. As a marriage is to a eunuch, as a show is to a blind man, so is this royal honor to you Madhusūdana, who are no king!"

The exposition is instructive by its very monotony: it reveals a dominating concept of the thought and ideology of Śiśupāla.

Bhīṣma's reply is grandiose. He rejects, without deigning to discuss it, this limited conception of *dharma*, opposing to it the greater truth: Kṛṣṇa is indeed more than a king, he is everything, he has everything:

> "It is in the full knowledge of his fame, his bravery, and his triumph that we offer the honor. . . . Of brahmins he is the elder in knowledge, of barons the superior in strength, and both these grounds to honor Govinda are found firm. Knowledge of the Vedas and their branches, and boundless might as well—who in the world of men possesses these so distinguishedly if not Keśava?"[10]

But Śiśupāla does not relent, and the assembly of the kings begins to react. For all of Bhīṣma's saying, "Look at these many kings older than you are: they consent to the honor paid Kṛṣṇa, and you should likewise forbear it" (1372), the audience is becoming more and more susceptible to this royalist demagogy which Śiśupāla pours forth in eloquent torrents. Sahadeva, the youngest of the Pāṇḍavas, is soon obliged to threaten to put his foot on the head of anyone who would challenge the decision, and at the sight of his foot none of the kings dares utter a word (1402–1405). But when Śiśupāla leaves the hall, they all follow him, and their wrath is great. One of them, Sunītha, incites them to attack those who have tried to humiliate them, and they make ready to prevent the sacrifice, *yajñopaghātāya* (1410–1412), so that, says the poet, "When they were being restrained by their friends, their appearance was like that of roaring lions that are dragged away from their raw meat. Kṛṣṇa then understood that the invincible sea of kings, surrounded by billowing troops, was making a covenant for war."

Things do not come to such a pass, however, and Bhīṣma, the Nestor of this epic, has good reason to say "Let these kings bark like a pack of dogs around a sleeping lion. . . ." And he hints at something quite interesting, which will lead us quickly towards the end, the death of Śiśupāla: this fine devotion to kings, this intransigence about the rights of kings, are they genuine? No, says Bhīṣma, repeating the image of dogs; Kṛṣṇa is for the moment like a sleeping lion, and before he wakes, the king of Cedi makes lions out of all these dogs. But in reality, unconsciously (*acetanaḥ*, 1427),

> ". . . he desires with all his being to lead them all to the abode of Yama . . . !"

And this accusation, which matches one of the well-known cruelties of Jarāsaṁdha, the king whom Śiśupāla has served as commander-in-chief, must have substance, for Śiśupāla protests vigorously (1433):

> "How is it you are not ashamed of yourself, decrepit defiler of your family, while you frighten all these kings with your many threats?"

In the last speech which he will give, in the face of the fate that awaits him, he will take up again the theme of offended royal dignity, and after another catalogue of kings who deserve to be honored, he will conclude by repeating the theme in the interrogative (1540–1541): "Why," he will say to Bhīṣma,

> "Why do you fail to praise such kings as Śalya and others, if as always your heart is set on praising, Bhīṣma?"

In the moments preceding the death of this overreacher, there occurs in the kings a change, a reversal. Kṛṣṇa has presented his grievances, has recalled the hundred offenses of which he has given five examples and which are affronts to the majesty and status of a king, and has called them all to witness the hundred and first which has been committed against him. The outcome is this (1575):

> All the assembled kings, upon hearing this and more from Vāsudeva, now began to revile the Cedi king.

In fact they watch without serious reaction the execution of Śiśupāla—and we shall see presently the remarkable mode of this death. Immediately after, when the body has been removed, Yudhiṣṭhira celebrates his *rājasūya* before the assembly of kings, as if no incident had marred the festivities. In the end, he dismisses his guests, including Kṛṣṇa, with honor, setting down the official version in his final proclamation (1604): "All these kings have come to us in a spirit of friendship."

Thus, in short, the rights of kings have been the subject of Śiśupāla's protest; afterwards the kings themselves, their loyalty and their choice have been at stake in the rhetorical debate; and finally, after coming close to an ill-timed insurrection, the kings have done what was expected of them, that for which they had been invited: their consenting presence has fully validated the rite.

The End of Śiśupāla; Śiśupāla and Kṛṣṇa

We left Kṛṣṇa and Śiśupāla, incarnate Viṣṇu and the "little Śiva," at the moment when Kṛṣṇa announces that the present offense, the hundred and first, is no longer covered by his promise of forbearance and will not be tolerated. Śiśupāla replies (1579):

> "Forgive me, if you have that much faith, or don't, Kṛṣṇa, what could possibly befall me from you, however angry or friendly?"

Defiance of the Commander? Resignation to fate? The end of a good loser? In any case, from this moment on, Kṛṣṇa's mind is made up. According to the Calcutta edition, he "thinks" of the *cakra (manasā 'cintayac cakram)*, the discus, his infallible weapon that has already punished the excesses of so many demons. The discus right away appears and positions itself in his hand. At this solemn moment Kṛṣṇa explains the situation once more, justifying his action. Then he acts (1582–1589):[11]

> ["Let the kings hear why I have put up with this: I have had to forgive a hundred of his offenses, at his mother's request. What she asked of me, I have given, and the tally is complete. Now I shall slay him before the eyes of all you earth-lords." So saying, at that moment the best of the Yadus,] scourge of his enemies, irately cut off his head with his discus. The strong-armed king fell like a tree that is struck by a thunderbolt.
>
> Thereupon the kings watched a sublime radiance rise forth from the body of the king of the Cedis, which, great king, was like the sun rising up from the sky; and that radiance greeted lotus-eyed Kṛṣṇa, honored by the world, and entered him, O king. When they saw that, all the kings deemed it a miracle that that radiance entered the strong-armed man, that greatest of men. In a cloudless sky heaven rained forth and blazing lightning struck and the earth trembled, when Kṛṣṇa slew the Caidya. There were kings there who did not say a word. . . .[12]

Thus, at the moment of the death of this madman who has never ceased, throughout his life, to pile up offenses and crimes against Kṛṣṇa, and who has just showered him once again with insolence, the best part of himself, his *tejaḥ agryam*, leaves his beheaded body in the form of a brilliant light and enters into his executioner, merging with him. It is indeed a miraculous spectacle, *adbhutam*, as the kings who are present all agree.

How is this miracle to be explained? The editors of the *Mahābhārata* see no difficulty here: Kṛṣṇa-Viṣṇu is the god who encompasses all, of whom all beings, despite appearances, are parts. His enemy Śiśupāla was therefore, in spite of himself, a part of this total Being. The total Being has simply wished to recover the part, and one may suppose that he has attracted him by some sort of hypnosis. Just before entering into the body of his killer, it seems that Śiśupāla has understood the meaning of the act: his *tejas* salutes the god, *vavande tat tadā tejo viveśa ca*. But until then he had not been in on the secret. During the final quarrel, he has been seized by a kind of intoxication, an irresistible need to reenter the womb of the incarnate All, a surprising variation on the maternal womb of the psychoanalysts. Consciously, he has rushed to his destruction, has provoked it, discarding all recourse. Unconsciously, it was something else: he was obeying the call, the will of Kṛṣṇa-Viṣṇu. Bhīṣma, the wise and experienced old man, had made a correct diagnosis when, some pages earlier, he ended his account of the birth and childhood of Śiśupāla with these words, which attempted to explain to the Pāṇḍavas the paroxysm of violence to which the challenger abandoned himself (1521–1522):

> "He of a certainty is a particle of the glory of Hari, strong-armed prince, and widely famous Hari wants to recover it.
>
> That is why this evil-minded king of Cedis roars fiercely like a tiger, tiger of the Kurus, without worrying about any of us."

This is in fact why he plunges into the hundred and first misdeed, which he could easily have avoided or held back. At the very time when he cries out his indifference to what Kṛṣṇa will or will not do—these, as we saw, are his last words—he is possessed by an unconscious need to make an end of it, to lose himself in the being whom he insults.

The Greek tragedians did not have to deal with this type of drama, but it is on a par with the loftiest situations which they encountered: Prometheus standing up to Zeus, Oedipus obstinately delving into his destiny. Śiśupāla is not a normal man; only thanks to Kṛṣṇa, to Viṣṇu, has he been freed from the bodily monstrosity that revealed him as a little Śiva. But, from the instant of this boon, the child's mother and Kṛṣṇa himself have foreseen the future: from this humanized Śiva to Viṣṇu incarnate, there will be, by an irresistible bent of nature—one might readily say, of theology—nothing but a series of insults, aggressions, and crimes; and Kṛṣṇa has determined, in his generous wisdom, to tolerate one hundred of them. In fact, there is no other aspect to their relationship: Śiśupāla—on his own behalf and undoubtedly on that of Jarāsaṁdha whose armies he commands—persecutes Kṛṣṇa and his family, and Kṛṣṇa, the divine Kṛṣṇa, until the credit is exhausted, endures, withdraws, retreats, even abandons his capital before this madman. And, in the end, we see that underneath this evil-minded and perverse conduct, Śiśupāla hoped in the depth of his being only to be reunited with Kṛṣṇa-Viṣṇu, only to be one with him, like a Saint Paul who would have awaited death and the hereafter to find his road to Damascus.

More mystical than the epic, more willing to meditate on the sublime absurdities of theology, the Purāṇas have repeated, exploited, and clarified its matter. In the *Viṣṇu Purāṇa*, for example, the belief in metempsychosis allows the conflict to be prolonged: from the standpoint of reincarnation, Śiśupāla is apparently a repeat offender with a checkered past. In previous lives, he has been the demon Hiraṇyakaśipu, and thereafter the demon Rāvaṇa, whom Viṣṇu killed in two of his incarnations. But it is in his new life as Śiśupāla that he has nursed against Kṛṣṇa, the incarnation of Viṣṇu, the most violent hatred. And precisely because of this violence, events this time around turn out differently, the routine of reincarnation has stopped, and another phenomenon occurs. In fact, all through his mature life Śiśupāla has only thought, spitefully to be sure, but in any case exclusively, of Viṣṇu; thanks to this obsession, in the end he is found ready, not for another random transmigration, but for the transformation which we have witnessed. The *Viṣṇu Purāṇa* explains[13] that, at the instant when he was killed by Viṣṇu, he was exposed for who he was, in his true nature; his furious hatred then evaporated, at the same time as the stock of sins he had accumulated, as if at will, was literally consumed by his venerable adversary. This made possible the happy, unexpected dénouement: total, definitive union of Śiśupāla and Kṛṣṇa-Viṣṇu, the reentry of the rebellious part into the immensely benevolent whole.

<The reader has surely felt, granted all the differences imposed by divergence in time, place, civilization, and belief systems, how much this complex career, replete with strangeness, parallels that of Starkaðr. We should now give more precision to this impression.>

Notes

1. The episode of Śiśupāla occupies ślokas 1307–1627 of the second book (*Sabhāparvan*) in the Calcutta edition (matching van Buitenen pp. 91–104). The late poem of Māgha has nothing to offer for our purposes; see *Bālamāgha, Māgha's Śiśupālavadha im Auszuge, bearbeitet von Carl Cappeller* (1915), and *Māgha's Śiśupālavadha, ins Deutsche übertragen von E. Hultzsch* (1926). For the Purāṇic accounts (particularly the *Bhāgavata Purāṇa*) see V. R. Ramachandra Dikshitar, *The Purāṇa Index*, III (1955), 423, s.v. "Śiśupāla."

2. Edward W. Hopkins, *Epic Mythology* (1915), pp. 51, 211.

3. This phrase does not pretend to solve the large

set of problems posed by the character of Kṛṣṇa in the *Mahābhārata*. My feeling is certainly that much of what is said of him is sufficiently explained as transposition of the mythology of an ancient Viṣṇu, a transposition of the same sort and scope as that which has produced the Pāṇḍavas from an archaic list of the functional gods. But of course, Kṛṣṇa is not only that. Here, it suffices that the equivalence Kṛṣṇa-Viṣṇu is explicitly stated in the course of the episode.

4. <See below, chap. IV.>

5. Edward W. Hopkins, *Epic Mythology*, pp. 220, 221.

6. Śl. 1497 (van Buitenen p. 100).

7. <See below, chap. IV.>

8. *Original Sanskrit Texts*, IV, 170–180.

9. *ME* I, pp. 213–222.

10. Śl. 1384–1387 (van Buitenen p. 95). The Poona edition, which is quoted here in translation, rightly omits the first line, which introduces the *vaiśyas* and *śūdras* into the matter.

11. The Poona edition rejects the end of Kṛṣṇa's speech and the following line.

12. Some of the kings to be sure, the text goes on (1590–1591), do indeed show their anger, wringing their hands and biting their lips, but they do not act, approval prevails and everything soon quiets down.

13. IV, 15, 1–5.

20. *Mater Matuta*

The following essay on the Roman dawn goddess Mater Matuta is the first of three appendices appearing in the third volume of Mythe et épopée, *Dumézil's* magnum opus *(most recently published as a single volume—1995, Paris: Gallimard). What does Roman Mater Matuta have to do with India? She has there a cognate deity in the form of the Vedic dawn goddess Uṣas. Dumézil demonstrates that curious and seemingly unrelated features of the Roman Matralia, festival of Mater Matuta celebrated annually on June 11, find a revealing explanation in Indic traditions of Uṣas. The work is a classic and compelling demonstration of the explanatory power and elegance of the comparative method applied to the study of Indo-European myth.* (RDW)

MATER MATUTA

Georges Dumézil

In memory of Jean Hubaux

The studies on Aurora belong to the second period of the new comparative mythology. Between 1935 and 1948 all comparative studies had been concentrated on the idea of the three functions—acknowledged in 1938—which is basic to Indo-European ideology. The main concern had been to take stock of living or fossilized expressions in the religious, epic, and social life of the different peoples of the language family. Only then could the procedures established for this core material be applied to other kinds of representations: the mythology of origins, of fire, of seasons, eschatology.

In several courses at the Collège de France, as early as 1952, the comparison of the Vedic Uṣas *with the Latin* Mater Matuta *produced results, and in 1955, in an article in the* Revue des études latines *33 (1955), 140–151, entitled "Les 'enfants des soeurs' à la fête de Mater Matuta," the second and most mysterious of the two known rites of the Matralia was confirmed. Then in 1956, following a lecture given at the University of Liège, I put forth an overview of the question in my short book* Déesses latines et mythes védiques *(Collection Latomus 24) (Brussels, 1956), pp. 9–43, together with a supplement on another no less remarkable and in some respects similar goddess, Diva Angerona. This publication gave rise to discussions; and on November 13, 1959, in a course at the Collège de France I, taking into account a critique of John Brough, corrected the interpretation of the first rite of the Matralia and, in so doing, justified the probable sequence of the two rites. Since then the dossier has scarcely been altered. It will probably be necessary to extend the study to include other parts of the Indo-European world. Concerning this I have only to indicate Johann Knobloch's very interesting article, "Der Ursprung von nhd.* Ostern, *engl.* Easter," Die Sprache 5 *(1959), 27–45 (the relationship between dawn and springtime, between night—or early morning—and daybreak in the Christian Easter rituals of the East and the West; etymology of the Lithuanian* aušrà-, *the Lettish* àustra *"dawn," the Old Church Slavic* za ustra *"at daybreak").*

I thank my friend Marcel Renard for allowing me to insert into this appendix the sections, improved and rearranged, from my 1956 exposé, which seem to me to retain their validity.

The Two Rites of the Matralia: Texts

On June 11, during the Matralia, the festival of the goddess Mater Matuta,[1] the Roman women—*bonae matres*[2]—who were in their first marriage—*uniuirae*[3]—performed two notable rites, which from antiquity to our day have not ceased to challenge historians of religion. On two occasions these two acts, apparently characteristic of the cult, are brought together in what has been preserved for us of Plutarch's work. They are assigned an analogy, an *interpretatio graeca*, common in antiquity, which is of no importance here. In the *Life* of Camillus, 5.2, we read:[4]

> For they [the Roman Women] take a servant-maid into the secret part of the temple, and there cuff her, and drive her out again, and they embrace their brothers'[5] children in place of their own.

The sixteenth and seventeenth *Roman Questions* are worded thus:[6]

> 16. Why is the temple of Matuta forbidden to slave-women; and why do the women bring in one slave-girl only whom they slap and strike in the face?
>
> 17. Why do they not pray this deity for blessings on their own children, but only on those of their sisters?

Elsewhere there is no mention of the first rite. In the *Fasti*,[7] Ovid contents himself with pointing out the prohibition made to the slave women without mentioning the exception. The second rite is noted in a third text of Plutarch, in the final lines of the treatise *De fraterno amore* (*Moralia, 492D*):[8]

> Whereupon the Roman dames even at this day, when they celebrate the feast of Leucothea (whom they name Matuta), carry in their arms and cherish tenderly their sisters' children, and not their own.

and in book 6 of the *Fasti*, 559 and 561:[9]

> Nevertheless let not an affectionate mother pray to her on behalf of her own offspring. . . . You will do better to commend to her care the progeny of another.

Everyone seems to agree that Ino-Leucothea[10] should be ruled out of the problem of origin. The moral reason for the second rite put forth in the seventeenth *Roman Question*[11] is no more binding. But the attempts at interpretation are very divergent. They have in common only the fact that they are linked to only one, or possibly two, of the elements of the dossier, as if each one could be independent of the others. There are four elements: the goddess' name, the date of her festival, and the two rites that are mentioned and that probably followed each other in the order in which Plutarch and Ovid describe them.

Actually, commentators have been interested above all in the rites, and in the second one more than the first, the former being indeed more notable in the religions of classical peoples taken as a whole. Let us briefly outline these comments, beginning with the second rite.

The Children of Their Sisters

The exclusive privilege enjoyed by the children of the sisters during this festival has been explained in five ways, three of which do not need much refutation despite the eminence of the scholars who formulated them. The first is a ritualization of the concern, verified in several historical cases, of the Roman aunts for their orphan nephews and nieces (J. A. Hild).[12] The second would be the remains of an archaic "system of kinship" (Georg Wissowa).[13] Finally, the third would be a nurses' rite, comparable to the Laconian *Τιθηνίδια* (M. Halberstadt).[14] There are solid objections to these attempts at an explanation, for the beneficiaries of the rite are not actually orphans (Halberstadt);[15] no known system of kinship, matrilineal or patrilineal, brings a woman closer to her sisters' children than to her own (H. J. Rose; James G. Frazer),[16] and the Matralia rite does not involve the relationships between nurses and their nurslings, but between aunts and their nephews.[17] The other two explanations must be discussed more carefully.

Frazer, without shutting his eyes to the dubiousness of the interpretation, assumed[18] that during the Matralia Roman women were scrupulously forbidden to utter the names of their children and that, consequently, they were prevented from recommending them to the goddess. The rite would thus fit into a well-documented category of ethnographic facts. Here are the objections:

(1) The ancients knew well what an "onomastic taboo" was and, when necessary, pointed it out in clear language.[19] Plutarch would not, therefore, be mistaken in his seventeenth *Roman Question*. (2) An "onomastic taboo" prevents only the uttering of a name, but in prayer it is easy to indicate the unnameable one with paraphrases. Yet here one's "own children" are excluded from both prayers and embraces. (3) Frazer himself recognized that, in his ethnographic dossiers, onomastic taboos generally apply to relationships by marriage (husband, wife, husband's father, wife's mother), rarely to blood relations (from children to parents, between brothers and sisters), and that they are uncommon from parents to children. In fact, the few examples he gives are all explained by special circumstances which have nothing to do with the Matralia.[20] (4) Frazer likewise recognized that in any case his proposition would not explain the positive part of the rite, that is, why the Roman women treated with consideration, carried in their arms, and recommended to the goddess their sisters' children.[21]

H. J. Rose proposed a more daring solution, one that aims no less at doing away with the problem, and which has the advantage of revealing it to its fullest.[22]

> All that we know of Rome [he wrote in 1934] forbids us to suppose that each woman present at the rite prayed for blessings on the offspring of any sisters she might have in such words as she chose to use. The worship of the goddess is old, belonging to the 'calendar of Numa,' and so not later than the end of the regal period and probably much earlier. In such a rite, old and obsolete Latin words may be confidently assumed, and I believe one of them can be, not indeed certainly restored, but guessed at with a tolerably high degree of probability. I suggest that the goddess was addressed in some such terms as these: *Mater Matuta, te precor quaesoque uti uolens propitia sies pueris sororiis.*

The whole explanation rests on the *pueri sororii*. This expression—which is fictitious—of the archaic prayer did not mean "sisters' children" but "adolescents." In fact Rose, after consulting Joshua Whatmough, distinguishes *sororius* from *soror* and sees in it the derivative of a **soros* theme—taken from an unconfirmed Indo-European root, **swer-*, doublet of **swel*, "to swell up," which is known with certainty only in the Germanic (Ger., *schwellen*, Eng., *to swell*). Now are not puberty and adolescence, like the ripening of grain, characterized by various "swellings"—and most especially in the case of young girls?[23] We thus arrive at a plausible meaning for this rite which, Rose says, would otherwise be absurd. During the festival of a goddess whose name, furthermore, is related to *maturescere*[24] the *bonae matres* simply asked her to bless the growth of the adolescents. In a word, from Ovid to Halberstadt, Romans and Latinists have based their speculations and labor on a misconception.

Rose has put forth this explanation no less than three times and rightly so. It provides a good example of the calm daring of the school of which he is the most articulate representative. But what a lot of unfounded claims! (1) The basic assumption is that the Roman women no longer understood at all the meaning and the purpose of what they did or said and that, thanks to the *Wald- und Feldkulte* and the *Golden Bough*, and especially to the Melanesian *mana*, modern scholars are able, in retrospect, to enlighten them. Nothing is more dangerous than taking such liberty. The primitivists compete in being arbitrary with the works of epigones who, three quarters of a century ago, discredited naturalistic mythology. (2) The expression *pueri sororii*, like the whole formula of this prayer, is no more than a fabrication of the English philologist who neglected to provide the reasons which confer on him "a tolerably high degree of probability." (3) Despite what Whatmough says, a Roman doublet **su̯er-* of **su̯el-* is difficult to accept. The adjective *sororius*,[25] where it is authenticated, like the slang verb *sororiare*,[26] can be well enough explained by "the sister" so we need not have recourse to the monster **soros*, "swelling" (which for inanimate things, furthermore, would be rather **sorus*, **soreris*). (4) In the ritual formula, what reason is there to devise the substitution of Rose's **sororii* for the ordinary and ancient expression *adolescentes*, together with the highlighting of the glandular "swelling" of puberty? (5) Two of Plutarch's three texts specify that the Roman women "take" the children for whom they pray "in their arms," *ἐναγκαλίζονται*. That is fine for babies, much less so for grown boys and girls.[27] It is true that the apt philologist has no trouble doing away with so imprudent a statement: "I suggest that Plutarch got his information in the *Q.R.* [in which there is no troublesome verb] from Verrius, that in the *de frat. amor*. [where the said verb is found] from hearsay, inaccurate memory, or some other inferior source, unless indeed *ἐναγκαλίζονται* is corrupt."[28] This liberty is enviable.

The Expulsion of the Intruding Slave Woman

The other rite of the Matralia—probably the first chronologically—has raised controversies.

Plutarch suggests that the poor treatment inflicted on a woman slave is no more than the illustration of the prohibition made against all of them, *σύμβολόν* ἐστι ποῦ μὴ ἐξεῖναι,[29] the only ban from then on that there is reason to justify. He justifies it by the *interpretatio graeca* of Matuta as Ino and by the legitimate complaint that this latter had against a slave woman. Until recent times, ancients and moderns were happy with this explanation by way of "symbol." In the *Fasti*[30] Ovid, already pointing out the prohibition that excludes women slaves, does not even mention the scenario of the expulsion, obviously because he, too, sees in it only a tangible expression, a dramatization, which adds nothing either essential or different to the prohibition. Frazer, his most recent annotator (1929), does not seem to hold a different opinion. What is important in his eyes is the general prohibition. As for the sole slave, admitted in, struck, and driven out, he simply notes that she is "a curious exception to the rule"[31]—an exception that dramatically reinforces the rule.

The general prohibition itself poses no difficulty. Greek and Roman antiquity, and on the whole civilizations based on slavery, offer analogous cases. It simply proves that Matuta's cult was a noble cult and that Roman society, in the strict sense, alone benefited from it.[32] But it is not so obvious that the expulsion scenario is tied to this prohibition. Rose (1924) and Halberstadt (1934) are the first to have expressed doubts, for which the latter gave strong grounds.[33] Among the well-documented records of cases where access to a sacred place is forbidden to beings considered impure or unworthy, Halberstadt notes that one would be at a loss to find such a staging having illustrative and pedagogic value. He thus formulates two objections. First, for this type of prohibition to be clear and effective there is no need of expression, of a symbolic ritual incorporated into the cult. It is enough to notify those concerned by word or in writing. Second, the symbolic ritual would result in the defilement that the prohibition is precisely designed to avoid. If indeed it is only a matter of a stronger warning to the servant class, the introduction of one of its representatives into the temple is jumping out of the frying pan into the fire. The two philologists thus looked for other interpretations.

The first[34] proposed that the thrashing of the slave resembles a fertility ritual more than a warning. Let us consider the well-known collection of facts—"das Schlagen mit der Lebensrute," as has been said since the *Wald- und Feldkulte*—where women are in fact struck, thrashed, and whipped with the purpose of encouraging the mysterious processes of maternity within them. Ten years later, Halberstadt proved that the Mannhardtian exegesis was not satisfactory.[35] In such scenarios it is the persons struck, not the floggers, whose flesh benefits from the violence done to them. Therefore, during the festival of Matuta, the matrons would have wanted, at best, to promote the fecundity of their slaves, which is improbable. Are we to surmise that the woman slave was there only as a substitute for the matrons, the latter feeling it inappropriate to allow themselves to be whipped, but reserving the benefit of the rite for themselves through a mystical transference? The example of the Lupercalia, when Roman women willingly gave themselves over to goat-whips,[36] is enough to prove that the supposed impropriety was not felt. We could add that the Romans, if through no more than the Lupercalia, were very familiar with these fertility rituals. Further: if, during the Matralia, it had been a question of such a ritual, they would not have made a mistake and would not have looked for another justification.

Halberstadt was less fortunate in developing his own theories than he was in critiquing those of others. Pushing aside the temptation of another analogy—the rituals of the Scapegoat, such as "the expulsion of Hunger," *βουλίμου ἐξέλασις*, described succinctly but clearly for Chaeronea[37] by Plutarch—he interpreted, explained the first rite of the Matralia in the same way as the second, looking for a link between it and the nurses. He thus compared Greek rituals—the Charila of Delphi[38] and the festival of Dionysus at Alea in Arcadia[39]—in which the nurses of Dionysus intervene, though indirectly and only occasionally. We need only to read with an open mind the descriptions of the two rituals to see all that separates them from the Roman facts. At Alea women are whipped, as are the Spartan ephebi during the festival of Artemis Orthia, but there is no expulsion rite.[40] At Chaeronea the ruling king presides over a novenial atonement ceremony in expiation for a sin committed in the past, during a great famine, by the king of the country, against a little girl named Charila. He distributes flour and vegetables to all those who present themselves. When the distribution is finished, he throws his shoe on a statuette representing Charila. Then the leader of the Thyiades—the sole link in all this with Dionysus—takes the statuette to the ravine where the little girl was buried after having choked to death, puts a rope around its neck, and buries it.

For the first as well as for the second rite, each of the proposals we have looked at contains at least one artifice that makes it lack credibility. Moreover, although many try hard to reconcile the interpretations of the two rites—Rose through life-producing whippings, Halberstadt through the nurses of Dionysus—the unity that they offer is no less obviously artificial. Finally, none of the proposals takes into account the significance of the other two facts: Mater Matuta's name and the date of the Matralia. When Halberstadt says that Mater Matuta is the goddess of nurses, he is forcing a role on her designed to fit his explanation of the second rite. He does not even try to match this function with the name. When Rose makes Matuta a goddess of fertility, this, too, is a result of his astonishing translation of the expression *pueri sororii*, that he began by inventing. From Hild to Rose everything takes place as if the exegetes had implicitly acknowledged that the gesture of the *bonae matres* in the second rite was self-sufficient, Mater Matuta being there only to preside over it without guiding it, without contributing a special meaning to the marks of affectionate attention showered on the children or to the specification of these children as "nephews."

As always we must work backwards and obtain an overall view that, bringing together all the facts, reveals what makes them equally useful or necessary, with each one having a different purpose. Let us look at what has been most misused or neglected in the dossier: the name and the date. First the name: what does *Mater Matuta* signify?

Mater Matuta, Goddess of Dawn

In Roman observance, for the "ordinary Roman" of the period with which we are familiar, Mater Matuta is the goddess of dawn or Dawn personified. The very classical derivative, *mātūtīnus*, means absolutely nothing other than "pertaining to early morning," just as *uespertīnus* refers only to the evening. Now none of the numerous Latin adjectives ending in *-īnus* (*diuinus, libertinus, equinus, Latinus*, and so on) changes anything in the concept to which it simply makes reference.[41] Were not *matutinus* and *uespertinus* accepted prior to Cicero? It was certainly not he who invented them. He used them with an ease that presupposes an accepted usage. The construction of the second term, analogical to that of the first, must on the whole have originated with the people. The first mention in literature of the goddess Matuta herself comes in the fifth book of Lucretius (650).[42] Here she is no more than a poetic designation of early morning, which seems "old hat," as much as a cliché in this passage as does "Aurora's chariot" in French writers of the age of Louis XIV. The atheistic poet Lucretius probably used her name only in conformity with the accepted meaning.

Why and how has this unquestionable meaning been contested for three quarters of a century by a certain number of authors? The reason appears to be simple. Matuta-Aurora has suffered from the general disrepute of naturalistic mythology. She had to be something else, something more acceptable to the new directions of the science of religions. An intemperate use of linguistics has provided not one, but at least two means of effecting this distortion.

The family of words to which *Mātūta* and *mātūtīnus* belong is vast. In addition to the archaic adjective *mānus*, "good," with its opposite *immānis* and the name of the *Mānes*, the ancient neuter form turned adverb *māne* "early," it includes the adjective *mātūrus* "ripe" and its derivatives. At the end of the last century, the linguist M. Pokrovskij studied it thoroughly[43] and showed that the meaning one must give to the root *mā*—which has given rise to these various concepts—is that of "passen, angemessen sein," to be ready: a "ready" plant or organism, a favorable season, and so on, are *maturus, -a, -um.* Something that happens "in the nick of time," a being adapted to its intended purpose, and so on, is *manus, -a, -um* (the general meaning of "good" has come from that). The awaited time in which one can again take up activities suspended during the night, "daybreak," is *mane*, presided over by *Matuta.*

But once we have acknowledged these relationships radiating out from a common central point, we do not have the right to establish arbitrarily other cross-filiations, and still less exchanges between the meanings of one and another of the terms in the family. Each one of these terms has taken on a precise and fixed meaning and cannot, on the pretext of an etymological relationship, be given the meaning of any of the others. In French *pommade* [pomade], *pommeau* [pommel], and *pommette* [cheekbone] are all derivatives of *pomme* [apple]. The cosmetic called "pomade" was originally prepared from the pulp of the apple. The pommel of a saddle and the cheekbones of the face call to mind in two different ways the shape of the apple. But who would dream of making a direct progression from *pommeau* to *pommade* or from *pommade* to *pommette?* However, the etymologists of antiquity sometimes did make just this kind of mistake, which the moderns have repeated. The former can be pardoned; the latter less. In the family of the *mā-* derivatives, *maturus* is "ripe,"[44] and not "good," in spite of the term *mānus*. Despite Saint Augustine[45] or his sources, and despite Rose,[46] *Matuta* has no need to take its meaning from *maturescere*, a secondary derivative of the primary one **matu-*. There are three ambiguous accounts found in Paulus Diaconus under "*Matrem Matutam,*" "*mane,*" and "*Mater Matuta,*" which go back to Verrius Flaccus.[47] Furthermore, in spite of these, *Matuta* does not, because of the adjective *manus* and still less because of the related Celtic adjectives with the same meaning,[48] have to exchange its own meaning for that of "Good Goddess, Good Mother."

On the other hand, it seems to me that scholars allow a little too much leeway to religious facts and cults when they coldly write that Mater Matuta was first the equivalent of "Bona Dea" and that once her name was no longer understood, she was "transformed" into a goddess of Dawn. A goddess of Dawn is not so easily invented by using as a model another divine type. Stylus or pencil in hand, Verrius Flaccus and his modern emulators can very well establish evolutionary diagrams—which, incidentally, they refrain from sharing with us. The concrete realities of religion—the traditional devotion of the faithful, the routine of the festival, the religious conservatism of these Romans who let so many cults and priesthoods weaken and die—would not have facilitated such a metamorphosis. From the beginnings to the principate, apart from the likenesses with the Greeks, the true Roman pantheon offers less evidence of change than impatient philologists would like to see or are willing to admit.

Strictly speaking, relatively few authors have pursued this path to the end. W. Warde Fowler, whose mind was strongly marked by Mannhardtism, in 1899 contented himself with voicing a doubt about the traditional, auroral meaning of Matuta.[49] In his commentary on the *Fasti* (1929), Frazer did not even go that far[50] and, with noticeable reluctance, followed the "good modern authorities," K. O. Müller, Theodor Mommsen, Ludwig Preller, Georg Wissowa, and even Alfred von Domaszewski, who agree that our goddess is Aurora. J. A. Hild, in Daremberg and Saglio, *Dictionnaire des Antiquités*,[51] Link in Pauly-Wissowa, *Real-Encyklopädie der classischen Altertumswissenschaft* (Stuttgart, 1928),[52] Carl Koch in his *Gestirnverehrung*,[53] Halberstadt in his monograph (1934),[54] did not think differently. But the French textbooks published recently (Albert Grenier, 1948; Paul Fabre, 1955) are less careful and even altogether careless.[55] In addition, Matuta has found a particularly determined restorer in the person of Rose. "That Mater Matuta was a dawn-goddess, as has been often enough asserted,[56] I may believe when I see some reason to suppose a cult of a dawn-goddess, not a mere appearance of an Eos or Aurora in mythology, in either Italy or Greece."

Here we are again in the midst of a philology of convenience. The adjective *matutinus*, the *Matuta* of Lucretius do not have any bearing, are no longer facts, but "suppositions" that should be supported by "reasons." We find ourselves above all at the very root of the fundamental illusion that harsh truth must confront: in its social structure and its religion ancient Rome did not have the affinity and special solidarity with neighboring Greece that Rose and many other experts of Greek and Latin imagine. Humanistic tradition and our academic formation, which closely link—and rightly so regarding the Golden Age—the two civilizations we call "classical," are poor teachers for the understanding of origins. Great progress was definitely made during the past century when the translations of Homer or of Euripedes no longer contained "Jupiter," "Minerva," and "Diana." Still today we must not think "Eos" when we study Matuta. In compensation young generations of Latinists must strive to place the ideas and things of most ancient Rome into the comparative structure indicated by linguists as early as 1918[57] and outlined by a half century of study. In religious matters especially, Vedic India, through striking, numerous, and well-structured analogies, provides the key to many of the most important Roman facts. Thus one of the most notable feminine figures of the *Rig Veda*, if not of the *Atharva Veda*,[58] is precisely the goddess Aurora, Uṣas. Likened to a mother for us mortals (7.81.4), compared also to the mother of the gods *mātā́ devā́nām* (1.119.19), she is very often invoked or celebrated. We must not, therefore, take the inconsistency of Eos as a pretext for rejecting a priori the authenticity of a goddess Aurora in Latium.

Significance of the Matralia

If Matuta is the goddess responsible for opening the "matutinal" hours, her festival date takes on great importance. June 11 falls a few days before the summer solstice, the day on which the balance between daytime and nighttime—in what is for us a "twenty-four hour day"—will shift. Ever since the winter solstice, through the spring equinox, diurnal time has unceasingly taken the advantage; dawn has continued to nibble away at the darkness, to come earlier. But then in June this daily gain dwindles, becomes unnoticeable, until the summer solstice. It then becomes a daily loss, a withdrawing of dawn, also unnoticeable at first, then more and more marked, through the autumn equinox, until the winter solstice.

Of course the summer solstice, which for us falls on June 21, does not have a fixed day in the poorly regulated luniscolar calendars of the days prior to Julius Caesar. The summation of months merely tallied was far from producing a total of "twenty-four hour days" coinciding with the exact, astronomical duration of one revolution of the sun. In order to reestablish a parallel or at least to prevent the scandal, for example, of a calendar summer encroaching on a natural winter, it was necessary to make adjustments from time to time—that is, to insert periods of time of varying length depending on the number of years that had passed since the prior adjustment. Have these intercalations always been periodic? Have they taken the form of supplementary days or months? Surely not, but they must have tended to become so in order to delimit accurately the section of the calendar within which the highlights of the sun's annual career—equinoxes and solstices—could reasonably vary. Finally, they did become cyclic while waiting for the Julian reform to reduce to its extreme limit the zone of mobility.[59]

In historical reality how did this system function? A reference by Livy to an eclipse in 191 B.C. bears witness to a discrepancy, readily cited, of nearly four months. He places it on July 11, while calculations show that it should have been recorded on March 14.[60] But this is probably a grossly extreme case caused by an extended malfunction of a generally better controlled mechanism. Obviously, it would be unwarranted to conclude that the Republican calendar did not relate to the seasons when many facts testify to the contrary. The war season framed by the war rituals of March and October could not have fallen normally in another season even if, through negligence or superstition, the pontifexes by way of exception had let the calendar drift for too many consecutive years. Festivals like the Consualia and the Opiconsivia which concern the gathering in of the harvest, the Volcanalia which turns aside the fires caused by the hot season, and many others that have fixed dates, *statae, statiuae*, in the calendar, are of necessity linked to the actual course of the seasons. Janus, who gave his name to January, is the god of beginnings, of transitions. Only exceptionally could his month, therefore, stray far from the "transition," from the beginning—the winter solstice. We must thus assume that during the first centuries of the Republic, when religious observance was certainly more demanding than it was during the last, competent authority was watchful. By the rather frequent insertion of cushions of time, it sought to keep within reasonable, thus conservative, limits the discrepancy between the unfolding of the calendar and the course of the sun, between the dates of seasonal festivals and seasonal realities.

That is particularly true of the solstices, which are, moreover, easy to situate through observation.[61] That the shortest days of the year, *angusti dies*, fall right at the time of the actual winter solstice, *breuissima dies, bruma*, does not depend on calendars. The goddess who steps in on this occasion, Diva Angerona, and who gives her name to these days has her festival, the Divalia, during the period in which, as a matter of fact, we await December 21. In ancient times, when theological definitions were still obvious to everyone, how could the Romans with their common sense have accepted for long the drifting of this festival with its goddess toward the springtime?

Let us thus be careful not to exaggerate the freedom of movement of the Republican calendar just because of the peculiarity of 191 B.C. From the beginning, the calendar by its very purpose was filled with festivals that were essentially seasonal, linked to the beginnings, heights, limitations, and characteristics of the real seasons. We can trust the Latin peasants; corrections perhaps by trial and error, perhaps more or less periodic, kept enough order to it all. Therefore, modern scholars should not be shocked when, to make a long story short, it is said that Angerona was "the goddess of the winter solstice," or that the festival of Aurora preceded the summer solstice only by a few days. In thus verbally assigning the ancient solstices to their proper place within the structure of Republican time, the inaccuracy is certainly less serious than in attributing to them mad deviations from their mark. Rome had common sense.[62]

It is certainly no accident that Aurora's festival is thus fixed—no more than that a festival consecrated to the Sun[63] precedes, in the same way, the winter solstice on December 11—that is, six months later to the day. We know beforehand how to interpret this fixing of the festival. In Rome more than elsewhere, a festival, *feriae, festus dies*, cannot be without purpose. Through it, through what takes place, the celebrants try to obtain a result, to influence the course of the hoped for or dreaded events that either depend on the current dispositions of a divinity or obey gestures or words formerly taught or exercised by a divinity or an august ancestor. On the occasion of the Matralia, during the slowing down and on the eve of Aurora's lengthy withdrawal, what can society hope for if not to help the goddess with a task that is becoming increasingly difficult for her? The scenes reenacted by the celebrants should tend toward this end. They accomplish in the temple what the goddess does in the sky. Just as each morning the duty of the goddess breaks down into two actions, so the celebrants "act out" two scenes. The first action, a negative one, consists of banishing the darkness that at one and the same time unduly and of necessity has invaded the sky; the other consists of receiving and revealing the young sun who has matured below the horizon. In the two corresponding scenes, the celebrants violently drive from the temple a slave woman whom they first unduly ushered in, and they show affection, concern, and respect for children.

The symbolism is immediately clear and easily extends to two characteristic details of the festival. If the celebrants in the two rites are multiple, probably numerous, it is most likely because they represent not "Aurora per se," but the throng of individual dawns that begin in succession the days of the year or the days of an indefinite period of time. If in the second rite the celebrants dote on and recommend to the goddess not their own children but "those of another," precisely those of their sisters (or brothers?), it is probably in order to signify on the one hand that Aurora, having only a brief moment at her disposal, cannot herself produce the Sun. She can only receive it after another entity, having the same nature as she, has prepared him. The action probably signifies, on the other hand, that Aurora and the Sun's real mother, whoever she be, work in harmonious collaboration.

This is and can only be a hypothesis since the mythology of Matuta as such has disappeared with the whole of Roman mythology. But it is a reasonable hypothesis, since it limits itself to deciphering the imprint that mythology has left on the rites, and to throwing light on this imprint both by the definition, in fact, by the very name of the goddess, and by the precise necessity that the date of her annual festival reveals.

The Vedic Aurora

This reconstitution is completely and coherently supported if, beyond the Greek Eos, we consider the Vedic Aurora. This is the Uṣas whom we called to mind earlier and of whom much is said in the hymns[64]—more in the hymns than in the rituals because Uṣas has no cult of her own. She does receive invocations or offerings under various circumstances, in morning liturgies or in marriage rituals, but always along with other divinities. The twenty hymns that are addressed to her, without mention of the numerous references to her in the rest of the collection, give reason, nevertheless, to think that this was not always the case.

In the hymns themselves, contrary to custom, no "myth of Aurora" as such is recounted. The daily service that she ensures gives rise to numerous vivid expressions, most of which do not seem to allude to connected narratives or even to consistent representations. They are simply rhetorical "games" among which the authors, even within a poem, do not worry, have no need to worry about maintaining coherence. For example, in regard to her appearance, if she is generally a woman, and a young woman, she is at times represented by a mare and more often by a cow. Still, a few representations statistically command attention.

First, we are struck by the frequency of the plural. Auroras are spoken of as well as Aurora, Daughters of heaven (4.51.1 and 10) as well as Daughter of heaven—and sometimes in consecutive stanzas of the same hymn. Louis Renou writes:[65]

> She is invoked at times in the singular—it is either a question of the present Uṣas, the last born, or of Uṣas generally conceived—at times in the plural. These are the "continually successive" Uṣas (*śáśvatī*), which group forms an entity that is simultaneously young and yet dates from time immemorial. . . . Nowhere does the Uṣas invoked seem to have a privileged position except for that resulting from the invocation itself.

"The Auroras" thus constitute a group equivalent to Aurora and are invoked collectively in the prayer of day as if all participated in the action of each one. We have seen that in Rome the multiple celebrants who act together and together mime the tasks of the unique Mater Matuta behave in like manner.

Another very natural expression recurs often. Since one of the aspects of the auroral phenomenon is to dissipate the darkness, which for several hours had been filling the sky, the poets speak often of hostility—but not of an equal contest. Aurora (or the Auroras) limit themselves to driving back darkness, *támas*, barely personified, but willingly laden with disagreeable epithets. Uṣas, for example, "chases away the mass of unshaped blackness" (*bā́dhate kr̥ṣṇám ábhvam, Rig Veda*, 1.92.5). "Driving back hostility and darkness, Aurora, Daughter of heaven, arrived with the light" (*ápa dvéṣo bā́dhamānā támāṃsi*, 5.80.5). "As a valiant archer (chases) the enemies, she drives back the darkness (*ápa . . . bā́dhate támaḥ*), like a swift driver (of a battle chariot)" (6.64.3); "The Auroras, leading the high sacrifice, repel the darkness of night by casting it aside" (*ví tā́ bādhante táma ū́rmyāyāḥ*, 6.65.2); "Aurora marches on, goddess, driving back (*bā́dhamānā*) with the light all the darkness, the dangers; here the brilliant Auroras appear, . . . the darkness, the unpleasant one, goes away toward the west (*apācī́naṃ támo agād ájuṣṭam*, 7.78.2 and 3)." Thus the obscurity is likened to the enemy, monstrousness (*á-bhva*), danger, and is repelled, pushed far away (one will note the frequency of the root *bādh*, which carries this meaning) by Aurora or by the troop of Auroras themselves described as *aryápatnīḥ* (7.6.5), *supátnīḥ* (6.44.21).[66] This is exactly what the *bonae matres* of Rome "perform" in the first rite of June 11 when they expel a slave woman who, unduly present in the temple of Aurora, must represent, in opposition to them, the bad, low-born element of society as well as the cosmic "enemy" of the goddess.

As for the other, positive, aspect of Aurora's work, her relationship with the Sun and the light, the Vedic poets express it as mentioned above through numerous images, in particular in terms of kinship that would be useless to attempt to reconcile. Most of these images, used only once or twice, certain of them also in enigmatic formulas, probably do not refer to a mythological tradition. Thus, one text signifies perhaps that she is the daughter of the night (3.55.12), another that "the great sun fathers her" (2.23.2); elsewhere she is called wife or lover of Agni, of the Sun. These isolated, banal images do not give evidence of stable representations. Certain more frequent texts are also too natural to be significant. Thus, she is consistently called *divó duhitṛ́* "daughter of heaven" (and not, in spite of what has been said, "daughter of the sun"). She is mother (4.2.15; 5.47.6), mother of prayer (5.47.1), as on occasion, mother of the sun or light, and even according to Louis Renou, "a type of universal mother, an Aditi, mistress of the world, called *mahī́*, 5.45.3."[67] This is probably explained by the same analogous reason that makes the Roman Aurora *Mater* Matuta, honored at the *Matr*alia.

But at least one expression, more original, exists whose usage statistically would suffice to prove the importance of Uṣas in the Vedic concept: *she is the sister goddess par excellence*. In the *Rig Veda*, the word *svásṛ* "sister" appears thirteen times applied to a divinity. Eleven times it is in reference to Uṣas or of a divinity called the sister of Uṣas.

It is with Rātrī, the Night, a divinity of the same style as Uṣas , that she forms a "sisterly couple," one that is particularly close and important. Of the eleven texts just mentioned, six concern Uṣas as sister of Rātrī or vice-versa. As for the binary form, in five examples the expression "the two sisters" designates Uṣas and Rātrī three times, the Heaven and the Earth two times. Moreover, whether in the composites of the couple (*náktoṣā́sā*, five examples; *uṣā́sānaktā*, ten examples), in the two joined but separated pairs (*uṣā́sā . . . náktā*, two examples), or in the dual form with one of the names equaling in itself the entire couple (dual form of *uṣás*, four examples; dual form of *nákta*, two examples), the link between the two "sisters" Night-Aurora is strongly emphasized.

This is not a matter of language artifice or of poetic cliché. Regardless of how fundamental the antithesis of dark and light may be, the Vedic Night and Aurora function mythically toward one another like respectful and devoted sisters, as has been brought out innumerable times. Abel Bergaigne very subtly says:[68]

> Nevertheless, this black cow (= Night) who comes among the bright cows (10.61.4) is considered the sister of dawn, a sister whom the latter thrusts aside and from whom she moves away (10.172.4; cf. 4.52.1), but who also moves away from her sister (7.71.1) by voluntarily relinquishing her place (1.124.8; cf. 113.1 and 2). These two sisters, *samānábandhū* (1.113.2), though they reciprocally efface their color (ibid.), no more quarrel than do they stop in the common path they follow one after the other (ibid., 3); though of opposite forms, they have only one and the same thought (ibid.). It is probably still dawn and night which are designated in verse 3.55.11 as those who take on their twin forms differently, one shining and the other dark and who, one being dark and one bright (cf. 1.17.1), are nevertheless sisters.

We may be surprised that, as darkness constantly belongs to the demoniacal and dangerous world, Night as a divinity is on the contrary a favorable goddess, the sister of the good Aurora, and that both are jointly called "the mothers of *ṛtá*," of ritual and moral cosmic Order (1.142.7; 5.5.6; 9.102.7). Certain individuals believed there was reason to distinguish here between starlit Night and dark nights, but Abel Bergaigne has aptly remarked that Night associated with Aurora, either explicitly or implicitly, in the pairs such as *uṣā́sā, náktā*, does not appear to include this nuance.[69] The explanation is elsewhere, in a trait that is strongly indicated by the hymnal and which throws light on the ritual rule of the Matralia: from the human point of view, Night and Aurora have a maternal work in common, a work more important than that which separates them. These sisters are mothers, and collaborating mothers at that. Either *they are, by a physiological wonder, the two mothers of the same child*, the Sun or the celestial Fire, *or Aurora takes delivery of the son from the Night alone and in turn cares for him.* Here are a few examples of these mythic presentations of one and the same cosmic act:

> 1.96 (hymn to Agni):
>
> 5. Night and Aurora, changing entirely their color, nurse in common (samī́cī) a single child. Between Heaven and Earth he shines afar (like) a golden jewel.
>
> 1.146 (hymn to Agni):
>
> 3. Both moving toward their common calf (*samānáṃ vatsám*) the two milk cows make their way separately, measuring carefully the distance so as not to cross. . . .[70]

On occasion the calf also changes color when passing from Night to Aurora:

> 1.9 (hymn to Agni):
>
> 1. Two cows of different colors, making their way straight to the objective, one after the other, nurse the calf (*anā́ynyā vatsám úpa dhapayete*). He becomes yellow near one according to his own will; beside the other he is brilliant, adorned with a beautiful luster.
>
> 3.55 (enigmatic hymn concerning various gods, where the stanzas 11–14 all seem to apply to the couple Night-Aurora). As happens in Vedic poetry, here incompatible conceptions are seen united: Night and Aurora as sisters (stanza 11), but also as mother and daughter (?stanza 12); a calf, probably their common calf, which they nurse together (stanza 12), but also the calf of one, which is licked by the other (stanza 13):[71]
>
> 11. The two twin (*yamíā*) sisters have put on different colors, one shines, the other is dark. The dark one and the pink one are two sisters (*svásārau*).[72]
> 12. There where the two good milk cows, mother and daughter, nurse together (their calf), I invoke them both to the seat of *ṛtá*.
> 13. Licking the calf of the other, she mooed (*anyásayā vatsáṃ rihatī́ mimāya*). Through what world has the cow hidden her udder? The *iḷā* (or *Iḷā* personified) swelled from the milk of *ṛtá*.
> 14. The multiform entity dresses in beautiful colors . . . [73] she remains upright, licking the calf of eighteen months. I glance over, I who know, the sojourn of *ṛtá*.

Throughout these variants we see that a key idea remains: Aurora nurses, licks the child who is either hers in common with her sister, Night, or is the child of the latter only, thanks to which this child, the sun (for whom can be substituted in the sacerdotal speculations, the fire of offerings), born first from the womb of the night, reaches the day's maturity for the good of mankind. This myth, which forms the notions of "mothers," of "sisters," and of "child of the sister," tangibly expresses the theologem that defines the essential kindness of the short-lived Aurora, the reappearance of the sun or of a fire that nevertheless precedes her, which was already formed when she came on the scene.

It is probably this same theologem, in the form most acceptable to positive minds—Aurora receiving, doting on the child of her sister the Night, and not in the enigmatic and monstrous form preferred by the *Rig Veda* in which the two sisters Aurora and Night are mothers of the same child—which intervened in the conception of Mater Matuta, of Mother Aurora, at the time when the exposure to the Greek gods had not yet led the Romans to disdain and forget their own theology. If the myth corresponding to the theologem has disappeared, the latter is nonetheless recalled, attested to by a ritual rule that transposes to men, or rather to women here, the very behavior of the divinity: at the Matralia when Mother Aurora is honored, the mothers do with the children of their sisters[74] what this sister of the Night does with the Sun, the child of the Night.

The Maternal Aurora

The agreement of Rome and Vedic India even to the point of making Night the *sister* of Dawn—which is found virtually throughout the Roman ritual and explicitly in the Indian myths—is remarkable. It is reinforced by the fact that, in the two mythologies, the dark sister exists only in terms of the luminous sister. Nothing supports the idea that Rome ever knew a practical personification, a cult of the night (Summanus is something else), and Rātrī, according to Renou's expression, is "only a pale reflection of Uṣas, without her own individuality."

In fact, despite this precise connection between Rome and Vedic India, the important element of the theologem is less the "sorority" of the two "mothers of the Sun"—she who ripens him in her bosom and she who receives him and rears him—than the principle of this "duality." We have proof of this in India itself. It has been shown elsewhere, in the wake of the memorable discovery of Stig Wikander, that not only the central group of heroes of the *Mahābhārata*—the five Pāṇḍava brothers—but also many other characters of the poem reproduce in their character, their behavior, and their lives the essential traits of the gods of whom they are the declared sons or incarnations. Further, just as the Pāṇḍavas, sons of canonical gods of the three functions, spread themselves among these functions, so their half-brother Karṇa, offspring of the Sun, took on two mythical representations of the Vedic Sun. His chariot, in combat, loses a wheel (and this accident is fatal to him); but before that he himself had two mothers: one according to nature, Kuntī, who abandons him at his birth and who much later will be the mother of the first three Pāṇḍavas, the other by adoption after this abandonment. It is this second one alone, Rādhā, whom he considers his mother. Kuntī and Rādhā are not sisters but successive mothers of the solar hero.[75]

What we have here is a representation of a myth that dates back at least to the Indo-Iranian period. This is borne out by the solar hero of the European

Iranians, the Ossets in the Caucasus, who are the latest descendants of the ancient Scythians. Soslan (Sosryko), in several situations, presents very clear solar traits, in particular at the time of his death, which was provoked by a wheel—the mythic representation of a kind of Saint John's wheel ("the wheel of Father John"). He also has two mothers. He was formed, an embryo, in a rock from which he was taken after nine months by her who would rear him, who would then constantly call him "my son whom I did not beget" and who, like the *bonae matres* of the Matralia, would show even more attention, more affection to him than to her own children. In this Caucasian tradition, the rock and Satana are not sisters either, but only collaborating and successive mothers.[76] These variants only make more noteworthy the fact that the *alterius proles*, "the child of another," whom the second "mother" takes in and cares for, should have been specified as "the child of the sister" in the myth put forth by the Matralia as in the *Rig Veda.*

Thus we have the four principal elements of the case of Mater Matuta completely and coherently explained, and her festival understood. The Roman ladies encourage, stimulate, and strengthen Aurora the night before the crisis that the summer solstice is about to open; they do so by sympathetic magic, by reproducing on earth the mythical acts that she accomplishes in heaven and which are expressed for us in the birth of successive days. But one must assume of course that this cosmic intention has a dual function. While they mime the solicitude of Aurora for her mythic *alterius proles*, the Sun, they themselves express an equal solicitude toward the little "extras" in this scene, their nephews, whom they hold in their arms; and, since they celebrate the festival of a goddess and can hope for her attention, they recommend them to this goddess who, beyond her concern for the celestial child, cannot fail to be interested in terrestrial children. Thus, in another connection, the maternal ex-voto found on the site of the sanctuaries that she possessed outside Rome are explained, as is the assimilation Matuta–Lucina that occurred in at least one of them.[77]

Notes

1. The goddess was common to the people of central Italy, but we know only of her Roman ritual. The word order is always *Mater Matuta,* except in Livy, 5.23.7, where the dative, *Matutae Matri,* is used.

2. Ovid, *Fasti,* 6.475: "ite, bonae matres, uestrum Matralia festum . . ."

3. Tertullian, *On Monogamy,* 17.

4. *καὶ γὰρ θεράπαιναν εἰς τὸν σηκὸν εἰσάγουσαι ῥαπίζουσιν, εἶτ' ἐξελαύνουσι καὶ τὰ τῶν ἀδελφῶν τέκνα πρὸ τῶν ἰδίων ἐναγκαλίζονται.* For the establishment and the meaning of this and the following texts, I refer the reader to the excellent article by Robert Flacelière, "Deux rites du culte de Mater Matuta, Plutarque, *Camille,* 5, 2," *Revue des études anciennes* 52 (1950), 18–27. Except for the point indicated in

the following note, I follow this translation. [The English translation is taken from the Dryden edition; <see "Note on the Translation," above.>]

5. The majority of interpreters—not Flacelière—have interpreted *τῶν ἀδελφῶν* as "sisters," even though the form could also be masculine. I believe they are right. James G. Frazer, *The Fasti of Ovid* (London, 1929), vol. 4, p. 280 n. 2, summarizes the question well: "In both the passages of Plutarch [= *Roman Questions*, 17 and *Camillus*, 5.2] the word translated 'sisters' (*τῶν ἀδελφῶν*) is ambiguous; it might equally mean 'brothers' or 'brothers and sisters'. It is only the analogy of Ino and Semele [in the *interpretatio graeca*] which seems to show that it was for their sisters' children alone that women prayed in the rites of Matuta." Cf. the first explanation of the *Roman Questions*, 17: *πότερον ὅτι φιλάδελφος μέν τις ἡ Ἰνὼ καὶ τὸν ἐκ τῆς ἀδελφῆς ἐτιθηνήσατο, ἡ δὲ περὶ τοὺς ἑαυτῆς παῖδας ἐδυστύχησεν* and the introduction to the last sentence of *De fraterno amore* (cited below at n. 8): *ἥ τε Λευκοθέα τῆς ἀδελφῆς ἀποθανούσης ἔθρεψε τὸ βρέφος καὶ συνεξεθείασεν· ὅθεν αἱ Ῥωμαίων γυναῖκες*. . . . The *alterius* of the *Fasti* (see below, n. 9) elucidated by its context, parallels this. But see below, "The Maternal Aurora," n. 74.

6. 16: *Διὰ τί δούλαις τὸ τῆς Λευκοθέας ἱερὸν ἄβατόν ἐστι, μίαν δέ μόνην αἱ γυναῖκες εἰσάγουσαι παίουσιν ἐπὶ κόρρης καὶ ῥαπίζουσιν;* 17: *Διὰ τί παρὰ τῇ θεῷ ταύτῃ τοῖς μέν ἰδίοις τέκνοις οὐκ εὔχονται τἀγαθὰ τοῖς δὲ τῶν ἀδελφῶν;* This text and those quoted in footnotes 8 and 9 alone prevent translating (Deubner, etc.) *πρό τῶν ἰδίων* of *Camillus*, 5.2 (see above, n. 4) as "*before* their own." It is, of course, "*instead of* [in place of] their own."

7. *Fasti*, 6.551–558.

8. *ὅθεν αἱ Ῥωμαίων γυναῖκες ἐν ταῖς τῆς Λευκοθέας ἑορταῖς, ἣν Ματοῦταν ὀνομάζουσιν, οὐ τοὺς ἑαυτῶν παῖδας ἀλλὰ τοὺς τῶν ἀδελφῶν ἐναγκαλίζονται καὶ τιμῶσιν.*

9. *non tamen hanc pro stirpe sua pia mater adoret:*
ipsa [= Leucothea] *parum felix uisa fuisse parens.*
alterius prolem melius mandabitis illi:
utilior Baccho quam fuit illa suis.

10. Ino-Leucothea and Semele, daughters of Cadmos, were sisters. It is said that after the death of Semele, Ino nursed her son Dionysus. On the contrary, among her own sons one, Learchos, was killed by his father in a fit of madness and the other, Melicertes, escaped from the paternal fury only to fall into the ocean and drown. According to a variant, his mother, who also went mad, plunged him into a cauldron of boiling water, then threw herself with the cadaver into the ocean. The link made between Matuta and Portunus is the result of a no less artificial assimilation between Portunus and Palemon-Melicertes and is not based on a Roman concept (Ovid, *Fasti*, 6.545–574).

11. *ἢ καὶ ἄλλως ἠθικὸν καὶ καλὸν τὸ ἔθος καὶ πολλὴν παρασκευάζον εὔνοιαν ταῖς οἰκειότησι;*

12. See "Mater Matuta" in Charles Victor Daremberg and Edmond Saglio, *Dictionnaire des antiquités grecques et romaines* (Paris, 1904), vol. 3, col. 1626a n. 7.

13. *Religion und Kultus der Römer* (Munich, 1902), p. 98 (= 2d ed. [Munich 1912], p. 111).

14. *Mater Matuta* (= Frankfurter Studien zur Religion und Kultur der Antike 8) (Frankfurt, 1934), pp. 58–59.

15. Ibid., pp. 60–61.

16. H. J. Rose, *The Roman Questions of Plutarch* (Oxford, 1924), p. 176; Frazer, *The Fasti of Ovid*, pp. 280–281.

17. "Les 'enfants des soeurs' à la fête de Mater Matuta," *Revue des études latines* 33 (1955), 142.

18. Frazer, *The Fasti of Ovid*, pp. 281–283, developing a suggestion by Lewis R. Farnell, "Sociological Hypotheses Concerning the Position of Women in Ancient Religion," *Archiv für Religionswissenschaft* 7 (1904), p. 84.

19. For example: Servius, *Commentary on the Aeneid*, 4.58: "Romae cum Cereis sacra fiunt, obseruatur ne quis patrem aut filiam nominet," quoted by Frazer himself, *The Fasti of Ovid*, p. 281 n. 1.

20. Frazer, *The Fasti of Ovid*, pp. 282–283. In certain northern regions of New Guinea, *if a child bears the name of the deceased paternal grandfather*, his mother must call him by another name. But this is only a particular instance of the general rule that forbids any woman from mentioning her in-laws by name. In northern Nigeria and elsewhere, parents avoid pronouncing the name of their *firstborn* child, pretending to despise it and to treat it like a stranger. This is because the firstborn is especially vulnerable to the ventures of evil spirits. Among the Halbas of central India, the child's name must not be pronounced *during the night* because if an owl

hears and repeats it, the child is liable to die.

21. Ibid., p. 283: "Similarly we may perhaps suppose that for certain reasons now unknown, it was deemed unlucky for women to pronounce the names of their own children in the rites of Mother Matuta, and that they were thus precluded from praying for their offspring to the goddess. Still this would not explain why they might pray for their sisters' children instead. No satisfactory solution of this problem has yet been found."

22. This interpretation is found in three studies by H. J. Rose: "De religionibus antiquis quaestiunculae tres," *Mnemosyne*, n.s. 53 (1925), 407–410 and 413–414 (summary of a personal communication from Joshua Whatmough): "Two Roman Rites," *The Classical Quarterly* 28 (1934), 156–157; *Ancient Roman Religion* (London, 1948) [see my note on this book in *Revue de l'histoire des religions* 139 (1951), 209], pp. 78–79 (see below, n. 77.1). In a prior work, *The Roman Questions of Plutarch*, p. 176, Rose had put forth another explanation (ethnographic facts where the maternal aunts, not the mothers, take care of young girls at the time of puberty), which he later retracted ("Two Roman Rites," 156 n. 5).

23. "Two Roman Rites," p. 157: "As regards the adjective which I have conjectured was used, I had occasion some years ago [= the article in *Mnemosyne*, 1925] to discuss it in another context, with the aid of Mr., now Professor, J. Whatmough. As a title of Iuno, I believe it to be connected with the verb *sororiare* [see below], not with the noun *soror*; this verb presupposes an adjective *sororius*, corresponding to it as *uarius* to *uariare*, and the adjective again a substantive **soros*, which, following Professor Whatmough, I would derive from a rt. *swer*, identical with that which gives rise to Germ. *schwellen* and Eng. *swell*; hence, applied to Iuno, the adjective means the goddess of swelling, ripening or maturing, in other words of adolescence or puberty, presumably that of girls. That epithets appropriate to worshippers of deities are often applied to the deities themselves is well enough known; for Rome, Fortuna Virgo may serve as an example, or Pudicitia Plebeia. Hence, there is nothing in the least unlikely in the supposition that this rare adjective, which if derived from *soror* makes no reasonable sense, witness the attempts of the Romans themselves to explain it by the aetiological story of Horatius and his sister, was applied, not only to Iuno, but to those for whom her protection, or that of any other goddess of fertility, was especially desirable, the younger generation, and especially the growing girls. However, *puer* being epicene, and Mater Matuata having apparently some connection with boys also, since she was identified with the nurse of Dionysos, and mother of Melikertes-Palaimon, it seems best to suppose that the *pueri sororii* on whose behalf I believe her to have been addressed were the adolescents of both sexes." I do not believe that any likely result can come from as loose a method as this, and as frivolous a reasoning. Rose alludes to an interpretation of the legend of the Horatii and the Curiatii which he also expounded several times, especially in his article "Mana in Greece and Rome," *Harvard Theological Review* 42 (1949), 165–169, with on p. 167 the most detailed presentation of the etymology of *sororius-sororiare* based on the alleged root **swer-* "to swell." The entry for *soror* is Alois Walde, *Lateinisches etymologisches Wörterbuch*, 3rd ed., rev. J. B. Hofmann (Heidelberg, 1954) does not even mention the etymology of *sororius, sororiare* put forth by Rose.

24. See below, n. 45.

25. In the name of *Juno Sororia*, linked to the legend of Horace killing his sister.

26. Festus, p. 381L[1] = p. 396L[2]: "sororiare mammae dicuntur puellarum, cum primum tumescunt, ut fraterculare puerorum." Slang willingly enlivens the parts of the body where the energy or the appeal of the sex organs is evident (cf. the refrain of a song sung at the front in 1918: "Oh, how much pleasure he gives me / Fernand's little brother!"). In an incomplete fragment of *Frivolaria* preserved by Festus, Plautus must have played with these expressions in speaking of a young girl barely in her puberty: [*tunc*] *papillae pri*[*mulum*] *fraterculabant,*——[*illud*] *uolui dicere, so*[*roriabant*], "It was precisely at the moment when her points began to 'become brothers'—excuse me, that is not what I meant to say: 'become sisters.'" The other gloss on *fratrare* (p. 80L[1] = p. 209L[2], with Lindsay's note; cf. *fratrescunt* in another glossary) does seem to prove that *sororiare* was created from verbs derived from "brother."

27. Rose's hypothesis is furthermore discredited

by the large number of ex-voto having the form of a diapered baby which were found in the non-Roman sanctuaries of Mater Matuta and which are sufficiently and naturally explained by the Matralia rite. Regarding the relationship between Mater Matuta and Ilithyia at Caere, <see above, chapter 4: "Juno and Mater Matuta.">

28. Cf. Flacelière, "Deux rites": "Concerning the text of *De fraterno amore, Moralia* 492 D, H. J. Rose, *Classical Quarterly* 28 (1934), 156 n. 1, notes that Plutarch is the sole author who says that, during the Matralia, children were carried in the arms of the matrons, and he wonders if *ἐναγκαλίζονται* is not corrupted. He forgets, though, that this word is verified by the parallel passage in the *Life* of Camillus where it is also found. Indeed, it is very likely that Plutarch made mistakes when speaking of institutions or rites that he learned of through Latin writers whose language he didn't know well. I think that is what happened, for example, regarding the statue of Juno Quiritus, *Romulus*, 29. But it is important, first of all, here as well as there, to determine exactly what he meant and to be careful not to correct or interpret his text in a way which would arbitrarily bring it into line with the other statements." See in Halberstadt, *Mater Matuta*, p. 56, the references establishing that *ἐναγκαλίζεσθαι* is used especially with regard to love and maternal care.

29. *Roman Questions*, 16: *ἢ τὸ μὲν ταύτην ῥαπίζεσθαι σύμβολόν ἐστι τοῦ μὴ ἐξεῖναι, κωλύουσι δὲ τὰς ἄλλας διὰ τὸν μῦθον;*

30. *Fasti*, 6.481–482.

31. *The Fasti of Ovid*, vol. 4, p. 279.

32. "Les 'enfants des soeurs,'" 150.

33. *Mater Matuta*, p. 15.

34. *The Roman Questions of Plutarch*, p. 175.

35. *Mater Matuta*, p. 16.

36. Plutarch, *Romulus*, 21.5: *αἱ δ' ἐν ἡλικίᾳ γυναῖκες οὐ φεύγουσι τὸ παίεσθαι, νομίζουσαι πρὸς εὐτοκίαν καὶ κύησιν συνεργεῖν.*

37. Plutarch, *Convivial Questions*, 6.8.1.

38. Plutarch, *Greek Questions*, 12.

39. Pausanias, 8.23.1.

40. *καὶ ἐν Διονύσου τῇ ἑορτῇ κατὰ μάντευμα ἐκ Δελφῶν μαστιγοῦνται γυναῖκες, καθὰ καὶ οἱ Σπαρτιατῶν ἔφηβοι παρὰ τῇ Ὀρθίᾳ.*

41. *Mythe et épopée III* (Paris, 1973), p. 42 n. 1.

42. *Tempore item certo roseam Matuta per oras*
aetheris aurora refert et lumina pandit
aut quia . . .
aut quia . . .

43. "Beiträge zur lateinischen Etymologie," *Zeitschrift für vergleichende Sprachforschung* 35 (1897), 233–237: "8. Maturus, Matuta, matutinus, manus (manis), manes, mane" quoting, other than *ὡραῖος, ἀκμαῖος*, semantic families of the same type, in particular in the Slavic languages (roots *dob-*, *god-*).

44. With numerous derived nuances: see for example Gellius, 10.11.1.

45. *City of God*, 4.8: *florentibus frumentis deam Floram, maturescentibus Matutam, cum runcantur, id est e terra auferunter, deam Runcinam. . . .* The text is ambiguous; certain manuscripts have *Maturam*. Perhaps, therefore, it is not even a matter of an approximation of *Matuta*. In the glosses of Pseudo-Placidus (Georg Goetz, *Corpus glossariorum latinorum* [Leipzig and Berlin, 1894], vol. 5, p. 221) this Matura reappears, but it carries, because of an inverted confusion, the personality of *Matuta*: "Matura dea paganorum quam Greci Leucotea[m] dixerunt." See below, n. 47.

46. See above, "The Children of Their Sisters."

47. Pp. 109, 112, 154L^{1} = pp. 248–249, 253, 278L^{2}; (1) Matrem Matutam "antiqui ob bonitatem appellabant, et *maturum* idoneum usuri, et *mane* principium diei, et inferi dii *manes*, ut suppliciter appellati bono essent et in carmine Saliari Cerus *manus* intelligitur creator bonus; (2) *mane* a diis *manibus* dixerunt, nam *mana* bona dicitur, unde et *Mater Matuta* et poma *matura*"; (3) Mater Matuta, manes, mane, matrimonium, materfamiliae, matertera, matrices, materiae "dictae, uidentur, ut ait Verrius, quia sint bona, qualia scilicet sint quae sunt *matura*, uel potius a *matre*, quae est orginis graecae." We see that Paulus (Festus, Verrius), having put together the accurate dossier of related words, goes too far and tries artificially to set up relationships (2: *mane* does not come from *di manes*). The first gloss (M. M. "ob bonitatem") is obviously only the same kind of hypothesis, having no more importance than many others of the *De significatione uerborum* (*genus* from *γῆν*, *gloria* from *κλέος*, *obliteratum* from *obliuio* or from *litus*, etc.). Priscian, *Institutiones grammaticae*, 2.53 (= vol. 2, p. 76, of Henrich Keil, *Grammatici Latini*

[Leipzig, 1855–1870]): matutinus "a *Matuta*, quae significat Auroram uel, ut quidam," *Λευκοθέαν*; but later (4.34) he gets caught in an incorrect derivation. He says that we should have **manumine*, from *mane*, and we have *matutine*! At the beginning of an account by Nonius Marcellus (see *manum*, pp. 66–67 of Quicherat), which is little less ambiguous than those of Paulus Diaconus, the adjective *manus* is incorrectly translated as "clarus" and thus made to explain *mane* and *Matuta*. We sense everywhere that this well-known family of words caused problems for the "prelinguists" of antiquity which were beyond their means: cf. above, n. 45. The definition of *Matuta* in the etymological dictionary of [Walde-] Hoffman, vol. 2, p. 53) strangely continues this confusion.

48. Gaulish *Mati-*, *Mato-* (*-matos*) in proper names, Irish *maith*, Gallic *mad* "good."

49. *The Roman Festivals of the Period of the Republic* (London, 1899), p. 156, after quoting Lucretius, 5.654: "We should, however, be glad to be more certain that Matuta was originally a substantive meaning dawn or morning. Verrius Flaccus [= Paulus, p. 109] seems to have believed that the words *mane, maturus, matuta, manes*, and *manus*, all had the meaning of 'good'contained in them; so that Mater Matuta might after all be only another form of the Bona Dea, who is also specially a woman's deity. But this cult was not preserved, like that of Vesta, by being taken up into the essential life of the State, and we are no longer able to discern its meaning with any approach to certainty." Strange logic. Having confidence in the etymological games of Verrius Flaccus, the philologist gratuitously bestows a prehistoric meaning on the cult, anterior and foreign to the known and clear historical meaning. He then states that no document informs us of this prehistoric meaning and concludes that we can never be certain of its "true meaning." One has only to eliminate these artificial detours to avoid difficulty. The "true meaning" of the cult is its historical meaning. There is no objective reason for finding its prehistoric meaning. Warde Fowler (with a bad translation of Plutarch's *πρό*, *Camillus*, 5.2: see Halberstadt, *Mater Matuta*, p. 56) writes wisely about the "sisters' children" rites (p. 155 n. 2): "I cannot explain the rule that a woman prayed for nephews and nieces before her own children, which is peculiar to this cult."

50. *The Fasti of Ovid*, p. 273.

51. Vol. 3, col. 1625a: see *Mater Matuta, Matralia*.

52. See *Matuta*, 14, col. 2326, refusing to follow Walter Otto, who had suggested the meaning "gute Göttin" in "Iuno," *Philologus*, n.s. 18 (1905), 212.

53. *Gestirnverehrung im alten Italien* (= Frankfurter Studien zur Religion und Kultur der Antike 3) (Frankfurt, 1933), p. 99.

54. *Mater Matuta*, p. 63.

55. See below, n. 77 (2) and (3).

56. "Two Roman Rites," 157. "Often enough" is tendentious: it is by far the most widely held opinion.

57. Joseph Vendryes, "Les correspondances de vocabulaire entre l'indo-iranien et l'italo-celtique," *Mémoires de la société de linguistique* 20 (1918), 265–285, specifying the meaning of a summary of the *Einleitung in die Geschichte der griechischen Sprache* of Paul Kretschmer (Göttingen, 1896).

58. N. J. Shende, "The foundations of the Atharvanic Religion," *Bulletin of the Deccan College Research Institute* 9 (1949), 235: "On the whole, the Atharvanic poets do not attach much importance to this deity. She has been neglected. There is not that charm and beauty of Uṣas as they are found in the *Rig Veda*. She is also not employed for magical purpose by the poet. It thus seems that in the Atharvanic mythology Uṣas is totally neglected." Is this loss of importance explained in part by the increasing importance of the god Savitar, "the Energizer" who, among other things, presides at sunrise? Cf. Giancarlo Montesi, "Il valore cosmico dell' Aurora nel pensiero mitologico del Rig-Veda," *Studi e materiali per la storia delle religioni* 24–25 (1953–1954), 111–132; and F. B. J. Kuiper, "The Ancient Aryan Verbal Contest," *Indo-Iranian Journal* 4 (1960), 217–281 at 217–242 (in particular, 223–242, "Uṣas and the New Year").

59. The few known facts are analyzed and discussed, moving back from the first to the fifth century, in the second part of Agnes Kirsopp Michels' book, *The Calendar of the Roman Republic* (Princeton, 1967). See in particular the discussion of the supposed change of the beginning of the year (from March 1 to January 1) in 153 B.C., pp. 97–101; p. 99: "It seems to me more probable that the republican calendar had always begun its year on the Kalends

of January. The calendar which it supplanted must, however, have begun on the Kalends of March."

60. Ibid., p. 102.

61. Ibid., p. 100.

62. See the discussion of the texts on the intercalation in ibid., pp. 160–172; in particular p. 169 (with n. 18): "It seems to me more probable that the pontifices followed the much simpler course of omitting an intercalation or two when they observed that the calendar was inconveniently behind the seasons. This would have kept the calendar in an approximately correct relation to the solar year, and it is clear that, until Caesar spoiled them, the Romans were quite satisfied with an approximate relation."

63. To "Forefather Sun": Ἀγωνάλια δαφνηφόρῳ γενάρχῃ Ἡλίῳ, Lydus, *Months, fragm. Caseol.*, p. 118 Beck. This correlation was emphasized by Koch, *Gestirnverehrung*, p. 99.

64. See the personal ideas of Kuiper about Uṣas in "Aryan Verbal Contest."

65. *Études védiques et paṇinéennes* (Paris, 1957), vol. 3, p. 6.

66. Ibid., p. 10.

67. Ibid., p. 9.

68. *La religion védique d'après les hymnes du Ṛig Véda* (Paris, 1878), vol. 1, p. 248. Cf. John Muir, *Original Sanskrit Texts* (London, 1870), vol. 5, p. 191; Alfred Hillebrandt, *Vedische Mythologie* (Breslau, 1899), vol. 2, pp. 44–47 (= 2d ed., 1927, vol. 1, pp. 45–49), and especially A. K. Coomaraswamy, "The Darker Side of Dawn," *Smithsonian Miscellaneous Collections* 94 (1935).

69. Contrary opinion again in Hillebrandt, *Vedische Mythologie*, p. 44 (= 2d ed., p. 46).

70. Renou, *Études védiques*, vol. 12, translates: "measuring interminable journeys." The meaning of *samānám*, "common," has been contested, although it is clear: see Renou, p. 42.

71. The commentator Sāyaṇa thinks that, if the eleventh stanza concerns "day and night," the following three concern "heaven and earth," and the fifteenth stanza one or the other of these pairs. This division is probably faulty. In the introduction and the notes of Karl Friedrich Geldner's translation, good reason is found to attribute the twelfth and fourteenth stanzas, like the eleventh stanza, to Night and to Aurora, and the fifteenth stanza to the neighboring couple Night and Day, but this interpretation must be extended to the thirteenth stanza. Not only does the presence of the calf, surely the same one, in twelve, thirteen, and fourteen advise against separating these three stanzas in the exegesis, but the poetic form itself, the *ṛtá* mentioned in the genitive at the beginning of the last verse of each (*ṛtásya . . . sádasi; ṛtásya . . . páyasā; ṛtásya . . . sádma*), proves that it is a unit, and a unit that the couple Night–Aurora fits very well since Night and Aurora are the two "mothers of *ṛtá*" (see above at n. 69). Bergaigne's objections to this unitary interpretation (*La religion védique*, vol. 2, p. 11 n. 2) are weak, and the principal one is erroneous. He says that Night and Aurora are never presented in the *Rig Veda* as mother and daughter; indeed, the "sisters" concept is predominant, and by a great deal (even here, stanza 11), but in 10.3.2 for example, "the dark" with which Agni fathers the "young woman" (*yóṣām*) is likely Night in the capacity of mother of Aurora.

72. I leave out the refrain common to twenty-four stanzas of the hymn, as it is not significant.

73. I refrain from choosing among all the artificial translations proposed for *pádyā;* Renou, *Études védiques*, vol. 5, p. 16: "(Aurora) placed at the feet (of the cosmos) . . ."

74. If the broadest meaning of "brothers and sisters" is given to the ἀδελφῶν of Plutarch's texts (see above, n. 5), we will acknowledge an extension, a generalization that is not improbable in a ritual. It can also be advanced that the deity who presides over certain phenomena in the second part of the night is masculine, Summanus; <see above, chapter 3: "Summanus.">

75. *Mythe et épopée I*, pp. 123–144 (concerning the two mothers, pp. 126–135).

76. See my *Légendes sur les Nartes, suivies de cinq notes mythologiques* (Bibliotheque de l'Institute Français de Léningrad 11) (Paris, 1930), pp. 75–77 (birth of Soslan) and 190–199 (solar elements of Soslan); *Loki* (Paris, 1948), pp. 227–246; *Le livre des héros* (Paris, 1965), pp. 69–71 (with the current bibliography).

77. <See above, chapter 4: "Juno and Mater Matuta," and, more generally, all of that chapter, on the relationship between Mater Matuta and Juno (cf. Uṣas and Aditi); on Mater Matuta and Fortuna

(cf. Uṣas and Bhaga), above, chapter 2; on Mater Matuta and Janus (cf. Uṣas and Savitṛ), above, chapter 3: "Summanus" and "The Pardon for the Tusculans."> The need for the celebrants of the Matralia to be married in a first marriage recalls the mention of the Auroras in the hymns and the Vedic marriage ritual (*Atharva Veda*, 14.2; 31.43, 44), where, moreover, Sūryā, daughter of Sūrya (the Sun), the prototype of every newly married girl, is perhaps only a variation of Uṣas. In order to measure the difference that separates the concepts and processes of the present study from those of recent manuals on Roman religion, I reproduce the lines that the three principal ones devote to Mater Matuta.

(1) H. J. Rose, *Ancient Roman Religion*, pp. 78–79: "In passing, a minor deity of the field should be mentioned, because her name has been much misinterpreted in ancient and modern times. This is Mater Matuta, who had a festival, the Matralia, on June 11, and a temple in the Cattle Market. A perfectly satisfactory explanation of her name has come down to us, and is due to Varro; she looked after the ripening (*maturescentia*) grains. This fits the time of her festival, not very long before harvest, also the fact that her feast was in the hands of free married women, for clearly her share in the provision of *numen* for the fields was important enough to demand the attention of these traditional practitioners of farm magic and doers of the lighter farm work. It equally explains why no slave-women might take part; slaves are foreigners, and what should they know of the way to approach the native goddess? Equally, it makes it clear why some Greek theologians thought she was the same person as their own Eileithyia, the goddess of birth; if she can ripen the fruit of the ground, why not that of the womb, seeing that the equation between Mother Earth and human mothers runs through all ancient religion and magic? But the same root which gives Latin its word for 'ripen', produces several words which signify 'early', especially early in the day. So the notion came about and is not yet quite departed that she was a dawn-goddess. It is refuted by the fact that she had a cult. Dawn—Eos in Greek, Aurora in Latin—is a pretty figure of mythology and folktales, whom no one is known to have worshipped in the whole ancient world." (This explanation of H. J. Rose was unfortunately adopted unreservedly in R. M. Ogilvie, *A Commentary on Livy, Books I–V* [Oxford, 1965], p. 680.)

(2) Albert Grenier, *Les religions étrusque et romaine* (= *Mana* 2.3 [1948]), pp. 116–117: "The Matralia, on June 11, is the festival of *Mater Matuta*, the goddess of happy beginnings and of the birth of beings. In this she singularly resembles Juno, and by virtue of this the matrons invoke her. As an attribute she has a key, because she facilitates deliveries, as *Juno Lucina* does later. The epithet Matuta that means "good, favorable" links her with Bona Dea, occasionally named *Fauna*, the favorable, and related to *Faunus*, the genie of fertility. . . . *Mater Matuta* had a temple in the Forum Boarium which probably was built by Camillus in 396 on the site of the old sanctuary whose foundation was attributed to Servius Tullius. Honored throughout Italy, she was one of the principal goddesses of Caere (Cervetri), the Etruscan port of Rome, and had a very ornate sanctuary there which was pillaged by Dionysius of Syracuse. Recent excavations have furnished numerous ex voto representing children in swaddling clothes. The findings had been the same at the temple of *Satricum* in Latium. *Bona Dea* and *Mater Matuta* were obviously Mother-Goddesses closely related to Juno and quite similar to the Gaulish Mother-Goddesses. Later assimilations made *Bona Dea* a *Hygie* and *Mater Matuta* the companion of *Portunus* or a relative of *Janus matutinus*." P. 132: "The epithet of *Matuta* means 'good, favorable': J. Vendryes, *Teutomatos* in *Comptes rendus Acad. Inscr.* (1939), pp. 466–480. The same root *matu* formed the word *matutinus* because morning is the favorable moment par excellence. *Mater Matuta* is 'the Good Mother'; her name has the same meaning as that of *Bona Dea*. Not understood, it transformed her into the goddess Aurora, associated with *Janus matutinus*, Hor., *Sat.*, 2.6.20. Mythologic speculation then assimilated her into the Greek Ino-Leucothea."

(3) Paul Fabre, *La religion romaine* in *L'histoire des religions* by Maurice Brillant and René Aigrain (Paris, 1955), vol. 3, p. 338: "Mater Matuta—again a nutritive *numen*; Matuta means 'good', 'favorable' [cf. Vendryes, *Teutomatos*, pp. 466–480]; *Mater Matuta* is thus the 'Good Mother'. She was

honored on June 11, the day of the *Matralia*, which was the festival of matrons, and only of those who had been married but once. The goddess received cakes baked in terra-cotta containers. At the time she was linked to Janus and was made a deity of beginnings who presided at the coming of dawn, probably through bringing together the epithets of *Matuta* and *Matutinus*. It is possible moreover that this coming together was not fortuitous. In any case, she presided, like Juno, with whom she seems to have more than one trait in common, at the birth of children. In short, she appears to be very much like a fertility goddess, very close to the other goddesses we have already encountered, but specialized above all it seems in the protection of the family. Her cult seems to have extended over all of central Italy."

It is remarkable that neither of the two specific and original rites of the Matralia that we have studied is mentioned in these presentations. Grenier and Fabre are wrong to quote Vendryes, *Teutomatos* to support their interpretation as "Bona Dea." Vendryes limited himself to noting correctly, as Porkrovskij had done, that the name of the Roman goddess of dawn, the derivative in *tu-ta* from the root *ma-*, rests on the concept of the type "of favorable hour"; he did not insinuate that *Matuta* ever specified "good" in general.

PART 5

IRAN

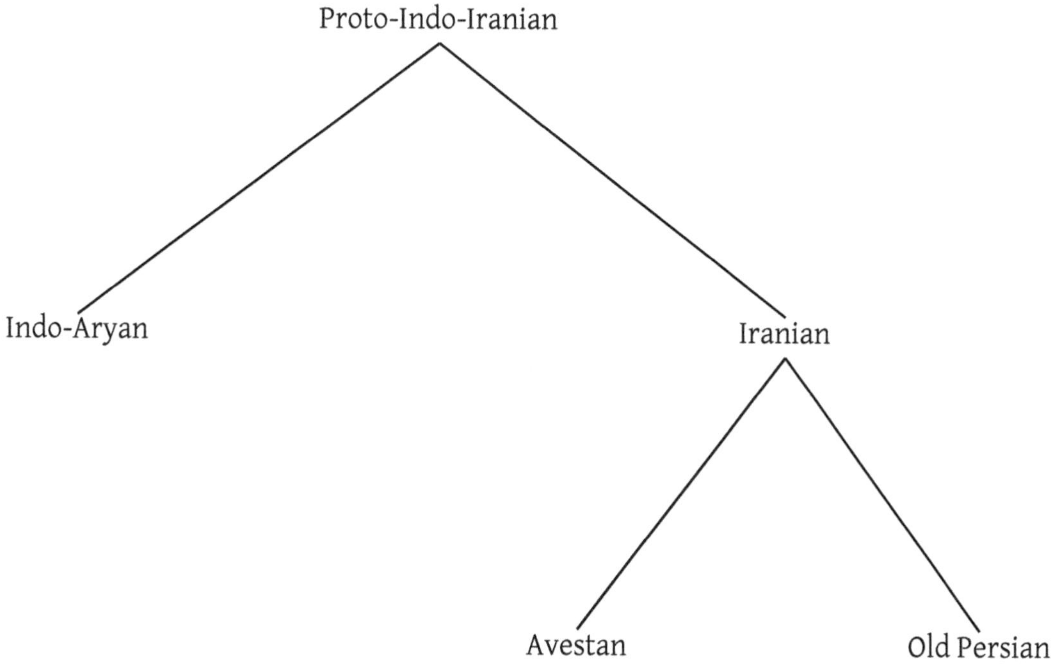

21. *Mithra and Ahura-Mazdāh, Mihrjān and Naurōz*

The religious reformer Zarathuštra (or, more generically, "the Iranian reformers," as Dumézil has it below) elevated one god, Ahura Mazdāh, to a position of preeminence far above all other gods. Ahura Mazdāh is clearly framed as such a supreme deity in that ancient set of Avestan hymns called the Gāthās. In later-produced portions of the Avesta (the Zoroastrian sacred book), however, the god Mithra emerges as a deity of enormous power and import. This "emergence" is very likely a "re-emergence" of a deity of pre-reform Iranian religion (pre-Mazdaism) who had been no less prominent than earlier Ahura: the Iranian divine pair named by the common dvandva *(a compound of two elements)—Mithra-Ahura—probably matches (linguistically, historically, theologically) the Vedic pair similarly denoted—Mitra-Varuṇa.*

In the short essay that follows (excerpted from a longer treatment of Ahura and Mithra), Dumézil adds to the body of evidence for the equation Mithra-Ahura = Mitra-Varuṇa a consideration of two Persian festivals: Naurōz (the New Year feast of Ahura Mazdāh) and Mihrjān (feast of Mithra). (RDW)

MITHRA AND AHURA-MAZDĀH, MIHRJĀN AND NAURŌZ

Georges Dumézil

In Iran, where the facts are more confused, and where one senses the purposeful hand of the reformers even in the earliest texts, I shall leave it to the specialists to prospect in their own territory. The Uppsala school, inspired by Mr. Nyberg, is already addressing itself, with happy results, to this question of the sovereign god (G. Widengren, *Hochgottglaube im alten Iran, Uppsala Univ. Aarsskrift*, 1938, VI). I shall therefore limit myself to a few observations made in the light of the Indian and Roman material we have been examining.[1]

It is certainly important, from a historical point of view, to record the ups and downs of Mithra's career; to note, for example, that he is absent from the *Gāthās* and to determine how he found his way back into the other parts of the *Avesta*. But the details of such misfortunes tell the comparatist very little, since his task is to search through the documents, of whatever kind, from any era and any source, for vestiges of the early state of the Indo-Iranian couple *Mitra-*Varuṇa, already present in the Mitani list of gods and so well preserved in India.[2] I have already referred, in this context, to the customary Avestic formula *Mithra-Ahura*, which, associating Mithra as it does with a "supreme Ahura" on an equal footing, is certainly anterior to Mazdaism proper. Is Ahura-Mazdāh the heir of this "preeminent Ahura" and, consequently, homologous with Varuṇa, the great Vedic Asura? This hypothesis, long accepted without argument, has subsequently been hotly disputed—wrongly, in my belief. On this point I regret being in disagreement with a mythologist of such standing as H. Lommel, but, since all my research has fully confirmed the validity of the description "sovereign" as applied to the Asura Varuṇa by Bergaigne, it seems to me more than probable that the rise of Ahura-Mazdāh derives precisely from the fact that he was an extension of the sovereign god of the premazdeans. The work of the Iranian reformers would then have consisted in a successful attempt to improve the morals of this ancient sorcerer, on the one hand, and, on the other, to isolate him in a position far above all other divine entities (cf. my *Ouranos-Varuṇa*, pp. 101–102).[3]

One consideration concerning Mithra strengthens this opinion still further. It is a fact that a religion's great annual festivals are less easily reformed than its dogmas. It is therefore probable that, like Christianity in other times and other places, Mazdaism was simply "sanctifying" the previous state of affairs when it balanced its year on two great festivals separated by the maximum interval (spring equinox to autumn equinox) and clearly antithetical in their meaning and their myths. And those festivals are placed under two invocations, one of Ahura-Mazdāh, the other of Mithra.

On the cosmic level, Naurōz, the Persian New Year and feast of Ahura-Mazdāh, celebrated "on the day Ohrmazd" of the first month, commemorates creation. The feast of Mithra (*Mithrakāna, Mihragān, Mihrjān . . .*), celebrated on "the day Mihr" in "the month Mihr," prefigures the end of the world. Why is this? Albiruni replies (*The Chronology of Ancient Nations*, 1879, p. 208): "Because, at Mihrjān, that which believes attains its perfection and has no more matter left to believe more, and because the animals cease to couple; at Naurōz it is the exact opposite." In this opposition between immobilized perfection and creative force, there is no difficulty in recognizing the theological adaptation of an old law-magic, conservation-fecundity opposition that we have seen expressed in

India by the couple Mitra-Varuṇa and in Rome—even apart from the opposite and complementary activities of flamines and Luperci—by Numa "perfecting" the "creation" of Romulus. There is an even more precise correspondence, however: this division of seasonal roles (the beginning of winter, the beginning of summer) between Ahura-Mazdāh and Mithra, in accordance with the "faculty of growth" and the "arrest of growth" that they express, clearly rests on the same symbolism as the assimilation of Mitra to the waning moon and Varuṇa to the waxing moon, which has sometimes been rather overhastily attributed to the "fancy" of brahman authors.

In epic terms, Naurōz was instituted by Yim (Yama), a king whose carnivalesque features leap to the eye, and who is specifically thought of as the father of the monster Gandarep (Gandarəva), just as the Vedic Yama is said to be the son of the Gandharva. Mihrjān, on the contrary, was instituted by Faridūn (Thraetaona), a law-abiding hero, who reestablished justice and morality after the tyrannical masquerade of the monster Aždahāk (Azhi-Dahāka), for whom Kndrv (again Gandarəva) acted as steward of royal entertainment. Here, once again, we find the distinction so clearly made in India between a "moon dynasty" and a "sun dynasty," between Gandharva kings (Purūravas, Nahuṣa) and the legislator king (Manu).

This comparison is reinforced even further by the fact that Yim's acting out of his triumph, commemorated annually during Naurōz, coincides exactly with that of Nahuṣa: he harnesses *devs* to an aerial chariot and has himself carried at tremendous speed through the sky; and men, "praising God for having raised their king to such a degree of greatness and power," institute this annual feast (Al Tha'ālibī, *Histoire des Rois de Perse*, trans. Zotenberg, p. 13). The scene commemorated by Mihrjān, on the contrary, is one of calm and serenity: Faridūn, having driven out Aždahāk, seats himself upon the throne, surrounded "near and far" by his vassals, and gives an audience to his people. "His physiognomy was illumined, from his mouth fell gracious words, the reflection of his divine majesty shone within him," and his subjects founded the feast of Mihrjān "to express that they had recovered through his justice the life that they had lost. . . ." Here we recognize a set of oppositions only too familiar by now: *celeritas* and *gravitas*, violent triumph and ordered organization, powerful king and just king.

These systems of antithetical representations, linked by a deeply rooted tradition to the two complementary feasts of Ahura-Mazdāh and Mithra—at the two equinoxes—seem to me to confirm that, before reform, the couple Mithra-Ahura had the same meaning, the same double orientation, the same balance, as the Vedic couple Mitra-Varuṇa, and that, consequently, the Ahurah Mazdāh of the Avesta is to be linked, typologically and genetically, with the Vedic Varuṇa.

Notes

1. Cf. *JMQ* III, ch. 2 and 3; M. L. Gerschel has also pointed out to me a significant linking of "Zeus" and "Helios" in Xenophon, *Cyropaedia*, VIII, 3, 11ff.; and 7, 3.

2. A curious lapse has led to these lines being taken as an admission that I am attempting to set up a jealously "comparative" method, in opposition to the "historical method" (R. Pettazzoni, *Studi et materiali di Storia delle Religioni*, XIX–XX, 1943–46, *Rivista bibliografica*, p. 7ff.). A close re-reading, however, will confirm that they simply draw a legitimate distinction between two problems, that of Mithra's *history* and that of the *vestiges* that subsist, within that history, from his *prehistory*. "Comparatist" in this context is merely a shorthand method to denote the scholar who is trying to reconstitute, like I am in this book, by means of comparisons, fragments of the religion of the Indo-Iranians or the Indo-Europeans. <The same observation applies to the other passage in this book (see the section on Dius Fidius: "It is of little importance, etc. . .") which Signor Pettazzoni also uses, with no greater justification, for the same purpose.>

3. *JMQ* III, p. 86ff.

22. Mihr Yašt (Yašt *10*)

The sacred book of the Zoroastrians, the Avesta, *is divided into three principal parts: the* Yasna, *a collection of liturgical hymns (of which the above-mentioned* Gāthās *form a portion); the* Yašts, *a set of hymns praising various deities individually; and the* Vidēvdāt, *a collection of anti-demonic texts. The importance and power of Mithra in post-reform Zoroastrianism is clearly demonstrated by this excerpt from* Yašt 10, *dedicated to Mithra.* (RDW)

MITHRA (MIHR) YAŠT (YAŠT 10)

Translated by William Malandra

I

1 Ahura Mazdā said to Zarathushtra the Spitamid: When I created Mithra of wide pastures, I made him, O Spitamid, as worthy of worship and praise as myself, Ahura Mazdā.

2 The knave who is false to a treaty, O Spitamid, destroys the whole country to the (same) extent as even one hundred kayadhas smiting the righteous (man). Do not break a covenant, O Spitamid, neither (the one) which you might conclude with a drugwant nor (one) with an ashawan belonging to the Good Religion, for the contract applies to both of you, to drugwant and to ashawan.

3 Mithra of wide pastures gives possession of swift horses to those who are not false to a covenant. Fire (Ātar), (the son) of Ahura Mazdā, gives the straightest path to those who are not false to a covenant. The good, strong, beneficent Frawashis of the Righteous give noble progeny to those who are not false to a covenant.

4 Because of his *rayi* and glory, I shall audibly worship Mithra of wide pastures with libations. We worship Mithra of wide pastures, who bestows peaceful and comfortable dwellings on the Iranian countries.

5 May he come hither to us in order to help (us). May he come hither

From *An Introduction to Ancient Iranian Religion*, by William W. Malandra, 1983. University of Minnesota Press. Reprinted by permission.

to us for spaciousness. May he come hither to us to support (us). May he come hither to us to (grant us) mercy. May he come hither to us to cure (us of disease). May he come hither to us so that we are able to defeat our enemies. May he come hither to us to (grant us) a good life. May he come hither to us to grant us possession of Truth. (May) strong, unshakable, undeceivable Mithra of wide pastures, who is worthy of worship and praise, (come hither) for the sake of the whole material world.

6 With libations I shall worship the powerful god, strong Mithra, strongest in the (world of) creatures; I shall pay homage to him with praise and reverence; with libations I shall audibly worship him, Mithra of wide pastures. We worship Mithra of wide pastures with haoma (mixed) with milk . . .

[Continue with Ny. 1.16 (p. 183)].

II

7 We worship Mithra of wide pastures, whose speech is correct, who is eloquent (in verbal contests), who has a thousand ears, is well built, has ten thousand eyes, is tall, has a wide outlook, is strong, sleepless, (ever)waking,

8 whom the rulers descending upon the battlefield worship (as they advance) against the bloodthirsty enemy armies, against those drawn up in battle lines between the two warring countries.

9 Whichever of the two (countries? rulers?) can worship him first, believingly, with understanding thought from a trusting mind—to that one, Mithra of wide pastures turns; at the same time, the victorious Winds (also turn to that one), at the same time Dāmōish Upamana (turns).

[Repeat sts. 4–6.]

III

10 We worship Mithra . . . [continue with st. 7];

11 whom the Warriors worship at (i.e., bending down close to) the manes of (their) horses, requesting strength for their teams, health for themselves, much watchfulness against enemies, the ability to retaliate

against foes, the ability to overcome unfriendly, hostile opponents at a blow.

[Repeat sts. 4–6.]

IV

12 We worship Mithra . . . [continue with st. 7];

13 who is the first supernatural god to rise across the Harā (mountain range), in front of the immortal swift-horsed sun, who is the first to seize the beautiful mountain peaks adorned with gold; from there he, the most mighty, surveys the whole land inhabited by Iranians,

14 where gallant rulers preside over many (offerings of) refreshments (to the gods), where high mountains rich in pasture lands and water provide fodder for cattle, where there exist deep lakes with wide expanses of water, where wide irrigation waters rush with eddies toward Parutian Ishkata, Haraiwan Margu, Sogdian Gawa, and Chorasmia.

15 Strong Mithra surveys (the continents) Arəzahī, Sawahī, Fradadhafshu, Widadhafshu, Wouru.barəshtī, Wouru.jarəshtī, and that splendid continent Xwaniratha, (the land of) village settlement and (of) healthy village habitation;

16 (Mithra) the supernatural god who drives over (throughout?) all the continents bestowing xwarənah, the supernatural god who drives over (throughout?) all the continents bestowing power. He secures victoriousness for those who, instructed (in religious matters), knowing Truth, worship him with libations.

[Repeat sts. 4–6.]

V

17 We worship Mithra . . . [continue with st. 7], who is deceived by no one, neither by the head of the house (ruling over) the house, nor by the village head (ruling over) the village, nor by the tribal head (ruling over) the tribe, nor by the head of the country (ruling over) the country.

18 If, indeed, the head of the house (ruling over) the house, or the village head (ruling over) the village, or the tribal head (ruling over) the tribe, or the head of the country (ruling over) the country is deceitful

toward him, Mithra, angered (at) having been treated with enmity, (comes) forth (and) smashes the house and the village and the tribe and the country, and the heads of the houses (ruling over) the houses, and the village heads (ruling over) the villages, and the tribal heads (ruling over) the tribes, and the heads of the countries (ruling over) the countries and the councils of premiers of the countries.

19 Mithra, angry (at) having been treated with enmity, will sally forth from (?) that direction in which, of the (possible) directions, the breaker of a covenant is least on guard in his mind.

20 Even the horses of the breakers of a covenant become loath to be mounted; running they do not get away, being ridden they do not take (their rider) forward, drawing (the chariot) they do not persevere (make progress). Back flies the spear which the covenant-breaker throws, in spite of (?) the evil spells which the covenant-breaker performs.

21 Even when his throw is a good one, even when he hits the body, even then they (?) do not hurt him (the opponent) in spite of (?) the evil spells which the covenant-breaker performs. The wind carries (away) the spear which the covenant-breaker throws, in spite of (?) the evil spells which the covenant-breaker performs.

[Repeat sts. 4–6.]

VI

22 We worship Mithra . . . [continue with st. 7], who (when) undeceived removes a man from anxiety, removes (him) from danger.

23 May you, O Mithra, undeceived (by us), remove us from anxiety, from anxieties. You induce fear for their own person(s) in men who are false to a covenant in this manner: (when) angered you are able to remove the power in their arms, the strength in their legs, the light of their eyes, the hearing of their ears.

24 (An enemy) does not hit with blades (?) of well-sharpened spear(s) or of far-flying arrow(s) him to whom Mithra comes with foreknowing thought to help, (Mithra) who, strong, having ten thousand spies, undeceivable, knows all.

[Repeat sts. 4–6.]

VII

25 We worship Mithra . . . [continue with st. 7], the profound, powerful Lord (Ahura), granting profit, eloquent (in verbal contests), pleased with (hymns of) praise, lofty, very skillful, *tanu.māthra*, the strong-armed warrior,

26 the smasher of the daēwas' heads, the especially evil punisher of guilty men who are false to a covenant, the suppressor of witches, who when not deceived leads the country to superior strength, who when not deceived leads the country to superior valor,

27 who carries away the straightest (paths) of the defiant country, obscures (its) xwarənah, removes (its) victoriousness; he harries them defenseless; he, strong, all-knowing, undeceivable, having ten thousand spies, deals out ten thousand blows.

[Repeat sts. 4–6.]

23. *The Root* *g^{u}hen-: *Avestan* jan-

The Proto-Indo-European verb root *g^{u}hen-, *'to slay', is widely attested among early Indo-European languages. In the following article, one of a set of essays treating a formulaic usage of this verb, Watkins examines the Avestan tradition of the slaying of a three-headed monster, an account closely matched by the Indic tradition of the slaying of the Tricephal Viśvarūpa—that event which Dumézil interprets as the first-function sin of the warrior god Indra (see Part 4, section 18: "Indra the Sinner" and "The Sins and Losses of Indra").* As in Rig Veda 2.11, *the hymn with which Watkins begins this essay, Indra is commonly presented as having an accomplice in the deed: Trita Āptya (the 'third' Āptya), who finds a structural homologue in Thraētaona, the Iranian dragon-slayer whom we have already briefly encountered in, among other places, Dumézil's discussion of the Persian New Year festival of Naurōz. Watkins argues cogently that lying behind the two traditions, Avestan and Vedic, is not only a parent Indo-Iranian myth, but a set of ancestral linguistic expressions, formulaic elements of an Indo-Iranian poetic tradition, as well.* (RDW)

THE ROOT *G^{U}HEN-: AVESTAN *JAN-*

Calvert Watkins

In RV 2.11.19 Indra is hymned by recalling his previous aid:

asmábhyaṃ tát tvāṣṭráṃ viśvárūpam
árandhayaḥ . . . tritā́ya

To us then you delivered the son of Tvaṣṭṛ,
Viśvarūpa, to Trita.

Trita is the legendary Trita Āptya, slayer of the three-headed, six-eyed dragon Viśvarūpa, with the aid of Indra. Benveniste (1934:195) pointed out the all-important structural similarity between this Indic dragon-slaying episode and the Iranian legend of the (mortal) hero Thraētaona, who slew the three-headed, six-eyed dragon Aži Dahāka, with the aid of Vərəϑraγna (Yt. 14.38,40):

amәmca vәrәϑraɣnәmca
. . .
yim ϑraētaonō taxmō barat̰
yō janat̰ ažīm dahākәm
ϑrizafanәm ϑrikamәrәδәm
xšuuaš.ašīm hazaŋrā.yaoxštīm . . .

The power and offensive force[1]
. . .
which brave Thraētaona bore
who slew the dragon Aži Dahāka,
the three-jawed, three-headed,
six-eyed one of a thousand skills . . .

<As we noted in the previous chapter,> using Jakobson's terms, the similarity is both syntagmatic and paradigmatic: syntagmatic in the sequential linkage of the two stories themselves, the aid brought by Vәrәϑraɣna to Thraētaona to enable him to slay Aži Dahāka, and the aid brought by Indra to Trita to enable him to slay Viśvarūpa (contiguity relations); paradigmatic in the near-identities of the names (*Thraēt-* ~ *Trit-*) of the hero and attributes (3-headed, 6-eyed) of the dragon, the protagonists of the two myths (similarity relations).

The basic formula in Old Iranian *yō janat̰ ažīm* is an exact cognate of Vedic *áhann áhim*, in both words; the phrase is relativized, but the marked word-order Verb-Object is preserved.[2] The relative verb phrase *yō janat̰ ažīm* is always sentence- or clause-initial in Avestan (further examples below). The word order is precisely that of the Vedic relative verb phrase *yó áhan píprum* 'who slew Pipru' in 1.101.2b cited above.

These names and phrases in both traditions recount traditional mythology which must be common Indo-Iranian patrimony, as has been recognized for over a century.[3] I note here only the linguistic equations. In Iran, as recounted in Yasna 9, the Hōm Yasht, *Vivaŋ^{v}hant* (= Vedic *Vivasvant*) was the first man to press *haoma* (= Vedic *soma*), and his reward was to beget *Yima* (= Vedic *Yama*), the first ruler, who presided over the golden age. The second man to press haoma was *Āϑβiia* (~ Vedic *Āptya*), whose reward was to beget *Thraētaona* (~ Vedic *Traitana*, on whom see further below), who slew *Aži Dahāka*. The third man to press haoma was *Thrita* (= Vedic *Trita*, both "third"), whose reward was to beget *Uruuāxšaiia*, a lawgiver, and *Kәrәsāspa*, the warrior hero who slew *Aži Sruuara*, the horned serpent.

Avestan *Thrita* and *Thraētaona* seem to be ablaut variants of the same name and identical with Vedic *Trita Āptya*, who is also associated with *soma*. *Āptya* itself is in origin identical with Avestan *Āϑβiia* < **ātpi̯a* (or *ātu̯i̯a* ?), remade with metathesis by association with *āp-* 'water'.[4]

Compare then, beside RV 2.11.19 cited above, the specifications in book 10 of the Rigveda about the legend of Trita Āptya and Viśvarūpa, 10.8.8:

> sá pítryāṇy ā́yudhāni vidvā́n
> índreṣita **āptyó** abhy àyudhat
> triśīrṣā́ṇaṃ saptáraśmiṃ[5] **jaghanvā́n**
> tvāṣṭrásya cin níḥ sasr̥je **tritó** gā́ḥ

> This one, **Āptya**, knowing his paternal weapons,
> set on by Indra, went forth to battle;
> **having slain** the three-headed, seven-bridled (Viśvarūpa),
> **Trita** let out even the son of Tvaṣṭr̥'s (Viśvarūpa's) cows.

Or 10.48.2 (Indra's self-praise):

> **tritā́ya** gā́ ajanayam **áher** ádhi

> **For Trita** I brought forth the cows from the **serpent**
> (i.e. which the serpent Viśvarūpa had swallowed).

Note the association of the two names with the perfect participle of *han-* (**gʷhen-*) and the word *áhi-* (**ogʷhi-*). For the same association in Avestan cf. Y. 9.7:

> **āβiiō** mąm bitiiō mašiiō
> . . . hunūta . . .
> tat̰ ahmāi jasat̰ āiiaptəm
> yat̰ hē puϑrō us.zaiiata
> vīsō suraiiå **ϑraētaonō**

> **Āϑβya** was the second mortal to press me (Haoma)
> . . .
> That fortune came to him,
> that a son was born to him,
> **Thraētaona**, of heroic family.

This is followed immediately by strophe 8:

> yō **janat̰ ažīm** dahākəm
> ϑrizafanəm etc. (Yt. 14.40 supra)

Who **slew Aži** Dahāka
the three-jawed, etc.

For the epithets compare RV 10.99.6:

sá íd **dā́saṃ** tuvīrávam pátir dán
ṣaḷakṣáṃ triśīrsā́ṇaṃ damanyat
asyá trító nv ójasā **vr̥**dhānó
vipā́ varāhám áyoagrayā **han**[6]

This lord in the house (Indra) overpowered
the loud-roaring, **six-eyed, three-headed dāsa**;
strengthened by his (Indra's) power, Trita **slew**
the boar with his iron-tipped arrow.

The MONSTER is here assimilated to a 'boar', *varāhá*; see below for the Iranian HERO Vərəϑraɣna in his furious onslaught also assimilated to a 'boar', the exact cognate *varāza-*. Further connections of this ancient Indo-Iranian word, borrowed into Finno-Ugric (see Mayrhofer, KEWA s.v.), are unknown. But the Indo-Iranian word is not only a shared lexical item; it is also a shared cultural and mythological icon.

With the similar description of the monster we have again Y. 9.8, of the hero Thraētaona:

yō janaṯ ažīm dahākəm
ϑrizafanəm **ϑrikamərəδəm**
xšuuaš.ašīm hazaŋrā.yaoxštīm
aš.aojaŋhəm daēuuīm drujim . . .[7]

Who slew Aži Dahāka
the three-mouthed, **three-headed,**
six-eyed one of a thousand tricks,
the very powerful Demoness, the Druj . . .

Note that Vedic *ṣaḷakṣa-* (*ṣaḍ-akṣ-a-*) 'six-eyed' and Avestan *xšuuaš.aš-i-* are exact cognates up to the suffixes. Note also the Avestan *ϑrikamərəδəm* (*ϑri-ka* + *mərəδa-*) is almost identical to Vedic *trimūrdhā́nam* (*tri-mūrdhan-*) 'three-headed', epithet of Agni (note 5 above).

Before continuing with Yasna 9.10 and the third presser of haoma we must examine another Indo-Iranian link. Mary Boyce in discussing the Iranian and Indic traditions around Avestan Thrita and Thraētaona son of Āϑβya, and Vedic Trita Āptya, notes that the Vedas mention once (RV 1.158.5) a Traitana, 'who appears obscurely, in a context which does not suggest any connection with the Avestan Thraētaona' <(p. 99)>.

Now the names are similar enough to arouse an interest (*trit-/ϑrit-, ϑraēt-/trait-*; for the suffix cf. Greek *κέρ-αυνος*, Slavic *Per-unЪ*, Hittite ^{D}IM-*unnaš*[*Tarḫunnaš*] beside Vedic *Parj-an-ya*), and when they are syntagmatically associated with other key lexical expressions of the myth, I would suggest the connection becomes perfectly real and self-evident.

The name is found in the Saga of the ṛṣi Dīrghatamas 'Of the long darkness', the blind poet, son of Ucathya and Mamatā.[8] It is one of the many examples of the Power of the Word in ancient India. The legend is told in Bṛhad-Devatā 4.21–24, and recalls that in MBh 1.104.23ff. As an old man Dīrghatamas' slaves bound him and threw him into a river. But his prayer saved him: one of the slaves, Traitana, tried to behead him with a sword, but instead cut off his own head, shoulder, and breast (Bṛh. Dev. 4.21, cited by Geldner). The waters carried Dīrghatamas safely to shore. RV 1.158.4–5 gives the words of his prayer: 'May the song of praise (*úpastuti*) save the son of Ucathya . . .'

(5) ná mā garan nadyò mātṛ́tamā
dāsā́ yád īṃ súsamubdham avā́dhuḥ
śíro yád asya **traitanó** vitákṣat
svayáṃ **dāsá** úro ámsāv ápi gdha.

The most mothering rivers will not swallow me.
When the **Dāsas** put him in, well bound,
when **Traitana** tries to hew off his **head**,
the **Dāsa** eats up his own breast and two shoulders.[9]

Traitana is a *dāsa* in the sense of 'slave', but he is at the same time a *dāsa* 'demon': the HERO has become the MONSTER. The power of Truth, of the spoken word, drives his WEAPON back on himself, and instead of Dīrghatamas' head (*śíras*) he cuts off his own 'breast and two shoulders' (1 + 2 = 3) in the Rigveda, or 'head and shoulders and breast' (1 + 1 + 1 = 3) in the Bṛhad-Devatā. The tone is grimly mock-heroic: Traitana has become precisely the three-headed serpent which Thraētaona slew, and the three-headed *dāsa* which Trita Āptya slew. Cf. RV 10.99.6 (quoted in full above) for the identical key words,

dāsám . . . triśīrṣāṇam . . . tritó . . . han,

or the same elements in Avestan (Y. 9.7–8) with a different order:

ϑraētaonō . . . janaṯ . . . ϑrikamərəδəm . . . dahākəm.

There should be no doubt that this legend is only another version of the same common Indo-Iranian myth, with its same formulaic diction.[10]

Yasna 9.10, with which we began, continues exactly parallel to strophe 7 quoted above, with Thrita, the third man to press haoma, whose fortune was

> yat̰ hē puϑra us.zaiiōiϑe
> uruuāxšaiiō kərəsāspasca
> t̰kaēšō **aniiō** dātō.rāzō
> āat̰ **aniiō** uparō.kairiiō
> yauua gaēsuš gaδauuarō
>
> That to him two sons were born,
> Urvāxšaya and Kərəsāspa:
> **the one** a judge, a lawgiver,
> **and the other** one of superior deeds,
> a young (hero), curly-haired, bearing the cudgel.

For the compound *gaδauuarō* in the last line note also Yt. 10.101, of Mithra, with a compound of *gan-* (*$g^{u̯}$*hen-*) and the weapon itself as object:

> hō paoiriiō gaδąm **nijaiṇti**
> aspaēca paiti vīraēca
>
> He first **strikes** his cudgel
> at horse and man.

As an illustration of a Common Indo-Iranian topos we may compare the figure of the two Iranians Urvāxšaya and Kərəsāspa, *aniiō* . . . *aniiō* . . . 'the one . . . the other . . .', with RV 7.83.9ab, to the gods Indra and Varuṇa:

> vr̥trā́ṇy **anyáḥ** samithéṣu **jíghnate**
> vratā́ny **anyó** abhí rakṣate sádā
>
> **The one smashes** the hostile defenses in battles,
> **the other** protects alliances always.

Even the second position of *aniiō/anyá-* is common to both.[11] Note in the Vedic the poetic antithesis under partial phonetic identity in the identically fronted *vr̥trā́ṇi* : *vratā́ni*. The figure is exactly that of ***last*** *but not* ***least***.

Kərəsāspa is with Mary Boyce 'the other great Avestan hero', and 'many more stories are told of him than of Thraētaona' (op. cit. 100). Yasna 9.11 continues immediately:

yō janat̰ ažīm sruuarəm
yim aspō.garəm narə.garəm
yim vīšauuaṇtəm zairitəm

Who slew the horned Aži,
the horse-swallowing, man-swallowing,
venomous, yellow-green . . .

With *aspō.gar-nərə.gar-* compare *aspaēca paiti vīraēca* 'against horse and man' of Yt. 10.101, together with the compound (ibid.) *aspa.vīraja* 'smiting (*gan-*) horse (and) man', also of Mithra.

We have already seen in the preceding section the enumeration of the other men or monsters slain by Kərəsāspa in Yt. 19.40–43, all in the identical formula *yō janat̰* NN. Again the subject Kərəsāspa is not overt in the sentences.

The verb phrase is nominalized to agent noun plus genitive in V.1.17 *θraētaonō* ***jaṇta ažōiš*** *dahākāi* 'Thraetaona slayer of Aži Dahāka'.[12] <For this and other Iranian nominal forms of *gan-* in the basic formula see chap. 51.>

The final Old Iranian example is furnished by three verses in Yt. 19.92 (cf. 93):

*vaδəm vaējō yim vārəθraγnəm
yim barat̰ taxmō θraētaonō
yat̰ **ažiš** dahākō **jaini**

Swinging the weapon which smashes resistance
which brave Tharaetaona carried,
when **Aži** Dahākā **was slain**.

Similarly in the continuation of the passage (describing the future coming of the Savior Astuuat̰.ərətō), 93 (*yim barat̰ . . .*) *yat̰ druuā̊ zainigāuš jaini . . . yat̰ turō jaini fraŋrase . . .* '(which NN bore) when evil Zainigu was slain . . . when the Turanian Fraŋrasyan was slain . . .' Note the variation in word order of the last, with the familiar distraction of noun (name) and adjective by intervening verb.[13]

The reading *vaδəm* for *vaēδəm* (anticipation of the following *vaējō*) is due to J. Schindler (p.c.). Avestan *vaδa-* equals Vedic *vadhá-* 'weapon, Totschläger', specifically Indra's cudgel in RV 1.32.6 et alibi.

We may juxtapose the Avestan sentence of Yt. 19.92 with the Vedic of RV 5.29.2 (cited in full above) to illustrate the close similarity of expression in the two languages:

vaδəm . . . yat̰ ažiš . . . jaini
vájram . . . yád áhiṃ hán.

All five collocations of *jan-* and *aži-* in Avestan are metrical; they are all octosyllabic verse lines.[14] There can be no doubt that these cognate verb phrases continue an ancient poetic tradition, a verbal flexible formula which is at least common Indo-Iranian in date.

We may illustrate the various forms of the root *gan-* in Avestan with a passage from Yt. 10.71, the hymn to Mithra, describing the onslaught of *vərəϑraγnō ahuraδātó* 'Ahura-created Vərəϑraγna' in the shape of a wild boar: a common and frequent image of the heroic deity,[15] which emphasizes his fearsome monstrous qualities. The verb *nijaiṇti* is in a relative clause, the syntactic definition of the hero, in accord with the pattern described at the end of the preceding section:

yō frąštacō hamərəϑāδa
. . .
stija **nijaiṇti** hamərəϑə̄
naēδa maniiete **jaγnuuå**
naēδa cim **γəną** sadaiieiti
yauuata aēm **nijaiṇti**
mərəzuca stūnō gaiiehe
mərəzuca xå uštānahe

Who, running before the adversary, . . .
smashes the adversaries in battle;[16]
he does not think that he **has struck**
nor has he the impression he **is striking** anyone,
until he **smashes**
even the vertebras, the pillars of life,
even the vertebras, the wellspring of vitality.

The echoic *stija nija(iṇti), naēδa . . . naēδa, mərəzuca . . . mərəzuca* form a counterpoint to the different forms of basic verb *gan-*: general present *nijaiṇti*, perfect participle *jagnuuå*, present participle *γəną*, repeated *nijaiṇti*. The metaphors with *stūna* 'pillar' are widespread[17] and those with *xå* 'wellspring' common in Indic as well: *rāyás khā́m* 'wellspring of riches' RV 6.36.4, and the Common Indo-Iranian *khā́m r̥tásya* 'wellspring of Truth' RV 2.28.5, *aṣ̌ahe xå* 'id.' Y. 10.4. Cf. note I above. Finally the parallel *gaiia-* 'life' and *uštāna-* 'vitality' recall the Italic merism in Latin *uires uitaque*, Oscan *biass biítam*, <discussed in chap. 18>.

Notes

1. Vərəθrayna's aid to Thraētaona can be compared to his aid to Zarathustra earlier in the same hymn (Yt. 14.29), giving him, in an arresting metaphor, *ərəzōiš xå̊ (bāzuuå̊ aojō, . . .)* 'the wellspring of the scrotum, (the strength of the two arms . . .)'

2. For the thematization of the Avestan 3sg. imperfect *janaṯ* beside Vedic *(á)han* = Old Persian *aja*, cf. Hoffmann 1975:73.

3. Cf. Reichelt 1968:95–7, and in greater detail Boyce 1975–82:1.85–108, esp. 97–104. Boyce is doubtless right (pp. 99–100) in assuming that Trita Āptya – Thrita Thraētaona, son of Āθβiia, were originally in Indo-Iranian times regarded as mortal rather than divine (as in India), though whether we should think of them as euhemerized "real" *Ātpi̯as living sometime before 2000 B.C. is open to question.

4. Gershevitch 1969:188–9, making more precise the identification long assumed. Cf. also Mayrhofer EWA s.v. *āptyá-*.

5. Cf. 1.146, 1a of Agni *trimūrdhā́nam saptáraśmim* 'three-headed, seven-bridled', and see below.

6. Note the triple alliterations **d**, **d**, **d**; **v**, **v**, **v**, the end-rhyme *dán* : *han*, and the two injunctives. The verb *damanya-* is a hapax in the Rigveda.

7. The Avestan lexicon includes synonyms opposed dualistically as applying to "good" and "evil" beings, Ahuric and Daēvic. These body parts are those of Daēvic creatures: *zafar/n-* 'mouth, jaws, set of teeth' (Vedic *jámbha-*, IE *ĝm̥bh- ~ *ĝm̥ph- as in Germ. *Kiefer*), *kamərəd-* 'head' (literally 'what a head' *ka-mərəd-*, Ved. *mūrdh-an-*), *aš-* 'eye' (Ved. *ákṣi, an-akṣ-*), opposed to those of Ahuric creatures, resp. *āh-* 'mouth', *vaγδana-* 'head', *dōiθra-*, *casman-* 'eye' (the cognate of Ved. *śiras, sarah-* 'head' is neutral). This part of the Iranian lexicon is of great theoretical and metalinguistic interest. It has received a fair amount of attention; the classic study is Güntert 1914, and the best recent studies (both with the intervening literature) are by Gercenberg 1972:17–40, and Toporov 1981:205–14. As Toporov notes in this seminal work, the question is complex, and still not settled.

8. Cf. RV 1.32.11 etc.

9. The present tense of the English translation of cd attempts to capture the Vedic injunctives. 'Put' of b is preterite, corresponding to the Vedic aorist.

10. Just *why* in India the original hero Traitana has become both monstrous and servile, an inept buffoon and the complete inversion of his heroic self, I cannot say. The mock-heroic is perhaps universally not far removed from the heroic, and perhaps coeval with it. Compare the beggar and anti-hero (W)Iros in *Odyssey* 18 (Ved. *vīrás* 'man, hero'), and Bader 1976.

11. Cf. also the similar 6.68.3. S. Jamison has shown that Vedic *anyá-* (. . . *anyá* . . .) in second position is definite, 'the one (. . . the other . . .)', while in first position it is indefinite, 'someone'. These examples would indicate the syntactic feature is Common Indo-Iranian.

12. For the agent noun with accusative construction cf. Yt. 17.12 *vītārəm paskāṯ hamərəθəm / jaṇtārəm parō dušmainiiūm* '(who is) the pursuer of the adversary from behind, the slayer of the enemy from in front' <see chap. 50 n. 3>. *hamərəθa-* and *dušmainiiu* are a figure of hendiadys.

13. The passage concludes with 'which Kavi Vīštāspa bore,' *aṣ̌ahe haēnaiiå̊ caēšəmnō* 'going to avenge Aša on the enemy army'. (Read *aṣ̌əm*; the error was induced by the line-initial *aṣ̌ahe* two lines later.) Here the participle of *kay-* 'avenge', IE *kʷei-, occupies a position parallel to *jaini* 'was slain', IE *gʷhen-. <For other examples from Avestan and especially Greek see chap. 49.>

14. For a recent discussion of YAv. metrics see Lazard 1984.

15. Cf. Benveniste and Renou 1934:34–5, 69, 73, and Gershevitch 1959:219.

16. The interpretation of *stija* is controversial. For discussion see Kellens 1974:84.

17. Cf. Watkins 1990:52–5<, and Hektor Τροίας . . . κίονα 'pillar of Troy' in the preceding chapter>.

24. *Aži Dahāka, Viśvarūpa, and Geryon*

The three-headed, six-eyed monster of the Indo-Iranian tradition that Watkins examined in the preceding selection—Iranian Aži Dahāka and Indic Viśvarūpa—provides the focus of the following essay. Watkins argues here that the monster may be attested farther afield in the Indo-European world. Geryon, the three-bodied giant slain by Heracles, whose cattle the hero drove off (see Part 3: Apollodorus, Bibliotheca *2.5.1-12), appears to be a Greek expression of the same proto-motif. Hence, Watkins suggests, the ancestral tradition of which the three-headed, six-eyed monster is a part is more ancient than the common Indo-Iranian period, belonging to an earlier era of Indo-European unity.* (RDW)

AŽI DAHĀKA, VIŚVARŪPA, AND GERYON

Calvert Watkins

<From the evidence surveyed in chap. 29> it is clear that a Common Indo-Iranian myth underlies the slaying of the dragon Aži Dahāka by Thraētaona and the slaying of Tvaṣṭṛ's son, the monster Viśvarūpa, by Trita Āptya. Thraētaona was a mortal hero, while Trita appears to have been a god. Both are enabled to perform their valorous deed by a god: Thraētaona by Vərəϑraɣna and Trita by the (higher) god Indra, whose epithet is *vṛtrahán-*. Both monsters, the Iranian and the Indic, share the same physical attributes: they have three heads (*ϑrikamərəδa-, triśīrṣán- / trimūrdhán-*) and six eyes (*xšuuaš.aši-, ṣaḷákṣa-*). The Indic monster kept cows, which Indra (or Trita? cf. Geldner ad loc.) carried off in RV 10.8.9:

> tvāṣṭrásya cid viśvárūpasya gónām
> ācakrāṇás trī́ṇi śī́rṣā́ párā vark
>
> Having driven off for himself some of the cows of Viśvarūpa son of Tvaṣṭṛ
> he twisted off the three heads.

While Iranian Aži Dahāka had no cows, the hero Thraētaona requested of the goddess Arəduuī Sūra Anāhitā in Yt. 5.34 (and of the goddess Aṣ̌i Vaŋ^{v}hī in

Yt. 17.34), and was granted, the boon 'that I may become the winner over Aži
Dahāka, the three-jawed, three-headed, six-eyed . . .' <(quoted in chap. 51)>,
moreover:

uta he vaṇta azāni
saṇhauuāci arənauuāci

And that I may carry off his (Aži Dahāka's) two beloved wives
Saṇhavac and Arənavac . . .[1]

On the passage see Hoffmann 1975:374–7. The two women were sisters of Yima
and had been carried off earlier by Aži Dahāka. The verb *az-* 'drive', cognate with
Vedic *aj-*, Greek ἄγειν, and Old Irish *agid*, is like them used with both cattle and
women as object, in the sense of 'carry off as booty'.[2] As we saw in the preceding
note, this Common Indo-Iranian myth has been compared, for almost a century
at least, with the Greek legend of the tenth labor of Herakles, the stealing of the
cattle of Geryon (Gēryoneus, Gēryonēs, Gāryonās). For references in classical
sources see Page 1973 and Fontenrose 1980:334ff. with n. 31. The myth is first
alluded to in Hesiod's *Th.* 287–94. Poseidon lay with Medusa, and when Perseus
cut off her head Chrysaor and the horse Pegasus sprang forth:

Χρυσάωρ δ' ἔτεκεν τρικέφαλον Γηρυονῆα
μιχθεὶς Καλλιρόηι κούρηι κλυτοῦ Ὠκεανοῖο.
τὸν μὲν ἄρ' ἐξενάριξε βίη Ἡρακληείη
βουσὶ παρ' εἰλιπόδεσσι περιρρύτωι εἰν Ἐρυθείηι
ἤματι τῶι, ὅτε περ βοῦς ἤλασεν εὐρυμετώπους
Τίρυνθ' εἰς ἱερήν, διαβὰς πόρον Ὠκεανοῖο.
Ὄρθον τε κτείνας καὶ βουκόλον Εὐρυτίωνα
σταθμῶι ἐν ἠερόεντι πέρην κλυτοῦ Ὠκεανοῖο

Chrysaor begot three-headed Geryoneus
joining in love with Kallirhoe, daughter of glorious Ocean;
him in might Herakles slew
beside his shambling cows in sea-girt Erytheia,
on that day when he drove the wide-browed cows
to holy Tiryns, having crossed the ford of Ocean
and killed (the monstrous dog) Orthos and the herdsman Eurytion
in the airy stead out beyond glorious Ocean.[3]

Hesiod repeats the story in condensed form in 981–3: 'Kallirhoe bore a son,
strongest of all men,'

Γηρυονέα, τὸν κτεῖνε βίῃ Ἡρακληείῃ
βοῶν ἕνεκ' εἰλιπόδων ἀμφιρρύτωι Ἐρυθείῃι

Geryoneus, whom mighty Herakles killed
in sea-girt Erytheia for the sake of his shambling cows.

The lines have two irregularities, *Γηρυονέα* and *βοῶν*, on which see West ad loc. The verb *ἐξενάριξε* of the first, longer version is a common lexical substitute for *πέφνε*, as we have seen; *κτεῖνε* in the second is neutral, and in the first version used for the ancillary killing of Geryon's dog and herdsmen. We may retain as central the epithet 'three-headed' (for the metrical lengthening *τρικέφᾱλος* see West ad loc.), and the formula *βοῦς*[4] *ἤλασεν* (*εὐρυμετώπους*) 'drove off the cows', which recurs in the *h.Merc.* 102 of Hermes rustling the cattle of Apollo, and *Il.* 1. 154.

Pindar shows the same words of the formula distracted in *fr.* 169a6–8; *ἐπεὶ Γηρυόνα*[5] *βόας . . . ἀπριάτας ἔλασεν* 'when he (sc. Herakles) drove off the unbought cows of Geryon.'

The poet Stesichorus, active from the latter seventh to the mid-sixth century, composed a mini-epic of over 1500 lines on this legend, the *Geryoneis*. The work is preserved only in a handful of fragments, fortunately augmented by extensive papyrus finds.[6] The sympathetic portrayal of Geryon is the most striking feature of the new text: his tragic sense of inescapable conflict and impending death, the colloquy with his mother and her passionate concern, and finally the infinite tenderness of the portrayal of the dying Geryon stricken by the poisoned arrow (SLG 15 ii 14–17):

ἀπέκλινε δ' ἄρ' αὐχένα Γαρ[υόνας
  ἐπικάρσιον, ὡς ὅκα μ[ά]κω[ν
ἅτε καταισχύνοισ' ἁπαλὸν [δέμας
  αἶψ' ἀπὸ φύλλα βαλοῖσα ν[

And Geryon bent his neck over to one side,
like a poppy that spoils its delicate shape,
shedding its petals all at once . . . (tr. Page).

Page notes (1973:152) that the model of the poppy is *Il.* 8.306ff. (well imitated by Vergil, *Aen.* 9.435ff.), but as he emphasized, 'the development of the drooping poppy is unique to Stesichorus'. We are a long way from a monster, and a long way from the topos of the adversary felled by the hero like a great tree <(chap. 47 n. 4)>. Though Geryon had three heads (Hesiod) and 'the body of three men joined at the waist, which became threeform at the flanks and thighs' (Apollodorus, *Bibl.* 2.5.10, probably taken from Stesichorus' poem [Page 1973: 144–5]), it is curious that in the attested fragments the words for 'head', 'helmet', and 'shield' are only singular: SLG 15 ii 3 *κεφαλά*, i 16 *τρυφάλει'*, i 12 *ἀσπίδα*, ii 10–11 *ἐπ' ἀκροτάταν κορυφάν*. Contrast the black-figured amphora, illustrated in Fontenrose 1980:335 (fig. 26), Br. Mus. B155, cat. II fig. 26, where Geryones (so labeled) has clearly three heads, three helmets, and three shields, as well as two wings and two feet.

We should note in the same representation that Athena (Αθε̄ναιε̄) stands directly behind Herakles and obviously brings him divine aid, as she does in Stesichorus *frg*. 3. Athena thus has the same functional role toward Herakles in the myth as Vərəϑraγna toward Thraētaona and Indra toward Trita.

Despite the singular 'head' in these fragments a three-form Geryon can be inferred for Stesichorus both because of Apollodorus' description above, and because a scholiast to Hesiod *Th.* 287 tells us that Stesichorus in an innovation presented Geryon winged and with six hands and feet: cf. PMG 186 *ἓξ χεῖρας ἔχειν φησὶ καὶ ἓξ πόδας*. The wings are attested on the Chalcydian vase painting illustrated in Fontenrose 1980:335, but Geryon there has two feet. According to Page 1973 this representation is clearly inspired by Stesichorus. Note that this vase has the expected Ionic spelling Γε̄ρυονε̄ς (it is Kretschmer, Vaseninschr. §40,9) whereas in the same scene illustrated in Kretschmer §4'0,2 (Schw. 797.2 and note 5 above), the spelling ΓαρυϝονεĪς would seem to be directly due to the influence of Stesichorus. Other forms on both vases are perfectly good Chalcidian Ionic. Combining the traditional epithet *τρικέφαλος* in Hesiod, the description in Apollodorus, the Chalcidian vase paintings, and the scholiast's statement we are justified in making the linguistic inference that Stesichorus in the Geryoneis described the adversary of Herakles as THREE-HEADED and SIX-somethinged. It may be that those somethings were 'feet', by an innovation of the poet; but I suggest that what they replaced was an earlier epithet 'six-eyed' identical in meaning to the Indic and Iranian epithets:

THREE-HEADED and SIX-EYED.

We may regard this as a poetic and mythographic formula common to Indo-Iranian and Greek, and resting on the semantic equations

tri-śīrṣán-	ṣaḷ-ákṣa-
tri-mūrdhán-	

ϑri-kamərəδa- xšuuaš-aši-

τρι-κεφαλο- ἑξ(α)-.

Such a formula is of course trivially easy to imagine on the plane of universals. To anchor it more firmly on the diachronic plane we can point to the association of the monster with wealth in cows, which are driven off by the hero as part of his exploit. Here the Vedic accusative plural *gā́s* (RV 10.8.8, 48.2) can be even morphologically equated, *mutatis mutandis*, with the Homeric and Hesiodic accusative plural *βοῦς* (*Th.* 291). We saw the forms in Pindar; and Stesichorus SLG 11.27–9 (PMGF S11, p. 156) adds the tantalizing fragment in broken context

περὶ βουσὶν ἐμαῖς
. . .
]κλέος[

. . . about my cows
. . .
]fame[.

We may then, however tentatively, suggest a specific late Indo-European (Greco-Indo-Iranian) myth whose semantic structure and signature formulas deploy the lexical items or names HERO (variable), SLAY (*g^{u}*hen-*, replaced in Hesiod by *ἐξενάριξε*), a MONSTER (**o*g^{u}*hi-*, not in Greek) who is THREE (**tri)*-HEADED (variable) and SIX (**su̯eḱs-*)-EYED (*h_3*ok*^{u}*p-*, not in Greek), with the aid of a GOD (variable). As a result HERO DRIVE OFF (*h_2*aĝ-*, replaced in Greek by *ἤλασε*) MONSTER's COWS (*g^{u}*ōs*, replaced in Avestan by WOMEN). A simple story perhaps, but one with enough arbitrary linkage (contiguity relations) for us to be unsatisfied with the explanation of mere fortuitous resemblance.[7]

The *names* of the actants in the three traditions are, as usual, variable and of little use, whether they are descriptive like Aži Dahāka 'the Serpent-D.', transparent like Viśvarūpa 'having many forms', or simply obscure, like Geryon. The name looks like the noun *γᾶρυς* 'voice, cry' as noted by Forssman, loc. cit., but the name 'Shouter' is without semantic relevance for the myth.

Notes

1. Reichelt, Av. Reader 103 and 96 (1911), where the comparison with Viśvarūpa's cows (and those of Geryon) is explicitly made. His explanation, on the other hand, that Thraētaona delivered wives instead of cows because Aši Vaŋ^{v}hī (Yt. 17) was 'the protectress of matrimony', seems farfetched. Heracles' taking of Geryon's cows was already compared with Indra's freeing the cows held by

Vr̥tra, or in the cave of Vala, by M. Bréal in 1863 (*Hercule et Cacus*) and later by L. von Schroeder in 1914 (*Herakles und Indra*).

2. Thraētaona's *vaṇta azāni* (lsg. subj.) 'that I may carry off his two beloved wives' is identical to Agamemnon's *ἐγὼ δέ κ' ἄγω Βρισηΐδα* 'I will take Briseis' *Il*, 1. 184.

3. The ring κλυτοῦ Ὠκεανοῖο in 288 and 294, first the god and then the place, indexes the remoteness of the island Erytheia; West points out wryly that the difficulty of capturing Geryon's cattle 'consisted in the remoteness of the ranch.' The name *Ἐρυθείη* is probably a derivative of 'red' or so understood, like *Loch Rudraige* in Ireland, scene of another drakontomakhia <(chap. 45)>. Such associations are fairly frequent, cf. the Vedic demon *Rudhikrā*, and the Avestan 'red serpent' *aži raoδita*, and probably not very significant. Cf. also <chapters 56 and 57>, for A. Kuhn, the Vedic worms, and the Germanic *red* : *dead* rhymes.

4. The monosyllabic acc. pl. is probably an archaism, equatable with Vedic *gā́s*.

5. For the non-appearance of the Doric form *Γᾱρυόνᾱς*, cf. Forssman 1966. He rightly notes the form *ΓαρυϜονες* on a sixth-century (Ionic) Chalcidian vase, Schwyzer 797.2 (Kretschmer, Vaseninschr. §40,2).

6. See the editions of Davies 1991, Page 1962 and 1972, as well as his 1973 study. Cf. also Lerza 1982, with bibliography.

7. We may also be unsatisfied with Fontenrose's conclusion, that Geryon is 'the king of the dead, a form of Thanatos of Hades' (1980:335). The new Stesichorus fragments (published after the appearance of the book) weaken the claim seriously for Greek, and the Indo-Iranian facts never fit it at all. <Cf. chap. 40.> Ours is only a variant of the same myth.

PART 6

IRELAND AND THE CELTS

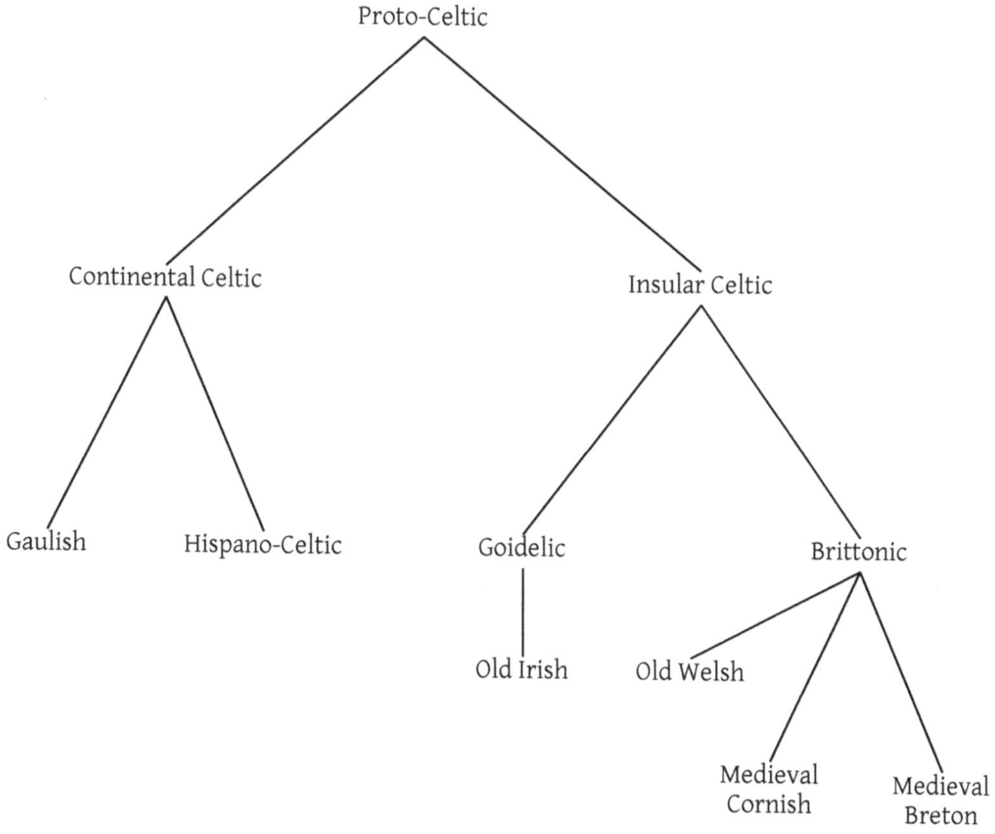

25. *The Indo-European Poet: His Social Function and His Art*

The poet, the *wek^{w}ōm tekson—*the "weaver of words" as the poet was known in the parent Indo-European language—was a person of singular importance in early Indo-European societies. "The function of the Indo-European poet was to be the custodian and the transmitter of . . . tradition. The totality of themes as expressed in formulas was in these preliterate societies entrusted precisely to the* PROFESSIONALS OF THE WORD, *the poets"—thus Watkins settles his readers into this study of the Indo-European poet.*

One of the historical Indo-European societies that supply the best evidence for the position and role of the poet is that of premodern Ireland. Watkins here masterfully provides us with a revealing glimpse into the world of the Celtic Bards, as well as that of their counterparts in, especially, Vedic India and in ancient Greece. (RDW)

THE INDO-EUROPEAN POET: HIS SOCIAL FUNCTION AND HIS ART

Calvert Watkins

<In chap. 3> we considered one of the two aspects of the study of Indo-European poetics, the formal question of the poet's *technique*. The second, to which we now come, concerns the social function of poetry and the poet in Indo-European times: his *purpose*. Both must be looked at together, complementarily. For the art of the Indo-European poet is to say something wholly traditional in a new and interesting, but therefore *more effective* way. It is verbal activity, artistically elaborated, but directed toward a more or less immediate, concrete goal.

We noted earlier in connection with the verbal formula <(chap. 1.2)> that formulas are the vehicles of themes, and that in the totality of these we find the doctrine, ideology, and culture of the Indo-Europeans. These formulas are collectively the verbal expression of the whole traditional culture of the Indo-Europeans.

The *function* of the Indo-European poet was to be the custodian and the transmitter of this tradition. The totality of themes as expressed in formulas was in these preliterate societies entrusted precisely to the PROFESSIONALS OF THE WORD, the poets.

The lexical expression of this function of custodianship and transmittal in the Proto-Indo-European language was **mnah*$_2$-(**mnā*-), a root derivative suffixed form (Benveniste's thème II) of the simple root **men*- expressing 'mental force'. The root **mnah*$_2$- exhibits a significant range of meanings in the languages which attest it:

> 'look at, see, experience' in Anatolian (Melchert 1993b:135), Cuneiform and Hieroglyphic Luvian *ma-na-a-du* (3 pl. ipv.) = Hittite *aušdu* 'let him see';
>
> 'be mindful of; remember' in Greek *μέμνημαι, μνάομαι*;
>
> 'commit to memory and hand down' in Vedic, Brāhmaṇas and Sūtras *ā-mnā*-.

The functional orientation is apparent in the figure of the Cretan law-court official *mnāmōn*, *μναμονευεν*, 'act as *mnāmōn*', the 'Remembrancer', as it is translated by Jeffery and Morpurgo Davies 1970:150. A passage with this verb in the Kauṣītaki-Brāhmaṇa 8.7 can well stand as a guiding principle of traditional Indo-European poetic culture:

> viparyasya dāśatayībhyaṃ vaṣaṭ kuryād iti haika āhur
> **yathāmnātam** iti tv eva sthitam
>
> Inverting the two verses from the Saṁhitā he should utter
> the call of *vaṣaṭ*, some say, but
> **'as it is remembranced'** is the established rule.[1]

The Italian school of students of Indo-European poetics, notably Durante and Campanile, has given considerable attention to the figure of the Indo-European poet, working in particular from the evidence of traditions of India and the Celtic British Isles, as well as Archaic Greece, and to some extent the Germanic world. Campanile 1977:27ff. presents a detailed survey of the figure and function of the traditional poet in Celtic and Indic society and defines him as 'the preserver and the professional of the spoken word. It is he who is by definition competent in all the areas where the word is, or is considered, operative.' This must be understood as a very concrete, practical notion. Those areas where the traditional spoken word is operative, and its control mandatory, impinge upon virtually the totality of the culture. Campanile 1987:26 noted that

> What we term Indo-European poetry was rather a society's sum of knowledge, which was orally transmitted. The features which our western tradition ascribes to poetry (feeling, inspiration, individualism, participation, etc.), and which the aesthetics of romanticism has particularly underscored, were for Indo-European poetry only a side issue, although they were present. The main thing was to preserve and increase cultural elements which presented something essential to the well-being, collectivity, and stability of the society. We are speaking of the magic spells which heal the sick, the legal formulas which settle disputes, the prayers which extort worldly goods from the gods, the genealogies which give to people consciousness of their past and pride in it, the eulogies which legitimize rulers by the celebration of their greatness. He who fulfilled such important functions held a position of the first rank in his society, but his traffic with the Muses was neither particularly frequent nor particularly necessary. For this kind of poetry one could prepare oneself only by years of study; what the Middle Irish Metrics texts tell us about the training of the Early Irish poet is basically valid for the Indo-European one as well.

B. Schlerath 1974 emphasizes the particular link between the activity of the poet and the priest: a religious poem, invocation, or hymn of praise to the gods is inextricably linked with the worship and all the paraphernalia of cult. The principal goal of the poem is the expression of that active, cosmic truth which is Indo-Iranian **r̥tá-*. Toporov 1981:200 puts the parallel function of poet and priest more loftily: 'Both combat Chaos, both strengthen Cosmic Order, its Law (**r̥tá*) and the safe, lasting place where the gods dwell . . . For society, the poet like the priest is indispensable. It is they who subdue the entropic tendencies of the universe, suppress or rework the elements of chaos, continually renew the world as cosmos, and assure increase, wealth, and continuity of offspring.'

Whether we choose to follow Toporov in this ideological assessment—cf. his further likening the poet, ancient and modern, to the first culture-hero, the Demiurge (1981:200 and 219–27)—is perhaps a question of taste. But one simple socioeconomic fact is clear: the Indo-European poet was the highest-paid professional in his society.

The concept and nature of the Indo-European poet cannot be separated from that of the society in which he operated. Indo-European tribal society was dominated by the Maussian principle of reciprocity and exchange or potlatch, of the gift entailing the counter-gift.[2] The *poet* did not function in that society in isolation; he had a *patron*. The two were precisely in an exchange or reciprocity relation: the poet gave poems of praise to the patron, who in turn bestowed largesse upon the poet. To the aristocracy of Indo-European society this reciprocal relation was a moral and ideological necessity. For only the poet could confer on the patron what he and his culture valued more highly than life itself: precisely what is expressed by the 'imperishable fame' formula.

Perhaps the clearest expression of this relation is the conclusion of a poem addressed by the 6th-century Greek poet Ibycus to the tyrant of Samos Polycrates (PMG 282 = SLG 151.47-8 = PMGF p. 243):

> καὶ σύ, Πολύκρατες, **κλέος ἄφθιτον** ἕξεις
> ὡς κατ' ἀοιδὰν καὶ ἐμὸν κλέος
>
> You too, Polycrates, will have **undying fame (kleos)**
> in accordance with my song and my **kleos.**

The two uses of *kléos* (IE **k̑léu̯os*) are the poet's pledge-token of reciprocity: the poet's *kléos* is the vehicle of the patron's. In this way we can understand the development of IE **k̑léu̯os* to the meaning 'word' in Old Iranian and Slavic (diffusion from Iranian?) and 'epic lay' already in Old Russian *slovo*.

The same reciprocity relation as between poet and patron existed between poet and the gods. We have the same eulogistic model: a good hymn of praise, saying something wholly traditional in a new and interesting way, is the gift of the poet to the god. This gift then *obligates* that deity to bestow as counter-gift that which is prayed for: prosperity, fecundity, long life. Poetry and poets were not a "frill" in Indo-European society but a necessity of life, a necessary condition for existence. The spoken word could produce a physical effect on the world, but only if properly formulated by the poet.

Typically the patron would commission a hymn by the poet to a god, to benefit the patron (in Vedic the *yajamāna*, 'he for whom the worship is performed'), for which the poet would be rewarded, i.e. paid. Most of the hymns of the Rigveda are so occasioned. It is a mark of the permansiveness of this system throughout the Indo-European world that 'a king without poets' was proverbial in Ireland for 'nothing', and that Aeschylus (*Ag.* 979) could call, wholly negatively, an unwanted fear

> ἀκέλευστος ἄμισθος ἀοιδά
>
> an uncommissioned, unrewarded song.

Greek *μισθός*, the base of negative *ἄμισθος* 'unrewarded', has already in Homer the sense of 'wages, hire'. Yet one of the self-designations of Greek and Indo-European poets is *ἐπέων τέκτονες* 'craftsmen of words', and like the journeyman the poet is worthy of his hire. Pindar freely uses *μισθός* for his compensation (*Pyth.* 1.75-77 *ἀρέομαι . . . μισθόν* 'I will earn as recompense') in a positive sense.[3] The word is a clear Indo-European inheritance, **misdhó*-, and its meaning 'honorific compensation for deed performed', as established by Benveniste 1969:1.163-9 on the basis of its Iranian (*mīždəm*) and Germanic (English *meed*) cognates. The word has a clean 'exchange value' in the Maussian system of reciprocity; note the related Avestan *miiazda*-, Vedic *miyedha*- 'offering, oblation'.

In Vedic the word for the poet's reward (or fee) was *dákṣinā*- (scil. *gáuḥ, dhenúḥ*), the *dákṣinā*-cow. The original force of the adjective is still a matter of dispute. For the aetiology see below.

Our knowledge of the socio-economic position of the Indo-European poet is inferential, from the daughter societies, especially India, Ireland, and Greece. The evidence from these three in turn will be considered in the following sections. The first two offer abundant evidence that poets belonged to a hereditary class or caste in an aristocratic society. Books 2 through 7 of the Rigveda are called the Family books because they are composed respectively by members of six families: Gr̥tsamada, Viśvāmitra, Vāmadeva, Atri, Bharadvāja, and Vasiṣṭha. In these books self-references by the poets are not uncommon.[4] In RV 4.4.10–11 we find a complex intertwining of the themes of the poet's genealogy, the power of the word, and the reciprocal gift-exchange relationship (Vedic *ātithyá*, Greek *xenía* 'guest-friendship', from *átithi, xénos* 'guest') of both poet with patron and patron (mediated by the poet) with god. The Vāmadevas of Book 4 were poets of the line of King Trasadasyu, one of whom is figured here returning from war laden with booty. The god Agni is addressed:

yás tvā sváśvaḥ suhiraṇyó agna
upayā́ti vásumatā ráthena
tásya trātā́ bhavasi tásya sákhā

yás ta ātithyám ānuṣág jújoṣat
mahó rujāmi bandhútā vácobhis
tán mā pitúr gótamād ánv iyāya
tváṃ no asyá vácasaś cikiddhi
hótar yaviṣṭha sukrato dámūnāḥ

He of good horses, good gold, who approaches you,
Agni, with wealth-laden chariot,
you become his protector, his friend,
he who duly enjoys your guest-friendship.

By my family, by the words of (my) great (father)
I smash (obstacles); that has come to me from my father Gotama.
Heed you this word of ours,
Hotṛ, o youngest, o wise one, as householder.

Note that *ātithyám* 'guest-friendship' is applied equally to the reciprocity relation between host and guest, poet and patron, and god and worshiper.

The reference of *rujāmi* 'I smash' is to the Vala-myth, a cosmogonic variant of the dragon-slaying myth (Vala and Vṛtra are from the same root *vṛ-*), which is narrated allusively in the preceding and difficult hymn 4.1, verses 13–17. Here the poet-priests (*náraḥ . . . uśíjaḥ*) by remembering (*manvata*, root **men-*) the thrice-seven highest secret names of the cows (a "skaldic" expression for the poetic language of the Rigveda: Geldner ad loc.) with their divine word (*vácasā dáivyena*) smash open the cave to release the captive cows, the light, the dawn's rays, the glorious milk of the dawn cows (*aruṇī́r yaśásā góḥ*). Geldner adds that the deeper meaning of the passage is that the act of remembering the cow's names is at the same time the birth of poetic inspiration, the 'divine word'. And from the released cows, the dawn's rays, the milk of the dawn cows came the first *dākṣinā*, the reward and recompense of the poet.

The "Mercenary Muse" who sings for hire (Pindar, *Isth.* 2.6, see below) is thus as old as creation, in the Indic view. That this myth in some form may go back to the proto-language is indicated on the one hand by the Irish myth of the *teora ferba fíra* 'three milk cows', with *fír* 'milk' cognate with Vedic *vā́r* in *usríyānām vā́r* (RV 4.5.8) 'milk of the dawn cows', (Watkins 1987d:402), and on the other by the isolated and much-discussed Greek expression *νυκτὸς ἀμολγός*, quasi 'milk of the night' (Lazzeroni 1971, cf. Campanile 1977:24).

The image of thrice-seven secret names of the cows as Vedic poetic language recurs in a hymn of a Vasiṣṭhid to Varuṇa, RV 7.87.4:

uvā́ca me váruṇo médhirāya
tríḥ saptá nā́mā ághnyā bibharti
vidvā́n padásya gúhyā ná vocad
yugā́ya vípra úparāya śíkṣān

Varuṇa said to me, the wise one:
"The cow bears thrice seven names.
He who knows the track should tell them like secrets,
if he would serve as inspired poet to the later generation."

The metaphor of the track (*padám*), which comes to mean 'word', is repeated in RV 4.5.2–3, a Vāmadevid hymn like those cited earlier:

mā́ nindata yá imā́m máhyaṃ rātím
devó dadáu mártyāya svadhā́vān
. . .
padáṃ ná gór ápagūḷhaṃ vividvā́n
agnír máhyam préd u vocan manīṣā́m

Do not blame him who gave me this gift,
the self-powerful god to a mortal . . .
Agni, having found the hidden word like the track of the cow,
made known to me the understanding.

For all that the poet attributes his knowledge to divine inspiration, he knows in practice that it had to be acquired by decades of laborious study. The same hymn continues (RV 4.5.6):

idám me agne . . . gurúm bhārám ná mánma . . . dadhātha

You have placed on me this knowledge, o Agni, like a heavy burden.

Though it confers privileged status the poet's wisdom is a heavy responsibility to bear.

Note that the words for the poet's understanding (*manīṣā́*) and wisdom (*mánma* = Old Irish *menmae* 'mind'), and the remembering (*manvata*) the 3 × 7 secret names of the cow which is Vedic poetics itself, are all derivatives of the root **men*- expressing active mental force, thinking, perceiving, remembering. So too is Greek *Μοῦσα* (Aeolic *Μοῖσα*) 'Muse', daughter of Zeus and Mnemosyne 'Memory': Proto-Greek **montwa* from **mon-tu-*h_2, cf. Vedic *mántu-*, *amantú-* '(un)caring, (un)mindful'. The inspiration of the divine Muse is thus only a personification of the trained mind of the poet.

Perhaps the single most telling indication of the common Indo-European origin of the reciprocal poet-patron relation as we have described it is the existence of a special literary genre in Vedic, Greek, Celtic, and Germanic, which we can call by its Sanskrit name *dānastuti* or 'praise of the gift'. The *dānastuti* is a short coda of one or more verses of thanks to the patron who commissioned the poem, praising his generosity and enumerating his gifts, which is incorporated into many Vedic hymns. These *dānastutis* regularly record such rewards (or fees) as 200 cows, 4 horses, and 2 wagons, like RV 7.18.22–25. The word for gift-chattels, masculine *dā́nās* (beside normally neuter *dā́nam* 'gift') is here and elsewhere linked by contiguity to the *śrávas* 'fame' of the generous patron. RV 8.46.23–24 records '10 chestnuts . . . the gift-chattels of Pr̥thuśravas ('Broad-fame')', and the poet plays there with his patron's name in another dimension: *várṣiṣṭham akr̥ta śrávas* 'he got for himself loftiest fame'.

RV 6.63.9-10, to the Aśvins, makes clear the nature of the process. The poet itemizes to the gods hymned the generosity of the patron(s): 'and for me two swift mares of Puraya's, a hundred (cows) with Sumīḷha, and cooked food with Peruka . . .'[5]

sáṃ vāṃ śatā́ nāsatyā sahásrā
áśvānām purupánthā giré dāt
bharádvājāya vīra nū́ giré dāt

Purupanthā gave together hundreds, thousands
of horses for your song of praise, o Nāsatyas,
To Bharadvāja he gave (them) for the song of praise, o heroes.

The poet of RV 5.61.17-19 dedicates his composition to a distant benefactor, the message—the hope of future reward—to be delivered by the goddess of Night, with an exact address. The *envoi* has a slightly Pindaric ring:

etám me stómam ūrmye
dārbhyā́ya párā vaha
gíro devi rathī́r iva

utá me vocatād íti
sutásome ráthavītau
ná kā́mo ápa veti me

eṣá kṣeti ráthavītir
maghávā gómatīr ánu
párvateṣv ápaśritaḥ

Carry this my song of praise, o Night,
to the descendant of Darbha,
my songs, o Goddess, like a charioteer.

And say for me thus
to Rathavīti who has pressed soma,
"My desire does not abate."

This generous Rathavīti
dwells along the Gomatī rivers,
hidden away in the mountains.

Examples of *dānastutis* from other Indo-European traditions are given below.

The reciprocal situation of poet and patron may have a negative side as well. Generosity leads to praise, but ungenerous payment can provoke blame, invective, and satire, the 'formidable weapon' (Binchy 1940:69) of poets from India and Greece to Ireland. A Vedic example with a thematically close parallel in Old Irish is given <in chap. 16>.

We pass now from the allusive and fleeting world of ancient Vedic India in the second millennium B.C. to the comparative clarity of Christian Ireland from the seventh to the seventeenth centuries. Despite the enormous differences in tone and cultural outlook the system, the structural position of the poet in each society, is remarkably similar in India and Ireland, and the Irish system remained basically static over the 1000 years from the beginning of our documentation to the collapse of the Gaelic world. For the early period compare the *Mittelirische Verslehren* (ed. Thurneysen, *Irische Texte* 3.1-182)[6] and the other legal texts edited and analyzed in Breatnach 1987 and for the Bardic poet of the Classical Modern Irish period Bergin 1970. For the Continental Celtic evidence from Gaul, as seen through Greek and Roman eyes, cf. the clear summary in MacCana 1970:14ff.

From the earliest times in Ireland the poet (Old Irish *fili*, Middle and Modern Irish *file*, plural *filid*) belongs to a poetic family for at least three generations. Compare *Uraicecht na Ríar* §§4 and 7 *amail as-beir fénechus: Ní tét acht lethdíre do ṡuidib, manip do chlaind genetar . . . Ceist, cuin as cland filed in chland? Ní hansae, fili a nathair 7 a senathair* 'as Irish law says: "Only half honor-price goes to sages if it is not to a family (of sages) that they are born" . . . Question, when is the family a family of poets? Not difficult; their father is a poet and their grandfather.' The ideal combination, as Breatnach shows (1987:96ff.), was family background, ability in poetry (*airchetal*, the actual poetic product, which the text speaks of having or not having), and study (*frithgnum*). With ability and study alone it was possible to become a poet, an *ánroth* 'splendid stream', second only to the *ollam* 'supreme', but it took again three generations, like most advancement to nobility or professions in medieval Ireland. The seven grades of *fili* in the eighth century are modeled on those of the 7th-century Irish church, as Breatnach notes. And the distinction between *fili* and *bard* (Welsh *bardd*), which is not found in Wales, seems also to be an innovation.

The patrons of the poets were the kings and nobles or the Church (Breatnach 1987:89). He cites there *Ériu* 13.17.20: *ní saora, ní sloinde acht righ no airigh, as doibh dligidh mormhainbhthe dia moaighid maoin* 'ennoble only, make known only a king or a noble, for it is from them that is due great wealth through which prosperity increases.'

Early Irish has a word *cerd* meaning both 'craft' and 'poetry', both 'craftsman' and 'poet'. Early Welsh has the same word *cerdd* meaning both 'craft' and 'poetry, poem'. In their synchronic semantics the two meanings of these Celtic words exhibit a *metaphor*, a *similarity* relation: poetry is like a craft, and the poet like a craftsman. But we have a *metonymy*, a *contiguity* relation projected back on the diachronic plane—reconstructed if you will—in the semantics of the Celtic words *cerd, cerdd* 'craft, poetry' and their unique cognate, Greek *κέρδος*, which means 'profit, gain'. The etymology is sure, but it rests on a metonymic figure: *craft—and poetry—is profit*. We can prove the etymology only by making explicit the cultural and pragmatic context in which such a metonymy was meaningful.

We see by this etymology just how arch Pindar was being in setting up as a foil[7] (one might think rather 'smokescreen') his "Mercenary Muse"—the word is *φιλο**κερδής***, 'profit-loving', from our *κέρδος*—in *Isth.* 2.6:

> *ἁ Μοῖσα γὰρ οὐ φιλο**κερδής** πω τότ' ἦν οὐδ' ἐργάτις*
>
> For the Muse then did not yet love **gain** nor work for hire.

For an analysis of the whole poem as *dānastuti* see below.

In Ireland right down to the collapse of the Gaelic world in the 17th century (and in Scotland in the 18th) the Gaelic poet, in Bergin's apt phrase, had to be *both born and made*. In his justly famous 1912 lecture on Bardic Poetry, Bergin (1970:3ff.) gives this description:

> For we must remember that the Irish *file* or *bard* was not necessarily an inspired poet. That he could not help. He was, in fact, a professor of literature and a man of letters, highly trained in the use of a polished literary medium, belonging to a hereditary caste in an aristocratic society, holding an official

> position therein by virtue of his training, his learning, his knowledge of the history and traditions of his country and his clan . . . At an earlier period he had been regarded as a dealer in magic, a weaver of spells and incantations, who could blast his enemies by the venom of his verse, and . . . a well-turned malediction.[8] He might be a poet, too, if in addition to his training he was gifted with the indefinable power, the true magic, of poetry. But whether he was a poet in this higher sense or not, he always composed in verse.

These sentences could be applied virtually without alteration to the Vedic *kavi* and to the mostly nameless composers, over hundreds of years, of the more than a thousand collected and preserved hymns, some good and some indifferent, which make up the Rigveda.

As illustration Bergin quotes from the description of a Bardic School by one who attended it in the early 17th century, in the *Memoirs of the Marquis of Clanricarde* (apparently the work of one Thomas O'Sullevane, see R. Flower, *British Museum Catalogue of Irish Manuscripts* 3.16 [editors' note]) which I excerpt:

> The poetical Seminary or School . . . was open only to such as were descended of Poets and reputed within their Tribes . . .
>
> The Structure was a snug low Hut, and beds in it at convenient Distances, each with a small Apartment without much Furniture of any kind, save only a Table, some Seats, and a Conveniency for Cloaths to hang upon. No Windows to let in the Day, nor any Light at all us'd but that of Candles, and these brought in at a proper Season only . . .
>
> The Professors (one or more as there was occasion) gave a Subject suitable to the Capacity of each Class, determining the number of Rhimes, and clearing what was to be chiefly observed therein as to Syllables, Quartans, Concord, Correspondence, Termination and Union[9], each of which were restrained by peculiar Rules. The said Subject (either one or more as aforesaid) having been given over Night, they worked it apart each by himself upon his own Bed, the whole next Day in the Dark, till at a certain Hour in the Night, Lights being brought in, they committed it to writing. Being afterwards dress'd and come together in a large Room, where the Masters waited, each Scholar gave in his Performance, which being corrected or approved of (according as it requir'd) either the same or fresh subjects were given against the next Day . . .
>
> Every *Saturday* and on the Eves of Festival Days they broke up and dispers'd themselves among the Gentleman and rich Farmers of the Country, by whom they were very well entertain'd and much made of . . . Nor was the People satisfied with affording this Hospitality alone; they sent in by turns every Week from far and near Liquors and all manner of Provision toward the Subsistence

> of the Academy . . . Yet the course was long and tedious, as we find, and it was six or seven years before a Mastery or the last Degree was conferred . . .
>
> As every Professor, or chief Poet, depended on some Prince or great Lord, that had endowed his Tribe, he was under strict ties to him and Family, as to record in good Metre his Marriages, Births, Deaths, Acquisitions made in war and Peace, Exploits, and other remarkable things relating to the Same . . .
>
> The last Part to be done, which was the *Action* and *Pronunciation* of the Poem in the Presence of the Maecenas, or the principal Person it related to, was performed with a great deal of Ceremony in a Consort of Vocal and Instrumental Musick. The Poet himself said nothing, but directed and took care that everybody else did his Part right.
>
> The Bard having first had the composition from him, got it well by Heart, and now pronounced it orderly, keeping even pace with a Harp, touch'd upon that Occasion; no other musical Instrumental being allowed for the said purpose than this alone, as being Masculin, much sweeter and fuller than any other.

This remarkable document probably comes as close as we will ever get to an eyewitness account of the formation of an Indo-European poet.

Another window on the Irish Bardic Poet's art and its mode of acquisition is furnished by the *Irish Grammatical Tracts*, edited by Bergin 1955, which contains myriads of quatrains cited as examples and described by such terms as *lochtach* 'faulty'. Whether these are 'detritus' from the schools or deliberately composed as such, it is clear that their assiduous study was part of the Bardic education. On these texts as a whole, and a beginning to the assessment of their place in the history of linguistics, see Bergin 1939 and Armstrong 1985 (rich bibliography p. 266). For they respond to the same sort of poetic challenge as did the nameless Hindu grammarians of the long tradition that culminated in the 'perfection' of the grammar of Pāṇini. Compare the words of Saussure cited from Starobinsky 1971:35 by Toporov 1981:216: "Le poète se livrait, et avait pour ordinaire métier de se livrer à l'analyse phonique des mots: que c'est cette science de la forme vocale des mots qui faisait probablement, dès les plus anciens temps indo-européens, la superiorité, la qualité particulaire, du *Kavis* des Hindous, du *Vātēs* des Latins, etc."

I close the account of Irish with some lines of Mathghamhain Ó Hifearnáin or Mahon O'Heffernan (Bergin 1970:145, 279), who belonged to the early 17th century, the time of confiscations and plantations, the collapse of the aristocratic Gaelic world, which brought along the ruin of its poets. He was the author of the well-known bitter verses beginning *A mhic, ná meabhraigh éigse* 'My son, cultivate not the poetic art':

1 Ceist! cia do cheinneóchadh dán?
a chiall is ceirteólas suadh:
an ngéabhadh, nó an áil le haon,
dán saor do-bhéaradh go buan?

4 Ceard mar so ní sochar dhún,
. . .
ga bríogh d'éinfhior dul re dán?

Question, who will buy a poem? Its meaning is genuine learning of scholars. Will any take, or does any lack, a noble poem that shall make him immortal? . . . Such an art (*ceard*, Old Irish *cerd*) as this is no profit to me . . . What use is it to anyone to profess poetry?

<For the rhyme scheme (end rhyme *b d*, internal rhymes *a b*, *c d*, 'consonance' *a c*) and alliteration see chap. 9.> Both the ideology and the vocabulary go back to Indo-European times.

For Germanic we need cite only some lines of the Old English *Widsith* which attest the institution of the mutual dependence, the reciprocity relation of poet and patron, and the genre of the *dānastuti*. Widsith the traveling court-poet of the speaking name ("Wide-journey") unlocked his word-hoard (*wordhord onleac*, 1) and told of meeting many peoples over the earth (*ofer eorþan* 2) and how (3–4)

oft he on flette geþah
mynelicne maþþum

Often did he in hall get desirable treasure.

In lines 64–7 of the first part of the poem, an ancient catalogue of peoples which the poet speaks in the first person, we find

Mid Þyringum ic wæs,   ond mid Þrowendum,
ond mid Burgendum,   þær ic beag geþah;
me þær Guðhere forgeaf   glædlicne maþþum
songes to leane.   Næs þæt sæne cyning!

I was with Thuringians and with Throwendians
and with Burgundians, where I received precious rings;
Gunther there gave me brilliant treasure
as reward for the song. That was no slow king!

'Reward for the song', *songes to leane*, shows the same word in the same construction as the expression

> sigores to leane
>
> as reward for the victory,

of the sword that Hrothgar son of Healfdene gave to Beowulf (line 1020) for slaying Grendel. The phrase is a Common Germanic formula, recurring in the Gothic compound *sigislaun* 'reward for victory, *Siegeslohn*'.

The victory-song composed by Hrothgar's poet to celebrate Beowulf's victory over Grendel (867ff.) included a narrative of the Common Germanic myth of Sigemund (Sigurðr, Sigfrit) slaying a dragon and gaining great glory. Lines 884–5:

> Sigemunde gesprong
> æfter deaðdæge **dom unlytel**
>
> To Sigemund came, after his death-day, **no little fame.**

Old English *dōm* is the moral and semantic equivalent of Greek *κλέος* and the litotic *dom unlytel* that of the Greek formula *μέγα κλέος*. But the Old English poet also gets *dom*. Widsith ends his moving composition with the lines (142–3)

> lof se gewyrceð
> hafað under heofonum heahfæstne dom.
>
> He who works praise has under heaven enduring fame.

The relation is precisely that expressed by Ibycus in the passage cited at the beginning of this chapter: both patron and poet get *κλέος*, and Widsith's enduring 'high-fast' fame is precisely Ibycus' *κλέος ἄφθιτον*.[10] Note finally that the poet by ring-composition effects the closure of the poem with the semantic frame *ofer eorþan* 'over earth' (2)—*under heofunum* 'under heaven' (144).

For the social context of the poet and his patron in ancient Greece I examine only a couple of representative passages of Pindar, some hidden formulas expressing themes of far greater antiquity than he.

Isthmian 2, of the famous "Mercenary Muse",[11] commemorates a chariot-victory in the 470's of the late Xenocrates of Akragas and is addressed to his son Thrasuboulos. Pindar had earlier celebrated Xenocrates' victory of 490, as well as Thrasuboulos, in *Pythian* 6, in which the theme of filial piety dominates. The whole poem—three triads and 48 lines—is an elaborate *dānastuti*, a memorial of prior munificence and a clear hint for more.

Pindar accomplishes his purpose by a set of echoes, recurrent words and phrases which serve to index and develop the essential idea. The theme is *xenía*, usually rendered 'guest-friendship', the mutual hospitality which Pindar viewed as the essence of the relation between himself and his patron. This is not merely 'traditional ties of religion, family, and society' (Woodbury 1968), but a reciprocal contractual relation.

The key recurrent words in the three triads which make up the ode are the following:

ἁ Μοῖσα γὰρ οὐ **φιλοκερδής** πω τότ' ἦν οὐδ' **ἐργάτις**

for the Muse then did not **love gain** nor **work for hire**.

taken up again in seemingly artless fashion, in the exact middle line of the ode, in the aside on the Elean heralds bearing the sacred Olympian truce, who recognized the charioteer Nikomakhos,

παθόντες πού τι **φιλόξενον ἔργον**

having experienced (from him) some **deed of hospitality**.

It is finally set forth again doubly in the praise of the late victor's hospitality:

οὐδέ ποτε **ξενίαν** / οὖρος ἐμπνεύσαις ὑπέστειλ' ἱστίον ἀμφὶ **τράπεζαν**

nor did a blasting wind strike sail about **his hospitable table**,

which is duly and properly praised by the poet's songs as he shifts to the first person:

οὐκ ἐλινύσοντας αὐτοὺς **ἐργασάμαν**

I did not **make** them to stand idle.

The whole is a message for the late victor's son Thrasuboulos, addressee of the poem, in the final line of the ode:

ταῦτα, Νικάσιππ', ἀπόνειμον, ὅταν
ξεῖνον ἐμὸν ἠθαῖον ἔλθῃς

Give this message, Nikasippos, when
you come to **my customary guest-friend**.[12]

Even the name of the victor Xenocrates echoes the *xénos*-theme, just as those of the charioteer Nikomakhos and the doubtless fictitious messenger Nikasippos echo the victory theme (*nī́kā*) and the phrase *ἵπποισι νίκαν* 'victory with horses'.

Victory requires a song of praise, which conveys the recompense of honor. This nexus is poetically expressed by the iconic phonetic figure in Pindar and other writers <discussed in chap. 3>: *nī́kā : tīmā́*. The vowels are identical and the sequence nasal consonant–oral unvoiced stop consonant is reversed. In *Isthmian* 2, where the whole poem is a *dānastuti*, the link binds the three stanzas in balance: *νίκα* 13, 26, *τιμά* 29, 34. The *nī́kā/tīmā́* theme is Pindar's pledge-token of his side of the contractual relation to his patron.

Xenía is a reciprocal notion, with what Benveniste called a 'valeur d'échange' in his programmatic work (1966:315) building on Mauss' *Essai sur le don*. And in *Pythian* 10, the earliest epinician ode of Pindar we possess (498 B.C.), we find a formula nestled between two iconically reciprocal grammatical and phonetic figures:

ἑτέροις ἑτέρων ἔρωτες ἔκνιξαν **φρένας**

as the age changes, new loves flutter the heart

πέποιθα ξενίαι

I trust in hospitality

φιλ**έων** φιλ**έοντ'** ἄγ**ων** ἄγ**οντα** προ**φρόνως**

friend to friend, leader to leader in kindness.

Pindar expresses by the stative perfect of the root **bheidh-* his trust and faith in the fundamental reciprocal social contract between guest/poet and host/patron. He repeats the formula at *Nem.* 7.65, again nesting and embedding it in the middle of a thoroughly traditional passage on his, the poet's, proper function in the traditional order, with such characteristic verbal themes as praise (*αἰνέσω*) and blame (*μέμψομαι*, *ψόγος*), oath (*ἀπομνύω*), glory (*κλέος*) for the patron, which is at the same time his reward (*μισθός*), which the poet brings to him like water to a plant. The formula itself is first indexed by the key word *ξεῖνος*, then echoed in a following personal name:

ξεῖνός εἰμι

I am a **guest-friend**

προξενίαι πέποιθα

I trust in hospitality

Εὐξένιδα πάτραθε Σώγενες

Sogenes, descended of **Euxenos**.

The formula is embellished by alliteration, ***pro*** ... ***pepoi*** ... That it means 'I trust in hospitality', just as in *Pyth.* 10.64, rather than 'I trust in proxeny', was seen and amply discussed by Pavese 1966.

Pindar even artfully echoes the lexical sequence of the formula without its semantics at *Ol.* 1.103–104:

πέποιθα δὲ **ξένον** / μή τιν'

I trust that no host . . .

Finally we may note the contiguity relation in the marked positioning (clause-initial and clause-final) of the same elements in fragment 94b (*Parth.*)

πιστὰ δ' Ἀγασικλέει
μάρτυς ἤλυθον ἐς χορόν
ἐσλοῖς τε γονεῦσιν
ἀμφὶ **προξενίαισι· τί-**

μαθεν γὰρ τὰ πάλαι τὰ νῦν
τ' ἀμφικτιόνεσσιν
ἵππων τ' ὠκυπόδων πο[λυ-
γνώτοις ἐπὶ **νίκαις**

As a **faithful** witness I have come to the dance, in honor of Agasikles and his noble parents, by reason of our **guest-friendship**. For of old as well as now they have been **honored** among their neighbors, both for the famous **victories** of swift-footed horses . . .

The identical placement of *τίμαθεν* and *νίκαις*, with the familiar Pindaric linkage, indexes and reinforces the linkage *πιστά*/*προξενίαισι*.

The true formulaic status of this Pindaric phrase *πέποιθα ξενίαι* is shown also by the attestation of the same collocation in the compound personal name Πιστόξενος attested from Mantinea in Arcadia (IG V 2.271.20, Schwyzer 662) and some 18 examples from the islands in vol. 1 of Fraser and Mathews 1987.

The root **bheidh-* recurs in reciprocal context in the Latin formula (Ennius, *Ann.* 32V.)

accipe daque fidem, foedusque feri bene firmum

give and take trust, and strike a treaty truly firm,

and significantly in the fundamental expression of the social contract among the Northern Albanians up to the 1930's, beside *be* 'oath',

besë 'pledge, truce, trust'.

In the *Fjalor i gjuhës shqipe* as translated by M. E. Huld (1984) 'A term for the freedom and security that the house of a murdered man used to give to the murderer or the men of his family with an assurance that it would not seek blood [n.b., *kërkoj gjak* = Hitt. *ešḫar šanḫ-* 'seek blood', C.W.] during a certain time'. The term *besë* was analyzed as **bhidh-tā-* by Eric Hamp 1961, who later (1985) proposed **bhidh-ti-* + *ā*, and brilliantly compared the 'Simonidean' (92 D.) epitaph for the Spartan dead at Thermopylae *ῥήμασι πειθόμενοι* 'obedient to (their) words'. Hamp is surely right in suggesting that *πειθόμενοι* here is used pregnantly in the contractual sense of the root **bheidh-*, in the Greek middle 'comply with, obey', perfect 'trust in, rely on'. But equally pregnant here is the use of *ῥήματα*, for it is a phonetic icon and etymological figure for the 'great *ῥήτρα*' (Dor. *Ϝρήτρα*), the 'covenant', the military as well as social contract of Sparta and of other Doric polities. The social contract of the soldier and that of the poet are two formulas expressing variants of a single theme of Indo-European antiquity, an all-important cultural nexus: Pindar's *πέποιθα ξενίαι* and 'Simonidean' *ῥήμασι πειθόμενοι* may be reconstructed as

TRUST (**bheidh-*) **gh(o)s-*

TRUST (**bheidh-*) **u̯reh$_1$-*.

The objects of TRUST are respectively HOSPITALITY as the total reciprocity relation between poet and patron, guest and host (**gh(o)s-*) and the covenant of the SPOKEN word (**u̯reh$_1$-*), which is the expression and the reification of the same relation.

Another formula with Indo-European **u̯reh$_1$-* in Greek is apt to reinforce the reciprocal contractual relation of gift exchange between poet and patron. In *Il.* 21.445 the gods Poseidon and Apollo were indentured for a year to King Laomedon of Troy, μισθῶι ἔπι ῥητῶι

at a specified wage.

The 'terrible' king (*ἔκπαγλος* 452) by welshing on the agreement robs them of their wage and thus breaks the covenant. Greek *μισθός* is also both the recompense of the poet and the reward of the patron in Pindar, as we have seen (*Pyth.* 1.76, *Nem.* 7.63). Nothing stands in the way of reconstructing an ancient, perhaps even Indo-European formula

COVENANTED (*$\hat{u}\textit{r̥}h_1$-*tó*-) RECOMPENSE (**misdhó*-),

where the covenant is precisely the all-powerful spoken word, *$\hat{u}\textit{r̥}h_1$-*tó*-, literally 'spoken'.

In the unifying and coherent Indo-European cultural nexus all three formulas, the Pindaric, the Simonidean, and the Homeric, lose their isolation and reveal themselves as deep archaisms. There exists a network of such formulaic contiguity relations, which lies partly below the surface; it is our responsibility to bring them to the light.

I conclude with a brief look at another of the many examples of the iconic phonetic figure linking the two words *νίκα* 'victory' and *τιμά* 'honor' in Pindar. It is a phrase in the author's prayer to Father Zeus at the conclusion of *Nemean* 9, lines 54–5: *τιμαλφεῖν λόγοις νίκαν* 'to do honor to victory by my words'. Honor (*τιμ-*) to victory (*νίκαν*) is conferred by the poetic message (*λόγοις*). The reciprocal gift of honor by the poet and the victory of the patron are linked by the verbal notion *-αλφεῖν*, from an Indo-European root **alg^{u}h-* which has precisely a Benvenistean 'valeur d'échange'—a semantic component of exchange and reciprocity: it means in Greek 'to fetch a prize in return for', in Indo-Iranian 'to be worth, to deserve'. The syntax, semantics, and derivational history of the Greek and Indo-Iranian forms are complex. Both verbs, Greek *ἀλφάνω* and Sanskrit *arhati*, select an accusative argument. Greek τιμαλφέω in the first instance is a denominative verb built on the compound adjective τιμαλφής[13] 'fetching a prize'. It is the victory which is worth the honor, and which fetches the prize of honor, but it is the victory (*νίκαν*) which is the accusative in our passage. The meaning of *τιμαλφεῖν λόγοις νίκαν* is thus 'make victory fetch the prize of honor by my words'. The phrase is a good illustration of the syntactic complexity of Greek and Indo-European compounds, but it is the pragmatics of reciprocal gift and exchange which makes it intelligible. The phrase remains a valid and powerful icon of the Indo-European poet, his art, and his social function.

Notes

1. Keith translates with periphrasis: 'but the rule is to follow the traditional text.'

2. As demonstrated at length by Benveniste 1949 and 1969:1.65ff., cf. also Watkins 1976b.

3. See the discussion in Nagy 1990b:188–90 for the 'Hellenization' of this Indo-European function.

4. For a detailed analysis of one such see Dandekar 1974.

5. The phonetic linkage with the names, *su**mī**ḷhé* ***śatám*** ***peruké*** *ca* ***pak**vā́*, is doubtless intentional, and the name *Sumīḷha* probably still carried a trace of its etymological meaning of 'reward, prize', IE **misdho-*, like Avestan *humižda-* 'bringing good reward'.

6. The text is in the process of being edited by D. Ó hAodha.

7. For the notion here of 'foil for the positive value of a transcendent reciprocity' see Nagy 1990:188, with references.

8. For a description of the fearsome satire called *glám dícenn*, which involves poets chanting the satire on the top of a hill before sunrise while piercing with a thorn of the whitethorn a clay image of the man against whom the satire is made, see Breatnach 1987:114–15, 140. See also Watkins 1993.

9. These all translate precise Irish technical terms<; see Chap. 9>.

10. For a perceptive appreciation and analysis of *Widsith*, its date, and the position it occupies in Germanic heroic poetry see Harris 1985.

11. Woodbury 1968 and Nagy 1990:188, as above.

12. For the pregnant meaning of *ἠθαῖος* (Ionic *ἠθεῖος*) 'customary' here as 'with whom one shares consecrated usage' (*ἦθος*, Vedic *svadhā́-*, Archaic Latin *suodālis*) see Watkins 1989:786–9.

13. The *s*-stem *-alph-es-* could well be an inheritance: cf. the Avestan *s*-stem noun *arəjō* 'worth' <**alg*$^{u̯}$*h-es-*.

26. Eochaid Feidlech, His Daughters and His Sons

Irish mythic tradition knows several feminine figures that are crucially linked to the acquisition of sovereignty by men destined or seeking to be king. Most conspicuous of these are the two Medbs: Medb of Cruachan, daughter of the great Irish king Eochaid Feidlech; and Medb Lethderg, queen of the province of Leinster. In the following essay, Dumézil argues that these Celtic female personifications of sovereignty closely and idiosyncratically match Indic Mādhavī, daughter of the famed ascetic and king Yayāti. More than that, Yayāti is himself a homologue of Eochaid Feidlech. Cursed by a Brahmin, Yayāti has become a frail old man; when four of his five sons refuse to surrender their own youth to him in exchange for his agedness, he exiles them to foreign lands—a tale told in Book One of the Mahābhārata. *Dumézil reveals that a remarkably parallel legend is recounted of Eochaid Feidlech, and that following these father-son struggles, both in Irish and Indic tradition, the daughters of the kings provide their fathers with invaluable assistance. In the case of Yayāti, this entails the conception of sons who will effect the return of their grandfather to heaven, from which place Indra had cast him down.* (RDW)

EOCHAID FEIDLECH, HIS DAUGHTERS AND HIS SONS

Georges Dumézil

Two Queens Named Medb

The most illustrious of the "queens Medb" is the one who comes from the province of Connaught, daughter of Ireland's supreme king Eochaid (or Eochu)[1] Feidlech. She is called "Medb of Cruachan" after the place of one of her residences. She plays a major role in *Táin Bó Cuailnge*; she is even at the bottom—as the cause—of the great conflict between her compatriots the men of Connaught and the men of Ulster, which is the subject of the epic. But that is only one episode among many others in her personal life: in fact, by her own

From *The Destiny of a King* by Georges Dumézil, 1973. The University of Chicago Press. Reprinted by permission of the University of Chicago Press.

decision or at the wish of her father, she had no less than four regular husbands, perhaps five, all of them kings.[2]

Her first husband was Conchobar, king of the Ulates; she left him "through pride of spirit," *tre uabar menman*, "in order to repair to Tara, where the (supreme) king of Ireland was," *co ndechaid chum Temrach in bail i raibe rí Erend*, that is, in order to return to her father's court.[3]

Her next suitor, Fidech son of Fiacc, was a native of Connaught (his name recalls Fidach, one of the departments, or "thirds," of this province), but he was eliminated by a rival, Tinde son of Conra Cass, also a man of Connaught. This is how it happened. Tinde was king of Connaught, but two princes had close ties to his kingship: Fidech son of Fiacc and Eochaid Dála (the latter belonging to another "third" of the province, that of the Fir Chraibe). Fidech went to Tara—the chief town in Mide, the Central Fifth, that of the supreme king—to establish his claim to the kingship, and there he asked the supreme king Eochaid Feidlech for the hand of his daughter Medb (*cur cuindidh Medb ar Eochaid Fedliuch*). Tinde caught wind of this scheme and set an ambush. The two troops met in the valley of the Shannon, and one of Tinde's men killed Fidech. Medb's father then degraded Tinde (he imposed on him an "untruth of nobility," *anfir flátha*),[4] exiled him to the wilderness of Connaught, and "placed Medb at Cruachan in place of a king," *ocus cuiris Medhbh a n-inadh rígh a Cruachain*; but this was not enough to keep Medb and Tinde from meeting later and marrying, *co mba céledach*. The only effect of this maneuver by Medb's father was that the place named Cruachan became, for a time, the place where the assembly-festivals of Ireland were held, *conidh a Cruachain dognítea áenuig Érenn*, and the sons of the kings of Ireland took up the custom, before engaging in battle with the province of Conchobar (Ulster), "of being at Cruachan with Medb," *ocus nobittís mic reig Érend hi Cruachain ic Meidhbh*. Before her marriage to Tinde, from the time when she was "in the place of a king" at Cruachan, there was, in Connaught province, no shortage of suitors representing the four other "Fifths" of Ireland. As she herself tells at the beginning of the *Táin*, "messengers came on behalf of Find son of Rus Ruad, king of Leinster, to ask for me in marriage; on behalf of Cairpri Nia Fer son of Rus Ruad, king of Tara; of Conchobar son of Fachtna Fathach, king of Ulster; and of Eochaid Bec [a kinglet of Munster]; and I did not go there." This reappearance of Conchobar has surprised some commentators, as has another more lively story which tells how, when Medb's father had brought his daughter to the festivals at Tara, Conchobar stayed behind after the completion of the games, lay in wait for Medb while she went to bathe herself in the river Boyne, and raped her. But did he not have an old account to settle with her?[5]

Tinde was killed opportunely in the battle that followed, and it was the second prince with close ties to this king—Eochaid Dála—who, not without a fight, brought Medb back safe and sound to her kingdom, together with the troops which had accompanied her. As a result, Eochaid Dála became king; more exactly, he was designated by the notables as king of Connaught, "Medb having consented to it on the condition that she would become his spouse," *do déoin Medba dia mbeth na chele dhi fen*. But this condition itself depended on another: not being herself the suitor, Medb reserved the right to accept or refuse. Now, it was her practice to refuse any partner who "was not without jealousy, without fear, and without avarice, for it was a *geis*—an interdiction under magical sanction—that she would accept as a husband only a man who combined these three qualities," *cen étt cen omun cen neoith do beth ann, uair ba ges disi beth ac ceili a mbeitís na trée sin*. Eochaid Dála presumably took on the triple obligation, or made the triple demonstration which it required, for "he became king in consequence of this, *doríghad Eochaid trit sin*, and was then for a time at Cruachan as the spouse of Medb, *ana chele icc Meidb*."[6]

But already the fourth husband had appeared, he who would have the honor of appearing in the *Táin*. At that time, in Connaught, a young boy called Ailill, son of Rus Ruad, king of Leinster, was being raised. His mother was a native of Connaught, so that the people of this province regarded him as one of their own. Moreover, "never were jealousy nor fear found in his heart," *ocus dano na frith et no omun inna chridiu*, an indication that he fulfilled at least two-thirds of Medb's standard requirements. She went to Leinster to take him with her to Connaught, and there, very quickly, he became an accomplished warrior. "And Medb loved him for his qualities and he was united with her and became her husband in place of Eochaid Dála." The latter made the mistake of showing his jealousy, *cur étluighi Eochaid*, which eliminated him once and for all. The clans interfered, but Medb held firm "because she preferred Ailill to Eochaid." There was a battle in which Ailill killed his predecessor; and then he became king of Connaught "with Medb's consent, so that he was the king of this province on two important occasions: at the coronation of Etarscéle, and at the beginning of the *Táin Bó Cuailnge*," Medb gave him three sons, the three named "Maine."[7]

There is sometimes a question of a fifth husband, supposedly the progenitor, with Medb, of a subordinate clan widely scattered over Ireland, that of the

Conmaicne. This Fergus was celebrated for the size of his penis.[8] The canonical list does not mention this last affair, but the rich get richer, and Medb herself had good reasons for saying, at the beginning of the *Táin*: "I have never been without one man near me in the shadow of another," *na raba-sa riam cen fer ar scáth araile ocum*.[9]

The second Medb, Medb Lethderg, daughter of Conán Cualann, was queen of Leinster, *rígain do Laignib*.[10] It is said of her that she gave two children to king Cú Corb—a descendant of Rus Ruad, one of the suitors, then a father-in-law of Medb of Cruachan—but that when Cú Corb was killed by Feidlimid Rechtaid, son of Tuathal Techtmhar, king of Ireland, she became the wife of the victor, who was famous above all as the father of Conn Cétcathach, "Conn of a hundred battles." "Truly great was the force and power of this Medb over the men of Ireland," one text says, "for she tolerated no king at Tara unless he took her as his wife, *roba mor tra nert ocus cumachta Meidhbha insin for firu Erenn, air isi na leigedh rí a Temair gan a beth feir aigi na mnái*; and it is for her that the royal *rath* (a kind of enclosure), the Rath Medba, was constructed near Tara, and there she made a building where the kings and the masters of all arts, *righa ocus ollamuin gacha dana*, came together."

She did not limit herself to these two husbands, but, at least for her regular partners, she did not seem to look beyond the dynasty. After Feidlimid, father of Conn, she married Art, son of Conn, and after him Cormac, son of Art. And, as one text specifies, it was this marriage, and it alone—not heredity—which allowed Cormac to assume royalty. "Cormac grandson of Conn," a text says, "lived at Kells before assuming the royalty of Ireland after the death of his father (Art). Medb Lethderg of Leinster had been the wife of Art and, after the latter's death, she took the royalty, *ocus arrobert side in rige iar n-ecaib Airt*."[11] A poem is specific on this point:

> The Leinstermen of the spears made over the sovereignty to the son of the king of Eire;
> not until Meadhbh [Medb] was united to the son [of the king of Ireland, i.e. of Cathaoir Mor] did Cormac become king of Eire.[12]

Medb, Sovereignty, and the Royal Virtues

The existence of two identically named doublets, one in the legends of Connaught, the other in the legends of Leinster, both diversely connected with the central Fifth, guarantees that the "Medb type" is indeed a variety of those feminine personifications of power, of *flaith*, of which Ireland presents other examples—sometimes under the simple name Flaith—and which have prospered down to the French and English romances of the Middle Ages. The most famous examples are found in the two stories of Niall and Lugaid Láigde. I mention them because they present a type of personification that is ruder than the type we see in Medb and, despite what has been said, not exactly its duplicate.

> In their youth, Niall and his four half-brothers, Brian, Fiachra, Ailill, and Fergus, having received weapons, went to try them out in the hunt. They lost their way and lit a great fire to cook the game they had killed. As they had nothing to drink, the last brother went in search of a water supply. He came before a spring guarded by an old sorceress who would not allow him to draw from it unless he gave her a kiss. He refused and came back with his bucket empty. One after another, the three intermediary brothers had the same experience, with the only exception that one, Fiachra, deigned to graze the woman with his lips, in reward for which she promised him "a brief contact with Tara," announcing to him thereby that only two of his descendants would become kings. When it came to the youngest, Niall's turn, he was less fastidious: he clasped the old woman and covered her with kisses. Presumably he closed his eyes for, when he looked, he saw himself in the grip of the most beautiful woman in the world. "Who are you?" he asked. "King of Tara," she answered—thus saluting him as "supreme king"—"I am Sovereignty and your descendants will be above every clan." And, sending him back toward his brothers, she recommended to him that he not allow them to drink before they had recognized his rights and his superiority.[13]

Very close to this story, with a supplement, is the story of the five sons of king Dáire.[14]

> It had been foretold to Dáire that a "son of Dáire," named "Lugaid," would attain the kingship of Ireland. For more assurance, to all the boys who were born to him he gave the same name, Lugaid. One day, at Teltown—a place where there were seasonal feasts and games—his sons were set to participate in a horserace, and there a druid specified to Dáire that his heir would be the one who succeeded in catching a fawn with a golden fleece who would enter the assembly. The fawn indeed appeared and, while it was being pursued, a magical mist separated the five brothers from all the other hunters. It was Lugaid Láigde who caught the animal. Then a great snow began to fall and one of the brothers set off in search of shelter. He was able to find a house with a great fire, food and ale, silver dishes, a bronze bed and a horrible sorceress. This latter offered the boy a bed for the night on the condition that she herself would share intimately in his repose. He refused, and she declared to him that in so

> doing he had just deprived himself of Sovereignty. The other brothers then came one after another to present themselves at the same house, but the sorceress asked nothing from them—until, last of all, came Lugaid Láigde who, with astonishment, saw the old body, under his embrace, become radiant like the rising sun in the month of May and fragrant like a beautiful garden. As he clasped her, she said to him: "Happy is your journey, for I am Sovereignty,[14] and you shall attain the sovereignty over all of Ireland."[15]

The story is interesting because it brings into play, in parallel—one confirming the other—two symbols or signs of sovereignty, the woman and the fawn, both of them encountered in the woods.[16]

Queen Medb, who conceals her beauty under no mask and lays no traps for the pretenders to royalty save her charms, symbolizes another aspect of power; she is no longer linked solely to a sometimes fortuitous conquest of royalty, but to a regular, controlled conquest and, above all, to the practice of royalty. It is she who defines royalty and rigorously sets its "moral" conditions. With her, it is no longer a question of chance, of boldness, of gallantry, but of merits. She does not satisfy herself with one partner but multiplies them, shamelessly delights in making them vie with each other under the pretext of assessing their qualities.

It may well have been the spectacle, the experience—unceasingly renewed—of the instability of the throne that oriented this figure, more and more, it would seem, toward a career of cynicism and debauchery. In the same way another experience, that of the waves of blood which flowed in the princely contests, appears to have earned for the other Medb, Medb of Leinster, her qualification *Leth-derg*, "of the red side" or "of the red half." That experience may also explain the epithet applied to the maidservant of Medb of Connaught's mother, passed on afterward to Medb's mother herself, Cruachu or Crochen *Chró-derg*, "of red skin," or "red blood."[17] So, too, the difficulties which marked the beginnings of the finest reigns gave rise—as the texts relating to Niall say quite plainly[18]—to the theme of the splendid woman who first presents herself under the guise of a horrible hag.

The close tie of the queens Medb with the practice of, and the "moral" conditions for, royalty follows from the three challenges which the more famous of the two threw out to anyone who aspired to become her husband, that is, to become king. These were mentioned above: the chosen one had to be, had to prove himself to be, and had to continue to be "without jealousy, without fear, and without avarice." In 1941, at the end of my first *Jupiter Mars Quirinus*,

I summarily proposed that this formula be understood as a psychological, almost Platonic expression of the structure of the three functions.[19] At the beginning of the *Táin Bó Cuailnge*, addressing her consort Ailill, the interested party herself enlarges upon the formula in very much the same way, except that she brings the most elevated term of the triad, jealousy, down to her own personal problems as a wife:

> " . . . for it is I," she says, "who exacted a singular bride-gift, such as no woman before had ever required of a man of the men of Ireland, namely, a husband without avarice, without jealousy, without fear.
>
> For should he be avaricious, the man with whom I should live, we were ill-matched together, inasmuch as I am great in largess and gift-giving, and it would be a disgrace for my husband if I should be superior to him in the matter of favors, and for it to be said that I was superior in wealth and treasures to him, while no disgrace would it be if one were as great as the other.
>
> Were my husband a coward, it would be equally unfit for us to be mated, for I by myself and alone brave battles and fights and combats, and it would be a reproach for my husband should his wife be more courageous than he, while there would be no reproach for our being equally brave, both of us brave.
>
> Should he be jealous, the husband with whom I should live, that too would not suit me, for there never was a time I had not near me one man in the shadow of another.
>
> Yet, I have found such a man: it is you, Ailill son of Rus Ruad of Leinster. You were not avaricious, you were not jealous, you were not a coward."[20]

In the practice of royal power, "jealousy" is a little more than this coquettish wife of so many kings has indicated here; or rather, the symbol calls for interpretation: to be jealous, to have a morbid fear of rivals, checks, and counterchecks, such are the spurs to tyranny in all its aspects, judicial as well as political. With this reservation, the justifications that Medb gives for her demands, speaking as a wife and not simply allegorically, are pertinent. They have been treated excellently by Alwyn and Brinley Rees in their *Celtic Heritage*.

> The three qualities essential to a king are defined in a negative way in Queen Medb's requirements in a husband. He must be "without jealousy, without fear, and without niggardliness." Jealousy would be a fatal weakness in a judge, as would fear in a warrior and niggardliness in a farmer. The higher the status, the more exacting are the standards that go with it, and it is noteworthy that the most reprehensible sin in each class is to indulge in the foibles of the next class below it. Meanness may be excused in a serf, but it is the denial of the farmer's vocation; fear is not incompatible with the peaceful role of the

> farmer, but it is the warrior's greatest disgrace; jealousy, as we have seen, is a trait of the warrior's character, the correlative of his virtue, but it can undermine the impartiality required in a judge. A king must have the virtues of all the functions without their weaknesses.[21]

Such was the mission of "Queen Medb," of Royalty personified: to see to it that the king, each new king, would have the assortment of qualities which had been demonstrated by a very early analysis—already present in the Indo-European tradition—to be an absolute necessity for the equilibrium of a society and the success of a reign; and also, once those qualities were ascertained in a prince, to give him the throne. Moreover, she herself, before formulating and expounding these three conditions at the beginning of the *Táin*, took care to claim credit for the corresponding qualities herself:

> . . . I was the most noble and the most distinguished (of my father's six daughters): I was the best of them in kindness and generosity (*bam-sa ferr im rath ocus tidnacul díb*): I was the best among them in battle, combat, and fighting (*bam-sa ferr im chath ocus comrac ocus comluid díb*). . . .[22]

She goes on, complacently, to add that the young nobles who formed her normal retinue numbered five hundred. Thus, to generosity and bravery, she added implicitly, as her third and highest advantage, her power to maintain about her in an orderly fashion—without jealousy!—a most illustrious outfit of courtiers.

Celticists have asked themselves how the essence of royalty came to be personified under a name which, drawn from that of the Indo-European mead, essentially expresses the power of intoxication.[23] They have collected texts in which the drink is highlighted in connection with either the practice or the acquisition or the exaltation of royal power. Few of these texts are really conclusive. For instance, an argument cannot be drawn from the metered praises of a king of Leinster:

> The sovereignty (*ind flaith*) is his heritage. . . . At the beer-drinking bout (*oc cormaim*) poems are recited. . . . The harmonious songs of bards make the name of Aed resound through the drinks of beer (*tri laith-linni*).

What could be more natural than for the king to be celebrated at the banquets he offers? More interesting is the obligation upon the king to offer them. A juridical text, enumerating the four activities of the king, begins with this obligation:

to drink beer (*do ól corma*) on Sundays, for there is no regular sovereign (*flaith techta*) who does not promise beer (*laith*) every Sunday.[24]

But that could still rest upon the assonance between the names for "power" (*flaith*) and "beer" ((*f*)*laith*).[25] The most noteworthy arguments are furnished by the fairly numerous legends which make the acquisition of royalty depend upon a certain drink, for instance the *derg-flaith*, "red beer" or "red sovereignty," which the personified Sovereignty of Ireland, in a dream, pours out for king Conn; or the "old beer" and the automatic drinking horns in the story of Lugaid Láigde; or the spring water which the sorceress Sovereignty allows to be drunk only in exchange for a kiss and which is at least the prelude to less harmless beverages, since the old woman turned young says to Niall: "May the drink (*linn*) that will flow from the royal horn be for you: it will be mead, it will be honey, it will be strong beer!" After citing these examples and several others, Josef Weisweiler adds the following, concerning one of the two Medbs directly:

> It is told of Medb of Cruachan that she intoxicated heroes to obtain their cooperation in the struggle against her enemies. The tragic duel between Fer Diad and his brother-in-arms Cúchulainn took place only because Medb made Fer Diad swallow, until he became drunk, "an intoxicating beverage, good, sweet to drink." She had already resorted to the same means in order to arm, put at her service, and send to his death Fer Báeth, foster brother of Cúchulainn, and Lárine mac Nois. There is obviously a connection between the intoxicating drink and the celebrated royal woman of Connaught.[26]

As to Medb of Leinster, she is called "daughter of Conán of Cuala" (*ingen Chonain Cualann*); now a medieval poet has written, evidently alluding to a tradition that was well understood in his time:

> niba ri ar an Erind, mani toro coirm Cualand.

> He will not be king over Ireland, unless the beer of Cuala should come to him.[27]

Thus the names for the two Medbs are justified, born perhaps from special royal rites which it would be as easy to imagine as it would be vain.

Medb and Mādhavī

We are now able to return to the Indian Mādhavī, daughter of the universal king Yayāti, wife and mother of multiple kings at an accelerated pace. If the account we have of her quadruple performance is fraught with pious thoughts and unfolded in conformity with the most respectable laws, both religious and civil, of brahmanic society, the story of the Irish Medb makes it likely that an extremely ancient notion has been conserved under this guise—proudly taking its place between the two other episodes in Yayāti's career. Let us put it bluntly: beyond the Indo-Iranian stage assured for the first and third episodes, this whole story continues to cast in poetic images an Indo-European theory of the nature, the chances, the risks of royalty and, above all, the qualities it requires. In particular, the trifunctional demands imposed by Medb upon all her royal husbands on the one hand, and the coherent trifunctional partnership formed by the royal sons of Mādhavī on the other, are two expressions of the analysis of these qualities in the most general framework of the Indo-European ideology.[28] And the synthesis is no less strongly delineated than the analysis: it is evident in the three demands of Medb, which are indissociable; and it is no less evident in the story of the sons of Mādhavī, who, although ruling over diverse lands, find themselves, against every custom and expectation, offering a common royal sacrifice on the very day that their own grandfather, formerly omnivalent in merits himself, needs them to reunite their merits and thus to recompose the complete trifunctional equipment he has lost.[29]

Behind Medb, behind both Medbs, there is a father, just as there is one behind Mādhavī: it is the father who gives Medb of Cruachan in marriage, at least to several of her husbands, and initially to the first, Conchobar, as part of the compensation for the wrong he had done him; it is the father of Medb of Leinster who disposes of the beer of sovereignty which appears to be inseparable from his daughter. And the supreme king of Tara is, by definition, the king of the "central Fifth" like Yayāti. Although the latter is in a position to divide up the surrounding lands between his five sons, he is properly the king of the good central land, since that is the "Fifth" which he reserves for the son whom he will make his successor.

Other features of the Indian legend are better explained in the light of the Irish phantasmagoria on sovereignty. Richer and more varied, this Irish tradition, in addition to Medb, presents Flaith, the beautiful young woman disguised as an old sorceress, and also the fawn which doubles for her in the story of Lugaid Láigde. It will be recalled that after her fourth child is born, Mādhavī, called upon to "make an end of it" in a socially dazzling way, that is, to marry herself "for good" to a decent prince, chooses at the height of the ceremony to unite herself not to a man but to the forest (*vana* being masculine), and that she in fact withdraws into the woods to devote herself to asceticism. Up to this point there is nothing noteworthy other than her decision to conserve from now on, away from all jeopardy, a virginity four times gambled. But the form of her asceticism, of her mystical marriage, is singular: she takes on the mode of life, the food, the lightness of a large *mṛga*, that is to say, of a gazelle or some animal of the same type, and it is presumably as such that she appears to her father the king and her four royal sons at that sublime reckoning of accounts which, in the providential plan whose existence we must take for granted, seems to be her final raison d'être.[30] We are truly close to Lugaid's fawn: here the two representations, the Beauty and the Beast, are united.

Just as the Irish have, on the one hand, the more concrete and more human Medb, a woman and a queen, and, on the other, the royal Power personified, Flaith, who, in a slightly different fashion, governs the rhythm of realms but, despite her technique of appearing at first repulsive and then seductive, remains more abstract, so in India the figure of Mādhavī is similarly akin, although without duplicating her, to the more abstract Śrī-Lakṣmī, "Prosperity," especially royal prosperity. Śrī-Lakṣmī has been rightly compared, by Alexander H. Krappe, Ananda Coomaraswamy, and Alwyn and Brinley Rees, to the Irish Flaith.[31] The acquisition of Śrī is also sometimes conceived of as a marriage. Śrī is the wife of Indra, seeks his protection, offers him the soma drink which she has caused to ferment by mastication, following an archaic technique. She is, like Flaith, an inconstant beauty, who, in an important episode of the *Mahābhārata*, passes from the demons to the gods, namely to the king of the gods, Indra.[32] At the time of the royal enthronement ceremony itself, she is connected with a rite which symbolizes that the *śrī*, the good fortune, of the king about to be consecrated, has escaped from him in its trifunctional component parts, later to be restored to him by a group of his queens.[33]

Finally, while Medb of Connaught scoffs at what will be said of her, parades her favors from one whim to the next, and expounds with complete frankness the theory behind her infidelities,[34] the pious Mādhavī passes from royal bed to royal bed out of duty and without licentiousness. But the fact is there, objectively, that she multiplies these experiences. Mādhavī's originality, of little importance for the two Medbs, is that she associates virginity with the intensive practice of remunerated unions, of temporary marriages by sale: four times she recovers her integrity, and it is with the obvious mark of innocence that she goes off as a gazelle in the forest of her choice.

Wide and deep as these correspondences are, they do not, of course, preclude considerable divergences, but the latter can in large part be accounted for by the different "ideological fields" of Ireland and India.

Thus, as we have seen, Mādhavī no longer bears any mark of drunkenness except in her name[35] and in the overwhelming desires which she arouses in all the kings to whom she is offered, whereas Medb, both Medbs, seem to be ritually associated with the practice of taking intoxicating drinks.[36] This is in conformity with the moral emphasis of the two societies: the Irish are always engaged in enormous drinking bouts, catalysts for acts of violence but also for exploits inconceivable in brahmanic India, which is hostile to the *surā*, to alcohol, and even—despite the example of the Vedic Indra—to the ritual abuse of the *soma*.

In the action of the two heroines, Ireland has highlighted the multiplicity of the husbands of Medb, making but few references to the offspring which result from these unions, a focus which accentuates the licentious aspect of her conduct. India, on the contrary, places the accent on the multiple sons of Mādhavī, on her efficacy as a mother, and also, with regard to Yayāti, on her daughterly piety. The only notes of voluptuousness in the account of her four unions are attributed to the royal buyers, not to Mādhavī, the innocent merchandise. In return, the western reader can boast that Medb, independent and proud, receives no fee for her services, while those of Mādhavī are paid for, although at a uniform rate—and not, of course, to her but to her rightful protector, who watches less over her than over the exactitude of the transactions.

Then too, the point at which Medb and Mādhavī apply that "royal virtue" which they have within them is not the same. Each of the Medbs, through her marriage, veritably creates kings in one of the provinces of the isle or, rather, at Tara, thus qualifying for the royalty of that province—or for the supreme royalty—men who, without her, would not have obtained such rank. Mādhavī, the good and beautiful dam, is commended, one after another, to three ruling kings and to a king emeritus, so that she may give them pleasure, certainly, but above all so that she may bear each a son who will become a king naturally, without her having to intervene.

In Mādhavī, India presents no equivalent to the rivalries, the conflicts sometimes ending in dispossessions, which occur again and again around the two Medbs—and, perhaps by way of compensation, this makes Mādhavī's sphere of action much larger. However fickle her Irish counterparts, they each operate in a single place and one of them, Medb of Leinster, in a single dynasty. Neither of the two Medbs, as long as her previous husband remains a king, tours the other royal beds of the island, and it is precisely because their virtue, if one can call it that, operates in a fixed and determined spot that all the rivalries, all the "palace revolutions," take place. On the contrary, Mādhavī's four clients are geographically and politically dispersed, and there is no risk of their succeeding each other on a single throne; thus, between them, there is neither competition nor jealousy. Two formulations make it clear that the successive embraces of the queen and the princess are different not in nature but in circumstances and consequences. Medb, for her part, says to one of her royal partners (the fourth): "There never was a time when I had not near me one man in the shadow of another," meaning that for the single throne with which she is concerned, there will always be a pretender ready to take the occupant's place;[37] on Mādhavī's part, one of her royal partners says to her venerable protector: "I will thus beget only one son upon her, I will tread in my turn the path that others have trod," showing thereby that, in these successive acts of common exploitation, none of the participants holds any threat for the others.[38]

On all these divergent points, one may be inclined to think that the Celts have retained in greater purity a system of concepts and images which, in the Indian version, is presented only as it has been domesticated by the brahmans, who were better casuists and more uncompromising moralists than the Druids.

Thus we are borne by the comparison well beyond Iran in space, and farther back than the second millennium B.C. in time. Between the conservative Ireland of the early middle ages and the conservative India of the epic, a direct, solid correspondence emerges here, to which a few scraps from Iran, though much paler and more distorted, may be added, recomposing the picture of a special accord between the extreme east and the extreme west of the Indo-European domain that has been exemplified so frequently. The correspondence, moreover, relates to the status of the **rēg*-, that is, to a figure whose name is attested only in the same two groups of societies.[39] To be sure, one must not draw hasty conclusions from this limitation, perhaps a provisional one,[40] but what we have just glimpsed is certainly important, and can perhaps be formulated briefly by reference to the episodes that make up the full-length saga of Yayāti.

1. In the first episode, we are struck by the coincidence of the division of Ireland into five Fifths—a central one, that of the supreme king, and four peripheral ones—with the Indian king's distribution of the lands among his five sons, establishing his heir at the center, exiling the four others to the circumference (and probably, in Vedic times, to the four quarters of the circumference). Although this "pattern," based on the cardinal points, is found

throughout the world, it is remarkable that, among Indo-European societies, only the Irish and the Indians (and probably the most ancient Iranians too) preferred it to tripartite patterns.[41]

2. In the second episode, there is a striking correspondence between the Irish Medb and Mādhavī, daughter of Yayāti, both successive wives of several kings and probable incarnations of royal power in the forms and within the limitations which have been specified.

3. Again in the second episode but with its continuation in the third, we note the insertion of the ideological structure of the three functions into the activities of both heroines: in Medb, through the qualities which she demands in her husbands (absence of avarice, absence of fear, absence of jealousy); in Mādhavī, through the excellences which are distributed naturally among her offspring (generous use of riches, valor in battle, liturgical exactitude, veracity).

Eochaid, His Sons, and His Daughter Clothru

To these concordances is added another, more important, perhaps, since it proves that the full extent of the saga of Yayāti—with its plan, a diptych presenting the sons on the one hand, the daughter and her sons on the other—is ancient, pre-Indian. For it is indeed a diptych, despite the three-part analysis we have just made of it. In the first episode, the universal king is involved only with his five sons, and, with one exception, it is a bad relationship: the sons fail to submit, or to show respect, to their royal father, the royal father then deprives the ungrateful or rebellious sons, as well as their descendents, of their natural heritage, and establishes, to their detriment and in favor of a single son who has shown himself dutiful, a revised order of succession to the central throne. In the second episode and in the third which is its sequel, the sons hardly appear and have no real roles; the protagonists are now the king's daughter and the grandsons she gives him, and all—they and she alike—manifest a vivid, total devotion to the king, their father and grandfather.

Now Medb occupies a homologous place in the total legend of her father Eochaid which, with the exception of an episode of sin and redemption, hardly conceivable in the ideology of Ireland, follows the same plan, gives the same lesson as that of Yayāti. Eochaid, supreme king of Ireland, appears first with his sons, then with his daughters and principally with Medb, in antithetical situations. The text which informs us most systematically about Medb's marriages and which was summarized earlier,[42] the *Cath Boinde*, in fact opens, after the inevitable biblical reference, with a double tableau:

> A king took kingship over Ireland once on a time: Eochaid Feidleach, the son of Finn, the son of Rogen Ruad, son of Easamain Eamna [. . .]. He was called Eochaid Feidleach because he was *feidil*, that is to say, just toward all.[43]
>
> 1. He had four sons: [first] the three Findeamna [*e(a)mna*, plural of *e(a)main*, "twin":[44] the "Finn triplets"], and they were born of one birth, Breas, Nar, and Lothar were their names. It is they who, in their own sister, engendered Lugaid-of-the-three-red-stripes [*Lugaid tri (sic) riab n-derg*] the night before they gave battle to their father, at Druimcriad. The three of them fell there by the hand of Eochaid Feidleach, and Eochaid Feidleach solemnly decided [on this occasion] that no son should ever rule Ireland [immediately] after his father—that which verified itself.[45] The [fourth] son of Eochaid Feidleach was Conall Anglondach,[46] who indeed did not become supreme king and from whom descend the Conailli, in the land of the men of Breagh.

As far as I know, no text explains the cause of the sons' coalition, but the battle fought by the sons against their father and lost by them is mentioned with more detail in other texts. Thus in an "explanation of place names" (*Dindśenchas*) under the heading of the place called Druim Criach:

> Druim nAirthir ["Ridge of the east"] was the name at first, till the three Find-emna gave battle to their father there, even to Eochaid Feidleach, king of Ireland. Bres and Nar and Lothar were their names. . . . They marched through the north of Ireland over Febal and over Ess Rúaid, and crossed [the rivers] Dub and Drobáis and Dall and Sligech, and over Senchorann and Segais and Mag Luirg and Mag nAi and Mag Cruachan, and there their sister Clothru sought them, and wept to them, and kissed them. And she said: "I am troubled at being childless," and she entreated them to lie with her. And thence was born Lugaid Red-stripes [*Lugaid Riab ndearg*], the son of the three Find-emna. This was done that they might not get "truth of battle" [?] from their father.
>
> Thereafter they marched from Cruachan over Áth Luain through Meath, over Áth Féne and Findglais and Glais Tarsna and Glais Cruind and Druim nAirthir.
>
> Thrice three thousand were then with Eochaid, and he ordered a fast against his sons to overthrow them, or to make them grant him a month's truce from battle. Nothing, however, was given him save battle on the following day. So then Eochaid cursed his sons and said, "Let them be like their names" [Noise and Shame and Trough]. And he delivered battle [to his sons and their troops], and crushed seven thousand of them; and the sons were routed with only thrice nine men in their company, to wit, nine with Nar, who

> reached Tír ind Náir in Umall, and there he fell at Liath na cor; and nine others with Bres at Dún Bres by Loch Orsben, and there he fell; and nine others with Lothar over Áth Lúain, and there he fell and, like his brothers, was beheaded.
>
> Then before nightfall their three heads came to Druim Criaich, and there Eochaid uttered the word, that from that time forward no son should ever take the lordship of Tara after his father unless some one came between them.[47]

The treatise on the "Fitness of Words," *Cóir anman*, also proposes to connect Eochaid's epithet, Feidlech, with this painful family conflict: the word, it is claimed, is contracted from *fedil-uch*, "long sigh," because "after his sons had been killed at the battle of Druim Críad, the pain never left his heart until he died."[48] This etymology, certainly false, attests at least to the importance of the episode in the traditions about this king.

After this destruction of the rebellious sons, the *Cath Bóinde* then passes, without transition, to Eochaid's daughters:

> 2. That king, Eochaid Feidlech, had a great family, namely:
>
> (a) Eile, daughter of Eochaid, wife of Fergal mac Magach; from her Bri Eili in Leinster takes its name; after Fergal she was wife to Sraibgend mac Niuil of the tribe of the Erna, and she bore him a son, Mata the son of Sraibgend, the father of Ailill mac Mata;
>
> (b) Mumain Etanchaithrech, daughter of Eochaid Feidlech, wife of Conchobar son of Fachtna Fathach,[49] the mother of Glaisne Conchobar's son;
>
> (c) Eithne, daughter of Eochaid Feidlech, another wife of the same Conchobar, mother of Furboide Conchobar's son [. . .];
>
> (d) Clothra [= Clothru], daughter of Eochaid Feidlech, mother of Cormac Conloinges, Conchobar's son [. . .];
>
> (e) Deirbriu, daughter of Eochaid Feidlech, from whom were named the "pigs of Deirbriu" [*muca Deirbrend*];
>
> (f) Mea[d]b [that is, Medb] of Cruachan, daughter of Eochaid Feidlech, another of Conchobar's wives, mother of Amalgad, Conchobar's son, so that Conchobar was Medb's first husband [*conad he Concobar cet fear Meadba*], but Medb forsook Conchobar through pride of mind, and went [back] to Tara, where the supreme king of Ireland was.
>
> The reasons that the supreme king [of Ireland] gave these daughters to Conchobar was that it was by Eochaid Feidlech that Fachtna Fathach [Conchobar's father] had fallen in the battle of Lottir-ruad in the Corann, so that it was as his eric [compensation] these were given to him, together with forcible seizure of the kingship of Ulster, over the children of the Clan Rudraidhe; and the first cause of the stirring up of the Táin Bó Cuailnge ["the Cattle-raid of Cuailnge"] was the abandonment of Conchobar by Medb against his will.[50]

Thus, like Yayāti, Eochaid is maltreated by his sons (in this text, by all but the fourth). He curses them and, still more unfortunate than Yayāti, has to fight them; and, instead of having to exile them by royal command, he makes them flee in three directions and sees them perish in their flight. Moreover, as Mādhavī does for Yayāti, his daughters make him happy in various ways. They are obedient girls. He uses several of them to pay compensation and thus avoid a showdown with Conchobar.[51] One of them, in particular, gives him a very odd grandson, Lugaid, whose body—thanks to his three fathers—is divided in three by circular red stripes; and, by so doing, she saves her father. Another daughter, the last and the most fully described, Medb, performs through her marriages, as we have seen, a role in the presentation and the transfer of royalty. Finally, at the conclusion of his conflict with his sons, Eochaid makes a general decision, but one whose primary effect is upon the succession of his own throne—a decision different from that one made by Yayāti in like circumstances, more serious but with the same meaning: Yayāti limits himself to removing his four eldest sons from the universal kingship, that with the central seat, which he transmits to his youngest; Eochaid, on the other hand, forever prohibits any son of a supreme king from succeeding directly, without an interim reign, to the supreme kingship of Ireland.

The role of Eochaid's daughters is particularly interesting. Most of them have been given as wives to Conchobar, like Medb, and in this capacity seem to be doublets for her. But one of them, it will be recalled, intervenes in an original way: under a specious pretext, she offers herself to the concupiscence of her brothers before they begin their unfilial battle against their father. One of the texts which has just been cited explains this action all too briefly, but in the right direction: the girl acts out of daughterly devotion, sacrifices herself in three incestuous unions in order to mystically and perhaps physically weaken her brothers, to put them at a disadvantage against their father. Another text, the *Aided Medba* of the Book of Leinster, which Françoise Le Roux has recently made available as additional documentation in this area, is more explicit.[52] The text also has the advantage of making it clear that Clothru is a double, or a duplication, of Medb: she is called "Clothru of Cruachan," as Medb is "Medb of Cruachan," and it is said that she was in fact queen of this place before Medb. And here we find, fully unveiled, the plan which Clothru conceives: when her three brothers undertake to dethrone their father, she at first tries to dissuade them. Unsuccessful, she uses the following bold scheme: "Come to me," she says, "in order to know whether I will have a descent, for it is the hour and the moment of conception!" And that is what they do. They approach her in succession, and she conceives a son, Lugaid of the Red Stripes, son of the three Findemna. Then she says to them: "Now you will not go forth against your father. You have committed enough evil by uniting with your sister. That will do: do not fight against your father." And so it is, the text of the *Aided Medba* concludes, that she prevents them from being triumphant in the upcoming battle. Mme Le Roux comments aptly: "The most likely interpretation is that Clothru paralyzes her brothers or deprives them of their martial vigor, all the while assuring her father of a male descendant"—a very necessary male descendant since, according to this text, Eochaid has no other sons than the three who have revolted, the three who will die in battle. This girl's heroic self-sacrifice, which involves her in a series of carnal, morally questionable relationships, thus has the goal and the effect of saving her father from defeat and from death. We are very close to the heroic self-sacrifice of Yayāti's daughter when she agrees to go from royal bed to royal bed in order to earn those rarest of horses which have been asked of her father and which her father cannot give—this kind of prostitution resulting in the birth of grandsons, who, in their turn, will save their grandfather from another still graver danger.

Lugaid Red-Stripes

Behind these correspondences and divergencies, common to the ancestors of Ireland and India and adapted to different circumstances, we perceive the epic illustration of a vast theory of kingship. This theory places in a fundamental opposition the behavior of the king's sons and that of the king's daughters. It contrasts the inevitable political risks inherent in the former with the commercial possibilities offered by marriages of the latter to other kings. It also contrasts the characters of the king's sons with the characters of his grandsons, that is, the sons of his daughters. It justifies a reform, temporary or lasting, in the order of royal succession. And finally, in the person of a princess named after the intoxicating drink **medhu-*, it presents a symbol, and a kind of guarantor or distributor, of the qualities—in accord with the three functions—which kings must synthetically possess.

Such an epic ensemble does not appear elsewhere. At most, in Iran, in the legend to which we alluded in connection with Mādhavī,[53] it was observed that the sons on the one hand, the daughter and her descendants on the other, have contrary destinies: the sons are eliminated, the *xvarrah* (*x*ᵛ*arənah*) does not enter into them; instead it enters the daughter, passes into her son and, through him, into the successive representatives of the Kayanid dynasty. But the role attributed to the father here is the inverse of what we find in Yayāti as well as in Eochaid: the father favors his sons, he does what he can to make the *xvarrah* enter them, and when the *xvarrah* has entered his daughter, he persecutes her and desires to kill her. Perhaps this is the result of a Zoroastrian reshaping of the old structure.

Between the Irish and the Indian treatments, the two principal differences—outside the plurality of Eochaid's daughters, perhaps doublets, as opposed to the single daughter of Yayāti—appear to be the following:

1. While Yayāti makes a distribution of the world between his sons dividing it between the good center, purely arya, and the less good or bad sections on the periphery, at least partially barbarian, the episode of Eochaid and his sons has no bearing on the division of Ireland into five Fifths (that of the center, reserved for the supreme king, and the four on the periphery). These Fifths preexist, and the sons, who are only three, or four (the rebellious triplets, and sometimes Conall) are neither in the beginning nor in the course of their lives connected with different territories. The only specification in this sense is the rule concerning the kingship in the center, which the indignant father decrees; but this rule bears (in the *Cath Bóinde*) upon the innocent younger brother, the fourth son, just as much as it does upon the guilty triplets (or their memories).

2. Medb's relation to the three functions is only a moral one, but it is self-conscious and willful and expresses itself in words and acts through her triple claim and the triple demand for qualities (a demand imposed upon her by a *geis*, a "fate" which weighs upon her) which she imposes upon royal candidates. In contrast, it is by carnal creations, in the assortment of grandsons which she gives to her father, by the unconscious mechanism of pregnancies and of what they transmit through heredity, that Mādhavī "expresses" the excellences, distributed among the three functions, which a complete king must normally possess. Another of Eochaid's grandsons, however—the child that another of his daughters, Clothru, has brought forth by her three wicked brothers in order to save her father—may perhaps retain the trace of a more discernible expression of the trifunctional structure. But if this is the case, we must recognize that the content of the three functions is no longer explicit in the texts, which are concerned only with the picturesque, the outer ap-

pearance of "Lugaid of the Red Stripes," and not with what these stripes, this bodily tripartition, may at first have signified. He had, says the *Cóir anman*, a circular stripe around the neck, another around the waist. And of the three sections thus marked off, his head resembled that of Nar, his torso that of Bres, and below the belt he was like Lothar.[54] There is certainly nothing functional in the meanings of the fathers' names or in the little that is known about the action of the son, but it should be pointed out that when such real or symbolic divisions of a human or animal body into three (or two, or four) parts are mentioned by some of the Indo-Europeans in their myths, rites, or speculations, they are generally connected with classification or the social expression of the functions. Without going into the political fable of Menenius Agrippa with his "patrician-stomach" and his "plebian-mouth, teeth, limbs, etc.,"[55] the Vedic hymn of the Primordial Man has the four *varṇas* (priests, warriors, tiller-breeders, and *śūdras*) born respectively from the mouth, arms, thighs, and feet of the human victim.[56] In the Indian ritual of the horse sacrifice, three queens perform unctions upon the head, the back, and the rump of the animal about to be immolated, the purpose of which unctions is to assure the royal sacrificer, respectively, of spiritual energy (*tejas*), physical force (*indriya*), and wealth in cattle (*paśu*).[57] Another Indian ritual, that of the *pravargya*, recently illuminated by J. A. B. van Buitenen,[58] presents a remarkable example of a correspondence between the three segments of the human body (head, trunk, lower body), the three social functions, and the three superimposed parts of the universe. At a certain moment in this ritual, the *adhvaryu* priest pours three oblations of butter while holding the ladle at the level of his face for the first, of his navel for the second, and of his knees for the third. On this occasion he pronounces three formulas, all addressed to a clay figurine called *Gharma*, "warm (milk)," and Mahāvīra, "Great Man." In the first formula, he names heaven and the *brahman* (neuter: principle of the first function and essence of the brahman class); in the second, he names the atmosphere and the *kṣatra* (principle of the second function and essence of the warrior class); and in the third, he names the earth and the *viś* (principle of the third function and essence of the tiller-breeder class). This triple equation certainly bears upon the form of the figurine: three balls of clay joined together, the lower portion flattened out to furnish a base, evoking a man seated in cross-legged position. The three segments marked by the congenital stripes on the body of Lugaid, which are very close to those which the Greek philosophers connected, or, rather, claimed to connect, from top to bottom, with the three functional aspects of the soul—the rational, the passionate, and the concupiscent—may thus initially have indicated that this young man was a perfect synthesis of the qualities which were enunciated a little differently in the triple requirements laid down by his aunt Medb.

The Indian account is in any case of wider scope, and is more harmonious, than the Irish. One may suppose that this latter, cut off from Druidic philosophy like all the epic Irish texts and conserving from the ancient symbols only the interplay of figures and their behavior, has reached us in an impoverished form. But the Indian comparison does afford a glimpse of its primary significance, its value as a structure.[59]

Will it be possible to propose a sociological or psychological interpretation of this structure? Today such an attempt holds only risks. But even now, precautions can be taken against one risk: to judge from the vocabulary of kinship, the oldest Indo-European societies were composed of families defined strictly in relation to the males, to fathers, and sons, and husbands. Accordingly, there is little chance that the conduct of the proud queen Medb, and that of her humble Indian sister Mādhavī, will carry us back to the nebula of matriarchy.[60]

Notes

1. *Eochaid*, or *Eochu*, genitive *E(o)chah*. On this name (**ivocatus*, "who fights with the yew"), see note and bibliography of Françoise Le Roux, *Ogam* 20 (1968): 393, n. 60. (Jaan Puhvel, *Myth and Law* . . . <[see above, chap. 4, n. 29]>, prefers to explain Eochaid by *ech*, "horse.") On principle, I conserve the orthography of each source.

2. The principal studies are: Tomás ó Máille, "Medb Cruachna," *Zeitschrift für Celtische Philologie* 17 (1928; volume dedicated to Thurneysen): 129–46; Rudolf Thurneysen, "Göttin Medb?" ibid. 18 (1930): 108–10, and "Zur Göttin Medb," ibid. 19 (1931–33): 352–53 (aligning it with a Sumerian *hieros gamos*); Alexander Haggerty Krappe, "The Sovereignty of Erin," *The American Journal of Philology* 63 (1942): 444–54; Josef Weisweiler, *Heimat und Herrschaft, Wirkung und Ursprung eines irischen Mythos* (1943), notably chap. 6 ("die Herrschaft über Irland"), pp. 86–120 (esp. pp. 91–104); Alwyn and Brinley Rees, *Celtic Heritage* (1961), pp. 73–75; Françoise Le Roux-Guyonvarc'h, *Celticum* 15 (1966), pp. 339–50 of her commentary on the *Tochmare Etaine* (pp. 328–74, with etymological appendices by Christian Guyonvarc'h, pp. 377–84). What follows here summarizes, with T. ó Máille, the basic text, the *Cath Bóinde*, edited and translated by Joseph O'Neill, *Ériu* 2 (1905): 173 (introduction), 174–84 (text), 175–85 (translation).

3. O'Neill, pp. 176–77; ó Máille, pp. 130–31.

4. See Myles Dillon, "The Act of Truth in Celtic Tradition," *Modern Philology* 44 (1946–47): 140.

5. O'Neill, pp. 176–80, 177–81; ó Máille, pp. 131–33.

6. O'Neill, pp. 176–82, 177–83; ó Máille, p. 134.

7. O'Neill, pp. 182–84, 183–85; ó Máille, pp. 135–36.

8. Thurneysen, pp. 108–9.

9. *Táin Bó Cuailnge*, ed. Ernst Windisch (1905): (version of the Book of Leinster), p. 6 (p. 7, transl.). At the beginning of the *Táin*, Medb also enumerates the four suitors whom she eliminated in her preference for Ailill: as to these five, they represent the five Cóiceds of Ireland, as underlined by Windisch, pp. 4 and 5.

10. ó Máille, pp. 136–39, where all the references can be found.

11. *Esnada Tige Buchet*, ed. and tr. Whitley Stokes, *Revue Celtique* 25 (1904): 23 (p. 24, transl.); cf. p. 34, variant.

12. Maura Power, "Cnucha Cnoc os Cion Life," *Zeitschrift für Celtische Philologie* 11 (1917): 43 (p. 48, transl.), distich 30:

doratsat Laighin na lann righi do mac righ Eirenn.
nocor fhaidh Medb lesin mac nirbo righ Eirenn Cormac.

13. On Niall, I summarize: Standish Ó'Grady, *Silva Gadelica* (1892), I, pp. 326–30 (text), II, pp. 368–73 (transl.); Maud Joint, "Echtra Max Echdach Mugmedoin," Érin 4 (1910): 104–6; Whitley Stokes, [same title] *Revue Celtique* 24 (1903): 190–207; Krappe, pp. 448–49.

14. A little later she renames herself: "I am the Sovereignty of Ireland," *missi banflaith hErenn.*

15. On Lugaid, I summarize: the *Cóir Anman*, ed. Whitley Stokes, in *Irische Texte* III, 2 (1897), §70, pp. 316–22 (317–323, transl.); cf. Krappe, pp. 444–45, with the variant of the *Dinśenchas* in verse.

16. Krappe, pp. 447–48, suggests a connection between some Greek and Iranian traditions that should certainly be kept apart: for example, the ram in the story of Ardašīr is something else, one of the incarnations of Vərəθrağna, the spirit of victory—as is also the boar.

17. ó Máille, pp. 142–43; Weisweiler, p. 92.

18. <For Niall's story, see above, sec. 2 and n. 13:> "I am Sovereignty," said the ravishing girl, "and just as you have at first seen me ugly, sodden, and repugnant, and beautiful only at the end, so will it be with royal power: only in hard combats can it be won, but in the end he who is king shows himself gracious and noble," *Silva Gadelica* I, p. 329, II, p. 372; "Royalty is harsh (*garb*) at the beginning, sweet (*blaith*) in the middle, peaceable (*saim*) at the end," *Ériu* 4 (1910): 106; cf. *Revue Celtique* 24 (1903): 200. Krappe misuses a poetic expression of Tha'alabī (ed. and tr. H. Zotenberg, p. 137), from which he artificially constructs a "tradition," in order to attribute a homologous legend to Iran: "[Zaw] had received the royalty from Afrāsyāb when it was like an old woman, ugly and toothless; he transmitted her to Kay Qobādh like a young bride"; the author simply notes, in his florid style, how the situation in Iran was ameliorated thanks to Zaw between the end of Afrāsyāb's usurpation and the advent of the founder of the Kayanid dynasty (on which, see *Mythe et épopée* II, p. 221).

19. P. 261.

20. Somewhat modified from Joseph Dunn, *The Ancient Irish Epic Tale Táin Bó Cualnge* (1914), pp. 2–3; cf. Windisch, p. 6.

21. A. and B. Rees, *Celtic Heritage*, pp. 130–31.

22. Windisch, p. 4.

23. Weisweiler, pp. 112–14, with discussion of the opinions on the meaning of Medb; <see above, chap. 4, sec. 4>.

24. Weisweiler, p. 113.

25. Ibid., p. 112.

26. Ibid., pp. 113–14. ó Máille, p. 144, interpreted one of the names for Connaught, *Cóiced (n-)Ólnecmacht*, as "The Province of the Drink of Powerlessness" (= intoxicating). But this explanation is contested: M. A. O'Brien, in *Ériu* 11 (1932): 163–64, interprets *Cóiced ól nÉcmacht* as "the province beyond the impassable tract of land," Connaught being separated from Ulster by a nearly insuperable series of lakes and marshes, obstacles referred to in ancient literature.

27. ó Máille, p. 145.

28. <See chap. 5, sec. 2, and chap. 2, sec. 1.>

29. <See chap. 2, sec. 1.>

30. Ibid.

31. *Celtic Heritage*, p. 75, with references to Krappe and Coomaraswamy.

32. *Mythe et épopée* I, p. 122.

33. Paul-Émile Dumont, *L'Aśvamedha* (1927), pp. 152–54.

34. But Medb is not a courtesan; rather, she pays her partners. On this idle moral debate, see most recently the appropriate remarks of Françoise Le Roux, *Celticum* 15: 341–42.

35. <See above, chap. 4, sec. 3.>

36. This means of intoxicating is not foreign to Medb, of whom the *Dindśenchas* in verse (ed. Edward Gwynn, IV [1913], p. 366) can say: "Such was the glory of Medb—and the excellence of her beauty—that two thirds of his valor he lost—every man who looked at her." F. Le Roux, *Celticum* 15: 343.

37. <See chap. 5, sec. 3.>

38. <See chap. 4, sec. 1.>

39. Most recently, see my *Archaic Roman Religion*, pp. 16–17, 582–85.

40. See *Mythe et épopée* II, part 1, developing a correspondence, concerning another aspect of the royal ideology, between India and two central parts of the Indo-European world, Scandinavia and Greece.

41. In Roman tradition, another quinquipartite "model" (in reality quadrupartite, with a subdivision) seems to have prevailed in an entirely different matter, where one would rather have expected a reference to the cardinal points. Varro, *De lingua latina* 5, 33, says that the *augures publici* distinguished five types of terrains: *ager Romanus*, evidently at the center; *a. peregrinus*, certainly the nearest to Rome (with its privileged variety *a. Gabinus*, which is indeed *peregrinus*, but has the *auspicia singularia*); *a. hosticus, a. incertus*.

42. See above, n. 2; O'Neill, p. 174 (transl. p. 175).

43. The Irish have proposed other etymologies.

44. The word is related to Indo-Iranian **yama* and to Old Scandinavian Ymir. The Vedic Yama and the Iranian Yima are also heroes in stories of incest with a sister (proposed by her and refused by him; or carried out; <see the end of the Introduction, above>). Lugaid had Cúchulainn for his master of arms, *Cóir Anman* §211 = *Irische Texte* III, 2 (1897), p. 374 (transl. p. 375). The taste for incest ran in the family, or at least in Clothra: she repeated the act with the son, Lugaid: *Eochadii f(eidhlech) filia Clothra mater Lugadii riab nderg, qui trium Finnorum filius; ipsa quoque mater Cremthanni, qui et eiusdem Lugadii filius*," Standish O'Grady, *Silva Gadelica* II, p. 544 (= XXIII, IV, c).—Another etymology explains *emna* by the town *Emain* (Macha).

45. *Corob e Eochaid Feidleach rochuindid in itchi næmda cen mac indeog a athar for Erind e obrath, cor firad sin.*

46. In other arrangements of the material (in *Aided Medba*, for example, see below, sec. 4 and n. 54), this Conall Anglondach is not a son, but a brother of Eochaid Feidlech, the latter having no other sons than the Triplets.

47. Whitley Stokes, ed. and tr., "The Rennes Dindsenchas, 1st Supplement," *Revue Celtique* 16 (1895): 148–49 (149–50, transl.).

48. *Irische Texte* III, 2 (1897), §102, p. 330.

49. It is she, for example, who is asleep by the side of Conchobar in *Tochmarc Ferbe* (Windisch, ed. and tr., *Irische Texte*, III, 2 1897, pp. 472–73) when a very beautiful woman appears who announces the events of the *Táin Bó Cuailnge*.

50. See above, n. 2; O'Neill, pp. 174–76 (transl. pp. 175–77). For the concluding paragraph, the text reads:

Is i cuis fa tuc rig Ereand na hingina sin do Concobar, air is le h-Eochaid Feidleach dothoit Fachna Fathach i cath Lithrechruaidi sa Corand, conad na eric tucad sin do, mailli re rigi n-Ulad do gabail do irreicin tar clandaib Rudraidi, conad he cet adbar comuachaid Thana Bo Cuailnge facbail Meadba ar Conchobar da a indeoin.

Cf. F. Le Roux, *Celticum* 15: 344.

51. As Mādhavī is handed over by her father to Gālava to avoid the dishonor of not giving the alms requested of him.

52. *Celticum* 15: 342–43, in her commentary on *Tochmarc Etaine* (see above, n. 46). According to this text, Eochaid has only three sons, the triplets, and three daughters, Eithne ("the Horrible"), Clothru, and Medb.

53. <See above, chap. 4, end of sec. 2, and n. 26.>

54. *Irische Texte* III, 2 (1897), § 105, p. 332 (p. 333 transl.); the preceding paragraph explains the common name of the three brothers by *emain*, "twin"; see above, n. 44.

55. Livy, II, 32,7–12, and parallel texts.

56. *R̥V* 10,90,12.

57. P.-E. Dumont, *L'Aśvamedha* (1927), pp. 152–54, 271–72, 329–30; my *Archaic Roman Religion*, p. 225.

58. *The Pravargya, an Ancient Indian Iconic Ritual*, Deccan College, Poona, Building Centenary and Silver Jubilee Series, 58 (1968), pp. 11, 124–25.

59. This does not contradict what has been said above, sec. 3, on one particular point (the attenuation of the theme of "the Intoxicating" in Mādhavī).

60. Cf. what was said of the Ossetic heroine Satana in *Mythe et épopée* I, pp. 562–63.

27. The Tuatha De Danann

*Prior to the arrival of the ancestors of the Celts, five successive groups of invaders had made their way to the shores of Ireland—so the tales of medieval Ireland tell. The fifth of these invaders were the folk known as the Tuatha De Danann, the 'People of the Goddess Dana (or Danu).' When they arrived in Ireland, the Tuatha De Danann encountered there the Fir Bolg (the fourth group of invaders), whom they battled and defeated in the First Battle of Mag Tuired, or Moytura. Much of the selection that follows, Marie Heaney's poetic retelling of medieval traditions, deals with the Tuatha De Danann and their oppression by those creatures called the Fomoire, whose domination is brought to an end at the Second Battle of Moytura. But the unraveling of Fomorian domination had begun with the mistreatment of a poet who was refused the poets' customary hospitality by Bres, the greedy half-Fomorian king who ruled despotically over the Tuatha De Danann. The poet, Cairbre mac Ethne, responded by composing a satirical poem (*glám*) against Bres, the first in Ireland, and Bres's sovereignty began to crumble. As Watkins observed above of patrons and poets: "Generosity leads to praise, but ungenerous payment can provoke blame, invective, and satire, the 'formidable weapon' (Binchy 1940:69) of poets from India and Greece to Ireland." Cairbre will subsequently wield power against the Fomorian army; he is a master of the* glám dícenn*—the satirical curse uttered by poets as they stand on one foot, one arm outstretched, one eye shut.* (RDW)

THE TUATHA DE DANAAN

Marie Heaney

Long ago the Tuatha De Danaan came to Ireland in a great fleet of ships to take the land from the Fir Bolgs who lived there. These newcomers were the People of the Goddess Danu and their men of learning possessed great powers and were revered as if they were gods. They were accomplished in the various arts of druidry, namely magic, prophecy and occult lore. They had learnt their druidic skills in Falias, Gorias, Findias and Murias, the four cities of the northern islands.

When they reached Ireland and landed on the western shore, they set fire to their boats so that there would be no turning back. The smoke from the burning boats darkened the sun and filled the land for three days, and the Fir Bolgs thought the Tuatha De Danaan had arrived in a magic mist.

The invaders brought with them the four great treasures of their tribe. From Falias they brought Lia Fail, the Stone of Destiny. They brought it to Tara and it screamed when a rightful king of Ireland sat on it. From Gorias they brought Lugh's spear. Anyone who held it was invincible in battle. From Findias they brought Nuada's irresistible sword. No one could escape it once it was unsheathed. From Murias they brought the Dagda's cauldron. No one ever left it hungry.

Nuada was the king of the Tuatha De Danaan and he led them against the Fir Bolgs. They fought a fierce battle on the Plain of Moytura, the first one the Tuatha De Danaan fought in a place of that name. Thousands of the Fir Bolgs were killed, a hundred thousand in all, and among them their king, Eochai Mac Erc. Many of the Tuatha De Danaan died too, and their king, Nuada, had his arm severed from his body in the fight.

In the end the Tuatha De Danaan overcame the Fir Bolgs and routed them until only a handful of them survived. These survivors boarded their ships and set sail to the far-scattered islands around Ireland.

When the Fir Bolgs had fled, the Tuatha De Danaan took over the country and went with their treasures to Tara to establish themselves as masters of the island. But another struggle lay ahead. Though they had defeated the Fir Bolgs, a more powerful enemy awaited them. These were the Fomorians, a demon-like race who lived in the islands to which the Fir Bolgs had fled.

Balor of the Evil Eye

Balor was the most powerful Fomorian king. Some of his followers were so ugly and rough they were frightful to look at, and some of them had only one hand and one foot. Balor built a shining tower on his island. It was made of glass, but shone like gold in the sun and from this tower Balor could watch out for ships and send his fierce pirates out to seize them if they came close. Not only did the Fomorians capture ships, but they sailed to Ireland and made raids there, seizing lands and slaves and levying taxes. Their druids had powerful magic spells, and it was through one of these spells that Balor got his power and his name.

One day when the young Balor was passing a house he heard chanting inside. He knew this place was out of bounds, for it was there the magicians gathered to work new spells, but curiosity overcame him. Seeing a window that was open high in the wall, he scrambled up and looked furtively through it, but he could see nothing for the room was filled with fumes and gases. Just as he peered through the window the chants grew louder and a strong plume of smoke rose in the air straight into Balor's face. He was blinded by the poisonous fumes and could not open his eye. He struggled to the ground, writhing with pain, and before he could escape one of the magicians came out of the house.

When the druid saw what had happened he said to Balor, 'That spell we were making was a spell of death and the fumes from it have brought the power of death to your eye. If you look on anyone with that evil eye it means they will die!' And so Balor got his name.

Among his own people his eye remained shut, but if he opened it against his enemies they dropped dead when he turned its deadly power on them. As he grew older his eyelid grew heavier and heavier until in the end he could not open it without help. An ivory ring was driven through the lid and through this ring ropes were threaded to make a pulley. It took ten men to raise the great heavy lid, but ten times that number were slain at a single glance. His evil eye made him of great importance to the Fomorians and he became the most powerful of them all. His ships raided Ireland again and again and Balor's pirates made slaves of the learned people of De Danaan.

But Balor had a secret fear. One of his druids had foretold that he would die at the hand of his own grandson. Balor had only one child, a daughter called Eithlinn, so he built another tower and shut the girl up in it with twelve women to guard her. He warned the women that not only should Eithlinn never see a man, but a man's name must never be mentioned in her presence. When this was done, Balor felt safe, for without a husband Eithlinn could not have a child and so he would not die.

He harried the Tuatha De Danaan more and more. He levied heavy taxes on them. They had to send him one-third of their grain, one-third of their milk, and, worst of all, one child in every three. So the Fomorians were feared and hated for their greed and cruelty and Balor was feared most of all.

Eithlinn grew up into a beautiful woman, a prisoner in the tower. Her companions were kind to her, entertained her and taught her skills, but Eithlinn felt lonely. As she looked out to sea from the high window of her tower, she would see long curraghs in the distance skimming over the waves and in these boats people unlike any she had seen before. In a dream, too, the same face would appear again and again and she felt a longing to meet this person. She asked the women who guarded her what they were called, these people that she had watched from a distance and seen in her dreams, but her companions remained silent. They remembered Balor's command that a man's name could not be mentioned in his daughter's presence.

The Birth of Lugh

Though he had cattle enough, Balor particularly coveted one wonderful cow, the Glas Gaibhleann, which never ran dry and belonged to a man of the Tuatha De Danaan called Cian. Balor would disguise himself in different ways and follow Cian and his marvellous cow around, waiting for a chance to seize it and bring it back to his island.

One day Balor saw Cian and his brother go to the forge of another brother, Goibniu, to get some weapons made by him. Cian had his cow with him on a halter because so many people had tried to steal her that she could not go loose, but had to be guarded night and day. Cian went into the forge to speak to Goibniu, while the other brother stayed outside with the Glas Gaibhleann. Balor saw his chance. Turning himself into a red-headed boy, he came up to the man who stood by the cow and began to talk to him.

'Are you getting a sword made as well?' he asked.

'I am,' said the brother, 'in my turn. When Cian comes out of the forge he'll guard the cow and I'll go into Goibniu and get my weapon made.'

'That's what you think,' said the boy. 'But there'll be no steel left for your sword. Your brothers have tricked you. They are using all the steel to make heavier weapons for themselves and you'll have none!'

When the third brother heard this he was furious. He stuffed the cow's halter into the boy's hand and ran into the forge to confront his brothers. Instantly Balor cast off his disguise and, dragging the cow behind him by the tail, he hurried to the strand and into the sea and headed back to the safety of his own island.

When his brother came storming into the forge yelling abuse at him, Cian realized he had been tricked. He raced outside just in time to see Balor pulling the Glas Gaibhleann behind him through the water, and as he watched cow and man became a speck on the horizon. It was Cian's turn to be angry now and he ranted at his brother for falling for such a trick, but it was too late. The cow was gone.

Cian went to a druid to ask for his help but the magician reminded him that no one could go near Balor without risking death, because of his evil eye. Cian was still determined to retrieve his cow, so he went to a woman druid called Birog, who had even greater powers. She disguised Cian as a woman and then she conjured up a wind so strong that Cian and she were carried off in a blast, high in the air, until they reached Balor's island.

The wind dropped and they landed safely at the foot of the tower where Eithlinn was imprisoned. Birog called out to the Eithlinn's guardians in the tower, 'Help us! Please help us! My companion is a queen of the Tuatha De Danaan. She is escaping from enemies who want to kill her. It's getting dark! Take pity on us and let us in!'

The women did not like to refuse another woman in distress and they let Cian and Birog in.

As soon as they were inside, Birog cast another spell and all the women fell fast asleep. All the women, that is, except Eithlinn herself. Cian, who had thrown off his women's robes, ran up the stairs and in a small room at the top of the tower found Eithlinn staring sadly out to sea. He thought she was the most beautiful woman he had ever seen. As he stared at her, Eithlinn turned round and there, in the room with her, was the figure she thought about all day long and dreamt about each night. Declaring their love for each other, they embraced with delight.

Because he and Eithlinn loved each other, it was Cian's wish to take his beloved from her prison and bring her home with him. He went to find Birog to persuade her to use her powers to help them to escape together. But Birog was afraid of Balor. She was terrified that the Fomorian king would discover them and kill them with his evil eye, so, in spite of Cian's protests, she swept him away from Eithlinn on another enchanted wind and took him back with her to Ireland.

Eithlinn was brokenhearted when Cian left her, but she was comforted when she discovered that she would give birth to his child. In due course the boy was born and she called him Lugh.

When Balor heard the news of his grandson's birth he made up his mind to kill the infant straight away so that the druid's prophecy could not come true. He gave orders that the baby be thrown into the sea. Despite the desperate pleading of Eithlinn, the child was snatched from her and carried to the shore. Wrapped in a blanket held in place by a pin, Lugh was cast into a current by Eithlinn's guardians. As the weeping women watched, the pin opened and the baby rolled into the sea, leaving the empty blanket spread over the waves. Balor was relieved to hear that Lugh had been drowned. Once more he felt safe. Now he had no grandson to bring about his end.

But Lugh had been saved. Birog, who had been riding the winds, saw what happened and lifted the baby out of the water and carried him with her through the air, away from the island and back to Ireland. Just as she had carried Cian to Eithlinn, so she carried Lugh safely back to his father. Cian was overjoyed that his son had been saved and fostered him out with a king's daughter who loved Lugh as if he were her own child.

In his foster mother's house Lugh learnt many skills. The craftsmen taught him to work in wood and metal, the champions and athletes performed amazing feats for him and invited him to join them in their training. From the poets and musicians he heard the stories of the heroes and learnt to play on the harp and timpan. The court physician taught him the use of herbs and elixirs to cure illness and the magicians revealed to him their secret powers. He got the name Lugh of the Long Arm and grew up as skilful as he was handsome. Moreover, though he did not know it, he had within him the power to slay his grandfather, Balor of the Evil Eye.

The Reign of Bres

While Lugh was growing up in the house of his foster mother and learning all the arts and crafts that were practiced there, another half-Fomorian was king of the Tuatha De Danaan and sat on the throne at Tara. He too was handsome, so handsome that he was called Bres the Beautiful. But he was greedy and cowardly as well.

Before Bres had been made ruler, Nuada had been the king of the De Danaan tribe. Nuada it was who had gained Ireland for his people by leading them in battle against the Fir Bolgs. His powerful army had driven the Fir Bolgs out of Ireland, then taken over the island and established the king's stronghold at Tara. In that battle Nuada lost an arm. It was severed from his body by the sword of Sreng and though he won the battle this accident cost Nuada his kingship. The Tuatha De Danaan had a law that only a man in perfect shape could rule them, and without his arm Nuada could no longer be king.

The people then chose Bres the Beautiful to be king [in] his place. Bres's father was a Fomorian and because of this the Tuatha De Danaan hoped that their new leader would form an alliance with Balor and put an end at last to the fierce Fomorian raids up the rivers and seas of Ireland. As it turned out the reign of Bres was disastrous for the Tuatha De Danaan. The Fomorians *did* form an alliance but their treaty was with Bres alone. Playing on his weakness and greed, they loaded heavier and heavier taxes on the Tuatha De Danaan and Bres added to his subjects' burden by imposing taxes of his own. He stripped the leaders of their wealth and power and made them do menial tasks. Ogma was set to chop wood and the Dagda to build fortifications around the king's stronghold.

As Bres grew greedier and more miserly the court at Tara became a cold and cheerless place. The poets and musicians were silent and the champions and heroes reduced to slavery. The chiefs who came to visit the king were given neither food nor drink and no entertainment was provided for them.

One day the poet Cairbre arrived at Bres's fort expecting the hospitality that poets were accustomed to receiving from their patrons. Instead he was shown into a narrow, mean, dark little house without a bed or a stick of furniture and no fire in the hearth. He was given three small dry cakes on a little plate and that was all. Cairbre was furious at Bres for this insulting treatment and the next morning as he crossed the enclosure on his way out of Tara, he composed a satirical poem against the king. This was the first satire ever made in Ireland, and through it the poet cursed Bres. 'Bres's prosperity is no more!' he cried, and his words came true. From that moment on, Bres's fortunes failed, his wealth dwindled and his people became poorer and more oppressed.

But Cairbre's satire had another effect as well; it gave the Tuatha De Danaan leaders the courage to rebel against their king. They made up their minds to depose Bres but their problem was they had no one suitable to put in his place. They would have loved to restore Nuada to the throne but while he had only one arm they could not.

Then something happened to help them. Nuada's arm was restored to him through the skill of two men, Dian Cecht, the chief physician of the Tuatha De Danaan, and his son Miach.

First of all Dian Cecht fashioned an arm out of silver for Nuada. It worked as well as a real arm, the elbow bent, the fingers moved, the wrist was flexible and Nuada was pleased to have the use of his limb again. He became known as

Nuada of the Silver Arm.

But he was still not perfect and therefore not fit to be king. So Miach, the physician's son, who had been taught the secrets of medicine by his father, decided to try to replace the silver arm with Nuada's real arm. He got Nuada's severed arm, which had been embalmed, and brought it to him. He removed the silver arm and set the severed arm into the socket. Then he said incantations over it:

> 'Joint to joint and sinew to sinew!
> Sinew to sinew and joint to joint!'

The operation took nine days and during that time Miach never left the king's side. For the first three days he bound Nuada's arm straight down along his side until it had rejoined the body at the armpit. For the second three days he bent the elbow and bound the arm across the king's breast and movement was restored. For the last three days he put a powder made of charred bulrushes on it and the arm was completely healed. It was as strong and flexible as it had ever been. Now Nuada could be king again and the De Danaan rejoiced.

But Miach paid a terrible price for his kindness and skill. His father became mad with jealousy that his student and his son, moreover, was now more powerful and skilled in medicine than he was himself. In a frenzy of rage and envy, he slashed at Miach's head with his sword. The first stroke cut into the skin and Miach healed himself on the instant. The second stroke reached the bone but Miach healed himself again. Though the third stroke went through the bone to the membrane of the brain still Miach was able to heal himself. With the fourth stroke, Dian Cecht cut out his son's brain and Miach fell dead.

Dian Cecht buried Miach on the plain outside Tara. By the next day a miraculous growth of herbs had sprung up, outlining Miach's body, every organ and bone and sinew. Each herb had special powers relating to the part of the body from which it had sprung. Airmed, Miach's sister, came to mourn for her brother and she saw the herbs, three hundred and sixty-five in all, growing out of his grave. She spread her cloak on the ground and started gathering the herbs to dry them, sorting them out according to their healing properties. But the jealous Dian Cecht came upon her as she was completing the task. He grabbed the cloak and scattered the herbs, mixing them all up together so that it was impossible to sort them out again, and to this day no one person really knows all the healing properties of herbs.

Lugh Comes to Tara

Nuada was perfect again and deemed fit to be king. The Tuatha De Danaan made up their minds to banish Bres and put Nuada back on the throne.

They went to Bres and, complaining bitterly to him about his cruel and miserly treatment of them, they told him to abdicate and restore the kingship to Nuada who was now whole again. Bres was very angry to be deposed, but he was too cowardly to resist so he agreed, and once more Nuada was king of the Tuatha De Danaan.

Bres was determined to take revenge for his humiliation. He left Ireland for the remote island where his Fomorian father lived to seek help from him.

'Why have you come here?' his father said. 'You were king in Ireland and had great power. What happened to bring you down?'

'It was my own fault. My injustice, arrogance and greed brought about my downfall!' Bres confessed. 'I put taxes on the people that they had never paid before, and I reduced them to poverty and hunger. I have only myself to blame for what has happened.'

'That is bad,' his father told him sadly. 'The prosperity of your people should have been more important to you than your own position. Their blessing would have been better than their curses. What do you want from me?'

'I have come to gather an army to take back the land by force,' said Bres.

'What you lost through injustice you shouldn't regain through injustice!' said his father, and though he would not help Bres himself, he sent him on to Balor's island to raise an army there.

When Balor heard Bres's story he rallied to his aid for he knew that without Bres on the throne of Ireland, his own tyranny and extortion would be threatened. He assembled a fleet so big it could form an unbroken bridge from his farthest island across to Ireland. He gathered a great army and started to prepare for war.

Nuada, reigning justly now in Tara, knew nothing of this. With Bres gone, he had restored the kingship to its full glory. The poets and musicians who had been silent in Bres's day now entertained the household. There was plenty to eat and drink, and once more Tara resounded to the noise of feasting and entertainments of all kinds. But Nuada was uneasy, nevertheless, for he knew that Balor's raiders would return.

One day, when a feast was in progress, a young warrior in the clothing of a prince appeared at the gate of the king's fort. He was as beautiful as Bres had been, but was nobler in bearing and he had with him a band of warriors.

As he rode up to the gates of Tara, his troops behind him, the two doorkeepers, Gamal and Camall, challenged him.

'Who are you?' they asked, and 'Why have you come here?'

'I am Lugh of the Long Arm,' the warrior said, 'son of Cian and Eithlinn and grandson of Balor. Tell the king I am at the gates and want to join his household!'

'No one finds a place in Nuada's household unless he has a special skill,' said Camall. 'So I must ask what skill you have.'

'Question me,' said Lugh. 'I am a carpenter.'

'We have a carpenter already named Luchta and we do not need you,' replied Camall.

'Question me. I am a smith.'

'We have a smith as well. Colum is his name and so we do not need another.'

'Question me. I am a champion, stronger than any other,' said Lugh.

'The king's own brother, Ogma, is a champion and one champion is enough. We do not need you.'

'Question me. I am a harper.'

'We have a harper of our own. He is called Abcan. You are of no use to us.'

'Question me, doorkeeper. I am a warrior.'

Camall answered, 'We do not need you. We have a warrior already. Bresal is his name.'

'Question me. I am a poet who can tell many stories.'

'We have a bard already. We do not need another.'

'Question me. I am a magician.'

'We have many druids and magicians. We need no more.'

'Question me. I am a physician.'

'Still we do not need you. Dian Cecht, our physician, is the best in the land.'

'I will bear the king's cup at table if you will let me in!'

'We have nine cupbearers and that is enough. We do not need you.'

'Question me for the last time! I am a skilled worker in brass and enamelling.'

'Credne is our metalsmith, famous for his skill. We do not need you.'

'Then,' said Lugh, 'go and ask the king if he has in his household any single person who can do all these things. If he has, I will leave these gates and will no longer try to enter Tara.'

Camall left Gamal at the gate and went with Lugh's message to the king.

'A young man is at the gate asking to be let in. His name is Lugh, but by his own account he is so gifted that he should go by the name Samildanach, that is, master of all the arts. He says he can do by himself all the arts, crafts and skilled work of this entire household.'

'Let us see if he is as talented as he claims,' the king ordered. 'Bring the chessboard out to him and let him compete against our best players.'

Camall ran off and did as he had been commanded. Lugh played against the best chess players in the land and won every game until there was no one left unbeaten.

When Nuada heard this he said to the doorkeeper, 'Let this young hero in! Samildanach is a fitting name for him. He *is* a master of all arts. His like has never been seen in Tara before.'

Gamal and Camall opened the gates and Lugh entered Tara. He went straight to the hall where Nuada sat, surrounded by chiefs and bards and champions. The four great leaders of the Tuatha De Danaan were there too, the Dagda, the chief druid, Dian Cecht, the physician, Ogma, the champion, and Goibniu, the smith. Lugh passed by them all and sat down on the Seat of Wisdom next to the king.

Ogma, the champion, was proud of his own great strength and annoyed by the young man's arrogance, so he decided to test Lugh and discover if he really had all the powers he had boasted about. He lifted a huge flagstone, one that had taken several yokes of oxen to put there, and hurled it through the thick wall of the fort and out on to the plain. Lugh walked out to where the flagstone lay, lifted it and cast it back through the gaping hole it had made. It landed in the hall and settled in the exact spot where it had been before. He lifted the piece of wall that the flagstone had carried with it and set it back in place so that Nuada's hall was sound again.

Then taking up the harp that was slung over his shoulder Lugh began to play. As he plucked the strings gently and soothingly Nuada and his company fell into a peaceful sleep. When they woke, Lugh played for them slow airs that made them weep. Then the music got faster and happier and, drying their tears, the whole company began to smile and laugh. Their laughter got louder and louder until the rafters rang with the sound.

Seeing that Lugh did indeed possess the mastery he claimed, Nuada decided to enlist his aid against Balor and his followers. He told Lugh about the evil of the Fomorians, about the tyranny of their taxes, their piracy round his shores and their cruelty to the captured sailors. He asked the young warrior to help him and Lugh agreed to be an ally. Then Nuada gave him the authority to rule by stepping off the throne while Lugh ascended it in his place.

Lugh was king of the Tuatha De Danaan for thirteen days and then, with Nuada and the four other leaders, he left Tara and went into a quiet place to plan the battle. They were in conference for a full year discussing their tactics and they kept their whereabouts and their plans secret so that the Fomorians would not suspect anything. Then, promising to meet again in three years, they left their hiding place. Nuada and the other leaders returned to Tara and Lugh went to seek the help of Manannan Mac Lir, the powerful ruler of the sea.

One day, nearly three years later, Nuada was looking out across the ramparts of his fort when he saw a troop of warriors coming towards him. His eyes were dazzled by a bright light as if he had looked full into the sun, but then he saw that the brilliant rays shone from the face of the leader of the troop and from his long golden hair. Darts of light came off the young man's armour and off his weapons and the gold-embossed harness of his horse. A great jewel blazed from the front of the golden helmet he wore on his shining hair, and Nuada knew that Lugh had come back to Tara.

This time Lugh was riding Manannan Mac Lir's magic horse that could gallop on the sea as if it were dry land and from whose back no one ever fell. He was wearing Manannan's breastplate that no weapon could penetrate, and in his hand he held Manannan's sword that was so deadly no one survived a blow from it.

Nuada, the king, and the De Danaan chiefs welcomed Lugh and brought him into Tara and they all sat down together. They had barely taken their places when another troop of men appeared on the horizon approaching Tara, but they were as different from Lugh and his noble followers as night is from day. Unkempt and surly, they slouched towards Nuada's fort as if they owned it. The doorkeepers who had questioned Lugh so closely when he had first arrived in Tara rushed to open the door for them, and without ceremony the slovenly crew shambled into the room where the king and Lugh were seated. Nuada and his household rose to their feet as soon as they entered while Lugh looked on in amazement and vexation.

'Why are you rising to your feet for this miserable, hostile rabble when you didn't stand for me?' he cried.

'We must rise,' Nuada replied, 'or they will kill us all, down to the youngest child! These are the Fomorians who have come back again to harry us as they did during Bres's rule. They have come to claim their taxes, a third of our crops and our cattle and a third of our children as slaves!'

Lugh was so furious when he heard these words that he drew Manannan's deadly sword and rushed at the Fomorian crowd and killed all but nine of them. 'You should be killed as well,' he told the cringing survivors, 'but I'll spare your lives so that you can return to Balor empty-handed and tell him what happened here!' The terrified messengers fled from Tara like hunted animals and made for the islands of the Fomorians as quickly as they could.

When they arrived at Balor's tower and told him about the fate of their companions, his rage was as great as Lugh's and he was determined to invade Ireland and regain his hold over the country and its inhabitants. He called a council of war and the most powerful Fomorians came to his tower, among them his wife, Queen Ceithlinn of the Crooked Teeth, his twelve sons, and his warriors and wise men. Bres, who had just arrived at Balor's tower to seek allies to regain his throne from Nuada, was there as well.

'Who is this upstart,' Balor roared, 'who dares to kill my men and send an insulting message back to me?'

Ceithlinn answered him. 'I know well who he is from the description these men give of him, and it is bad news for us. He is our own grandson, the son of our daughter Eithlinn, and he is known as Lugh of the Long Arm. It has been foretold that he will banish the Fomorians from Ireland for all time and that it will be at his hand, the hand of your grandson, that you, Balor, will meet your end.'

When Bres heard this he said to Balor, 'I came to you here to ask you to help me recover my throne. Now we can help each other. Get ready ships and men and arms for me and pack our boats with provisions and I'll go to Ireland and meet Lugh in battle myself. I'll cut off his head and bring it back to you.'

'Do that if you can,' said Balor, 'but I will come too, and for all his skills I'll overcome my insolent grandson. When that's done, I'll tie that rebellious island to the stern of my ship and tow it back here where none of the De Danaan will dare to follow. And where Ireland once lay there will be empty ocean.'

Then marshalling his fearsome army and accompanied by Ceithlinn and his warriors, he made for the harbour. Every ship in the huge fleet raised a bright sail and, catching the wind, set out for Ireland.

The Battle of Moytura

As soon as the Fomorian messengers had fled from Tara, Lugh and Nuada began to make plans for battle too, for they knew that Balor would seek revenge for the men who had been killed, and would try to gain control over the Tuatha De Danaan and impose the same taxes as before. They called together the magician and cupbearers, the druid and craftsmen, the poet and physicians, all the people who possessed special skills, and Lugh asked each one of them what contribution he would make to the struggle.

The magician told him he would topple the mountains of Ireland and cause them to roll along the ground towards the Fomorian army, but these same mountains would shelter the Tuatha De Danaan during the fight.

The cupbearers promised to bring a great thirst on the Fomorians and then drain the lakes and rivers of Ireland so that there was no water for them to drink. But there would be water for Nuada's army even if the war lasted seven years.

The druid said he would send a shower of fire to fall on the heads of the Fomorians and rob them of their strength, but every breath the Tuatha De Danaan drew would make them stronger.

Then Lugh questioned the craftsmen and the wise men in the same way as to what special powers they would bring to battle.

Goibniu, the smith, promised to make swords and spearheads that would never miss their mark and to supply them to the Tuatha De Danaan for as long as the battle raged.

Credne, the worker in brass, said he would provide rivets and sockets for spears and swords and rims for shields as long as they were needed, and Luchta, the carpenter, swore he would make the strongest spearshafts and shields and would do so until Lugh's army was victorious.

Then Lugh questioned Cairbre, the poet who had cursed Bres, about his contribution to the struggle.

'The weapons I use are invisible,' Cairbre replied, 'but no less strong for that. I attack the mind. At daybreak I will compose a satirical poem about the Fomorians and because of this poem they will be full of shame and will lose heart and their will to win.'

Lugh addressed Dian Cecht last of all and the physician answered, 'My daughter Airmed and I will go to the battlefield each evening and bring back the injured. We will treat their wounds with herbs and bathe them in our miraculous well and unless they have been mortally wounded they will be cured. In the morning they will join the ranks more eager than ever for battle and fight more fiercely than before.'

As he finished speaking, the Morrigu, the fierce goddess of battlefields, appeared in the shape of a crow. She spoke to the leaders of the Tuatha De Danaan and promised them that she would help them when they most needed her, at the hour of their greatest danger, and she foretold a victory for them.

'But you must prepare yourselves immediately,' she said, 'for I have seen the warriors of Balor's mighty army stream off the ships at Scetne. They have already started marching across Ireland towards Tara!'

Lugh marshalled his troops and told them everything he had heard. He spoke to every man in turn, encouraging them and exhorting them to fight and he filled them full of battle fury.

But Lugh himself was so precious to the Tuatha De Danaan that the king and his advisers imprisoned him behind the lines and left nine champions with him to keep him there. Nuada and the other leaders stayed with Lugh while the battle lines were drawn and the ordinary soldiers made ready to fight. Then the two armies marched towards each other and met on the Plain of Moytura. Though they had been fired for battle by Lugh's encouragement and fought fiercely and bravely, Nuada's army could not overcome the countless men the Fomorians sent out to meet them. Day after day the battle raged and each morning the De Danaan soldiers who had been injured in the action the day before were back in battle file, their wounds healed and their weapons intact. The Fomorians noticed this and were angry at the tactics the Tuatha De Danaan were using against them, but they fought all the more fiercely and held fast. The struggle went on for days with heavy losses on both sides and no side gaining the upper hand. As the troops became more and more war-weary the Fomorians decided to make a final assault.

Balor himself, with Bres and Ceithlinn at his side, went to the head of the Fomorian army, and led the horde, vast still in spite of the losses, on to the Plain of Moytura. Helmeted and well-armed, they marched in their thousands in close formation, men and women side by side.

The Tuatha De Danaan closed ranks and moved against them. Lugh could bear it no longer. Using all his strength he escaped from his guards and raced to the front of the line to lead the De Danaan army. Nuada and the Dagda and all the champions joined him, while the Morrigu, the Battle Crow, hovered above them to watch the battle. Lugh stood facing his troops as the plain behind him grew dark with the Fomorian warriors.

'You must fight now and fight to the death,' he shouted, 'for if we lose this battle we will lose everything and live in slavery for all time!'

He turned towards the advancing host and with a great shout the two armies rushed to meet each other. The battle was fierce and bloody. There was no time now for the physicians to heal the wounded or the smiths to repair weapons. The warriors fought hand to hand. Sword clashed against sword, spears whistled through the air and battle-axes thudded against shields.

The warriors roared as they fought and the wounded screamed as they fell. The tumult rolled over the Plain of Moytura like thunder and the ground became slippery with blood. Still the two sides fought on. Face to face they fought and when they slipped and fell to their knees they continued to hack at each other, forehead braced against forehead. The river carried away the dead, friend and enemy side by side. Ceithlinn of the Crooked Teeth hurled a spear at the Dagda, inflicting a terrible wound. Other De Danaan leaders fell, men and women together, and it seemed as if the Fomorians would be victorious. But Nuada rallied his forces and led them afresh into battle. He marched at the head of his troops and at last the two leaders met. Balor raised his sword over his head and felled Nuada with one blow. When the Tuatha De Danaan saw their king dying at Balor's feet a groan of despair arose from them and they faltered. At that instant the black crow shape of the Morrigu appeared above the battle lines screaming the encouragement she had promised them at their darkest hour and fresh courage surged into the De Danaan troops.

Lugh rushed to the side of the dying Nuada and angrily taunted Balor. His abuse drove his grandfather into a rage.

'Lift up my eyelid so I can see this gabbling loudmouth who dares to insult me like this!' he roared. A terrified hush fell over the multitude for everyone knew the dreadful power of the Evil Eye. Ten Fomorian champions pulled on the ropes to raise the heavy lid as those nearest to Balor fell to the ground to escape his deadly stare. Lugh stood his ground, put a stone in his sling, took aim and let fly directly at Balor's eye as it opened. The force of the stone drove the eye back through Balor's head and it landed in the midst of the Fomorian lines. Balor fell dead and hundreds of his followers were killed by the eye's fatal power.

Then Lugh cut off Balor's head and led the Tuatha De Danaan in a fierce assault against the Fomorians. With the Morrigu hovering above them, they broke through their enemy's lines, and what had been a battle became a rout. The Fomorians were beaten back to the sea by Lugh and his army. They fled to their ships, boarded them in great haste and speedily set sail for their islands, never to return to Ireland. Bres survived the battle and was captured by the Tuatha De Danaan but Lugh, who had become king in Nuada's place, spared his life on condition that he would share with him his knowledge of husbandry and farming. So Bres taught the Tuatha De Danaan when to plough and sow and reap and, when they had mastered these crafts, he too left Ireland for good.

The Tuatha De Danaan survivors cleared the battlefield of the dead who were as countless as the stars in the sky or the grass underfoot, as countless as flakes of snow in the air or Manannan's horses, the white-capped waves of the sea.

When this sad task was done the battle goddess, the Morrigu, declared victory to the Tuatha De Danaan. Then, from the mountain summits and riverbanks and estuaries, she proclaimed peace to the land of Ireland:

'Peace in this land
From the earth up to the skies
And back down to the earth.
Honey and mead in abundance
And strength to everyone.'

28. The First Battle of Moytura

At the beginning of the previous selection, Marie Heaney provided us with a succinct summary of the First Battle of Moytura, or Mag Tuired. What follows is an excerpt from M. J. Fraser's translation of the account of this epic confrontation between the Fir Bolg and the Tuatha De Danann, as recorded in a medieval Irish manuscript from the collection of Trinity College, Dublin. The story here begins on the third day of battle, a carnivalesque carnage of streaming color and flashing light—warrior frenzy is unleashed in a maelstrom of destruction, as seers work their spells on the enemy ranks, and poets chronicle glorious deeds of doom. Here we meet Nuada, king of the Tuatha De Danann, and Sreng, a mighty hero of the Fir Bolg, and read of their fight face-to-face: "Each of them inflicted thirty wounds on the other. Sreng dealt a blow with his sword at Nuada, and, cutting away the rim of his shield, severed his right arm at the shoulder; and the king's arm with a third of his shield fell to the ground." (RDW)

THE FIRST BATTLE OF MOYTURA

Translated by M.J. Fraser

43. Next day it was the turn of Sreng, Semne, and Sithbrug, along with Cirb, to lead the Fir Bolg. They rose early in the morning. A flashing penthouse of shields and a thick forest of javelins they made over them, and the battle-props then moved forward. The Tuatha De saw the Fir Bolg approaching them in that fashion across the plain from the east. 'With how much pomp,' they said, 'do those battle-props enter the plain and draw towards us.' And it was then that the plain got its name of Mag Tured, the Plain of Props.

44. The Tuatha De asked who should lead them on that day. 'I will,' said the Dagda, 'for in me you have an excellent god;' and, thereupon, he went forth with his sons and brothers. The Fir Bolg had firmly stationed their props and columns, and marshalled their battalions on the level of Mag Nia (which, henceforth, was called Mag Tured, the Plain of Props). Each side then sprang at the other. Sreng, son of Sengann, began to dislodge the hosts of the enemy. The Dagda set to breaking the battalions and harrying the hosts and dislodging

From *Ériu* 8 by J. M. Fraser, Royal Irish Academy, 1915.

divisions and forcing them from their positions. Cirb, son of Buan, entered the fray from the east and slaughtered brave men and spirited soldiers. The Dagda heard Cirb's onset, and Cirb heard the Dagda's battering blows. They sprang each at the other. Furious was the fight as the good swords fenced, heroic the heroes as they steadied the infantry, and answered the onslaughts. At last Cirb fell before the Dagda's battering blows.

Sreng, Sengann's son, was pressing back the hosts from their places when he came on three sons of Cairbre Cas of the Tuatha De, and the three sons of Ordan. Cairbre's sons with their three columns fell before the sons of Ordan, as Sreng drove in the hosts. The enemy fell before him on every side, and the fury of the combat grew behind him.

45. After the fall of Cirb the Fir Bolg were driven into their camp. The Tuatha De did not pursue them across the battle-field, but they took with them a head and a stone pillar apiece including the head of Cirb, which was buried in the Cairn of Cirb's Head.

46. The Fir Bolg were neither happy nor cheerful that night, and as for the Tuatha De, they were sad and dispirited. But during the same night Fintan came with his sons to join the Fir Bolg, and this made them all glad, for valiant were both he and they.

47. In this cheerful mood the morning found them. The signals of their chiefs roused them on the spacious slopes of their camping-ground, and they began to hearten each other to meet danger and peril. Eochaid, the High-king, with his son, Slainge the Fair, and the soldiers and chiefs of Connaught, came forth to join them. Sengann's three sons with the hosts of Curoi's province, took their place at one side of the line. The four sons of Gann with the warriors of Eochaid's province marched to the centre of the same army. Buan's sons Esca and Egconn ranged themselves with the men of Conchobar's province on the other wing. The four sons of Slainge with the host of the Gaileoin brought up the rear of the army. Round Eochaid, the High-king, they made a fold of valour of battle-scarred, blood-becrimsoned braves, and juggling jousters, and the world's trustiest troops. The thirteen sons of Fintan, men proven in courageous endurance of conflict, were brought to where the king was.

A flaming mass was the battle on that day, full of changing colours, many feats and gory hands, of sword-play and single combats, of spears and cruel swords and javelins; fierce it was and pitiless and terrible, hard-packed and close-knit, furious and far-flung, ebbing and flowing with many adventures. The Fir Bolg, in the order told, marched boldly and victoriously straight westwards to the end of Mag Tured till they came to the firm pillars[1] and props of valour between themselves and the Tuatha De. The passionate Tuatha De made an impetuous, furious charge in close-knit companies with their venomous weapons; and they formed one mighty gory phalanx under the shelter of red-rimmed, emblazoned, plated, strong shields. The warriors began the conflict. The flanks and the wings of the van were filled with grey-haired veterans swift to wound; aged men were stationed to assist and attend on the movements of those veterans; and next to those steady, venomous fighters were placed young men under arms. The champions and serving men were posted in the rear of the youths. Their seers and wise men stationed themselves on pillars and points of vantage, plying their sorcery, while the poets took count of the feats and wrote down tales of them. As for Nuada, he was in the centre of the fight. Round him gathered his princes and supporting warriors, with the twelve sons of Gabran from Scythia, his body-guard. They were Tolc, Trenfer, Trenmiled, Garb, Glacedh, Gruasailt Duirdri, Fonnam, Foiriscm, Teidm, Tinnargain and Tescad. He would have no joy of life on whom they made a gory wound. ('Twas they that killed the sons of Fintan, and the sons of Fintan killed them.) Thus they delivered their assault after fastening their bodies to rough-edged stones with clasps of iron; and made their way to the place appointed for the battle. At that moment Fathach, the poet of the Fir Bolg, came to his own pillar, and as he surveyed the armies to the east and west, said:

'Swiftly advance the hosts marshalling on Mag Nia their resistless might; 'tis the Tuatha De that advance and the Fir Bolg of the speckled swords.

'Methinks the Fir Bolg will lose some of their brothers there—many will be the bodies and heads and gashed flanks on the plain.

'But though they fall on every side (?), fierce and keen will be their onset; though they fall, they will make others to fall, and heroes will be laid low by their impetuous valour.

'Thou hast subdued (?) the Fir Bolg; they will fall there by the side of their shields and their blades; I will not trust to the strength of any one so long as I shall be in stormy Ireland.

I am Fathach, the poet; strongly has sorrow vanquished me, and now, that the Fir Bolg are gone, I shall surrender to the swift advance of disaster.'

48. The furies and monsters and hags of doom cried aloud so that their voices were heard in the rocks and waterfalls and in the hollows of the earth.

It was like the fearful agonising cry on the last dreadful day when the human race will part from all in this world. In the van of the Tuatha De advanced the Dagda, Ogma, Alla, Bres, and Delbaeth, the five sons of Elatha, together with Bres, grandson of Net, the Fomorian, Aengus, Aed, Cermad the Fair, Midir, Bodb Derg, Sigmall Abartach, Nuada the High-king, Brian, Iuchar and Iucharba, the three sons of Turenn Bigrenn, Cu, Cian and Cethenn, the three sons of Cainte, Goibnenn the Smith, Lucraidh the Joiner, Credne the Craftsman, Diancecht the Physician, Aengaba of Norway, the three queens, Ere, Fotla and Banba, and the three sorceresses, Badb, Macha and Morigan, with Bechuille and Danann their two foster-mothers. They fixed their pillars in the ground to prevent any one fleeing till the stones should flee. They lunged at each other with their keen sharp spears, till the stout shafts were twisted through the quivering of the victims on their points. The edges of the swords turned on the lime-covered shields. The curved blades were tempered in boiling pools of blood in the thighs of warriors. Loud was the singing of the lances as they cleft the shields, loud the noise and din of the fighters as they battered bodies and broke bones in the rear. Boiling streams of blood took the sight from the grey eyes of resolute warriors. It was then that Bres made an onset on the Fir Bolg army, and killed one hundred and fifty of them. He struck nine blows on the shield of Eochaid the High-king, and Eochaid, in his turn, dealt him nine wounds. Sengann's son, Sreng, turned his face to the army of the Tuatha De, and slew one hundred and fifty of them. He struck nine blows on the shield of the High-king Nuada, and Nuada dealt him nine wounds.

Each dealt dire blows of doom, making great gory wounds on the flesh of the other, till under their grooved blades shields and spears, heads and helmets broke like the brittle branches hacked with hatchets wielded by the stout arms of woodsmen. Heroes swayed to this side and that, each circling the other as they sought opportunity for a blow. The battle champions rose again over the rims of their emblazoned shields. Their courage grew, and the valiant virulent men became steadfast as an arch. Their hands shot up with their swords, and they fenced swiftly about the heads of warriors, hacking their helmets. For a moment they thrust back the ranks of the enemy from their places, and at the sight of them the hosts wavered like the water flung far over its sides by a kettle through excess of boiling, or the flood that, like a water-fall, an army splashes up over a river's banks, making it passable for their troops behind them. So a suitable space was cleared for the chiefs; the heroes yielded them their places, and agile combatants their stations; warriors were dislodged by them, and the serving-men fled for horror of them. To them was left the battle. Heavily the earth was trodden under their feet till the hard turf grew soft beneath them. Each of them inflicted thirty wounds on the other. Sreng dealt a blow with his sword at Nuada, and, cutting away the rim of his shield, severed his right arm at the shoulder; and the king's arm with a third of his shield fell to the ground. It was then that the High-king called aloud for help, and Aengaba of Norway, hearing him, entered the fray to protect him. Fierce and furious was the attack Aengaba and Sreng made on each other. Each inflicted on his opponent an equal number of wounds, but they were not comparable as an exchange, for the broad blade of Sreng's lance and his stout spear-shaft dealt deeper, deadlier wounds. As soon as the Dagda heard the music of the swords in the battle-stress, he hastened to the place of conflict with deliberate bounds, like the rush of a great water-fall. Sreng declined a contest with the two warriors; and though Aengaba of Norway did not fall there, it was from the violence of that conflict that he afterwards died. The Dagda came and stood over Nuada, and, after the Tuatha De had taken counsel, he brought fifty soldiers, with their physicians. They carried Nuada from the field. His hand was raised in the king's stead on the fold of valour, a fold of stones surrounding the king, and on it the blood of Nuada's hand trickled.

Note

1. *Coirthi* means 'stone pillar,' used to mark a grave, &c., in §§ 35, 37, 39, 47. In at least two passages the word seems to refer to a stone, forming part of the soldier's equipment, which he planted on the ground to rest against in fighting.

PART 7

SCANDINAVIA AND THE GERMANIC TRIBES

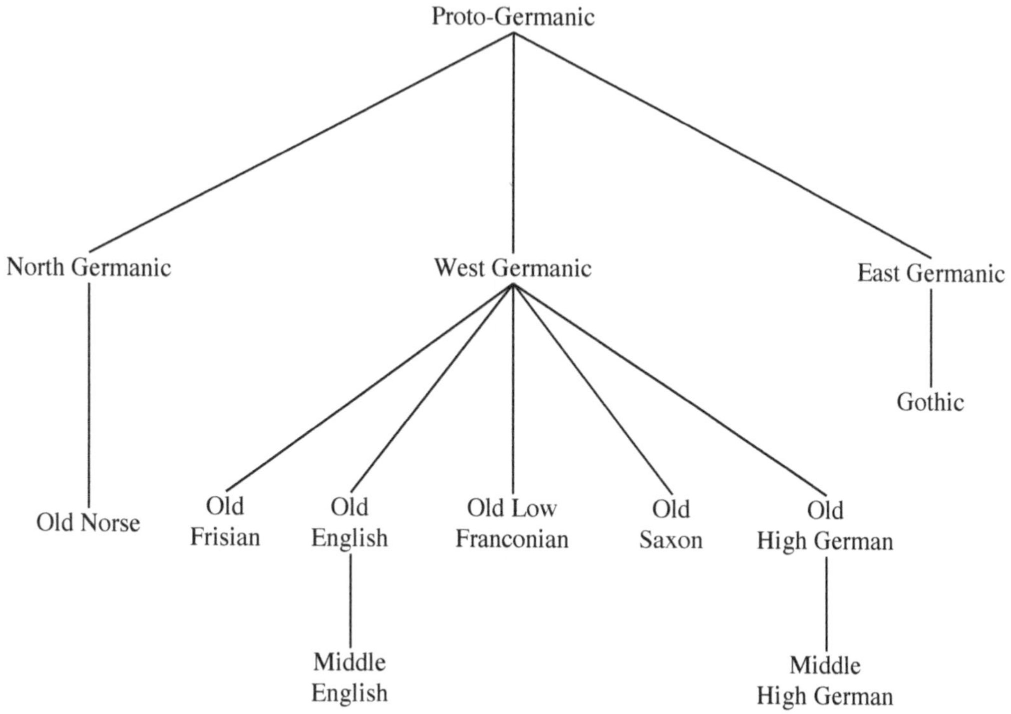

29. The One-Eyed God and the One-Handed God

Two of the chief deities of the early Indo-Europeans of Scandinavia are Odhinn (or Odin) and Tyr, gods widely known among the Germanic peoples. Of their own volition, both gods experienced bodily mutilation—Snorri Sturluson, the thirteenth-century Icelandic author of the Prose Edda, *knows their stories: Odin gave up an eye to acquire wisdom; Tyr lost a hand to the wolf Fenrir in order to secure the safety of the gods. Dumézil argues that these figures—the one-eyed god and the one-handed god—are of primitive Indo-European origin. Homologous figures survive in both Italic and Celtic myth, heroic figures playing salient roles in crucial military engagements, appearing in traditions, Roman and Irish, with remarkably parallel structures. In Rome's mythic history, they are Horatius Cocles and Mucius Scaevola, heroes of the young Roman Republic's war waged against Etruscan forces. In Irish lore, they are Nuada, king of the Tuatha De Danann, who lost his arm in the First Battle of Moytura, and Lug, the multitalented member of the Tuatha De who comes to their rescue as they suffer oppression at the hands of the Fomoire.* (RDW)

THE ONE-EYED GOD AND THE ONE-HANDED GOD

Georges Dumézil

Thus Tyr's disfigurement, like Odhinn's, is directly related to his divine function and permanent mode of action. It is possible that, in its earliest form, the myth from which Snorri's story derives had as its object the *justification* of Tyr's already-recognized juridical nature. In that case, there would be strict symmetry between the two gods, the one being the Magician because he has dared to lose his eye, the other being the Jurist because he has dared to pledge his hand. They would have become what they are in the same way that specialists were prepared for their tasks in China—a comparison much loved by Marcel Granet—by adaptive mutilation. However, even in its attested state, the tradition already gives us enough without that hypothesis. Perhaps it was not *in order* to become the divine lawyer that Tyr lost his right hand, but, it was at the very least *because* he was the lawyer that he, alone among the gods, was the one who did in fact lose his hand.

In sum, alongside **Thunraz-Thôrr* (who wins wars without resorting to finesse, by infighting, by relying on his strength alone), the two sovereign gods represent two superior techniques. **Wôdhanaz-Odhinn* terrifies the enemy, petrifies him with the glamor of his magic, while *Tyr-*Tîwaz* circumvents and disarms him with the ruses of the law. We do not know who, on the earthly level, the "men of Tyr," the guardsmen of the Germanic armies, actually were, but we have already seen who "Odhinn's men" were: the *berserkir*, the beast-warriors, invulnerable and wild, of whom Odhinn himself is the prototype, since we read of him (*Ynglingasaga*, 6): "He could make his enemies blind and deaf, or like stones with fear, and their weapons could no more cut than sticks. . . ." Such are the various but equally efficient—one might almost say "equally elegant"—privileges of the one-eyed god and the one-handed god.

The symbolism here is probably very ancient, since Roman epic literature has preserved an invaluable variant, linked not to two "sovereigns" (the Republican orientation of these stories would not permit that), but to two "saviors of the state." I am thinking of the two famous episodes that together constitute the greater part of the Republic's first war: that of Horatius the Cyclops and that of Mucius the Left-handed. Twin episodes, one of which irresistibly summons up the other among both the historians and the moralists of antiquity, and whose interdependence is underlined even further by the fact that Cocles and Scaevola, at the conclusion of their exploits, both receive exceptional, and to some extent similar, public recognition—a last vestige, possibly, of the "sovereign" value originally attached to their modes of action and their careers.

Cocles is the one-eyed hero, the famous Horatius, who, when Lars Porsenna is about to take the city by assault, single-handedly holds the enemy in check by his strangely wild behavior, and thus wins the first phase of the war. When the city has finally been besieged and famine threatens, Scaevola is the hero who goes to Porsenna and of his own free will burns his own right hand before him, thus persuading Porsenna to grant the Romans a friendly peace that is the equivalent of a victory. The traditions relating to Odhinn and Tyr give us the key to these two little "historical" mysteries. The selfsame concept is apparent in the guise of mythical tales among the Germans and of historical narratives in Rome: above the equipoise of fortune in an ordinary battle, we have the certain victory gained by the "demoralizing radiance" of someone with "the gift," on the one hand, and, on the other, a war terminated by the heroic use of a legal procedure. Let us examine these two stories more closely.

Cocles[1]

Little inclined as they were to the supernatural, the Romans have nevertheless made it very plain that Cocles, in this combat, was more than an ordinary man; that he mastered his enemies more by the force of his personality and good luck than by any physical means; and that his enemies were unable to get near him.

Polybius, for example (*Histories*, VI, 55), even though he is the only writer to accept that Cocles was badly wounded and died after the battle, is clear on this point, despite his generally rather slapdash wording: "covered with wounds, he [Cocles] stayed at his post and checked the assault, the enemies being less struck (stupefied, *καταπεπληγμένων*) by his strength than by his courage and his daring."

Livy's account (II, 10) is more circumstantial and gives us a very clear picture of a situation unique in "Roman history." He depicts Cocles, amid the general debacle, rushing to the head of the bridge that is the sole access to Rome, which the Romans, taking advantage of this respite, then begin to demolish. "He stupefied the enemy by this miracle of daring" (*ipso miraculo audaciae obstupefecit hostes*). Then, remaining alone at the entrance to the bridge, he casts terrible and menacing looks at the Etruscan leaders (*circumferens truces minaciter oculos*), challenging them individually, insulting them collectively. For a long while no one dares to attack him. Then they shower him with javelins (*undique in unum hostem tela coniiciunt*); but all stick bristling in his shield, and he, stubborn and unmoved, continues with giant strides to hold the bridge (*neque ille minus obstinatus ingenti pontem obtineret gradu . . .*). Eventually, they decide to hurl themselves upon him, but just then the thunder of the collapsing bridge and the joyful shouts of the Romans fill them with a sudden fear and stop them in their tracks (*fragor . . . clamor . . . pavore subito impetum sustinuit*). Mission accomplished, Cocles commends himself to the god of Tiber, hurls himself fully armed into the river, and swims across it under a hail of ineffective missiles, all of which fail to hit him (*multisque superincedentibus telis incolumis ad suos tranavit*). Thus, in Livy, Cocles controls events throughout, with his terrible grimaces, which paralyze the enemy, and with his good luck, which wards off all weapons.

Dionysius of Halicarnassus (V, 24), who is more verbose and concerned with verisimilitude, at least adds the detail that Cocles was a *iunior*. He also retains this feature: "The Etruscans who pursued the Romans did not dare engage him in hand-to-hand combat (while he was occupying the bridge), regarding him as a madman and as a man in the throes of death" (*ὡς μεμηνότι καὶ θανατῶντι*). There then follows a lengthy description of the fight, conducted at a distance, during which the unapproachable Roman victoriously returns all the projectiles with which the enemy vainly attempts to overwhelm him.

This unanimity among our authors makes it plain enough that there was something superhuman about Cocles in this battle. Properly speaking, his "gifts" are not, even in Livy, magical "eye-power" and invulnerability; but they are almost that, and they would have been precisely that if the source were not a narrative with historical pretensions, and if we were not in Rome.

It must be remarked upon that this terrible hero who blasts the Etruscans with his gaze, thereby reversing the normal course of battle, is called "Cocles," which is to say (if we follow the usual Roman interpretation), the one-eyed. It is no less remarkable that the mutilation is constantly presented as prior to the exploit. He had lost an eye, all the authors simply tell us, during a previous war. Plutarch alone (*Publicola*, 16), after having quoted this opinion first, adds an extremely interesting variant: "other writers say he owed this appellation [a distortion of the Greek "Cyclops"] to the fact that the upper part of his nose was so flattened, so deeply recessed, that there was no separation between his eyes, and his eyebrows met" (*διὰ σιμότητα τῆς ῥινὸς ἐνδεδυκυίας, ὥστε μηδὲν εἶναι τὸ διόριζον τὰ ὄμματα καὶ τὰς ὀφρῦς συγκεχύσθαι*).

In my *Mythes et dieux des Germains* (p. 105 and n.2), I drew attention to the fact that the great warriors of northern Europe—the Irish Cuchulainn, the Viking chiefs—practiced a heroic grimace that was the certificate of their power, as it were, and the proof of their victory. In Cuchulainn's case, this grimace is only one of the "signs," one of the monstrous "shapes" or "forms" (*delba*) that came upon him immediately after his initiation combat and that were manifest thereafter whenever he was gripped by warlike fury. It took the following form: "he closed one of his eyes," one text says, "until it was no bigger than the eye of a needle, while opening the other until it was as big as the rim of a mead cup" (*iadais indara suil connarbo lethiu indas cro snathaiti, asoilgg alaile combo moir beolu midchuaich*); or, according to a variant, he "swallowed one of his eyes into his head, until even a wild heron could scarcely have brought it back from the depths of his skull to the surface of his cheek," while "the other leapt out and placed itself on his cheek, on the outside" (*imsloic in dara suil do ina* *chend, issed mod danastarsed fiadchorr tagraim do lar a gruade a hiarthor achlocaind, sesceing a seitig co m-boi for a gruad sechtair*: for these texts and other variants see M.-L. Sjoestedt-Jonval, *Etudes Celtiques*, I, 1936, pp. 9, 10, 12, 18; also, analogous data concerning Gallic coins that I interpret differently from the author; cf. E. Windisch, *Tain Bo Cualnge*, 1905, p. 370, n.2). In the case of the Viking Egill, the grimace forms part of a heroic gesture that is, apparently, traditional, since it is understood by the person at whom it is directed. He presents himself in this grimacing shape before the king, who is bound to pay him the wages of his victories, and who, in fact, does continue to pay for as long as the Viking's countenance has not regained its natural composure: "When he sat down, he caused one of his eyebrows to leap down as far as his cheek, and the other up to his hairline; and Egill had black eyes and eyebrows that met" (*er hann sat . . . tha hleypdhi hann annarri bruninni ofan a kinnina, en annarri upp i harraetr; Egill var svarteygr ok skolbrunn*). It is not until he is satisfied with the payment that he abandons this "shape," and that "his eyebrows return to their places" (. . . *tha foru brynn hans i lag:* See *Egils Saga Skallagrimssonar*, LV, 9). These grimaces amount to a monstrous widening of one eye, while occluding the other. Both form part of a terrifying mimicry, doubtless based on a principle well known to the Harii, who, according to Tacitus (*Germania*, 43), won battles by terror alone: *terrorem inferunt, nullo hostium sustinente novum ac velut infernum adspectum; nam primi in omnibus proeliis oculi vincuntur* ("they strike terror; no enemy can face this novel and, as it were, hellish vision; in every battle, after all, the feeling of being conquered comes to the eye first"). This "ghostly army" (*feralis exercitus*) of the Harii leads us back to the Einherjar (**Aina-hariya-*) and the *berserkir*, presided over by their prototype, Odhinn (cf. *Mythes et dieux des Germains*, p. 80ff.). It also seems to me probable, albeit unprovable, that Odhinn's ocular disfigurement, of which we have already seen the "civil" magic value, as it were, must also, in "military" actions, have contributed to the paralyzing terror that the *Ynglingasaga* (section 6) attributes to him as his principal weapon. In times of peace, his single eye was the pledge and the proof of his clairvoyance; in times of war, the god undoubtedly cast "the evil eye" upon those whose fate he had quite literally decreed. Ultimately, there seems little doubt that this, too, was one of the objectives shared by the ocular contortions of Egill and Cuchulainn. The congenital, or acquired, malformation attributed by Roman epic literature to its terrorizing champion, Cocles, doubtlessly is maintaining the memory of analogous and very ancient beliefs or practices in the Latin world.

Scaevola

Scaevola's links with Fides and Dius Fidius have long been recognized. I cannot do better than to reproduce the reflections of W.-F. Otto (Pauly-Wissowa, *Encyclopédie*, VI, 1909, col. 2283, under *Fides*): "Several scholars have noted that the story of Mucius Scaevola must have been connected, in some way, with the worship of Fides, and particularly with the custom, specific to that cult, of swathing the right hand. Ettore Pais has drawn attention to the fact that the temple of Dius Fidius, who is certainly akin to Fides, was located on the *collis Mucialis*, the name of which calls to mind the *gens Mucia*, and he has concluded that the myth of the burnt right hand originated in some variety of ordeal. According to Salomon Reinach (*Le voile de l'Oblation, Cultes, Mythes et Religions*, I, 1905, p. 308; though the work originally dates from 1897), the swathing of the right hand in the cult of Fides is a symbolic offering of that hand to the goddess, and the story of Scaevola would thus refer to a time and a case in which such offerings were still made. This second interpretation seems to me inadmissible; but I cannot resign myself to separating the story of Mucius burning his right hand from the custom of swathing the right hand in the cult of Fides. Although unable to explain the legend, I should like to point out that the tradition concerning Claelia and other hostages, a tradition closely linked with that of Mucius Scaevola, is recounted as outstanding evidence of the *Fides publica populi Romani. . . .*"

Basing himself on W.-F. Otto, M. F. Münzer (*op. cit.*, XVI, 1933, col. 417, under *Mucius Scaevola*) has made the following accurate observations: "Dionysius of Halicarnassus himself, even though his rationalism and incomprehension caused him to suppress Scaevola's self-mutilation, does draw attention to the fact that, when face-to-face with Porsenna, Mucius swears an oath forcing himself to tell the truth (V, 29, 2: *πίστεις δοὺς ἐπὶ θεῶν*), and that he receives a guarantee from Porsenna, also under oath (29, 3: *δίδωσιν αὐτῷ δἰ ὅρκων τὸ πιστόν*). Dionysius also adds that Mucius tricks Porsenna, and that his oath is a ruse, a matter that the other authors leave in the air, failing to make clear whether the revelations that Mucius makes (about the plan drawn up by three hundred young Romans to relay one another, in successive attempts to stab the enemy king—he, Mucius, being only the first to make the attempt, and to fail) are true or false. Here, perhaps, lies the original reason for the loss of Mucius's right hand: out of patriotism, and with full awareness of his action, he swore a false oath and voluntarily received the punishment for his false swearing. Thus, what could have once been celebrated as an act of heroic abnegation later came to lose any clear motivation, or ceased to have any motivation at all, when it began to seem impossible to accept the treachery and the false oath."

It is certain that Münzer is correct here, and that the central thrust of the story was originally as he describes it. But perhaps the "prototype" tradition, on which the historians of Rome were at work, with their varying sets of moral susceptibilities, was even simpler still. Let us remember the mutilation of Tyr: that mythological fiction is easily superimposed on the fragment of epic history we are considering here. For Mucius, as for Tyr, the object is to inspire trust in a threatening enemy, to make him believe something false—in both cases by sacrifice of a right hand—which will persuade that enemy to adopt a stance favorable to their own side. In risking—and thereby inevitably sacrificing—his hand, Tyr gives the gods' enemy the wolf reason to believe that the leash they wish to put on him is not a magic bond (which is false) and thus to agree to the trial. Once bound, the wolf will not be able to free itself, Tyr will lose his hand, but the gods will be saved. By voluntarily burning his hand before Porsenna, Mucius is giving Rome's enemy, the Etruscan king, reason to think that he is being truthful (even if he is lying) when he tells him that three hundred young Romans, all as resolute as himself, could very well have sacrificed their lives in advance and that, in consequence, he, Porsenna, stands every chance of perishing by one of their daggers. The fear, and also the esteem, the king suddenly feels for such a people leads him to conclude the peace treaty that saves Rome. It is true that the "pledge" mechanism is not the same in both cases; the hand that Tyr previously risks is a genuine *bailbond* for his honesty, whereas the hand that Mucius destroys then and there is a *sample* of Roman heroism. But the result is the same: both hands provide the *guarantee* of an affirmation that, without the hand, would not be believed, and that, by means of the hand, is in fact believed and thus achieves its effect on the enemy's mind.

I hasten to acknowledge that Mucius Scaevola's act, whether sullied by trickery or not, is the nobler of the two (or at least produces nobler effects): Porsenna is not deprived of the capacity, merely of the intention, to do harm. As befits a representative of the series "Mitra-Fides, etc.," Mucius is a true peacemaker who diverts the enemy's mind onto the path of an honorable truce, a durable friendship, so that the treaty concluded between the young Republic and the Etruscan king is certainly not fraudulent, and was even to be famously respected (cf. the story of Claelia), and to serve, as Mommsen and Münzer (*op.*

cit.) have observed, as a model and reference point for the treaties of friendship that historical Rome was to conclude with foreign sovereigns.

This mythological consonance between Rome and the Germanic world is reinforced by a linguistic one: the Latin *vas* (genitive *vadis*), the legal term for the "pledge that stands surety for," has no corresponding word except in Germanic and Baltic, and there the corresponding word is precisely the one to be found in the Snorri text, quoted earlier: Tyr's hand is placed in the wolf's mouth *at vedhi*, "as surety," so that he will permit himself to be bound. This word (*vedh*, neuter) is the same one that still subsists in the modern German *Wette*, "wager," in the Swedish *staa vad*, "to wager," and even in the French *gage*, *gager*, "pledge, to wager"—a curious contamination of the Latin and Germanic forms. (On *wadium, Wette*, etc., on "the amphibology of the wager and the contract," and on the relation between *wadium* and *nexum*, cf. Mauss, *The Gift*, p. 60ff.).

Roman Mythology[2]

These two stories—which I have not coupled arbitrarily, since they were always consciously regarded by the Romans themselves as inseparable—are clearly seen to illuminate the Nordic facts. And this fact, in its turn, is justification for the procedure I have adopted of constantly searching in the earliest "Roman history" for the equivalent of what, under other skies, presents itself as "divine myths." It is not my concern here to take sides as to the fundamental veracity of this history. It is of little consequence to me whether, for example, kings named Romulus and Numa actually did exist, whether Romulus was assassinated, whether the Tarquinii were later "driven out," whether Lars Porsenna did besiege Rome, whether the plebeians did secede to the Sacred Hill, and so on. I am not interested in arguing about the reality of Brutus the Consul, or Publicola, or the importance that the gens Horatia and the gens Mucia might or might not have had in distant times. For me, the important thing is that the Romans should have linked certain edifying or symbolic scenes to their epic narratives of these events, and to the biographies of these characters, whatever their degree of historicity; and that the purpose of those scenes is the justification either of periodic feast days or rites (such as the Lupercalia, the *poplifugium*, the *regifugium*, the festival of Anna Perenna, etc.), or of moral behaviors or "systems of representations" still familiar in the classical era, all of which are naturally very much earlier than the real or fictitious events seen as "establishing themselves" in "history," since they are as old as, and older than,

Roman society itself. We must accustom ourselves to the notion that, given such wan gods who are almost wholly lacking in adventures—as Dionysius of Halicarnassus observed in his *Roman Antiquities* (II, 18)—the true Roman mythology, the mythology articulated in narratives, in circumstantiated events, is a mythology of heroes, epic in form, and little different—its weighty concern for verisimilitude apart—from the Irish mythology of the Middle Ages. Let none of my critics attempt to saddle me with the ridiculous thesis that the "Roman-Etruscan" or "Publicola-Porsenna" conflicts were the "historicization" of an ancient mythology of the Indian or Greek type, in which gods struggle against demons. No, Scaevola's opponent has not "taken the place" of a demon! What I do think is that, from its very beginnings, from the time when it acquired those specific characteristics that led to its success, Rome conceived its myths on the terrestrial plane, as a dynamic balance between terrestrial actors and forces.

Nuada and Lug

A moment ago I mentioned Irish mythology; and it is by no means out of place in this investigation, since it too presents us with a version of the "one-eyed sovereign" and the "one-armed sovereign" antithesis. In the epic representation of the successive invasions and settlements of Ireland, the Tuatha De Danann, which is to say, the ancient gods, on whom the Irish concentrated what they had retained of the Indo-European myths, conquered the island from the demonic Fomorians and their allies the Fir Bolg, the Fir Domnann and the Galioin. Their two leaders in this conquest were Nuada (or Nuadu) and Lug, two ancient and well-known gods. One had been the *Nodens, Nodons*, whose name occurs in Latin inscriptions in Great Britain; the other is the great *Lug samildanach* ("sym-poly-technician"), who gave his name to Lugnasad, the Irish seasonal festival, and to the Gallic city of Lugdunum.

Tradition describes the installation of the Tuatha De Danann in Ireland as occurring in two phases. There were two successive battles, two victories, achieved a few years apart in the same place, on the plain called Mag Tured; the first over the Fir Bolg, the Fir Domnann and the Galioin, and the second over the Fomorians. Philologists, however, are generally of the opinion that this chronology is the result of a late and artificial doubling, and that there was originally only a single battle, that which became "the second." On the face of it, their argument is that the two earliest catalogues of Ireland's epic literature, as well as the "Glossary of Cormac" (about 900 A.D.), mention only "a" battle of

Mag Tured, and that it is not until texts of the eleventh century that two battles are mentioned and expressly differentiated (d'Arbois de Jubainville, *The Irish Mythological Cycle*, Dublin, 1903 pp. 84–86; cf., with slight attenuation, *L'Epopée celtique en Irlande*, 1892, p. 396). But the real and underlying reason is that this duality of battles seems, to them, both nugatory and meaningless, and that, in addition, the epic material of the first battle is as jejune and insignificant as that of the second is fertile and original.

The philological argument is a weak one. First, it might well be that the first battle was in fact known at an early date, *without giving rise to autonomous epic narratives* such as those recorded in the early catalogues, and that it was referred to in narratives dealing with the second battle solely in order to clarify a detail or a situation. Second, the *fragment* inserted in the "Glossary of Cormac" does certainly refer to the "second" battle, waged against the Fomorians (d'Arbois de Jubainville, p. 85 n. 3); but how does that prove that the existence of the first battle was unknown in about 900 A.D.? Was Cormac obliged to mention everything? Similarly, the Cinaed poem contains a brief allusion to a well-known preliminary of the second battle and situates it, without further clarification, "before the battle of Mag Tured" (*ria cath Maigi Tuired*); but why *should* he specify "before the *second* battle"? Third, a poet contemporary with Cinaed, Eochaid ua Flainn (died, 984), was already aware of the first battle, since he says of that battle, in which a hundred thousand warriors were slain, that it ended the royal line of the Tuath Bolg (i.e., clearly, the Fir Bolg). And this presupposes that the division explicitly indicated in the later tradition was already acquired (first battle: Tuatha De Danann versus Fir Bolg; second battle: Tuatha De Danann versus Fomorians).

As for the philologists' underlying reason for eliminating the first battle, the considerations of this present chapter annul it, or rather provide a very serious argument against it. If there are two successive victories at Mag Tured, it is because, as in the war against Porsenna and the exploits of Cocles and Scaevola, there are two types of victorious warrior to be given individual prominence: in the first, Nuada leads his people to victory, but *loses his right arm in so doing*—and this accident is immediately made use of in *a ruse based on the law of war*, which in turn leads to *a compromise peace and a pact of amity* between the adversaries. In the second battle, Lug ensures success for the selfsame people *with magic*, by circling around his army *while taking on the appearance of a one-eyed man*, and this time *the victory is total, without compromise.*

The second of these episodes is well known (*Second Battle of Mag Tured*, ed. W. Stokes, *Revue Celtique*, XII, 1891 p. 96ff.). The Tuatha De Danann are already partially established in Ireland as a result of the first battle, but, feeling themselves oppressed by Bress and the Fomorians, they have shaken off their yoke. The great battle is about to begin. The Tuatha De Danann, who have designated Lug as their commander-in-chief (section 83), are unwilling to place in peril a life and a fund of knowledge so invaluable to them (section 95). Then (section 129), "the Tuatha De Danann, on the other side, rose up, left nine of their comrades to guard Lug, and went to do battle. Then, when the combat had begun, Lug, together with his driver, escaped from the guard under which he had been placed, so that he appeared at the head of the Tuatha De Danann army. A hard and fierce battle was fought between the Fomorians and the men of Ireland. Lug strengthened the men of Ireland (*boi Lug og nertad fer n-Erenn*), exhorting them to fight bravely so that they might live in servitude no longer; it was better for them to meet death defending their country than to live in subjugation and pay tribute, as they had been doing. That is why Lug then sang this song, while he circled the men of Ireland on one foot and with one eye (*conid and rocan Lug an cetul so sios for lethcois ocus letsuil timchall fer n-Erenn*; cf. above Cuchulainn's one-eyed *delb*):

> *A battle shall arise. . . .*

(Section 130): "The armies let out a great shout as they went into combat, and so on." And then comes victory (sections 131–138), dearly bought but crushing and final, for the army of Lug, who is made king, Nuada having been killed at the very outset.

The first episode is less famous, doubtless because of the prejudice against it noted earlier. Here it is, as recounted in the unique and late manuscript published by M.J. Fraser (*Eriu*, VIII, 1916, pp. 4–59), which, despite its verbose form conforming to the taste of decadent epic literature, might of course retain early material. The Tuatha De Danann have just landed in Ireland. They have requested that the natives, the Fir Bolg, cede one half of the island. The Fir Bolg have refused, and a fierce battle ensues. In the course of battle (section 48), the Fir Bolg named Sreng "struck the 'paramount king,' Nuada, with his sword; he cut through the edge of his buckler and the right arm at the shoulder, so that the arm fell to the earth with a third of the buckler" (*dobert Sreang bem cloidimh don airdrigh .i. do Nuadhaid gur theasg bile an sgeth ogus an laimh ndes ac a ghualaind, gu ndrochair an lamh gu triun an sgeth le for talmain*). The Tuatha De Danann carry Nuada from the battlefield and fight on so valiantly that they end that day victorious. So victorious, apparently, that should the struggle be resumed the next day, the Fir Bolg face certain extermination. During the night, despondent and downcast, the Fir Bolg hold council. Should they leave Ireland? Accept partition? Or fight on (section 57)? They agree on the third option. But Sreng appears to deplore this bloody and futile resistance: "Resistance, for men, is destruction," he says in verse, "the plains of Ireland are filled with suffering; for its forests we have met with misfortune, the loss of many brave men." As a result (section 58), when the two armies are drawn up, Sreng challenges his victim of the previous day, Nuada, to single combat. "Nuada looked at him bravely, as if he were sound in body (*atracht Nuada co nertchalma, amail dobeth slan*), and said to him: 'If what you seek is a fair fight (*comlann comadais*), strap down your right arm, for I no longer have mine (*cengailter luth de laime desi, uair nach fuil sin oramsa*); in this way, the fight will be fair!' Sreng replied: 'Your state implies no obligation on my side (*ni tormaig sin fiacha etir oramsa*), for our first fight has been canceled out (*uair robo comthrom ar cetchomrag*), that is the rule agreed between us!'" This threat to Nuada, this blackmail, as it were, leads the Tuatha De Danann to take the initiative in reaching a compromise that will limit their success. After meeting in council, they offer Sreng the choice of any province in Ireland for himself and his people. Thus peace is concluded, "peace and agreement and friendship" (*sith ogus comand ogus cairdine*). Sreng and the Fir Bolg choose the province of Connaught, the province of the paramount king, which consoles them for their real defeat with the appearance of "success" (*co haindinid aithesach*). As we have seen, Nuada survives, but is forced to give up his kingship to a temporary king (Bress), while he has an artificial arm made in order to reclaim his kingship. Hence, his appellation "Nuada Airgetlam," or "Nuada of the Silver Hand."

If we now go back to the diptych of legends that makes up the war of the Romans against Porsenna, the differences between it and the paired Celtic narratives are easily perceived. First, the order of the episodes is reversed: Cocles and his wild looks preceded Scaevola and his burned hand, whereas Nuada and his severed arm precede Lug and his magic grimace. Second, the episodes of Cocles and Scaevola are two episodes in a single war, which, thanks to Scaevola, is definitively ended by the pact of peace and friendship, whereas the Tuatha De Danann fight two successive wars, the first ended by a peace pact, the second by the extermination of their enemy. Third, Scaevola's mutilation is voluntary, calculated; it is Scaevola himself who makes juridical use of it, persuading Porsenna to come to terms, despite his imminent victory: whereas Nuada loses his arm by accident, and the exploitation of that accident is initiated by the Fir Bolg, who are facing disaster, rather than by the Tuatha De Danann, who, while facing a threat to their king's life, are nevertheless in practice already victorious.[3]

All this is true; but the analogies are no less perceptible. First, the chronological reversal of the episodes in no way alters their meaning. Second, although the Irish epic speaks of two wars, those wars are waged with only a short interval between them, and are merely two complementary, interdependent episodes in the Tuatha De Danann's settlement of Ireland. Moreover, the second war is declared in the name of liberty (cf. Lug's exhortations to his troops quoted earlier), as the Tuatha De Danann have thrown off the yoke of a semi-alien and wholly tyrannical king, Bress, whom the Fomorians wish to replace—which is precisely the situation of the Romans in relation to Porsenna, who wants to reinstate Tarquinius Superbus (cf. the insults hurled by Cocles at the Etruscans in Livy, II, 10). Third, however dissimilar the "exploitations" of Scaevola's burnt hand and Nuada's severed arm might be, the fact remains that this exploitation takes place, that it culminates in a compromise peace and friendship (as in the case of Porsenna) which is, above all, juridical: using legalistic arguments, and rejecting the case against it formulated by Nuada, Sreng demands his *right in law*, which is to resume the duel begun the day before, with its "score" exactly as it was at the end of the first "set," which he had won, as it were, "hands down." And it is under pressure from this harsh but legitimate requirement that the Tuatha De Danann, after deliberation, make peace with the Fir Bolg.

Therefore, it seems to me that the two battles of Mag Tured are early; that, from the viewpoint of a philosophy of sovereignty inherited by the Celts, as by the Latins, from their Indo-European ancestors, they are necessary; and that they preserve, in an original fictional form, the double symbolism of the one-eyed sovereign and the one-handed sovereign. Additionally, such a stance also avoids the serious difficulties that arise if one accepts the argument that there originally was only a *single* battle of Mag Tured. I will give one example. Unless we suppose (and where would that lead us?) that the story of the single original battle had a quite different structure from the narrative that has come down to us of the second battle, how are we to situate within that single battle the *mutilation* of Nuada, since he also, we are told, *perishes* in it and must of necessity perish in it? His appellation "of the Silver Hand" clearly requires an interval between the loss of his hand and his death. Yet how can we accept that Nuada survived a battle constructed wholly in honor of Lug, which had as its consequence, both logical in itself and asserted by tradition, that Lug became the new king of the Tuatha De Danann and, therefore, Nuada's successor?

It is from this new point of view we ought to resume the old argument, always conducted on shaky grounds, for and against the linking of "Nuada of the Silver Hand" with the one-handed Tyr (In favor: Axel Olrik, *Aarb. f. oldk.*, 1902, p. 210ff.; J. de Vries *Altgerm. Religionsgesch.*, II, 1937, p. 287. Against, with very weak arguments or most improbable hypotheses: K. Krohn, *Tyrs högra hand, Freys svärd*, in *Festsk H.F. Feilberg*, 1911, p. 541ff.; Al. H. Krappe, *Nuada à la main d'argent*, in *Rev. Celt.*, XLIX, 1932, p. 91ff.); the link holds good.

We know that a late Mabinogi conserves, in the form "Lludd of the Silver Hand," *Lludd Llaw Ereint* (a description without explanation today),[4] the Welsh equivalent of *Nuada Airgetlam*. It is worthy of note that this Mabinogi, *The Adventure of Llud and Llevelys*, (Loth, *Les Mabinogion*, ed. of 1913, I, pp. 231–241) presents Lludd not just on his own, but as a couple, two brother-kings, Lludd (king of Britain) and Llevelys (king of France). King Lludd is a great builder (of London), a fine warrior, a generous distributor of food, but he is unable to solve the problem of three mysterious scourges that invade and lay waste his island. He consults Llevelys, "known for the excellence of his councils and his wisdom," and it is Llevelys who explains to him the magic origin of the three scourges, as well as providing him with the magic means to be rid of them. Ought we to see, concealed by a final distortion behind Llevelys, an equivalent of the Irish Lug (who is certainly to be found in the *Mabinogi of Math*, under the name of *Lleu*)?

Notes

1. On the various Horatii heroes, cf. *Horace et les Curiaces*, p. 89ff.

2. Cf. *JMQ* I, p. 36ff.; *Horace et les Curiaces*, p. 61ff.; *Servius et la Fortune*, p. 29ff., p. 119ff., p. 125ff.; *JMQ* II, p. 123ff., and all of ch. 3 (*Histoire et mythe*).

3. In other words, although the "one-armed sovereign," Nuada, is king of the Tuatha De Danann, it is their adversaries who benefit from the legalistic exploitation of that mutilation. In turn, this throws into prominence another situation relating to the "one-eyed sovereign": the other leader of the Tuatha De Danann, Lug, is indeed "one-eyed" as we have seen, but he is so only for a brief period, of his own free will, while assuming a grimace with magic effects. Now, in the battle that is in the offing, Lug's *adversary*, the most terrible of the enemy chiefs (who is, moreover, his own grandfather, whom he will strike down), is "Balar (or Balor) of the piercing

gaze" (*Birugderc*), who is authentically one-eyed, and whose power, entirely magical, is linked precisely to that physical disfigurement, which is itself of magic origin. Of his two eyes, the story says (section 133), one, habitually closed, sprang open only on the field of battle, when it shot death at those unfortunate enough to be struck by his gaze. And we are also told the origin of this fearful privilege: one day, when his father's druids were busy concocting spells, Balar came and looked through the window; the fumes of the brew rose so that they reached his eye. (Cf. A. H. Krappe, *Balor with the Evil Eye*, Columbia Univ., 1927.) All these facts seem to indicate that the Irish tradition hesitated, at some point, as to whether the one-eyed and one-armed couple (and the advantages gained by the two mutilations) were to be placed in the Tuatha De Danann camp or in that of their enemies.

4. The epithet *Llaw Ereint* is applied to Lludd only in another Mabinogi, that of *Kulwch and Olwen*; but the same personage is certainly involved.

30. *The Eddic* Völuspá

Snorri Sturluson's Prose Edda, *introduced in the final reading of the previous chapter, is complemented by a second medieval source of Germanic mythic tradition, the anonymous* Poetic Edda, *earliest attested in an Icelandic manuscript of the thirteenth century called the Codex Regius. The* Poetic Edda *is a collection of early Norse poems, or lays, one of the most important of which is the* Völuspá, *its title sometimes rendered in English as "The Sibyl's Prophecy." The lay begins with a poetic synopsis of the Norse creation account and the history of the gods, which soon leads on to a prophecy of the doom of the gods, punctuated periodically by the haunting refrain, "Seek you wisdom still?"* (RDW)

VÖLUSPÁ

Translated by Patricia Terry

Hear my words, you holy gods,
great men and humble sons of Heimdall;
by Odin's will, I'll speak the ancient lore,
the oldest of all that I remember.

I remember giants of ages past,
those who called me one of their kin;
I know how nine roots form nine worlds
under the earth where the Ash Tree rises.

Nothing was there when time began,
neither sands nor seas nor cooling waves.
Earth was not yet, nor the high heavens,
but a gaping emptiness nowhere green.

Then Bur's sons lifted up the land
and made Midgard, men's fair dwelling;
the sun shone out of the south,
and bright grass grew from the ground of stone.

The sun climbed; the moon's companion
raised its right hand over heaven's rim.
The sun did not know where its hall would stand,
the stars did not know where they would be set,
the moon did not know what would be its might.

Then all the gods met to give judgement,
the holy gods took counsel together:
they named night and night's children,
gave names to morning and noon
afternoon and evening, ordered time by years.

until three of the Æsir assembled there,
strong and benevolent, came to the sea;
they found on the shore two feeble trees,
Ash and Embla, with no fixed fate.

These did not breathe, nor think or speak,
they had no hair, no fairness of face;
Odin gave life's breath, Hoenir gave mind,
Lodur gave hair, fairness of face.

Then the Æsir in Idavöll
built altars, temples, high timbered halls,
set up forges to fashion gold,
strong tools and well-shaped tongs.

Sitting in meadows, smiling over gameboards,
they never knew any need of gold,
but there came three maidens monstrous to look at,
giant daughters of Jotunheim.

She remembers war, the first in the world.
Countless spears were cast at Gullveig,
her body burned in Odin's hall;
three times burned, three times born,
again and again, yet even now alive.

Witch was her name in the halls that knew her,
a sorceress, casting evil spells;
she used magic to ensnare the mind,
a welcome friend to wicked women.

Then the mighty gods met to give judgement,
the mighty gods took counsel together:
should the Æsir accept great losses,
or all the gods be given what was due?

Odin's spear shot into the host—
that was the first war fought in the world.
The wall of Asgard proved too weak—
the victory was won by Vanir magic.

Then the mighty gods met to give judgement
the holy gods took counsel together:
who had filled the air with evil speech,
offered to a giant the goddess Freyja?

Thor alone struck, swollen with anger—
never idle when he heard such news;
vows were broken, promises betrayed,
the solemn treaties both sides had sworn.

There is an ash tree— its name is Yggdrasil—
a tall tree watered from a cloudy well.
Dew falls from its boughs down into the valleys;
ever green it stands beside the Norns' spring.

Much wisdom have the three maidens
who come from the waters close to that tree;
they established laws, decided the lives
men were to lead, marked out their fates.

She knows that Heimdall's hearing is hidden
where the holy tree rises to the heavens;
she sees a rushing turbid river
pour from Odin's pledge. Seek you wisdom still?

She sat alone outside; the old one came,
anxious, from Valhalla, and looked into her eyes.
Why have you come here? What would you ask me?
I know everything— where you left your eye,
Odin, in the water of Mimir's well.
Every morning Mimir drinks mead
from Warfather's tribute. Seek you wisdom still?

Valhalla's lord gave gold and treasure;
she looked far into the future,
spoke with wisdom of all the worlds.

She saw valkyries come from far away,
ready to ride to the lands of men;
Hild had a shield, so did Skogul,
Gunn was there, Gondul, Geirskogul.

I saw Balder stained with blood,
I saw the fate of Odin's son:
above the fields, fragile and fair,
stands the slender mistletoe.

From that same plant which seemed so frail
the fatal shaft came to Hod's hand;
and Frigg wept in Fensalir
for Valhalla's sorrow. Seek you wisdom still?

She saw in chains under the kettle-wood
someone who looked like guileful Loki;
there sits Sigyn— she doesn't seem
happy for her husband. Seek you wisdom still?

A river bears westward through a baneful valley
spears and swords; its name is Fear.

Far from sunlight stands a hall
on the Shores of the Dead; its doors face north.
Deadly poisons drip through its roof,
snakes were woven to form its walls.

She saw men wading through heavy streams;
some were oath-breakers, others had murdered,
some had lured women to love.
There the Serpent sucks on corpses,
the Wolf rends dead men. Seek you wisdom still?

He sat on a grave-mound, striking a harp,
Eggther, glad to guard the giants' herds;
close to him, the bright red cock,
Fjalar, crowed from the gallows tree.

And in Asgard Gold-comb crowed,
the cock who wakes Odin's warriors;
another is heard beneath the earth,
a soot-red cock in the halls of Hel.

Garm is howling from the Gnipa Cave,
the rope will break, and the Wolf run free.
Great is my knowledge, I can see
the doom that awaits almighty gods.

Brothers will die, slain by their brothers,
kinsmen betray their close kin;
woe to the world then, wedded to whoredom,
battle-axe and sword rule, split shields asunder,
storm-cleft age of wolves until the world goes down,
only hatred in the hearts of men.

Mimir's sons play; now fate will summon
from its long sleep the Gjallarhorn:
Heimdal's horn clamors to heaven,
Mimir's head speaks tidings to Odin.

Lofty Yggdrasil, the Ash Tree, trembles,
ancient wood groaning, the giant goes free;
terror harrows all of Hel,
until Surt's kinsman comes to consume it.

How fare the Æsir? How do the elves fare?
Jotunheim seethes, the Æsir assemble;
at the stone doorways of deep stone dwellings
dwarfs are moaning. Seek you wisdom still?

Garm is howling from the Gnipa Cave,
the rope will break, and the Wolf run free.
Great is my knowledge, I can see
the doom that awaits almighty gods.

Westward drives the giant, Hrym, his shield high;
the world-girding Serpent rises from the water,
lashing at the waves; the bright-beaked eagle
rends corpses, screaming; Naglfar sails free.

Westward the ship sails, Loki steers;
ruin by fire flies across the sea
with Muspell's demons, monsters, and the Wolf.
Byleist's brother, Loki, leads them.

Surt moves northward, lord of the fire giants,
his sword of flame gleams like the sun;
crashing rocks drag demons to their doom,
men find the way to Hel, the sky splits open.

Garm is howling from the Gnipa Cave,
the rope will break, and the Wolf run free.
Great is my knowledge, I can see
the doom that awaits almighty gods.

A second sorrow comes to Odin's wife:
Odin goes forth to fight the Wolf;
Frey, who killed Beli, battles with Surt.
Lifeless has fallen Frigg's beloved.

Odin's son Vidar goes forth to fight the Wolf;
that carrion eater, Loki's evil son,
feels the hero's sword inside his heart—
thus is avenged the Æsir's lord.

Far-famed Thor, the son of Earth,
the son of Odin, goes forth to fight the Snake.
Midgard's defender dies tiumphant,
but the human race no longer has a home:
nine steps beyond the Serpent's body,
Thor, wounded, walks in pride.

The sun turns black, the earth sinks below the sea,
no bright star now shines from the heavens;
flames leap the length of the World Tree,
fire strikes against the very sky.

She sees the earth rising again
out of the waters, green once more;
an eagle flies over rushing waterfalls,
hunting for fish from the craggy heights.

The Æsir meet in Idavöll;
they speak together about the Serpent,
consider all that came to pass,
the ancient runes offered to Odin.

Later they will find a wondrous treasure,
gold gameboards, lying in the grass
where they had left them so long before.

Barren fields will bear again,
Balder's return brings an end to sorrow.
Hod and Balder will live in Odin's hall,
home of the war-gods. Seek you wisdom still?

She sees a hall, fairer than the sun,
thatched with gold; it stands at Gimlé.
There shall deserving people dwell
to the end of time and enjoy their happiness.

There comes the dark dragon flying,
flashing upward from Nidafells;
on wide swift wings it soars above the earth,
carrying corpses. Now she will sink down.

Notes

This translation of *Völuspá* is based on an edition of the text recently published by Paul Schach. Meaningless passages have been omitted, and what seems a more satisfactory order has been restored. In addition, Professor Schach's explanatory notes have provided many valuable interpretations, including indications of probable gaps in the narration, shown here by large spaces between stanzas.

I have preferred to return to the Norse title of this poem because the supernatural being, the *völva*, who reluctantly speaks prophetic words to Odin, cannot really be named in English. "Witch" would perhaps be closest, but, despite *Macbeth*, it primarily suggests evil rather than prophecy. "Sibyl" is too tame, too intellectual, coming from Greece. I have also restored the pronouns by which the original text refers to the *völva*, sometimes in the first person, sometimes in the third. This leaves open the possibility, incorporated into the Vigfusson-York edition, that there is more than one narrator. It also makes a connection with the final "she" of the poem, the *völva* who "sinks down" into her shadowy dark domain.

These notes<, in addition to the glossary of proper names,> will provide information about Norse mythology. But understanding of the underlying cosmology simply brings the mysterious to a deeper level. The inseparability of chaos and form is the very subject of the poem, the doom of creation inherent in the violence of the beginning. The battle is lost in advance, *Ragnarök*, the doom of the gods, the battle for which the warriors were brought by the valkyries to Valhalla, because it cannot be won, is the ideal of Germanic heroism.

Professor Schach gives convincing reasons for deleting the reference to Ymir which occurs at the beginning of *Völuspá* in other editions. This has the disadvantage, however, of making the creative activity of "Bur's sons" seem more peaceful than it was. Contemporary readers, being familiar with Norse cosmology, would have known what Snorri Sturluson already felt it necessary to explain in his thirteenth-century handbook for poets. According to Snorri, Ymir was the first creator, himself created out of the union of opposites, frost meeting warmth in the primordial void. No deity was involved in this quite modern idea of life's beginning. Descendants of the Frost Giant, "Bur's sons," one of whom was Odin, killed Ymir and created the world: its waters from his blood; earth from his flesh; mountains from his bones; Midgard, the home of humans, from his eyebrows. It is clear that "giants" (*jotuns*) and "gods" (the Æsir) are interrelated, but giants, as seen by the gods, are evil. The *völva*, a giant, and constrained to speak by Odin's superior powers, is thus a precarious source of knowledge.

The sea that surrounds Midgard is the home of the Serpent who will ultimately emerge to participate in *Ragnarök*. Beyond the sea is Jotunheim or Utgart, home of the giants. Below Midgard is Niflheim, "Mist-home," the realm of the dead, ruled by Loki's daughter Hel. In the center of Midgard is Asgard, dwelling place of the Æsir. The Æsir created the human race from two trees. One is, like the World Tree, an ash; the identity of the "embla" is uncertain. Heimdall, mentioned in the beginning of the poem as the father of humans, has a prominence not far from Odin's. He too made a sacrifice for wisdom, leaving his particularly acute hearing, or an ear in some readings, in Mimir's Well where Odin left his eye. In contrast, the principal attribute of Thor, defender of humans against the giants, is unthinking strength.

Odin grew old and anxious about the fate of the gods, although he must already have known their future when he consulted the *völva*. She hints at possible causes, the recurrence of evil in the relations of the Æsir, warrior gods, with the Vanir, the older fertility gods who win a temporary victory through magic. There is also the attempt to kill Gullveig, who may be the sorceress casting her evil spells in the next stanza. Her name, however, refers to the power of gold.

Later, when the Æsir and Vanir have been united, the goddess Freyja is promised to a giant by Loki who then breaks his word. Thor's Hammer completes the betrayal. Loki's crimes were of such magnitude that they could be evoked by brief allusions now quite obscure. In fact, he is evil itself, sometimes in the disguise of simple mischief. Although he often acts as the ally, even the intelligence, of the gods, he is a giant whose offspring, in addition to Hel, include the Wolf and the Serpent. Loki not only finds a way to kill the god Balder, protected by all living things except the mistletoe, but uses as his agent Balder's brother, the blind and innocent Hod. Snorri describes Balder as the best, the wisest, and the most beautiful of the gods. Loki is punished, but the ordering moral factors in society break down. The valkyries assemble, the warriors in Valhalla hear the cocks crowing to announce the final battle. Naglfar, the Ship of the Dead, begins its mysterious journey; the Wolf and the Serpent are free.

The Ash Tree referred to in the beginning of the poem is difficult to locate even in mythological space. Everything is in some sense "below" it: the home of giants; Midgard, Middle Earth, the home of men; and Hel. Below it also live the Norns, the source of human destiny. These may be the giant maidens whose arrival is the first indication that the tranquility of the Æsir will not be permanent. The Tree, Yggdrasil, is also called the World Tree. Its Norse name means "Odin's Horse," in reference to Odin's hanging himself on the Tree in order to obtain secret runes of wisdom, a story related in "Sayings of the High One." The Ash Tree is also life itself, its greenness in opposition to the "nowhere green" of the primordial void. According to recent, and compelling, readings of the text, it remains visible, like a flaming torch against the sky, after the earth and the stars have been destroyed.

When the earth rises again from the waters, the Æsir, but not their opponents, reappear. Balder lives again, at peace with Hod. There are people again as well, some of them destined, by their virtue, to live in a hall called Gimlé in happiness forever. Snorri refers to this as a pagan heaven; more recent commentators see here, and elsewhere in the poem, a Christian meaning. These will be more inclined to accept as genuine the defective stanza which follows the present stanza 49 in one manuscript, and which Schach includes. A literal translation carries so many inevitable, but perhaps inappropriate, connections with Christian terminology that I prefer to place it here. It seems in any case hard to fit into the chronology and what seems to me the spirit of the poem, at least without the lost passages which must have accompanied it.

> The mighty one comes down   on the day of doom,
> that powerful lord   who rules over all.

The final stanza has also been the subject of much conflicting interpretation, in which the dragon is seen in a variety of functions from purifying to threatening. Like Peter Hallberg and Paul Schach, I see its presence as a reminder that good cannot be disentangled from evil; to separate light from the darkness is to intensify the darkness.

31. *The Gods: Æsir and Vanir*

In Norse traditions the gods are of two sorts: the Æsir and Vanir. Prominent among the Æsir are Odin, Tyr, and Thor (the great champion, affiliated with thunder, whose weapon is the hammer Mjollnir); while the chief members of the Vanir are Njord and his two children—son Frey and daughter Freya. In much of Scandinavian tradition the two sets of gods are depicted as forming an organic whole—a complete divine community—so that the gods can be collectively denoted by formulas such as "Odin, Thor, Frey." There was a time, however, when the gods Æsir and Vanir were at war with one another—the conflict of which the sibyl makes mention in the Völuspá*: "I remember war, the first in the world."*

Dumézil, in the excerpt that follows, examines these words from the Völuspá *and accounts of the conflict as preserved in three other medieval Germanic sources: Snorri Sturluson's* Prose Edda*; the* Heimskringla*, Sturluson's history of the kings of Norway; and the* Gesta Danorum *of Saxo Grammaticus. This war, argues Dumézil, is the Scandinavian expression of that primitive Indo-European motif of a conflict between the functions. In part 2 we encountered the Roman homologue of the Scandinavian tradition, the war that Romulus fought with the Sabines after his abduction of the Sabine daughters. Now Dumézil demonstrates, identifying idiosyncratic structural parallels, that the motif survived in Indo-European Asia as well, far beyond the boundaries of Scandinavia and the Italian peninsula.* (RDW)

THE GODS: ÆSIR AND VANIR

Georges Dumézil

Mythology frequently joins the same characters [Odin, Thor, and Frey] in a triad. Among them alone are divided the three treasures forged by the dwarfs after losing a bet with the malicious Loki: Odin gets the magic ring, Thor the hammer that is to be the instrument of his battles, and Frey the wild boar with the golden bristles.[1] It is they, and only they, whom the *Vǫluspá* (strs. 53–56) describes as being joined in the supreme duels and deaths of the eschatological battle.[2] More generally, it is they—and the goddess Freya, closely associated with Frey and Njord—who dominate, who indeed monopolize almost all the mythological material. It is no less significant that the three gods who split the property of the dead—the last two under rather obscure conditions—are Odin, who consigns to himself the nobles or "half the dead" from the battlefield, Thor, to whom go the thralls (more correctly, no doubt, the nonnobles), and Freya, who according to one text[3] takes the other half of those killed in battle and according to another text takes the dead women.[4]

Such is the present situation. But this union and this happy harmony, founded on a clear analysis of human wishes, have not always existed, according to the legend. In a far distant past the two divine groups lived at first separately, as neighbors; then they fought a fierce war, after which the most distinguished Vanir were associated with the Æsir, with the rest of their "people" living somewhere away from the struggle and the cares of their cult. Four strophes from that breathless poem, the *Vǫluspá*, in which the sibyl relates quite allusively the entire history of the gods; two texts of the erudite Snorri; and finally an unadroit plagiarism by his contemporary Saxo Grammaticus—these inform us of this initial crisis of the gods, which is presupposed also in several passages from other Eddic poems. These documents are not homogeneous: two present the event in mythological terms, two transpose it into historical and geographical terms. The first group includes strophes 21–24 of the *Vǫluspá* and a passage in Snorri's mythological manual written for the use of poets, the *Skáldskaparmál* (chap. 4); the second includes chapters 1, 2, 4, and 5 of the *Ynglingasaga*, discussing the *Ynglingar*, supposed descendants of Frey, and chapter 7 of the first book of Saxo's *Gesta Danorum*, a fragment of the "saga of Hadingus" which fills chapters 5 through 8 of that book.

a) *Vǫluspá* 21–24. I have elsewhere[5] made an extended analysis of this passage, which the hypercritical Eugen Mogk[6] sought to eliminate from the dossier on the Æsir and Vanir. The order of events—described as "the first war of armies in the world"—seems somewhat confused in these rapid and discontinuous strophes, which do not narrate, but content themselves with evoking episodes already known to the listeners. There is extensive reference to a female being called *Gullveig*, literally, "gold-drink, gold-drunkenness," sent by the Vanir to the Æsir, who, despite metallurgical treatment, cannot rid themselves of her. A sorceress, she sows corruption, particularly among women. There is also reference (24) to a spear, apparently magic, thrown by Odin against an enemy army, which does not prevent that "broken was the wall of the stronghold of the Æsir" and that "the warlike (?) Vanir were able to trample the plains." But nothing decisive results from these contrary movements, because (23) the gods hold an assembly for peace where they discuss eventual compensation.[7]

b) *Skáldskaparmál* (chap. 5, *Prose Edda*) (The response of Bragi to the question "Whence comes the art called poetry?"):

> The beginning of it was that the gods were at war with the people known as the Vanir and they arranged for a peace meeting between them and made a truce in this way: they both went up to a crock and spat into it. When they were going away, the gods took the truce token and would not allow it to be lost, and made of it a man. He was called Kvasir. He is so wise that nobody asks him any question he is unable to answer. He travelled far and wide over the world to teach men wisdom and came once to feast with some dwarfs, Fjalar and Galar. These called him aside for a word in private and killed him, letting his blood run into two crocks and one kettle. The kettle was called Óðrörir, but the crocks were known as Són and Boðn. They mixed his blood with honey, and it became the mead which makes whoever drinks of it a poet or a scholar. The dwarfs told the Æsir that Kvasir had choked with learning, because there was no one sufficiently well-informed to compete with him in knowledge.[8]

(There follows the story of the acquisition of the mead by Odin, who is to be its greatest beneficiary).

c) *Ynglingasaga* (the beginning of the *Heimskringla*) (chaps. 1, 2, 4, 5):

> 1. Of the Three Continents.—The earth's round, on which mankind lives, is much indented. Great seas cut into the land from the ocean. We know that a sea goes from the Norva Sound [the Strait of Gibraltar] all the way to Jórsalaland ["Jerusalem Land," Palestine]. From this sea a long arm extends to the northeast which is called the Black Sea. It separates the three parts of the world. The part to the eastward is called Asia; but that which lies to the west of it is called by some Europe, by others Eneá. North of the Black Sea lies Svíthjóth the Great or the Cold.
>
> Some men consider Svíthjóth the Great not less in size than Serkland the Great ["Saracen Land," North Africa], and some think it is equal in size to Bláland ["Blackman's Land," Africa]. The northern part of Svíthjóth is uncultivated on account of frost and cold, just as the southern part of Bláland is a desert because of the heat of the sun. In Svíthjóth there are many large provinces. There are also many tribes and many tongues. There are giants and dwarfs; there are black men and many kinds of strange tribes. Also there are animals and dragons of marvellous size. Out of the north, from the mountains which

are beyond all inhabited districts, a river runs through Svíthjóth whose correct name is Tanais [the Don River]. In olden times it was called Tana Fork or Vana Fork. Its mouth is in the Black Sea. The land around the Vana Fork was then called Vana Home or the Home of the Vanir. This river divides the three continents. East of it is Asia, west of it Europe.

2. Of Ásgarth and Óthin.—The land east of the Tana Fork was called the Land or Home of the Æsir, and the capital of that country they called Ásgarth. In this capital the chieftain ruled whose name was Óthin. This was a great place for sacrifices. The rule prevailed there that twelve temple priests were highest in rank. They were to have charge of sacrifices and to judge between men. They are called *díar* or chiefs. All the people were to serve them and show them reverence.

Óthin was a great warrior and fared widely, conquering many countries. He was so victorious that he won the upper hand in every battle; as a result, his men believed that it was granted to him to be victorious in every battle. It was his habit that, before sending his men to battle or on other errands, he would lay his hands on their heads and give them a *bjannak* [benediction]. Then they believed they would succeed. It was also noted that wherever his men were sore bestead, on sea or on land, they would call on his name, and they would get help from so doing. They put all their trust in him. Often he was away so long as to be gone for many years.

4. The War between the Æsir and the Vanir.—Óthin made war on the Vanir, but they resisted stoutly and defended their land; now the one, now the other was victorious, and both devastated the land of their opponents, doing each other damage. But when both wearied of that, they agreed on a peace meeting and concluded a peace, giving each other hostages. The Vanir gave their most outstanding men, Njorth the Wealthy and his son Frey; but the Æsir, in their turn, furnished one whose name was Hœnir, declaring him to be well fitted to be a chieftain. He was a large man and exceedingly handsome. Together with him the Æsir sent one called Mímir, a very wise man; and the Vanir in return sent the one who was the cleverest among them. His name was Kvasir. Now when Hœnir arrived in Vanaheim he was at once made a chieftain. Mímir advised him in all things. But when Hœnir was present at meetings or assemblies without having Mímir at his side and was asked for his opinion on a difficult matter, he would always answer in the same way, saying, "Let others decide." Then the Vanir suspected that the Æsir had defrauded them in the exchange of hostages. Then they seized Mímir and beheaded him and sent the head to the Æsir. Óthin took it and embalmed it with herbs so that it would not rot, and spoke charms over it, giving it magic power so that it would answer him and tell him many occult things.

Óthin appointed Njorth and Frey to be priests for the sacrificial offerings, and they were *díar* [gods] among the Æsir. Freya was the daughter of Njorth. She was the priestess at the sacrifices. It was she who first taught the Æsir magic such as was practiced among the Vanir. While Njorth lived with the Vanir he had his sister as wife, because that was the custom among them. Their children were Frey and Freya. But among the Æsir it was forbidden to marry so near a kin.

5. Gefjon Ploughs Zeeland Out of Lake Mælaren.—A great mountain chain runs from the northeast to the southwest. It divides Svíthjóth the Great from other realms. South of the mountains it is not far to Turkey. There Óthin had large possessions. At that time the generals of the Romans moved about far and wide, subjugating all peoples, and many chieftains fled from their possessions because of these hostilities. And because Óthin had the gift of prophecy and was skilled in magic, he knew that his offspring would inhabit the northern part of the world. Then he set his brothers Vé and Víli over Ásgarth, but he himself and all *díar*, and many other people, departed. First he journeyed west to Garthríki [Russia], and then south, to Saxland [northwestern Germany]. He had many sons. He took possession of lands far and wide in Saxland and set his sons to defend these lands. Then he journeyed north to the sea and fixed his abode on an island. That place is now called Óthinsey [Óthin's Island], on the island of Funen.

Thereupon he sent Gefjon north over the sound to seek for land. She came to King Gylfi, and he gave her a ploughland. Then she went to Giantland and there bore four sons to some giant. She transformed them into oxen and attached them to the plough and drew the land westward into the sea, opposite Óthin's Island, and that is [now] called Selund [Zeeland], and there she dwelled afterwards. Skjold, a son of Óthin married her. They lived at Hleithrar. A lake was left [where the land was taken] which is called Logrin. The bays in that lake correspond to the nesses of Selund. Thus says Bragi the Old:

> Gefjon, glad in mind, from
> Gylfi drew the good land,
> Denmark's increase, from the
> oxen so the sweat ran.
> Did four beasts of burden—
> with brow-moons eight in foreheads—
> walk before the wide isle
> won by her from Sweden.

But when Óthin learned that there was good land east in Gylfi's kingdom he journeyed there; and Gylfi came to an agreement with him, because he did not consider himself strong enough to withstand the Æsir. Óthin and Gylfi vied

> much with each other in magic and spells, but the Æsir always had the better of it.
>
> Óthin settled by Lake Logrin, at a place which formerly was called Sigtúnir. There he erected a large temple and made sacrifices according to the custom of the Æsir. He took possession of the land as far as he had called it Sigtúnir. He gave dwelling places to the temple priests. Njorth dwelled at Nóatún, Frey at Uppsala, Heimdall at Himinbjorg, Thór at Thrúthvang, Baldr at Breithablik. To all he gave good estates.[9]

d) Saxo Grammaticus, *Gesta Danorum*, I, 7.[10] This brief passage is clarified by the texts of the *Vǫluspá* and of Snorri, but in itself clarifies nothing. It gathers and alters radically several features of the legend of the war and of the reconciliation of the Æsir and the Vanir, notably the gold statue (*Vǫluspá*), the beheading of Mímir (*Ynglingasaga*), and the murder of Kvasir (*Skáldskaparmál*). "Othinus" here too is a king, whose capital is "Byzantium," but who willingly spends time *apud Upsalam*.[11]

Indo-European parallels help to explain not only the formula of the composition of the triad, but also the legend of the initial separation and war, as well as the reconciliation and fusion of the Æsir with the Vanir. To be sure, the Vedic hymns say nothing about this, oriented as they are toward eulogy and prayer: they are hardly proper for recalling the delicate episodes of divine history. The later literature, the epic, knows that the gods Indra and the Nāsatya, whose association is so necessary and so close, were nevertheless not always joined in one unified society. By chance an Iranian legend confirms that several essential traits of the material in this story, which probably comes from the "fifth Veda," the oral corpus of legends, were pre-Vedic, indeed Indo-Iranian. Originally the gods of the lower level, the Nāsatya or givers of health and prosperity, were apart from the other gods. The gods, headed by Indra (for such is the state of the divine hierarchy in the epic), whose weapon is the lightning, refused them what is the privilege and practically part of the credentials of divinity, participation in benefits of the oblations, under the pretext that they were not "proper" gods, but rather some kind of artisans or warriors who were too much mixed in with men. On the day when the Nāsatya raised their claims and tried to enter into divine society, a bitter conflict ensued.

We see how this entrance is substantially parallel to the initial separation of the higher Æsir—the masters of magic and lightning—and the lower Vanir—

givers of richness and fecundity. In India, let us note without delay, the heterogeneity of the two groups of gods could not be explained by the contact and conflict of religions or of different peoples, as is proposed in Scandinavia for the Æsir and Vanir: Mitra-Varuṇa and Indra on the one hand, the Nāsatya on the other, grouped together at the same time and with the same hierarchical order, were brought by the Indo-Iranian conquerors to the bend in the Euphrates as well as into the Iranian plateau and the basin of the Indus in the fourteenth century B.C. But the correspondences between Snorri and the *Mahābhārata* do not stop there. They extend to a group of rare and complex traits which permit the comparativist to be more positive.

We recall from the *Skáldskaparmál* the birth and death of Kvasir: at the moment when peace is concluded between the divine adversaries, they all spit into the same vessel. Out of this "pledge of peace" the gods fashion a man named Kvasir who has extraordinary, absolutely enormous, wisdom. He travels about the world, but two dwarfs kill him, distributing his blood among three bowls, mixing honey with it and thus concocting the "mead of poetry and wisdom." Then they tell the gods that Kvasir has choked with learning, no one having been able to compete with him in knowledge.

The name *Kvasir* in this legend has long been interpreted: since 1864 K. Simrock, then R. Heinzel (1889), and then E. Mogk (1923) have shown that it is an onomastic personification of an intoxicating drink which recalls the *kvas* of the Slavs.[12] It is natural that the precious intoxication given by the mead of poetry and wisdom should have honey as an ingredient. It is equally natural that a drink fermented from squashed vegetables (Dan. *kvas* "crushed fruits, wort of those fruits") should be made to ferment by spittle. This technique is frequently attested; it is at least conceivable, as we are here dealing with a ceremonial or communal drink, sanctioning the agreement between two social groups, that such fermentation should be caused by the spittle of all concerned. Furthermore, on this point E. Mogk has gathered sufficient ethnographic parallels.

What is less common is that the intoxicating drink prepared with the spittle and called upon to enter as a component of the other intoxicating drink, the mead of poetry, between its two stages as a drink, should take on a completely different form, that of a man or superman, and this by the will of the gods. Furthermore, this theme is not only rare (the "King Soma," and Dionysos-Zagreus, are something else again); it is inserted in a complex and precise whole, which must not be dislocated. It was not under just any circumstance, nor without design, that this man-drink was created. He was created at the conclusion of the war between the Æsir and Vanir, to seal the peace. Then he was put to death, and his blood, spread among the three recipients, served to make another drink, more durable in that it still inebriates Odin, poets, and visionaries.

Let us return now from Scandinavia to India, where we have left the higher gods and the Nāsatya in a great conflict, Indra already brandishing his thunderbolts against the latter. How does this crisis turn out? An ascetic allied with the Nāsatya who, as part of their usual services, have restored his youth to him, creates, through the force of his asceticism—the great weapon of Indian penitents—a gigantic man, who threatens to swallow the world, including the recalcitrant gods. This enormous monster's name is *Mada* "Drunkenness": he is drunkenness personified. Even Indra gives in, peace is made, the Nāsatya definitely join the divine community, and no allusion will ever be made to the distinction among gods or to the initial conflict. But what to do with this character, Drunkenness, whose task is finished and who is now only dangerous? The one who created him, this time with the accord of the gods, cuts him into four pieces and his unitary essence is split up into the four things that, literally or figuratively, are indeed intoxicating: drink, women, gaming, and hunting.

Such is the story to be read in the third book of the *Mahābhārata*, sections 123–125. An Iranian legend that I called attention to in the last section of my *Naissance d'archanges*[13] and which Professor Jean de Menasce has further scrutinized,[14] that of the *Hārūt-Mārūt*, confirms the linkage of drunkenness with this affair from the beginning of Indo-Iranian mythology. The reader will not have failed to notice the analogy between the fabrications and the liquidations of Kvasir and Mada, an analogy that it is easy to delimit and define. Here is how the balance sheet was formulated in my *Loki*:

> Certainly the differences between Germanic and Indic myth are striking, but so is the analogy between their fundamental situations and results. Here are the differences: among the Germanic peoples, the character "Kvas" is formed *after* the peace is concluded, as a *symbol of that peace*, and he is made according to a precise realistic technique, fermentation with spittle, whereas the character "Drunkenness" is made as a *weapon, in order to* force the gods into peace, and he is made *mystically* (we are in India), by the force of ascetism, without reference to a technique of fermentation. Then, when "Kvas" is killed and his blood divided in thirds, *it is not done by the gods* who made him, but by two dwarfs, whereas in India, it is his creator who at the order of the gods

dismembers "Drunkenness" into four parts. Further, the dismemberment of "Kvas" is simply *quantitative,* into three homogeneous parts (three vessels receiving the blood, all of the same value, though one happens to be larger than the others), whereas that of "Drunkenness" is *qualitative,* into differentiated parts (four sorts of drunkenness). In Germanic legend, it is simply as a lying explanation that the dwarfs afterwards tell the gods of an intolerable force (of a purely *intellectual* kind), out of proportion with the human world, which *would* have led to the suffocation of "Kvas," whereas in the Indian legend the excess of force (*physical,* brutal) of Drunkenness is *authentically* intolerable, incompatible with the life of the world, and as such leads authentically to his being dismembered. Finally the Germanic legend presents "Kvas" as a *benefactor* from the beginning, well disposed toward men—a sort of martyr—and his blood, properly treated, produces that most valued thing, the mead of poetry and wisdom, whereas in India "Drunkenness" is a *malefactor* from the beginning and his four fractions are the scourge of mankind.

All this is true, but it would only prove, if there were need of it, that India is not Iceland and that the two stories were told in civilizations that in content and form had developed in almost diametrically opposite directions. Notably their ideologies of insobriety had become just about inverse. There exists nevertheless a common pattern. It is at the moment when divine society is with difficulty but definitively joined by the adjunction of the representatives of fecundity and prosperity to those of sovereignty and force, it is at the moment when the two hostile groups make their peace, that a character is artificially created incarnating the force of intoxicating drink or of insobriety and is named after it. When this force proves to be excessive for the conditions of this world—for good or for evil—the person thus made is then killed and divided into three or four intoxicating parts that either aid or threaten man.

This pattern is original. It is not met with anywhere in the world but in these two cases. In addition, its principle is easily understood, if one pays attention to the social conditions and conceptions which must have existed among the Indo-European peoples. In particular, intoxication under various names and shapes would have been of use to all three social functions. On the one hand, it is one of the fundamental stimuli in the life of a sorcerer-priest and of a hunter-warrior in this culture, and, on the other hand, it is procured through plants that the farmer must *cultivate* and *prepare.* It is thus natural that the "birth" of intoxication and all that goes with it should be situated at that moment of mythological history when society is formed through reconciliation and the union of priests and warriors on the one hand with farmers and all the powers of fecundity and nourishment on the other. There is a profound harmony between this sociomythological event and the appearance of intoxication, and it is not superfluous to remark here that neither the poets

> of the *Mahābhārata* nor Snorri could still have been aware of this, which lends a strange air to their tales. For the poets of the *Mahābhārata*, the Nāsatya are no longer what they were at the time of the Vedic compilation, typical canonized representatives of the third function. However well Snorri in his various treatises portrays the differing characters of Odin, Thor, and Frey, he surely does not understand the reconciliation of the Æsir and the Vanir as a myth concerning the origin of the harmonious collaboration of the diverse social functions.[15]

This correspondence is not the only one. We have also a Roman tradition that presents a new pattern for the events of the war between the Æsir and the Vanir given by the sibyl in the *Vǫluspá*, one that confirms the meaning of the entire story. In Rome, as we know, there is no more mythology, and the earliest lore is deposited in the epic of origins. Further, the "complete society" whose creation interested the very matter-of-fact Romans could only be their own. It is in fact the tradition about the birth of the city which offers the Germanist the parallel of which we speak. Rome, says the legend, was constituted by the union of two groups of men, the purely masculine companions of the demigod Romulus, maintainers of the *promises of Jupiter* and strong in their *military valor*, and the Sabines of Titus Tatius, *rich farmers* and, through their *women*, the only ones capable of giving fecundity and durability to the nascent society. But the happy union of these two complementary groups, like that of the Æsir and Vanir, was brought about at the conclusion of a difficult and long-contested war, in the course of which each adversary in turn gained the upper hand. The union was affirmed in a scene and by means that would well illustrate its "functional specialty." The Sabines, the "rich ones," nearly won by occupying the capitol, but how did they occupy it? By bribing Tarpeia, a *woman*, with *gold*—or with *love*, according to another version. Later, in the battle of the forum, when his army fled in disorder, Romulus not only restored order, but even drove the Sabine army out of the capitol back to their camp. How did he achieve this result? With his eyes and hands to the sky, he addressed himself to the *sovereign Jupiter*, reminding him of his promises, imploring a miraculous suspension of panic; and Jupiter granted it. It is notable that the two episodes of the war of the two divine clans in the *Vǫluspá* correspond to these two, with the same functional features. The rich and voluptuous Vanir send among the Æsir as a scourge the woman called Gullveig, "insobriety (or power) of gold," who corrupts their hearts, especially those of the women. Further, Odin *throws his spear* in a gesture that the sagas know well, where it regularly has the effect of throwing the enemy army into a fatal panic. In the conflict of Indra and the Nāsatya which was treated at some length above, and which does not achieve the dignity of a war of peoples, the conduct of the two parties is no less clearly significant of their functional levels. The Nāsatya have as their ally the ascetic *Cyavana*, whom they obtained by restoring his *youth* and *beauty* and by permitting him to keep his *wife* whom they had first intended to take for themselves. And it is with brandished thunderbolt that Indra responds to their audacity.

Even if all the picturesque details of Snorri's narrative have not found equally striking correspondences outside Scandinavia (I am thinking of the stories of Hœnir and the decapitation of Mímir), those just recited should suffice to establish that the war of the Æsir and the Vanir is indeed a myth that is *older* than the Germanic peoples, *older* than the dispersion of their ancestors and those of the Italic, Indo-Iranian, and other Indo-European peoples. It is a myth whose apparently strange elements still preserve, though not fully understood by its narrators, the complex elements and nuances of a "lesson" on the structure of Indo-European societies.

Notes

1. *Edda Snorra Sturlusonar*, ed. Finnur Jónsson (Copenhagen, 1931), p. 123 (*Skáldskaparmál*, chap. 44). References to Snorri's *Edda* (also known as *The Prose Edda*) are to this edition. Abbreviated: *Snorra Edda* (Jónsson). *The Prose Edda* is divided into parts with separate chapter numbering: *Gylfaginning, Bragarœður, Skaldskaparmál, Háttatal.*

2. *Edda* (Kuhn [Heidelberg: Carl Winter, 1962]), pp. 12–13; *Edda* (Bellows [New York: The American-Scandinavian Foundation, 1923 and later]), pp. 22–23. References to individual poems of the *Edda* are frequent in the text and are not separately footnoted except for direct quotations.

3. *Grímnismál*, str. 14: *Edda* (Kuhn), p. 60; *Edda* (Bellows), pp. 90–91.

4. *Egils saga*, chap. 78.

5. Dumézil, *Tarpeia* (Paris: Gallimard, 1947), pp. 249–291.

6. Mogk, E., *Die Gigantomachie in der Völuspá. Folklore Fellows Communications* 58 (Helsinki, 1924).

7. *Edda* (Kuhn), p. 5; *Edda* (Bellows), pp. 10–11.

8. *The Prose Edda of Snorri Sturluson*, trans. Jean I. Young (Berkeley and Los Angeles: University of California Press, 1964), p. 100. Translations from the *Snorra Edda* are taken from this version, abbreviated *Prose Edda* (Young).

9. *Heimskringla: History of the Kings of Norway*, trans. Lee M. Hollander (Austin, Texas: University of Texas Press, 1964), pp. 6–10. Abbreviated: *Heimskringla* (Hollander).

10. Cited from the edition of J. Olrik and H. Ræder (Copenhagen, 1931).

11. Dumézil, *La saga de Hadingus* (Paris: Presses Universitaires de France, 1953).

12. For references see the bibliography in Jan de Vries, *Altgermanische Religionsgeschichte*, 2d ed., 2 vols. (Berlin: Walter de Gruyter, 1956–1957), pp. ix–xlix. Abbreviated: *AGR* 2 (the first edition, Berlin 1935–1937, is *AGR* 1).

13. Dumézil, *Naissance d'archanges* (Paris: Gallimard, 1945), pp. 158–170.

14. Menasce, Jean de, in *Revue de la Société Suisse d'Études Asiatiques* 1 (1947), 10–18.

15. Dumézil, *Loki* (Paris: G.-P. Maisonneuve, 1948), pp. 102–105.

32. *The* Rígsþula *and* *Indo-European Social Structure*

Another of the lays of the Poetic Edda, *the* Rígsþula, *serves as the focal point of the following essay by Dumézil. A curious aspect of early Germanic society—human society, that is, as opposed to divine society—is the disappearance (from the perspective of Indo-European inheritance) of a priestly class. Dumézil finds at least an ideological survival of human social tripartition, along primitive Indo-European lines, in the story of the god Heimdall, his journeys among humankind, and the children he engenders in those journeys, as preserved in the* Rígsþula. (RDW)

THE *RÍGSÞULA* AND INDO-EUROPEAN SOCIAL STRUCTURE[1]

Georges Dumézil

Since the beginning of research into the three Indo-European functions (magic and juridical sovereignty, physical force, fecundity) and their expressions, a characteristic fact has emerged concerning the Germanic domain which doubly opposes it to the Celtic domain.[2] The Celts, as well the Gauls as the Irish, present in their social organization a formula almost superposable on the Indo-Iranian structure (druids, *flaith* or warlike nobility, *bó airig* or breeders-farmers). But in their theology one observes a complex picture in which it is not easy to find the equivalent Vedic and pre-Vedic lists of patron gods of the same three functions ("Mitra-Varuṇa, Indra, Nāsatya"). On the contrary, the Germanic peoples profess a clear trifunctional theology (presented in Scandinavia as "Odin, Thor, Frey"), but do not divide their societies according to these three functions. Caesar, who knew the Gauls well, was struck by this difference.[3] The Germans, he remarked, have no class comparable to that of the Druids and show little interest in ritual. As they no longer apply themselves to agriculture, only one type of man exists among them, the warrior: *vita omnis in venationibus atque in studiis rei militaris consistit.*[4]

This statement, assuredly too simple and too radical, nevertheless brings together the essentials of Germanic originality, at least on the Continent and near the Rhine, for, as far back as one goes, Scandinavia has nourished a peasant mass, conscious of its function, under the sign of the gods Njord and Frey. But even in the north the absence of a sacerdotal class keeps the social structure from being superposable on the Indo-Iranian or Celtic model. In looking more clearly at *Rígsþula*, the famous Eddic poem in which this structure is exposed, or rather formed under our eyes, I should like to show that it can nevertheless be explained on the basis of the Indo-European functional tripartition.

Traveling incognito throughout the world under the name of Rig (ON Rígr)[5] the god Heimdall presents himself in a first house, a very poor one, in which he is met by the couple Great Grandfather and Great Grandmother. He spends three nights there in the conjugal bed and leaves after begetting a son. At his birth this son is named *þræll* "slave (thrall)." His descendants, boys and girls, bear only pejorative names. Rig then presents himself in a second house, more wealthy, where he receives the hospitality of the couple Grandfather and Grandmother. After three nights, he again goes off, leaving Grandmother with child, a son who at his birth receives the name *Karl*, "freeholder." The children fathered by Karl bear names the majority of which make allusion to peasant life and one of which, *Smiðr*, is even the word meaning "artisan (smith)."[6] The names of his daughters, less characteristic, are flattering. Finally Rig appears in a third house, this one luxurious, where Father and Mother receive him sumptuously. Here the product of his passage receives the name *Jarl*, "noble (earl)." In an action contrasting with the way he treated his other children, Rig does not abandon this one, but assists in his education and adopts him as a son. To this "Rig-Jarl" only male descendants are attributed, who all have names signifying "boy, son, heir," and who live like their father. Only the last, the young Konr, "Konr ungr," detaches himself from the mass and becomes the first king (*konungr*).

This social structure has long been confirmed by juridical documents from the most diverse parts of the medieval Germanic world:[7] *adalingus, liber, servus* (Angles); *edhilingi, frilingi, lazzi*; or, *nobiles, ingenui, serviles* (Saxons); *satrapa* (or *nobilis*), *ingenuus, servus* (Danish: Saxo Grammaticus). We are certainly concerned here with a tradition, almost a Germanic theory. But it must be noted right away that in the *Rígsþula*, þrǽll and his descendants remain heterogeneous with the superior classes. The derisory or even defamatory names they bear are proof of it. They are not only found secluded at the bottom, but are even outside of the "good" social division, just like the *śūdra* of classical India in relation to the three superior *varṇa*; such that the following equivalence can be established, with a gap in the first term only:

——	brāhmaṇa
Jarl	kṣatriya
Karl	vaiśya
——	——
þræll	śūdra

In fact, the description that the poem contains (strs. 22–23) of the life Karl leads corresponds, *mutatis mutandis*, to the definition of the Indian breeder-farmers, the *vaiśya*:

Hann nam at vaxa oc vel dafna;
øxn nam at temia, arðr at gørva,
hús at timbra oc hlǫðor smiða,
karta at gørva oc keyra plóg.

Heim óco þá hanginluclo,
geitakyrtlo, gipto Karli;
Snør heitir sú; settiz undir ripti;
biuggu hión, bauga deildo,
breiddo blæior oc bú gørðo.

He began to grow, and to gain in strength,
Oxen he ruled, and plows made ready,
Houses he built, and barns he fashioned,
Carts he made, and the plow he managed.

Home did they bring the bride for Karl,
In goatskins clad, and keys she bore;
Snör was her name, 'neath the veil she sat;
A home they made ready, and rings exchanged,
The bed they decked, and a dwelling made.

Similarly, the occupations of Jarl—and also of Father, in whose house he is born—are those of the Indian *kṣatriya*; it is said about the Father (str. 28):

Sat húsgumi oc sneri streng,
álm of bendi, ǫrvar scepti.

There sat the house-lord, wound strings for the bow,
Shafts he fashioned, and bows he shaped.

Then about Jarl (str. 35):

Upp óx þar Iarl á fletiom;
lind nam at scelfa, leggia strengi,
álm at beygia, ǫrvar scepta,
flein at fleygia, frǫccor dýia,
hestom ríða, hundom verpa,
sverðom bregða, sund at fremia.

To grow in the house did Jarl begin,
Shields he brandished, and bowstrings wound,
Bows he shot, and shafts he fashioned,
Arrows he loosened, and lances wielded,
Horses he rode, and hounds unleashed,
Swords he handled, and sounds he swam.

As for the first term of the Scandinavian and Indian table, consideration of the precise kind of royalty represented by "Konr ungr" reduces considerably the difference, at first glance irreducible, produced by the absence in one group and presence in another of a sacerdotal caste. "Konr ungr" in effect is and can only be defined as a *magician*, with the notable exclusion of the warrior traits that still characterize his father and his brothers. He owes his promotion and success solely to his magic knowledge (strs. 43–46):

Upp óxo þar Iarli bornir;
hesta tǫmðo, hlífar bendo,
sceyti scófo, scelfðo asca.

Enn Konr ungr kunni rúnar,
ævinrúnar oc aldrrúnar;
meirr kunni hann mǫnnom biarga,
eggiar deyfa, ægi lægia.

Klǫc nam fugla, kyrra elda,
sæva of svefia, sorgir lægia,
. . . .
afl ok eliun átti manna.

Hann við Ríg iarl rúnar deildi,
brǫgðom beitti oc betr kunni;
þá ǫðlaðiz oc þá eiga gat
Rígr at heita, rúnar kunna.

Soon grew up the sons of Jarl,
Beasts they tamed, and bucklers rounded,
Shafts they fashioned, and spears they shook.

But Kon the Young learned runes to use,
Runes everlasting, the runes of life;
Soon could he well the warriors shield,
Dull the swordblade, and still the seas.

Bird-chatter learned he, flames could he lessen,
Minds could quiet, and sorrows calm;
. . . .
The might and strength of twice four men.

With Rig-Jarl soon the runes he shared,
More crafty he was, and greater his wisdom:[8]
The right he sought, and soon he won it,
Rig to be called, and runes to know.

Thus the first function, magic sovereignty, if it does not have for support a whole class of men opposed to the class of warriors and to that of breeder-farmers, does at least appear, and in the expected hierarchical place. It is concentrated, however, in the person of the king, whom the function has colored even to the point where there remains in him only "the" magician par excellence.[9] The *konungr* is thus clearly distinguished from the Indian *rājan*, coming in general, like "Konr ungr," from the warrior class, but who, pre- or juxtaposed to the class of priests, is characterized by temporal power more than by talent or knowledge, and must double, for the purpose of religious acts, with the priest par excellence who is his chaplain, the *purohita*.

The picture the *Rígsþula* gives in "Konr ungr" of royalty is in any case schematic and insufficient.[10] If one turns to the mythology, which is doubtless closer to social reality, one sees that the god of the first function, Odin, is to be sure a king-magician similar to "Konr ungr," but that he is also (and how could it be otherwise in the Germanic world?) a warrior god, even the great ruler of combats and fighters, the patron of the *jarlar* as well as of the *konungar*, and in the other world, of the *einherjar*, dead heroes skilled in combat whom the Valkyries bring to him. I have shown on several occasions how certain Scandinavian peoples or groups, while maintaining the Indo-European structure of the three functions in the triad Odin-Thor-Frey, modified the distribution of conceptual material among the three levels.[11] This is true first for Odin, with whom the accent is often placed on the warrior aspects at the expense of the magical aspects of his province. But this is also true for the one who strikes, the thundering and lightening Thor. He, in return, often lost his contact with the warriors, and interested society instead, and especially the peasants, with the fecund result of the atmospheric battle that he produces through rain. This confusion has either brought Thor closer to the proper, terrestrial gods of fecundity, Frey and Njord, or it has pushed these two, in turn, into the parts of their province where Thor does not compete, such as human fecundity and voluptuousness. The following were, for example, according to Adam of Bremen, the values of the three gods associated with the temple at Uppsala: *Wodan, id est furor, bella gerit*, says this keen observer, *hominique ministrat virtutem contra inimicos; Thor praesidet in aera, qui tonitrus et fulmina, ventos imbresque, serena et fruges gubernat*; and Fricco—the god *ingenti priapo*—has no more to himself than *pacem voluptatemque*. Consequently, one addresses oneself to Wodan *si bellum imminet*, to Thor *si pestis et fames*, and to Fricco *si nuptiae celebrandae sunt*.

Even in Norway, where the former dominion of Frey has been largely preserved, and where Thor, in the literature, has certainly remained the "one who strikes," modern folklore and Lapp borrowings attest nevertheless to a clear and ancient evolution of this god, through the benefits of storms, toward fecundity and the service of peasants. This can easily be seen in the verses of the *Hárbarðsljóð* (str. 24) in which Odin hurls into Thor's face the celebrated insult:

> Odin has the *jarlar* who fall in battle,
> And Thor has the race of the *þrælar*.

Jan de Vries has plausibly surmised[12]—for Thor has nothing to do elsewhere with the *þrælar*—a caricature, a parody of a more exact saying, where, corresponding to Odin, patron of *jarlar*, one should find Thor the patron of the *karlar*: is not *karl* the stereotyped surname that Thor bears in Lapp mythology (*Hora Galles* < **Kar(i)laz*)? And, in folklore from the South of Sweden, is the god not designated by a quasi-synonym of *karl, go-bonden, korn-, åker-bonden*?

These breaks and overlappings in divine functions permit a justification of the parallel displacement which is observed in the attribution of symbolic colors that the *Rígsþula* makes to the social classes.

We know that this usage is very old, even Indo-European; it is well known among the Indo-Iranians (with whom the notion of "class, caste," is expressed by the words, *varṇa, pištra*, which are connected with color). This has recently been reported among the Hittites, and has also left clear traces in Rome.[13] In these various domains the colors retained were white (first function: priests, the sacred), red (second function: warriors, force), and dark blue or green (third function: breeder-farmers, fecundity). Only post-Rigvedic India, which placed a fourth class, that of the servant *śūdra*, below the three *ārya* classes, adjusted this system at the same time, attributing yellow to the *vaiśya* and reserving for the *śūdra* the dark color in its extreme form, black.[14] The *Rígsþula*, too, associates colors with the eponyms of the Germanic social classes.[15] It presents the baby Thrall, at his birth (str. 7), as *svartan*, black. Then it describes the baby Karl (str. 21) as *rauþan ok rjóðan*, red of hair and face; and finally the baby Jarl (str. 34) is *bleikr*, a bright white. And apparently "Konr ungr," for whom color is not indicated, is himself also *bleikr*, in his quality as the son of Jarl. We see that, if the black attributed to Thrall and his slave descendants is no more surprising than the black of the Indian *śūdra*, in return the white and red, attributed respectively to the noble warriors and freeholders, are lowered by one level in comparison with Indic and also with the Indo-European prototype. The table below will show how the overflowing of Odin into the warrior function and that of Thor into the function of fecundity can explain this "descent" of white and red:

Indo-European State	Scandinavian Theology	Rígsþula
White ~ Magic → Odin	{ Magic	Konr ~ ungr
	{ War	Jarl ~ white
Red ~ Force, War → Thor	{ Atmospheric Combat	
	{ Fecund Rain	} Karl ~ red[16]
Blue ~ Fecundity → Frey	Terrestrial Fecundity	}
		Thrall ~ black

In other words, the aspect of Odin (war) incorporated with Jarl and the aspect of Thor (fecund rain) incorporated with Karl caused the transfer to Jarl and Karl, respectively, of symbolic colors that, originally, were associated with aspects of Odin (magic) and Thor (atmospheric combat) which were not incorporated in Jarl and Karl. The transfer could only have been facilitated by the fact that the magic function, being no longer assured to a class of men but only to an individual "Konr ungr," was no longer felt to be homogeneous with the functions assured to Jarl and the *jarlar*, Karl and the *karlar*, and could, without opposing an already broken symmetry, remain outside the play of colors.[17]

These reflections permit the *Rígsþula* to be put into the dossier of our study and afford a glimpse of the simple and coherent evolution that transformed the Indo-European prototype into an original structure among the Germanic peoples.

"*La Rigsþula* et la structure sociale indo-européenne,"
Revue de l'histoire des religions 154 (1958), 1–9.

Notes

1. These remarks were made in a course at the Collège de France, March 1, 1958. For the text of *Rígsþula* see *Edda* (Kuhn), pp. 280–287; *Edda* (Bellows), pp. 201–216.

2. Georges Dumézil, *Mythes et dieux des Germains* (1939), pp. 6–13.

3. Caesar, *De bello gallico*, VI, 21, 1; 22, 1.

4. *Ibid.*, VI, 21, 3.

5. On the god Heimdall in his Indo-European perspective, see Dumézil, *Les dieux des Indo-Européens* (1952), pp. 104–105; J. de Vries has written on "Heimdallr, dieu énigmatique" in *Études germaniques* 10 (1955), 257–268, and in *Altgermanische Religionsgeschichte*, 2d ed. (1957), II, 238–244. Also see my article <below, chapter 8>, where one will find a justification of the use of *Rígr*, a foreign (Irish) name for king, which does not imply, contrary to what is often said, that the poem is of Celtic inspiration. In particular, the social division presented in the *Rígsþula* is certainly Germanic.

6. See my article "Métiers et classes fonctionelles chez divers peuples indo-européens," *Annales, Économies, Sociétés, Civilizations* 13 (1958), 716–724.

7. J. Grimm, *Deutsche Rechtsalterthümer*, A. Heusler and R. Hübner, eds., 4th ed. (1899), pp. 312–314. N. Wittich, "Die Frage der Freibauern, Untersuchungen über die soziale Gliederung des deutschen Volkes in altgermanischer und frühkarolingischer Zeit," in *Z. d. Savigny-Stiftung, Germ. Abt.* 22 (1901), 262–263.

8. It has been stated above that Rig (Heimdall) taught Jarl, beside the art of war, "the runes." But with Jarl this magic science did not prosper; it was retained as a seed that only flowered with Konr ungr.

9. This seemed so astonishing that it was supposed that the poem was broken off, and that the last strophes, lost, told of the exploits of war of "Konr ungr." In fact, nothing supports this hypothesis.

10. J. de Vries, "Das Königtum bei den Germanen," *Saeculum* 7 (1956), 289–309, brings a solution to the difficult problem proposed by Tacitus, *Germania*, 7, *reges ex nobilitate, duces ex uirtute summunt.*

11. In the latest place, see my *Les dieux des Indo-Européens*, pp. 25–26; also my *L'idéologie tripartite des Indo-Européens* (collection "Latomus," vol. 31) (1958), chap. 2, pars. 19–22.

12. Jan de Vries, "Über das Wort Jarl und seine Verwandten," *La nouvelle Clio* 6 (1954), 468–469: "Hier möchte ich an eine bekannte Verszeile des Harbardliedes erinnern:

Óðinn á Jarla þá er i val falla
en þórr á þræla kyn.

Damit beschimpft der góttliche Fährmann den Weitgewanderten Thor. Dass Odin der Gott der Jarle, der Fürsten im allgemeinen war, wissen wir schon längst, aber ebensosehr war Thor der Gott der Karle, hiess er ja selber *þorrkarl*, wie uns die lappische Entlehnung *Horagalles* bezeugt. Der Spotter des Harbardliedes hat sich nicht gescheut, den biedern Bauerngott als den Schutzherrn der Sklaven zu verunglimpfen; aber das war nun eben die Bösartigkeit seines Witzes. Ich vermute, dass er eine alte Verszeile, die ursprünglich *þórr á karla kyn* lauten mochte, umgebildet hat. Dann wurde der Gegensatz *jarl: karl* auch hier zutage treten und sogar seine Entsprechung im Götterpaar Odin: Thor finden."

13. See Dumézil, *Les rituels indo-européens à Rome* (1954), III, "Abati russati virides," IV: "Vexillum caeruleum," pp. 45–72; also my *L'idéologie tripartite des Indo-Européens*, chap. 1, pars. 20–21.

14. There are ritual traces of the ancient system (white-*brahmaṇa*, red-*kṣatriya*, black-*vaiśya*): *Gobhila G. S.*, IV, 7, 7; *Khādira G. S.*, IV, 2, 12.

15. On the precise value of these adjectives of color, see the notes of H. Gering and B. Sijmons, *Kommentar zu den Liedern der Edda* (1927), 349, 354, 360.

16. Among the continental Germanic peoples in the Middle Ages, the colors of the peasant are brown (or grey), blue on holidays. O. Lauffer, *Farbensymbolik im deutschen Volksbrauch* (1948), pp. 20–22; G. Widengren, "Harlekintracht und Mönchskutte, Clownhut und Derwischmütze," *Orientalia Suecana* 2 (1953), 53 n. 3 (in all of this work, several valuable indications and corrections on the symbolism of blue and brown will be found).

17. It was rather as a fighter, and as the Scandinavian equivalent of Indra, that Thor had a red beard—which passes, with the hammer, to Saint Olaf; cf. also the red shields of the Vikings, and, on the continent, the red-tinted hair of certain Germanic warriors (Tacitus, *Histories*, IV, 61). But red has several other values: J. T. Storaker, *Rummet i den norske folketro, Norsk Folkeminnelag* 8 (1923), 51–54, par. 14 (significance of the color red). Along with red, blue too was a color of Thor: J. T. Storaker, *Elementerne i den norske folketro, Norsk Folkeminnelag* 10 (1924), 113 n. 1.

33. The Germanic World

The dragon-slaying motif is well known in Germanic literary tradition. In the essay that follows, Watkins examines early Germanic occurrences of the theme and demonstrates that Germanic shares with other Indo-European traditions the inherited primitive Indo-European formulas of heroic combat, making plain in the process the rightness of "the proposition that linguistics needs poetics." He ends his essay, and this collection, with an examination of the use of the dragon-slaying theme in an Old English charm in which the apple—"an Indo-European fruit" (see the Preface of the present work)—serves as a homeopathic defense against snake venom. (RDW)

THE GERMANIC WORLD

Calvert Watkins

Myth and Hero

The earliest Germanic literature, Old English, Old High German, Old Saxon, and Old Norse, knows a great many combats between heroes and dragons or heroic adversaries, epical conflicts which have continued to seize popular imagination from the Dark Ages right down to the 19th and 20th centuries, in the response to the operas of Richard Wagner, the still unabated vogue of the literary creations of the distinguished philologist J. R. R. Tolkien, and the immense success of the game Dungeons and Dragons. The themes of all these epic poems and tales have been repeatedly studied, catalogued, and analyzed by philologist and folklorist alike, and their similarity to the themes of Greek, Indic, and other legendary material has been noted since the 19th century.[1] The thematic similarities may be presumed as given; our concern here is language.

A number of verbal parallels among the various Germanic dragon-slaying legends have been adduced,[2] which prove, by the tenets of the comparative method, that they are genetically related and common inheritance. Such is the remarkable and methodologically indispensable agreement in what Meillet (1925:3) would term the critical 'détail singulier', the *hepti-sax* 'hilted knife',

WEAPON of Giant adversary in the *Grettissaga* (§66) and a hapax in Old Norse, and the *hæft-méce* 'hilted sword' Hrunting which Unferth loaned to Beowulf (1457) and which was useless against Grendel's mother (1523 *bitan nolde* 'would not bite'). The equation of the compounds is notable for two reasons. The first is that both contexts refer to the antiquity of the weapon: *Beowulf* 1458 *án foran ealdgestréona* 'foremost of the ancient treasures'; *Grettissaga* §66 metalinguistically as *þat kolluðu menn þá heptisax* 'such men called then heptisax'. The second is that *Beowulf* and *Grettissaga* come respectively at the beginning and the end of the attested Old Germanic heroic literary tradition. The two are separated by nearly 600 years (8th to 14th century), yet they are very close to each other, perhaps identical, in theme and message, i.e. in "meaning". It is a remarkable testimony to the tenacity of the Germanic tradition.

Perhaps the clearest evidence for a common Germanic (at any rate West and North Germanic) dragon-slaying myth are the respective genealogies of the heroes Sigemund in *Beowulf* and Sigmundr-Sigurðr ("Siegfried") in Old Norse:

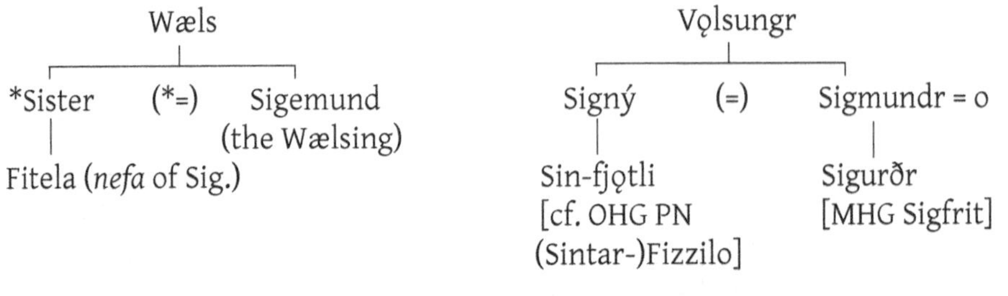

The identity of the names and their relations, the mythopoeic incest motif (probably reconstructible for Old English as well), all point unequivocally to a common Germanic mythographic background, whether the dragon-slayer is Sigemund as in *Beowulf*, or his son Sigurðr/Sigfrit as elsewhere. It is with this myth that we may begin.

Sigemund's exploit is narrated as part of the victory song composed to celebrate Beowulf's victory over Grendel (867ff.). In this victory song we have a treasure house of the metalanguage of Old Germanic poetry. 'Mindful of lays' (*gidda gemyndig*) the poet 'found another poem, truly bound [i.e. rightly alliterative]' (*word óðer fand / sóðe gebunden*). (With the neuter plural *word* compare Greek *ἔπεα*.) He began to 'vary words' (*wordum wrixlan*), as Klaeber puts it (ad 874) 'in the customary manner of Germanic poetry', and told of the deeds of Sigemund:

884–7 Sigemunde gesprong
æfter déaðdæge **dóm unlýtel,**
syþðan wíges heard **wyrm ácwealde,**
hordes hyrde.

To Sigemund came, after his death-day, no **little fame,**
since the handy battler **killed a serpent,**
the guardian of a treasure.

'Great fame' is expressed in the ancient figure of litotes, literally '*un*little fame' (*dóm unlýtel*), like Greek *κλέος ἄφθιτον* and Vedic *ákṣiti śrávaḥ* '*im*perishable fame'; compare also with the same semantics, Greek *μέγα κλέος* and Vedic *máhi śrávas* 'great fame'.[3] And embedded in the phonetic figure ***heard... hordes hyrde*** we find one of the traditional Old English dragon slaying formulas: *wyrm ácwealde* 'killed the worm'.

Germanic has no cognate of *áhi-*, *aži* -, *ὄφις*; the word for 'worm, serpent, dragon' is Old English *wyrm*, Old Norse *ormr*, Old Saxon and Old High German *wurm*, Gothic *waurms*: Germanic **wurmiz*, exactly cognate with Latin *uermis*, and presupposing Indo-European **u̯r̥mis*. The word is a rhyme formation in Indo-European to **k$^{u̯}$r̥mis*, probably for reasons of tabu; **k$^{u̯}$r̥mis* is found in Celtic, Balto-Slavic, Albanian, and Indo-Iranian. The usual meaning of **k$^{u̯}$r̥mis* is just 'worm' in most traditions, but in Middle Iranian it is also the word for 'dragon'; compare the Pahlavi version of the familiar Indo-European formula: *kirm ōzad būd* 'had slain the dragon' (chap. 29). There can be no doubt that in **u̯r̥mis/k$^{u̯}$r̥mis* we have two variants of the same alternative designation of the Indo-European mythological serpent-adversary.[4]

Old English here uses *cwellan* as the unmarked verb for 'kill', the causative of *cwelan* 'die': Indo-European **g$^{u̯}$el(h_1)-*, Cuneiform and Hieroglyphic Luvian *wal-* 'die', Old Irish *at-baill* 'dies', Greek *βάλλω* 'throw'. The causative formation **kwaljan*, anachronistically **g$^{u̯}$ol(h_1)-éi̯e-*, appears to be confined to Germanic, and its use in the dragon-slaying formula is apparently an innovation confined to Old English.[5] *Beowulf* furnishes two further instances, both precisely in that formula:

1053–5 ond þone ǽnne heht
golde **forgyldan** þone þe Grendel ǽr
máne **ácwealde**

and he ordered the compensation **to be paid**[6]
for the one whom Grendel wickedly **killed,**

1334 þé þú gystran niht Grendel **cwealdest**

(the fight) in which **you killed** Grendel last night.

The two well illustrate the inherited bidirectionality of the formula

→
KILL SERPENT,
←

even where the lexical expression of KILL has been renewed, from IE *g^{u}hen- to Germanic **kwaljan*, Old English *cwellan*.

Other verbs as well are associated with the narration of dragon combat in both West and North Germanic. The Old Norse verb *vega* 'fight' pret. *vá* < IE **u̯oik-* (**u̯eik-*) is attested in the fragments of the *Vǫlsungasaga* (3. Brunnhildr to Gunnarr): *sigurðr* ***vá*** *at Fáfni/ormi* 'Sigurd fought with Fáfni/the serpent'. In the *Vǫluspá* (53), the Sybil's prophecy, Odin will fare forth

við úlf **vega**

to fight the Wolf,

and perish in the attempt. But he will be avenged: as the next stanza relates, the 'mighty son of Sigfadir' *mikli mǫgr Sigfǫður* ("Victory-Father", epithet of Odin) will come

vega at valdyre

to fight with the corpse-monster (the wolf Fenrir),

and spear him through the heart. Formulaically note the same collocation of the verb and the epithet in *Lokasenna* 58: Loki taunts Thor that he will not dare fight with the wolf (*við úlfinn* ***vega***) and the latter will swallow Odin (***Sigfǫður***). The verb is found only once in *Beowulf* (2400), but in the identical context and again a prophecy of doom: 'So he survived (*genesan*) every battle

oð ðone ánne dæg
þé hé wið þám **wyrme** **gewegan** sceolde

till that one day
when he had to **fight** against that **serpent**.

The verb is IE **u̯eik-*, with an old athematic ablauting paradigm with shifting accent **u̯éik-ti*/**u̯ik-énti* which accounts for the Germanic hesitation in root final consonant, Gothic *weihan*, but Old English, Old Norse (-)*wegan*. Among cognates note Old Irish *fichid* 'fights', Old High German *ubarwehan* 'conquers', with nasal infix Latin *uincō* 'conquers', perfect *uīcī* < **u̯oik-* = Old Norse *vá*, and Homeric Greek *οὐκ ἐπίεικτον* 'unconquerable, insuperable', which if correctly transmitted in vocalism looks like the obscure Old Irish form *fíacht* (Thurneysen 1946:422).

Old Norse provides us with a precious piece of evidence for the channel for the renewal and replacement of IE **gʷhen-* by other verbs like Germanic **kwaljan* or **wigan* (**weihan*), which we can only present now; the explanation will come in the pages immediately following. In the *Vǫlundarkviða* 33, one of the oldest of the Eddic poems, the smith Vǫlundr makes the King Niðuðr swear an oath, 'by ship's sides, shield's rim, horse's withers and sword's edge', *at skips bordi ok at skialdar rǫnd/at mars bógi ok at mækis egg*, clearly traditional language. Ship and horse, shield and sword are together the warrior's transport and arms; compare the instruction in the Sanskrit laws of Manu (8.113) that the man of the warrior caste (*kṣatriya*) must swear by his 'chariot and weapons' (*vahanāyudhais*), and with the arms alone, the Old Irish oath *tar mo scíath ⁊ tar mo c[h]loidim* 'over my shield and over my sword' (*Fled Bricrenn* §99). Vǫlundr makes the Norse king swear

> at þú **kveliat** kván Vǫlundar
> né brúði minni **at bana verðir**
>
> that you will not **kill** Vǫlundr's wife,
> nor **become the bane** (= killer) of my bride.

Here *kvelja* and the periphrasis *at bana verða* (on which see below) are semantically identical; the choice of each is governed by the alliteration.

The Old English noun *bona (bana)*, Old Norse *bani* 'slayer, killer', is frequent in poetic texts in both languages. In *Beowulf* it is applied both to heroes and to monsters; the dragon is the subject. Cf. Grendel in 1743 *bona swíðe néah* 'a killer is very near', 2082 *bona blodigtóð* 'the bloody-toothed killer', and of the Worm who killed Beowulf and was killed by him, 2824 *bona swylce læg* '(his) killer also lay dead'. In Old Norse the dragon is the object. It is used twice with the dragon Fáfnir as object, once of the WEAPON and once of the HERO.[7] *Grípisspá* 15:

> þú munt hǫggva hvǫsso sverði
> brynio rísta með **bana Fáfnis**

You will hew with sharp sword,
cut her byrnie with **Fáfnir's bane** (the sword Gram),

Oddrúnargrátr 17:

iǫrð dúsaði ok upphiminn
þá er **bani Fáfnis** borg um þátti

Earth and Up-heaven shook
when **Fáfnir's bane** (Sigurðr)
looked at (Brynhildr's) fortress.[8]

We find finally the collocation with the generic word for serpent in a kenning for the god Thor. *Hymiskviða* 22:

orms einbani uxa hǫfði

The serpent's single bane (used as bait) the head of an ox.

Here the compound *ein-* is there only to alliterate with *orms* and *uxa*; the underlying phrase is *orms bani*, which nominalizes the familiar formulaic verb phrase

KILL SERPENT.

The noun phrase 'serpent's killer' is itself here a definition of the Germanic divine HERO par excellence, the warrior god Thor himself, Nordic counterpart of Indra.

There is in fact no primary, non-derived verb in Germanic which is related to the noun of Old English *bona* etc.[9] To express such a notion verbally by this root all the early North and West Germanic languages have recourse to a periphrasis meaning literally 'become slayer to', which semantically means just 'slay' : Old English *tó bonan weorðan* (+ dat.), Old Norse *at bana verða* (+ dat.), Old High German *ti banin werdan* (+ dat.), Old Saxon *te banon uuerðan* (+ dat.). This periphrastic verb phrase is regularly used of more than ordinary killings: it is semantically marked. It is found characteristically in narration of killing of or by a dragon or other monster (bidirectionality), of fratricide or other kin-slaying, of awesome exploits of the hero, or of awesome victims. The context is not indifferent. The examples from *Beowulf* are the following:

1330–1 **Wearð** him on Heorote **tó handbanan**
wælgǽfre

A wandering murderous sprite (Grendel's mother)
slew him in Heorot.

Note the sentence-initial verb and the postposed, indefinite subject, who is not identified by name.

2078–9 him Grendel **wearð**
mǽrum maguþegne **tó múðbonan**

him, the famous young retainer, Grendel **slew by mouth.**

The first compound members *hand-* and *múð-* are for alliteration. Beowulf taunts Unferth:

587 þéah ðú þínum bróðrum **tó banan wurde**

though you **killed** your brothers,

and the same verb describes the primeval fratricide in

1261–2 siþðan Cáin **wearð**
tó ecgbanan ángan bréþer

since Cain **killed** his only brother by the sword,

and the death of Hygelac's son in

2202–3 ond Heardréde hildeméceas
under bordhréoðan **tó bonan wurdon**

and battle-swords **killed** Heardrede under shield-covering.

After Heardrede's death Beowulf legitimately succeeded to the kingship of the Geats:

460 **wearð** hé Heaþoláfe **tó handbonan**

He (Beowulf's father) **slew** Heatholaf,

2501–2 syððan ic for dugeðum Dæghrefne **wearð**
to handbonan Húga cempan

since I (Beowulf) in the presence of the hosts
slew Dæghrefne, champion of the Franks.

From the Old Norse *Poetic Edda* we may cite the following. Of dragons (*Grípisspá* 11):

þú munt báðom **at bana verða**
Regin ok Fáfni

You will **slay** both, Reginn and Fáfnir.

Of brothers (*Reginsmál* 5):

brœðrum tveim **at bana verða**

to **slay** the two brothers,

Helgakviða Hundingsbana I.36 (a taunt, as in *Beowulf* 587 above):

(þú hefir . . .) brœðr þínom **at bana orðit**

you have **slain** your brother.

And finally Odin's question and the witch's answer in *Baldrs Draumar* 8–9:

hverr man Baldri **at bana verða**?
hann man Baldri etc.

Who will **slay** Baldr?
He (Baldr's blind brother Hoðr) will etc.

In Old High German note only the single but telling example of the periphrasis, of tragic adversaries doomed to an ineluctable conflict. Hildebrand says of his son Hadubrand, who does not recognize his father (*Hildebrandslied* 54):

eddo ih imo **ti banin werdan**

or I (shall) **kill** him.

The construction is finally found in Old Saxon Christian poetry as well; for examples, see the work of Rosemarie Lühr cited below.

Old Norse knows another periphrasis with the same word *bani* in the same meaning 'slay': *ban(a)orð bera af* (+ dative), literally 'bring the killer('s) word from', the 'death message'. The expression is explained by Gering s. v. as derived from the legal obligation of a murderer to acknowledge himself as such.[10]

Compare *Fáfnismál* 39 *at Reginn skuli / mitt* ***banorð bera*** 'that Reginn should slay me'; *Landnámabók* iv. 17 (the forge-song of the smith Vǫlundr):[11]

Ek **bar** einn af ellifu
banaorð. Blástu meirr!

I **killed** eleven alone. Blow harder!

Atlakviða 43:

hon hefir þriggia þiódkonunga / **banorð borit**

She **killed** three kings.

In the *Prose Edda* of Snorri Sturluson the description of Ragnarök, the Twilight of the Gods, presents the whole gamut of Old Norse phrases with *bani* in the space of a few lines: the hound Garmr will fight Tyr, *ok **verðr** hvárr ǫðrum **at bana*** 'and each will kill the other', *Þórr **berr banaorð** af Miðgarðsormi* 'Thor will slay the Miðgarð serpent', *Ulfrinn gleypir Óðin; **verðr** þat hans **bani*** 'the wolf will swallow Odin; that will be his death'. Note once again the role of Thor as formulaic dragon-slayer: *berr banaorð af ormi* is equally

KILL SERPENT

like *orms einbani* above.

The construction 'became the bane' in Old English *to bonan weordan*, Old High German *ti banin werdan* etc. is discussed by Rosemarie Lühr 1982: 2.652–4, in her exhaustive study with rich comparative material and secondary literature. She shows that it is common West and North Germanic. Lühr rightly explains the meaning 'death, destruction, *bane*' found in all the medieval Germanic languages as a development of this construction, where the subject is not a person but a thing. (Compare the rich proliferation of Medieval and Early Modern English plant names like *henbane, wolfbane, cowbane, dogbane, fleabane.*)

On the other hand, Lühr's identification of this construction with certain others in Germanic misses the point. Old English and Old High German constructions like Laws *Grið* 21.2 *þræl wearð to ðegene* 'slave became noble', *Tat.* 15,2 *steina zi brote uuerden* 'stones to become bread' are not equivalent to a finite verb, and *Otfr.* III 19,25 *uns zi frúmu wurti* '(that) it become of use to us' is just the equivalent of a Latin (etc.) "double dative" (*nobis auxilio*) construction. OHG *ti banin werdan*, OSax. *te banon uuerðan*, OEng. *to bonan weorðan*, ON *at bana verða* are not 'fientive'; they are periphrases which mean 'to slay'. As such they are the exact semantic equivalent of the primary finite verb from the root which produced the Germanic **banan-* 'slayer, bane': a primary verb which does not exist in Germanic.

We have seen the contexts where we find the phrases *to bonan weorðan* and cognates (for convenience I will use the Old English formula as a portmanteau form) or Old Norse *bera ban(a)orð:* slaying of or by a "dragon" (bidirectionality!); killings of heroic dimension; fratricide. These are precisely the context for the appearance of the Indo-European formula

HERO SLAY (**g^{u}hen-*) SERPENT/$HERO_2$,

and we pose as equivalent Germanic

to bonan weorðan

HERO SERPENT/HERO$_2$.

bera ban(a)orð

In Germanic as well the subject HERO is frequently not overt, the more readily since he is the *bona*.

The equivalence *g$^{u̯}$hen-: *tó bonan weorðan* and *bera ban(a)orð af* must finally be recognized as not merely a typological semantic parallel, but a genetic equation. For E. Seebold and others have made a convincing case for *b* as the typical reflex of Indo-European *g$^{u̯}$h*,[12] citing the family of Old English *bona* as part of the evidence; we may equate *bona* exactly[13] with Greek *φóνος* and Vedic *ghaná-*: Indo-European *g$^{u̯}$hon-o-*, *o*-grade of the root *g$^{u̯}$hen-*. Indeed, it should be emphasized that the *poetic* equation *g$^{u̯}$hen-: *tó bonan weorðan* is additional and independent evidence for the correctness of Seebold's *phonological* equation and of the sound law. It is yet another argument for the proposition that linguistics needs poetics.

Skeptics of the equation like Meid 1984:104, who prefer to regard the equation as reflecting a borrowing into Germanic from a related "Northwest block" Indo-European dialect would have to assume that the traditional phrasing of the dragon-slaying mythology of the Germanic peoples was also borrowed at the same time from this mysterious source. I doubt they would find that a congenial hypothesis.

Note finally that in the expression *φóνος γενέσθαι* (+ dative) of *Od.* 21.24

αἳ δή **οἱ** καὶ ἔπειτα **φóνος** καὶ μοῖρα **γένοντο**

but thereafter these **became** his **death** and doom,

we can see in Greek the precise syntactic conditions for the development of the Germanic periphrastic construction 'become the bane' of Old English *tó bonan weorðan* (+ dative). A similar phrase is found in *Od.* 11, when the shade of Agamemnon says (444),

ἀλλ' οὐ **σοί** γ', Ὀδυσεῦ, **φóνος ἔσσεται** ἔκ γε γυναικός

and yet **you**, Odysseus, will never **be murdered** by your wife.

Lattimore's translation clearly captures the verbal force of the periphrasis. Compare also the legal formula in a fifth-century Arcadian inscription, Schwyzer 661.25–6 (Buck 17):

> ει **Ηις** ιν το(ι) ιεροι τον τοτ[ε απυθανοντον]/ **φονες εστι**
>
> If anyone (present) in the temple is a murderer of those
> who were killed at that time.

We may add Germanic to those branches of the Indo-European family which continue the ancient mythological and heroic formulas

HERO	SLAY (*$g^{\underline{u}}$*hen-*)	SERPENT

and

$HERO_1$	SLAY (*$g^{\underline{u}}$*hen-*)	$HERO_2$

The Germanic innovations are only to lose the verbal root *$g^{\underline{u}}$*hen-* and to develop, using inherited morphological, syntactic, and poetic means, a periphrasis with the agent noun derivative *$g^{\underline{u}}$*honó-*, and to utilize the inherited **u̯r̥mi-*, rhyme-form to *$k^{\underline{u}}$*r̥mi-*, for the serpent. The Indo-European asymmetry of the formula is well attested in Germanic, and the bidirectionality is perhaps more prominent in this family than any other due to the pessimistic Germanic view of "final things": Beowulf slays the Worm and is slain by him; at Ragnarök Thor will slay the Miðgarð Worm and die of its poison.

Applied Myth as Charm

We may examine here briefly<, as a sort of appendix in anticipation of part VII below (From myth to charm),> an Old English dragon-slaying narrative that is incorporated into a longer metrical piece known as the Nine Herbs Charm. It is edited by Dobbie 1942: 119–21, 210, from the unique manuscript Harl. 585, dated by Ker to the 10th/11th century.[14] The relevant episode in the edited text begins with an introduction (27–30):

> Þis is seo wyrt   ðe wergulu hatte;
> ðas onsænde seolh   ofer sæs hrycg
> ondan attres   oþres to bote.
> Ðas viiii magon   wið nygon attrum
>
> This is the plant that is called *wergulu* (crabapple);[15]
> a seal sent it over the sea's ridge[16]

to compensate for the malice of other venom.
Those nine are efficacious against nine venoms.

The narrative of the dragon myth proper (31–35) begins a new folio page (161b) and is demarcated by a cross before the first word of 1.31 and another cross at the beginning of line 36.[17] The text then runs:

Wyrm com snican, toslat he man;
ða genam Woden viiii wuldortanas,
sloh ða þa næddran, þæt heo on viiii tofleah.
Þær geændade æppel and attor,
þæt heo næfre ne wolde on hus bugan

A worm came sneaking, it bit someone;
then Woden took nine glory-twigs,
he smote then the adder, so that it flew in nine (pieces).
There the apple ended (it) and (its) venom,
so that it never should go into house.

I translate thus in the light of common sense (the 'apple' as direct object is much more difficult) and the cross-linguistic commonplace of a third person object unexpressed or expressed by a zero sign. Joseph Harris (p.c.) very tentatively suggests as an Old English parallel *Andreas* 1221–2 *bæron ut hræðe / ond þam halgan þær handa gebundon* 'they quickly carried (him) out and bound the saint's hands'. The alliteration requirement (*halgan : handa*) may have entailed a movement from the more expected '. . . carried the saint out and bound his hands', leaving the pronoun as a trace. For a similar zero subject with a conjoined noun phrase compare Old Irish *téit ⁊ a máthair* '(he) goes and his mother' = 'he and his mother go'.

The text has given rise to considerable discussion and some controversy. The medical historian Charles Singer (1920: 15) recognized the notion that diseases arose from the nine fragments into which Woden smote the reptile. The healing virtues of the nine herbs mentioned in the text before and after our passage are then to be understood as directed each against a particular 'venom' (*áttor*). The arithmetic of the nine herbs is itself unclear, as noted by H. Meroney,[18] who points out that even for an Old English botanist the (crab)apple is hardly an 'herb'.

In my view (partly building on Meroney) at least two originally distinct metrical charms have been combined by the compilator of ms. Harl. 585 or its source: an 'apple charm' with the dragon-slaying narrative of Woden and a 'nine herbs charm'. The link is either just the magic number nine or the apple pulp (*þæs æpples gor*), which along with 'old soap' (*ealde sapan*) provides in the prose 'recipe' the base into which the ground herbs are mixed. The 'nine herbs charm' will no longer concern us here; we are interested in the other, whose text has been given.

The name of the pagan god Woden is very rare in Old English literature; aside from genealogies Bosworth-Toller cite only this passage and one other from the Exeter Book (Krapp and Dobbie 1936:161, Maxims 1, line 132):

> Woden worhte weos, wuldor alwalda,
> rume roderas
>
> Woden wrought idols, the Almighty (wrought) glory,
> the heavens far and wide.

That both this passage and the 'apple charm' should show the collocation *Woden . . . wuldor* 'Woden . . . glory, fame' is probably more than coincidence, the more so since the Old Norse cognate of the latter, *Ullr*, is a divine name or epithet, 'eine Form des alten idg. Hochgottes' (de Vries, s.v.). Like Woden (IE **u̯et-* 'see, be cognizant of', Latin *uātēs* and Old Irish *fáith*), *wuldor* and *Ullr*, Goth. *wulþus* '*δόξα*, splendor' are derivatives of a root meaning 'see', IE **u̯el-*, with close links to poetry and mantic prophetic wisdom as well, Old Irish *fili* 'learned poet'. <See on these the discussion in chap. 9.>

The narrative itself is 'classical' basic formula, with lexical renewal of the basic verb of violent action. First comes the preliminary victory of the serpent,

SERPENT (*wyrm*) *toslítan* 'lacerate by biting' MAN,

then the reciprocal, the hero's smiting of the beast with a weapon:

HERO (*Woden*) SMITE (*sléan*) SERPENT(*næddre*) with WEAPON (*tān*).

The verb is precisely Modern English *slay*; the Old English *sléan* is also used reciprocally with the snake as subject, *gif næddre sléa man* 'If a serpent bites a man' (Cockayne 1961: 2.110.14).

The weapon is a magical twig (*tán*). The Old Norse cognate *teinn* appears notably in the compound *mistil**teinn***, English *mistleTOE*, the sinister twig which is the WEAPON with which blind Hǫðr will kill—become the bane of, *at bana verða*—Odin's son Baldr (*Vǫluspá* 31, *Baldrs Draumar* 9). The word is also used for a twig cast as a lot, and we know from Tacitus, *Germania* 10.1, that these were cut from fruit trees (*virgam frugiferae arbori decisam in surculos amputant*)—and *agrestia poma* 'wild fruit' along with fresh game and curds were alleged to be the principal diet of the ancient Germans (ibid. 23.1).[19] Such are the overtones of Woden's weapon against the serpent in this ancient Germanic myth narrated as part of the charm.

The brief and formulaic myth is framed, both preceded and followed, by the reference to the apple: first under the name of *wergulu*, mediated by the mysterious seal over the sea's ridge to remedy venom, then as the *æppel* which finished off the serpent and his venom. What is the connection, or more simply, what is the apple doing in this charm?

The apple is an Indo-European fruit; see the discussion of Gamkrelidze and Ivanov 1984: 2.637–43, with attention to language, botany, ethnography, and mythology. The apple is prominent in several myths among various Indo-European peoples, such as the apple of discord, or the golden apples of the Hesperides (guarded by a dragon), or the golden apples conferring eternal youth and immortality which belong to Idunn, wife of Bragi, the Norse god of poetry (: Vedic *bráhmaṇ-* 'formulation', perhaps Iranian *brazman-*). For Slavic and Baltic compare the references cited by the Georgian and Russian scholars in their work.

I suggest, however, that a much simpler and humbler homeopathic image underlies the function of the apple in this Old English charm against venom (*áttor*). Venom is conveyed by the serpent's tooth; elementary observation teaches that it is the bite of the serpent which is toxic.

Consider then a formulaic curse in Hittite, attested from Old Hittite times down into texts of the New Kingdom and recently discussed by Soysal 1989. KBo 3.46 + Ro. 12′–13′:

> ^{GIŠ}]šamluwanza gakuš=(š)muš [dāu
>
> May the apple take your (or their) teeth!

The reference is clearly to the danger of eating an unpeeled apple for one with poor teeth or ailing gums: one may leave one's teeth in the apple.[20]

As such the apple is a natural homeopathic symbol of defense against the serpent's tooth and its venom. The worms and their venom (Old English *áttor*) are at the same time a metaphor for diseases in Germanic (and Atharvavedic) thought <(chap. 56)>. Add that diseases in the Germanic Middle Ages were themselves metaphorically known as wolf's tooth; compare from Middle High German, Wolfram von Eschenbach, *Parzifal* 7591 *ir truogt den eiterwolves zan* 'you bear the toothmark of the pus-wolf', with *eiter* the German cognate of Old English *āttor*.[21]

The logic of the whole charm then becomes perfectly clear and perfectly natural. It begins with an 'external' narrative:

> The apple is sent against venom.

Then the 'internal' narrative, the myth proper:

> The Serpent bites Man;
> Woden smashes the Serpent into nine pieces with magic twigs.

The pieces are venoms, diseases; the venoms are (wolf's) tooth; the apple takes the tooth. Therefore, returning to the 'external' narrative,

> The apple ends (the Serpent) and the venom.

The terms *apple, serpent* (both *adder* and *worm*), and *Woden* are all Common Indo-European as well as Common Germanic, and *venom* (*áttor*) and magic *twigs* (*tánas*), and the 'external' verbs *send* and *end* (rhyming!) and the 'internal' verbs *bite* (*slítan*) and *smash* (*sléan*) are all Common Germanic. The Old English charm as we have it lexically may thus be legitimately projected back into, that is, reconstructed for, Proto-Germanic. We are that much closer to the goal expressed by Gamkrelidze and Ivanov 1984: 2.643, that the commonality of motifs about the apple in the various traditions may point to a 'reflexion of Common Indo-European ritual and mythological concepts'.

Notes

1. Compare the bibliography in Klaeber 1950. Perhaps the finest appreciation is still Tolkien 1938. For extra-Germanic comparisons cf. recently, and in some detail, Fontenrose 1980: Appendix 5.

2. Cf. Klaeber 1950:xv–xviii and note to line 1457. That the Germanic names of the dragon-slaying hero in their first element (cf. Gothic *sigis* 'victory') have the same root **seĝh-* 'overcome, conquer' as the Greek name *Ἕκτωρ* (Hektor) is perhaps accidental, but still worth pointing out. The semantics of the formation of the name *Ἕκτωρ* are older than those of the synchronic verb *ἔχω* in Homeric Greek. Cf. Ved. *sáhate* 'conquers, overpowers, wins over'.

3. See on these Schmitt 1967:79ff.

4. See further below <(chap. 56)> on the Charm.

5. Likewise proper to Old English is the use of the verb *overcome* with the dragon as object. It is used twice of Grendel: *Beowulf* 845 *niða ofercumen* 'overcome by the fight', 1273 *þy he þone feond ofercwom* 'then he (Beowulf) overcame the adversary'. Since Grendel is only the first of Beowulf's monstrous adversaries we could see in *ofercuman* here the continuator of IE *$terh_2$-, expressing the preliminary victory of one of the protagonists. IE **seĝh-* shows a similar meaning; compare n. 2 above, and recall only that Hektor too won a preliminary victory.

6. Compare the Greek *τίνω, ποινή* below in the same context.

7. *inn fráni ormr* 'the speckled snake' *Fáfnismál* 19, 26; for the perseverance of this frequent Eddic

formula cf. Faroese *frænorormur*, New Norw. dial. *franarormen* 'the snake with yellow spots'. Cf. Greek *ἀργῆν ἔπεφνεν* <and chap. 39>.

8. 'Earth and Up-heaven' is itself an old formula in the Old Norse tradition, indeed probably of Indo-European age. The connection is natural enough, to be sure, but compare in Hittite such collocations, all from mythological or ritual texts, as *Ù* DUMU ^{D}IM ^{MUŠ}*illuyankaš katta nu* ***šarā nepiši*** *attišši ḫalzāiš* 'But the Storm God's son was with the Serpent; and he called up in heaven to his father . . .' (Illuyankas §25); ***šarā nepiši*** *kuwat šakueškizzi* 'Why does it keep looking up to heaven?' (KUB 7.41 Ro. 10–11). Both probably originally would have showed the directive case *nepiša*; for the locative cf. *šēr=a=ššan nepiši šiunaleš ueškanta* 'up in heaven the divine ones are shrieking' (KBo 10.24 iii 13–14). The topos of the stormy agitation of Earth and Heaven is widespread in early Indo-European literatures.

9. Old Norse does show the denominative weak verb *bana* (+ dat.), already once in the *Poetic Edda* (*HHv* 26). It is comparable to the Greek creation *φονεύω*, which as we have seen increases dramatically in frequency in the course of the fifth century B.C.

10. One might also however imagine a directly created metaphor, the act of killing itself being the word, the message. In RV 8.101.3 the missile of Mitra and Varuṇa is called their 'swift messenger' *ajiró dūtás*. The 'swift messenger' is formulaic in Vedic, *dūtó ajirás* RV 10.98.2, *āśúṃ dūtám ajirám* 3.9.8. It is also in Greek *ταχὺς ἄγγελος Od.* 15.526 and especially Sappho 44.3L-P, where it is line final in the same metrical slot as that occupied by *κλέος ἄφθιτον* in the next line. See on the latter Nagy 1974:117. Greek *ἄγγελος* 'messenger' lacks an etymology; should we equate it with Vedic *ajirás* 'swift', via the transferred epithet? A mechanical preform **h_2n̥ĝ$h_1$lo-* will account for both. <For examples of the transferred epithet in etymology see chap. 12.>

11. Cited from Gordon 1949:134. For the meter see ibid. 294. Note also the enjambment which permits a "vertical" as well as "horizontal" alliterative linkage in *b*-, and the "Irish" rhyme (by consonant-class) *einn : meirr*.

12. Seebold 1967, 1980. Note also Cowgill 1980:53, 65, citing with approval Martinet 1972: 89–93.

13. Gmc. **bana-* + *n*-, cf. Lühr 1982:651. Strictly the equation is with the oxytone agent noun *ghaná-* rather than the barytone action noun *φόνος*. But Indo-European and Germanic could well have had both, as was conjectured by Wackernagel for Greek (*ἡ φονός*, <chap. 36>).

14. I am indebted to Daniel Donoghue for this and many of the references cited below, and am particularly indebted to Joseph Harris for corrections and suggestions, not all of which—at my peril—I followed.

15. So Cockayne 1961:3.34, and the lexica, most recently Bierbaumer 1976:127–8. The word is found only here. Cockayne's justification for the meaning 'crabapple' is presented at 3.348.

16. The reference to the seal is obscure. With the metaphor in *ofer sæs hrycg* 'over the sea's ridge, back' compare the Old Irish phrase *fairrge al druim* 'over the sea's ridge, back' from the 7th-century poem on St. Columba <discussed in chap. 9>. We may have diffusion here. The same Archaic Irish poem attests the kenning *nemeth mbled* 'whales' sanctuary' for 'ocean', like Old English (*Beowulf* et passim) *hronrád, hranrád* 'whale-road'.

17. As can be learned from Cockayne's original edition.

18. Meroney 1944. I cannot follow him in his eventual equation of *wergulu* with *lombescyrse* 'lamb's cress'.

19. Cf. the edition and commentary of Anderson 1938, and Much 1959.

20. Rather than Soysal's view that it is the sourness of the wild apple which is envisaged. Apples and corn on the cob are routinely proscribed to those with dentures.

21. Cited in Gerstein 1974.